Reform of the International Monetary System

Chinese Perspectives and Strategies

Reform of the International Monetary System

Chinese Perspectives and Strategies

Xiao Li
Jilin University, China

Translated by
Yong Jiang
Guangdong University of Foreign Studies, China

World Scientific

NEW JERSEY • LONDON • SINGAPORE • BEIJING • SHANGHAI • HONG KONG • TAIPEI • CHENNAI • TOKYO

Published by

World Scientific Publishing Co. Pte. Ltd.

5 Toh Tuck Link, Singapore 596224

USA office: 27 Warren Street, Suite 401-402, Hackensack, NJ 07601

UK office: 57 Shelton Street, Covent Garden, London WC2H 9HE

Library of Congress Cataloging-in-Publication Data

Names: Li, Xiao, 1963 April 23– author.
Title: Reform of the international monetary system : Chinese perspectives and strategies /
Xiao Li, Jilin University, China ; translated by
Yong Jiang, Guangdong University of Foreign Studies, China.
Other titles: Guo ji huo bi ti xi gai ge. English
Description: New Jersey : World Scientific, [2020] | Includes bibliographical references and index.
Identifiers: LCCN 2020032968 | ISBN 9789811218866 (hardcover) |
ISBN 9789811218873 (ebook) | ISBN 9789811218880 (ebook other)
Subjects: LCSH: International finance. | International economic relations. |
Foreign exchange. | Foreign exchange--China. | Monetary policy--China.
Classification: LCC HG3881 .L477613 2020 | DDC 332.4/5--dc23
LC record available at https://lccn.loc.gov/2020032968

British Library Cataloguing-in-Publication Data

A catalogue record for this book is available from the British Library.

Sponsored by Chinese Fund for the Humanities and Social Sciences

国际货币体系改革: 中国的视点与战略
Originally published in Chinese by Peking University Press

For any available supplementary material, please visit
https://www.worldscientific.com/worldscibooks/10.1142/11785#t=suppl

Desk Editors: Ramya Gangadharan/Lixi Dong

Typeset by Stallion Press
Email: enquiries@stallionpress.com

Preface

This preface is a statement on the basic research ideas and background of the reform of the international monetary system and China's position and strategy. Since the outbreak of the global financial crisis in 2008, the call for reform of the international monetary system has far outweighed its actual actions. What is even worse, we have not seen any significant progress in the much-anticipated reform of the international monetary system in addition to reform proposals and actions related to transnational financial supervision and the distribution of voting rights of international financial organizations, etc.

After the global financial crisis broke out, domestic studies on American hegemony and the reform of the international monetary system mainly put forward the following views:

(1) The huge blow to American hegemony marks the decline of American hegemony, the significant and even fundamental progress in the reform of the international monetary system, and the restraint on the hegemony of US dollar.
(2) With the rise of the status of emerging economies, especially the "BRICS" in the world economy, world multi-polarization is taking shape, which will become an important force to check and balance the American hegemony and conflict with international reserve currencies, leading to collapse of the hegemony of the US dollar.

(3) China's status and role will be greatly enhanced, and it has unconsciously become the core force to promote the reform of the international monetary system. Some scholars believe that the modern international system has entered a transition period, that is, a period of alternation between "the falling of the West" and "the rising of the East," and the world is entering the "post-Western international system era."

We believe that the aforementioned understanding is still based on traditional thinking. It is incomprehensive or even wrong to ignore the current changes in the US economic structure and their impact on the global economic and political structure. So far, there are clearly some problems in the research of Chinese academia on the reform of the international monetary system. Two points stand out: one is that it only focuses on economics, international economics and other professional perspectives, and lacks a comprehensive analysis of international political economy; the other is that it pays too much attention to the current situation and problems but less attention to summarize the historical experience. The former problem is prone to in-depth prejudice and the latter lies in its shortsightedness.

It should be noted that the problem of a hegemonic system and its replacement takes priority in the current international monetary system as well as the many problems it faces. Compared with the previous hegemony, namely, the hegemony of the British Empire, this hegemonic system and its structure have two distinct differences: one is that the nature of the hegemonic country (not only the scale) is different, and the other is the structure and nature of the hegemonic system has greatly changed.

In the past more than 30 years of reform and opening-up, China's international political and economic status has rapidly risen along with the development of social economy of China, and our perception of the world has also undergone significant changes. Especially after the end of the Cold War, Chinese government and academia have a more rational understanding of the United States, which dominates the rule-making power of international politics and economics at this stage, and its hegemony. Accordingly, a wealth of research results has been produced. But it must also be acknowledged that there are still many misunderstandings in our perception of American hegemony. They are mainly manifested in three aspects: first, based on the long history of China, the United States is considered to be a country with a history of only more than 200 years. It ignores not only the immigration process of the British Puritans but also the long-term accumulation of European civilization; second, based on China's own history since modern times, American hegemony tends to be analyzed with a narrow nationalist prejudice, and it is difficult to understand "hegemonic neutrality" from the perspective of international political economy. Consequently, while trying to advocate resisting American hegemony, China began to be regarded as a new regional hegemony by the surrounding countries, and fell into an extremely embarrassing situation. Third, the process of industrialization and the characteristic of a "trade country" make it difficult to understand the politics, economic policies or strategies of the United States, which has already become a "financial country." To view the "financial country" from the perspective of a "trade country" is doomed to be erroneous. Obviously, these three misunderstandings are extremely detrimental to China, which has become the world's second largest economy, and even lead to the corresponding strategic misjudgment and unnecessary strategic passiveness.

We believe that it is very necessary to clarify the following three points when China is actively participating in the reform of the international monetary system.

(1) In the new international division of labor system, financial revenue and the US dollar system have become the core interests of the United States, and reform of the international monetary system has been beset with difficulties.
(2) The nature of China's rise at this stage must be calmly understood.
(3) Where exactly does China's core security pressure come from at this stage? Is it military or monetary or financial? Based on

this idea, strategic countermeasures should be formulated and implemented.

At present, in the course of participating in the reform of the international monetary system, China must unswervingly follow four points:

First, due to the existence of the US dollar system, currently, there is no real "currency politics" around the world. China must avoid proactively and independently challenging the core interests of the United States (in fact, the fundamental reform of the international monetary system goes against the national interest of today's China). Therefore, in view of the risks and costs of the US dollar system at this stage, China's main goals for participating in and promoting the reform of the international monetary system should be: on the one hand, to actively participate in global financial governance and promote the reform of the international monetary system in a direction that restrains the United States from benefiting itself; on the other hand, strive to "control imbalances" and "control exchange rate fluctuations," and promote the international community to build a global mechanism to control the risks and costs of the existing system.

Second, spare no efforts to retard the process of fully opening capital account. Since the reform and opening-up, China has always considered opening-up as a controllable process. Therefore, the main consideration for joining the World Trade Organization (WTO) is whether it can "dance with wolves," but it has not realized that the opening-up of market and technology is controllable and their competition is, in nature, among some industries or sectors. However, financial opening-up and its consequences are difficult to be controlled since its competition is comprehensive. Once it makes a mistake, it loses all. At this stage, a lot of deficiencies and weaknesses exist in the financial development of China in terms of the level, idea and system. Under the US dollar system, efforts should be, in particular, made to avoid the rush to fully open capital account on the condition that the related system is not completely constructed yet.

Third, make all-out efforts to promote the regionalization of RMB, which is a measure that can avoid the risks and costs of the US dollar system at this stage. Regarding the internationalization of RMB, recent years have witnessed numerous research results in domestic academia. Based on the aforementioned analysis, our specific arguments are: on the one hand, the internationalization of RMB has no direct relationship with the reform of the international monetary system. Its goal is not to reform the international monetary system, but to control or mitigate the costs and risks the system brings to us; on the other hand, the internationalization of RMB cannot be achieved overnight. It will undergo a long, complicated and difficult process. Therefore, we must first realize the regionalization of its various functions and finally achieve the goal of internationalization through regionalization. To this end, we must consider the following three questions: the first one is whether we can build a domestic demand-driven economic growth model through structural adjustment and reform, and become the final commodity market for East Asia and even the world; the second one is, through reform, whether we can construct an institutional framework for the development of the modern financial industry; the third one is, whether a variety of political, economic and diplomatic measures can be used to formulate and firmly implement a regional strategy of "harmonious neighborhood"; fourth, in the longer term, the key to China's real rise is striving to build a regional and even global capital control system.

World history proves that monetary power, namely, the ability to control currency and capital flows, is the key to a country's rise and fall. The rise of any major country would never be achieved only by relying on its own reserve resources and its own capital. Currently, the United States has unprecedented global monetary power, while other countries are facing tremendous challenges and realize unprecedented pressure. In order to support the real rise of China in the future, as well as avoid repeating the historical mistakes of weakening or losing monetary sovereignty, we must take a long-term view and think about how to establish a regional and even global capital control system. Otherwise, China's economic and military expansion cannot continue, and the rise of a great power would be nothing more than empty talk under the framework of the US dollar system in the contemporary era. It is for this reason that the book is titled "Reform of the International Monetary System: Chinese Perspectives and Strategies."

Finally, on behalf of all members of the research group and translation group, I would like to express my sincere gratitude to the National Fund for Philosophy and Social Sciences for its appreciation of this research result and the funding for publication, and thanks also to all the editors of the publishing house for their active and earnest attitude, and efficient work!

About the Author

Li Xiao is Dean and Professor of the School of Economics and the School of Finance of Jilin University. In 2004, he was selected as one of the "New Century Excellent Talents" by the Chinese Ministry of Education, and was given the title of Distinguished Professor of "Yangtze River Scholars" and "Kuang Yaming Distinguished Professor" of Jilin University. He was also part of the first batch of "Changbai Mountain Scholars" and a "Leading Professor of Economics." He is the Vice President of the China World Economics Association, the Director of the China Institute of International Finance, an Expert of China–Japan–Korea Think Tank Network and a member of the National Social Science Fund Evaluation Committee. He has won the Outstanding Achievement Award of the Humanities and Social Sciences of the Ministry of Education, the "Pushan Economics Outstanding Thesis Award" of the World Economic Association of China, "Liu Shibai Economics Award" and the National Golden Finance Book "Golden Sheep Award" and the First Prize for Outstanding Achievements in Social Science.

About the Translator

Jiang Yong, Professor of Guangdong University of Foreign Studies, is currently the Deputy Dean of the School of English for International Business. His research interests include International Economics and academic translation of economic literatures. In recent years, he has published nearly 20 papers, including nearly 10 papers in the core journals of International Economics. He has participated in editing two textbooks and won two teaching awards. He is the Director of one National Social Science Fund project, one project of Ministry of Education and four provincial-level research projects.

Contents

Chapter 1

The Main Problems and Sustainability of the Current International Monetary System

1.1 The Current International Monetary System and Its Relationship with the Global Economic Cycle

The international monetary system is arranged based on certain common practices or agreements among countries in international economic relations, with reference to exchanges of currencies, exchange rate systems, adjustment of international payments, supply of reserve assets and international capital flows. It is a general term for the principles, measures and organizational forms for a certain currency to function as a world currency in an international context. Its role is to ensure the orderliness and stability of the foreign exchange market, address problems in international payments settlement and facilitate countries or regions that have suffered destructive impacts to obtain international credit (Eichengreen, 1996).[1] A reasonable and effective international monetary system can promote global financial stability and world economic growth. It is an important condition for the sustained, stable and healthy operation of the global economy, and

[1]Eichengreen, Barry, and Jeffrey A. Frankel, On the SDR: Reserve Currencies and the Future of the International Monetary System. Berkeley: University of California, 1996:15–26.

also a guarantee for the socio-economic development of all countries, including China. The emergence of the current international monetary system has its reasons to exist, and it does play a positive role in the global economic cycle, promoting the rapid development of economic and financial globalization and the integration of the global economy. At the same time, it offers changes in the world economic structure and globalization in the economy and finances. On the one hand, the imbalance in global payments has become a prominent issue plaguing the dollar system.[2] On the other hand, the global financial crisis in 2008 caused great damages to the real economy and reduced global welfare. Although the current international monetary system is not a direct cause of global economic imbalances and the international financial crisis, it has sown the seeds of global economic imbalance and international financial crisis, which have further exposed the deficiencies of the current international monetary system and thus revealed the necessity for its reforms and improvement in structures and operating mechanism. However, various factors in the meanwhile indicate a certain degree of sustainability of the current US dollar-centered international monetary system, and little probability of fundamental changes in the short term. This presents the basic environment for China to actively participate in the reform of the international monetary system.

[2]Since the collapse of the Bretton Woods system in the early 1970s, although the international currency system has shown a trend of diversification of reserve currencies, the cutoff of the link between US dollar and gold has not really weakened the former's status. In fact, it still plays a central role and occupies a dominant position in the international monetary system, transforming itself from an alternative of the world currency to an actual world key currency. The Bretton Woods system actually became an underlying dollar system, which, to be specific, was an international currency system where the US dollar, though not exchangeable with gold, still played a key role and furthermore, became a dollar-centered international financial system based on a worldwide credit system with all turnover periods (refer to: Li, X. and Ding, Y. *Transcendence in Asia-Constructing East Asian Regional Monetary System and "Asianization of RMB."* Beijing: Contemporary China Publishing House, 2005, 3–9 (in Chinese)).

1.1.1 *The Framework, Nature, Characteristics and Operation of the Current International Monetary System*

1.1.1.1 *The Framework of the Current International Monetary System*

The Jamaica Agreement of 1976 and the Second Amendment of the International Monetary Fund's (IMF) Constitution marked the end of the Bretton Woods system and the start of the current international monetary system. Since the collapse of the Bretton Woods system, the reform of the international monetary system has entered a long journey. The Jamaica Agreement passed by the IMF in 1976 confirmed the legitimacy of the floating exchange rate system adopted by major countries following the collapse of the Bretton Woods system and maintained the principles of global free multilateral payment. Since then, although the status of the US dollar as the core currency and the international reserve currency has been weakened, its leading position in the international monetary system and the function as an international reserve currency have continued. Therefore, it became possible for the IMF's original organizational structure and functions to continue. However, the criteria and norms under the Bretton Woods system determined by its five basic elements have been fragmented. Thus, the existing international monetary system is called an "inefficient system." The weakening of the rules has led to numerous contradictions. In particular, the globalization of the financial market had been further strengthened in the 1990s under the influence of an overall economic globalization, which brought new features to the components and operation of the system. As shown in Figure 1.1, the development of financial globalization closely linked the economies of all countries.

Based on the aforementioned overall structure of the international financial market, the main functions of the international monetary system include the following five aspects:

First, establish international currency or reserve assets. It provides necessary means of repayment for global trade and guarantees

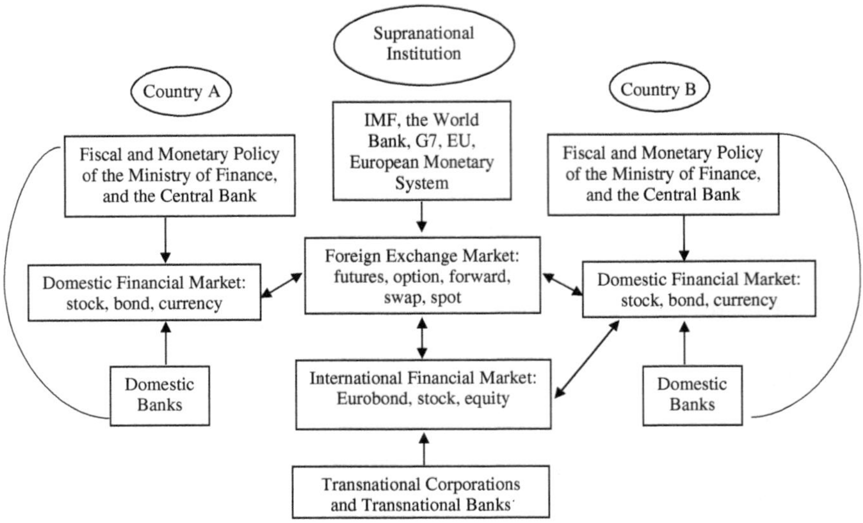

Figure 1.1. The Framework of the Current International Monetary System

the normal foreign economic activities of all countries amidst a relatively stable currency system.

Second, establish an international exchange rate system. It is supposed to encourage all countries and regions to reach a consensus on currency exchange rates, regulate exchange rate movements worldwide according to reasonable principles and adopt an exchange rate mechanism to prevent unnecessary competitive devaluations.

Third, form an effective balance of payments adjustment mechanism. Through an effective regulatory mechanism, it shall redress the imbalances in international payments caused by factors at home and abroad.

Fourth, build and operate international financial institutions. In order to establish a stable international currency system and promote cooperation, some international financial institutions represented by the IMF and the World Bank were established after World War II. They have played an active role in maintaining the operation of the international monetary system and promoting cooperation among currencies. At the same time, they also play an important part in the international capital cycle as supranational players.

Fifth, build a multinational financial supervision system. With the integration of domestic and international financial markets, the tendency of financial risks to transfer and spread among countries is continuously increasing. Therefore, it has become increasingly urgent to strengthen international cooperation in financial supervision. The transnational financial supervision system has also become an integral part in ensuring the stable operation of the international financial system.

1.1.1.2 *The Nature and Special Features of the Current International Monetary System*

The opinions of domestic and foreign academics are not consistent on the definition of the current international monetary system. Some scholars believe that the current "international currency system" cannot be called a system because it has neither a clear standard currency nor a unified exchange rate. The behaviors of various countries cannot be effectively regulated, and that is, "the inefficiency of our current 'system'."[3] However, the system does maintain many of the characteristics of the Bretton Woods era. For example, the Bretton Institutions (IMF and the World Bank) still exist and play a certain role, and the US dollar is still in a dominant position. A considerable number of currencies have a relatively fixed exchange rate with the US dollar, etc. Therefore, some people call the current system the "post-Bretton Woods System,"[4] and others call it the "Resurrection of the Bretton Woods System,"[5] or "New Breeze" Forest System.[6]

[3]Mundell, Robert, "Currency Areas, Exchange Rate Systems and International Monetary Reform," *Journal of Applied Economics* 3, no. 2 (2000): 217–256.

[4]Bayoumi, Tamim, and Eichengreen, Barry, "Shocking Aspects of European Monetary Integration," In *Adjustment and Growth in European Monetary Union*, edited by Torres, G. and Giavazzi, F., 193–235. Cambridge: Cambridge University Press, 1993.

[5]Dooley, Michael P., David Folkerts-Landau and Peter M. Garber, "An Essay on the Revived Bretton Woods System," *NBER Working Paper*, no. 9971 (September 2003).

[6]Eichengreen, Barry, "Global Imbalances and the Lessons of Bretton Woods," *Economie Internationale* 100, no. 4 (2004): 39–50.

Despite the different titles, scholars unanimously recognize that the current US dollar still plays a role of the standard currency, and thus the current international monetary system is also known as the "dollar system." The demonetization of gold has made the current international currency system the first one in history to use a pure credit currency as the standard. Since the contemporary international currency system is based on the country's credit currency, the United States, the country issuing international currency, serves the role as the world central bank to provide liquidity for international exchanges.

This nature of the current international monetary system determines its uniqueness clearly in various aspects such as the supply of international reserve assets, the choice of exchange rate system, adjustment of international payment balance, international capital flow and the operation and evolution of the system.

First, from the perspective of the supply of international reserve assets, the dollar is the most important reserve currency, but the euro and the yen (especially the euro) also partly function as international currencies. In reality, the US dollar has the strength to become the standard currency under the current system, which, however, is not explicitly justified in the legal sense. This essentially results in the absence of a nominal monetary anchor under the current international monetary system, meaning that the US's monetary policy behaviors are not bound by laws, and behaviors of other countries are also more arbitrary.[7] The demonetization of gold and the preparation of the US currency issuance system in 1980 became a preparation for securities issuance, which further weakened the control of international liquidity. The excessive privilege of the United States has enabled it to obtain indefinite credit at a low cost from other countries and has also undermined the dollar's anchor role.[8]

[7]Dooley, Michael P., David Folkerts-Landau and Peter M. Garber, "An Essay on the Revived Bretton Woods System," *NBER Working Paper*, no. 9971 (September 2003).

[8]McKinnon, Ronald I., *The Unloved Standard: From Bretton Woods to the Rise of China*. Beijing: China Financial Publishing House, 2013, 1–10.

Second, from the perspective of the choice of the exchange rate system, the current system clarifies the legitimacy of the free floating exchange rate and the illegality of "manipulating the exchange rate." However, because it is extremely difficult to define what "manipulating exchange rate" is, it is virtually impossible to effectively regulate countries' exchange rate policies. Under the current international monetary system, the dollar's standard currency nature makes it a (*quasi*) currency anchor for most countries outside of Europe. However, although short-term informal pegging to the US dollar is common in Asia, America and many other regions, it is basically "soft pegging" which lacks credibility, especially in the long run. This makes the current dollar system ineligible to ensure the stability of exchange rates.[9] In the absence of a clear international standard currency and a floating exchange rate, it is inevitable that the real exchange rate will be diversified and exchange rates of major currencies will become volatile. Most developed countries and emerging market countries implement floating exchange rates or managed floating exchange rates, but there are also many countries' central banks actively intervening in the forex market to prevent excessive exchange rate fluctuations.

Third, from the perspective of international payment balance adjustments and global cooperation, the mechanism has been diversified so that member states can flexibly adjust payments balance with the exchange rate mechanism, interest rate mechanism, IMF's short-term loans and intervention, financing of international financial markets and commercial banks, etc. The development of economic globalization has also added new content to the autonomic adjustment, that is, the valuation effect.[10] At the same time, currency and exchange rate management have shown increasingly obvious tendencies of joint management and group management

[9]McKinnon, Ronald and Gunther Schnabl, "The East Asian Dollar Standard, Fear of Floating, and Original Sin," *Review of Development Economics* 8, no. 3 (2004): 331–360.

[10]Obstfeld, Maurice, "External Adjustment," *Review of World Economics* 140, no. 4 (December 2004): 541–568.

(Li and Zhang, 1994),[11] which has been manifested by the advocation and development of the European Monetary System (EMS) at the end of the 1970s, the birth of the Euro in 1999, East Asia's monetary cooperation, the establishment of BRICS Bank, the Free Trade Area of the Asia-Pacific and other regional currency cooperation.

Fourth, from the perspective of international capital flows, the overwhelming majority of countries have achieved the liberalization of capital projects, with little limits in cross-border capital flows. The interaction between cross-border capital flows (as well as international speculative capital) and changes in exchange rates makes both of them more prone to fluctuations. In order to maintain the stability of exchange rates and capital flows, many emerging market economies represented by East Asian countries have had to keep large amounts of reserve assets to intervene in the foreign exchange market when needed. And under the current dollar system, US Treasuries naturally become the main form of such reserve assets.

Fifth, from the perspective of international financial institutions, the IMF provides loans with strict conditions for countries suffering from payment imbalances crises due to insufficient reserve assets. However, the pro-cyclicality of its loan terms and its lack of representativeness increases the international community's pressure on its reforms.

Sixth, from the perspective of international financial supervision, existing international financial institutions (IMF and (Bank for International Settlements) BIS, etc.) can neither implement country-specific supervision nor effective cross-border supervision for developed countries' financial markets. Although Basel III proposed new rules for global supervision after the international financial crisis, its implementation was difficult. When the United States announced that it would not be able to implement the new rules as scheduled on 1 January 2013, whether or not the agreement could be fully implemented in 2019 was uncertain. Until 2 July 2013, the Federal Reserve Board (FRB) approved the US banking industry's implementing the

[11]Xiao, Li, and Xianji Zhang, "On the Integration of World Economy and Regional Grouping of World Economy," *World Economy* 4, (1994): 37–43.

capital regulations of Basel III and promoted the further implementation of the new rules of financial supervision. This reflects the complexity of the game between member states over international financial supervision.

1.1.1.3 *Operation of the Current International Monetary System*

Under the condition in which the contemporary international currency system is based on the countries' credit currency and the country issuing the international currency plays the role of the world's central bank to provide liquidity for international exchanges, there are two ways in which the world currency flows provide liquidity; firstly, the currency flow behind the real economic flow, and secondly, directly generated by capital flow. A simple analysis of the international currency operating mode can be conducted based on this position (Figures 1.2 and 1.3).[12]

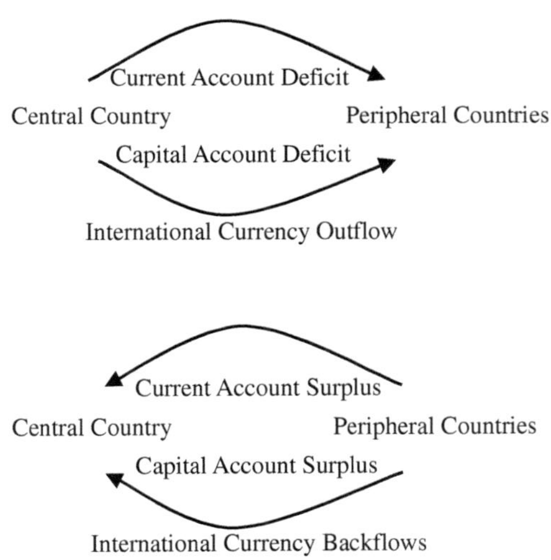

Figure 1.2. International Currency Flow

[12]For the sake of research, countries that do not have international currency are collectively referred to as "peripheral countries"; countries whose national currency is international are called "central countries."

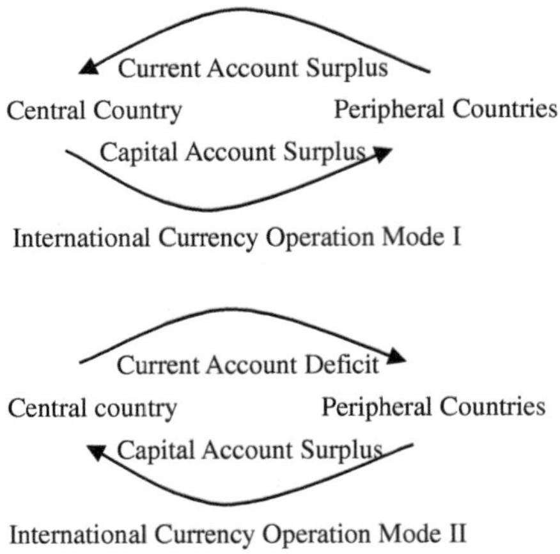

Figure 1.3. Two Modes of International Currency Operation

Outflow of international currencies can be achieved by the peripheral countries' importing real resources into the central country or through the central country investing currency capital into peripheral countries. From the perspective of the central country, the international money supply is completed through the current account deficit or the capital account deficit. The return of international currency inflows can be achieved through the central country's exporting real resources or investing currency capital in the peripheral countries. From the perspective of the central country, the international currency return is accomplished through the current account surplus or the capital account surplus.

Since only one net effect can be produced by operation under a certain account, there are two modes of international currency operation.

Under International Monetary Operation Mode I, the outflow of international currencies is realized through the central country's capital project deficit; the return of international currency inflows is realized through the current account surplus. Under the International Monetary Operation Mode II, the outflow of international currencies is achieved through the current account deficits of the central country; the inflow of international currencies is achieved through the surplus of capital accounts. Theoretically, both of the aforementioned methods can ensure the smooth operation of the international monetary system.

In addition, we can also obtain some simple but useful inferences from the following models:

Inference 1: For peripheral countries without rights to issue international currencies, the acquisition of international currency can only be achieved through net exports or net international capital inflows.

Inference 2: For the central country, since its national currency has a dual nature as an international currency and the national currency, the acquisition of international currency can be achieved through net exports or net inflows of international capital as in peripheral countries, or it can also increase liquidity through the central bank's currency issuance.

Inference 3: International economic exchanges must be based on the interaction between the central and peripheral countries. Only in this way can its supply meet demand.

Inference 4: Due to the nature of the credit currency of the current international currency system, there is an inverse relationship between the degree of liquidity and credit. The more effective the international currency operation model, the more it can limit the money amount in the international currency system and maintain its stability.

Given the nature of the "dollar system" in today's international monetary system, the operation mode of the current international monetary system can be easily understood by examining changes in the United States' payment balance (Inference 3).

Under the Bretton Woods system, the US payment account balance showed current account surpluses and capital account deficits before 1970 (see Figures 1.4 and 1.5). During this period, the international monetary system operation mode was Model I, in which the US dollar outflows were achieved by capital account deficits, and the return of the US dollars was realized through the current account surpluses. Judging from the actual situation, in the early post-war period, when Western European countries and Japan were not able to

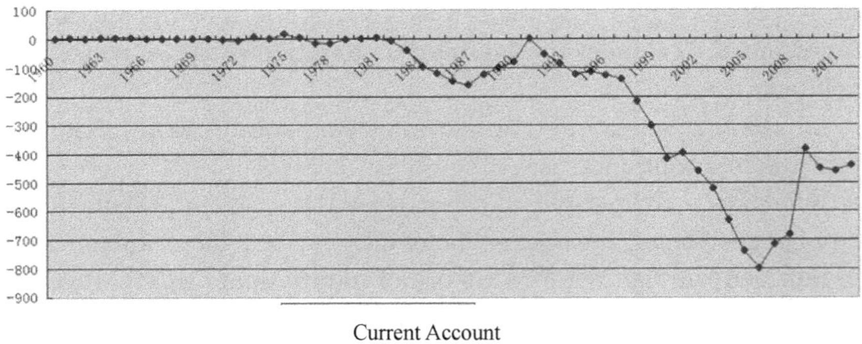

Figure 1.4. The US's Balance of Current Accounts 1960–2012 (in US$ 100,000,000)

Source: Bureau of Economic Analysis, US.

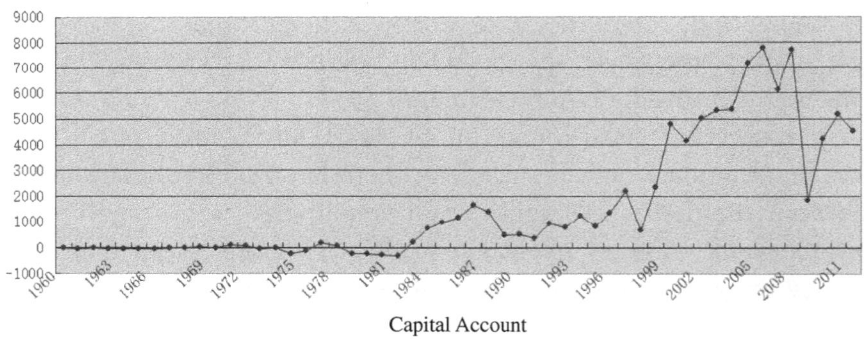

Figure 1.5. The US's Balance of Capital Account 1960–2012(in US$100,000,000)

Source: Bureau of Economic Analysis, US.

export to the United States, the United States mainly provided Western Europe and Japan with substantial US dollar liquidity through financial aids such as the Marshall Plan, while Japan and Western European countries imported from the United States all kinds of materials and technological products necessary for economic development with a limited amount of foreign exchange. The flows of the international currency have supported the recovery and development of the world economy.

However, from the 1970s onward, as Western Europe and Japan's economy gradually revitalized, their products grew in competence and faced fierce competition from the American products in the international market. As a result, the US current account surplus gradually shrank. A deficit began to appear. Although the US's overseas investment has not weakened but increased during this period, the supply of US dollars (for outflows) can only be achieved by domestic currency supply, for the dollar return model is no longer effective. That means, the increasing demand for liquidity by the expansion of global trade can only be met by printing money (Inference 2). In this situation, the gold constraint eventually led to the collapse of the Bretton Woods system.

After the Bretton Woods system collapsed, although the status of the US dollar did not decline, the international currency operation mode changed from mode I to mode II. That is, the US achieved currency outflows through current account deficits and inflows through capital account surpluses (see Figures 1.1 and 1.2). The following are several reasons for the smooth operation of mode II:

First, the real economy's structure is symmetric. Dooley and some other scholars believe that the current international monetary system is a revived Bretton Woods system.[13] Although this theory has been questioned, there is indeed some symmetry in the world's economic structure.

From the perspective of peripheral countries, Asian countries and regions, especially those in East Asia, as well as some countries in the former Soviet Union and Eastern Europe undergoing economic transitions, have formulated and implemented export-oriented economic development strategies since the 1980s. On the one hand, it solved the problem of domestic labor surplus, thus stabilizing the society.

---

[13] Dooley, Michael P., David Folkerts-Landau and Peter M. Garber, "The Revised Bretton Woods System," *International Journal of Finance and Economics* 9, no. 4 (October 2004): 307–313. According to the currency, the US is "the central country," and other countries are "peripheral countries," among which the EU is "the alternate central country," China, Japan and other emerging economies are core peripheral countries, and the rest of the world are general peripheral countries.

On the other hand, due to the low labor costs of these countries, their products have a strong cost advantage. The products surplus caused by a weak domestic demand was alleviated through a significant amount of exports. This has promoted economic development.

From the perspective of the central country, the United States acts as a huge market for world products. With strong technical support, the United States continues to upgrade and transform its industrial structure, and imports labor-intensive products to the US market. At the same time, manufactured goods from transnational companies investing overseas at a low cost have also become a part of the US market's imports, which rely heavily on the US's economic structure. The US has a typical consumer-oriented economy, in which personal consumption expenditures have always been around 2/3 of the gross domestic product (GDP). Stimulated by the wealth effect of the US's "Internet bubble" in the 1990s and the low interest rate caused by an influx of Asian funds, US residents' investment continued to maintain a strong momentum, which promoted the increase in the value of assets such as stocks and real estate, raising the propensity of consumption. Since 2001, the proportion of personal consumption expenditure in the United States has been stable at around 70% of its total GDP, compared with 68% in 2013; the contribution of individual consumption to GDP growth has also consistently ranked in first place, surpassing investment, net exports and government spending (see Table 1.1).

Due to the symmetrical economic structure, peripheral countries are willing and able to export and produce their surplus products while the central country is willing and capable of importing and consuming them. Thus, the US dollars' worldwide outflow has been achieved through these current accounts.

Secondly, the demand of international currency is balanced. From the perspective of the peripheral countries, international currency demand can be classified into several levels. The first is the demand for international economic exchanges. Economic development in emerging countries is in its infancy, and importing resources and technology for development requires sufficient foreign exchange reserves.

Table 1.1. Contribution to the Real GDP (%)

	2002	2003	2004	2005	2006	2007	2008	2009	2010	2011	2012	2013
Real GDP	1.8	2.8	3.8	3.4	2.7	1.8	−0.3	−2.8	2.5	1.8	2.8	1.9
Personal consumption expenditures	1.70	2.08	2.58	2.35	2.02	1.51	−0.24	−1.06	1.34	1.74	1.52	1.37
Fixed investment	−0.64	0.69	1.18	1.24	0.37	−0.37	−1.22	−2.77	0.21	0.85	1.17	0.66
Net export	−0.62	−0.42	−0.64	−0.32	−0.06	0.59	1.12	1.14	−0.51	0.10	0.10	0.12
Government expenditures	0.81	0.42	0.31	0.12	0.29	0.30	0.54	0.64	0.02	−0.68	−0.20	−0.43

Source: Bureau of Economic Analysis, US.

The second is the demand for economic development models. Since most of the peripheral countries have adopted the export-orientated development model, a stable or even underestimated exchange rate remains beneficial to expanding exports and the developing economy. In order to maintain the stability of the exchange rate, countries need to have sufficient foreign exchange reserves, for intervening at any time in the foreign exchange market. In addition, due to the frequent international financial crises, especially after the East Asian financial crisis, governments in various countries' that have increased foreign exchange reserves have had new functions such as preventing financial turmoil and currency crisis.

From Table 1.2, it is easy to see that when it comes to the size of foreign exchange reserves, among the top 10 countries or regions, the BRICS countries and East and Southeast Asia (including Japan) occupy 8 places. Singapore and Thailand follow closely, ranking 11th and 15th. The foreign exchange reserves held by all these emerging economies and export-oriented countries or regions amount to about US$8 trillion, accounting for nearly 60% of the world's total.

From the perspective of the central country, the back flow of US dollars is a guarantee and resource for its operations around the world.

If the US dollars cannot return to the United States effectively, liquidity can only be achieved by currency supply, which, however, will probably detach from the US dollar's position as an international currency (Inference 4). This is the key reason for the collapse of the operational mode I of the international monetary system.

In addition, the high fiscal deficit of the US government also makes overseas financing necessary. After the mid-1970s, the United States' fiscal deficit continued to increase. It did not begin to decrease until prolonged economic prosperity after 1995. In 1998–2001, the fiscal deficit was even eliminated for the short term. However, since the "dotcom bubble" burst in 2001, the economic growth decelerated. Plus, the expansion in military expenditure during the Iraqi war contributed to the US fiscal deficit, which has increased rapidly since 2002.

Table 1.2. Ranking of Foreign Exchange Reserves of Major Countries

Rank	Country or Region	Foreign Exchange Reserves (in million US dollars)	Time
	World	13, 381, 748	—
1	China*	3, 887700	2014.9
2	Japan	1, 288, 206	2014.2
3	Saudi Arabia	725, 685	2014.1
4	Switzerland	543, 758	2014.2
5	Russia	493, 326	2014.2
6	Taiwan, China	423, 059	2014.2
7	Brazil	362, 691	2014.2
8	Korea	351, 792	2014.2
9	Hong Kong, China	315, 919	2014.2
10	India	306, 648	2014.4
11	Singapore	273, 996	2014.2
12	Germany	210, 554	2014.2
13	Algeria	192, 500	2013.12
14	Mexico	183, 763	2014.2
15	Thailand	168, 081	2014.2

Note: *Excluding Hong Kong, Macau and Taiwan.

Source: http://en.wikipedia.org/wiki/List_of_countries_by_foreign_exchange_reserves. http://www.pbc.gov.cn/publish/html/kuangjia.htm?id=2014s09.htm.

During 2006–2008, the deficit remained stable at about US$240 billion. After 2009, affected by the global financial crisis, it has increased substantially and reached a record of US$1,412.688 billion in 2010. The huge deficit is mainly made up by the issuance of US Treasuries. However, domestic savings in the United States have always been insufficient. The government bonds have to rely on the purchase of foreign funds, and the US dollar therefore has another layer of significance (Figure 1.6).

The United States has the world's most advanced financial capital market with great depth and breadth. Not only financial derivatives and other innovative products but government bonds, stocks, corporate bonds and other securities are also issued in great numbers. In addition, the degrees of financial and capital liberalization and internationalization of the United States are all high. The market rules are sound, fair and highly transparent. Investors from all over

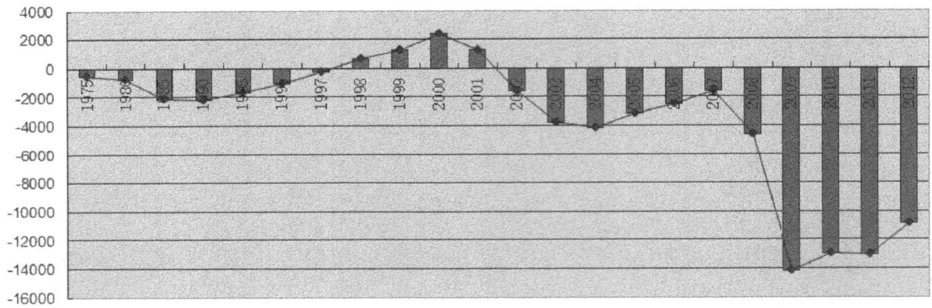

Figure 1.6. Changes in US Fiscal Deficit (in US$100 million)
Source: Bureau of Economic Analysis, US.

the world are provided with an ideal environment and diverse investment products in the US. As a result, foreign capital investment in the United States is most active.

Under the circumstance of balanced international currency demand, peripheral countries are willing to accumulate foreign exchange through export, while the United States aims to continue to attract the return of the dollars through the provision of asset and securities products. In this way, the demand of the US dollar has remained basically balanced and its position as the international currency has been maintained.

Within the mentioned operating mode, the current international currency system also shows different operational characteristics in content from the past. The specific characteristics are as follows:

(1) A diversified exchange rate system with floating exchange rates: According to the classification in the IMF Annual Report 2005, eight real exchange rate arrangements coexist under the current international currency system: exchange arrangements with no separate legal tender, currency board arrangements, other conventional fixed peg arrangements, pegged exchange rates within horizontal bands, crawling pegs, exchange rates within crawling bands, managed floating with no predetermined path for the exchange rate and independently floating. At present, the major exchange rate adopted by countries are the independently

floating arrangement, managed floating arrangement, conventional peg arrangement and arrangement of no separate legal tender. The currencies with floating exchange rates in real terms are the US dollar, euro, yen, pound sterling and Swiss franc. A system with the exchange rate pegged to the dollar at a low frequency is adopted in developing countries and many emerging market economies. Dynamically, since the 1990s, the number of countries with the freely floating exchange rate system have not decreased but increased. The number of countries with a managed floating exchange system have increased significantly. From the perspective of the relation between exchange rate system and the IMF voting rights, the countries with independently floating and managed floating exchange rates as well as the Eurozone countries have a clear advantage. This has highlighted the three exchange rate arrangements which are dominant in the current international monetary system.

(2) Autonomous balance of payments adjustment mechanism: Under the current international monetary system, an autonomous international payments adjusting mechanism still relies on the relative changes of bilateral and multilateral exchange rates, which mainly exist between countries adopting a completely free floating exchange rate system. When a country experiences a trade deficit, the demand for its currency will fall and that of the foreign currency will rise in the global foreign exchange market. This will result in a currency depreciation, which, will subsequently increase to drive the country's exports and improve its trading accounts. Changes in exchange rates, foreign currency reserves, relative prices and short-term capital flows can all autonomously regulate the payment balance to a certain degree. Therefore, member states can flexibly use the exchange rate mechanism, interest rate mechanism, IMF short-term loans, financing tools at international financial markets and commercial banks to adjust the payment balance. It is worth noting that, in the context of economic globalization, a new feature shows up in the autonomy payment balance adjustment mechanism — the

valuation effect.[14] It refers to a sharp increase in foreign assets or liabilities that drive the foreign exchange rates and other asset prices to change; the capital value as well as the overseas investment will fluctuate (up or down, dramatically) when their foreign position is so large, that is, a transfer of wealth will be generated. When the wealth is transferred from the surplus country to the deficit country (requiring the currency of the surplus country to appreciate and that of the deficit country to depreciate), the external economy is automatically adjusted. This effect enhances the self-regulating international payments mechanism in the globalization context. However, this effect happens only based on certain premises. In a country with a given amount of external assets and liabilities, the valuation effect can play a role only when the exchange rate changes cannot be speculated. For most emerging market countries, the adjustment of foreign accounts is mainly achieved through trade. However, this does not mean that the valuation effect is not important in these countries. On the contrary, it reveals that the effect has some negative impacts. For example, depreciation in exchange rates will often lead to a permanent deterioration to the net foreign asset positions, so that the external equilibrium shall be achieved through improving net exports. In some industrial countries, especially the United States and Japan, the valuation effect has played a critical role: when there is a long-term divergence between the performances of foreign net assets and net exports, the assets evaluation will change, thus systematically preventing this divergence.[15] For all countries, in the short term, the adjustment is

[14]For more research on the valuation effect and its application, please refer to Xiao, Li, and Zhou Xuezhi, "The Sustainability of US Foreign Liabilities: The Expansion of External Adjustment Theory," *World Economy Study* 12 (2012): 130–155 (in Chinese); Xiao, Li and Zhou Xuezhi, "The US Net External Liabilities Outlook and US Dollar Exchange Rate Adjustment," *Studies of International Finance* 2 (2014): 29–42 (in Chinese).

[15]Gourinchas, Pierre-Olivier and Helene Rey, "International Financial Adjustment," *Journal of Political Economy* 115, no. 4 (August 2007): 665–703.

generally achieved through long-term changes in trade. In the long run, it is also crucial to reach equilibrium in the foreign accounts through trade. However, valuation effect does help the short-term adjustment in the United States, and has also played an important role in the short-term external equilibrium adjustment of other industrialized countries.[16]

(3) The diversified international reserve currency pattern with the US dollar at its dominant position: Under the current international monetary system, the recognized international currencies mainly include the US dollar, the euro and the Japanese yen, while the US dollar is the key currency. Many currencies, such as GBP, Canadian dollar and Australian dollar, cannot easily be defined as international currencies or regional international currencies in the general sense. Their "internationality" is obviously lower than the aforementioned three currencies and they are quite "regional."[17] Therefore, the current international reserve currency pattern is diversified, and also dominated by the US dollar, which features the dollar system.

(4) International financial institutions — IMF and the World Bank: There are currently two major organizations responsible for international financial affairs, established under the Bretton Woods system, the IMF and the World Bank Group. With the formation of new international currency relations and changes in the world economic situation, the two major organizations have also undergone a series of reforms and now still play an active role. The IMF is mainly responsible for monetary and financial affairs, fostering consultation and collaboration among member countries on international currency issues, promoting exchange rate stability and orderly arrangements to avoid competitive

[16]Corsetti, Giancarlo and Panagiotis Th. Konstantinou, "Current Account Theory and the Dynamics of US Net Foreign Liabilities," *CEPR Discussion Paper*, no. 4920 (February 2005).

[17]Chinn, Menzie David and Jeffrey A. Frankel, "Will the Euro Eventually Surpass the Dollar as Leading International Reserve Currency?" *NBER Working Paper*, no. 11510 (August 2005).

devaluation. It has also established a multilateral payment and exchange system for current accounts, striving to eliminate foreign exchange controls that hinder the development of world trade. It provides member countries with a temporary financial intermediation so that they can redress international payments imbalances without resorting to measures that harm domestic and international economic prosperity. It also helps to shorten the duration and length of payment imbalances among member countries, so as to strike a balance in international trade, improve employment and income and expand the production capacity. The World Bank has served as a supporter of global development. It not only provides a large amount of financial aid to the developing countries but also explores new trails of world economic development by studying the various aspects of the world economic development theories and policies; so, it helps to promote effective flow of its financial aid. The policies of the World Bank have gradually changed in the past few years. For example, it has put more emphasis on universal development connections, comprehensive development framework and some non-economic development factors. In terms of poverty reduction policies, it gives more priority to direct poverty alleviation projects compared with indirect ones. It emphasizes the guidance of policies and knowledge transfer. At the same time, it downplays its function in currency transfer, and tightens project policies (additional conditions), increases borrower's financial costs, implements national standards and rules, supports global public products and so on. Despite all these changes, the World Bank continues to play an important role in promoting social and economic development, and improving people's lives in all countries around the world.

(5) International financial supervision: In the process of financial globalization, free cross-border capital flow has promoted the growth of the global economy, but at the same time it may also increase its disorder and accelerate the spread of international

financial crises. Against this background, strengthening international cooperation in financial supervision and unifying national financial regulatory legislation has become necessary. The Basel Committee has played an important role in the global supervision unification from the Principles for the Supervision of Banks Foreign Establishments in 1975, to the Core Principles for Effective Banking Supervision in 1997 and the New Basel Accord in 2003. The accord has established the core principles of financial supervision. Basel III in 2013, as a benchmark for global banking supervision, further adjusted and reorganized international financial regulatory guidelines. In addition, some international financial regulatory organizations, such as those of securities commissions, insurance supervision and payment and settlement system committees of banks for international settlements, as well as the IMF, have taken steps to deal with specific multinational financial supervision issues by strengthening cooperation. However, due to the lack of a global coordination mechanism for multinational financial supervision, there is currently no systematic cross-border financial supervision system. The IMF is responsible for monitoring the global macro economy; the BIS, for payments settlement between the Central Bank and international organizations, and the information exchange and cooperation among central banks; the international standard setting bodies such as the Basel Committee, for setting industry operating standards for specific financial institutions such as the capital adequacy ratio for commercial banks; and the financial supervisory departments, for the supervising work in domestic financial markets. Due to the lack of a unified communication platform and a coordination mechanism, it is tough to carry out effective and systemic monitoring for global risks. International coordination for dealing with these risks and the cross-board financial supervision of them remains weak. This has become one of the major reasons for the frequent outbreaks and rapid spread of financial crises in recent years.

1.1.2 *A Theoretical Interpretation of the Global Economic Imbalance and the Role of the International Monetary System*

The global economic imbalance was a topic proposed by the IMF in early 2005, referring to a phenomenon that has existed in the world for numerous years, that is, the US's regular deficit grows rapidly and accumulates a huge amount of debt, while countries including those in Asia such as Japan and China, other emerging market countries and OPEC countries hold large trade surpluses, accordingly accumulating a large amount of foreign exchange reserves. The reason why this phenomenon arouses so much concern is mainly because, due to long-term trade surpluses in relatively underdeveloped countries, developed countries hold deficits for a long time, causing a trade mode circuit of capital, which features the former exporting products as well as capital to the latter. This mode, however, reaches an abnormal equilibrium. It is of course questionable in its rationality, while its sustainability is even more worrying.[18] There is a general concern that the global economy will fall into a deep crisis if this fragile equilibrium is broken. Therefore, redressing the global economic imbalance has become a common goal for the world's major countries in making policies.

In view of the current global economic imbalances, academics at home and abroad have conducted analyzes from various theoretical perspectives. Some scholars believe that global economic imbalances are caused by national investment–savings gap resulting from different savings rates in terms of the savings–investment relationship. Specifically, the root cause of the imbalance is the gap between low saving rate in the United States and the high savings rate in countries including Japan and China. (Naik, 2005)[19] The former Chairman of the Federal Reserve, Ben Bernanke, also believes that the US current account

[18]McKinnon, Ronald I., "The International Dollar Standard and the Sustainability of the US Current Account Deficit," *Brookings Papers on Economic Activity* 2001, no. 1 (2001): 227–239.

[19]McKinnon, Ronald and Gunther Schnabl, "China's Exchange Rate and International Adjustment in Wages, Prices and Interest Rates: Japan Deja Vu?" *CESifo Economic Studies* 52, no. 2 (2006): 276–303.

deficit is mainly caused by the world's "saving surplus."[20] Some scholars pointed out that the root cause of the US current account imbalances lies in the US fiscal and monetary policies.[21] Other scholars claim that some countries such as China undervalued its currency to stimulate exports, which becomes the main reason for global payment imbalances in terms of the exchange rate. (Frankel, 2006)[22] Yet other scholars argued that the imbalance and the dominant position of the US dollar in the international monetary system have led to an overvaluation of the US dollar, leading to the US's constant current account deficit.[23] Some scholars analyze the causes of imbalances from international trade and division of labor. Some believe that the changes in manufacturing trade flow caused by manufacturing advantages are key reasons for the global economic imbalances.[24] Some scholars believe that the international flow of production factors has changed the traditional international labor division and formed a new pattern in which manufacturers concentrated production factors in some countries and regions, and produce based on demands of the whole world. This is manifested by the development of multinational outsourcing and the

---

Naik, Vasant, Amitabh Arora, Srivaths Balakrishnan, and Alexei Jiltsov, "Global Savings-Investment Imbalances: A Look through the Life-Cycle Model," New York: Lehman Brothers, Fixed Income Research (September 2005): 35–47.

[20]Bernanke, Ben S., Jean Boivin and Piotr Eliasz, "Measuring the Effects of Monetary Policy: A Factor-Augmented Vector Autoregressive (FAVAR) Approach," *The Quarterly Journal of Economics* 120, no. 1 (2005): 387–422.

[21]Roubini, Nouriel and Brad Setser, "Will the Bretton Woods 2 Regime Unravel Soon? The Risk of a Hard Landing in 2005–2006," Unpublished manuscript, New York University and Oxford University, 2005, 6.

[22]Goldstein, Morris, "China's Exchange Rate Regime," Testimony before the Subcommittee on Domestic and International Monetary Policy, Trade, and Technology Committee on Financial Services, 2003.

Frankel, Jeffrey, "On the Yuan: The Choice between Adjustment under a Fixed Exchange Rate and Adjustment under a Flexible Rate," CESifo Economic Studies 52, no. 2 (2006): 246–275.

[23]Xiaolong, Huang, "Global Imbalances, Excessive Liquidity, and Currency Crisis: An Analysis Based on an Unbalanced International Monetary System," *Financial Research* 45, no. 8 (2007): 31–46 (in Chinese).

[24]Mann, Catherine L., "Breaking Up Is Hard to Do: Global Co-Dependency. Collective Action, and the Challenges of Global Adjustment," *Paper of CESITO Forum* 6, no. 1 (2005): 16–23.

extension of the global supply chain. Consequently, companies adopting manufacture–export pattern gradually concentrate in East Asia, so the trade imbalance would become long term.[25] Some scholars pointed out that during the aforementioned changes in the pattern of international labor division, the formation of comparative advantages of countries such as China and the United States are not synchronous. "Trade imbalance" or "current account imbalance" may appear when the former's comparative advantages emerge.[26] Therefore, the current global economic imbalance is temporary and will be compensated with the future growth in the export of the US comparative industries.

We believe that the current global economic imbalance is not temporary. It is an inevitable result of the long-term adjustment of global economic structure and international labor division. After the Second World War, the world formed a new labor division between virtual and real economies based on countries' comparative advantages. Represented by the United States, its comparative advantages in financial and service sectors make it a typical hegemonic "financial country."[27] Correspondingly, developed countries such as Japan and developing countries such as China have become trading countries with a developed manufacturing industry. Therefore, the imbalance between "financial countries" and "trading countries" is essentially

[25] Zhang, Youwen, "The Historical Impact of Factor Flows and Global Economic Imbalances," *International Economic Review* 2 (2006): 43–45 (in Chinese).

[26] Wang, Yu, "The Imbalance of the World Economy is a Dynamic Equilibrium," *International Economic Review* 3 (2006): 10–12 (in Chinese).

[27] The so-called "financial country" refers to a country with "financial hegemony." Its domestic currency is a world currency, and its financial market is capable of regulating and controlling global financial resources and formulating corresponding market rules. In a certain sense, modern "financial countries" are hegemonic powers. The term "trading countries" has two meanings: on the one hand, they are countries whose domestic financial markets are closed and underdeveloped, which cannot lead the development of international financial markets and formulate rules; on the other hand, it refers to those who rely on exports to spur economic development and earn foreign currencies. Of course, it can also refer to those countries without "financial hegemony." See Xiao, Li, and Ding Yibing, *Asia's Surpassing-Building an East Asian Monetary System and "Asianizing the RMB."* Beijing: Contemporary China Press, 2006, 14–18 (in Chinese).

a structural problem caused by the long-term labor division. The industrialization of export-oriented East Asian economies is also a result of international labor division. Therefore, it is decided by endogenous factors. Solely changing the international monetary rules or the economic growth models of some countries cannot redress the global economic imbalance. Similarly, even without "financial hegemony," some other countries will gain comparative advantages in financial markets. Global economic imbalances are not related to dollar hegemony or the dominance of the US dollar.[28] After the Second World War, the change in the international labor division determined that there must be a serious economic imbalance between "financial countries" and "trading countries."

In addition, the current international monetary system has helped to alleviate the predicament of the "Triffin Dilemma" to a certain extent, and maintain the "dollar system" of today. An important reason for this is that at the current stage of the international labor division's evolution, the United States has formed a trade-capital circulating mechanism with other countries on the world. The formation of this mechanism relies greatly on the major changes in the international labor division as well as the spontaneous market forces in global industrial restructuring and transmission, market liberalization and financial liberalization. All of the above are prompting the spontaneous flow of official reserves from trade surplus countries to the United States (Figure 1.7).

Emerging market economies, those in East Asia in particular, obtain dollars through export surpluses with the United States. Some of these dollars are then used for importing capital goods, and some others invested in the US Treasuries and then restored as their foreign exchange reserves in the United States. Since the 1990s, about 60% of the US capital account surpluses have come from public sector funds. Except for Japan, almost all of these public assets originate

[28]Xu, Jianwei and Yao Yang, "A New Form of International Division of Labor, Financial Market Development, and Global Imbalances," *World Economy Study* 3 (2010): 3–30 (in Chinese).

Figure 1.7. The Worldwide Credit Revolving System with US Dollar as the Center

from developing countries, mainly East Asian emerging market countries. As a result, East Asian countries not only rely heavily on the US commodity market, but also on the "dollar system" — the more they want to maintain their exports to the United States, the more they strive to peg their currencies to the US dollar. Whereas the more they wish to maintain the peg to the dollar, the more US dollar-dominated exchange reserves they should keep. As a result, the external funds attracted by the United States are constantly increasing, which not only helps to solve the current account deficits but also to gain capital surpluses available for export. With the attraction of high returns on assets in East Asian countries and regions, a considerable part of the exported capital has flowed back to these countries and regions. This part of capital finally becomes investment in the United States in the form of foreign exchange reserves of these countries. In this way, the scale of the US dollar credit circulation system continuously expands worldwide, promoting the large-scale and frequent fund flows. On the one hand, the United States provides an ever-expanding commodity export market, and on the other hand, it provides increasing financial assets. This works to maintain the US dollar's stability and the balance of its relative supply and demand on the international market, solving the "Triffin Dilemma" to some extent. The global economic imbalance is long term and sustainable because it is supported by the trade-capital circulation between the United States and East Asia. China plays a key role as the intermediary for capital circulation as well as the site for final polymerization. In the short term, due to the difficulty to change countries' investment and saving preferences, the transfer of private capital from developed countries to surplus countries and the existence of the "dollar system," global economic imbalances can be maintained without serious disruptive consequences. Thus, there shall not only be relevant policy adjustments made between China and the United States, multilateral negotiations and coordination in the global trade and finance are also obligatory.[29]

Therefore, judging from the global economic cycle, the current international labor division determines the basic characteristics of the international monetary system. The differences between "financial countries" and "trading countries" determine their status and role in the system. The system has an impetus to increase, but does not directly result in, the global economic imbalance. It is difficult to solve the global imbalance by totally repudiating or overthrowing the current international monetary system. In a sense, it can be fair to classify the current global economic imbalance as an essential structural problem, which cannot be solved completely by simply adjusting the order of the international monetary system.

1.1.3 *The Relationship between the Current International Monetary System and the Global Financial Crisis*

There is much debate among scholars about the relationship between the current international monetary system and the global financial crisis. Some scholars believe that the root causes of the crisis are the problems existing in the international monetary system, that is, the oversupply and unrestrained status of the US dollar, making the current "dollar system" difficult to sustain. Correspondingly, China's strategic response should be to take this historic opportunity to have

[29] Xiao, Li, and Ding Yibing, "Global Economic Imbalances at Present and the Role of China," *Journal of Jilin University Social Sciences* 1 (2007): 17–26 (in Chinese).

a greater say in, and promote the adjustment and reform of, the international monetary system and the re-establishment of the international economic order.[30] We agree on this view that the fundamental reason for the outbreak of the crisis lies in the fact that, with highly advanced technologies, we have neglected supervision that is necessary of the financial sector which is using new financial derivatives to generate huge profits, or in other words, related innovation in the system fails to catch up with that of technology. The financial innovation represented by financial derivatives is overdeveloped, whereas risk management and measurement capabilities fail to keep up with it and the market-based credit intermediaries. This has made the financial derivatives market go out of control, and regulatory systems have been impacted.[31] Consequently, imprudent operations and fraudulent activities are hard to detect as are the loopholes in the financial supervisory system. This has indulged the "shadow banking" system and the hyper-expansion of its financial leverage ratio outside the traditional commercial banking system, resulting in a financial system extremely vulnerable to falling prices.[32] The current international monetary system is not a direct cause of the global financial crisis, but it does have indirect effects on global liquidity. Therefore, the corresponding countermeasures should be taken to strengthen national and global financial supervision and institutional innovation, and to cooperate globally.[33]

[30] Xia, Bin, "China's Opportunities in the Global Economic Recession," *New Finance* 1 (2009): 18–20 (in Chinese); Wu, Guihua, "American Financial Crisis and the International Monetary System," *Jiangxi Social Sciences* 5 (2009): 90–96 (in Chinese).

[31] Maskin, Eric S., "Mechanism Design: How to Implement Social Goals," *The American Economic Review* 98, no. 3 (June 2008): 567–576.

[32] Zheng, Liansheng, "Shadow Banking System: Development, Connotation and Prospect," International Financial Research Center of the Institute of World Economics and Politics of the Chinese Academy of Social Sciences, *Policy Brief No.* 09035 (18 May 2009) (in Chinese).

[33] Xiao, Li, and Fu Jinghui, "The Reform of the International Monetary System at the Current Stage: East Asia's Dilemmas and Strategies," *Forum of World Economics & Politics* 4 (2010): 62–75 (in Chinese).

1.2 The Main Defects of the Current International Monetary System

1.2.1 *Structural Defects of the Current International Monetary System*

As mentioned earlier, while the current international monetary system provides support for world economic growth, it also brings many constraints to the world economy. By examining the framework of the current international monetary system and its operating characteristics, we can further understand its major problems and deficiencies.

To examine the major problems in the international currency system, it is natural to refer to the Bretton Woods system established after World War II. The fundamental feature of this system is the dominance of the US dollar as a reserve currency. The ability of the dollar to become a reserve currency is attributive to the fact that, being linked to gold, the dollar became a universally accepted pricing unit, settlement method and value storage method. The various functions are generated by the country's power in terms of politics, economy and military strength. With the dollar as a reserve currency, and the US. Treasury securities as a reserve asset, the US is able to dominate and utilize global resources at the lowest costs, which in turn strengthens its superpower status. Since countries with non-reserve currencies must accumulate dollar-denominated reserve assets, the United States can obtain Seigniorage from all over the world. Because of the existence of the "Triffin Dilemma," the proliferation of the US dollar has shaken the trust of creditors (the holders of dollar reserve currency) who used the US dollar as a value restoration tool, which eventually led to the collapse of the Bretton Woods system.

After the collapse of the Bretton Woods system, the fluctuations of exchange rates among the US dollar, German mark, yen, pound, etc., became normal. The world economy has withstood a series of crises and events such as the oil shocks, petrodollar recycling, the Latin American debt crisis, the Plaza Accord, the Japanese financial crisis, the Mexican financial crisis, the East Asian financial crisis and the collapse of the US IT bubble. The Jamaican System characterized by floating exchange rates and free capital flow is also called "a system without systems." It seems the system has merely affected the rapid development of the world economy and international trade. Moreover, as foreign investors' pursuit of dollar-denominated assets largely offset the currency's depreciation pressure caused by the US trade deficit, the "Triffin Dilemma" has been alleviated for a while.

However, judging from the basic structural characteristics of the international currency system, the operating mode under the Bretton Woods system (the aforementioned operating mode I) is actually more stable than the current operating mode (operation mode II). In addition to the hard constraints, that the dollar is linked with gold, the dollar supply under operation mode I is actually closely linked to the US economy. The United States has become a supplier and creditor to the world by exporting products and capital. The strong dollar reflects the US's real economy. In particular, the return of the dollar is actually subject to the international supply of US products and services. Therefore, the US domestic economy will be negatively influenced by an oversupply of its currency. A soft constraint can be observed.

In comparison, under the current international monetary system (operation mode II), although the international position of the US dollar is inextricably linked with the country's overall economic strength, it is more closely related to the financial fictitious economy. Since the oversupply of the US dollar can be digested worldwide through financial product channels, the consequences of the depreciation of the US dollar and inflation are shared the world over. Therefore, the result of sharing is the weakening of the internal soft constraint. There is neither an external hard constraint of the gold nor an internal physical economic soft constraint. It can be seen that operation mode II has natural defects and the equilibrium it reaches is unsteady. Former US Treasurer Somerset even called the world economy under this international monetary system a "balance of financial terror." It is reflected that there is a fundamental structural flaw in the current international monetary system.

1.2.2 *The Specific Defects of the Current International Monetary System*

There are a series of specific defects in the current international monetary system, which can be classified into five aspects.

1.2.2.1 *The Asymmetry of the International Monetary System and the Global Economic Circulation*

The international currency system dominated by the US dollar is unequal and asymmetric. It can neither promote the diversification of international reserves, provide a stable international currency with super sovereignty, nor does it automatically adjust international payment imbalances or guarantee a normal international capital flow.[34] Under this system, countries with non-reserve currencies are at a disadvantage in the global economic cycle. On the one hand, these countries are offering their own low-cost resources to the US in order to obtain the necessary international reserves; on the other hand, they have to retain their international reserves by holding dollar-denominated securities, bonds and other assets. The right of use is therefore transferred to the United States, resulting in a situation where "the richest and most capitalized country obtains financing from poor countries by creating an international reserve currency."[35] The diversification of international reserves under the current international monetary system is conducive to alleviating or solving the "Triffin Dilemma," lowering the possibility of a dollar trust crisis under the Bretton Woods system, and maintaining the system's normal operation. However, there is still a new "Triffin Dilemma," that is, the stability of the international currency system depends on the stability of the US dollar, which mainly depends on the country's payment balance. However, the global solvency supply depends on

---

[34]Ba, Shusong and Yang Xianling, "Studying the Future Reform of the International Monetary System from the Perspective of Financial Crisis," *Contemporary Finance* 11 (2009): 51–56 (in Chinese).

[35]Teunissen, J. J., "The International Monetary Crunch: Crisis or Scandal?" *Alternatives: Global, Local, Political* 12, no. 3 (1987): 359–395.

the US payments deficit, and the US's "privilege of seigniorage," which has also been enlarging its current account deficits.[36]

1.2.2.2 *The Failure of Solving the Problem of Greater Volatility of the Exchange Rates in Tripolar Multiple Exchange Rate System*

Under the current floating exchange rate system, the instability of exchange rates among various currencies has increased. The coexistence of multiple exchange rate systems has added to the complexity in the operation of the exchange rate system. Exchange rate fluctuations and the "currency war" have broken out frequently, contributing to international financial speculative activities. The high liquidity of international capital and the global economic integration have in turn generated mutual influences among exchange rates of various countries. The risk of financial crisis has greatly increased.[37] Especially in the framework of the central–peripheral exchange rate system, large countries can often take advantage of small ones. This has caused the conflict of interests to become more tense and complicated between developed and developing countries.[38] By analyzing the exchange rates among the major currencies of the US dollar, the euro and the yen, we have found that exchange rates among these three currencies are also highly volatile, although under certain conditions, fluctuations in exchange rates are conducive for open economies, especially those of developed countries, to pursue autonomic monetary policies and realize automatic adjustment of the external economy. However, large fluctuations in exchange rates between major currencies have impaired the growth of the world economy. Moreover, due to the difficulties in coordinating international exchange rates, capital flows and exchange rate fluctuations

[36]McCauley, R., Unifying Government Bond Markets in East Asia, *BIS Quarterly Review* (December 2003).

[37]Mussa, Michael, Paul Masson, Alexander Swoboda, Esteban Jadresic, Paolo Mauro and Andrew Berg, Exchange Rate Regimes in an Increasingly Integrated World Economy, *IMF Occasional Paper No. 193*, 2000.

[38]Huang, Da, "The Rise of the RMB: Challenges and Opportunities," *Economic Research Journal* 7 (2004): 4–8 (in Chinese).

are often mutually promoted in the context of free capital flows, causing huge financial instability in related countries.

1.2.2.3 *Asymmetry of the Balance of Payment Adjustment Mechanism*

Although the current payments adjustment mechanism is diversified, there are lots of problems about its soundness. Although the payments can be adjusted through multiple channels, these channels have their own defects. For example, the exchange rate adjustment mechanism is limited by the elasticity of export commodities and the side effects of interest rate mechanisms. The competition of commercial banks may loosen the constraints of loans and result in debt accumulation of developing countries. The mutual coordination is difficult to achieve. In particular, the current payments adjustment mechanism is asymmetric. The developed countries represented by the United States have mature financial markets with strong self-recovery capabilities in responding to external shocks, while the imperfect financial systems in emerging market countries such as those in Asia have resulted in limited ability to self-balance. The financial systems in these countries are more fragile. On the other hand, faced with the financial crisis and global economic imbalances, the United States, as a reserve currency issuer, can force other countries to share the costs by expansionary monetary policies. In this context, emerging market countries need to bear more costs of adjustment. In addition to the resources and capital provided by the emerging market countries to the developed countries in the trade and financial cycle, the spillover effect achieved by emerging countries' purchases of international reserves has made part of these funds flow back to these countries by purchasing production facilities and financial assets with private capital in the developed countries.[39] Even if the time value of these funds is not taken into account, inflation and devaluation of the US dollar caused by the deregulation will also cause enormous risks

[39]D'Arista, Jane, "Financial Regulation in a Liberalized Global Environment," In *International Capital Markets: Systems in Transition*, edited by Eatwell, John and Taylor, Lance, 75–76. New York: Oxford University Press, 2002.

and losses to these countries. It can be said that the costs of current payment adjustment are mainly borne by countries with non-reserve currencies.

1.2.2.4 *Loss and Failure of Multinational Financial Supervision*

Although some international financial supervisory organizations and institutions have already proposed some unified standards, international financial supervision is still carried out independently in countries. The globalization of finance and the independent supervision are extremely disproportionate, and will inevitably trigger great contradictions. Over a long period of time, the international financial regulatory system has been adopting the mode "regulatory issues arise — take remedial measures — new regulatory issues arise — take "new remedial measures." This mode brings about a lagging effect of the international financial regulatory framework and at the same time results in the absence or dislocation of major international financial regulatory agencies (FSA, 2009).[40] Existing key institutions in international financial regulatory and coordination systems include the IMF, the World Bank (WB), the Basel Committee on Banking Supervision (BCBS), the Financial Stability Forum (FSF), etc. However, in practice these institutions have failed to effectively perform their supervision functions. Before the outbreak of the Asian financial crisis in the late 1990s, the IMF and the World Bank played insignificant roles in global financial supervision. The IMF only paid attention to the health of its member countries' financial systems according to the fourth article in the negotiations, and the World Bank only supervised financial institutions in some technical assistance projects. These two important international regulatory agencies did not play a central role in financial supervision. The absence or dislocation of the functions has led to the failure of the existing international financial regulatory framework to effectively implement supervision.

[40]Financial Service Authority — FSA, UK., Annual Report. 2009. http://svgfsa.com/fatca-crs-ird-memo-april-22nd-2009/

The global financial crisis triggered by the US subprime mortgage crisis has profoundly exposed defects in the framework and philosophies of the Anglo-Saxon free-market financial supervision system. Zhang pointed out that the major problems existing in the current international financial supervision system include: First, the difficulty for regulatory systems in specific fields to accurately monitor the cross-industry operations of the financial institutions that operate in the mixed industries; second, a supervision system of multiple regulatory agencies may leave a vacuum at the overlap of regulated territory; third, the lack of additional strict and specific supervision for financial institutions with systematical significance, such as Lehman Brothers, Fannie Mae and Freddie Mac, AIG Group, etc.; fourth, the lack of basic information disclosure and supervision for certain types of financial institutions (such as hedge funds); fifth, under the New Basel Accord, the capital adequacy ratio and the method of asset and liability management Value at Risk (VAR), and the accounting method for prices marked to market, all have a considerable degree of pro-cyclicality, which makes it easy to amplify the impact of market fluctuations on the financial institution's balance sheet and earnings; sixth, both the risk management departments and the regulatory agencies of financial institutions have underestimated the systematic damage of the tail risk; seventh, the regulatory authorities have neglected the supervision for off-balance-sheet investment entities or the Structured Investment Vehicles (SIVs), etc.[41]

From the perspective of the global financial system, the biggest flaw in the multinational financial supervision lies in the lack of a systematic cross-border financial supervision system, which in turn leads to the failure of transnational financial supervision. First of all, the financial supervisory authorities of each country are working separately and there are significant differences in the regulatory standards

[41]Zhang, Ming, "International Monetary Reform: Background, Causes, Measures and China's Participation," *International Economic Review* 1 (2010): 114–137 (in Chinese).

and strength. This leaves room for institutional arbitrage of financial institutions; second, there is no such coordination mechanism for transnational financial supervision, leading to the fragmentation of the current global financial regulatory system: the IMF is responsible for monitoring the global macro economy; the BIS is responsible for payment settlement between the central banks and international organizations as well as the information and cooperation among the central banks; the international standard setting bodies such as the Basel Committee are responsible for setting industry operating standards for specific financial institutions such as the capital adequacy ratio for commercial banks; and the financial supervisory departments, for the supervising work in domestic financial markets. Due to the lack of a unified communication platform and a coordination mechanism, it is tough to carry out effective and systemic monitoring for global risks. International coordination for dealing with these risks and across-the-board financial supervision remains weak. The chaotic financial markets in Europe and America since the subprime crisis, have fully revealed the necessity of creating a new global financial supervision system.[42]

1.2.2.5 *Inadequate Representation of International Financial Governance Institutions*

An important flaw in the current international monetary system is the inadequate representation of international financial institutions. Take the establishment of the IMF after the Second World War as an example. This institution, whose main duty is to maintain the operation of the international monetary system, has flaws in the following aspects:

First of all, the quota share allocation system of the IMF member countries is seriously flawed. It has in fact become an institutional basis for the developed countries to obtain primary control of the

[42]Zhang, Ming, "International Monetary Reform: Background, Causes, Measures and China's Participation," *International Economic Review* 1 (2010): 114–137 (in Chinese).

institution. According to the Bretton Woods Agreement, the voting power of the IMF member countries depends mainly on their contributions and the basic voting power. In the current structure of IMF's quota share allocation, the proportions of a few developed countries represented by the United States are too large, leading to an excessive concentration of voting rights. Most developing countries and emerging economies have no power because of low quota shares (see Table 1.3). Prior to the IMF vote reform in 2008, G7 countries' share and voting power accounted for 46% and 44%, respectively; the proportion of China, Russia, Brazil, India, and South Africa (the so-called "BRICS") are 11% and 10%.[43] Although the IMF experienced several rounds of share and voting power reforms after the global financial crisis, the basic pattern in which the developed countries form an absolute monopoly has not changed fundamentally. The US, in particular, is in an intact "dominant" position.[44]

Second, the basic voting power of the IMF member states did not help promote national sovereign equality. For safeguarding the equal status of sovereign states and avoiding deficiencies in governance, IMF member countries have an equal number of basic votes (250). However, from the time of its inception until the global financial crisis in 2008, the weight of the basic votes in the final voting power has continuously decreased (from 11.3% to 2.1%), which makes the basic votes fail to achieve its purpose of equality. In other words, although the majority of developing countries and emerging economies have obtained the same basic votes as the developed countries, they have not gained a fair share in decision-making. Although the IMF decided to triple all countries' capital votes in 2008 (that is, to 750) and

[43] Chen, Tianyang and Tan Yu, "The Dilemma and Countermeasures in IMF's Reform of Quota and Voting Power System," *Studies of International Finance*, no. 8 (2013): 22–32 (in Chinese).

[44] In fact, an important premise for the US to join and lead the international political and economic system after the Second World War is to gain veto power in any of the international systems (institutions) or organizations. In this way, for a long time in the future, the US's absolute control of the various international financial organizations will lose or even vanish.

Table 1.3. Changes in Shares and Voting Rights of G7 and BRICS Countries in Recent Years (Unit: %)

	Quota Shares			Voting Power		
	2008, pre-reforms	2008, post-reforms	2010, post-reforms	2008, pre-reforms	2008, post-reforms	2010, post-reforms
The United States	17.071	17.670	17.398	16.732	16.727	16.470
Japan	6.118	6.556	6.461	6.000	6.225	6.135
Germany	5.978	6.110	5.583	5.863	5.803	5.305
France	4.935	4.505	4.225	4.842	4.286	4.002
United Kingdom	4.935	4.505	4.225	4.842	4.286	4.022
Italy	3.242	3.306	3.159	3.185	3.154	3.015
Canada	2.927	2.672	2.311	2.876	2.554	2.213
China	3.718	3.996	6.390	3.651	3.806	6.068
Russia	2.732	2.494	2.705	2.686	2.386	2.585
India	1.911	2.442	2.749	1.882	2.337	2.627
Brazil	1.395	1.783	2.315	1.377	1.714	2.217
South Africa	0.859	0.784	0.640	0.852	0.770	0.634

Source: Chen, T. and Yu, Y. "The Dilemma and Countermeasures in IMF's Reform of Quota and Voting Power System," *Studies of International Finance*, no. 8 (2013): 22–32 (in Chinese).

increase its weight from 2.1% to 5.5%, the absolute monopolistic voting power of the developed countries remains unchanged. In fact, the 5.5% will have almost no influence in real voting. Some studies have pointed out that even if the proportion of existing basic votes is restored to 11.3% as when the IMF was founded, it is still only a solution that may look good but is actually useless and costly. Because it requires a revision of the IMF agreement, and the proportion of the 24 countries with the biggest voting power in Africa in total has only risen from 1.99% to 2.81%, their basic votes have no real impact. This embarrassing position of the developing countries in the IMF's voting process will likely remain well into the foreseeable future.

Third, the formulas for calculating the contribution of the IMF member countries are unscientific. Since 1944, the IMF has developed a total of six formulas for quota calculation. The first five formulas have been criticized by a large number of developing countries for being complex and not transparent. The sixth formula, which has been currently adopted (see Table 1.4), is thought to be simple and transparent. It also reflects the rising economic status of emerging markets and developing countries. Thus, it is still in use. In the current formulas listed in Table 1.5, four variables are included and shown in shares. They are namely GDP, openness, variability and reserves, with weights of 50%, 30%, 15% and 5%, respectively. The variable GDP is a mix of 60% GDP at market exchange rate and 40% GDP at purchasing power parity. These several variables can reflect the trend of world economic development, but its drawbacks still exist. As an indicator of economic development scale, GDP not only reflects the economic strength and contribution capability of a country but also shows the relative economic status of the country. To some extent, it can reflect the potential needs of funding. It is an ideal comprehensive indicator. And the purchasing power parity is also a scientific method to assess economy scale. Because it can reflect the true value and long-term exchange rate of a certain currency, it is more stable. In contrast, GDP calculated based on the market exchange rate may cause price deviations and fluctuations, underestimating the GDPs of developing countries, and overestimating those of developed countries. The formula thus cannot truly reflect

Table 1.4. Formula of the Quota Share of the IMF Member Countries

Formula	CQS	Y	O	V	R	K
CQS = (0.5 × Y + 0.3 × O + 0.15 × V + 0.05 × R)K	Calculated quota shares	Average GDP of 3 years, blending 60% market and 40% PPP exchange rates	Average sum of current-account income and expenses in 5 years	Fluctuations of the sum of current account income and net capital inflows (standard deviation between the actual value over the past 13 years and average in 3 years)	The average official reserves in 12 months, including foreign exchange, SDR, fund reserve positions and currency gold	Compression factor

Source: Chen, Tianyang, and Yu Tan, "The Dilemma and Countermeasures in IMF's Reform of Quota and Voting Power System," *Studies of International Finance* 8 (2013): 22–32 (in Chinese).

Table 1.5. List of IMF Managing Directors

No.	Dates	Names	Nationality
1	May 1946–June 1951	Camille Gutt	Belgium
2	August 1951–October 1956	Ivar Rooth	Sweden
3	December 1956–May 1963	Per Jacobsson	Sweden
4	September 1963–September 1973	Pierre-Paul Schweitzer	France
5	September 1973–June 1978	Johannes Witteveen	Netherlands
6	June 1978–January 1987	Jacques de Larosiere	France
7	January 1987–February 2000	Michel Camdessus	France
8	May 2000–March 2004	Horst Kohler	Germany
9	March 2004–May 2004	Anne Krueger*	The United States*
10	May 2004–November 2007	Rodrigo Rato	Spain
11	November 2007–May 2011	Strauss Kahn	France
12	June 2011–present	Christine Lagarde	France

Note: *Anne Krueger as IMF's Acting President from March to May 2004.
Source: Collected by the author.

the countries' economic strength. However, in this formula, 60% of GDP is calculated at market exchange rate, which also requires some improvement. The variable openness in the formula may actually drive member countries to subsidize export in order to obtain more IMF quotas, or to increase tariffs on imported goods, which will boost trade protectionism and unfair competition. Those relatively unopened economies that benefit from the stable global economic environment might be ignored, which may adversely influence the world economy. Also, the formula is still not simple and transparent enough. It is difficult for member countries to determine the number of quotas they deserve based on domestic data. What is particularly widely resisted by the developing countries is that the formula excludes factors such as the population, the demand for IMF funds, etc., which they believe should be fully considered.[45]

[45]Chen, Tianyang, and Yu Tan, "The Dilemma and Countermeasures in IMF's Reform of Quota and Voting Power System," *Studies of International Finance* 8 (2013): 22–32 (in Chinese).

Fourth, Europe and the United States have for long forcibly occupied the leadership in the IMF. Traditionally, the presidents of the IMF are appointed by European countries (Table 1.5). In exchange, the presidents of the World Bank are American, and the US has long played the role of vice president in the IMF. In addition, the IMF's Executive Board, which is responsible for making policies and most decisions, is composed of 24 Executive Directors whose appointments are determined by the five IMF countries with the largest shares (the United States, Japan, Germany, France and the United Kingdom). This has caused the developing countries to be underrepresented in the IMF, and thus there is a lack of representativeness of dynamic reality of the world economy in this organization. In the context of the global financial crisis, economic growth in the United States and Europe are facing a recession, and the "BRICS" (India, China, Russia, Brazil and South Africa) representing emerging market countries are rapidly rising. The IMF should provide more voices from the emerging market countries.

Finally, the crisis management capacity is inadequate. At present, assistance provided by the IMF is mainly post-crisis, which only helps to reduce losses at most, but cannot avoid them beforehand. Four historical defects in the IMF's assistance can be observed from examining financial crises: first, financial rescue is not timely and the funds are inadequate; second, aid plans are too rigid and are not made based on the characteristics of specific countries; third, the conditions of the rescue mechanism are harsh, forced and bundled. Countries undergoing crisis sometimes face a worse situation in the prolonged negotiations with the IMF after they seek assistance from it with no other choices. Fourth, the practice of favoring creditors in the crisis has encouraged speculative activities.

1.3 Sustainability of the Current International Monetary System

Given the serious problems existing in the current international monetary system, is it difficult for it to sustain? Are there mature conditions to carry out fundamental and comprehensive reforms of the current system?

To answer these questions, there should be a comprehensive and in-depth analysis of the sustainability of the system which covers the foundation and main influencing factors, as well as the sustainability of its specific components.

1.3.1 *Features and Sustainability of the US Hegemony Structure — A Foundation of the Current International Monetary System*

Given the fact that the formation and development of the global monetary system in the past 500 years is not only an international economic issue but also an issue concerning political economy, especially during modern times, the trends of the international currency are often the result of the changes in the global hegemony. It is necessary for us to conduct an analysis of the hegemonic position of the US dollar as a topic in international political economy.

After the Second World War, the argument that the US hegemony will decline appeared about every 10 years. After the "New Economy" in the 1990s, the "9.11 Terrorist Attack" in 2001, the global financial crisis in 2008–2009 and the rapid rise of the BRICS in recent years, the argument has become popular again. Correspondingly, it has also put forward that the current international monetary system dominated by the US dollar cannot sustain; therefore, a fundamental reform must be carried out on the existing international monetary system. Historically, however, none of the predictions of this decline has become a reality. The United States still maintains its lasting strength around the globe in fields such as military, production, trade, currency and finance, and even in knowledge, ideas and systems.

From the perspective of power structures, the academic community has provided detailed lists of the US's power resources. In particular, Nye put forward the concept of "soft power," noting that the United States not only possesses more power resources than Spain, the Netherlands, France and Britain in history but also stronger

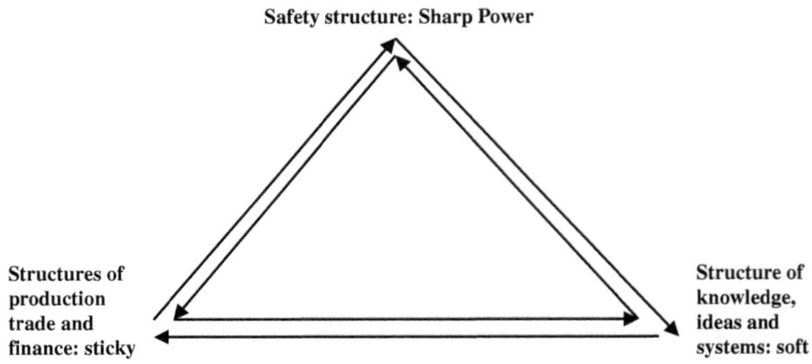

Figure 1.8. The US's Three-Dimensional Power Structure

"soft power."[46] Mead pioneered the concepts of "sharp power" and "sticky power" while referring to "soft power." The first refers to its military power and the second corresponds to its economic policies and systems that attract other countries to rely on it without military coercion or reached consensus.[47] Therefore, based on its multidimensional power structure, the United States can offset the negative effects of a decline or temporary decrease in a certain kind of its power resources by strengthening other power resources and promoting mutual support and reinforcement among all of these resources.

Specifically, the basic framework of the US power structure as shown in Figure 1.8, consists of 3 parts, sharp power, sticky power and soft power, which respectively refer to the security structure, the production-trade-finance structure and the knowledge-ideas-systems structure. All of these three power structures can support, reinforce and strengthen each other.[48] Among them, the "sharp power" means that the United States can provide its allies with the necessary military guarantees apart from its own, and can also effectively deter or attack potential and realistic attackers. This

[46] Nye, J. S., "The Changing Nature of World Power," *Political Science Quarterly* 105, no. 2 (1990): 177–192.

[47] Mead, W. R., "America's Sticky Power," *Foreign Policy* 141 (March 2004): 46–53.

[48] Strange, S., *States and Markets*. London: Pinter Publishers, 1988, 45. However, we believe that Susan Strange placed the "trade structure" in the position of "secondary power structure," which is not suitable for analyzing the US's case.

power originates from the country's strong military power, nuclear competence, extensive overseas military deployments and huge military expenditures. "Sticky power" refers to the US's ability to generate a "gravitational effect" on other countries through its competitive advantages in production, trade and finance. It also refers to its capability of attracting other countries or regions to the international system it leads. This power derives from the US's strength in multinational corporations, technological capability in research and development, the added value in manufacturing, status in international trades especially import, its currency's international status, development of financial markets, etc. "Soft power," or the assimilative capacity, refers to the ability to realize its desired achievements by attraction rather than coercion or purchase.

First of all, in today's global system, the United States holds structural power in security issues. The significance of this power to its hegemony lies in the following aspects: First, it acts as a guarantee for the overseas economic expansion and political infiltration of the US multinational corporations as well as the development of its financial institutions and markets.[49] Second, the military protection of important sea lanes and the military presence in key strategic areas are essential to safeguard US interests of oil and ultimately military hegemony.[50] Third, the security protection to its allies lowers their defense costs and promotes long-term post-war prosperity. Therefore, they are more willing to follow the US in politics and diplomacy. Finally, protection to its allies justifies its coercion of them to adjust, assist or follow it by economic or monetary policies, and thus to obtain safe and guaranteed currency rights,[51] as well as easy entry

[49]Muzaffar, Chandra, "The Empire: What it is and What it Means for all of Us," *Global Research* (30 December 2005), http://www.globalresearch.ca/the-empire-what-it-is-and-what-it-means-for-all-of-us/1681, accessed 3 December 2013.

[50]Statement of James Schlesinger before the Committee on Foreign Relations United States Senate, 16 November 2005, http://planetforlife.com/oilcrisis/oilschlesinger.html, accessed 3 December 2013.

[51]The US has taken this approach toward West Germany. Gavin, Francis J., *Gold, Dollars & Power: The Politics of International Monetary Relations 1958–1971*. Translated by Yan Rong. Beijing: Social Sciences Academic Press, 2011.

of multinationals into labor and commodity markets during the Cold War period.[52]

Second, the "sticky power" of the United States is reflected in its competitive advantages in production, trade and financial structure. "Production structure" can be defined as all the arrangements used in production, who produces items, whom it is produced for, how it is produced and under what conditions it is produced.[53] The sticky power of the United States in this area is generated by three factors: the strength of its multinational corporations, R&D capability and the added value in its manufacturing.

The strength of a US multinational corporation can be measured in three ways: first, its ranking among the top 500 in the world. As of March 2013, there were 132 US multinational corporations that were shortlisted in the world's top 500 companies, outnumbering China (including Hong Kong and Taiwan) at the second place by 37.[54] Second, from the industrial distribution of these shortlisted US multinationals, the competitive advantages of the US multinationals are widely distributed in different industrial sectors compared with those with relatively concentrated industrial distribution. Third, in terms of the status of the US multinationals in the global value chain, in order to save costs and improve profitability, the US multinational corporations tend to keep high value-added activities such as product design and R&D in the country, while outsourcing lower value-added activities such as components production to other developed countries, and those even lower value-added ones such as processing and assembling to developing countries or regions.

[52]In the early post-war period, one important condition for the US to be able to change the previous principles of global multilateralism and non-discrimination, as well as promoting Western European countries, which were then discriminating the US products to sign "the Rome Statute" was that European countries had guaranteed the US companies' that subsidiaries in Europe will enjoy "national treatment." See Gilpin, Robert, *Multinational Corporations and American Hegemony*. Beijing: The Oriental Press, 2011, 86–87 (in Chinese).

[53]Strange, Susan, *States and Markets*. London: Pinter Publishers, 1988, 62.

[54]http://www.fortunechina.com/fortune500/c/2013-07/08/2013G500.htm, accessed on 3 December, 2013.

The technological R&D is the second factor of the US's Sticky Power. In spite of being slightly inferior to Germany and Japan in the field of automobiles, and less competitive than Germany in the field of environmental protection, the United States is at the leading position around the world in fields including agriculture, food production, commercial spacecraft, military spacecraft, chemistry, energy, life sciences, information, communications and instrumentation.[55] This has a close connection with the country's high investment in R&D. The US's R&D expenditure in 2013 was estimated to be the highest in the world, amounting to US$423.7 billion, which is higher than the total of 34 European countries and equivalent to the total of China, Japan and India. As for the specific sources, private enterprises especially multinational ones, are the mainstay of the funds for the US's R&D activities, with a cumulative amount of US$261.7 billion, growing at a rate of 2.3%, and contributing 61.8% of the total.[56]

The strength of multinationals and technological R&D is a guarantee from the US's high-value-added manufacturing industry. From 1970 to 2011, the US's share of value-added manufacturing has been over 20% of the world's total. Japan, at the second place in the long term, continued to fall after its peak of 17.95% in 1991. In 2011, its added value in manufacturing industry dropped to 10.58%. The added value of China's manufacturing surpassed Germany in 2005 and Japan in 2008. In 2011, it accounted for 16.87% of the world's total, 3.65 percentage points less than that of the United States.[57]

[55]Battelle, *2013 Global R&D Funding Forecast* (December 2012), http://www.rdmag.com/sites/rdmag.com/files/GFF2013Final2013_reduced.pdf, accessed on 3 December, 2013.

[56]There are two points worth noting in terms of the implementers of these R&D activities: first, the industry is the main recipient of funds from the federal government and its agencies. The total amount is estimated to reach US$293.6 billion or 69.3% of the total; second, academic institutions are another major bearer of US scientific innovation, and a recipient of funds from all sources just as the Fed-funded R&D center. The funds it received are estimated to reach US$66.6 billion or 15.7% of the total, second only to the industry.

[57]United Nations, "National Accounts Main Aggregates Database," http://unstats.un.org/unsd/snaama/selbasicFast.asp, accessed on 3 December, 2013.

However, due to the gap with the US in terms of science and technology, the realization of high added value can neither compete with that of the US nor are the high-value-added sectors as wide as those of US.

"Trade Structure" refers to the flow, content and terms of international trade.[58] Trade content involves the composition of goods and services traded between the United States and other countries. Trade conditions include mainly the price indexes of the imported and exported goods, which depends on the trade content and the US's monopoly on international trade rules. Specifically, the US engages in intra-industry trade with countries at close development levels under relatively fair conditions, and engages in inter-industry trade with developing countries. Its monopoly on international trading rules can even make its own trade laws soar over the international laws, making the trade conditions favorable to it.

In measuring its "sticky power," we shall look into how much it exports, rather than how much it imports. From 1948 to 2012, the share of US exports to the world kept falling from 21.7% to 8.4%. Over the same period, the US merchandise imports remained relatively stable, dropping slightly from 13.0% to 12.6%.[59] Two phenomena are particularly noteworthy behind all these figures: first, after the Second World War, the low-tariff and zero-tariff policies of the US made it a major market for manufactured goods in Japan and Western Europe, which were undergoing an economic recovery. After other developing countries started industrialization, demand from the United States also made it a strong market for them. To date, the role of the United States as a "market for final consumer goods" has not changed.

Here, we can further understand the "sticky power" of the US by comparing its trade mode with that of the UK. Historically, "current account surplus + capital account deficit" has been an important

[58]Susan Strange, *States and Markets*. London: Pinter Publishers, 1988, 161.

[59]WTO, *International Trade Statistics 2012, World Trade Report 2013: Factors Shaping the Future of World Trade*.

mechanism for maintaining British hegemony. It benefited the short-term prosperity, but was not conducive to the long-term stability of its hegemonic position. The UK's current account surplus in the long term has suppressed the development of the colonial economies, and also caused discontent in latecomer industrialized countries. Deficits of the capital account in the long term have not only contributed to the UK's investment returns but also added to the burden on colonies, further exacerbating the completion between latecomer industrialized countries and Britain in the colonial investment market. In the days of colonial systems, the ultimate solution to these contradictions was the hegemony warfare, which however, has led to tremendous damage to British hegemony. Today, the US hegemony is mainly based on the mode of "current account deficit + capital and financial accounts surplus." In the era of economism,[60] the attraction of such a mechanism for other countries is that by exporting large amounts of goods to the United States, they can realize external demand-oriented development without being constrained by weak domestic demand. They can also make a profit by investing export revenue in the US (through foreign exchange reserves). The strategic benefits of this mechanism for the US are: on the one hand, the deficits in the current account effectively include a large number of peripheral countries or regions in the US-centered international economic system; the return of the US dollar lowers the interest rate, stimulates US economic growth and at the same time drives the external exports by promoting consumption demand. On the other hand, the surplus in capital and financial accounts inject external funds into the financial market, consolidating the hegemony of the US dollar and the position of the US as a world financial center. It also works to intensify the "financial countries vs trading countries" labor division between the United States and periphery countries.

[60]For further information of the concept of "territorialism" and "economism" and their differences, please refer to Xiao, Li, "China–Japan Relations in the Era of Economism," *International Economic Review* 2 (2006): 55–60 (in Chinese).

"Financial structure" can be defined as an umbrella term of all the arrangements that determine the availability of credit and all the factors that influence the currency exchanges.[59] The "sticky power" of the United States stems from two key sources; the international status of its currency, and the development of its financial market. The US dollar is a dominant international currency, which can be reflected from four aspects. First, dollars are the world's major foreign exchange reserve assets. By the second quarter of 2013, the US dollar accounted for 61.9% of the foreign exchange reserves of all countries, wherein the situation was stable. The euro, in second place, weakened after it reach a peak at 2009 (27.7%) and has subsequently fallen to 23.8%. The third-place yen accounted for only 3.8%.[61] Second, the dollar is the main "anchor" currency. Since 1995, the number of countries that linked their local currency with the US dollar has remained stable. In 2010, eight countries adopted the dollar-based or dollar-linked currency board arrangement, 90 countries pegged their currencies to the dollar, and nine countries maintained a managed floating exchange rate system using the US dollar as the reference.[62] Third, the US dollar has long been the main currency for international trade transactions. Until September 2013, the US dollar has been the most used settlement and payment currency in international trade (36.85%), while euro, pound and Japanese yen ranking next on the list account for 36.13%, 8.79% and 2.49%, respectively. The RMB, ranked 12th, accounts for only 0.86%.[63] In the sector of international finance, the US dollar accounted for 87.0%, 85.5%, 52.4%, 60.1% and 56.5% of the currencies used in foreign exchange transactions, foreign exchange derivatives transactions, international bonds,

[61] IMF, *Currency Composition of Official Foreign Exchange Reserves* (COFER) (30 September 2013), http://www.imf.org/external/np/sta/cofer/eng/, accessed on 3 December, 2013.

[62] Goldberg, Linda S., The International Role of the Dollar: Does it Matter if this Changes? Staff Report, Federal Reserve Bank of New York, 2011.

[63] SWIFT, "Will Europe Overtake Asia in RMB Trade Settlement?" https://www.swift.com/news-events/press-releases/will-europe-overtake-asia-rmb-trade-settlement, accessed on 3 December, 2013.

international deposits and international loans. The euro and the yen cannot compete with it.[64] Fourth, the US dollar is a key currency for bailout (worldwide relief). In the early stages of the global financial crisis when the currency swap agreement had not yet expanded, the amount of US dollars available in the international market was less than US$70 billion. By the beginning of 2008, with the expansion of the US dollar swap agreement among the central banks and the surge in the US overseas financing demand, the available liquidity of central banks in various countries reached US$560 billion.[65] In this sense, the Fed has actually played the role of the world central bank, or the "final lender" during the whole process of global financial crisis and afterward.

The US's developed financial markets also added to the attractiveness of the dollar to peripheral countries. The World Bank has compared the development of financial markets in various countries between 2008 and 2010 based on four indicators: depth, access, efficiency and stability. Except for a relatively lower stability (28.8), the US financial market is significantly superior to other financial markets in terms of depth (219.7), degree of access (72.6) and efficiency (342.7).[66] In particular, the development of the US capital market considerably surpassed other countries or regions. As for the stock market, none of these countries can compete with the United States in terms of scale, liquidity and selectivity.By 2012, the turnover of the NYSE Euronext was 3.9 times that of the Tokyo Stock Exchange, 6 times that of the London Stock Exchange and 10.5 times that

---

[64] BIS, *Triennial Central Bank Survey: Foreign Exchange Turnover in April 2013: Preliminary Global Results*, September 2013, www.bis.org/publ/rpfx0 (12 December 2014); BIS, *Statistical Release: OTC Derivatives Statistics at End-December 2012* (May 2013) www.bis.org/publ/otc (12 December 2014); ECB, *The International Role of the Euro*, July 2013, http://www.ecb.europa.eu/pub/pubbydate/2013/html/index.en.html (12 December 2014).

[65] Goldberg, Linda S., "Is the International Role of the Dollar Changing?" *Current Issues in Economics and Finance* 16, (2010): 6.

[66] World Bank, *Global Financial Development Report 2013: Rethinking the Role of the State in Finance*, Washington, DC: International Bank for Reconstruction and Development / World Bank, 2012.

of the German Stock Exchange; the transaction value of the NASDAQ is 2.8 times, 4.5 times and 7.7 times those in the three stock exchanges.[67] From the perspective of the bond market, the US bond issuance volume far exceeds that of other countries. The total bond issuances of major developed countries such as Japan and the UK (US$32.41 trillion) are lower than that of the US (US$35.68 trillion).[68] When it comes to the security holders, the US securities held by foreign investors reached as high as US$13.26 trillion up to June 2012. Among them, long-term securities reached US$12.45 trillion and short-term debt, US$0.81 trillion.[69]

The significance of "sticky power" to the US hegemony has many components: First of all, it promotes the mutual support, reinforcement and strengthening among the production, trade and finance sectors in the structure. To begin with, the US's advantages in its production structure increases its "sticky power" in trade and financial structures. US multinationals will include more countries and resources in its trade by improving its international competence via technological R&D and strengthening its global value chain. Its overseas investment can also trigger greater demand for the dollar, creating conditions for the broader circulation of US dollars.[70] Second, the advantages of the US's trade structure will reinforce its "sticky power" in terms of production and financial structure. Imports from peripheral countries lowered the wages of industrial workers, enabling

[67]World Federation of Exchanges, "2012 WFE Market Highlights," http://www.world-exchanges.org/files/statistics/2012%20WFE%20Market%20Highlights.pdf, 3 December, 2013.

[68]*BIS Quarterly Review*, September 2013, Statistical Annex, Table 3B.

[69]Department of the Treasury, Federal Reserve Bank of New York and Board of Governors of the Federal Reserve System, "Foreign Portfolio Holdings of US Securities, as of 30 June 2012," April 2013, http://www.treasury.gov/resource-center/data-chart-center/tic/Documents/shla2012r.pdf, 3 December 2013.

[70]In Gowan's view, "the United States must build its dominance over its control of the production process in the global economy; otherwise its control of international monetary finance will be very fragile." See Gowan, Peter, *The Global Gamble*, translated by Gu Wei and Jin Fang. Nanjing: Jiangsu People's Publishing House, 2003, 94 (in Chinese).

multinationals to use part of the revenue for R&D. By importing low value-added products from other countries, US multinationals have dragged developing countries into a "trap of comparative advantages." By exporting high value-added products and services, they can invest part of the revenue into the R&D of new technologies and new products, so as to maintain their competitive advantage in key technology areas. The more peripheral countries export to the United States, the more US dollars flow back to its financial market, and thus the stronger the market is, and the more capable the market is in creating credit. Third, the United States' advantage in financial structure has maintained its "sticky power" in the production and trade structures.[71] The international status of the US dollar and the breadth and depth of the US financial market provide a large amount of funds for multinationals' technological R&D and overseas direct investment at low costs. The US government can control the currency's exchange rate, facilitating assistance to the overseas M&A activities and direct investment in other forms. The US can directly pay for foreign trades in dollars. It can even lower the costs of payment by appreciating the US dollar. This is a self-evident attraction of the US market to other countries.

Second, the "sticky power" in the production, trade and financial structures has consolidated the "sharp power" of the United States. Judging from the production structure, the overseas investment return of multinationals provides funds for global military hegemony. Moreover, some large multinationals are engaged in military R&D and production themselves, while high-tech multinationals

[71] After the collapse of the Bretton Woods system, there has been no real equilibrium of exchange rates in the international monetary system. The exchange rates of almost all countries are controlled by the United States. Any monetary policies adopted by the US will influence the value of other currencies no matter these countries' economic status. Therefore, countries are gaming with the US, rather than with the market in terms of exchange rates. The so-called equilibrium of exchange rate in the current international monetary system is only a "sovereign equilibrium of exchange rate" determined by the United States. See Hua, Min, "Global Economic Imbalance: Concepts, Causes and China's Choices," *Journal of Jilin University-Social Sciences Edition* 1 (2007): 15 (in Chinese).

have maintained close cooperation with the US military.[72] From the perspective of trade structure, exports of high value-added military products and services provide financial support for further military development. Also, providing military products and services to its allies on a priority basis can strengthen the ties with those countries. As for the financial structure, international status of the US dollar brings substantial revenues of seigniorage. By virtue of this, "the United States can establish expensive military bases abroad without foreign currency restrictions."[73] The breadth and depth of the US financial market has attracted constant back flows of the US dollars, providing funds for the country's huge military expenditures and supporting the US's global military hegemony.

Third, "sticky power" has raised the US's "soft power" in fields of knowledge, ideas and systems. Among them, the functions of production structure and financial structure are very obvious. The strong financial and technological strength has attracted outstanding talents abroad to the US multinationals and financial institutions. While enjoying good working conditions, these talents have accepted the technical standards and financial rules of the United States, and have also recognized its values of free competition and its open and inclusive cultural atmosphere.

The "soft power" of the United States is mainly embodied in its knowledge, ideas and systems. These are considered by international political economists as important factors affecting the subject's power. Strange[74] stressed that the knowledge structure determines what knowledge is to be discovered, who discovers it, by what means it is discovered, how it is stored and to whom it is imparted. In the knowledge structure, power and authority are given to those who are recognized as having "rights" to obtain appropriate knowledge,

---

[72]Typical cases are the so-called Eight Guardian Warriors of America: Cisco, IBM, Google, Qualcomm, Intel, Apple, Oracle, Microsoft. Except for Qualcomm, these companies are all listed in the Fortune 500.

[73]Gowan, Peter, *The Global Gamble*. Jiangsu: Jiangsu People's Publishing House, 2003, 35 (in Chinese).

[74]Strange, Susan, *States and Markets*. London: Pinter Publishers, 1988, 117.

those who are striving for it, those who are entrusted with knowledge storage and those who control the channels by which knowledge and information are transmitted.[75] Antonio Gramsci stressed the importance of cultures, ideas and ideologies for hegemony. In his opinion, hegemony is built on consent or consensus. Such consent or consensus needs to be established in the cultural life of media and universities and religious institutions.[76] Nai classifies knowledge, culture, ideas, institutions, etc., into the category of "soft power." He believes that they have the ability to assimilate the expectations and behaviors of other countries. If a country can use its resources to justify its power to other countries, it will be less likely to undergo resistance from them.

Judging from the knowledge structure, US universities have always held the most abundant knowledge resources around the world. They not only undertake the tasks of carrying out scientific research and development but also act as producers and disseminators of cutting-edge and mainstream theories. They not only attract scholars by their excellent teaching and experimental facilities but also shape their understanding of human development such as by the concepts of political democracy, economic freedom and market competition. When these ideas are brought back to or even implemented by scholars and policymakers in China, the soft power of the United States, in terms of knowledge, emerges. Typical cases are the "the Third Wave of Democracy"[77] and the economic marketization and financial liberalization from 1970 to 1990.

From the cultural and conceptual perspectives, the United States is a young immigrant country with no local vested interest groups.

---

[75]Huntington, Samuel Phillips, *The Third Wave: Democratization in the Late Twentieth Century*, translated by Liu Junning. Beijing: China Remin University Press, 2013, 2 (in Chinese).
[76]Heywood, Andrew, *Political Ideas and Concepts: An Introduction*. London: Palgrave Macmillan, 1994, 100–101.
[77]Huntington, Samuel Phillips, *The Third Wave: Democratization in the Late Twentieth Century*, translated by Liu Junning. Beijing: China Remin University Press, 2013, 2 (in Chinese).

Therefore, its culture is innately open and tolerable. People of different colors, races and nationalities have strong sense of belonging in the United States. The US is also a country with assimilation power in values and ethics. On the one hand, the American-style market economy encourages free competition and opposes government intervention. This economic style nourishes entrepreneurship and innovation, and makes them the impetuses and source of the country's international competence. On the other hand, the United States values salvation and self-salvation. John Winthrop's sermon "City Upon a Hill,"[78] Thomas Woodrow Wilson's statement "Fourteen Points,"[79] and Franklin Roosevelt's speech "The Four Freedoms,"[80] have all reflected American people's inherent sense of fate and mission, thereby fortifying the United States' stand on the commanding heights of human morality and ethics.

In terms of the institutional structure, similar to British hegemony, the United States also promotes liberal international rules. However, unlike British liberal orders, the US international orders are highly institutionalized. Peripheral countries enjoy trade expansion, economic growth and convenient transactions with international economic and monetary orders set by the United States. Thus, this order is more inclusive, malleable and embedded. For emerging powers, they "are not simply facing a US-dominated order or a Western

[78]Boorstin, Daniel J., *The Americans: The Colonial Experience*, translated by Shi Yinhong *et al.* Shanghai: Shanghai Translation Publishing House, 1997, 5 (in Chinese).

[79]On 8 January, 1918, Wilson proposed the "Fourteen Points" in his address at Congress. These principles construct a post-war world order from aspects including diplomacy (open diplomacy), economics (freedom navigation, elimination of international trade barriers), military (armament reduction), and politics (impartial handling of colonial issues, national self-determination, and the establishment of an international alliance, etc.).

[80]On 6 January 1941, Roosevelt first stated his determination of achieving "the four freedoms of humans" to American people in the State of the Union address at the Congress. The four freedoms are: freedom of speech and expression, freedom of worship, freedom from want and freedom from fear. Since then, Roosevelt has reiterated these four freedoms in his "fireside chats," making them engrained in American people.

system. They are faced with a comprehensive international order shaped by struggle and centuries of innovation. This order is highly developed, expanded, inclusive, institutionalized and deeply embedded in the society and economy of the developed and developing countries. Moreover, in the past half century, this order has successfully attracted emerging powers, and has become more politically and culturally diverse."[81]

In short, the significance of "soft power" for the US hegemony is as follows: First, it can reduce the probability and cost of its "sharp power." Knowledge, cultural ideas and systems can assimilate the thinking and behavior of other countries, making them followers of the US. "When the sense of cultural superiority is successfully silently maintained and recognized, it helps to reduce the country's reliance on military power to maintain the empire's central strength."[82] Second, international rules and institutions of liberalism can effectively maintain the US's "sticky power" in production, trade and finance structures. The rules and regulations made by the IMF, the World Bank and the World Trade Organization (WTO) on financial liberalization, economic development and multilateral trade negotiations all follow those of the United States. Guaranteed by them, US multinationals and financial institutions have gained more access to products, services and capital markets in other countries. US traders also acquire more favorable trade terms and higher profits. And the financial market is also more attractive for foreign capital.

The aforementioned characteristics make the US's hegemonic position sustainable. From the perspective of international political economics at least, the current dollar-led international monetary system based on the US's hegemony will sustain for a considerably long period of time.

---

[81]Ikenberry, John, "The Future of the Liberal World Order: Internationalism after America," *Foreign Affairs* 90, no. 3 (May/June 2011): 56–68.

[82]Brzezinski, Zbigniew Kazimierz, *The Grand Chessboard: American Primacy and Its Geostrategic Imperatives*. Shanghai: People's Publishing House, 2007, 29 (in Chinese).

1.3.2 *The Foundation of the Dollar Hegemony at Present*

Under the traditional Bretton Woods system, the hegemonic position of the US dollar was based on "double-pegging": the US dollar pegged to gold, and other currencies pegged to the US dollar. However, the closing of the "Gold Window" in 1971 and the Smithsonian Institute Agreement on 17–18 December of the same year broke the formal rules of the system: the former freed the dollar from the hard constraints of the "official price of gold," and the latter put an end to the adjustable peg system. In spite of this, the dollar's hegemony has been strengthened rather than weakened. More and more peripheral countries or regions have been involved in the "dollar system." This study found that compared with the basis of the dollar hegemony in 1944–1971 (a strong manufacturing industry and sufficient gold reserves), the foundation for the US dollar's hegemony since the 1970s has undergone profound changes. The financial industry has already become an important basis for the currency's hegemony (or US financial hegemony). Correspondingly, since the 1990s, the United States has gradually adopted a permissive attitude toward its deficit in its balance of payments, which also contributes to the current economic imbalance of the world.

On the whole, currently there are four pillars supporting the "dollar system": the commodity dollar return mechanism, the mechanism to pay foreign debts by domestic currency, the dollar pricing mechanism for petroleum trades and the dollar rescue mechanism for the financial crisis.

1.3.2.1 *The Mechanism of the Back Flow of Commodity Dollars*

Ever since the 1970s, from the 1980s especially, the financial modernization process of the US economy has markedly accelerated. This has created a new international labor division pattern between the US and other countries: the US has become a "financial country" with its advantages in financial industries, while other countries have become "trade countries" with advantages in manufacturing industries (including countries and regions that are advantageous at technology-intensive, capital-intensive and labor-intensive manufacturing industries such as Germany, Japan, Korea and China). In this pattern, these "trade countries" achieve export-oriented economic growth relying on trade surpluses with the United States, while the US as the "financial country" obtains a great amount of resources from the "trade countries" by the deficits of its international balance of payments. Ultimately, "trade countries" have to invest their dollars in the US Treasuries and other financial instrument under the pressure of maintaining their competence in export and the value of their foreign exchange reserve (in US dollars). In this way, the dollars flow back to the US, funding its trade and fiscal deficits. Thus, a circulation of dollars has taken shape between the "financial country" (the US), and many "trade countries."

1.3.2.2 *The Mechanism to Pay Foreign Debts by Domestic Currency*

Traditionally under the Bretton Woods system, the United States paid its debts to other countries in gold. Since Nixon announced the closure of the "Gold Window," the gold that was used by other countries as a tool of value storage and risk avoidance has been replaced by the credit currency of the United States, the US dollar. The US has gained an "exorbitant privilege" over other countries with its mechanism to pay foreign debts by the US dollar, pushing these countries to invest the huge amount of dollars they have accumulated in the US's financial market, which is advanced, secure and of high liquidity. The channels are mainly purchases of domestic securities, especially the US. Treasuries. Up to December 2014, the total US. Treasury securities held by foreign investors amounted to as much as US$6.1537 trillion, of which the official holdings amounted to US$4.1131 trillion. The "dollar system" has already become a "debt standard" based on these Treasury receipts, for the purposes of loans (IOUs).

1.3.2.3 *The Mechanism to Price Oil in Dollars*

The monopoly of pricing oil, the international commodity, is also important in order for the US to maintain the dollar hegemony. After the collapse of the Bretton Woods system, it was virtually impossible for the dollar, disconnected with gold, to hold its position as an international reserve currency. After the Middle East wars and the Oil Crisis in 1973, an "unchangeable agreement" was reached between the US and Saudi Arabia, the world's largest oil producer. This eventually removed the pound's pricing rights in the oil trades of Middle East oil producers. What came after was a dollar pricing mechanism in oil trades, closely linking the dollar with the world's most traded commodity — oil — after its disconnection with gold. In this way, the currency's position as an international reserve currency was sustained, and the US's global hegemonic status has also been strengthened: First of all, by using the dollar for oil production, any country should have abundant dollar reserves if they want to trade for oil. This generates a great demand for dollars among the peripheral countries, bringing about a huge amount of seigniorage revenue for the United States. Second, by using the US dollar in oil pricing, the US can easily manipulate the price trend by monetary policies and exchange rate policies so as to seek benefits for its own manufacturing groups, energy giants or financial interests. Third, a unique mechanism of the "petrodollar" and its circulation will be formed in the world economy. On the one hand, the great number of petrodollars can flow to the dollar market in Europe through its hub, London financial market, strengthening the position of the US dollar as a denominated currency, settlement currency and trading currency in the international financial market. On the other hand, oil exporters can make dollars flow back to the US through financial investment and commodity trades. The back flow of dollars helps to fund the trade deficits and fiscal deficits, supporting the development of the US financial markets.

1.3.2.4 *The Mechanism of Financial Assistance by US Dollar*

In the major post-war international financial crises, the US dollar has almost always been the most frequently used bailout currency. On the one hand, no matter in the traditional Bretton Woods system or in today's "dollar system," the IMF, as a multilateral financial institution, provides relief loans to its crisis-stricken member countries in US dollars. On the other hand, the United States has also provided large-scale bilateral credit to countries at crisis in the local currency, such as in the Latin America's debt crisis in the 1980s, the Mexican financial crisis in 1994–1995 and the Asian financial crisis in 1997–1998. In particular, in the global financial crisis in 2008, the US dollar played a key role in the bailout. During that period, the Fed provided US$240 billion swap arrangements to countries including Australia, Canada, South Korea, Mexico, Singapore, Sweden, Brazil, Denmark, Norway and New Zealand, and without amount limits on the swaps with the Eurozone, Japan, the UK and Switzerland. Though swaps agreements with crisis-stricken countries have been signed by the European Central Bank, the Swiss National Bank, the Central Banks of Scandinavia, the People's Bank of China and the Bank of Japan to offer non-dollar liquidity support, their scale cannot compete with that of the Fed's.

With its currency's hegemonic status in the world, the United States seldom encounters restrictions on the balance of international payments as do other countries. It can put off its adjustment of payment imbalances, and it can transfer the responsibility and pressure for imbalances to other countries. More importantly, the back flow of commodities and petrodollars not only acts as stable sources for funding the US's huge trade deficits and fiscal deficits but also support its military, economic, and financial hegemony: in the military aspect, the US can establish and maintain the huge amount of widely distributed military bases in the long run, without concerns about foreign exchanges. Economically, US multinationals can acquire and merge a great number of foreign companies or make other direct investment without payment restrictions. Financially, the US financial capital can be invested at great amounts into investing quoted securities or acquiring financial assets of other countries without concerns about liquidity. Because of this, the hegemony of the dollar constitutes the main body of the US hegemonic structure, and it is the core of the US national interests. Any country or region that may threaten or challenge this core interest shall definitely face constraints, suppression or attacks from the United States.

1.3.3 *The Sustainability of Specific Mechanisms of the Current International Monetary System*

1.3.3.1 *The Sustainability of Global Economic Imbalances*

As mentioned earlier, the root cause for the "dollar system" to have arisen and been maintained over time is the international labor division between the United States and other countries: one with comparative advantage in financial industries and the other in manufacturing industries. One feature of such a division pattern shown in the balance of payments is global economic imbalances.

Since the formation of the Bretton Woods system, trade between the United States and other countries has been the basis of the world economy. The first-generation Bretton Woods system was led by the US–European trade (1950–1960); the second-generation, by the US–Japan trade and trades of "Four Asian Tigers" (1970–1980); the third-generation Bretton Woods system, by the US–China trade (since the 1990s). It seems that it is the trade between these countries that supports this system, but in fact, what acts as a foundation for the system is the trade–investment circulation between the US and Asia, the trade of which is centered on China's export processing trade.

It is a country's import scale, rather than the export scale, that determines the country's power in formulating global economic rules. Even during the process of financial crises, the United States still holds surpluses, the size of which is far bigger than those of the European Union. Japan and China, however, are faced with deficits. On the one hand, the United States provides dollar liquidity to the world by purchasing commodities. On the other hand, it achieves the back flow of the dollar through issuing financial products. The US seizes the initiative in the global economy by its demand for commodities. It influences the formulation of the global economic rules. Maintaining a trade surplus with the United States in the short term is a path for the "trade countries" to follow. Artificially eliminating this imbalance may do harm to the world economic growth.

The innovation in the US financial market drives its consumption growth, and also maintains its role as the market of final products. Over the past 10 years, the growth of US financial assets far exceeds that of savings. The net foreign debts of the US can also fund its deficits in current accounts. Consider that the foreign debts of the US are mainly in the form of equity, the yield of which reaches nearly 9%, while its foreign liabilities are mainly in the form of debts, the cost of which is only 1%. Some scholars have pointed out that if this situation continues, by 2017 the US will achieve a balance between foreign assets and liabilities.[83]

Specifically, after World War II, the US trade accounts and current accounts for goods and services have maintained surpluses. Nevertheless, in 1971, they showed a first deficit after the war. By 2011, the trade deficit of US goods and service reached US$559.88 billion, accounting for 3.7% of its GDP of that year. The deficit in current accounts needs to be funded by surpluses in the financial accounts, which is often generated by increases in foreign liabilities. The constantly increasing deficit in the US's trade deficit directly resulted in accumulation of its net foreign liabilities. By 2011, its net foreign liabilities reached US$2,473,599 billion, nearly 26.7% of the GDP. The foreign liabilities of the US influence the future of the "dollar system." Since the "dollar system" established after the dollar's disconnection with gold after 1971 was based on the country's national credit, the way the US makes use of the dollar hegemony to maintain domestic consumption by debts and repay old debts with new debts

[83] Takeshi, Masaharu and Zhang Hu, "The Sustainability of US Foreign Liabilities and the Future of the International Monetary System," *International Economic Review* 4, (2011): 84–102.

after the outbreak of the global financial crisis has been increasingly doubted and heckled. The international community has paid more attention to the sustainability of the US foreign debts. Once these debts are no longer sustainable, the international position of the US dollar will be greatly impaired. And the study found that the United States' foreign liabilities are still somewhat sustainable.

First, the trade is no longer the only channel to adjust foreign liabilities. With the dramatic increase in the depth and breadth of the international financial market, the sizes of foreign assets or liabilities of many countries have increased dramatically. The change in the value of international investment positions increasingly influences a country's external wealth. An important means to adjust the United States' foreign liabilities stock is to change the assets prices and the exchange rate of the dollar, which is the so-called the "valuation effect." With the increase in the amount of global investment positions, the "valuation effect" has a greater impact on the value of a country's foreign assets and liabilities.

Overall, only to analyze the US's net foreign liabilities through trade accounts can often lead to permissive findings that actually have already been proved to be true. The United States has not undergone drastic adjustments due to huge foreign liabilities. In the rapidly developing global financial markets, the adjustment of countries' external wealth has become more diversified. Research on the adjustment of the US's foreign liabilities stock has given optimistic conclusions and expectations.

Research on the adjustment of the US's foreign liabilities stock flourished during the 2008 global economic crisis from the mid-2000s to 2008. In this period, the net foreign liabilities of the United States kept growing, but drastic adjustments that many scholars had previously anticipated did not appear. Therefore, a new research perspective to study the sustainability of the US foreign liabilities from the changes in value of the US international investment positions and investment returns has merged.

With the increases in the amount of global international investment positions, the so-called "valuation effect," which refers to change the value of foreign assets and liabilities by adjusting asset prices and dollar exchange rates, has generated an increasing influence on countries. Its significance is no less than that of the current account.[84]

Among the studies on the change in the US international investment position stock, most claim that there is a difference in the return rates of the US's foreign assets and liabilities (hereinafter referred to as the foreign asset–liability return gap). Therefore, even when the United States holds net liabilities, it can still make a profit from it. Masaharu researched the prospects of the United States' foreign liability under three different assumptions.[85] Under the first assumption, if the US economic indicators such as the future trade deficit and economic growth rate keep the average performance during 1989–2009, then the country's pure foreign debt will disappear in 2017. The second assumption shrinks the foreign asset–liability return difference to 3%, and it shows that a balance between assets and liabilities will appear in 2030. Under the third assumption, when the foreign asset–liability return difference disappears, the adjustment for the US's foreign liabilities will be very difficult. Compared with the third, the first and second assumptions were held to be more likely to happen by the author.[86] The United States' foreign debt has a low cost, so it can afford a net debt for a certain period. In the future, the return of US foreign assets will still be higher than that of those held by foreign investors; thus, we can call the US a "shrewd capitalist," not a "sharecropper."[87] Compared with the traditional analysis of trade channels, Gourinchas and Rey pioneered a model of external

---

[84] Lane, Phillip and Milesi-Ferretti, Gian Maria, "The External Wealth of Nations Mark II: Revised and Extended Estimates of Foreign Assets and Liabilities, 1970–2004," *Journal of International Economics* 73 (2007): 223–250.

[85] Takeshi, Masaharu and Zhang Hu, "The Sustainability of US Foreign Liabilities and the Future of the International Monetary System," *International Economic Review* 4, (2011): 84–102.

[86] *Ibid.*

[87] Kitchen, J., "Sharecroppers or Shrewd Capitalists? Projections of the US Current Account International Income Flows, and Net International Debt," *Review of International Economics* 5 (2007): 1036–1061.

imbalance. It assists a comprehensive analysis of trade channels and valuation channels under intertemporal constraints.[88] The formula is as follows:

$$nxa_{t+1} \approx \frac{1}{\rho} nxa_t + r_{t+1} + \Delta nx_{t+1}.$$

In this formula, nxa measures the overall status of international investment positions. It is a variable that includes import, export, foreign assets and foreign liabilities. ρ is a long-term ratio between trade channels and the amount of international investment positions:

$$\rho = 1 + \frac{\bar{X} - \bar{M}}{\bar{A} - \bar{L}}.$$

Δnx_{t+1} represents the increase in net import in the short run. r_{t+1} is the return rate of net foreign assets. In this equation, nxa increases as export and foreign assets amount grow, and decreases as import and foreign liabilities rise. The significance of this model is that a higher return on net foreign assets will drive up nxa, alleviating external imbalances. Therefore, with intertemporal constraints, the US can redress external imbalances by filling up its trade deficit, or by increasing the rate of return of foreign assets through a valuation effect. On this basis, a calculation with VAR equation, the regression equation concluded that 27% of the US's periodic external imbalances could be erased by the valuation effect. The contribution of the study by Gourinchas and Rey is: first, it redefined the external imbalance and claimed the external imbalances should not be measured solely by current accounts, but should also take into account the foreign assets and liabilities; second, it expanded the channels to adjust external imbalance from trade to valuation.[89]

Experience has shown that many factors may contribute to the foreign asset–liability return difference.

---

[88] Gourinchas, P.-O. and Rey, H., "International Financial Adjustment," *Journal of Political Economy* 4 (2007a): 665–703.

[89] *Ibid.*

As early as the 1960s, some scholars discovered that the US can benefit from the special position of the dollar. As the center of the international financial system, the US acts as a "world bank." Therefore, it can lend medium and long-term assets to other countries, and borrow short-term assets. The US government can acquire a kind of liquid discount by providing this international currency as well as pay less in the international bond market (Kindleberger, 1976; Despres *et al.*, 1966).[90] In this way the US makes extra benefits by providing liquidity to the world, a method that has strengthened over time, especially after the collapse of the Bretton Woods system together with the fixed exchange rate system (Portes and Rey, 1998).[91] The study by Gourinchas *et al.* (2010) further outlined the "exorbitant privilege" of the US as the central country in the international monetary system, which is, a return on the foreign assets higher than the costs of foreign liabilities.[92] However, they also pointed out that the US has borne an exorbitant duty while enjoying this privilege. It exported a great amount of capital during the global financial crisis in 2007–2009, which protected the world economy to a certain extent.[93]

Exchange rate changes are integral in the valuation effect. With the increase in the amount of foreign assets and liabilities, small changes in exchange rates can lead to massive transfer of transnational assets.[94] Tille attributed the debt surge in 1999–2001 to the appreciation of the US dollar, which is roughly 1/3 of the new debt.[95]

---

[90] Kindleberger, Charles P., "Lessons of Floating Exchange Rates," *Carnegie-Rochester Conference Series on Public Policy* 3, no. 1 (February 1976): 51–77.

[91] Despres, E., Kindleberger, C.P., and Salant, W.S. (1966). "The Dollar and World Liquidity: A Minority View", *The Economist*, 526–529.

[92] Gourinchas, P.-O.; Rey, H. and Govillot, N., "Exorbitant Privilege and Exorbitant Duty," *IMES Discussion Paper Series* 2010-E-20, 2010.

[93] *Ibid.*

[94] Gourinchas, P.-O., "Valuation Effects and External Adjustment: A Review, in Kevin Cowan," *Series on Central Banking, Analysis and Economic Policy*, edited by Sebastian Edwards and Rodrigo Valdes, Vol. X II, 195–236, Banco Central de Chile, 2008.

[95] Tille, C., "The Impact of Exchange Rate Movements on U. S. Foreign Debt. Federal Reserve Bank of New York," *Current Issues in Economics and Finance* 1, no. 9 (2003): 1–7.

In his opinion, since the valuation effect is so strong, there is no need to worry about debt as it will decrease when the dollar starts to depreciate.[96] Then, in 2005, he further studied the impact of changes in the dollar's exchange rate on the US's foreign liabilities. First, Tille resolved the US's foreign assets and liabilities from their denominating currencies. It was found that a half of foreign assets held by American investors were denominated in the US dollars, a small part in Asian currencies. Therefore, the dollar's depreciation against the euro will generate a huge valuation effect. On this basis, he used a general equilibrium model of open economics to study the impact of changes in exchange rates on welfare in the valuation effect. The results show that changes in the exchange rates will cause changes in the value of the United States' foreign assets and liabilities, and the welfare effects that it brings will even outweigh the effects in the current account. If we relax the assumption of price rigidity, the valuation effect caused by a depreciation of the dollar will bring even greater benefits. However, this study also has its defects: First, the investor's currency proportion in its international asset portfolio is predetermined, while in practice how investors allocate currencies in their portfolios requires further study; second, holding assets denominated in foreign currencies is risky, but lacked close scrutiny in this study.[97] Obstfeld and Rogoff also established a model of the United States, Europe, and Asia. They analyzed the valuation effect brought about by changes in exchange rates on the U.S.'s foreign liabilities.[98] They believe that the devaluation of the US dollar has little effect on improving international investment positions.[99] In this regard, Cavallo and Tille (2006) believe that such a pessimistic conclusion is drawn under the "swift adjustment." If it is a gradual adjustment process, the impact of the dollar's depreciation on foreign liabilities

[96] *Ibid.*

[97] Tille, C., Financial Integration and the Wealth Effect of Exchange Rate Fluctuations, *FRBNY Staff Report 2005*, No. 226.

[98] Obstfeld, M. and Rogoff, K., Global Current Account Imbalances and Exchange Rate Adjustment, *Brookings Papers on Economic Activity* 1 (2005): 67–123.

[99] *Ibid.*

will be very large. Cavallo and Tille further considered the valuation effect of European and Asian foreign assets and liabilities, and the results showed greater benefits of the US's valuation effect, which can help the country's adjustment in foreign liabilities.[100] Therefore, as the global financial integration deepens, the United States can increasingly add value to its capital by depreciating its currency. This will alleviate its external imbalance, preventing the hard landing put forward by Obstfeld and Rogoff.[101]

More generally, Lane and Shambaugh (2010a, 2010b) extend the factors that influence the exchange rate of a currency.[102] The changes in a country's net foreign assets can be measured by the following formula:

$$NFA_t - NFA_{t-1} = CA_t + VAL_t.$$

In it, *NFA* is the foreign asset, *CA* represents the current account, and *VAL* is the return on net assets, which can be further denoted as

$$VAL_t = KG_t^A - KG_t^L = kg_t^A A_{t-1} - kg_t^L L_{t-1}.$$

kg_t^A and kg_t^L represent the return rates on foreign assets and liabilities, when transferred to the level of currency, as follows:

$$\frac{\partial VAL_t}{\partial E_t} = \frac{\partial kg_t}{\partial E_t} A_{t-1} - \frac{\partial kg_t^L}{\partial E_t} L_{t-1}.$$

In this equation, E is the exchange rate. This formula indicates that it is necessary to include the pricing currencies of foreign assets

---

[100]Cavallo, M. and Tille, C., Could Capital Gains Smooth a Current Account Rebalancing? *Federal Reserve Bank of New York Staff Reports* No. 237 (2006).

[101]Obstfeld, M. and Rogoff, K., Global Current Account Imbalances and Exchange Rate Adjustment, *Brookings Papers on Economic Activity* 1 (2005): 67–123.

[102]Lane, P. R. and Shambaugh, J. C., "Financial Exchange Rates and International Currency Exposures," *American Economic Review* 1, no. 100 (2010a): 518–540; Lane, P. R. and Shambaugh, J. C., "The Long or Short of It: Determinants of Foreign Currency Exposure in External Balance Sheets," *Journal of International Economics* 1, no. 80 (2010b): 33–44.

and liabilities into the study.[103] To this end, Lane and Shambaugh established a weighted average[104] exchange rate indicator.

$$I_{it}^{A} = I_{it-1}^{A} \times \left(1 + \sum \omega_{ijt}^{A} \times \%\Delta E_{ijt}\right) \quad \omega_{ij}^{A} = \sum_{k=1}^{k=N} \lambda_{it}^{Ak} \times \omega_{ijt}^{Ak},$$

$$I_{it}^{L} = I_{it-1}^{L} \times \left(1 + \sum \omega_{ijt}^{L} \times \%\Delta E_{ij}\right) \quad \omega_{ijt}^{L} = \sum_{k=1}^{k=N} \lambda_{it}^{Lk} \times \omega_{ijt}^{Lk}.$$

The former is the effective exchange rate index of country i's foreign assets. ω_{ijt}^{A} is the currency j's ratio at period t. λ_{it}^{Ak} represents the proportions of stock, foreign direct investment (FDI), equity and foreign exchange reserve in the total foreign assets. E_{ijt} are the nominal exchange rates of countries i and j.

Similarly, the latter represents the effective exchange rate index of foreign liabilities. On this basis, a comprehensive weighted average exchange rate indicator can be calculated, as follows:

$$I_{it}^{F} = I_{it-1}^{F} \times \left(1 + \%\Delta I_{it}^{A} \times \frac{A_{it-1}}{A_{it-1} + L_{it-1}} - \%\Delta I_{it}^{L} \times \frac{L_{it-1}}{A_{it-1} + L_{it-1}}\right).$$

It can be further concluded based on previous equations, as follows:

$$\frac{\partial VAL_t}{\partial E_t} = \left(\omega_{ijt}^{A} \times \frac{A_{it-1}}{A_{it-1} + L_{it-1}} - \omega_{ijt}^{L} \times \frac{L_{it-1}}{A_{it-1} + L_{it-1}}\right) \times (A_{it-1} + L_{it-1}).$$

Thus, an indicator can be calculated as

$$VAL_{it}^{XR} = \%\Delta I_{it}^{F} \times (A_{it-1} + L_{it-1}).$$

[103] Lane, P. R. and Milesi-Ferretti, G. M., "The External Wealth of Nations Mark II," *Journal of International Economics* 2, no. 73 (November 2007a): 223–250. Lane, P. R. and Milesi-Ferretti, G. M., "Europe and Global Imbalances," *Economic Policy* 22, (2007): 519–573.

[104] To facilitate understanding and save space, the derivation process of Lane and Shambaugh (2010a) will be modified slightly and simplified thereinafter.

Changes in the exchange rates will influence the price of international investment position, not only through changing nominal exchange rates but also by altering the ratio of pricing currencies of assets or liabilities. VAL_{it}^{XR} is an indicator of the sensitivity of net international investment position to currency movements.[105] The significance of VAL_{it}^{XR} can be stated in two aspects: first, it gives a clear view of factors that influence the foreign exchange in the valuation effect, and thus helps to better study the impact of the exchange rate on the value of the international investment position. Second, unlike the traditional tools to solely consider the changes in exchange rates, the weighted average exchange rate index can not only reflect changes in exchange rates but also the pricing currency of assets (or liabilities). The currency movements will produce the wealth effect, which cannot be fully reflected by the traditional trade-weighted average exchange rates. The finance-weighted average exchange rate can better reflect the adjustment on international investment position by currency movement. Lane and Shambaugh have created a database of currency combinations in international investment portfolios of 117 countries.[106] They found that the trends of finance-weighted and trade-weighted exchange rates are not consistent. The net foreign-currency positions of many developing countries are negative. Depreciating their local currency will produce a huge negative wealth effect. Although developing countries have been improving their foreign-currency exposure in recent years, the wealth effect brought about by currency movements will make this effect hard to reverse in the short term. The developed countries will still benefit from the currency movements.[107] Lane and Shambaugh (2010b) further factor

[105]It appears to be influenced by exchange rates, but it is in fact under the impact of the currency portfolio of international investment positions. When VAL_{it}^{XR} rises, the sensitivity of net international investment position to exchange rate changes will increase.

[106]Lane, P. R. and Shambaugh, J. C., "Financial Exchange Rates and International Currency Exposures," *American Economic Review* 1, no. 100 (2010a): 518–540.

[107]*Ibid.*

the foreign-currency exposure based on $FX_{it}^{AGG} = \omega_{it}^{A} \times \frac{A_{it}}{A_{it}+L_{it}} - \omega_{it}^{L} \times \frac{L_{it}}{A_{it}+L_{it}}$,[108] the formula proposed by them (2010a)[109]:

$$FX_{it}^{AGG} = \left(\frac{NFA_{it}}{A_{it}+L_{it}}\right) + \left(\omega_{itDC}^{L} \times \left(\frac{L_{it}}{A_{it}+L_{it}}\right)\right.$$
$$\left. -\omega_{itDC}^{A} \times \left(\frac{A_{it}}{A_{it}+L_{it}}\right)\right]$$

$$FX_{it}^{AGG} = \left[\left(\frac{A_{NRit}-L_{it}}{A_{it}+L_{it}}\right) + \frac{FXR_{it}}{A_{it}+L_{it}}\right] + \left[\left(\frac{PEQL_{it}+FDIL_{it}}{A_{it}+L_{it}}\right)\right.$$
$$\left. + \left(\frac{DEBTI_{it}^{DC}}{A_{it}+L_{it}}\right) - \left(\frac{A_{NRit}^{DC}}{A_{it}+L_{it}}\right)\right]$$

$$FX_{it}^{AGG} = \alpha + \phi_t + \gamma \times COV(Y_{it}, E_{it}) - \varphi_H \times VOL(\pi_{it})$$
$$-\varphi_F \times VOL(E_{it}) + \rho \times OPEN_{it}$$
$$+\beta \times VOL(Y_{it}) - \sigma \times F_{it} + \varepsilon_{it}.$$

The former equation shows the two parts of foreign-currency exposure, one is the position of net international investment, and the other is the liability reduction right in local currency.[110] The former equation can be further decomposed to the latter, in which, $A_{NRit} - L_{it}$ is the net non-reserve assets, FXR is the foreign exchange reserve. $PEQLFDIL, DEBIT^{DC}, A_{NR}^{DC}$ are stock portfolio, FDI, foreign liabilities in the narrow sense in local currency, foreign assets in local currency. When related with some major economic variables, the

[108]For the meaning of ω, please refer to the formula of the finance-weighted foreign exchange indicator.

[109]Lane, P. R. and Shambaugh, J. C., "The Long or Short of It: Determinants of Foreign Currency Exposure in External Balance Sheets," *Journal of International Economics* 1, no. 80 (2010b): 33–44; Lane, P. R. and Shambaugh, J. C., "Financial Exchange Rates and International Currency Exposures," *American Economic Review* 1, no. 100 (2010a): 518–540.

[110]Lane, P. R. and Shambaugh, J. C., "The Long or Short of It: Determinants of Foreign Currency Exposure in External Balance Sheets," *Journal of International Economics* 1, no. 80 (2010b): 33–44. In extreme cases, when both foreign assets and liabilities are denominated in foreign currencies, the foreign-currency exposure is $\frac{NFA_{it}}{A_{it}+L_{it}}$.

equation can be expressed as

$$\begin{aligned} FX_{it}^{AGG} &= \alpha + \phi_t + \gamma \times COV(Y_{it}, E_{it}) - \varphi_H \times VOL(\pi_{it}) \\ &\quad -\varphi_F \times VOL(E_{it}) + \rho \times OPEN_{it} \\ &\quad +\beta \times VOL(Y_{it}) - \sigma \times F_{it} + \varepsilon_{it}. \end{aligned}$$

Among them, Y_{it} is the economic growth rate of country i at period t, E_i is the nominal exchange rate, π_i is the domestic inflation rate, $OPEN_i$ is the openness of trade and F_{it} measures the capability to borrow in local currency and acquire assets in foreign currency.

Lane and Shambaugh concluded that net foreign asset $(\frac{NFA_{it}}{A_{it}+L_{it}})$ is the most critical factor for foreign-currency exposure. In the asset portfolio, the stock asset in foreign liabilities ($PEQL$) has the largest influence on the foreign-currency exposure.[111] While the scope of the currency combinations' influence is rather limited, because the countries that are able to borrow in their own currencies tend to have much foreign assets denominated in local currencies. The debts and assets offset each other and narrow the foreign-currency exposure. From a cross-section view, countries that are wealthier (higher in Y) and more open (higher in $OPEN$) often have more foreign-currency positions, which make them prone to benefit from a currency depreciation. An implication of Lane and Shambaugh's study to the research of the sustainability of the US foreign liabilities is that the US can benefit from a depreciation, but mainly based on the currency combinations in its investment portfolio.[112] Further, the currency combination is only part of the foreign-currency exposure, which is composed and determined by more factors. Therefore, what

[111]Lane, P. R. and Shambaugh, J. C., "The Long or Short of It: Determinants of Foreign Currency Exposure in External Balance Sheets," *Journal of International Economics* 1, no. 80 (2010b).

[112]Lane, P. R. and Shambaugh, J. C., "Financial Exchange Rates and International Currency Exposures," *American Economic Review* 1, no. 100 (2010a): 518–540; Lane, P. R. and Shambaugh, J. C., "The Long or Short of It: Determinants of Foreign Currency Exposure in External Balance Sheets," *Journal of International Economics* 1, no. 80 (2010b): 33–44.

Lane and Shambaugh have done is to further expand factors that influence the exchange rates in the valuation effect.[113] The general conclusion they obtained actually proves and recognizes the US's advantages in international investment.

However, the foreign asset–liability return difference cannot be achieved solely by the US dollar's international status and altering foreign exchanges. Gourinchas and Rey attempted to examine the "exorbitant privilege" of the United States in the long run.[114] They believe that theoretically a country's accumulation of current account deficits should be equal to the reduction in its international investment positions at that period. However, the decrease in the US's international investment positions is much smaller than the accumulation of its current account deficits. The gap in between is called the "valuation component." The scholars first factored the return rate on external assets (the interest rate of liabilities) in the model, as follows:

$$r^a = \mu^{ae} r^{ae} + \mu^{ad} r^{ad} + \mu^{af} r^{af} + \mu^{ao} r^{ao}$$
$$r^l = \mu^{le} r^{le} + \mu^{ld} r^{ld} + \mu^{lf} r^{lf} + \mu^{lo} r^{lo}.$$

In it, μ^{ae}, μ^{af}, μ^{ao} and μ^{ad}, respectively, represent the weight of stocks, FDI, other foreign assets and the assets in the form of foreign liabilities in the asset portfolio. r represents the return rate.[115] After recognizing the return difference between the US's foreign assets and liabilities, the scholars further factor the expectation as

$$\begin{aligned} E(r^a - r^l) &= E[\bar{\mu}^o(r^{ao} - r^{io})] + E[\bar{\mu}^d(r^{ad} - r^{ld})] + E[\bar{\mu}^e(r^{ae} - r^{le})] \\ &\quad + E[\bar{\mu}^f(r^{af} - r^{lf})] + E[(\mu^{ad} - \mu^{ld})(\bar{r}^d - \bar{r}^o)] \\ &\quad + E[(\mu^{ae} - \mu^{le})(\overline{r^e} - \bar{r}^o)] + E[(\mu^{af} - \mu^{lf})(\bar{r}^f - \bar{r}^o)]. \end{aligned}$$

Among them, the first four factors are "return effect," which indicate whether the US investors can gain higher return from its

[113] *Ibid.*

[114] Gourinchas, Pierre-Olivier, and Helene Rey, "International Financial Adjustment," *Journal of Political Economy* 115, no. 4 (August 2007): 665–703.

[115] The same for foreign liabilities.

foreign investment than their foreign counterpart's gain from their investment in the US; the last three refer to the "composition effect," showing the US's foreign asset-liability return difference generated by the disparity in asset portfolios. The results show that the "return effect" is the major cause of the foreign asset-liability return difference. Though the impact brought by the "composition effect" is relatively small, it grows as time passes by. The decomposition they make implies that in the adjustment of the US's foreign liabilities, besides the benefits brought about by a currency depreciation based on the dollar's status, the structural advantages of the country's international investment position and the technical advantages in its investment also contribute to the expansion of its foreign liabilities. Take bonds as an example, the US bond yields are lower than those of foreign bonds held by the US investors.[116]

Today, in the deepening global financial integration, countries have different developments in financial industries. Mendoza *et al.* established a dynamic stochastic general equilibrium model with the development level as a factor in order to investigate the relationship between a country's net foreign assets amount and its financial industry development.[117] Although countries with higher financial development levels tend to have greater foreign liabilities, they can still gain high returns from those foreign assets, most of which are risky and highly profitable. Therefore, for the United States with its financial market highly developed, it can sustain high foreign liabilities without triggering a global financial crisis. From a microscopic perspective, Hung and Mascaro attributed the US's high returns on overseas investments to FDI.[118] They concluded three major reasons

---

[116]Habib, M. M., Excess returns on Net Foreign Assets -the Exorbitant Privilege from a Global Perspective. *Working Paper Series* 1158, European Central Bank, 2010.
[117]Mendoza, E. G., Quadrini, V. and Rios-Rull, J. V., "Financial Integration, Financial Development and Global Imbalances," *Journal of Political Economy* 3, no. 117 (2009): 371–416.
[118]Hung, J. H. and Mascaro, A., "Return on Cross-border Investment: Why Does U.S. Investment Abroad Do Better?" *Economic and Budget Issue Brief* 17, (2004): 32–41.

for the returns: first, with a longer history in FDI, the US companies have many first-mover advantages; second, the FDI of the US is often of higher risks, and thus also of higher returns[119]; third, it is not rare for the US companies to exaggerate the return they gain from direct foreign investment, while companies in other countries often conceal the return on investment in the US. Taking the stock market as an example, foreign investors in the United States often rush into the market when it is high, which leads to a position that may be relatively low when the market goes lower, causing a loss or low gain.[120]

The aforementioned analysis shows that as a "financial country," the United States can effectively adjust its international investment position by the dollar's international status, the breadth and depth of its developed financial markets and relatively high investing skills, so as to improve the sustainability of its foreign liabilities.

Compared with other methods, those adopted by the US in adjusting its foreign liabilities through foreign exchange rates are relatively more controllable and feasible. In fact, since the early 1970s, the US dollar has been depreciated against the currencies of the world's major countries, but it has not worked to reverse and has deteriorated the imbalances in the country's trade. It is, therefore, fair to state the depreciation of the dollar is not done for improving its trades or current accounts, but for the transfer of wealth by revaluating the dollar based on its hegemony status. In the next 10 years, it is very likely for the US to adjust its international investment positions by moderately depreciating the US dollar. Otherwise, it will be facing more serious foreign liability problems. Therefore, after the collapse of the Bretton Woods system, a floating exchange rate system will help it to adjust the foreign liabilities and also make the current

[119] *Ibid.*

[120] Curcuru, S. E., Dvorak, T. and Warnock, F. E, "Decomposing the U.S. External Returns Differential," *Journal of International Economics* 80, no. 1 (2010): 129–143.

US dollar-led international currency system more flexible. By this it is clear that:

First, the "weak dollar" policy (depreciating the US dollar or forcing other major currencies to appreciate) will remain the core in the US's financial strategy for a long period of time in the future. Advantages of the US financial market and its rule-making will still play an active role in promoting the global financial liberalization and encouraging other countries or regions to further open up their financial markets and transfer a huge amount of wealth to the United States. Only in this way can the US keep or improve its foreign liabilities' status, and thus maintain the dollar's as well as the US financial market's hegemony.

Second, the "weak dollar" policy must be controllable. That is, it shall be implemented based on the international community's confidence in the US dollar. It is therefore not certain that the US dollar will appreciate at any period. Both appreciation and depreciation are likely to be adopted to carry out this policy.

Third, because of the reasons mentioned earlier, the rise and fall of the dollar has nothing to do with its status. The depreciation does not indicate a decline or fall of the dollar's position. The dollar hegemony is a result of the development of American politics, economy, society and also a structural choice over the past 200 years. The decline or collapse of its hegemony can also be the result of a series of major international political, economic and military events, or other major countries' development and the changes in their relations with the US. It looks like it will take a long time for the current situation to change. However, the consequences of the "weak dollar" policy are obvious. They are a global liquidity excess, along with an inflation, and financial risk, which will all challenge a country's formulation and implementation of its financial strategies and the international monetary system reform.

In sum, we believe that the global economic imbalance under the "dollar system" can be sustained for quite a long time. It is rather unlikely for the imbalance to cause a major crisis. However, the future frequent financial crises brought about by the "weak dollar" policy will substantially threaten the world economy.

1.3.3.2 *Sustainability of the US Dollar's Position as a Reserve Currency*

The financial crisis causes people to question the dollar system and raises questions about the dollar's position as a key currency. Some scholars believe that the euro will replace the US dollar in the future. For example, Chinn and Frankel believe that even if Britain does not join the Euro-zone, as London gradually becomes an offshore euro trading center, the euro used in foreign exchange markets will exceed the dollar by 2025 when 20% of transactions in the London foreign exchange market are to be made in euros.[121] It also suggests that the future international monetary system will be led by the competition among dollar, euro and RMB, and the internationalization of the RMB may help that currency to replace the dollar.[122]

As for the reform of the international currency system, we believe that although the future of the US dollar remains uncertain, there is no currency that has the strength to surpass the US dollar at present, and the "dollar system" will be sustainable. After the global financial crisis broke out, many scholars believed that the system was unsustainable and strongly advocated a fundamental reform of the current international monetary system. However, we shall make two clarifications: one, what do we need? A reform of the entire international monetary system or just the adjustment of some of its defects; two, if adjustment is what is actually needed, the system must be sustainable for a considerably long time, and efforts should be made by promoting the regional monetary and financial

[121]Chinn, M. D. and Frankel, J. A., "The Euro May over the Next 15 Years Surpass the Dollar as Leading International Currency," *National Bureau of Economic Research Working Paper* No. 13909 (2008).

[122]Huang, Haizhou, "US Dollar and RMB: Where to Go," *International Economic Review*, 34, no. 2 (2010): 7–15 (in Chinese).

cooperation to avoid risks. But, if a drastic and complete reform is to be carried out, we should answer four questions. First, is there a perfect international monetary system? Second, has the dollar really declined? Third, as experience shows that the reform or adjustment often comes with hegemony replacement (or a major change in the international structure), or we shall say that the latter is the premise of the former, then, is it probable for the US hegemony to fall or be replaced during the current period? Last but most importantly, after the crisis, can East Asian economies, as important supporters of the "dollar system," quickly get rid of it?

First of all, there is no perfect international monetary system. Neither the past gold standard nor the current "dollar system" is ideal. Any international economic system that ever existed, including the monetary system, has contradictions and problems. There is no international monetary system that is only beneficial, but not contradictory. The gold standard system centered on the pound sterling, and like the Bretton Woods system and the "dollar system" it was a typical "central–periphery" structure. Comparatively, the current "dollar system" features the globalization of capital flows. Under the gold standard system, the main means of international economic exchanges is international trade. In a limited, or a fragmented, or even blocked market, the competition in trades often leads to "zero-sum" results. Countries benefit from their rivals' losses. This has been one of the key reasons for two World Wars. However, with the liberalization of capital flows, especially financial liberalization after the Second World War, major changes have taken place in the means of international economic exchanges. Under the current "dollar system," the results of competition among countries are often "positive-sum," with the costs and benefits highly correlated. One of the major features of the 2008 global financial crisis was that the major countries and regions in the world had to share the costs and losses. This shows the environment and conditions of hegemony replacement have changed in the economic globalization. These changes may benefit the US's hegemony, especially its "financial hegemony" on the world for a long period.

Second, during and after the several global financial crises since the 1970s, the dollar has remained strong. Since the 1960s, the long-term depreciation trend of the US dollar has become a hotly debated topic. But every time a crisis breaks out, regardless of its cause and home, the dollar remains a "straw" for governments and investors to ensure asset safety and avoid risks. The US dollar has not been weakened but strengthened.[123] This situation has not changed at the birth of the euro. In fact, the damage to the Eurozone has been even greater than that to the US. The dollar's sharp rise during any crisis indicates that at present it remains the leader in the current international monetary system, and the euro is not yet as competitive.

Again, taking into account the US's political, economic, military and cultural strengths of today, despite the so-called "one superpower and several strong countries" pattern having emerged, none of these strong countries has the capacity to replace America to be the "superpower" in the current period. Unlike the previous hegemonic countries Portugal and the Netherlands who grabbed and conquered the colonies, or the British Empire that "developed" its colonies, the US did not become a superpower by warfare, establishment, control and plundering colonies. Instead, its rise was based on a free market system with extremely highly efficient resource allocation. It utilizes and allocates resources of the whole world, driving other countries to rely on it economically and financially. Today, with its developed and open financial market with great breadth and depth, the United States has created a new "central–periphery" structure, namely the international division of labor between "financial countries" and "trade countries." This structure can help it easily formulate monetary policies to reach domestic economic goals, without worrying about the balance of payments and exchange rates. The "trade countries" will sustain most of the pressure of adjustment. Moreover, the US can make use of the monopoly status of the dollar,

[123]Xiao, Li, "The Path Choices for East Asia in Monetary and Financial Cooperation in the Global Financial Crisis," *Northeast Asia Forum* 5 (2009): 3–25 (in Chinese).

the major currency for international transactions, to obtain higher seigniorage income by pushing up inflation or depreciating the dollar. At the same time, the US acts as the world's market to maintain the backflows of the dollars. This not only strengthens its position in international negotiations by adding to other countries' reliance on the dollar but also enables the US to occupy resources, commodities and wealth under an imbalanced economic structure. One might comment that the dollar (or the US) has kidnapped the world by holding countries' export commodities and resources as hostages — they are forced to voluntarily maintain the competitive position of the dollar.[124] Although the dollar system is not widely favored, it is impossible for another currency to replace it as an international currency.[125]

Finally, for a quite long period time in the future, East Asian economies will still rely on the US market. The US's position as the "final product market" for East Asia will not change in the short term. Since the 1990s, despite the rapid growth of the regional trade in East Asia, due to the decentralized production process, most of the products of this region are semi-products, components and capital goods. The markets of final products are still foreign countries and regions such as the United States. The statistics (Table 1.6) show that the US remains the "final product market" of East Asia despite its shares of final products imported from this region having generally declined since 1999. Although Japan's share of the final products exported to most of these also fell, it still holds an advantage over China in the ASEAN. From the absolute amount of final products imported, the gap between China and the US in the proportions of the final products they imported is still noteworthy. It is clear that, with the exception of Singapore, the proportional differences between

[124]Hua, Min, "The Trigger Mechanism of Global Economic Imbalances and China's Choices," *International Economic Review* 2 (2006): 45–49 (in Chinese).
[125]Ronald, I. Mckinnon, *The Unloved Dollar Standard-from Bretton Woods to the Rise of China*. Beijing: China Financial Publishing House, 2013, 1–10 (in Chinese).

Table 1.6. Changes in the Proportions of China, Japan and the United States in the Final Product Exports to East Asian Economies (Unit: %)

Importer	China			Japan			The United States		
Exporter	1999	2003	2008	1999	2003	2008	1999	2003	2008
South Korea	2.63	4.14	5.20	16.59	8.49	4.81	30.29	36.62	22.59
Singapore	3.08	4.57	9.29	11.45	6.61	6.20	16.43	14.37	9.95
Philippines	0.70	1.99	1.07	13.83	11.60	11.83	57.04	47.89	37.31
Thailand	1.43	1.77	2.17	16.73	16.70	11.34	30.97	27.69	17.74
Malaysia	0.59	1.22	2.07	13.18	9.93	6.32	28.25	26.42	17.40
Indonesia	1.47	0.91	1.83	11.62	11.92	7.55	29.97	31.85	31.28
Hong Kong, China	9.53	11.65	12.47	7.16	8.09	6.32	38.21	36.96	28.87

Note: 1. The final product counted here includes only consumer products. The BEC codes: 112, 122, 51, 522, 61, 62, 63. 2. South Korea's data in the year of 2008 are not available. Data of 2007 are therefore listed here.

Source: Compiled from data from UN Commodity Trade Statistics Database.

the two countries' final products imported from the remaining countries have all reached 15%, or even 36% (Philippines). Moreover, since the adjustment of economic structure is expected to take much time and effort, in the short term, there will not be an alternative to the US as the "final products market." Neither Japan nor China is equipped with such capability.

It is noteworthy that the outbreak of the global financial crisis has made East Asian economies more eager than their pre-crisis counterparts in their desire and motivation to drive economic growth by maintaining an export surplus. Experience has shown that export has always been the best path for East Asian economies to restore and stimulate economic growth. No matter what changes have taken place in the US's domestic savings rate and consumption pattern during or after the crisis, the country will still remain the most important market for these economies.

In summary, after any crisis, the operating capacity of the US dollar-centered global credit revolving system will remain strong. East Asian economies still have to rely on this final product market, and therefore will support this system. There will not likely be a fundamental change taking place in the "dollar system."[126] And this also indicates the complexity and gradualness of any reform in the international monetary system.

1.3.3.3 *Sustainability of the Current Mechanism for Adjusting Balance of Payment*

In dealing with the severe global economic imbalances, governments no longer rely solely on their autonomous mechanisms for balance-of-payments adjustment.

The two sides of the imbalance, represented by the US and China, are making efforts in adjusting the structures. They are also trying to improve the effectiveness of external balancing through international cooperation and coordination. International organizations such as the IMF, the World Bank, WTO, APEC, G8 and G20 have also undertaken duties to ensure steady growth of the world economy. To stabilize the world economy in redressing imbalances, countries should reach a consensus to try to maintain main macroeconomic variables and ensure a stable growth of demand, thus to fuel steady development. Emerging market economies in East Asia are striving for consumption-led growth. They are trying hard to change the status of a GDP growth, mainly driven by investment and exports, whereas developed countries are considering increasing savings and reducing deficits.[127] Although restructuring the economy is a long-term task, efforts of developed and developing countries have achieved some results indeed. In a certain period of time, the willingness to cooperate between the two parties will even weigh more than the actual results. At the same time, it should be noted that as China strengthens its trade and industrial connections with other East

[126]Xiao, Li, "The Sustainability of the 'Dollar System' and the Path Choices of East Asian Monetary and Financial Cooperation," *Academic Monthly* 6 (2010): 69–77 (in Chinese).

[127]Dooley, Michael P., Folkerts-Landau, D. and Garber, P., "Bretton Woods II still Defines the International Monetary System," *NBER Working Paper No.* 10332 (2009).

Asian economies, it is not impossible for it to become the new final product market of East Asia. The stable growth of China's economy, structural changes in economic growth patterns and moderate monetary policies will also help to stabilize regional economic development and "anchors" for regional monetary policies.[128] This implies that the in-depth regional economic cooperation will improve the adjustment mechanism of the international balance of payments, coordinate the development of the international economic system and thus alleviate the global economic imbalances. By coordinating international economic policies and promoting in-depth regional economic cooperation, the existing balance-of-payments adjustment mechanism will help to explore feasible paths for reform and adjustment.

1.3.3.4 *Feasibility and Effectiveness of Multinational Financial Supervision*

After a financial crisis, as global economic uncertainty increases, international cooperation in financial supervision can help policymakers control the imported spillover volatility and add to the benefits of cooperative supervision. The supervision of various countries is actually a trade-off between stabilizing and strengthening the competitive position of the domestic financial sector. The impact of the financial crisis on investors' confidence will lead to countries' increased attention to financial stability, which advocates a coordination of financial supervision.[129] Therefore, theoretically, the financial crisis will improve financial supervisory authorities' coordination and cross-border supervision. In fact, strengthening global financial supervision has been advocated after the last crisis broke out. International financial regulatory organizations and countries'

---

[128]Xiao, Li, "The Sustainability of the 'Dollar System' and the Path Choices of East Asian Monetary and Financial Cooperation," *Academic Monthly* 6 (2010): 69–77 (in Chinese).

[129]Masson, P. R. and Pattison, J. C., "Financial Regulatory Reform: Using Models of Cooperation to Evaluate Current Prospects for International Agreement," *Journal of Economic Asymmetries* 3, no. 6 (2009): 119.

regulatory agencies have all put forward new plans and proposals. The IMF published the report *Global Financial Stability Report* in the context of the financial crisis.[130] The report's contents are as follows: promulgate macro and prudential supervision measures, appoint managers with clearer minds to stabilize the system, expand the scope of financial supervision to detect systemic risks caused by inadequate or inefficient supervision in a timely manner; ensure the institution is prudent and can promote the stability of the system, crack down on arbitrage and maintain effective supervision; deal with the pro-cyclicality and other conditions of capital adequacy in the crisis, pay more attention to rules as the foundation and counter-cyclicality; narrow the information gap, especially for financial structures and off-balance-sheet transactions with loose supervision; improve information disclosure for regulators and investors; remove political and legal obstacles to cross-border supervision; facilitate the Central Bank to provide liquidity and respond to systemic shocks; improve the response of country agencies to systemic crises and so on. The suggestions put forward by the IMF shed a new light on the future construction of a multinational financial supervision system.[131] In response to the existing problems in the new agreement, the Basel Committee on Banking Supervision has also begun to revise documents and issue stricter rules for supervision on the bank operations, and improve capital quality. The regulatory agencies in various countries have already raised suggestions and are paying more attention to the pro-cyclicality of the capital system, gradually introducing counter-cyclical mechanisms and other tools to improve their responses to economic cyclical fluctuations.[132]

---

[130]International Monetary Fund, *Global Financial Stability Report. Navigating the Financial Challenges Ahead.* Washington, DC: IMF, 2009, http://www.imf.org/external/pubs/ft/gfsr/2009/02/index.htm, accessed on 12 December 2014.

[131]*Ibid.*

[132]Mao, Qianru, "Cooperation and Coordination in Financial Crisis Management and International Financial Supervision," *Forum of World Economics & Politics*, 12, no. 3 (2009): 54–57 (in Chinese).

At present, the major countries have shifted their attitude from actively promoting the liberalization of international capital flows to establishing international financial supervision and risks detection mechanisms, whose aim is to ensure the orderly international funds flows. The EU put forward the financial "100-day reform" plan during the Washington Global Financial Summit. President Obama also put forward higher requirements for the global financial supervision system. Although the supervision put forward by the EU is stricter than that of the United States, there are different opinions about the unified market supervision within the EU. But all of these discrepancies show that the international community has been actively constructing a new international financial monitoring system. After the enactment of the Dodd–Frank Wall Street Reform and Consumer Protection Act in the United States, the Obama administration is also actively building a unified legal system for financial supervision reforms, and laying the foundation of domestic laws for a more dominant position in the global financial regulatory system.[133]

The evolution of the Basel Accord fully demonstrates that it is a set of international financial regulatory frameworks and rules set up under the leadership of the United States. It reflects the interests of major developed countries represented by the United States. The intention of the United States to construct this institution was not to deal with potential financial risks, but to curb the over-lending of its commercial banks while limiting the expansion of their competitors. Countries including Japan, Germany and France all have to follow the US to avoid larger losses. Therefore, the establishment of the current international financial regulatory framework is not a Pareto improvement. Gaming with the powers has featured several adjustments and reforms of the current international financial regulatory framework.

[133]Wang, Da, "On the Latest Progress in International Financial Regulatory Reform: The Global Financial Market LEI System," *World Economy Study*, 29, no. 1 (2013): 10–28 (in Chinese).

Facts have proved that the fundamental flaws of the current international financial regulatory framework are not at its technical level, but at levels such as procedure rules, governance structure and implementation efficiency. Under the current framework, the formulation of international financial supervision rules depends on the United States and the interests balanced between major developed countries. The efficiency of the new rules also depends on the game process. In this process, academic and technical factors often give way to interest claims of core countries. Regulatory measures are often taken on the basis of major nations' negotiations rather than technical considerations. Take Basel II as an example, one of its much-criticized flaws is pro-cyclicality, which is inextricably linked with the credit rating system and internal rating method, promoted by the US. Although some scholars had pointed this out in the mid-1990s, and scholars and institutions had also noted it during the second drafting of Basel II in 2001, there were no measures formulated in the final draft under the strong dominance of the United States.[134] In fact, many of Basel II's terms and risk weight parameters were formulated based on the compromise between the US and Germany, instead of on considerations of regulatory techniques. The complex game around Basel II among major developed countries has made the introduction and implementation of the new rules extremely inefficient. Many of the terms have been revised numerous times, or been continuously delayed. It is not so much that the technical defects of Basel II make it unable to prevent the global financial crisis. It would be better to say that the tedious decision-making process has prevented it from playing its role.

The gaming and wrestling among major developed countries in the implementation of Basel III fully demonstrate that regulatory

[134]It is widely acknowledged that the US has the most developed and perfect credit rating system. It has three most influential global credit rating agencies (Standard & Poor's, Moody's Investors Service and Fitch Ratings). Obviously, restrictions on the credit rating systems will undoubtedly affect the core interests of the United States.

measures, even if they are technically optimal, once they threaten the interests of core countries, cannot be carried out effectively. Coordination of all countries' interests is important and more complex than fixing technical flaws in the implementation of new regulations. Obviously, in the short term, it is still difficult to completely solve this problem under the framework of the Basel Accord.

After the global financial crisis, major developed countries represented by the United States have reflected on the concept and practice of financial supervision. Judging from the supervision theories and guiding ideologies, the concept of regulatory intervention has replaced the previous *laissez-faire* market and overstates market regulation mechanisms as the global financial supervision's dominant ideology.

It has become a global consensus to build a macro prudential supervision framework on the basis of constant strengthening of supervision. From the standpoint of regulatory interests, financial regulation places greater emphasis on protecting financial consumers and the public interest of taxpayers. From the perspective of the organizational structures, it seems a good choice to improve the effectiveness by establishing legal regulation and coordination agencies and narrowing the overlap or gap of supervision in the long system. As for the regulatory content, it is imperative to comprehensively supervise financial innovation activities such as shadow banking systems and asset securitization. For regulatory coordination mechanisms, all countries emphasize on the strengthening of international financial regulatory cooperation, improving standards and jointly combating systemic risks. Obviously, Basel III, the current international financial supervision framework, has not done enough to achieve those changes mentioned earlier. In particular, it does not explicitly answer the core question of how to build a compatible macro prudential supervision framework around the world.

At present, major developed countries still hold different opinions on how to deepen the reform of the international financial regulatory framework. There is still a long way to go. The focuses of these discrepancies include:

First, it is debated whether to limit the scale and scope of commercial banks. The "Volcker Rule," as one important part of the Dodd–Frank Wall Street Reform and Consumer Protection Act, explicitly proposes restrictions on the scale and high-risk self-operating businesses of commercial banks. However, this restriction caused widespread disputes and doubts at home and abroad. At present, both the Eurozone and the United Kingdom have stated that they will not introduce such a regulation, which undoubtedly places the United States in a dilemma.

Second, it is not clear whether tax measures are to be formulated to strengthen supervision. Although the United States abandoned the plan to impose taxes on banks in 2010, and it is even more unlikely to collect bank taxes on a global scale, Germany and France have shown strong attitudes concerning taxation as the European debt crisis escalates. These two countries rigorously led the European Commission to pass a new rule to impose taxes first on 11 EU countries in February 2013, regardless of the opposition of the United States and the risk of breaking up with the UK and the EU. The rule was planned to come into effect in January 2014 (later postponed until January 2016). This unilateral act undoubtedly casts a shadow over the prospects of international financial regulatory reforms.

Third, countries should also consider the supervision of hedge funds. Hedge funds are used in furious speculative bets against the euro in the global financial crisis, which has pushed Germany and France to strengthen the regulations on them. In October 2010, the EU finance ministers' meeting passed a draft on hedge fund supervision (AIFMD). The draft stipulates that non-EU funds can only be operated within the EU after obtaining a "EU passport." This document with obvious discrimination and protectionism has been ardently opposed by the UK and the US. Since more than 80% of the EU hedge funds are headquartered in London, the UK particularly opposes the rule which may influence London's status as a global financial center. However, under the strong promotion of Germany and France, the European Parliament and the European Commission passed the bill in June 2011 and it took effect in July 2013.

The two countries' aggressive act undoubtedly worsened the contradictions on this issue.

Finally, countries should also figure out how to carry out and advance international financial regulatory cooperation. Although the major developed countries all emphasize the importance of cooperation, there are still many different opinions on relevant strategies. The EU under the leadership of Germany and France has advocated a regulatory model operating beyond sovereignty, while Britain tries to maintain its influence on international financial affairs without EU's constraints. As a financial superpower and the leader of international financial regulatory reforms, the United States cannot accept this model either. As a matter of fact, as argued by Ba (2009), the United States not only refuses to be constrained by international financial regulatory cooperation but also always tries to export its regulatory standards and measures.[135] It can better protect its interests by making it the world's standards. Therefore, while the international community is emphasizing cooperation, there are many interesting conflicts behind the scenes. It remains a tough journey to achieve international financial regulatory cooperation. To sum up, the key to the US's reconstruction of the current international financial regulatory framework is to bridge or eliminate differences in all parties' opinions on this issue. In the short term, it is still a daunting task.[136]

1.3.3.5 *Sustainability of the Functions of International Financial Institutions*

Since the 1960s, both the IMF and the World Bank have undergone many reforms. They have continuously adjusted their focus after changes occurred in the international economic situation. For example, in the acute transformation of the Soviet Union and Eastern Europe, providing financial aid and guidance on policies to transition countries became IMF's main task; in terms of the frequent financial

[135] Ba Shusong, "The Trend and Outlook of Global Financial Supervision in the Financial Crisis," *Southwest Finance*, 58, no. 10 (2009): 11–14 (in Chinese).
[136] *Ibid.*

crises, preventing future outbreaks, strengthening supervision and arranging aid funds became the main functions of the IMF. Changing functions enables the IMF and the World Bank to maintain their active and major roles in the new international currency relations. As long as it's being granted legitimacy and trust through relevant reforms, the IMF can still effectively implement many of its functions, namely: formulate and supervise policies on exchange rates among member states, the current accounts, payment and currency conversion; provide emergent funds to member countries with difficulties in the balance of payments, minimizing the influences on other countries; and provide meeting places for member countries on international currency cooperation and negotiation.[137] The main functions of the World Bank are still mainly to help improve the productivity of developing countries, promote social and economic development and people's livelihood. Although the specific rules as well as the policies of these two financial institutions may change, their core functions will not. After the global financial crisis, the international community has different requirements for the reforms of the IMF and the World Bank. Developed countries require these organizations to cut their operation scope, improve the effectiveness of rescue and assistance, attach more importance to government governance and strengthen the restrictions on the two institutions. Whereas the developing countries require them to abandon dogmatic policies, keep the autonomy of developing countries, mobilize more funds to alleviate poverty and realize the Millennium Development Goals.[138] However, the main objective is to ease the imbalance and disorder in the international economic system and to promote a balanced and orderly global economy through institutional arrangements. Therefore, the IMF's function to stabilize international monetary and financial systems

[137]Eichengreen, Barry, "A Blueprint for IMF Reform: More than just a Lender," *International Finance* 2, no. 10 (2007): 153–175.
[138]Zhong, Hong, "A Research on the Direction of International Monetary System Reform and China's Countermeasures," *Studies of International Finance*, no. 10 (2006): 18–26 (in Chinese).

and World Bank's role to support global economic development will sustain.

Of course, under the current framework of international financial supervision, the positioning of international financial institutions and their roles are faced with a series of challenges. Take the International Monetary Fund as an example:

First of all, the original missions and goals of the IMF are challenged by foreign exchange control and exchange rate fluctuations. Increasing speculation and frequent financial crises have prompted some countries that have realized the free convertibility of capital accounts, especially emerging markets and developing countries, to resume control of capital accounts under the impact of hot money. Some developed countries have also imposed some restrictions on short-term capital flows. Capital controlling measures to some extent deviate from the goals that the IMF and the international monetary system enumerate.

Second, the stability and fairness of the credit currency standard system led by the IMF are facing challenges. The current credit currency standard enables America, the issuer of the reserve currency, to enjoy many privileges. It can dump its currency onto the world, and generate a greater number of financial derivatives in the form of financial innovation, thus challenging the stability of the reserve system and the fairness of international economic development. In addition, the unique status of the US dollar makes the US in fact a central bank and exchange rate setting agency for many countries. The US benefits from influencing the value of other currencies by manipulating that of the dollar. It is a major challenge for the IMF to solve these problems.

Third, IMF's monitoring and prevention of financial risks are disturbed by frequent speculations. In the accelerating global financial integration, the bonds between countries' financial institutions become increasingly tight. The financial markets are also more interdependent. Any errors in the financial system will challenge the security of the entire financial network. Frequent global financial crises since the 1990s have demonstrated the "counter-party risk" in the international financial sector and the lack of control and effective supervision. In the wake of the new global financial crisis, the IMF faces challenges including maintaining the security of the global financial system, strengthening financial supervision, preventing risks and resolving the international transmission effects of these risks.

Fourth, the IMF's monopoly in decision-making is challenged by the cooperation mechanism required in financial integration. Ever since its establishment, the IMF has been manipulated by interest groups and has only represented the interests of a few countries. In fact, the IMF is actually a special company aiming at making the world's finances more prosperous. The voting power depends on the member countries' shares in the IMF. However, the voting power system of the IMF cannot take proper care of the interests of the developing countries and emerging economies. Faced with the prospects of a global financial crisis, the credibility and leadership of the IMF are challenged by major issues including strengthening the mechanism of international financial cooperation and better responding to the risks and crises.

Finally, the strategies of the IMF in crisis management face challenges. On the one hand, since the 1990s, the poor performance of the IMF in dealing with financial crises drew doubts on its crisis management strategies and capabilities. Its credibility and reputation are severely challenged. On the other hand, the way IMF responds to financial crises and its strategies are obviously limited. Its strategies include: austerity in fiscal and monetary policies, floating exchange rates and economic liberalization reforms. However, the results often turn out to be counter-productive, and may even trigger an economic recession.

Of course, major international financial institutions such as the World Bank, WTO and the Bank for International Settlements also face new problems and challenges in their own fields. The sustainability of the current international financial institutions and their functions depends mainly on how to effectively respond to these issues. Undoubtedly, there is a long and arduous way to go.

Chapter 2

Reform Objectives, Plans and Progress of the Current International Monetary System

2.1 Reform Objectives of the Current International Monetary System

2.1.1 *Promote Global Economic Development and Free Trade*

As the most important monetary system arrangement in the world, the international currency system's primary goal is to maintain and promote the sustained and healthy development of the global economy. The Bretton Woods system, established after the Second World War, and the current "dollar system" reflect the world economic structure established after the war, that is, they mainly support the major developed countries represented by the United States (or represented by the "Group of Seven") interests. Since the outbreak of the global financial crisis, a series of significant changes have taken place in the global economic landscape. One of the most prominent phenomena is that a large number of emerging and developing economies have become important drivers of global economic growth (Figure 2.1 and Table 2.1). In particular, developing countries represented by China have made important contributions to the world

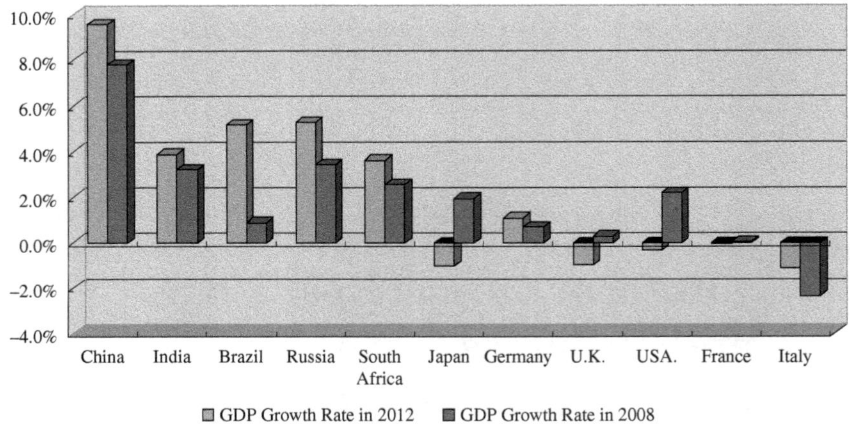

Figure 2.1. Economic Growth Rates of Major Countries in 2008 and 2012
Source: World Bank World Development Indicator database.

economic growth.[1] To this end, promoting the steady growth of the global economy, especially the vast number of emerging economies, is

[1]Analysis of a large amount of data has proved that after the outbreak of the global financial crisis, China has become the engine of global economic growth, major demand supporter, exchange-rate ballast and new source of capital. Statistics from the International Monetary Fund (IMF) show that during the period from 2008 to 2012, China's economy grew at an average annual rate of 9.3%. In five years, the net economic growth in China accounted for 29.8% of the global economic increase; China's economic growth was 7.8%, and the net increase in GDP accounted for 60.9% of the global net increase for the year 2012. At the same time, China's current account surplus as a share of GDP has fallen sharply from 10.2% in 2007 to 2.3% in 2012. According to statistics from the World Trade Organization (WTO), the share of China's imports in global imports increased from 6.9% to 9.5% during the period from 2008 to 2012. In the three years (2008–2010) when the financial crisis raged, global imports contracted by 8.4%, while China's imports increased by 23.3%. At present, China is the second largest importer in the world. In the near future, with the overall leap in Chinese household income and the popularity of new business models such as E-commerce, China may become a "world market" and play the role of a global product buyer and a supporter of world demand. In addition, since China started to reform the exchange rate system in 2005, the nominal exchange rate of the RMB against the US dollar has appreciated by about 33%, the real effective exchange rate has appreciated by about 34%, the RMB exchange rate fluctuation range has continued to expand, and the formation mechanism has gradually become clear.

Table 2.1. Commodity Imports and Exports of Major Countries in the World (Unit: US$10 Billion)

Country	Index	2003	2004	2005	2006	2007	2008	2009	2010	2011	2012
Global	Export	758.9	922.2	1050.8	1213.0	1402.3	1616.0	1255.4	1528.3	1831.9	1840.1
	Import	786.9	957.1	1087.0	1246.3	1432.9	1657.1	1277.8	1550.3	1849.9	1860.1
Brazil	Export	7.3	9.7	11.9	13.8	16.1	19.8	15.3	20.2	25.6	24.3
	Import	5.1	6.6	7.8	9.6	12.7	18.2	13.4	19.2	23.7	23.3
China	Export	43.8	59.3	76.2	96.9	122.0	143.1	120.2	157.8	189.8	204.9
	import	41.3	56.1	66.0	79.1	95.6	113.3	100.6	139.6	174.3	181.8
France	Export	39.2	45.2	46.3	49.6	56.0	61.6	48.5	52.4	59.6	56.9
	Import	39.9	47.1	50.4	54.2	63.1	71.7	56.1	61.1	72.0	67.4
Germany	Export	75.2	91.0	97.1	110.8	132.1	144.6	112.0	125.9	147.4	140.7
	Import	60.5	71.6	77.7	90.7	105.5	118.5	92.6	105.5	125.5	116.7
Japan	Export	47.2	56.6	59.5	64.7	71.4	78.1	58.1	77.0	82.3	79.9
	Import	38.3	45.5	51.6	57.9	62.2	76.3	55.2	69.4	85.5	88.6
Russia	Export	13.6	18.3	24.4	30.4	35.4	47.2	30.3	40.1	52.2	52.9
	Import	7.6	9.7	12.5	16.4	22.3	29.2	19.2	24.9	32.4	33.5
South Africa	Export	3.6	4.6	5.2	5.8	7.0	8.1	6.2	8.1	9.8	8.7
	Import	4.0	5.3	6.2	7.9	8.8	10.2	7.4	9.4	12.2	12.4
United Kingdom	Export	30.6	34.7	39.1	45.1	44.2	47.2	35.5	41.6	50.3	47.4
	Import	39.9	47.1	51.9	61.3	63.8	65.8	51.9	59.1	67.4	69.0
United States	Export	72.5	81.5	90.1	102.6	114.8	128.7	105.6	127.8	148.0	154.6
	Import	130.3	152.6	173.3	191.8	202.0	216.9	160.5	196.9	226.6	233.6

Source: WTO database.

one of the important goals of the current reform of the international monetary system.

Another goal of the international monetary system reform is to promote the development of international trade. David Hume proposed the automatic adjustment and balance mechanism of the balance of payments under the gold standard, which is the "Price–Specie Flow Mechanism." Under the gold standard, gold, as the only international reserve currency, can have a free international cross-border circulation, which makes it difficult for a country to maintain its balance of payments deficit for a long period of time, and changes in the money supply will play a role in automatically adjusting the balance of international payments. However, under the current "dollar system," the core currency of the US dollar and the Fed's monetary policy have lost their ability to adjust to the US trade deficit and global economic imbalances, which in turn has caused the United States to have no fear of its own growing trade deficit (Figure 2.2). Although we cannot make a clear judgment on the causal relationship between the current imbalance in the international monetary system and the imbalance in international trade, it goes without saying that the current "dollar system" is quite relevant to global trade imbalances (Figure 2.3). In the context of international trade imbalances, the development of international trade has been hampered. On the one hand, the exchange rate risk of settlement currencies has increased, and the risk of foreign exchange reserves accumulated by export surpluses has increased. Countries have adjusted their export-oriented economic strategies and have had to give up their comparative advantages for national security. At the same time, in order to reverse the trade deficit, the deficit countries frequently use trade protectionism to safeguard their own narrow interests, which in turn greatly hinder

---

The proportion of China's foreign direct investment (FDI) in the world rose from less than 0.5% in 2002 to 4.4% in 2011, and China's share of foreign exchange reserves increased from 8.6% in 2000 to 31.2% in 2011. The role of China in the world investment is undergoing a historic transformation. The data are from *Xinhua* News Agency, http://news.xinhuanet.com/fortune/2013-09/05/c_117242532.htm.

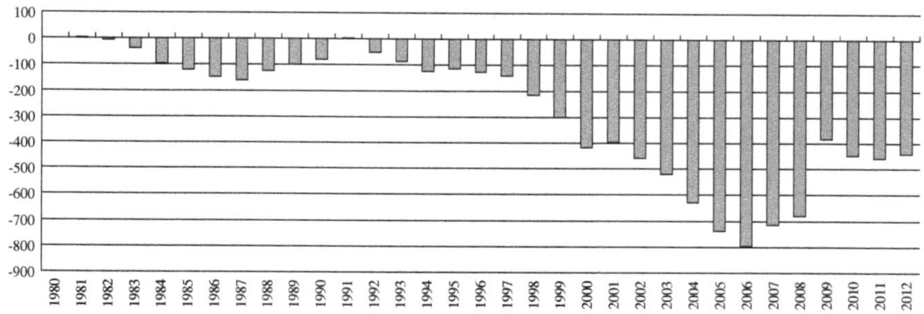

Figure 2.2. Current Account Balances in the United States (Unit: US$1 Trillion)
Source: Federal Reserve Economic Data, St. Louis Fed.

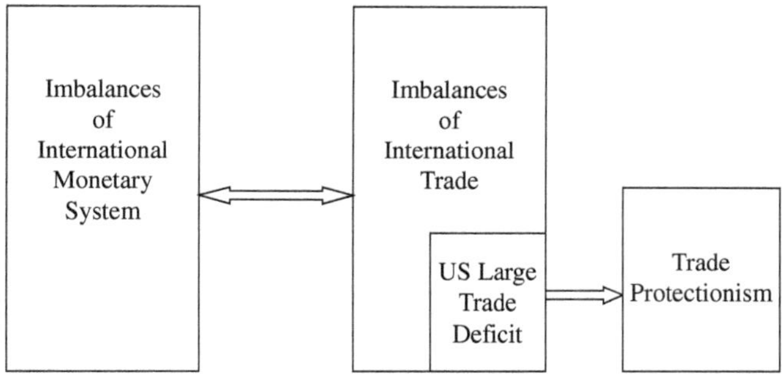

Figure 2.3. Protectionism in the Current International Monetary System

the development of international free trade.[2] Therefore, the elimination of barriers to trade protectionism and the establishment of an international monetary system that can effectively promote

[2]The current "dollar system" cannot provide strong support for the development of international trade from the monetary and financial system level, and there is a serious lack of effective balance of payments adjustment mechanisms. As countries cannot effectively negotiate and coordinate their balance of payments problems under a unified framework, various hidden protectionist methods have become the best means for countries to safeguard their own interests. Especially after the outbreak of the global financial crisis, the developed economies, such as the United States and European countries, which bore the brunt of the crisis, have resorted to the banner of trade protectionism and pointed to China as the "world's factory." For details, refer to Wang, Da and Bai Dafan, "US Export Control Policy and Its Impact on US–China Trade," *Northeast Asia Forum* 5 (2012): 65–71.

the sustainable development of international trade on a global scale should be the common goals and visions pursued by all countries.

2.1.2 *Establish an Orderly and Stable Cycle of Global Capital*

After the collapse of the Bretton Woods system, the international monetary system entered the era of the Jamaican system. Since the "Jamaica Accord" does not have strict regulations on the currency exchange rate and reserve currency, the system is also called a "system without system" or a "*de facto* dollar standard system." In this context, the increasingly active international capital flows have brought great risks to the stability of the international capital market. Another purpose of reforming the current international monetary system is to reduce the risk of capital flows to countries and increase the stability and efficiency of capital flows.

First, the current system of using the currency of a single sovereign country as the major currency for international reserve asset valuation must be reformed, and a more fair and reasonable international reserve asset management system should be explored. Export demand is one of the important reasons for stimulating the economic development of many countries. However, another issue that "trade countries" have to face while earning foreign exchange through exports is how to effectively manage their foreign exchange reserve assets. In the post-Bretton Woods era, the dollar, which was the most widely distributed and internationalized currency, naturally took the role of the most important international reserve asset valuation currency. However, in fact, in the current international monetary system, foreign exchange assets accumulated by export-oriented countries are inefficiently used, and are mainly used for investment in the US financial market rather than returning to their real economies. The large number of US dollar-denominated foreign exchange reserve assets (Table 2.2) held by the "BRICS countries" (including Brazil, Russia, India, China and South Africa) and Japan cannot be used effectively at the real economy level and naturally form a leakage of currency flow (Figure 2.4). The consequence of this is that a large

Table 2.2. Foreign Exchange Reserves of Major Countries in the World (Unit: US$1 Billion)

Country	2004	2005	2006	2007	2008	2009	2010	2011	2012
China	619	826	1073	1534	1953	2426	2876	3213	3341
Japan	845	847	895	973	1031	1049	1096	1296	1268
Brazil	53	54	86	180	194	239	289	352	373
India	130	136	176	274	254	275	298	298	298
Russia	125	182	304	479	426	439	479	499	538
Germany	97	102	112	136	138	181	216	239	249
United States	87	65	66	71	78	131	132	148	150

Source: United Nations database.

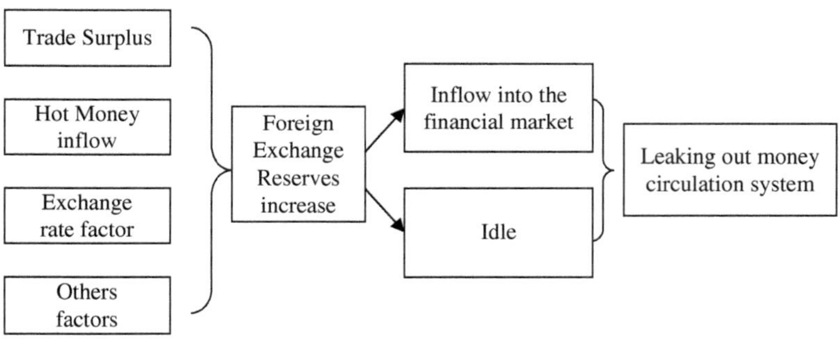

Figure 2.4. Sketch Map of Foreign Exchange Reserve Leakage

number of foreign exchange reserves in developing countries that are in urgent need of funds cannot be effectively allocated. However, in developed "financial countries," the United States has ample liquidity despite its book deficit. Such a deformed pattern of international capital flows is a product–capital division between the United States as a "financial country" and a "trade country" represented by East Asian countries (i.e. the center under the "dollar system" — periphery) under the global economic imbalance pattern. The prominent representative of the "double-cycle" model.[3]

[3]Xiao, Li, and Ding Yibing, "The Imbalance of Global Economy at This Stage and the Role of China," *Journal of Social Science of Jilin University* 1 (2007): 17–26.

Second, strengthening the supervision and coordination mechanism for capital flows and transnational financial activities can effectively prevent financial turmoil caused by international hot money speculation. The current international monetary system cannot effectively regulate the large-scale capital flow. At present, international financial resources are mainly in the hands of a few countries. Under the international monetary system with financial liberalization as the guideline, developed countries, especially the United States, can not only pose a threat to the financial security of other countries through capital flows but can also acquire bonuses from capital penetration from developing countries. After the outbreak of the global financial crisis, the drastic changes in the international capital flow pattern had a tremendous impact on developing countries and emerging economies. Specifically, the deterioration of the global financial crisis in 2010, especially the full-scale outbreak of the European sovereign debt crisis, caused international capital to flow to emerging economies with better economic conditions, which in turn helped to form the bubbles of these countries' domestic asset price and seriously intensified the domestic inflationary pressure.[4] However, with the slow recovery of the economies of major developed countries such as the United States and Europe, especially after the Federal Reserve expressed its intention to withdraw from the quantitative easing monetary policy in June 2013, the expectation of international capital flows reversed. Large-scale inflows into developing countries and emerging economies occurred. The bulk of the international capital has returned to the developed countries on a large scale, which again has a severe impact on the economic condition of these countries.[5] Therefore, one of the important objectives

[4]China was facing severe inflationary pressure in 2010. Xiang, Weixing and Wang Da, "On the Asymmetry in the Financial Interdependence between China and the United States," *World Economic Research* 7 (2011): 10–16.

[5]After the United States released a signal to withdraw its quantitative easing monetary policy in June 2013, Brazil, one of the BRICS countries, experienced a serious capital outflow, which in turn led to a significant depreciation of its local currency. At the same time, due to the lack of domestic investment and

of the current reform of the international monetary system should be to strengthen the supervision over international capital and to formulate corresponding rules to restrict the free flow of international capital and reduce its threat to the economies of developing countries, that is, to effectively solve the problem of the effect of disorderly international capital flow to the economies of peripheral countries. In addition, strengthening international financial regulatory cooperation and building a unified international financial regulatory framework should also be one of the important goals of the current international monetary system reform. The fact that the global financial crisis has broken out proves that transnational mixed operations of systemically important financial institutions are important causes of systemic risks in the global financial system. The differences in regulatory systems and regulatory standards in various countries have led to the regulatory arbitrage of multinational financial institutions. Motivation, in turn, greatly weakens the effectiveness of macroprudential supervision by financial supervisory authorities in various countries. As mentioned earlier, under the current "dollar system," international financial regulatory cooperation is still fragmented and weak. Under the background of commercial banks' continuous development of financial innovation tools under the mixed business model, the core of the international banking regulatory framework of Basel II and Basel III has increasing difficulty dealing with potential systemic risks.[6] Therefore, building a unified regulatory framework and

the decline in exports, Brazil's economic situation has deteriorated drastically. The specific performance is: First, the economic growth rate dropped sharply; second, the inflationary pressure rose; third, the "double deficit" status of the fiscal and current accounts experienced further deterioration; fourth, the currency devaluation and capital outflow became serious; fifth, the financial leverage has been continuously enlarged; sixth, the scale of foreign debt has expanded rapidly. For details, please refer to Gao, Yi: "Analysis and Prospect of Recent Economic Situation in Brazil," *Policy Brief No.* 201341, Institute of World Economics and Political Science, Chinese Academy of Social Sciences.

[6]Wang, Da, "The Current International Financial Supervision Framework Led by the United States: Evolution, Defects, and Reconstruction," *International Finance Research* 10 (2013): 33–44.

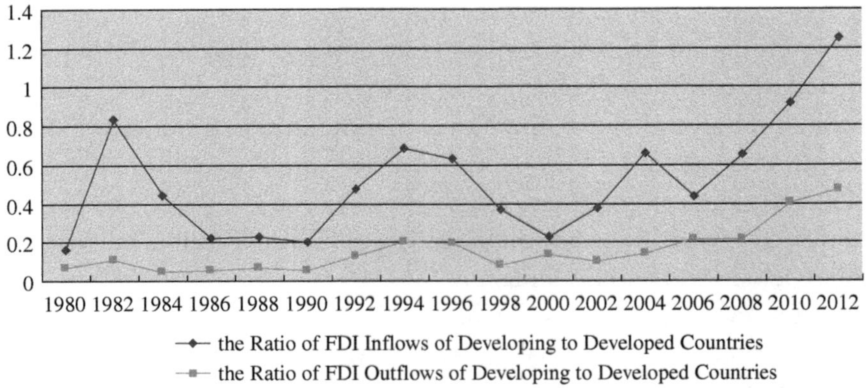

Figure 2.5. Inflow and Outflow of FDI in the Developing and Developed Countries

Source: Calculated from http://stats.unctad.org/FDI/data.

strengthening regulatory cooperation on a global scale should become an important goal of the reform of the current international monetary system.

Finally, the international monetary system should expand its inclusiveness. At present, the direction of international capital flows is mainly from developed countries to developing countries. Figure 2.5 shows that in the period from 1980 to 2010, the FDI flow rate in the developing countries was always lower than that in the developed countries, mainly because the ratio of FDI inflows and outflows between the developing countries and developed countries was smaller than 1. Until 2012, FDI inflows from the developing countries exceeded that of the developed countries. However, the outflow of FDI in the developing countries has been far lower than in the developed countries (the former was always less than 20% of the latter before 2010). It is not difficult to infer that the pattern of international capital flows in more than 30 years is mainly due to the influx of developed countries' large amounts of capital to developing countries. Of course, this has, to a certain extent, promoted the development of developing countries, but at the same time it also exposed negative aspects of the country's currency system: the current flow of international capital is a one-way flow from developed countries to developing countries. Therefore, one of the goals of the current reform of the international monetary system is to open up the channels for capital flows from developing countries to developed countries and to achieve an orderly flow of international capital. This aspect will be conducive to the optimal allocation of capital to developing countries, especially those countries that hold a large amount of foreign exchange reserves. On the other hand, the developing countries can share the fruits of economic growth with the developed countries in the process of outbound investment, and through the spillover effect of direct investment these countries have driven the upgrading and transformation of related domestic industries, improved the level of technological development and accumulated management experience, thereby further enhancing the connotative development. In other words, an inclusive international monetary system should allow and encourage most developing countries and emerging economies to play a greater role in the international capital flow pattern, and not merely be passive recipients of the transnational capital transfer of the developed countries.

2.1.3 *Dealing with the Occasional Impact with a Certain Degree of Flexibility*

After the collapse of the Bretton Woods system in the mid-1970s, regional financial and currency crises under the current "dollar system" frequently had different degrees of impact on the global financial system (Table 2.3). In responding to these crises, the current system seems to be powerless. In the Asian financial crisis that broke out in 1997, the actions of the IMF had been questioned. At present, the international community has two main views on the reform of the international monetary system. One view is that in light of the serious imbalance between the global economy and the monetary system, a comprehensive and thorough reform of the current international monetary system should be carried out; another view is that the international monetary system will be sustainable for a long time. The core problem of the reform is to reduce the occasional

Table 2.3. Loss and Recovery Time Caused by Currency Crisis (1975–2001)

Currency Crisis	Number of Countries	Average years of Recovery[a]	Average Loss[b]	Average Loss Ratio[c]	Total Average Loss[d]
	158	1.6	4.3	61	7.1
Industrial countries/	42	1.9	3.1	55	5.6
Developing countries	116	1.5	4.8	64	7.6
Currency crisis/	55	2.0	7.1	71	10.1
Industrial countries/	13	2.1	5.0	62	8.0
Developing countries	42	1.9	7.9	74	10.4
Bank crisis/	54	3.1	11.6	82	14.2
Industrial countries/	12	4.1	10.2	67	15.0
Developing countries	42	2.8	12.1	86	14.0
Currency crisis[e]	32	3.2	14.4	78	18.5
Banking crisis[f]	6				
Industrial countries		5.8	17.6	100	17.6
Developing countries	26	2.6	13.6	73	18.8

Notes: [a]The number of years before the GDP returns to crisis; [b]the difference between the expected growth rate of GDP and the real growth rate in each crisis (%); [c]the proportion of the number of crises times causing the loss of GDP growth (%); [d]The average value of the GDP growth loss (%) caused by all the losses that constitute GDP growth; [e]the currency crisis in the foreign exchange market pressure index which accounts for more than 75% of the currency crisis; [f]The banking crisis occurred during the currency crisis.

Source: IMF, *World Economic Outlook*. Washington, DC: The Fund, May 2002.

financial risk of the system, and it should be used as a goal to make necessary adjustments to the current international monetary system. We believe that the gradual adjustment and reform of the current international monetary system is a more pragmatic choice.

Many scholars critique the current international monetary system on the grounds of global economic imbalances, arguing that it is the current international monetary system that has led to an increase in imbalances. As shown in Figure 2.6, compared with the previous gold standard system and the Bretton Woods system, the current international monetary system does not impose stringent restrictions on member states, especially on the dominant countries, in terms of impact adjustment and control of currency issuance. There is a moral

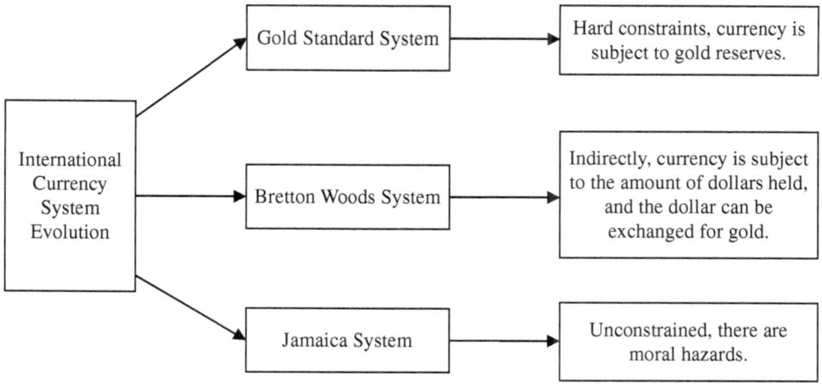

Figure 2.6. Evolution of International Monetary System and Currency Constraints

Source: Zhang, Lan, "The Attributes of the International Monetary System: A Study Based on International Monetary Contracts," *World Economic Research* 126, no. 1 (2010): 27–32.

hazard in force, and this moral hazard does increase international economic imbalances. However, it needs to be pointed out that the Bretton Woods system was also based on the global economic imbalance at the beginning of its establishment, or it can be said to have resulted from global economic imbalances.[7] The important reason for the formation of the "dollar system" lies in the division of labor between the United States and other countries that form "financial countries" and "trade countries." Given that this basic pattern of international division of labor is unlikely to change radically at this stage, there are no fundamental conditions for a fundamental or thorough reform of the current international monetary system.[8]

The current international monetary system was created in the 1970s. The earlier Bretton Woods system was created after World War II. With the changes in the world situation, the existing

[7]Xiao, Li, "The Path Choice of East Asian Monetary and Financial Cooperation under the Global Financial Crisis," *Northeast Asia Forum* 45, no. 5 (2009): 3–25.

[8]Xiao, Li, and Wang Qian, "The Goal of the Reform of the International Monetary System in the Post-Crisis Era," *Journal of Economics* 32, no. 12 (2011): 56–68.

institutional arrangements have lagged behind changes in the world economic landscape. The former Federal Republic of Germany and Japan joined the IMF in 1953 and the economies have experienced a rapid miraculous rise in the following decades. The economic growth of other developing countries has also been quite rapid. After entering the 1980s, China gradually integrated into the world economy in the context of accelerating the process of reform and opening-up. The total economic output of China has increased from ¥364.5 billion in 1978 to about ¥50 trillion in 2012, and the total economic output has even surpassed Japan's to become the second largest in the world in 2010. At the same time, the economic status of the United States has declined. In 1960, the GDP of the US accounted for 35% of the world's GDP, and in 2012 it dropped to about 23%. The sharp decline in the US economic status is a true reflection of the tremendous changes that have taken place in the world economic structure in the past half-century or so. Judging from the institutional design of the IMF, voting rights of the IMF are still mainly concentrated in the hands of a few developed countries represented by the United States. To a certain extent, it reflects the will of the great powers of the post-World War II era. "The contract rules of the current international monetary system are incapable of real constraints on the countries within the system. When the political and economic relations of major countries change, or when a major country is making major adjustments in economic decision-making or strategic orientation, the characteristics and mechanisms of system operation may change accordingly."[9] In this context, the response mechanism of the current international monetary system to sporadic shocks lacks flexibility, and it shows severe asymmetries in the process of salvaging regional crises. In other words, when there are crises in the peripheral countries of the current international monetary system (such as the East Asian financial crisis of 1997), the IMF's response is often

[9]Zhang, Lan, "The Attributes of the International Monetary System: A Study Based on International Monetary Contracts," *World Economic Research* 1 (2010): 27–32.

very slow and the rescue is quite weak. However, if there is a crisis in a core country or a major advanced economy, the IMF's response and rescue will be sufficiently large (such as the European sovereign debt crisis that broke out in 2010). This lack of flexible and asymmetric crisis relief mechanisms is not only contrary to the principle of fairness but is also not conducive to maintaining the stability of the global financial system. Therefore, it is necessary to reform the IMF-centered crisis relief and response mechanism in the current international monetary system from the perspective of institutional arrangements to make it more flexible.

2.2 Options for International Monetary System Reform: Foreign Scholars' Perspectives

The reform of the international monetary system is a broad topic. Many foreign scholars have conducted considerable analysis and research on this issue from different perspectives. The relevant literature is mainly reflected in the following five aspects: international reserve currency reform, exchange rate system reform, reform of international balance of payments adjustment mechanism, reform of international financial supervision system and reform of international financial organization.

2.2.1 *Literature Review of International Reserve Currency*

At present, the international monetary system has evolved from the Bretton Woods system with the "US dollar linked to gold, and foreign currencies linked to the US dollar" to the current Jamaican system. The Bretton Woods system collapsed due to the "Triffin dilemma," but the current Jamaican system still does not completely solve this problem. Triffin once pointed out: "the reserve of gold of United States exceeds the amount of short-term liabilities (including bonds and securities) to foreign countries .... This tendency to decrease obviously cannot continue forever. It will undermine the confidence of foreigners to regard the US dollar as a safe accumulation of reserves."[10] This clearly shows that under the Bretton Woods (gold exchange standard system), the international reserve currency faces the external constraint of the amount of gold reserves. With the collapse of the Bretton Woods system and the non-monetization of gold, the conflicts of the dollar's functions between international key currencies and a national sovereign currency have been weakened, making it less difficult to choose between the stability of the dollar's value under the Bretton Woods system and international liquidation methods. The dilemma is no longer sharp. However, under the current Jamaican system, the US dollar remains the main international reserve currency, and the "Triffin puzzle" has not been fundamentally resolved. If the value of the dollar is to be stable, it cannot be used as an international currency; if the dollar is to be used as an international currency, its value cannot be stabilized. That is, if the US dollar becomes the world currency, it must maintain the trade deficit under the current accounts, thus making the dollar flow out of the US and allowing other countries to obtain enough US dollars. On the other hand, with the continuous outflow of the US dollar and the consistent growth of deficits, it will affect the confidence of the holders of US dollars. Once there are any fluctuations, they will panic and sell their US dollars.[11] Although it is a choice of the market rather than a policy for the US dollar to be the main international settlement currency and reserve currency, a public good such as the international monetary system that affects the interests of all countries in the world cannot be established on the basis of only one certain type of sovereign currency. A sovereign currency, as a reserve asset, will inevitably lead to internal instability of the reserve system,

[10]Triffin, R., *Gold and the Dollar Crisis; The Future of Convertibility*. New Haven: Yale University Press, 1961, 65.

[11]Obstfeld, Maurice, "The International Monetary System: Living with Asymmetry," *NBER Working Paper* no. 17641 (December 2011).

leading to imbalances in international payments and turmoil in the world financial system.[12]

In order to solve the current dilemma caused by the US dollar as the main international settlement currency and reserve currency, many scholars, such as Eichengreen, believe that it is necessary to reform the pattern of the current international reserve currency.[13] From the viewpoint of the supply of reserve currency, the emergence of the euro constitutes strong competition for the US dollar, which changes the monopoly position of the US dollar against the international reserve currency. From the perspective of demand, the developing countries' trading partners and capital controls have changed. New requirements for the composition of the reserve currency must be put forward. All the signs show that the composition of the international reserve currency is changing. Moreover, from a historical point of view, the simultaneous sharing of one major currency by several nations is also conducive to the stability of the international monetary system.[14] Mundell predicted that the most important thing that took place in the 21st century was the harmonious coexistence of the US dollar and the euro, pointing directly at the direction of the future development of the international monetary system — the multi-currency standard.[15]

Regarding the development direction of the multi-currency standard, there are currently three possibilities for replacing the US dollar or becoming the world's reserve currency along with the US dollar:

[12] Ocampo, J. A., "The Instability and Inequities of the Global Reserve System," *International Journal of Political Economy* 4, no. 36 (2007): 71–96.
[13] Eichengreen, Barry, "Sterling's Past, Dollar's Future: Historical Perspectives on Reserve Currency Competition," *National Bureau of Economic Research* (2005).
[14] *Ibid.*
[15] Mundell, R. A., "EMU and the International Monetary System, A Transatlantic Perspective," *Oesterreichische Nationalbank (Austrian Central Bank) Working Papers*, 1993.

the euro, the special drawing rights (SDRs), and the sovereign currencies of emerging economies (RMB as a representative).

Some scholars believe that the euro is more likely to become the new world reserve currency. Frankel believes that the euro is very likely to replace the US dollar as the world's leading reserve currency by 2022, but it depends on two points: (1) whether there are enough EU countries to join the Eurozone, making the total economic output of the EU exceed that of the United States; (2) Whether the United States adopts macroeconomic policies of inflation and devaluation, which will cause people's confidence in the exchange rate of the US dollar to fluctuate.[16]

In addition to the euro, another interesting international reserve currency is the SDR.[17] However, the view on the development direction of the SDR is not yet unified. Some scholars believe that the SDR is a key method that may be used in solving the current international monetary system issues, but its implementation still requires a complicated process; other scholars believe that the SDR does not have the advantage as an international reserve currency. Stiglitz and Greenwald believe that the current reform of the international monetary system can begin with the transformation of the SDR: (1) Using the SDR as a non-reserve currency in international reserves on a solid and reasonable basis; (2) the SDR is used as a unit of price for commodities, such as oil; (3) the distribution of SDR should be partially served to offset the externalities of the surplus countries.[18] Fiorentini and Montani analyzed the international monetary system reform after the financial crisis from the perspective of the US dollar as a reserve currency and pointed out that in order to solve the current "Triffin problem," there are two aspects of the reform trend that

[16]Frankel, Jeffrey A., "No Single Currency Regime Is Right for All Countries or at All Times," *National Bureau of Economic Research Working Paper* No. w7338 (September 1999).

[17]Clark, P. B. and J. J. Polak, "International Liquidity and the Role of the SDR in the International Monetary System," *IMF Staff Papers* (2004): 49–71.

[18]Stiglitz, Joseph E. and Bruce Greenwald, "Towards a New Global Reserve System," *Journal of Globalization and Development* 1, no. 2 (2010): 78–91.

are imperative: one is that industrialized countries adopt a unified global monetary target, and the other is the issuance of UN bonds so that US dollar reserves can be effectively converted into SDRs.[19] Kenen believes that the international reserve system has fundamental flaws,[20] so the SDR should be used as the main international reserve asset, and the development of a super-sovereign currency should be promoted step by step through the establishment of an alternative account. Since the weight of the SDR's constituent currency will be adjusted as the currency value changes, the SDR is a convenient reserve decentralization tool and a stable value reserve carrier. However, Mundell believes that the establishment of a super-sovereign currency will solve many difficult issues, including how to determine the price of a country's currency relative to the world currency, the speed of issuing world currencies, how to transfer currency sovereignty, how to determine the world's central bank, how to allocate seigniorage taxes, how to ensure the credibility of world currencies in crisis and so on; second, the currency and the central bank system up to this point has been based on a certain political system. It is not clear if the future monetary system will be completely independent of the political system.[21] However, many scholars are not optimistic about the prospect of SDR. Eichengreen and Frankel believe that the SDR does not have the advantage as an international reserve currency relative to the US dollar, the German mark and the Japanese yen. The diversification of the reserve currency is a viable option.[22]

---

[19]Fiorentini, Riccardo and Guido Montani, "Global Imbalances and the Transition to a Symmetric World Monetary System," *Perspectives on Federalism* 2, no. 1 (2010): 82–98.

[20]Such as the Triffin dilemma and arrogant privilege. Kenen, P. B., *Substitution Account as a First Step toward Reform of the International Monetary System.* Washington, DC: Peterson Institute for International Economics, 2010.

[21]Robert, Mundell, On One World Currency and Africa, http://www.blackelectorate.com/articles.asp?ID=240.

[22]Eichengreen, Barry, and J. A. Frankel, *On the SDR: Reserve Currencies and the Future of the International Monetary System.* Berkeley: University of California, 1996.

Taking the sovereign currency of emerging economies (represented by RMB) as a part of the international reserve currency constitutes a possibility for the development of the international reserve currency in the future. The growing relative economic quality of emerging market economies in the global economic system will increase the importance of their currencies. Among the existing emerging economies, the most advantageous reserve currency candidate is the renminbi (RMB). However, most scholars believe that even with the assumption that China's economic growth and financial development will remain optimistic in the future, RMB has a long wait before it can become a new reserve currency.[23] In particular, the gap in the financial development between China and other countries is very obvious. For example, the proportion of RMB bonds and deposits in Hong Kong in total RMB bonds and deposits is very small; the development of China's domestic financial market has just started and is still highly regulated; domestic systems are in a state of "financial suppression"; cross-border capital flows are tightly controlled. Some scholars even suggested that because of the low level of development of China's financial markets, the prospect of RMB becoming a reserve currency is relatively low.[24] However, some scholars are very optimistic about the prospect of the RMB becoming the new national reserve currency. Subramanian believes that the RMB will become the major international reserve currency by 2022.[25] However, its theoretical model omits financial development variables, but uses the government policy variable instead. This means that the RMB internationalization policy of the government will help to increase the international status of RMB even after considering the reality

---

[23]Chinn, M., A Note on Reserve Currencies with Special Reference to the G20 Countries. written for the International Growth Centre (IGC), India Central Programme (2012).

[24]Prasad, E. and L. Ye, "The RMB's Role in the Global Monetary System," Discussion Paper Series, Forschungsinstitut zur Zukunft der Arbeit (2012).

[25]Subramanian, Arvind, "Renminbi Rules: The Conditional Imminence of the Reserve Currency Transition," *Peterson Institute for International Economics Working Paper Series*, no. 11–14 (September 2011).

of the backwardness of China's financial development.[26] Mundell predicted that "the future of the RMB may be to become a reserve currency even if the Chinese government does not do anything about it ⋯ The process of the RMB becoming an international currency is inevitable."[27] Although the predictions are different, foreign scholars have roughly the same view of the prospects of RMB. As Eichengreen concludes: one day, the RMB will perhaps exceed the dollar. However, for the foreseeable future, it is difficult to see that it can compete with the still larger economy, and the US currency (US dollar). Will the RMB become a regional reserve currency? Yes. Is it an auxiliary reserve currency? Yes. But it is unimaginable that it could become the dominant reserve currency.[28] In response to the RMB internationalization policy measures, McCauley found that Chinese government authorities have not attempted to develop offshore markets while controlling cross-border capital flows.[29] Prasad and Ye further pointed out that China's attempt to promote the development of RMB offshore financial centers in Hong Kong will not help promote the internationalization of the RMB. China needs to relax capital controls.[30] As the internationalization of the RMB will eventually mean a "perforation hole" in China's capital controls, it will ultimately challenge the government's control of currency and credit in the country.[31] In order to make the RMB a reserve currency, China

---

[26] *Ibid.*

[27] Mundell, R. A., "EMU and the International Monetary System, A Transatlantic Perspective," *Oesterreichische Nationalbank (Austrian Central Bank) Working Papers* (1993).

[28] Eichengreen, Barry, "The Renminbi as an International Currency," *Journal of Policy Modeling* 33, no. 5 (September–October 2011): 723–730.

[29] McCauley, R., The Internationalization of the RMB. Speech to the Second Annual International Conference on the Chinese Economy, Macroeconomic management in China: monetary and financial stability issues, Hong Kong Institute for Monetary Research, Hong Kong SAR (2011).

[30] Prasad, E. and L. Ye, "The RMB's Role in the Global Monetary System," *Discussion Paper Series, Forschungsinstitut zur Zukunft der Arbeit* (2012).

[31] McCauley, Robert, "Internationalizing the Renminbi and China's Financial Development Model," a Council on Foreign Relations/China Development

should learn from the historical experience of the current reserve currency and strengthen institutional development (improve the rule of law and reduce corruption),[32] open domestic financial markets and allow legalized capital inflows.[33] The order of opening of a proper capital account should first allow limited exchangeability for trade purposes, and then use greater exchange rate flexibility as a prelude to full convertibility of the capital account.[34] Although Ronald McKinnon recognized the potential of the RMB as an international reserve currency, he also pointed out the liquidity trap in the developed countries where the "almost zero" interest rates have become an obstacle for the RMB to become an international currency. The high inflation rate in the developing countries forces them to maintain higher interest rates than those in the developed countries. For example, when China's interest rate cannot fall below 4%, the interest rates in Japan and the United States are close to zero. If China does not regulate capital accounts, there will be opportunities for arbitrage. In order to avoid arbitrage, China's financial liberalization reform cannot be carried out completely, which will hinder the internationalization of the RMB.[35]

At present, Western scholars have basically reached a consensus on the necessity of the reform of the international monetary system, but they have different opinions on how to carry out international reserve currency reforms. Eichengreen believes that the future of the

---

Research Foundation Symposium, The Future of the International Monetary System and the Role of the Renminbi, Beijing, 2011, 1.

[32]Chinn, Menzie David and Hiro Ito, "What Matters for Financial Development? Capital Controls, Institutions, and Interactions," *Journal of Development Economics* 81, no. 1 (October 2006): 163–192.

[33]Frankel, Jeffrey, "Historical Precedents for Internationalization of the RMB," Council on Foreign Relations/China Development Research Foundation Symposium, The Future of the International Monetary System and the Role of the Renminbi, Beijing (2011).

[34]Eichengreen, Barry, *Managing a Multiple Reserve Currency World.* University of California, Berkeley, 2010.

[35]Mckinnon, Ronald and Gunther Schnabl, "China's Exchange Rate and Financial Repression: The Conflicted Emergence of the RMB as an International Currency," *China & World Economy* 22, no. 3 (2014): 1–35.

international financial system will be more diversified; the dollar, the euro and the RMB will eventually become more or less equally important.[36] In response to this diversified system, the central bank will reconfigure the amount of money it owns to obtain the highest return, resulting in the inherent instability of the multiplex system. Eichengreen put forward the opposite opinion. He believes that this view confuses the functions of central banks and hedge funds, and that the central bank's goal is usually long term rather than short term. The currency of the RMB and other emerging markets will diversify the supply of reserve currencies and resist the financial shock by limiting the excessive issuance of the US dollar and allowing the central bank to maintain a larger buffer zone. Therefore, a multiple financial system will be more stable than the current "dollar system." However, the adjustment of the international reserve currency is an extremely complicated process. Even if the economic scale of the Eurozone exceeds that of the United States, the euro can hardly replace the international position of the dollar in the near future. However, there are still many problems in using the SDR. Theoretically speaking, the transformation of the SDR can make the international monetary system reach a relatively ideal state, but the negotiation cost during the period is relatively high, and the type of SDR countries can accept is inconclusive.[37]

On the whole, after the collapse of the Bretton Woods system more than 40 years ago, the reform of the international reserve currency structure has become an important development direction of the current international monetary system reform. In the process, although the euro, SDR and RMB all have the potential to become major international reserve currencies, the final results will certainly vary.

---

[36]Eichengreen, Barry, *Managing a Multiple Reserve Currency World*. University of California, Berkeley, 2010.

[37]Eichengreen, Barry, *Exorbitant Privilege, The Rise and Fall of the Dollar and the Future of the International Monetary System*. New York: Oxford University Press, 2010.

2.2.2 *Literature Review on the Reform of Exchange Rate Regime*

After the Bretton Woods system collapsed, many countries adopted the floating exchange rate system, and the international currency system entered the era of a parallel system of fixed exchange rate system and floating exchange rate system. At present, the international exchange rate system can be roughly divided into three types: free float exchange rate, pegged exchange rate and dirty-floated exchange rate.

Traditional exchange rate system theorists are still arguing over the merits of the floating exchange rate system and the fixed exchange rate system. At present, the aim of discussion in the international academic community is mainly focused on the two-tier exchange rate system and the central exchange rate system. Eichengreen was an earlier scholar who proposed bipolarism.[38] Concerning the European exchange rate crisis at that time, he believed that it was difficult to succeed in the crisis by relying on gradually reducing exchange rate fluctuations to achieve a transition to a currency union.[39] Obstfeld and Rogoff made it clear that there is no comfortable middle ground between the floating exchange rate and the adoption of a common currency.[40] However, Frankel emphasized that the so-called "endpoint solution" is not a universally used method.[41] It is only applicable in certain countries at a specific time. For the three major currencies in the world, namely, the US dollar, euro and yen, Mundell believes that the sharp fluctuations in exchange rates between them have brought serious instability to the economy of the

[38]Eichengreen, Barry, *International Monetary Arrangements for the 21st Century.* Washington, DC: Brookings Institution Press, 1994.

[39]*Ibid.*

[40]Obstfeld, Maurice and Kenneth Rogoff, "The Mirage of Fixed Exchange Rates," *National Bureau of Economic Research Working Paper* no. w5191 (July 1995).

[41]Frankel, Jeffrey A., "No Single Currency Regime is Right for All Countries or at All Times," *National Bureau of Economic Research Working Paper* no. w7338 (September 1999).

three major currency regions. If a "World Currency" can be established in the future, this problem can be better solved. However, this proposal may be seen as too idealistic and not feasible in the short term.[42]

Although the discussion on the exchange rate system is inconclusive, it cannot be denied that regardless of the exchange rate system adopted by countries, the goal of the exchange rate reform in the international monetary system should be to establish a stable and orderly exchange rate system. It is necessary to formulate an exchange rate system appropriate to the economic development of a country, keeping in mind the actual conditions of different countries.

One of the IMF's initial functions was to monitor the implementation of fixed exchange rates in various countries. With the birth of the Jamaican system, this function has been weakened. A document of the IMF summarizes the current exchange rate monitoring mechanism and concludes that: (1) There is no exchange rate system that suits all countries; (2) Countries can choose their own exchange rate system to perform their duties, but they cannot peg to gold; (3) The IMF provides clear and concise recommendations within the scope of member states' performance, which are mainly based on policy stability; (4) Analysis and policy recommendations on exchange rate issues will conflict with the economic and policy situation of member countries.[43]

In 2011, a research group led by former IMF President Michel Camdessus brought together officials from major countries (including deputy governor of China's central bank), academics and former senior executives of international financial institutions, and released a proposal with the title of "International Monetary System Reform: Proposal for the 21st Century Cooperation Approach." The proposal clearly stated that since the implementation of the floating

[42]Mundell, Robert, *The Euro as a Stabilizer in the International Economic System* (Springer US, 2000), 57–84.

[43]Mundell, Robert, "The Euro and the Stability of the International Monetary System," In *The Euro as a Stabilizer in the International Economic System*, edited by Robert Mundell, and Armand Clesse, 57–84. Boston: Springer, 2000.

exchange rate in 1973, the exchange rate fluctuations between the major currencies in the system have been enlarged, reflecting that strong and unpredictable speculative forces are often inconsistent with the economic base. The current exchange rate arrangements do not respond well to large-scale international capital flows, and unconstrained cross-border capital flows are the main source of instability. They can lead to drastic economic fluctuations that will affect the country's ability to maintain macroeconomic and financial stability. Camdessus advocates that the IMF and the Bank for International Settlements (BIS) jointly establish an analytical method that can better measure and monitor global liquidity and formulate globally consistent exchange rate "standards" to help identify important exchange rate instability and misalignment.[44]

At present, the controversy over the choice of the international exchange rate system is still very large, and different countries have chosen different exchange rate systems because of their different circumstances and interests. Under the current international monetary system, regardless of the exchange rate system chosen by a given country, any analysis of the system cannot be conducted in isolation. At present, there is no research result that can uniformly process the exchange rate system of various countries, and this task is quite difficult. According to specific national conditions, the reform of the international exchange rate system should be started from the "microscopic point of view" and formulate strategies. It is unrealistic to begin global exchange rate cooperation at the "macro" level in the short term. As for the idea of a fixed exchange rate guarantee and implementation of a single global currency, we believe that it will not be realized in the foreseeable future.

2.2.3 *Literature Review of Adjustment Mechanism of International Payments*

The reform of the balance of payments adjustment mechanism is an important part of the current reform of the international monetary

[44]Camdessus, M., "The Future of the IMF," *The World in Words*, Frac Press, February 12, 2000.

system. The "Triffin puzzle" has not been completely resolved with the collapse of the Bretton Woods system. Under the current international monetary system, the "New Triffin Paradox" has formed. Dooley *et al.* believe that the current international monetary system and the Bretton Woods system are very similar in nature. They analyzed the imbalance of international payments from a European point of view and believe that the European initiative to reduce the dollar position will make the euro appreciate against the US dollar, so that competitors from Asia may be able to replace the European market share in the United States. In the final part of the research paper, Dooley and others made a questionable assumption: If the euro can replace the dollar and thus form two central currencies, how long will it take for the capital account to separate the trade account from the capital account? Although the authors did not give a definitive answer, this type of questioning is instructive.[45] The analysis of current account deficits by Bernanke *et al.* shows that: (1) the US national savings rate is negatively correlated with the US current account deficit; and (2) the US short-term interest rate increases are conducive to reducing current account deficits; (3) investment recovery in Asian countries and oil-producing countries other than China has a good effect on resolving current account issues; (4) the increase in real GDP in Japan and the euro area can reduce the current account deficit of the United States.[46] Eichengreen believes that the United States is not enthusiastic about improving the current account deficit, so Asia should make its own efforts to improve current account imbalances: for example, to achieve a balanced development of the trade sector and the non-tradable sector; to increase investment in education; encourage the development of regional bond

[45]Dooley, Michael P., David Folkerts-Landau and Peter M. Garber, "The Revised Bretton Woods System," *International Journal of Finance and Economics* 9, no. 4 (October 2004): 307–313.
[46]Bernanke, B. S., J. Boivin and P. Eliasz, "Measuring the Effects of Monetary Policy: A Factor-Augmented Vector Autoregressive (FAVAR) Approach," *The Quarterly Journal of Economics* 1, no. 120 (2005): 387–422.

markets and so on.[47] Cooper emphasized that the growth of US foreign investment and returns is the source of its trade deficit.[48] Bergsten believes that China's trade surplus is due to China's underestimation of exchange rates, but China has no incentive to improve the current balance of payments.[49] Greenwald and Stiglitz pointed out that the sovereignty and credit of the international reserve currency arrangement are the root causes of global imbalances in the international balance of payments. It is inaccurate for the United States to attribute the external imbalance to the undervaluation of the RMB exchange rate. It will only allow the United States to redirect imports to other Asian countries, and it will not fundamentally reverse the external imbalances of the United States.[50] Noyer also advocates the establishment of an effective and stable "International Financial Architecture."[51]

At the same time, as mentioned previously, under the background of economic globalization, the autonomy adjustment mechanism of the balance of payments has produced. a new feature — the valuation effect. In some industrial countries, especially the United States and Japan, the valuation effect has played a big role: when there is a long-term divergence between foreign net assets and net exports, the valuation of assets will change, and this systematic deviation will be prevented.[52] Although the short-term production cycle fluctuations

[47]Eichengreen, Barry, "Global Imbalances and the Lessons of Bretton Woods," *Economie Internationale* 48, no. 4 (2004): 39–50.

[48]Cooper, R. N., The Future of the Dollar, *Policy Brief in International Economics* no. PB09-21 (September 2009).

[49]Bergsten, C. F., *Correcting the Chinese Exchange Rate. Testimony before the Hearing on China's Exchange Rate Policy*, Committee on Ways and Means, US House of Representatives (2010).

[50]Greenwald, B. C. and Stiglitz, J. E., "A Modest Proposal for International Monetary Reform," In *Time for a Visible Hand: Lessons from the 2008 World Financial Crisis*, edited by S. Griffith Jones, J. A. Ocampo and J. E. Stiglitz. Oxford:Oxford University Press, 2010.

[51]Noyer, C., "The G20 and the Role of Emerging Markets in the New Financial Architecture," BIS (2009), http://www.bis.org/review/r090902a.pdf.

[52]Gourinchas, Pierre-Olivier and Helene Rey, "International Financial Adjustment," *Journal of Political Economy* 115, no. 4 (August 2007): 665–703.

will cause the output to fluctuate in the short term and thus affect the balance of payments, the fundamental factor affecting the balance of payments is the technical impact. Long-term technical impact increases the fluctuation of the balance of payments deficit. Technical shocks will fundamentally affect a country's output and consumption and thus determine the state of international payments.[53]

In short, we believe that the main causes of the failure of the current international balance of payments adjustment mechanism are multiple factors, such as trade imbalances, imbalances in the global industrial structure and the disorder of hot money resulting from the imbalances in the global financial system. Therefore, the reform of the balance of payments adjustment mechanism cannot be discussed concerning this matter, but discussions should start with the economic fundamentals and consider the impact of global technology shocks on the balance of international payments, and from the standpoint of the international financial system to avoid the international flow of funds and disorderly flow of balance of payments.

2.2.4 *Literature Review of International Financial Regulatory Issues*

The discussion of international financial supervision by foreign scholars is mainly from the perspective of international financial institutions. Their views can be roughly divided into two categories: some scholars believe that it is difficult to establish an effective multinational regulatory agency in the short term; the outbreak of an international financial crisis in 100 years has led some other scholars to advocate the establishment of specific institutions responsible for global financial supervision and control.

First, it is not feasible to establish an effective international financial regulatory agency in the short term. All countries should first communicate and cooperate on specific financial affairs. Only when

[53]Corsetti, G. and P. T. Konstantinou, "Current Account Theory and the Dynamics of US Net Foreign Liabilities," *CEPR Discussion Papers* (2005).

financial and monetary cooperation reaches a higher stage can high-level transnational financial supervision be realized and be more effective. Each round of regulatory reforms may gradually improve the regulatory framework and correct past loopholes or mistakes, but they may also have a negative impact on the sustainability and efficiency of the financial policy framework.[54] Crockett believes that establishing a global supranational regulatory agency is not feasible, because no authority is willing to transfer its own power to this super-sovereign organization. Therefore, the best way to reform international financial supervision now is to strengthen risk sensitivity based on the existing regulatory framework, adopt flexible monitoring mechanisms and strictly obey market rules.[55]

On the other hand, scholars who strongly advocate the strengthening of multinational financial supervision and cooperation point out that under the impact of the financial crisis, global economic uncertainties have increased. Strengthening international cooperation in financial supervision will help policymakers to control the fluctuation of spillovers from foreign countries and increase the gains of the cooperation supervision. Cross-border supervision is actually a trade-off between maintaining stability and strengthening the competitive position of the domestic financial sector. The common impact of the financial crisis on investor confidence will lead countries to focus more on financial stability, which will increase the incentive for financial regulation and coordination.[56] However, some scholars have pointed out that after the financial crisis, countries have successively strengthened financial control. However, such strengthening of financial supervision does not mean the development of international financial regulatory cooperation. In fact, compared with the era of

[54]Veron, N., "Financial Reform after the Crisis: An Early Assessment," *Bruegel Working Paper* (2012).

[55]Crockett, A., "Issues in Global Financial Supervision," *General Manager of the Bank for International Settlements and Chairman of the Financial Stability Forum, at the 36th SEACEN Governors' Conference held in Singapore* (2001).

[56]Masson, Paul R. and John C. Pattison, "Financial Regulatory Reform: Using Models of Cooperation to Evaluate Current Prospects for International Agreement," *The Journal of Economic Asymmetries* 6, no. 3 (December 2009): 119–136.

financial liberalization, in the era of strengthening financial supervision in all countries, it is intrinsically more difficult to achieve integration of international supervision.[57]

In the current stage of international financial supervision, the G20 is undoubtedly playing an increasingly important role. On the one hand, the G20 is continuously expanding its influence. On the other hand, it puts forward a series of innovative proposals for global financial supervision. Of course, as Denters pointed out, the current G-20 international financial supervision measures are mainly based on political statements. There is no substantial progress in the establishment of the organization and the construction of the framework; the financial system is inherently unstable, and a global financial supervision system should be produced under the World Financial Organization (WFO). The WFO is responsible for running this set of supervision systems to supervise the operation of international financial markets and national finances.[58]

In addition, some scholars have analyzed other relevant factors of financial supervision. Based on a review of the trends in the financial regulatory system, Masciandaro and Quintyn believe that there is a concentrated trend in financial power in the developed countries, especially in Europe. Through comparative analysis of 68 countries around the world, they believe that the strength of financial supervision is not relevant to institutional factors.[59] De Luna-Martinez and Rose studied 15 countries that have conducted financial joint supervision, and concluded that financial joint supervision is a new phenomenon and its effectiveness has not been fully exerted, regardless of the forms of the regulators, who need to have strong

[57]Rottier, S. and N. Veron, *Not All Financial Regulation is Global.* Washington, DC: Peterson Institute for International Economics, 2010.

[58]Denters, Erik, "Regulation and Supervision of the Global Financial System: A Proposal for Institutional Reform," Lecture in International Economic Law, VU University Amsterdam (2009).

[59]Masciandar, D. and M. Quintyn, "Regulating the Regulators: The Changing Face of Financial Supervision Architectures before and after the Crisis," *European Company Law* 5, no. 6 (2009): 187–196.

comprehensive planning capabilities and management capabilities.[60] Cline's related research shows that continuous supervision of global financial integration can significantly affect the economic development trend.[61]

2.2.5 *Literature Review of International Financial Organization Reform*

At present, the IMF is one of the most representative international financial organizations. Overseas scholars' discussion of the reform of international financial organizations mostly starts with the reform of the IMF. As the IMF is an international organization that is involved in a wide range of areas, its reform also involves many aspects. Here, we mainly carry out the necessary literature review on the reform of share and voting rights, supervision functions and loan functions.

Rapkin and Strand believe that the reform of IMF voting rights is an important way to improve the status of the majority of developing countries in the IMF.[62] In 2008, the IMF proposed a new voting right reform plan by which China, South Korea, Mexico and Turkey will be the first group of countries to enjoy more voting rights, although some countries hope that the list would be increased to a maximum of 10. At the same time, the initial adjustment may be between 1.5% and 2.5%. The second phase of the reform was completed before 2008, when the depth and scope of adjustment was further increased. The adjustment of the quotas is based on the proportion of each member country's economy relative to the global economy. The second phase of the adjustment will also include the increase of basic voting rights. The main beneficiaries are African countries because these countries fear that the adjustment of the entire system will weaken

[60] De Luna-Martinez, Jose and Thomas A. Rose, *International Survey of Integrated Financial Sector Supervision.* Washington, DC: World Bank Publications, 2003.

[61] Cline, W. R., *Financial Globalization, Economic Growth, and the Crisis of 2007-09.* Washington, DC: Peterson Institute, 2010, 10–35.

[62] Rapkin, D. P. and J. R. Strand, "Reforming the IMF's Weighted Voting System," *The World Economy* 29, no. 3 (2006): 305–324.

their right to speak in the foundation. For such a calculation method based on the GDP of member countries, some scholars have made clear objections.[63] Bryant believes that the new formula will not increase the share of developing countries, but will have the opposite result.[64] Cooper and Truman believe that the openness index should not be included in the formula, because the openness of many countries is positively correlated with GDP, and this will lead to double counting.[65]

After the crisis, the voice for strengthening global financial supervision has been increasing. International financial supervision organizations and national regulatory agencies have all put forward new financial supervision plans and proposals. The IMF (2009)[66] published a report on the "Lessons of Financial Institution Supervision, Financial Market Regulation, and Liquidity Management in the Future" in the context of the financial crisis. The report puts forward regulatory recommendations from regulatory bodies, scope of supervision, regulatory rules, etc., which provides a positive signal for the construction of a multinational financial supervision system in the future. In response to the problems in the new agreement, the Basel Committee on Banking Supervision has also revised a series of documents and issued more stringent rules for the supervision of bank operations to improve the quality of capital. The regulatory agencies of various countries have also made a number of recommendations, the most notable of which is *The Turner Review* published by Lord Turner, Chairman of the Financial Services Authority (FSA). After dissecting the main causes of the current global financial crisis,

---

[63] *Ibid.*

[64] Bryant, R. C., *Reform of Quota and Voting Shares in the International Monetary Fund: "Nothing" is Temporarily Preferable to an Adequate "Something."* Washington, DC: Brookings Institution, 2008.

[65] Cooper, R. N. and E. M. Truman, "The IMF Quota Formula: Linchpin of Fund Reform," *Policy Briefs in International Economics* no. PBO7-1 (2007).

[66] International Monetary Fund IMF, Lessons of the Financial Crisis for Future Regulation of Financial Institutions and Markets and for Liquidity Management, Prepared by the Monetary and Capital Markets Department, Approved by Jaime Caruana, February 4, 2009. https://www.imf.org/external/np/pp/eng/2009/020409.pdf

the 120-page report boldly proposed reconstruction of the global financial system (Turner, 2009).[67] Cooper clearly pointed out that international organizations such as the IMF should play a more important role in reducing the impact of the international financial crisis on the global economy.[68] In short, due to lack of independence and authority resulting in inadequate supervision and funding, the legitimacy and effectiveness of the IMF have been questioned to a large extent.

Therefore, how to improve and effectively play the IMF's supervisory function has also become one of the topics discussed by overseas scholars. James examined the development of the supervisory function since the establishment of the IMF and considered that "information" is very important in supervision. When conducting multilateral surveillance, having reliable information can help avoid a crisis.[69] Morck, after analyzing the organizational structure of the IMF, believes that the reform of the IMF "Board of Directors" will help the IMF's supervision function.[70] Lavigne *et al.* (2009) believe that the reform of the IMF's supervisory mechanism is fruitful.[71] If the decision-making process can be simplified and mutual adjustments can be made with the SSP, better results can be achieved. In addition, in view of the current serious global imbalances, the IMF's supervisory function on exchange rates has also received extensive attention.[72] Bergsten believes that the trade imbalance between

[67] Turner, Adair, The Turner Review: A Regulatory Response to the Global Banking Crisis. London: Financial Services Authority, 2009: 56–62.

[68] Cooper, Richard N.., "Is There a Need for Reform?" *The International Monetary System: Forty Years after Bretton Woods* (1984): 21–39.

[69] James, H., *The Historical Development of the Principle of Surveillance*, Staff Papers-International Monetary Fund (1995): 762–791.

[70] Morck, R., "Behavioral Finance in Corporate Governance — Independent Directors and Non-Executive Chairs," *National Bureau of Economic Research* (2004).

[71] Lavigne, Robert, and Lawrence L. Schembri, "Strengthening IMF Surveillance: An Assessment of Recent Reforms," Bank of Canada Discussion Paper, no. 2009–10 (July 2009).

[72] Levy-Yeyati, Eduardo and Federico Sturzenegger, "Classifying Exchange Rate Regimes: Deeds vs. Words," *European Economic Review* 49, no. 6 (August 2005): 1603–1635.

China and the United States is a major manifestation of global economic imbalances. It is therefore suggested that the IMF supervise the exchange rate of the RMB.[73]

The loan provision is one of the IMF's three major functions. Member states must have certain "conditions" for lending to the IMF. Marchesi and Thomas believe that the IMF's preparation of loan conditions is to promote the balance of payments of member states.[74] Stone believes that the IMF's loan program can improve the balance of payments of member states.[75] Among the countries that received the loans, Oatley and Yackee found that countries with close ties to the United States were generally able to obtain loans. The IMF aims to not only accomplish its risk-sharing function but to also address the challenges it faces due to political and scale constraints. The IMF's borrowing capacity must be expanded and credit lines must be guaranteed to be free from policy or political manipulation. However, this is a contradiction. The primary goal pursued by the IMF is to provide insurance and stabilize the international monetary system. Therefore, the separation of insurance funds and control mechanisms has become the focus of controversy.[76]

2.3 Progress and Trend of the Reform of International Monetary System

2.3.1 *Status of International Reserve Currency Structure*

After the collapse of the Bretton Woods system, although the status of the US dollar has fallen drastically, and the international statuses

---

[73]Bergsten, C. F., "The Dollar and the Global Imbalances," *CESifo Forum* 8, Institute for Economic Research at the University of Munich, no. 4 (2007): 3–5.

[74]Marchesi, Silvia and Jonathan P. Thomas, "IMF Conditionality as a Screening Device," *The Economic Journal* 109, no. 454 (March 1999): 111–125.

[75]Stone, Randall W., *Lending Credibility: The International Monetary Fund and the Post-Communist Transition.* Princeton: Princeton University Press, 2002; Oatley, Thomas and Jason Yackee. "American Interests and IMF Lending." International Politics 41, no. 3 (September 2004): 415–429.

[76]Oatley, Thomas and Jason Yackee, "American Interests and IMF Lending," *International Politics* 41, no. 3 (September 2004): 415–429.

Table 2.4. Comparison of Major World Currency Positions

	Proportion of Foreign Exchange Reserves in the World (%)			Daily Average Transaction Volume in Each Currency (%)			
	Year 1999*	Year 2003*	2013 Q1*	1998	2004	2010	2013Q1
USD	71.0	65.9	62.2	86.8	88	84.9	87.1
EUR	17.9	25.2	23.7	—	37.4	39.1	33.4
JPY	6.4	3.9	3.9	21.7	20.8	19	23.0

Note: *Annual data are from the end of the year or at the end of the quarter. Based on the data for April each year, since each foreign exchange transaction involves two currencies, the sum of the proportion of each currency transaction is 200%.
Source: IMF, Annual Report 2009, *BIS Quarterly Review* (June 2010), http://www.imf.org/external/np/sta/cofer/eng/index.htm. BIS. Foreign exchange turnover in April 2013: preliminary global results.

of the federal deutsche mark, the yen and the SDRs have clearly increased, the international status of the US dollar has not been fundamentally shaken (Table 2.4).[77]

From the perspective of pricing currency, the US dollar is still the world's most important currency, mainly in two aspects: First, the international oil, agricultural products and other commodities are priced in US dollars. The fluctuation of the exchange rate of the US dollar has a great impact on the prices of these commodities; second, the exchange rates of various countries are mostly based on the US dollar, and the US dollar is still the currency anchor for many countries. In particular, for countries that adopt a pegging exchange rate system against the US dollar, exchange rate fluctuations have become important regulatory targets.

From the point of view of the settlement currency, the US dollar is still the world's most important settlement currency, but the euro has had a greater impact on the US dollar settlement status. About 50% of the Eurozone's foreign trade is settled in euros, and some countries (such as Iran) have indicated that they are willing to use

[77]Xiao, Li, and Ding Yibing *et al.*, *Study on Problems of RMB Regionalization.* Beijing: Tsinghua University Press, June 2010, 63–101.

Table 2.5. Imports and Exports of Countries (Regions) in World Total Exports (%)

	Import		Export	
Year	1948	2011	1948	2011
World	100.0	100.0	100.0	100.0
United States	13.0	9.81	21.7	13.76
Japan	0.6	4.12	0.9	3.33
China	1.1	9.43	0.4	10.38
EU	—	38.8	—	37.5

Source: www.WTO.org.

the euro to settle their oil exports. At present, the proportion of international trade in the Eurozone has exceeded that of the United States, which is an important guarantee for the euro to increase its status as a settlement currency (Table 2.5).

From the standpoint of reserve currency functions, the US dollar is still the world's first reserve currency. In general, the United States still holds a large proportion of foreign exchange reserves held by countries in the world, which remains above 60% (Figure 2.7).

It can be seen that the financial crisis that began in the United States and spread to the world has not shaken the foundation of the US's hegemonic position. By providing liquidity support to central banks in all countries, the Fed has effectively acted as the "lender of last resort" in the international financial market.[78]

The financial competitiveness of the United States, especially the development of the capital market, is far ahead of other countries or regions, which in turn supports the international status of the US dollar. From the perspective of the stock market, no financial market can approach the United States in terms of scale, liquidity

[78]Goldberg, Linda S., "Is the International Role of the Dollar Changing?" *Current Issues in Economics and Finance* 16, no. 1 (2010): 2–7. Allen, W. A. and R. Moessner, *Central Bank Co-operation and International Liquidity in the Financial Crisis of 2008–9*. Basel: Bank for International Settlements, Monetary and Economic Department, 2010. McGuire, Patrick and Peter von Goetz, "The Dollar Shortage in Global Banking and the International Policy Response," *International Finance* 15, no. 2 (2012): 155–178.

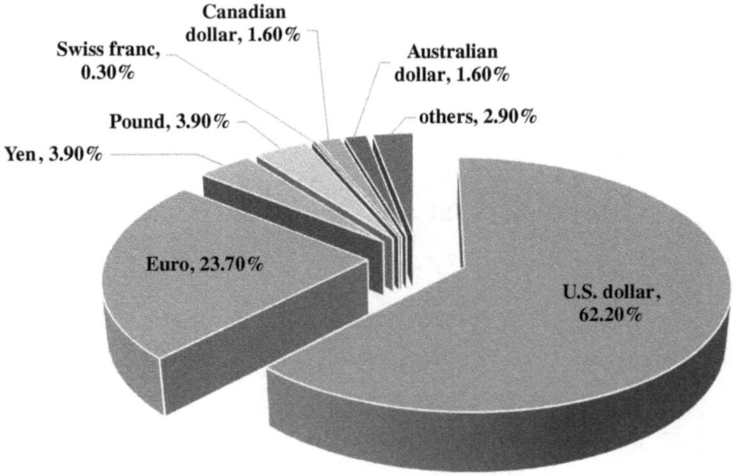

Figure 2.7. World Savings Currency Composition (End of Q1 2013)
Source: IMF Statistics Department COFER database and International Financial Statistics. https://www.imf.org/en/Data.

and selectivity. As of the end of 2012, the market capitalization of only one NYSE Euronext stock exchange reached US$14.09 trillion, an increase of 19.4% from the end of 2011. The US stock market is also more liquid than other markets. In 2012, NYSE Euronext trading was 3.9 times larger than the Tokyo Stock Exchange, 6 times higher than the London Stock Exchange, and 10.5 times higher than the German Stock Exchange; the transaction value of the NASDAQ in New York was the three certificates 2.8, 4.5 and 7.7 times the exchange.[79] The US stock market also provides investors with diversified investment opportunities. By the end of 2012, there were 2,577 companies listed on NASDAQ in New York and 2,339 listed on the NYSE Euronext. The total number of listed companies in both markets exceeded the number of issuers in any other country or regional

[79]World Federation of Exchanges, "2012 WFE Market Highlights," http://www.world-exchanges.org/files/statistics/2012%20WFE%20Market%20Highlights.pdf, December 3, 2013.

stock market.[80] From the perspective of the bond market, the US's bond issuance volume far exceeds that of other countries. Even the total bond issuances of major developed countries such as Japan and the United Kingdom (US$32.41 trillion) cannot compete with the US (US$35.68 trillion).[81] From the perspective of security holders, as of June 2012, the total amount of US securities held by foreign investors was as high as US$13.26 trillion. Among them, long-term securities were US$12.45 trillion and short-term debt was US$0.81 trillion.[82] The foreign official's increase in the shareholding of the US Treasury Department's securities is significant, with the most significant being China and Japan.[83] This is due to the fact that foreign investors have passively returned the US dollars to the United States, and that the developed financial markets in the United States have a strong attraction.

Based on the aforementioned analysis, we believe that the US dollar will remain the world's largest currency for a long time, followed by the euro. Although the euro did not fundamentally replace the dominance of the US dollar, it has already competed against the US dollar. The pound and the yen belong to the third group. The RMB is not yet an international currency and its position in the international currency system is still relatively low.

2.3.2 *Status of the International Exchange Rate System*

Since the disintegration of the Bretton Woods system in the 1970s, the international monetary system has entered the era of the coexistence of a fixed exchange rate system and a floating exchange rate

[80]World Federation of Exchanges, *2012 Annual Report & Statistics.* http://www.world-exchanges.org/statistics/

[81]*BIS Quarterly Review* (September 2013), Statistical Annex, Table 3B.

[82]Department of the Treasury, Federal Reserve Bank of New York and Board of Governors of the Federal Reserve System, "Foreign Portfolio Holdings of US Securities, as of June 30, 2012," April 2013.

[83]See http://www.treasury.gov/resource-center/data-chart-center/tic/Documents/mfh.txt, accessed on 3 December 2013.

system. The current exchange rate system arrangement in the international currency system lacks the inherent stability of the Bretton Woods system. In fact, the seemingly free exchange rate system has many problems. At the same time, the international debate on the exchange rate system of developing countries has continued. The developed countries have accused individual developing countries of undervalued exchange rates and manipulation of exchange rates. In particular, after the Asian financial crisis, developing countries represented by Southeast Asian emerging market countries, in order to achieve the accumulation of international reserve currencies, requested their central banks to continuously intervene in the foreign exchange market, resulting in a fixed exchange rate system or a managed floating exchange rate system (Table 2.6).

According to the IMF survey, as of 1 April 2008, 66 countries in the world chose the US dollar as their nominal anchor, while only 27 countries chose the euro.[84] The main reason is that the US dollar is still the most stable choice for a country's foreign exchange reserves, and the US still has the most developed financial market.

In 2007, the IMF adopted the new "Bilateral Supervision Decision" (hereinafter referred to as the "New Decision") to replace the 1977 "Exchange Rate Policy Supervision Decision." The resolution does not add new responsibilities and obligations to the member states, but instead makes necessary additions and updates to the 1977 resolution. The "New Decision" defines the concept of "exchange rate manipulation" more clearly. Irrespective of the purpose of the member country's exchange rate, changes caused or prevention of its changes in violation of the provisions of Article 4, Section 1, Subsection 3 (Article IV, Section 1 (iii)) can be considered manipulation of the exchange rate. After the US subprime mortgage crisis triggered the global financial tsunami in 2008, due to the country's commitment to economic recovery, the legalization of the floating exchange rate enabled a global competitive devaluation

[84]Eichengreen, Barry, "The Dollar Dilemma — The World's Top Currency Faces Competition," *Foreign Affairs* 88, no. 5 (September/October 2009): 53–68.

Table 2.6. Distribution of Exchange Rate Regimes in Various Countries

Exchange Rate System		Country and Region
No independent fiat money	Other national currency as legal currency (9)	Panama, East Timor, Ecuador, Kiribati, Marshall Islands, Micronesia, Palau, El Salvador, San Marino
	Eastern Caribbean Currency Union (6)	Antigua and Barbuda, Dominica, Grenada, Saint Kitts and Nevis, Saint Lucia, Saint Vincent and the Grenadines
	African Franc District (14)	Benin, Burkina Faso, Togo, Guinea Bissau, Côte d'Ivoire, Mali, Niger, Senegal, Equatorial Guinea, Congo, Gabon, Cameroon, Chad, Central Africa
	Eurozone (12)	Ireland, Austria, Belgium, Germany, France, Finland, Netherlands, Luxembourg, Portugal, Spain, Greece, Italy
Currency board (7)		Estonia, Bulgaria, Bosnia and Herzegovina, Djibouti, Lithuania, Brunei, Hong Kong, China
The traditional pegging	Staple single currency (47)	United Arab Emirates, Aruba, Egypt, Ethiopia, Antilles, Barbados, Bahamas, Pakistan, Bahrain, Belarus, Bolivia, Belize, Bhutan, Eritrea, Cape Verde, Guyana, Netherlands, Honduras, Zimbabwe, Qatar, Comoros, Kuwait, Latvia, Lesotho, Lebanon, Rwanda, Maldives, Malta, Macedonia, Mauritania, Namibia, Nepal, Sierra Leone, Seychelles, Saudi Arabia, Swaziland, Suriname, Solomon Islands, Trinidad Tato and Tobago, Turkmenistan, Venezuela, Ukraine, Syria, Iraq, Jordan, Vietnam, China

(*Continued*)

Table 2.6. (*Continued*)

Exchange Rate System	Country and Region
Peg currency basket (5)	Fiji, Libya, Morocco, Samoa, Vanuatu
Wave pinning (6)	Denmark, Cyprus, Slovakia, Slovenia, Tonga, Hungary
Management floating (51)	Algeria, Afghanistan, Argentina, Angola, Papua New Guinea, Paraguay, Burundi, Dominica, Russia, Gambia, Colombia, Georgia, Kazakhstan, Haiti, Kyrgyzstan, Guinea, Ghana, Cambodia, Czech Republic, Croatia, Kenya, Laos, Liberia, Romania , Madagascar, Malawi, Malaysia, Mauritius, Mongolia, Bangladesh, Peru, Myanmar, Moldova, Mozambique, Nigeria, Serbia, Sao Tome and Principe, Sudan, Sri Lanka, Tajikistan, Thailand, Tunisia, Guatemala, Uruguay, Uzbekistan, Singapore, Jamaica, Armenia, Yemen, India, Zambia
Independent floating (25)	Albania, Australia, Brazil, Iceland, Poland, Philippines, Democratic Republic of the Congo, South Korea, Canada, United States, Mexico, South Africa, Norway, Japan, Sweden, Switzerland, Somalia, Tanzania, Turkey, Uganda, New Zealand, Israel, Indonesia, United Kingdom, Chile

Sources: Zhang, Weiping and Wang Yiming, "The Classification of Exchange Rate Systems, Country Differences, and Historical Evolution," *International Finance Research* 5 (2007): 54–60.

of currencies, which has greatly hindered the recovery of the world economy.

The Chinese government is not entirely convinced about the "new decision" and believes that:

> The current changes in the international monetary and financial system have gradually evolved under the background of fundamental changes in the global economy and the allocation of production factors. The Fund's policy toward member states should fully consider the economic globalization, the adjustment of the industrial division of labor, the basic influence of scientific and technological progress on the current global economy, attach importance to the relationship between domestic economic stability and external stability, look at the role of exchange rate policy in achieving external stability in a country, and strengthen the supervision on member countries that issue major reserve currencies and have a key influence on the global systematic stability.[85]

Some Chinese scholars believe that the "new decision" of the IMF was led by the US and other developed countries and aimed at promoting their own national interests. The "New Decision" mainly reflects the interests of developed countries and is unfavorable to developing countries.[86]

Against the background of global economic imbalances, the issuance of the "New Decision" cannot completely solve the global economic imbalance represented by the trade imbalance between China and the United States. As mentioned earlier, we believe that the root cause of the global economic imbalance lies in the major changes in the pattern of international division of labor after the Second World War. Therefore, exchange rate factors have a very limited role in correcting this imbalance.

China announced the reform of the exchange rate system in 2005 and implemented a managed floating exchange rate system based on market supply and demand and adjusted with reference to a basket of currencies. China will not completely liberalize capital controls and

---

[85]The website of the Central People's Government of the People's Republic of China: http://www.gov.cn/gzdt/2007-06/20/content_654543.htm.

[86]Liang, Yanfen and Lin Li, "Comments on the IMF's Exchange Rate Supervision, New Decisions," *International Trade* 7, (2008): 45–50.

adopt a floating exchange rate system for the time being. Increasing the flexibility of the RMB exchange rate within a limited range is a road that is in line with the reality of China's economic development, and is also a positive move in conjunction with the reform of the international exchange rate system. Under the impact of the financial crisis, in order to avoid the disorderly flow of international capital and distortion of the exchange rate as a price mechanism, China re-selected a stable pegged exchange rate system in July 2008. The US dollar and the RMB exchange rate stabilized at 6.83. This provides a stable external environment for China's export-oriented enterprises. However, with the economic recovery and the stabilization of the international financial situation, China relaunched a managed floating exchange rate system that pegged a basket of currencies in June 2010. In response to changes in the economic and financial situation at home and abroad, the flexible adoption of an adaptive exchange rate system is conducive to the promotion of China's economic recovery and stable growth, and also reduces the possibility of transnational infections should market failure result in a crisis.

Then, how does a country choose an exchange rate system that will contribute to its own economic development? Scholars have different answers to this question, but it is certain that regardless of the exchange rate system adopted by countries, the goal of the reform of the international currency system should be to establish a stable and orderly exchange rate system. This is because the existing SDRs do not have the condition of being the only currency anchor because of design flaws, and any type of sovereign currency has no evasion of the "Triffin puzzle" as a monetary anchor. The 2008 global financial crisis and its impact were not enough to completely change the current exchange rate system. The revised plan should seek a stable exchange rate mechanism under the current framework of the exchange rate system.[87]

[87]Wang, Lirong and Lijun Liu, "The Role of China in the Future Reform of the International Exchange Rate System," *Contemporary Economic Research* 12, (2012): 71–74.

2.3.3 *Status Quo of Adjustment Mechanism of International Payments*

At present, the serious imbalance in the balance of payments has become a global fact. It is mainly reflected by the high debt and high deficits of the "financial countries" and high surpluses and huge claims of the "trade countries" (such as China and Japan). No effective adjustment mechanism in the current international monetary system can change this situation. In this context, the strengthening of monetary policy coordination across countries and regions and the promotion of international financial market development will be an important trend in promoting the reform of the international payments adjustment mechanism.

Because of the special status of the US dollar in the world economy and the international monetary system, US economic conditions and monetary policies will have a major impact on the economies of other countries. For example, the recession of the US economy after the financial crisis reduced its demand, and caused many negative impacts on the economies of other countries through various channels including trade channels, which spread the financial crisis to the world. At the same time, the highly expansionary quantitative easing monetary policy of the United States has also kept the exchange rate down while avoiding further deterioration of the financial crisis. This helped to achieve Obama's goal of 5% growth in US exports, but this balance of payments adjustment mechanism is at the expense of other countries' economic slowdown and the shrinkage of foreign exchange reserve assets. Therefore, when countries use macroeconomic policies to adjust their balance of payments, strengthening coordination and cooperation among macroeconomic policies and jointly alleviating current account imbalances will become the direction of future balance of payments reforms. In this regard, the G20 and international financial institutions should provide a platform for cooperation to promote international macroeconomic policy cooperation and reduce global fundamental imbalances.

In addition, international economic organizations should also play an active role in this aspect. As the world's three major economic organizations, the IMF, World Bank (WB) and WTO have an indispensable role in the reform of the balance of payments adjustment mechanism. At present, the IMF has already made important efforts in the coordination of international currency issues: providing theoretical guidance, enhancing information exchange and promoting international coordination and cooperation. The WB and WTO have also made their own contributions in other areas.

In addition to strengthening the coordination of monetary policy, the establishment of an international financial market is also an important way to improve the balance of payments adjustment mechanism. The emergence and development of international financial markets provide a channel for the balance of payments deficit countries to regulate the balance of payments, that is, countries with deficits can borrow or raise funds from international financial markets, so that they can plan their economic development more flexibly, and they can ease the pressure on the balance of international payments to a large extent.

At present, the trend of international financial market integration is obvious. China should actively participate in the reform of the international financial market. China is committed to working hard to create a stable international financial market.

2.3.4 *Proposals and Measures for International Financial Supervision*

In April 2009, the former Financial Stability Forum (FSF) was upgraded to become the Financial Stability Board (FSB), an important event in the field of international financial regulatory reform. In March 2009, the European Commission proposed the establishment of a pan-European financial regulatory agency. A written statement released by the Swiss National Bank in 2009 showed that Philipp Hildebrand, the Vice Chairman of the Central Bank's management committee, called for improving the financial market infrastructure based on the experience gained from the most recent financial crisis. The improvement of financial market infrastructure will be conducive to international financial supervision. At present, the international call for international financial supervision is increasing.

Since the outbreak of the global financial crisis, the Basel Committee has issued three important regulatory guidelines. The "Principles of Robust Liquidity Risk Management and Supervision" published in December 2008 proposed eight guiding disciplines, such as the establishment of liquidity risk capacity, maintaining liquidity at a sufficient level, allocating liquidity costs, benefits and risk, identification and measurement of all categories of liquidity risk, design and use of various stress testing programs, seeking a dynamic, actionable and contingent financing plan, strengthening the management of risk assets and collateral, and promoting public disclosure on market opinions. Two other documents issued in December 2009, "Strengthening Resilience of the Banking Sector" and "International Framework for Measuring, Standardizing, and Monitoring Liquidity Risk," covered five key areas: improvements in the quality, consistency and transparency of the capital base, strengthening the risk coverage of the capital framework, the introduction of leverage ratio as a supplementary measure under the Basel II risk-based framework and the use of a series of measures to enhance the capital shock absorber that was accumulated for use at the proper time during the crisis. They also introduced global minimum liquidity standards for banks with international operations. On 12 September 2010, the management meeting of the Basel Committee on Banking Supervision was held in Switzerland. The representatives of the central banks of 27 member states agreed on Basel III to strengthen banking supervision. The reform program mainly involves the minimum level of capital requirements, including raising the minimum requirement for the proportion of common shares from 2% to 4.5%, establishing a 2.5% capital retention buffer and 0–2.5% of the countercyclical capital buffer. In Article 10 of the G20 Washington Summit Declaration in 2008, it was mentioned that "after consulting with other economies and existing institutions and drawing on the advice of well-known independent experts, we will ask our Treasurer to give more opinions on strengthening the flexibility and transparency of the credit derivatives market to reduce systemic risks and improve over-the-counter market infrastructure."[88] The joint communique issued at the G20 London Summit in 2009 stated that all financial institutions, markets and tools must receive appropriate supervision and management. At the meeting, it was also decided to strengthen financial supervision and regulation, and include the shadow banking system that was previously in the gray zone.

On the other hand, the outbreak of the subprime mortgage crisis in the United States exposed the huge deficiencies of the US rating agencies and the loopholes in their supervision. Both the United States and the European Union have also decided to strengthen the supervision of rating agencies. On 21 July 2010, President Obama formally signed the Financial Supervision Reform Act and introduced an "accountability system" for rating agencies. On 21 July 2010, he signed the Dodd–Frank Wall Street Reform and Consumer Protection Act (DF Act). The bill aims to protect consumers and solve systemic risks in the financial industry. It aims to prevent the recurrence of the financial crisis in 2008. Nearly 400 political, economic and academic people related to this legislation attended the meeting. At the ceremony, Obama pointed out: "This reform represents the most powerful consumer financial protection in history." The program was implemented by a new consumer protection agency that has only one mission: to protect the common people in the financial system; not a large bank or a lender, or an investment institution. Obama also said that this reform will stop the rescue of large banks and benefit the US economy. The signing of the bill marks the completion of the US financial regulatory reform legislation that lasted for nearly two years, and it officially opened the prelude to a new financial era of Wall Street. The financial regulatory reform bill is considered to be another legislative achievement of the Obama administration following the signing of the US Medicare reform bill in March 2010.

[88]G20 Declaration Summit on Financial Market and the World Economy, 15 November 2008 http://www.g20.org/Documents/g20_summit_declaration.pdf pp. 3.

However, there is still a lot of controversy about the effectiveness of the bill in terms of the effectiveness of crisis prevention.

In the context of international financial regulatory reform, China is also actively signing financial regulatory agreements with other countries. As of 31 October 2008, China has agreements with 33 countries, which promote the legal and stable operation of bilateral agreements.

2.3.5 *Effectiveness of Reform of International Financial Institutions*

The IMF and WB are the world's leading international financial institutions. After the crisis, the IMF made major reforms to the original loan mechanism, canceling the Supplement Reserve Facility (SRF) and the Compensation and Contingency Facility (CCFF), and setting up short-term loan arrangements (Short-Term Liquidity Facility (SFL)) to alleviate the liquidity problems faced by emerging economies in crisis. Due to the limited effect of SLF, in February 2009, the Flexible Credit Line (FCL) was introduced to replace SLF. The IMF also amended the conditions for the Exogenous Shocks Facility (ESF) to make the IMF's loan assistance to less developed countries more effective. In 2010, the IMF increased quota again, but the US share still reached 16.5%.[89]

The WB recently conducted reforms mainly focusing on equity reforms, anti-corruption reforms, information disclosure systems and loan systems.[90] In October 2009, the World Bank Group's High-level Committee on Governance released the report "Injecting New Momentum for the World Bank in the 21st Century," also known as the "Zedillo Report." The report proposes five suggestions for the reform of the WB: reform of the right to speak and participation,

---

[89]International Monetary Fund, "Quota and Voting Shares Before and After Implementation of Reforms Agreed in 2008 and 2010," http://www.imf.org/external/np/sec/pr/2011/pdfs/quota_tbl.pdf.

[90]Xiong, Aizong, "World Bank Recent Reform: Progress and Evaluation," *International Economic Cooperation* 1 (2010): 60–65.

election reform of executive board seats, reform of electoral procedures, strengthening accountability for management and strengthening the resource base of the WB.

Although the IMF and WB have carried out positive reforms on their own, the issue of the "lender of last resort" has not been fundamentally resolved. Neither the IMF nor the WB can currently become a true "lender of last resort." This will not solve the risks that crises will bring to countries, and will force countries to accumulate large amounts of foreign exchange reserves to cope with them.

While the original international financial institutions are advancing reforms, the newly established international financial organizations are also actively playing their part. After the financial crisis, as mentioned earlier, in order to solve the problem of the lack of a coordinated implementation platform for cross-border financial supervision across the globe, participating member states at the G20 London Summit in April 2009 agreed to reform, expand FSB and design a relevant institutional plan, which might give the Financial Stability Commission more power and a broader role in promoting financial stability. In addition, the FSB is also responsible for assessing the fragile links in the financial system, proposing action programs for the fragile links, promoting coordination and exchange of information between financial supervisory authorities, formulating guidelines, establishing multinational regulatory agencies and providing flexible solutions for cross-border crisis management. At the same time, the FSB also needs to cooperate with the IMF to establish a joint early warning mechanism for the accumulation of macroeconomic and financial risks, and has the right to take targeted actions when necessary. The FSB will act as a coordinator for the transmission of information by countries and help promote international financial cooperation.

2.3.6 *Progress in Regional Currency Cooperation*

In general, the progress of regional monetary cooperation in Asia and Europe will help promote the development of the current international monetary system reform.

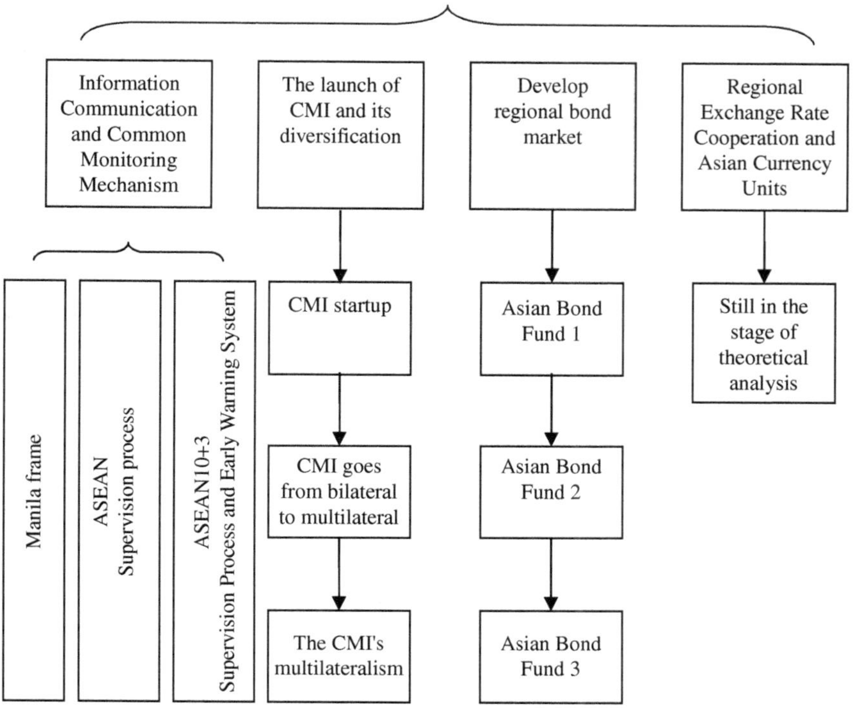

Figure 2.8. Schematic Diagram of East Asian Monetary Cooperation

At present, the process of monetary cooperation in East Asia can be roughly summarized in Figure 2.8 (see details in Chapter 4).

Regional currency cooperation in Europe was relatively successful. A new currency, the euro, was created to allow European countries to achieve a higher degree of monetary cooperation. However, there are still many problems in European currency cooperation. During the subprime mortgage crisis, the Eurozone economy and the euro suffered a heavy blow, exposing the weaknesses of countries in policy and financial coordination. Especially in the coordination of financial issues, the performance of countries is inconsistent, and the euro reform is imperative. Herman Van Rompuy, EU President, said that the strength of the Eurozone in the 11th year after its debut has hidden the financial problems in the euro area. This sovereign debt crisis has caused the euro to be hit hard. The major reform of the monetary and financial system in the Eurozone is imperative. The Lisbon Treaty may also need to be amended.[91] Under the impact of the crisis, Europe established a banking alliance to cut off the interaction between sovereign risk and bank risk, and proposed establishing a single supervision mechanism to prevent risk concentration at the EU level; to establish a single clearing mechanism to solve transnational banks' risk contagion problems; and to establish a deposit insurance mechanism to solve the banking crisis. The process of harmonizing economic policies in the countries of the Eurozone determines, to a large extent, the future of the euro.

[91]Fang, Liping and Liang Wang, "Eurozone Currency Reform is Imperative," *Guangzhou Daily*, 27 June 2010.

Chapter 3

Prospects for the Future of International Monetary System Reform: China's Vision

3.1 International Reserve Currency System Reform Program

The global financial crisis once again exposed major flaws in the international monetary system. There is a new upsurge in discussions of domestic scholars on the international monetary system reform. Chinese monetary authorities have also expressed their own opinions in various ways in response to the reform of the international monetary system. Looking at the recent literature on the study of the reform, the main focus is on aspects of the international reserve currency, the international exchange rate system, international financial institutions, multinational financial supervision, East Asian monetary and financial cooperation and the reconstruction of the balance of payments coordination mechanism. A more in-depth analysis and research was conducted, and to a great extent provided an important theoretical premise for China's active participation in the reform of the international monetary system.

3.1.1 *Overview of the International Reserve Currency System Reform Program*

Under the current situation, the international reserve currency system with the US dollar as the core can no longer adapt to the healthy development of the global economy. Especially after the financial crisis in 2008, the risks and drawbacks that the system brings to the world economy have become increasingly evident. Following the collapse of the Bretton Woods system, the United States used the trade deficit to meet the demand of other countries for the US dollar, so as to maintain the dominance of the US dollar in the international monetary system. However, with the increase in global liquidity demand, the United States' foreign liabilities have increased, and people's confidence in the US dollar has faltered, causing drastic fluctuations in the exchange rate of the US dollar. After the global financial crisis, the US Federal Reserve Committee implemented a quantitative easing monetary policy, which further exacerbated the instability of the international monetary system.[1] Huang and Xiong believe that the US dollar as a credit currency acts as both the domestic currency and the international currency, as well as fulfilling the dual functions of domestic currency and international currency, making the rights and obligations of the US dollar extremely unequal. This is the main flaw exposed by the US dollar as the core currency in the international reserve currency system.[2] For many years, the reason why the world has always accepted the United States to maintain its current account deficit is precisely that the dollar still serves as the world's leading settlement currency and reserve currency. The dollar-centric international monetary system laid the institutional foundation for the United States' debt consumption model.[3] Under

[1]Yu, Yongding, "International Currency System Reform and Preservation of China's Foreign Exchange Reserve Assets," *International Economic Review* 3 (2009): 12–18.

[2]Huang, Meibo and Aizong Xiong, "International Monetary System and Financial Crisis," *Economist* 7 (2009): 57–64.

[3]Li, Xiangyang, "The International Financial Crisis and Prospects for the World Economy," *Finance and Trade Economics* 1 (2009): 12–17.

the international reserve currency system with the US dollar at its core, it cannot meet the growing demand of non-reserve countries for international currencies due to the inability to use net capital outflows from reserve currency countries, and there are no third parties of super-sovereign countries, so they can only pass reserves. The current account deficit of the currency countries meets the demand of the non-reserve countries for international currencies, resulting in the current account deficits of the reserve currency countries and serious global economic imbalances. As long as the total demand for international reserves by non-reserve currency countries continues to grow, it will be impossible to make exchange rate adjustments to resolve trade deficits and global economic imbalances in reserve currency countries. At the same time, under this kind of international monetary system, regardless of the form of the balance of payments policy that the reserve currency country chooses, it is very easy to trigger financial crisis and global economic instability.[4]

Needless to say, if we want to make the world economy develop in a healthy and stable direction, we must reform the current international reserve currency system. The domestic academic community has put forward many ideas and suggestions on the reform of the international reserve currency system. To sum up, it can be divided into three aspects or six main points, as shown in Figure 3.1.

The first thing that needs to be pointed out is that there is no realistic basis for establishing a physical currency system, whether it is to restore the gold standard system or establish a commodity reserve currency system. The turbulence in the international monetary system at the end of the gold standard has shown that the monetary system based on physical reserves is no longer adapted to the development reality of human society.

With the restoration of the US economy, the view of maintaining the US dollar standard system may become more prominent.

[4] Wang, Daoping and Xiaoyun Fan, "Whether the Current International Monetary System is the Cause of Global Economic Imbalance and Financial Crisis," *World Economy* 1 (2011): 52–72.

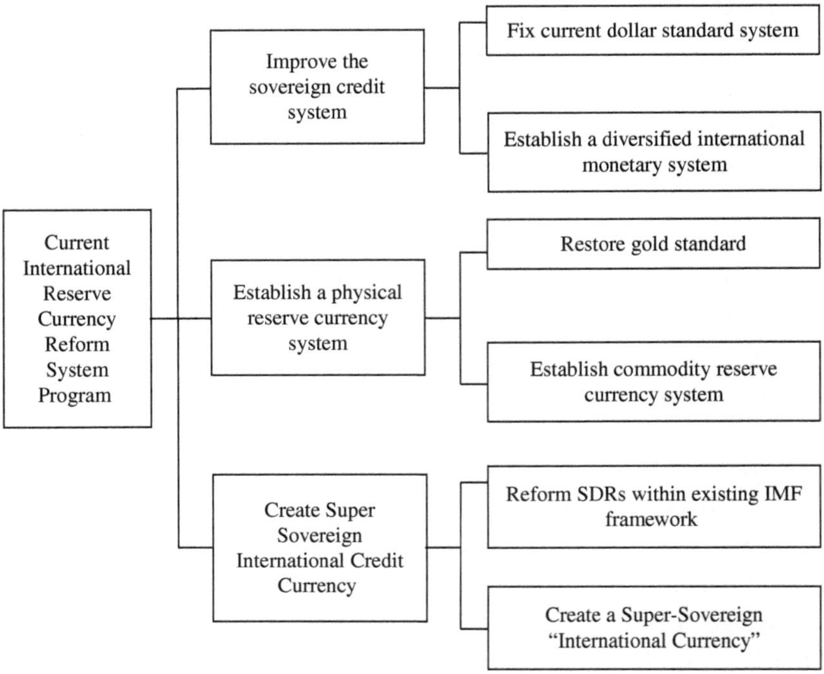

Figure 3.1. Current Reform of the International Reserve Currency System

However, the continuation of this "dollar system" that led to the "new Triffin puzzle" depends on the world's highly self-disciplined trust in the operations of the US monetary policy and fiscal policy. This is a pair of contradictions. This virtually unconstrained mechanism and trust in "self-discipline" are difficult to sustain in the long term.

At present, domestic scholars have focused on the creation of a super-sovereign international credit currency and improved the sovereign credit and monetary system in the specific reform plans for international reserve currencies.

3.1.2 *Super Sovereign Reserve Currency*

Historical experience shows that relying on the currency of a sovereign nation to act as a monetary system for international solvency is bound to cause serious instability and even collapse of the system. Therefore, the Special Drawing Right (SDR) was created by the International Monetary Fund (IMF) in 1969 to ease the inherent risks of sovereign currencies as reserve currencies have become the main targets of the super-sovereign reserve currency proposition. The superiority of the super-sovereign reserve currency is that it not only overcomes the problem of the "Triffin puzzle" and the instability of the value of reserve assets caused by the use of a country's sovereign credit currency as a liquidity measure but also helps reduce the exchange rate risk that exists under the exchange rate system of free choice. When a country's sovereign currency no longer serves as a yardstick and benchmark for global trade, the country's exchange rate policy will greatly enhance its economic imbalance. Unfortunately, the role of SDRs has not been fully realized due to limitations in the distribution mechanism and scope of use. However, Zhong believes that the idea of SDRs can still serve as a reference for the future reform of the international reserve system, replacing a variety of currency reserve systems with a basket of currencies universally accepted by all countries in the world. In this way, it is possible to fundamentally solve the problem of using a national currency as a reserve asset.[5] Shao believes that SDRs have the basic characteristics and potential of super-sovereign reserve currencies, and the IMF should use SDRs, which is a super-sovereign reserve currency, as the main direction and focus of reserve currency reform, and continue to promote and improve the use of SDRs.[6]

After the outbreak of the US subprime mortgage crisis, the Governor of the People's Bank of China, Zhou Xiaochuan, wrote an article on the eve of the London G20 Financial Summit and called for the reform of the international monetary system and the creation of a "super-sovereign international reserve currency" that can replace

[5]Zhong, Hong, "Research on the Direction of International Monetary System Reform and China's Countermeasures," *International Finance Research* 10 (2006): 18–26.

[6]Shao, Li, "Special SDR Reform Direction: Super Sovereign Reserve Currency," *China Finance* 4 (2011): 86–87.

the dollar hegemony status.[7] In his article "Reflections on Reforming the International Monetary System," he pointed out that the use of national currencies as world currencies will face contradictions between the domestic policies of the reserve-issuing countries and the needs of world economic development, in order to fundamentally solve the "Triffin Dilemma." The article proposed creating a super-sovereign reserve currency to replace the US dollar. Considering that "rebuilding a new reserve currency that has a stable fixed-value benchmark that has not been accepted by all countries may be a long-term goal," Zhou proposes to expand the scope of SDRs' issuance and use in the short term to reduce the degree of dependence of the global economy on the US dollar. The proposal was supported by the governments of emerging market powers such as Russia and Brazil. As a result, the super-sovereign reserve currency has once again become a hot topic. Of course, SDRs still have various difficulties in replacing the US dollar as an international reserve currency.[8] These difficulties were summarized by Xiang, and include the difficulties involved in the transformation of the IMF, the establishment of SDRs bond asset markets, the conversion of SDRs as a currency for valuation and settlement, and the political support and cooperation of large countries such as the United States.[9]

Wang summarized the recommendations of the academic community regarding the expansion of the use of SDR: increase the size of official SDRs and expand their use as reserve assets; add new SDR assets; assign the role of SDR as a bookkeeping currency; adjust the currency basket of SDRs to increase its appeal.[10] In addition, the alternative account surrounding SDR has also become an entry point for the establishment of a super-sovereign reserve currency.

[7]Zhou, Xiaochuan, "Reflections on Reforming the International Monetary System," *China Finance* 4 (2009): 8–9.

[8]*Ibid.*

[9]Xiang, Songxi, "International Monetary System Reform: Thoughts and Strategies," *International Monetary Review* 1 (2010): 1–21.

[10]Wang, Xin, "Analysis of Prospects for Reforming the International Monetary System and Exploiting SDR Roles," *Diplomacy Review* 3 (2011): 33–43.

A substitution account mechanism is essentially a global foreign exchange reserve open-end fund based on SDR. This account allows member countries to replace dollar assets with alternatives. The SDR assets in the account provide interest income. In other words, the member countries that do not want to hold dollar assets are not obliged to sell in the capital market, but instead they save assets in the form of SDRs at the IMF.[11] Zhang and Sheng supported the alternative account scheme, arguing that it has created the basis for SDRs to become the international currency, and it is the scheme with the smallest differences among all parties. Therefore, it is currently the most possible reform program to be adopted.[12]

Following the idea of SDRs, Lin proposed that "paper gold" be issued as a super-sovereign currency and believes that "paper gold" is a complete credit currency with the characteristics of gold and can avoid the disadvantages of gold, whose circulation growth can be determined in accordance with the need for economic growth. On the one hand, this kind of super-sovereign currency can avoid the conflict between national interests and global interests brought about by using the national currency as a reserve currency. On the other hand, it retains each country's own currency, enabling it to have independent monetary and fiscal policies. Countries that have avoided crises in the Eurozone do not have the drawbacks of their own currency and policy options for devaluation.[13] However, Ma emphasized that the fundamental difficulty of the gold standard is that its supply cannot support global economic growth and thus will cause deflation. "Paper Gold" has many difficulties in replacing the US dollar: (1) "Paper Gold" as a super-sovereign reserve currency will face the same international coordination difficulties as SDRs; (2) "Paper Gold" cannot be linked directly to gold, otherwise it will suffer from the restrictions of international gold supply; (3) If "Paper Gold" is

---

[11]Huang, Wei, "Reform of the International Reserve Currency System for Global Economic Governance," *International Finance Research* 12 (2012): 12–27.

[12]Zhang, Yiping and Bin Sheng, "Replacement of Alternative Accounts and the International Monetary System," *International Trade Issues* 1 (2011): 129–138.

[13]Lin, Yifu, "A Talk on Global Economy," *Scientific Development* 3 (2013): 3–13.

also linked to a basket of international currencies, then there is no essential difference between it and SDRs; (4) If you want "Paper Gold" to follow a rule of given quantity (for example, according to the proportion of the total global GDP), then there may be problems with adverse selection in different countries, and so on.

However, some scholars doubt or even reject the SDRs' reform strategy. Ma proposed that SDRs were originally designed to replace the US dollar as an international reserve currency design, but have not been successful so far: It faces two problems: (1) Difficulties in issue: If it is issued by the IMF, the scale is too small; if issued by the United States, it has no enthusiasm; if a certain fund issues SDRs-denominated assets, it will be considered as a basket of currencies that can be copied by other financial organizations, and it will lose its value as an independent reserve currency. Especially because of its lack of liquidity, it is even less attractive to investors. If SDRs are a new currency decoupled from any currency, the issuer becomes the new central bank, but at this stage there is no such central bank with world government significance to determine the global monetary policy. If SDRs are linked to a basket, the liquidity of newly issued SDRs will lead to more global liquidity rather than to replace the liquidity of the existing major currencies. (2) Problems of coordination: The establishment of a super-sovereign international currency actually requires that all countries renounce their monetary policy. This kind of global coordination is very difficult when the performance of the real economy has distinctive features.[14]

At present, there is another view in the academic community that advocates the creation of a super-sovereign "international currency" that does not rely on SDRs. Li proposed that there is another way to build a super-sovereign international currency — the super-sovereign international currency issued by the IMF with guarantees of gold, foreign exchange and local currency assets paid by member states.[15]

[14]Ma, Jun, "Suboptimal Selection of International Institutions: from 'Bounded Rationality' to 'Uncertainty'," *Diplomatic Review* 4 (2013): 128–142.

[15]Li, Wei, "On the Path and Prospect of Establishing a Super-sovereign International Currency," *Academic Research* 2 (2010): 91–96.

The value of the super-sovereign international currency can refer to SDRs or European currency units (ECUs). It can be used for the settlement of various international economic activities, and unlike SDRs, it can only be used for settlement between governments or international organizations. The use of super-sovereign international currencies for valuation and settlement will effectively reduce exchange rate risks, because currencies involved in the determination of super-sovereign currency will reverse the exchange rate changes between currencies to some extent due to the relative appreciation and devaluation of each other. The currency of the international currency is relatively stable. The super-sovereign international currency will gradually occupy the international currency circulation field with advantages unmatched by various foreign exchanges. The reformed IMF, as a world central bank, can adjust the amount of super-sovereign international currency by adjusting the statutory reserve ratio and the loans to central banks of various countries. At present, the United States is not active in establishing a super-sovereign international currency and other major economies in the world (such as the Eurozone countries, Japan and the United Kingdom) politically follow the policy of the United States, so the establishment of a super-sovereign international currency is difficult to achieve in the short term. However, Li Chong[16] believes that calls for the promotion and establishment of a super-sovereign international currency are necessary, ensuring it become a consensus of human society.[17]

Different from the concept of the above-mentioned super-sovereign currency, Pan[18] proposed the idea of the US-dominated single-world currency, that is, the joint construction of world currencies by the currencies of sovereign nations. She believes that the United States has the inherent requirements for the introduction of a single world currency and has explored two specific models: the first

[16]Li, Chong, "On the Path and Prospect of Establishing a Supersovereign International Currency," *Academic Research* 32, no. 2 (2010): 45–57.

[17]*Ibid.*

[18]Pan, Liquan, "Reform of International Monetary System and RMB Internationalization," *East China Economic Management* 20, no. 4 (2000): 12–28.

one is the catastrophic emergency plan by Mundell. After the financial crisis, Mundell suggested building a world currency based on the currencies of the five major economies: the US dollar, the euro, the Japanese yen, British pound and the Chinese yuan, and reorganizing the IMF into a world central bank that can issue currency. Mundell said that the single world currency is priced by a basket of currencies and issued by the IMF. International currency used for international balance sheet pricing and settlement may act as a reserve asset of the central bank. The second model is the single-world monetary commission scheme, which originates from Morrison Bonpasse's 3G plan. The plan requires establishing a global central bank (GCB), a global monetary union (GMU) and a single global currency (SGC). Pan believes that the single world monetary scheme between Mundell and Bonpasse reflects the intention of the US government to escape from the existing "dollar system."

In the adjustment of the real financial system, no matter what kind of new super-sovereign currency is created, it is necessary to balance the interests of different countries and regions. The high coordination costs, especially the different claims of various countries' interests, make the realization of this concept a long-term and arduous process. The creation of a super-sovereign currency is an economic issue, however, to a greater extent, it is also an international political issue.

3.1.3 *Diversification of the International Monetary System*

Because the US dollar supply under the current international monetary system is unrestrained, the US can continuously export the US dollar to the world through the trade deficit. When the US economy is brought into crisis, it also brings instability to the world's economies. After the last crisis, the promotion of the diversification of the international monetary system has become one of the most important directions for the reform of the current international monetary system. Chinese economists believe that the issue of diversification of the international monetary system not only relates to the long-term goals and direction of China's domestic financial reform but also relates closely to China's participation in Asian monetary and financial cooperation and the future global positioning of the RMB. For some economists, the diversification of the international monetary system is not only a tendency, it is in fact a reality that has already begun to emerge. Cao and Zhou believe that the development of a diversified international reserve currency may gradually restrict the US dollar from excessive amount of currency issue. When the currencies of major exporting countries gradually become internationalized and functional in international settlement, their use and reserves of US dollars will be gradually reduced. The issue forms a soft constraint rather than a hard constraint.[19] Lu believes that the currency truly capable of changing the hegemonic position of the US dollar would be a diversified international currency system. A diversified international currency system is conducive to the formation of a number of competing international regional currencies, free from excessive dependence on a country's currency.[20] Li and Xingzhong believe that the multi-pillar international monetary system is in fact the current default option and a realistic improvement plan. The evolution from the existing international monetary system to the multi-pillar one will largely follow the path of market-oriented development, so the economic and political resistance it encounters will also be relatively small and therefore it will be the most favorable scenario.[21] Xiang briefly summarized the seven major conditions for the international reserve currency and compared the US dollar with

[19]Cao, Honghui and Zhou Liping, "The Direction of International Monetary System Reform and Related Mechanisms," *International Finance Research* 9 (2009): 8–14.

[20]Lu, Qianjin, "Dollar Hegemony and the Reform of the International Monetary System—and on the Issue of RMB Internationalization," *Journal of Shanghai University of Finance and Economics* 1 (2010): 61–69.

[21]Li, Daokui and Xingzhong Yin, "The New Framework of the International Monetary System: A Study of Post-Finance Crisis Era," *Financial Research* 2 (2010): 31–43.

potential competitors based on these seven conditions. The results are shown in Table 3.1.[22]

Xiong and Jinping pointed out that the impact of the European debt crisis on the international currency status of the euro shows that the international currency status of the US dollar has apparently rebounded. The diversification of the international monetary system has been temporarily curtailed, and the diversified international reserves are indeed a choice or trend after the US dollar crisis, but it must be a long-term process.[23] Ma believes that with the development of diversified world economy and trade, the diversification of the monetary system is an inevitable trend, and a diversified monetary system can better realize the transaction medium of the international reserve currency under the normal economic state. Functionality and the ability to provide liquidity are imperative for the global financial system in times of crisis. At the same time, it can avoid the inequality caused by the super strong position of a single reserve currency to other countries and overcome the inefficiency of the super-sovereign reserve currency in international coordination. However, there are some inherent problems with the system of multiple reserve currencies: (1) Compared to a single reserve currency, transaction costs may increase; (2) International capital flows between different reserve currencies may be large and frequent; (3) In the event of a major economic shock, international capital could suddenly abandon a reserve currency, which may cause market volatility. From another perspective, however, these problems can be tolerated compared to a single "dollar system," SDRs or "Paper Gold."[24]

There are two main points about the specific forms of diversification of the international monetary system: the first is a multi-reserve

---

[22]Xiang, Songxi, "International Monetary System Reform: Thoughts and Strategies," *International Monetary Review* 1 (2010): 1–21.

[23]Xiong, Aizong and Dai Jinping, "European Debt Crisis and Diversification of the International Monetary System," *Guangdong Social Sciences* 6 (2012): 36–43.

[24]Ma, Jun, "Suboptimal Selection of International Institutions: From 'Bounded Rationality' to 'Uncertainty'," *Diplomatic Review* 4 (2013): 128–142.

Table 3.1. Seven Required Conditions for International Reserve Currency

	Current Ratio (%)	Political Stability	Powerful Economy	Bond Market	Stock Market	Foreign Exchange Market	Free Convertibility	Currency Stability
USD	64	10	24	10	10	10	Free convertibility	8
EUR	28	9	22	8	8	9	Free convertibility	10
RMB	Nil	10	7.40	4	4	4	Non-free convertibility	8
JPY	Less than 3	10	8	5	5	5	Free convertibility	7
GBP	Less than 3	8		5	5	5	Free convertibility	7
Swiss franc	Less than 1	10		5	5	5	Free convertibility	9
SDRs	Nil	Nil		Nil	Nil	Nil	Non-free convertibility	Nil

Note: "Nil" in the table indicates that the quantity is negligible. The gap between the United Kingdom and Switzerland is small, and SDRs are not suitable for measuring the size of the economy.

Source: Xiang, Songxi, "International Monetary System Reform: Thoughts and Strategies," *International Monetary Review* 1 (2010): 1–21.

currency system that is mainly based on the US dollar and supplemented by multiple currencies; the second is the combination of US dollar, euro and some emerging economies. The currency constitutes a situation of tripartite confrontation of the reserve currency system, including the three major international currency systems of the US dollar, the euro and the RMB. Table 3.2 lists domestic scholars' representative views.

Although the outbreak of the financial crisis has raised the demand for diversification of the international reserve currency, in fact, the current international reserve currency pattern cannot be fundamentally changed. When a currency becomes the international reserve currency, it must have three basic conditions — a stable currency value, a low transaction cost and a high degree of transparency. In Table 3.1, compared with the US dollar, there is still a clear gap between the other major currencies and the international reserve currency. The outbreak of the global financial crisis and its consequences show that the crisis does not weaken but, to a large extent, strengthens the dominant currency status of the US dollar and proves that it is difficult for the US dollar hegemony to fundamentally change in the short term. As the US economy recovers, the idea of repairing the "dollar system" may become more prominent. However, it is clear that the continuation of this "dollar system" with a profound "new Triffin problem" depends on the trust of highly self-disciplined US monetary and fiscal policy operations by countries and regions in the world. Therefore, the key issue is that under the condition that there is no restraint mechanism, the US monetary policy and fiscal policy can be "self-disciplined" and this kind of trust in "self-discipline" can be maintained for a long time.

3.1.4 *The Combination of Reserve Currency Diversification and Super-Sovereign Reserve Currency*

As mentioned earlier, after the international financial crisis, more and more domestic scholars believe that the super-sovereign reserve

Table 3.2. Comparison of the Views of Domestic Academia on the Diversification of the International Monetary System

US Dollar-Based Multi-Reserve Currency System		Three-Pole and Multi-Reserve Currency System	
Chen (2008)	This financial crisis has created conditions for breaking the hegemony of the dollar and establishing a diversified international monetary and financial system with "dollar-led and multiple currencies" which is conducive to maintaining the stability of the international market.	Zhang (2010)	From 2010 to 2030, humans will most likely see a "ternary" international currency system, that is, an international monetary system that is constructed from the three pillars of the US dollar, the euro and the Asian dollar or the currency of an Asian economy.
Wang (2009)	The goal of the current stage of the international monetary system reform is to break the monopoly position of the US dollar and establish a multi-reserve system that is mainly supplemented by US dollars and other major currencies.	Zhang and Qi (2005)	The single-centric framework of the international monetary system does not have system compatibility. Therefore, the multi-centric framework in which regional currencies act as world currencies will become the evolutionary direction of the future international monetary system.

(*Continued*)

Table 3.2. (*Continued*)

US Dollar-Based Multi-Reserve Currency System		Three-Pole and Multi-Reserve Currency System	
Cheng (2009)	In the short term, the US dollar will continue to support the unipolar system as the only core currency; in the medium term, the mainstream currencies such as the euro will increasingly share the responsibility of the world's currencies; and a multi-level "diversity" international currency with internal binding and external coordination. The establishment of the system will be completed in the long term.	Wu (2009)	It is envisaged that the future international monetary system will present the situation in which the US dollar, the euro and the RMB compete side by side. Through system arbitrage, fiscal discipline is imposed on major international currencies.
Guan (2009)	In the future, the US dollar may continue to dominate the international monetary system. This is supported by the US comprehensive and super-comprehensive national power for a long period of time. In the long run, the reserve currency diversification does not exclude US dollar guidance.	Zhang (2010)	Compared with the continued use of the US dollar as a global reserve currency and the creation of a super-sovereign reserve currency on the basis of the SDR, the multi-polarization of the international reserve currency as the evolution direction of the international monetary system may be more realistic and reasonable. In the future international monetary system, there may be a tripartite situation with the US. dollar, the euro and some Asian currency (which may be either the RMB or a basket of currencies consisting of major Asian currencies).
Dai (2011)	After a decade or more, a diversified monetary system consisting mainly of the US dollar, the euro, the RMB, etc., is formed, and the exchange rate can be coordinated, which is beneficial to the stability of the global economy. It is also more realistic and feasible.	Xu (2011)	At present, the "one American hegemony" international monetary system is extremely unreasonable and extremely unstable. It is urgent to establish a new system of world currency that has "three pillars." Due to various complicated reasons of history and reality, the establishment of a single

		currency "Asian dollar" in East Asia lacks a realistic basis. The internationalization of the RMB and a foothold in the "three pillars" are the general trend.
Ma (2013)	The single dollar-dominated currency, SDRs and paper gold have many flaws in the international monetary system. Although multi-currency systems are also flawed, countries can overcome these deficiencies through coordination. Major national policies need to be coordinated to reduce market volatility in the process of partial replacement of the US dollar by the RMB. In the current turbulent international environment, there is a special need for greater efforts by the G20, especially the long-term coordination between the United States, China and Europe.	

Source: Author, based on data.

Chen, Zhiwu, *Why Chinese Are Hardworking But Not Rich*. Beijing: CITIC Publishing House, 2008.
Wang, Songqi, "On the Reform of the International Monetary System," *The Banker* 45, no. 4 (2009).
Zhang, Haibing, "The Trend and Impact of the G20 Mechanism," *World Economic Research* 23, no. 9 (2010).
Zhang, Ming, and Donghai Qin, "Analysis on the Resource Flow of the Evolution of the International Monetary System," *World Economy and Politics* 15, no. 12 (2005).
Cheng, Shi, "Future Development of the International Monetary System: After the Subprime Crisis: Standard Choice, Direction and Path," *Economist* 19, no. 7 (2009).
Guan, Tao, "International Financial Crisis and Reserve Currency Diversification," *International Economic Review* 22, no. 3 (2009).
Wu, Guihua, "American Financial Crisis and International Monetary System," *Jiangxi Social Sciences* 39, no. 5 (2009).
Zhang, Lan, "The Attributes of the International Monetary System-A Study Based on the International Monetary Contract," *World Economic Research* 43, no. 1 (2010).
Dai, Jinping, *International Monetary System: Where to Go from Here*? Xiamen University Press, 2011.
Ma, Guonan, and Robert N. McCauley, "The Evolving Renminbi Regime and Implications for Asian Currency Stability," BIS Working Paper, no. 321 (September 2013).
Xu, Mingqi, "On the Reform of the International Financial System and the Reinvention of the Bretton Woods Institutions," *International Financial Research* 1, (2006).

currency is the ultimate goal of the reform of the international monetary system, but in reality there are various difficulties. The future reform of the international currency system is likely to be parallelism.

Qiao and Xu believe that the ultimate goal of the reform of the international monetary system is the global management of global credit, and its transitional path is from a managed multi-reserve currency system to a super-sovereign reserve currency system with the supporting mechanism of regional monetary cooperation.[25] It is believed that by strengthening the status and role of SDRs in the international monetary system and gradually making it a super-sovereign world currency, the transformation of the IMF into a "World Bank" (WB) is most likely to fundamentally resolve the problem of the instability of the international monetary system. Thus, this path is the most ideal progressive line of reform. In the specific operations to strengthen the function of SDRs, they put forward four suggestions: First, issue and distribute SDRs in a reasonable manner. Second, increase the SDRs' basket of currencies in emerging countries and adjust the proportion of each currency according to economic conditions. Third, set up an alternative account. Fourth, broaden the scope of application of SDRs. In the specific operations to improve the governance structure of the IMF, their recommendations are as follows: First, the functions of the IMF in international financial supervision and global currency management should be clarified; second, a group of currency experts should be established; third, the SDRs issuance mechanism should be reformed to meet the global economic balance; fourth, adjust the constituency of the Executive Committee to reflect the status of emerging market countries in the world economy; fifth, strengthen the IMF's ability to coordinate and supervise the operation of international reserve assets.[26]

Xiong and Meibo believe that under the current international currency system centered on the US dollar, reforms can begin with

[25]Qiao, Yide and Mingqi Xu, "Strengthening the Role and Role of SDR in the International Monetary System," *International Economic Review* 5 (2011): 52–65.
[26]*Ibid.*

the restriction of US dollar power and the strengthening of US dollar liability. From the perspective of restricting the US dollar power, there is currently no realistic basis for changing the international currency status of the US dollar. A super-sovereign currency as a good alternative to the US dollar also does not have practical advancing conditions, so the direction of short-term reforms can only be the patch of the existing international monetary system, not a fundamental change. In terms of strengthening the responsibility of the US dollar, direct and indirect constraints can be used. Due to the economic sovereignty of the United States, most of the direct constraints are not operative, but they can strengthen international economic coordination and cooperation from stabilizing the US dollar exchange rate, and to a certain extent ensure that the existing system does not deteriorate any further, and serve as a follow-up reform. The indirect constraints on the US dollar can be achieved through currency diversification. However, there are variables and risks related to the regional currency cooperation or direct internationalization of sovereign currency. Therefore, the reform of the international monetary system in the short and medium term can only proceed slowly and gradually.[27] The authors provided clearer ideas for reform in a follow-up document.[28] After analyzing the path of the super-sovereign currency for the reform of the international monetary system, they proposed that the world will move toward a unified currency and will rely on "two paths" and "a hub." The "two paths" are the path of super-sovereign currency development and regional monetary cooperation, respectively. "A hub" refers to the alternative account. Because the speed of development of the two paths will be different and there will be crossovers, it is faced with the question of how super-sovereign currencies replace the currencies of various countries (regions). Through the substitution of accounts, the

[27]Xiong, Aizong and Huang Meibo, "The Dilemma and Way Out of the Reform of the International Reserve Currency System," *China Market* 46 (2011): 8–16.

[28]Xiong, Aizong, and Meibo Huang, "An East-Asian Perspective on the Reform of the International Reserve Currency System." Changce Think Tank Global Macroeconomic Policy (GMEP) Series of Research Reports, no. 2010-007.

foreign exchange reserves of all countries (except the United States) are completely replaced by SDRs, and all foreign exchange reserves would be fully concentrated in the IMF's replacement account. At this time, under the condition of stabilizing the exchange rates of various currencies and SDRs, countries can surrender the issuance right of the national currency, then the SDRs can be fully introduced and eventually move toward world currency status.

Xu believes that the establishment of a multinational international reserve currency system is a general trend, but this system is still unstable: First, although several international currencies are jointly available as a reserve currency, its nature has not fundamentally changed and sovereign currency acts as a reserve currency. The "Triffin puzzle" brought about by this situation has not been solved; second, deflationary tendencies still exist; third, global exchange rate fluctuations and capital flows have intensified, so international financial markets may be more volatile; fourth, competitive currency devaluation may occur, leading to global inflation; fifth, inequality will not be eliminated by the diversification of reserve currencies, non-reserve currency countries will still be self-protected and will implement export-oriented economic strategies to accumulate foreign exchange reserves.[29] The only difference is that the "coinage tax" revenue of the issuing country of reserve currencies will no longer only be enjoyed by a single country, and other reserve currency issuers will benefit from it. Therefore, Xu believes that in the future, the international monetary system will inevitably be a new system that takes into account both the multiple reserve currency and the super-sovereign common reserve currency, namely, the "3+1+n" system ("3" is the US dollar, the euro and the RMB, floating between each other and competing for reserve currency status; "1" refers to SDRs, as the global common reserve currency, jointly exercising the international reserve currency functions together with

[29] Xu, Hongcai, "The Mode of Future International Monetary System Reform," *China Finance* 4 (2013): 81–82.

the US dollar, euro and RMB; "n" refers to other sovereign currencies pegging to US dollar, the euro and RMB, respectively). At the same time, Xu believes that the inherent defects of the current mechanism of SDRs have determined that they can only act as assets of international reserves and cannot be used as international reserve currency for super-sovereignty. Therefore, it is proposed to amend the IMF-related rules and authorize the IMF to issue SDRs autonomously in accordance with market demand, with IMF mandating the function of "open market operations" as "The World's Central Bank."[30]

3.2 International Exchange Rate System Reform Program

3.2.1 *Selection of Exchange Rate System*

At present, the structure of the exchange rate and exchange rate system in the world is based on the principle of free choice established by the Jamaican system. Since the 1990s, the number of countries that have chosen the free floating exchange rate system has substantially decreased, and the number of countries that have chosen the managed floating exchange rate system has increased significantly. The exchange rate arrangement mainly focuses on systems such as independent floating, managed floating, traditional nailing and no independent legal currency. In general, most developed countries such as the United States, Japan and the euro countries have adopted a floating exchange rate system, while China and other developing countries have mostly chosen a fixed exchange rate system or a managed fixed (floating) exchange rate system.

Then, how does a country choose an exchange rate system that will contribute to its own economic development? Scholars have different answers to this question, but it is certain that regardless of the exchange rate system adopted by countries, the goal of exchange

---

[30] *Ibid.*

rate reform in the international currency system should be to establish a stable and orderly exchange rate system. This is because the existing SDRs do not have the condition of being the only currency anchor due to the flaws of their original design, and any type of sovereign currency does not evade the "Triffin puzzle" as a monetary anchor. Therefore, the compromise solution should be to seek a stable exchange rate mechanism under the current international exchange rate framework.[31] Dai believes that the choice of a country's exchange rate system should comprehensively consider the various economic conditions in the country and the development of the international exchange rate system.[32] And within the development phase changes, the exchange rate system should reflect the development strategy. Zhong's research shows that the choice of exchange rate system should be a dynamic adjustment process. Different countries should choose an exchange rate system that suits their economic development strength and financial management level according to their national conditions. In different regions, there may be arrangements for currency closely linked to regional trade, namely a "regional flexible exchange rate system." Differentiated exchange rate systems will be the mainstream of international exchange rate system arrangements for a long period of time. All countries should retain their free choice, and adjust the autonomy of the country's exchange rate system.[33] Gong *et al.*[34] named the fixed exchange rate system or managed exchange rate system selected by developing countries

---

[31]Wang, Lirong and Lijun Liu, "The Role of China in the Future Change of International Exchange Rate System," *Contemporary Economic Research* 12 (2012): 71–74.

[32]Dai, Jinping, Aizong Xiong, and Shushi Tan, *International Monetary System: Where to Go from Here*? Xiamen University Press, 2012.

[33]Zhong, Hong, "Research on the Direction of International Monetary System Reform and China's Countermeasures," *International Finance Research* 10 (2006): 18–26.

[34]Gong Gang. "The Choice of Exchange Rates and Exchange Rate Regimes for Developing Countries under Non-international Currencies: On the Reform of the RMB Exchange Rate System and RMB Internationalization." 24 June 2010. ht tp://www.cfrn.com.cn/getPaper.do?id=2593.

that issued non-international currencies as the "reserve exchange rate system." Under this system, in order to achieve the accumulation of international reserve currencies, the constant intervention in the foreign exchange market of the central bank in these countries has resulted in the long-term undervaluation of the currency and a continuing trade surplus. They believe that under the current international monetary system, the system should be the best choice for developing countries.

Domestic scholars have studied the influence of different factors on the choice of exchange rate systems from different perspectives. For example, Li *et al.* used a simple monetarism model and foreign exchange reserve demand influencing factor model to find that the foreign exchange reserve required for a new market, adopting the intermediate exchange rate system arrangement, requires more foreign exchange reserves than that required by emerging markets with a fixed exchange rate regime and a floating exchange rate regime.[35] Wang analyzed, from the perspective of political economics, and stated that the nature of hegemony, domestic political systems and social interest groups all have important influence on the choice of the national exchange rate system, which broadens the research vision for the choice of exchange rate systems in various countries. Based on the international exchange rate of developed countries, the research results suggest that the choice of a country's exchange rate system should focus on two aspects: First, changes in the exchange rate system must take into account the effectiveness of government intervention in economic policy instruments; second, the choice of exchange rate system must be consistent with the development of domestic industries.[36] Huang (2012) analyzed the system from the perspective of currency mismatch. For East Asian emerging market countries,

[35]Li, Jie, Yu Chen and Liqing Zhang, "Management of Foreign Exchange Reserves and Choice of Real Exchange Rate System," *Journal of Central University of Finance and Economics* 5 (2012): 24–29.

[36]Wang, Zhengyi and Bo Qu, "Political and Economic Analysis of Exchange Rate Regime Selection: Comparison of Three Research Approaches and Their Implications," *Journal of Jilin University-Social Science* 5 (2006): 59–65.

the implementation of a flexible exchange rate system will help ease the risk of currency mismatches and bring higher benefits.[37] To this end, East Asian emerging market countries should first take steps to reduce the degree of currency mismatches and create the necessary conditions for the conversion from a pegging exchange rate system to a flexible exchange rate system.

3.2.2 *Reform of the International Exchange Rate System*

From the aforementioned analysis, it can be concluded that the central exchange rate system will have difficulty surviving for a long time, and the two-pole exchange rate system has its own defects. Therefore, the common dilemma faced by all countries and regions is: as long as the defects of the current international monetary system still exist, regardless of the exchange rate system they choose, most countries and regions cannot fundamentally eliminate large fluctuations in currency or even financial crisis, except for a few countries such as the United States.[38] Therefore, domestic academic researchers have made many suggestions on the reform and further arrangement of the international exchange rate system.

Based on the analysis of the characteristics of the combined pattern of real exchange rate arrangements in terms of regional distribution, country distribution, evolutionary trends and monetary policy framework, Geng (2007) believes that the future framework of exchange rate arrangements will move toward a coexistence of floating and fixed exchange rate systems.[39] Li (2000)[40] believes that there

---

[37] Huang, Wei, and Dongmin Liu, "G20 and Global Economic Rebalance," Analysis And Forecast Of World Economic Situation In 2012. Ed. Luolin Wang and Yuyan Zhang. Social Science Literature Press, 2012.

[38] Jiao, Jijun, "Research on RMB Internationalization," Liaoning University, 2004.

[39] Geng, Shengxin, *The Reform of the Current International Monetary System and the RMB Exchange Rate System*. Beijing: China Financial and Economic Publishing House, 2007.

[40] Li, Chong, "On the Reform of the International Monetary System," *Economic Review* 4 (2000).

will be no major changes in the international exchange rate system for a considerable period of time in the future, and countries will still have greater flexibility in the choice of exchange rate systems.[41] Xu also believes that because there are huge differences in interests between the developed and the developing countries, it will be difficult to achieve breakthroughs in reforms of core content in the short term, but it will be possible to make progress in reform areas that have already been put on the agenda. The G20's promotion of the reform of the international financial system is encouraging, and China will make more and more contributions toward promoting reforms.[42]

Zhong predicts that the euro will become a natural anchor currency for Eastern European countries, the dollar will become the natural anchor currency for Latin American countries and Asia will retain the freedom of each country's chosen exchange rate for a long period of time.[43] It may be possible to develop a regional currency framework. From the perspective of Asian monetary cooperation, Li proposes the concept of the exchange rate system in the future international monetary system and believes that Asia will become an important pole in the future international currency system and occupy an important position in the international exchange rate system.

Regarding the choice of exchange rate system, Gong studied the choice of developing countries' exchange rate regimes under non-international currencies development, and concluded that the depreciating fixed exchange rate is the system of choice.[44] This is

[41]Li, Chong, "On the Path and Prospect of Establishing a Supersovereign International Currency," *Academic Research* 2 (2010): 91–96.
[42]Xu, Mingqi, "On the Reform of the International Financial System and the Restructuring of Bretton Woods Institutions," *International Finance Research* 1 (2006): 54–60.
[43]Li, Yang, "Reform of the International Monetary System and China's Opportunities," *China Finance* 24, no. 13 (2008): 67–79.
[44]Gong, Gang, The Choice of Developing Countries' Exchange Rate and Exchange Rate System under Non-International Currency: Concurrently Discussing the Reform of RMB Exchange Rate System and the Internationalization of RMB, http://www.cfrn.com.cn/getPaper.do?id=2593,2010-06-24.

mainly due to its ability to assist developing countries to continuously accumulate international currency reserves in order to maintain their economic security. At the same time, the surplus labor force in developing countries also means that their depreciating fixed exchange rate system is not only conducive to the developing countries' catch-up with the developed countries but also conducive to the optimal allocation of resources worldwide. Of course, this choice of developing countries is actually a natural reaction to the current asymmetrical (or even unfair) international economic order. If developing countries want to abandon the choice of depreciating fixed exchange rates and completely transfer to a floating system, they must meet the following two conditions: First, the surplus labor in the developing countries must be used up; developing countries are or will soon become developed countries; second, it is the currencies of the developing countries that must become internationalized to become one of the world's major currencies.[45] Zhu and Chen believe that the developing countries should ensure the stable development of their economies by setting exchange rate target zones or adopting a managed floating system without prior announcement of interventions (Table 3.3).[46]

To sum up, most Chinese scholars believe that due to the unbalanced global economic development, different economic foundations, and huge institutional and cultural differences, all countries should retain the freedom to choose and adjust the autonomy of their own exchange rate regimes. Therefore, on a global level, it is difficult to return to a fixed exchange rate system or implement a comprehensive floating exchange rate system for a considerable period of time. The differentiated exchange rate system will remain the mainstream international exchange rate system.

---

[45] *Ibid.*

[46] Zhu, Mengnan and Wenqi Chen, "Difficulties in the Selection of Exchange Rate Systems in Developing Countries and Countermeasures," *Asia Pacific Economics* 2 (2004): 94–96.

Table 3.3. Domestic Scholars Suggestions for Exchange Rate Reform

Directions of Exchange Rate System Reform	Representative Scholar
Exchange rate system arrangements that remain flexible over a period of time	Li (2000), Xu (2006), Ran (2007), etc.
Exchange rate system arrangement under multi-polar currencies	Zhong (2006), Li (2008), etc.
Exchange rate system choice for developing countries	Gong (2010), Zhu and Chen (2004), etc.

Source: Author based on data.

Li, Chong, "On the Path and Prospect of Establishing a Supersovereign International Currency," *Academic Research* 2 (2010).

Li, Yang, "Reform of the International Monetary System and China's Opportunities," *China Finance* 13 (2008).

Ran, Shengxin, Current International Monetary System and Reform of RMB Exchange Rate System. China Finance and Economic Publishing House, 2007.

Xu, Mingqi, "On the Reform of the International Financial System and the Reinvention of the Bretton Woods Institutions," *International Financial Research* 1 (2006).

Gong Gang. "The Choice of Exchange Rates and Exchange Rate Regimes for Developing Countries under Non-international Currencies: On the Reform of the RMB Exchange Rate System and RMB Internationalization." 24 June 2010. http://www.cfrn.com.cn/getPaper.do?id=2593.

Zhong, Hong, "Research on the Reform Direction of International Monetary System and China's Countermeasures," *International Finance Research* 10 (2006).

Zhu, Mengnan, and Wenqi Chen, "Difficulties and Countermeasures of Exchange Rate System Selection in Developing Countries," *Asia Pacific Economy* 2 (2004).

3.3 Reform Program for International Financial Institutions

The current imbalance and disorder in the international monetary system poses a direct challenge to the functions of international financial institutions. In particular, the IMF, which was the most important aid agency during the global financial crisis, exhibited some degree of failure in the rescue and handling of the crisis. This has resulted in calls for reform of international financial institutions.

Domestic scholars have studied the issue of reform, especially of the IMF and the Financial Stability Board (FSB), which just begun its operations in 2009.

3.3.1 *Proposals for IMF Reform*

The IMF is the most important international financial organization in the international currency field and it plays an extremely crucial role in the development and reform of the international monetary system. Of the six proposals made by China's President Hu Jintao in his speech on changing the international financial order, given at the London G20 Financial Summit, four were directly related to the IMF, including: increase China's capital support for the IMF, with new funds prioritized for underdeveloped countries; strengthen the supervision over the currency issuance policy of major reserve currency issuing economies; improve the governance structure of the IMF and the WB and increase the representation and voice of developing countries; improve the international monetary system and the regulatory mechanism for the issuance of reserve currencies, and maintain the stability of main reserve currencies, promote the diversification of the international monetary system, and so on. Domestic scholars' research on the IMF reform mainly focused on the IMF's internal decision-making mechanisms, loan policies and conditions, supervision mechanisms and the response to the financial crisis.

In the study of the IMF's internal decision-making mechanism and its reform, Meibo believes that developing countries have a disadvantageous position in the IMF's share and voting rights, and reform of the IMF's internal decision-making mechanism is an important part of IMF reforms.[47] He further clarified the specific reform direction of the IMF: reform allocation formulas, and increase the share of developing countries; reduce the number of seats in the EU; increase the basic voting rights. The meeting of G20 finance ministers and central bank governors in September 2009 put forward the need to

[47]Huang, Meibo, "International Monetary Fund's Internal Decision-making Mechanism and Its Reform," *International Forum* 1 (2006): 54–59.

urge the rapid implementation of the reform plan of the international financial institutions in 2008 and to conduct a new review of the quotas of the IMF by January 2011.[48] However, Zhang believes that even if the new share allocation formula can be passed unanimously, the reformed IMF share structure still cannot change the US veto power and dominance of the IMF decision-making right of the US and European countries. To make the IMF's share and voting power more inclined to emerging market countries, reform formulas alone cannot be achieved and more significant system innovation must be pursued.[49]

Regarding the reform of the IMF's loan policies and conditions, Yu believes that the IMF's loan conditions have many defects, such as lack of constraints on speculative capital, lack of an effective monitoring system and equal participation rights.[50] Zhang believes that since the outbreak of the subprime mortgage crisis, the IMF has responded to the critique of emerging markets on the IMF loan by improving the loan response rate and loan size, thus enhancing the flexibility and adaptability of loan conditions, but the scale of credit resources available to the IMF is still far from enough to meet the financing scale needed to overcome the global systemic financial crisis. Therefore, it is imperative to supplement the IMF's loan resources by various mechanisms.[51]

In studies of the IMF's oversight mechanism and its response to the financial crisis, Zhao and Huang reviewed the historical evolution of the IMF's supervisory mechanisms, and discussed the latest developments and trends of this mechanism, including improved

---

[48]He, Dong, "On the Reform of Decision Mechanism of the International Monetary Fund," *Hubei Rural Finance Research* 6 (2007): 53–57.

[49]Zhang, Ming, "International Monetary System Reform: Background, Causes, Measures, and China's Participation," *International Economic Review* 1 (2010): 114–137.

[50]Yu, Yongding, "Witness Imbalances-Double Surplus, RMB Exchange Rate and US Dollar Trap," *International Economic Review* 3 (2010).

[51]Zhang, Ming, "International Monetary System Reform: Background, Causes, Measures, and China's Participation," *International Economic Review* 1 (2010): 114–137.

transparency, enhanced sense of responsibility, the development and assessment of standards, guidelines and crisis prevention mechanisms.[52] Cao believes that in the medium and long term, the IMF should invest more effort in the preventive diagnosis of member economies and eliminate the crisis in the bud, thus strengthening its function of maintaining the supervision of the global financial order.[53] Zhang believes that it is imperative to reform the macroeconomic monitoring function of the IMF.[54] The IMF should expand bilateral monitoring of member states to multilateral monitoring of global macroeconomic and financial markets; increase the transparency and binding force of macroeconomic monitoring results; in particular, improve the function of IMF in macroeconomic monitoring and its binding force on the developed countries that do not raise a request for a loan from the IMF. Integration of the IMF's macroeconomic monitoring with the financial market monitoring of the Financial Stability Committee is also a major challenge facing the international community.

In addition, in the reform proposal of internal governance of the IMF, some domestic scholars such as Yu, Huang and Xiong, and Zhang have given strong support to foreign scholars on the idea of creating an alternative account for the IMF.[55] They believe that the creation of an alternative account will not only help the IMF concentrate foreign exchange reserves to strengthen global liquidity management and reduce the risks faced by the international monetary system but also guarantee the safety of international foreign

[52]Yu, Yongding, "Reform of the International Monetary System and Preservation of China's Foreign Exchange Reserve Assets," *International Economic Review* 35, no. 5–6 (2009).

[53]Huang, Meibo, and Aizong Xiong, "On the Space and Opportunity of RMB Internationalization," *Journal of Shanghai University of Finance and Economics: Philosophy and Social Science Edition* 11, no. 2 (2009).

[54]Zhang, Ming, "International Monetary System Reform: Background, Causes, Measures, and China's Participation," *International Economic Review* 1 (2010): 114–137.

[55]*Ibid.*

exchange reserves with huge reserves of dollar assets. However, creating a replacement account faces a crucial institutional obstacle, which is who will bear the loss of the depreciation of the dollar in the alternative account. Even if the exchange gains and losses arising from the substitution of the IMF member countries are the greatest beneficiaries of the countries' alternative account scheme for countries with large foreign exchange reserves (such as China) and the United States, it is unfair for those countries with a basic balance of international payments. If it is possible to agree on the sharing of exchange gains and losses in the alternative account, the alternative account will still be difficult to implement (Table 3.4).

3.3.2 *Functional Analysis of the Financial Stability Committee*

The biggest flaw of the international financial supervision system exposed by the subprime mortgage crisis is the lack of a unified coordination agency responsible for financial supervision on a global scale. The IMF, the Bank for International Settlements, the Basel Committee, the various accounting standards committees and the financial supervisory authorities of various countries are fighting each other in the supervision of cross-border operations of financial institutions, resulting in overlapping supervision, regulatory vacuums and complex interventions because of the inconsistency of standards. In order to address the lack of a coordinated implementation platform for cross-border financial regulation across the globe, the G20 summit in London, April 2009, decided to establish a global financial supervision system. The FSB came into being in this context and officially began operations on 27 June 2009. The FSB's member institutions include central banks, finance ministries, and regulatory agencies and major international financial institutions and professional committees in more than 20 countries. The Chinese Ministry of Finance, the People's Bank of China, the China Banking Regulatory Commission and the Hong Kong Monetary Authority of China are members of the committee. The specific functions of the FSB include:

Table 3.4. Domestic Scholars' Suggestions on IMF Reform

Suggestions for IMF Reform	Representative Scholar
Internal decision-making mechanism reform	Huang (2006), He (2007), Zhang (2010), etc.
Reform of IMF loan policies and conditions	Yu (2010), Zhang (2010), etc.
The IMF's oversight mechanism and the reform of the financial crisis function	Zhao and Huang (2005), Cao (2008), Zhang (2010), etc.
Reform of IMF internal governance	Yu (2009), Huang and Xiong (2009), Zhang (2010), etc.

Source:
Huang, Meibo, "International Monetary Fund's Internal Decision-making Mechanism and its Reforms," *International Forum* 1 (2006).
He, Dong, "On the Reform of the Decision-making Mechanism of the International Monetary Fund," *Hubei Rural Finance Research* 6 (2007).
Zhang, Ming, "Reform of the International Monetary System: Background, Reasons, Measures and China's Participation," *International Economic Review* 1 (2010).
Yu, Yongding, "Witness Imbalances-Double Surplus, RMB Exchange Rate and US Dollar Trap," *International Economic Review* 3 (2010).
Zhao, Guojun, and Meibo Huang, "An Overview of the Supervision Mechanism of the International Monetary Fund," *International Information* 9 (2005).
Cao, Jing, "Strengthen the Supervision Function of the International Monetary Fund," *Business Culture* 9 (2008).
Yu, Yongding, "Reform of the International Monetary System and Preservation of China's Foreign Exchange Reserve Assets," *International Economic Review* 5–6 (2009).
Huang, Meibo, and Aizong Xiong, "On the Space and Opportunity of RMB Internationalization," *Journal of Shanghai University of Finance and Economics: Philosophy and Social Science Edition* 11, no. 2 (2009).

assessing the fragility of the global financial system; supervising countries in improving actions; promoting cooperation and exchange of information among national regulatory agencies; providing advice on national regulatory policies and regulatory standards; coordinating the work of international standard setting agencies; formulating emergency plans, etc. Zhang believes that the most important function of the FSB is to become a platform for information communication and exchange among governments, international organizations, international standard setting agencies, and various agencies responsible for specific financial supervision and regulation.[56] All types of regulators are able to communicate and monitor regulatory concepts and regulatory practices in the framework of the FSB, thereby suppressing regulatory arbitrage to the greatest extent and preventing the outbreak of systemic risks through global prudential supervision.

The outbreak of the global financial crisis has prompted the lack of cross-border financial regulatory mechanisms, which in turn will shape the FSB as an important platform for the implementation of cross-border financial supervision in the future. This is of great significance for the introduction of a series of measures for cross-border supervision in the future. However, whether this platform can play the role expected by the founders depends upon resolving key issues.

There is the integration of overlapping functions with existing international organizations. Huang pointed out that the current FSB is a new form of cooperation organization outside the UN framework.[57] Cooperation and links with existing UN financial institutions such as the IMF and WB need to be established. Mechanisms for giving the original cooperation institutions new functions, allowing them to play an important role in the new international financial order, must be solved urgently. For a concrete example, after the establishment of the FSB, the overall monitoring task of the international financial market that originally belonged to the IMF appeared to be borne more by the FSB. Interfacing the macroeconomic monitoring of the IMF with the financial market monitoring of the FSB became a major international problem in the short term.

In terms of the formulation of regulations, the FSB distinguishes itself from an important aspect of the previous Financial Stability Forum, in that it has a charter to clarify the basic operating rules and

[56]Zhang, Ming, "International Monetary System Reform: Background, Causes, Measures, and China's Participation," *International Economic Review* 1 (2010): 114–137.

[57]Huang, Fanzhang, "G20 and Reform of International Monetary System," *Financial Studies* 2 (2010): 44–51.

thus provide the institution with a more adequate and stable institutional basis. According to the statutes, the goal of the FSB is to coordinate the work of competent national authorities and international standard setting bodies at the international level in order to formulate and promote the implementation of effective regulatory policies and other financial policies, and to work with international financial institutions to address the fragility of the financial system. To this end, the main responsibilities of the FSB include: (1) assessing issues that affect the vulnerability of the global financial system, identifying and reviewing regulatory actions and other related actions that need to be taken in a timely and sustained manner and their results; (2) promoting the cooperation and information exchange between competent authorities accountable for financial stability; (3) monitoring market development and its impact on regulatory policies, and making related recommendations; (4) making recommendations on best practices for meeting regulatory standards and conducting supervision; (5) conducting joint strategic reviews; the policy development offices of international standards setting bodies ensure that their work is timely, effective and focused on priorities; (6) establishing guidelines and providing support for the establishment of supervisory colleges; (7) supporting the development of supervisory colleges; (8) collaborating with the IMF to establish early warning exercises.

The internal governance structure of the FSB is divided into four levels: the plenary session, the steering committee, the chairman and the secretariat. There are also three standing committees and three special working groups. Its membership is broader than the Financial Stability Forum and is divided into the following three categories: (1) Member States (Regions) Competent Authorities responsible for the maintenance of financial stability, namely the Ministry of Finance, the Central Bank and the Financial Supervisory Authority, including members of the G20 and the corresponding competent authorities of Switzerland, Spain, Singapore and Hong Kong; (2) International financial institutions, including IMF, WB, Bank for International Settlements and Organisation for Economic Co-operation and Development (OECD); (3) International standard setting bodies, including the Basel Committee, the Payment and Settlement System Committee, Global Financial Systems Committee, International Accounting Standards Board, International Association of Insurance Supervisors and International Securities Regulatory Commission, etc. The international standard setting bodies that are members of the FSB remain independent, but work closely with the former and report to the FSB without compromising existing reporting arrangements or independence. International financial institutions participate in the FSB as members, subject to their respective legal frameworks and policies.[58]

In addition, regarding the distribution of discourse power, it can be seen from the candidates of the committee's director that the FSB has expanded European discourse power, but the discourse power of emerging countries has not been reflected. This financial crisis reflects the lack of self-regulation by the United States that has the absolute right to speak. It is clear that the distribution of this discourse power of the FSB is not beneficial to eradicating the ills of the global monetary system.

3.4 Multinational Financial Supervision System Reform Plan

3.4.1 *Overall Direction of Multinational Financial Regulatory Reform*

For financial supervision under the conditions of financial globalization, the academic community has always had two different orientations: regulatory competition and regulatory cooperation. Chen obtained an analysis based on a two-nation game model indicating that the long-term cooperation strategy will be the best strategy choice for the game player. This provides theoretical support for international financial regulatory cooperation. The two suggestions

[58]Liao, Fan, "The New Development of International Financial Supervision: From the Perspective of G20 and FSB," *The Review of International Law — Wuhan University* 1 (2012): 176–191.

on the international financial regulatory system put forward by Hu Jintao at the Pittsburgh summit in September 2009 also showed that China is moving forward with regulatory cooperation. The specific content of the proposal is: first, the reform of the international financial supervision system should touch upon the most fundamental regulatory principles and objectives. The future financial regulatory system must be simple and easy to implement. Second, the world should strengthen financial supervision and cooperation, expand the coverage of financial supervision, and quickly formulate universally accepted financial regulatory standards.[59]

Song believes that the "dollar system" will not change in the short term, and that countries have different national conditions. Therefore, the most feasible method at this stage is to establish an international multilateral governance mechanism consisting of bilateral governance, regional multilateral governance and global multilateral governance.[60] Jiang proposed nine improvements for the reform of the international financial supervision system under the background of the global financial crisis: (1) reform the unipolar international currency system and steadily promote the diversification of the international monetary system; (2) expand the scope of financial supervision, and achieve fair supervision of all financial institutions, financial products and financial markets; (3) strengthen the supervision of compensation incentive mechanisms to avoid short-term risk-taking behaviors of market operators and financial institutions; (4) improve the financial regulatory coordination mechanism and focus on preventing cross-industry and cross-border risks; (5) re-examine the accounting standards accompanying the market, avoid bubbles in economic prosperity and shortage of funds in times of economic hardship; (6) promote a rational return of business models for financial institutions, from selling risk to active risk

[59]Chen, Qiqing, "Competition or Cooperation: A Game Theory Analysis of International Financial Supervision," *Financial Studies* 10 (2008): 187–197.

[60]Song, Xianwei, "Multilateral Governance Mechanism of International Financial Supervision — A Multi-layered Framework of Vision," *Journal of Fujian Institute of Public Administration* 3 (2009): 93–97.

management; (7) improve bank risk management to ensure transaction transparency; (8) dialectically treating financial product innovations to ensure that financial innovations are compatible with risk management capabilities; (9) changing the competitive model in the financial market from a free competition model to a responsible competition model.[61] Huang also proceeded from this financial crisis and believed that the internationalization of financial supervision should be implemented. That is to say, international cooperation in financial supervision should reach consensus and make commitments on the concepts, principles and methods of financial regulatory cooperation, forming a powerful and consistent cross-border, trans-regional or even global regulatory cooperation mechanism, and establishing effective and timely information sharing mechanisms and risk early warning mechanisms.[62] Guo and Mengnan pointed out that from the perspective of China, it is difficult to strengthen its own financial supervision and China should take corresponding measures from five aspects: (1) actively participate in the international financial regulatory organization and strive to make international regulatory standards; (2) promote cooperation and exchanges between bilateral supervisory authorities and improve the stability of the financial system; (3) strengthen coordination and cooperation among domestic regulatory authorities and improve supervision efficiency; (4) strengthen supervision of online banking and prevent illegal online transactions; (5) enhance Asian currency cooperation and increase the flexibility of the RMB exchange rate.[63]

Domestic academics have reached a consensus on whether to choose supervisory cooperation. However, due to the late start of research on international financial issues, especially the reform of the

[61]Jiang, Dingzhi, "The Problem of Improving Financial Supervision under the Crisis," Peking University (CCISSR) Forum (2009).

[62]Huang, Fanzhang, "G20 and Reform of International Monetary System," *Financial Studies* 2 (2010): 44–51.

[63]Guo, Chunsonga and Zhu Mengnan, "Strengthening International Coordination and Cooperation in Financial Supervision," *Shanghai Finance* 10 (2004): 28–30.

international monetary system, the fact that China's capital projects have not yet been opened means most of the domestic studies are less targeted, with lower operability (Table 3.5).

In short, as a developing country that is gradually integrating into financial globalization and continuously opening its financial system, China should actively participate in the reform of the international financial supervision system. The Chinese government should actively participate in the activities of BIS, the Basel Committee and other international financial multilateral organizations, and these should be integrated into the global financial supervision system as soon as possible. As a member of the G20 and FSB, the Chinese government should actively participate in the formulation and implementation of future international financial regulatory standards and exert its due influence in the standard setting process.

3.4.2 *Macro-prudential Regulatory Issues*

Ding pointed out that macro-prudential supervision should include five aspects: First, the financial system's supply of funds to the real economy, credit pricing, the leverage ratio of borrowers and the degree of risk assumed by both parties. Second, the asset structure, the form of the transformation of the maturity of different assets and related liquidity risks, such as the extent of bank asset maturity mismatches, and banks' reliance on wholesale financing. Third, whether the price of assets such as housing, stocks and credit securitization is consistent with its long-term equilibrium value. Fourth, the level of leverage of the financial system. Fifth, the impact of some new types of financial institutions, especially financial institutions that have not yet been prudently monitored, such as hedge funds, on systemic financial risks. The Financial Services Authority of the United Kingdom proposed that macro-prudential supervision tools should include such regulatory indicators as capital adequacy ratio, provision for loan losses, liquidity and leverage. At the same time, in the application of macro-prudential supervision tools, the UK Financial

Table 3.5. Domestic Academics Discussions on International Financial Supervision and Reform

Problems	Representative Scholar	Conclusions
Should international financial regulatory cooperation be implemented?	Chen (2008)	Yes.
What is the background of financial supervision cooperation and reform?	Song (2009)	Under the dollar system.
	Jiang (2009)	To promote the diversification of the international monetary system and propose nine reforms.
How should China participate?	Guo and Zhu (2004)	(1) Actively participate in the international financial supervision organization, make efforts to bring the regulatory standards into line with international standards; (2) Promote the cooperation and exchanges between the bilateral supervisory authorities and improve the stability of the financial system; (3) Strengthen the coordination and cooperation of domestic regulatory authorities and improve the efficiency of supervision; (4) Strengthen the supervision of online banking to prevent various risks brought about by online transactions; (5) Improve Asian currency cooperation and increase the flexibility of the RMB exchange rate.

Source: Authors, organized according to relevant data.

Services Authority believes that monetary and fiscal policies can also refer to the results of macro-prudential supervision.[64]

Regarding macro-prudential management, Xia pointed out that the subprime mortgage crisis, the global financial crisis and the global economic recession caused all countries to face the problem of systemic risk, that is, not a single country but the entire global system.[65] For the understanding of macro-prudential management, the first is macro-prudential management from a global perspective, then followed by internal macro-prudential management of a country. In financial practice, different countries and different periods have different understandings and concerns for macro-prudential management. For example, due to the inconsistent degree of openness under capital projects in various countries, countries are also inconsistent with the objectives and policy measures for macro-prudential management.[66] Since Basel III was formulated under the conditions of complete liberalization of capital projects, some provisions of macro-prudential management may not be fully applicable to the developing countries, especially countries that have not yet fully opened up under capital projects. From a global perspective, the maturity of financial systems in various countries is inconsistent, with the characteristics of structuralism and inequality. Therefore, emerging market economies must follow the principle of gradual and orderly progress in macro-prudential management. Therefore, Xia believes that the current macro-prudential regulatory framework discussed by the international community should be viewed objectively, rationally and dialectically, avoiding the same mistakes as those used only by foreign countries. It should be noted that the current macro-prudential management systems and mechanisms are incomplete and have a process of constant exploration.[67]

[64]Ding, Desheng, "Research on the Modes and Models of Financial Supervision at Home and Abroad after the Subprime Mortgage Crisis," PhD thesis of Liaoning University (June 2013).

[65]Xia, Bin, "Macro-Prudential Management: Framework and Improvement," *China Finance* 22 (2010): 30–32.

[66]*Ibid.*

[67]*Ibid.*

Li analyzed the problem of macro-prudential supervision from the pro-cyclical perspective of the financial system and pointed out that the pro-cyclicality of the financial system is mainly reflected in three aspects: pro-cyclicality of capital adequacy ratio supervision, pro-cyclical provision of loan losses and pro-cyclicality for fair value accounting. The first two aspects are reflected in the fact that when the economy is in an upswing, the financial system will increase the supply of credit to the real economy. On the other hand, when the economy is in a recession period, it will reduce the supply of credit to the real economy. The third aspect is reflected in the amplification effect of the financial system on asset price fluctuations. In order to change the effect of pro-cyclical development on the economic and financial development, he suggested that the financial system should be reformed in three areas in a pro-cyclical manner: first, a counter-cyclical capital buffer mechanism should be established, that is, the capital adequacy ratio should be appropriately increased when the economic prosperity increases. Contrarily, when the economic situation is bad, the demand for capital adequacy ratio is lowered. Second, the provision for counter-cyclical loan losses is established to prevent possible financial risks. Third, the fair value of accounting reforms is reformed so that the asset value can be more in line with its long-term value.[68]

Shi[69] systematically reviewed domestic scholars' research on macro-prudential supervision issues and related policy recommendations. As mentioned, Li and Bin summarized the evolution of the financial supervision system in the United States, the United Kingdom, the European Union, Germany, France and Japan, focusing on the reform and development of financial supervision in various countries after the crisis broke out. The main trends in future financial regulatory reforms include the following: first, adjusting financial regulatory structures; second, establishing a macro-prudential

[68]Li, Wenbiao, "Discussion on Counter-cyclical Policy under the Macroprudential Supervision Framework," *Financial Studies* 7 (2009): 7–23.
[69]Shi, Jianping, and Yu Gao, "A Summary of the Research on Macro-prudential Supervision Theory," *International Finance Research* 12, no. 8 (2011): 34–45.

regulatory framework to prevent systemic risks; third, reaching a consensus on strengthening the intervention in the financial industry; fourth, assessing financial institution's balance sheet; fifth, promoting financial information exchange; sixth, strengthening the protection of the interests of investors and consumers; seventh, restructuring financial executive compensation system; eighth, promoting coordination and cooperation in global financial regulations. They also clearly pointed out: "The new changes in the economic and financial system require a more comprehensive financial supervision system, and macro-prudential supervision will be a key part of this."[70] Cao believes that China should establish the long-term goal of a unified financial system for supervision, division, collaboration and umbrella management, establish a unified financial regulatory agency (China Financial Supervision and Management Commission) to conduct comprehensive financial management, and propose that reform of China's financial supervision system can be divided into three phases.[71] Xia also pointed out that it is necessary to establish a macro-prudential management team or institution on the basis of existing institutions, collect relevant data, formulate specific selection targets, design for a series of policy indicators and participate in international cooperation of macro-prudential management, then take the unified responsibility for decision-making to the State Council.[72] On the other hand, Li Yu *et al.*[73] hold different viewpoints. They stressed the importance of central banks in the framework of macro-prudential supervision, and considered that the nature of macro-prudential supervision is macro-liquidity management, and

---

[70]Li, Yang and Hu Bin, *Global Financial Regulatory Reform in the Background of the Financial Crisis*. Beijing: Social Science Academic Press, 2010.

[71]Cao, Fengxi, "Enlightenment of the Global Financial Crisis to China," *International Finance Research* 5 (2009): 3.

[72]Xia, Bin, "Macro-prudential Management: Framework and Improvements," *China Finance* 22 (2010): 30–31.

[73]Li, Wei, "Macro-prudential Supervision and Financial Stability," *Financial Research* 8 (2009): 52–59.

there is inherent consistency of the functions of the central banks, monetary and credit policy instruments, independence, etc., so the central bank is assumed to take the responsibility of macro-prudential supervision.

3.4.3 *Revision and implementation of Basel III*

After the global financial crisis broke out, the developed countries such as the United States began to revise the existing international financial regulatory framework. Basel II, which was adopted in 2004, bears the brunt. The introduction of international financial supervision has entered the era of Basel III. In this regard, domestic scholars have conducted more in-depth research, and put forward some new insights from different perspectives.

He Fan pointed out that as witnessed from the outbreak of the financial crisis, the Basel Accords have serious flaws in at least the following aspects: (1) Focusing solely on capital adequacy ratios and ignoring liquidity risks. In this financial crisis, due to the credit crunch, many banks with sufficient capital are still unable to obtain liquidity and are forced to "close down." (2) Miscalculation of risk. Due to the different capital adequacy ratios of the Basel Accord for different business requirements, the capital requirements for mortgage loans are lower than those for large enterprises, which leads banks to be keen to save capital. Under Basel II, foreign banks' loans to Icelandic banks require less capital compared to their loans to higher-trust multinationals because the Icelandic government has a very high credit rating. The Basel New Capital Accord also encourages banks to have greater impulse to asset securitization, because it can also reduce their capital requirements. (3) Over-reliance on the self-risk assessment of large banks. The Basel Capital Accord allows large banks to evaluate their capital requirements based on their own internal risk models. The financial crisis has proved that this practice has completely failed. The entire Basel framework is based on a blind belief in market forces, but the banks that could provide the highest returns to shareholders before 2007 have suffered the most damage in this financial crisis. Equity investors prefer banks that are more willing to taking a risk, rather than relatively conservative banks.[74]

Zhong pointed out that Basel III aims to encourage commercial banks in all countries to reduce their high-risk businesses, improve their ability to resist financial crises and ensure that banks have enough reserves to deal with the crisis alone without relying on government assistance in the event of a financial crisis. Its implementation will have a profound impact on the global banking industry as follows: (1) the global banking industry will face greater financing pressure, especially the European banking industry; (2) the new standard of bank capital is too harsh and will have a large impact on the economy and may inhibit the supply of capital that is crucial to economic growth and new employment; (3) the new capital structure will affect the business model and operation model of the financial sector; (4) the new agreement may lead to international regulatory short-term arbitrage. However, the impact of Basel III is limited for the banking sector of China in the short term. The specific reasons are as follows: First, the current regulatory standards for capital adequacy in China's banking industry and the actual capital adequacy ratio for commercial banks are all at a relatively high level. Second, China's bank supervision requirements will increase significantly with the implementation of the new agreement. The commercial banks will then face the pressure of supplementary capital. Third, other regulatory indicators of Basel III such as leverage, buffer capital and liquidity indicators will also have an impact on the Chinese banking industry.[75]

The series of studies on Basel III indicate that Basel III aims to strengthen global financial risk supervision of both the individual banking and financial systems. At the level of a single bank entity (micro-prudential), it intends to increase the ability of banks and

[74]He, Fan, "Unscrupulous International Financial Regulatory Cooperation," *International Economic Review* 3 (2010): 155–156.

[75]Zhong, Wei, *Basel III The New Developments and Preliminary Impacts*, edited by Xie Ping, editor-in-chief of Financial Transformation. Beijing: China Economic Publishing House, 2011.

other financial institutions to recover during periods of market fluctuation, so that banks can better withstand the pressure of economic and financial risks.[76] The main contents include the improvement of the original capital supervision requirements and the establishment of liquidity standards. At the level of the entire financial system (macro-prudential), it seeks to reduce the impact of banks with potential systemic risks on the entire financial industry, so as to support global long-term financial stability and economic growth. Therefore, Basel III represents the general trend of international financial regulatory reform.[77] As one of the members of the G20, China has an obligation to implement the supervision of high capital requirements in line with Basel III. At the end of April 2011, the "Guiding Opinions on the Implementation of New Regulatory Standards for the Chinese Banking Industry" issued by the China Banking Regulatory Commission became a programmatic guideline for the implementation of new international regulatory requirements in China. This guideline for the implementation of new regulatory standards, which includes the four regulatory tools, is based on the new regulatory ideas such as counter-cyclical supervision in Basel III's capital framework.[78] From a practical perspective, China should, in light of its own financial development and the actual situation of financial institutions, effectively implement the prudential supervision concept that combines the regulatory framework established by Basel III.[79]

---

[76]Ba, Shusong and Yuanqian Zhu, *New Basel Capital Accord in the Financial Crisis: Challenges and Improvement*. Beijing: China Financial Publishing House, 2010.

[77]Ba, Shusong, *Basel III Represents the General Trend of International Financial Regulatory Reform* (*China Economic Times*, January 4, 2012).

[78]Ba, Shusong, Lingling Jin and Yuanqian Zhu, "The Impact of Capital Supervision under Basel III on China's Banking Industry," *Rural Finance Research* 6 (2011): 12–16.

[79]Ba, Shusong, Lingling Jin and Yuanqian Zhu, "The Reform of the Basel III Market Risk Capital Framework and the Application of Commercial Banks in China," *Study on Financial Development* 1 (2013): 3–7.

3.4.4 *International Financial Regulatory Cooperation*

Chen analyzed the current two orientations of international financial supervision: regulatory competition and regulatory cooperation.[80] On the basis of sorting out existing literature, he utilized the game theory method to build a game model for countries to cooperate in financial supervision. The research shows that if we give up the hypothesis of a game and extend the game process, the (cooperation, cooperation) strategy is a subgame perfect Nash equilibrium for an infinite number of repeated games. The equilibrium path is that the two players choose the cooperation strategy at each stage. In other words, the cooperation strategy will be the optimal tactical choice for the players in the long run. International regulatory cooperation is theoretically established and is the best choice for international supervision. At the same time, it can also be observed in reality that international financial regulatory cooperation is constantly being promoted in the race for short-term interests and long-term interests. Because of the short-term benefits of national self-interest and opportunism, the form of international financial supervision and cooperation is more important than the essence. Bilateral regulatory coordination lacks a stable mechanism to guarantee the resolutions, while principles and criteria adopted by international financial cooperation organizations also tend to be kept only in the ideological discussion. However, based on consideration of long-term interests, the international community has taken important steps in international financial regulatory cooperation. International financial regulatory cooperation organizations such as the Basel Committee, the International Securities Commission and the International Association of Insurance Supervision have been established one after another, and many international regulatory standards have been introduced in an attempt to promote the integration of financial regulatory practices in various countries. Therefore, as financial globalization continues

[80]Chen, Qiqing, "Competition or Cooperation: A Game Theory Analysis of International Financial Supervision," *Financial Studies* 10 (2008): 187–197.

to advance, the interests and needs of regulatory cooperation will increase, and international financial regulatory cooperation will also achieve greater progress.[81]

Tan and Li believe that inaccurate understanding of financial regulation, lack of timely action and inadequate measures are important factors in the outbreak of the crisis. They suggested that the authority should consider strengthening international regulatory cooperation in coping with the subprime mortgage crisis. International regulatory cooperation is an inevitable and realistic choice to deal with the financial crisis. At the same time, strengthening international and national financial supervision is the key to coping with the financial crisis. In all measures, seeking financial breakthroughs in regulatory theory and new policy practices are fundamental requirements for preventing and resolving the financial crisis. In the future development of financial supervision theories, they pointed out that the Great Depression in the 1930s gave birth to Keynesianism, and that the subprime mortgage crisis in the early 21st century heralded in a comprehensive reflection on the current economic and financial theories aimed at improving the existing theoretical system, by seeking more effective solutions to the current characteristics of economic development.[82]

3.5 Plan for Monetary and Financial Cooperation in East Asia

After the outbreak of the Asian financial crisis, the monetary and financial cooperation within the East Asian region has gradually been highly valued by regional governments and academia. In the past decade or so, regional financial and monetary cooperation has made some progress in Asian financial markets, East Asian foreign

---

[81] *Ibid.*

[82] Tan, Yong and Meng Li, "From the 'Great Depression', China and the United States Deal with the Current Financial Crisis," *Journal of Shanghai University of Finance and Economics* 6 (2008): 65–71.

exchange reserves, the Chiang Mai Initiative (CMI), and regional cooperation mechanisms for policy dialogue. In terms of regional exchange rate cooperation, a variety of initiatives have also been proposed. However, East Asian monetary and financial cooperation still faces many difficulties: the supervision mechanism in the region is still difficult to put into practice. The bilateral exchange in the CMI lacks uniform rules and substantial binding force, and the size and depth of the East Asian bond market are inadequate. In addition, the official dialogue mechanism within the system is not effective. At the same time, the East Asia region is facing new challenges such as global imbalances in the balance of payments, devaluation of the US dollar, rising oil prices, and monetary and financial cooperation issues. What needs to be pointed out in particular is that East Asian monetary and financial cooperation has not been able to make breakthroughs and has failed to develop to the level of exchange rate coordination and cooperation. Although the 2014 APEC Beijing meeting once again put forward the idea of further promoting the Asia-Pacific free trade zone, and enhancing further cooperation between relevant countries in the fields of national investment and currency, there are still many problems hampering cooperation in the region.

3.5.1 *East Asian Financial Market Construction*

East Asian currency cooperation should be gradual and cannot be accomplished overnight. At present, the main purpose of the East Asian monetary and financial cooperation is to rescue and prevent a crisis. In a discussion on the time framework of East Asian financial cooperation, Shi divided the regional financial cooperation in East Asia into three stages: short term, medium term and long term. In the short term, East Asia should still focus on monetary and financial cooperation in the region's "lender of last resort." With regard to the establishment and improvement of the emergency rescue mechanism, the focus of the medium-term work is on the development of regional capital markets, especially the long-term bond market. East

Asia exchange rate cooperation can only be realized in the longer term.[83]

The governments of East Asian countries have made considerable contributions to the development of the East Asian bond market. Huang and Lin in the book "Study on the Development of the East Asian Emerging Bond Market," discuss the four initiatives that governments have reached for in the construction of the East Asian Bond Market — Asian Bond Market Initiative (ABMI) and Asian Bond Fund (ABF). A detailed and systematic introduction was made to the Regional Bond Market Development Initiative (RBMDI) and the Asian Bond Market Development Initiative (ABMDI). The book gives a positive assessment of the East Asian bond market's achievements in improving currency mismatch, stabilizing the financial system and promoting regional financial integration.[84]

However, in recent years, East Asian countries have basically moved more than they take in the regional bond market. This is mainly because the plan needs to resolve too many contradictions and problems in the process of the East Asian bond market construction. Specifically, it includes: first, the lack of a unified legal framework, accounting standards, regional credit guarantee system, and regionally recognized credit rating agencies in the bond market; second, to avoid marginalized non-cash currency countries, the regional bond market should define an appropriate Asian currency basket as the bond fixing currency. In case it is difficult to advance the cooperation of the exchange rate mechanism, this kind of "Asian" bond issuance will be difficult; third, the currency swap market in each country is not yet sound. In the absence of effective coordination, the function of the Asian bond market to resolve currency mismatches is greatly limited; fourth, and more importantly, the domestic bond market in the region is underdeveloped, and capital controls exist in almost all

[83]Shi, Jianhuai, "East Asian Financial and Monetary Cooperation: Short-term, Medium-term, and Long-term," *International Economic Review* 6 (2010): 56–60.
[84]Huang, Meibo and Yang Lin, *Research on the Development of East Asian Emerging Bond Markets: From the Local Currency Bond Market to the Asian Bond Market.* Beijing: Economic Science Press, 2008.

low-income countries. The level of financial ties is much lower than the degree of financial correlation between Asian and European and American markets. These are important obstacles to the development of regional financial markets.[85] Li and Ding pointed out that according to the stronger financial correlation between Asia and European and American markets, the development of a regional international currency (such as US dollars) bond-bonded market is only one of the conditions in which the currency in the region is not fully convertible. The transitional measures and the development of the US dollar bond market in the region will allow the US dollar funds of each country to be more allocated to the local market, which will help reduce the dependence on US domestic investment vehicles.[86]

As Asia's largest developing economy, China faces basic characteristics of the small size of the domestic financial market, the limited depth and breadth of the financial market, the backwardness of the financial sector and the extent of financial liberalization. Regarding promotion of China's participation in the development of regional financial markets, Gao believes that the real consideration is to realize the overseas issuance of RMB bonds through this developed market in Hong Kong. The RMB corporate bonds issued in Mainland China from 2007 to 2008 are an important practice in this area.[87] Zhang also put forward similar proposals, arguing that there are two main paths for the development of the regional bond market: one is to develop the domestic bond market, and the other is to develop the regional bond market. On the one hand, the Chinese government

[85]Li, Yang, "Development of Bond Market: The Challenges of Asia," *International Finance Research* 11 (2003): 10–16; Gao, Haihong, "The Role of China's Asian Regional Financial Cooperation," *International Economic Review* 3 (2009): 25–36; Hu, Ying and Jie Hu, "The Focus of Asian Financial Cooperation: Developing the Asian Bond Market," *International Finance Research* 5 (2004): 25–31.

[86]Xiao, Li, and Ding Yibing, "East Asian Financial Cooperation under Global Financial Turmoil: Policy Options and Recommendations," *International Economic Review* 6 (2008): 45–49.

[87]Gao, Haihong, "The Role of China's Asian Regional Financial Cooperation," *International Economic Review* 3 (2009): 25–36.

should integrate the internationalization of the Chinese bond market with the internationalization of the RMB, and at the same time promote the development of the offshore RMB bond market in Hong Kong and the domestic panda bond market. On the other hand, we must devote ourselves to integrating domestic government debt and corporate bond markets.[88]

3.5.2 *East Asia Reserve Bank*

The concept of the East Asian foreign exchange reserve originated from the Asian Monetary Fund (AMF), proposed by Japan. The proposal was once suspended because of opposition from the United States, the European Union and the IMF. In May 2000, ASEAN 10+3 finance ministers signed an agreement to establish a regional currency swap network in Chiang Mai, Thailand, that is, the Chiang Mai Protocol (CMI). The ASEAN 10+3 finance ministers' meeting in May 2007 decided to establish a self-managed regional foreign exchange reserve as a concrete form of the Chiang Mai Initiative Multilateralization (CMIM). The central banks of each member state set a certain amount of foreign exchange reserves to establish the regional foreign exchange reserves with the value of US$80 billion. The reserve fund is used for short-term liquidity support to member countries under the conditions of financial crisis. In February 2009, under the prevailing global financial crisis, ASEAN 10+3 finance ministers announced the "Asia Economic and Financial Stability Action Plan." The planned scale of the reserve fund was increased to US$120 billion and it was proposed to establish an independent regional monitoring entity. In May 2009, the ASEAN 10+3 parties reached consensus on all elements of the reserve pool and determined the time when the reserve bank would begin to operate.

[88]Zhang, Ming, "The Easy-going Difficulty of Structural Transformation in Asian Countries," The International Finance Research Center, Institute of World Economics and Politics, Chinese Academy of Social Sciences, 2010.

The multilateralization of the CMI mechanism means significant progress in the cooperation of the East Asian reserve. Gao believes that the multilateralization of CMI has actually laid the foundation for the further construction of the East Asian Monetary Fund. The future development is mainly to further institutionalize the current multilateral CMI mechanism, but its function still remains to provide short-term financing support. The specific progress of the East Asian foreign exchange reserve is shown in Table 3.6.[89]

The conclusion of the "Foreign Exchange Reserve Pool" agreement is a major breakthrough in financial cooperation in East Asia. Zheng[90] pointed out that the "Foreign Exchange Reserve Pool" will cope with financial issues in East Asian countries when summarizing the significance of the "Foreign Exchange Reserve Pool Plan."[91] The crisis will effectively ease the liquidity difficulties of some member countries. It will complement the existing international financial institutions and promote the reform and improvement of the international financial system. At the same time, what is more important is that the establishment of the "Foreign Exchange Reserve Pool" is the beginning of East Asian monetary and financial integration. It will upgrade regional currency funds at the right time, and create conditions for the initiation of Asian currency units (ACUs) and ultimately the unified currency.

The future development of East Asian foreign exchange reserves is a matter of greatest concern to the international community. This issue involves two levels: first, whether the foreign exchange reserves

[89]Gao, Haihong, "Common Foreign Exchange Reserve Funds of ASEAN, China, Japan and South Korea: An Important Measure to Move towards Asian Monetary Funds," *Working Paper of International Finance Research Center, Chinese Academy of Social Sciences, Policy Brief No.* 08030, www.ricf.org.cn, 2008; Gao, Haihong, "The Role of China's Asian Regional Financial Cooperation," *International Economic Review* 3 (2009): 25–36.

[90]Zheng, Haiqing, "Regional Response to the Financial Crisis: East Asian Foreign Exchange Reserve Bank," *World Economic Research* 12 (2009).

[91]Zheng, Haiqing, "Regional Response to the Financial Crisis: East Asian Foreign Exchange Reserve Bank," *World Economic Research* 12 (2009).

Table 3.6. Progress of East Asian Foreign Exchange Reserves

Time	Meeting	Progress
2007.5	10th ASEAN+3 Finance Ministers' Meeting (Kyoto, Japan)	The participating parties agreed in principle that the CMI will be changed frequently and established self-managed foreign exchange reserve arrangements.
2007.11	11th ASEAN+3 Leaders' Meeting (Singapore)	Signed the Second Joint Statement on East Asia Cooperation and the 2007–2017 Cooperation Work Plan between ASEAN and China, Japan and South Korea.
2008.5	11th ASEAN+3 Finance Ministers Meeting (Madrid, Spain)	The parties reached a consensus on the size of the East Asian foreign exchange reserve pool: at least US$80 billion, and the ratio of the three countries of China, Japan and the Republic of Korea to ASEAN is 80:20, and agreement was reached on key issues such as the conditions for the use of loans and the initiation mechanism.
2008.11	ASEAN+3 Finance Ministers and Central Bank Governor Deputy Meeting (Hakone, Japan)	A preliminary consensus was reached on specific measures to deal with the financial crisis, such as accelerating the establishment of the reserve bank, expanding the scale of the reserve pool and strengthening regional economic monitoring, and the drafting of the "Asia Economic and Financial Stability Plan of Action" was begun.
2009.2	ASEAN+3 Special Finance Ministers' Meeting (Phuket, Thailand)	The "Asia Economic and Financial Stability Action Plan" was submitted; the original scale of the East Asian foreign exchange reserve database has been expanded to US$120 billion; countries have further strengthened the regional testing system and established an effective and reliable monitoring mechanism to ensure the timely start of the East Asian foreign exchange reserve; the aforementioned monitoring mechanism, after effective operation, will guide the percentage of loans that have been delinked from the existing IMF terms, which can be increased.
2009.4	ASEAN+3 Finance Ministers and Central Bank Governors Deputy Meeting (Thailand, Thailand)	A consensus was reached on such factors as the capital contribution structure, loan quotas, monitoring mechanism and borrowing conditions. ASEAN countries also reached a preliminary consensus on their share of investment; Hong Kong, China joined the East Asia Foreign Exchange Reserve.

(Continued)

Table 3.6. (*Continued*)

Time	Meeting	Progress
2009.5	12th ASEAN+3 Finance Ministers' Meeting (Bali, Indonesia)	Consensus was reached on all major elements of regional foreign exchange reserves, including share of capital contribution, amount of borrowing and monitoring mechanism; all parties agreed to formally establish a foreign exchange reserve bank in East Asia by the end of 2009; they agreed to establish an independent regional monitoring agency as soon as possible for the East Asian region. The internal economy in the region is monitored and analyzed, and it provides support for the decision-making mechanism of the East Asian foreign exchange reserves. Hong Kong, China officially participate in the East Asia foreign exchange reserves.
2010.5	13th ASEAN+3 Finance Ministers Meeting (Tashkent, Uzbekistan)	On 24 March 2010, CMIM officially came into effect. All parties agreed to adjust the share of capital contribution from Indonesia, Malaysia, the Philippines, Singapore and Thailand so that the five countries' share of foreign exchange reserves is equal.
2011.5	14th ASEAN+3 Finance Ministers Meeting (Hanoi, Vietnam)	In favor of the "Guidelines for Enhancing the Effectiveness of CMIM," this guideline is a currency swap operating manual specified in accordance with the CMIM protocol.
2012.5	15th ASEAN+3 Finance Ministers Meeting (Manila, Philippines)	The size of foreign exchange reserves has doubled, from US$120 billion to US$240 billion; the proportion of non-connected IMF has increased from 30% in 2012 to 40% in 2014.
2013.5	15th ASEAN+3 Finance Ministers Meeting (Delhi, India)	The parties agreed to further study "improving the use of local currencies under CMIM" and "jointly dealing with capital flows under ASEAN+3."
2014	APEC Beijing Conference	The establishment of the Asian Infrastructure Investment Bank entered a substantive stage and helped promote the rational allocation of regional foreign exchange reserves.

Source: Zhao (2010) and the official website of the Association of Southeast Asian Nations: http://www.asean.org/.
Zhao, Jin, "G20: New Mechanism, New Issues and China's Propositions and Actions," *International Economic Review* 5 (2010).

managed independently by each country eventually evolve into a unified account of centralized management, and the focus of this step is the transfer of the reserve bank to the Asian Currency Fund; second, whether the reserve bank will evolve into AMF, and an independent agency is set up to manage, operate and use these foreign exchange assets, forming regional crisis response mechanisms and institutions at the same time. Regarding the aforementioned issues, Li and Ding proposed the establishment of an Asian Cooperative Investment Fund (ACIF) that will mainly invest in financial assets in the region. This fund will transform the self-management of multilateral CMI into joint management.[92] This step will complete the first-level problem. Then, the fund is combined with the functions of the ABF, which is used to invest in sovereign and semi-sovereign bonds denominated in international currencies in the region. This move enables the unified management and operation of foreign exchange assets in the fund. There are two major advantages of ACIF over the multilateral CMI and the "Foreign Exchange Reserve Pool Program": first, ACIF can effectively achieve the goal of diversifying the risk of reserve assets in various countries, relocating funds within the region, and combining reserve resources in East Asia with East Asian financial market development; second, ACIF can play the role of issuing preparations and guarantees for issuing regional currency or currency basket-denominated assets, thereby further strengthening the development of Asian regional financial markets.[93]

The "Foreign Exchange Reserve Pool" and its further development as regional currency funds have provided conditions for the creation of the ACU. Although ACU has no direct connection with CMI, they can complement each other. In 2005, the Asian Development Bank created the ACU with reference to the ECU. However, its

[92]Xiao, Li, and Ding Yibing, "East Asian Financial Cooperation under Global Financial Turmoil: Policy Options and Recommendations," *International Economic Review* 6 (2008): 45–49.
[93]*Ibid.*

start-up plan has been postponed indefinitely because of the inability to determine the weight of each currency in the currency basket, especially due to various complex political and economic conflicts. At present, ACU is only an index of exchange rate stability. However, if ACU can be supported by smooth regional economic development, its function is likely to expand to the ACU-denominated bond issuance, and expand to be the currency of trade and investment, and the valuation currency of financial assets such as stocks and bonds, leading to widespread use in the private sector. By then, ACU will use the "Foreign Exchange Reserve Pool" or the regional currency fund platform to prevent devaluation of the currencies of neighboring countries, promote the coordination of regional exchange rates, maintain relatively stable regional currency values, reduce the dependence of US dollar of East Asian countries and reduce the size of large-scale regional foreign exchange asset reserves in East Asia, help to ease global imbalances in the balance of payments, and promote economic integration in East Asia.

At present, the majority of domestic scholars' researches on ACU focus on its use as a basket currency in the economic region and it is used in the research of regional exchange rate cooperation mechanisms. The two-layer currency basket structure proposed by Ou and Zhang includes exchange parity between ACU and ERMTPCB (the currency basket formed by the currencies of major trading partners outside the region) and the exchange rate parity between East Asian currencies and ACU.[94] Ogawa and Zhizhong summarized the advantages and disadvantages of the currency basket: pegging the currency basket can eliminate frequent changes in the exchange rate and reduce the impact; the fluctuation of the pegging currency against other single currencies is conducive to the formation of stronger exchange rate risk for residents and enterprises. It is also conducive to the cultivation of awareness of forward markets and the creation of hedging instruments in the foreign exchange

[94]Ou, Minggang and Kun Zhang, "Study on the Structure of Double Currency Baskets in East Asia," *International Financial Research* 6 (2010): 15–23.

market, facilitating the transition to a more flexible exchange rate system. However, its disadvantage is that it increases the cost of international contacts; it does not evade foreign exchange shocks. This is a passive intervention and requires the central bank's regulation, so it cannot completely avoid the impact of foreign exchange reserves on monetary policy.[95] Zhang and Fan (2006) believe that to further exert the influence of ACU on regional exchange rate cooperation, it is urgent to work in two aspects: firstly, the issuance of ACU-denominated bonds; secondly, monetary authorities in the regional economies should complete ACU's parity design in the process of exchange rate adjustment. This will lay a solid foundation for further East Asian exchange rate cooperation.[96]

3.5.3 *Currency Interchange between Central Banks*

The bilateral currency swap agreement in East Asia originated from the CMI established after the Asian financial crisis in 1997. Chen believes that during the Asian financial crisis, the performance of the IMF prompted the East Asian countries to strengthen cooperation. The AMF plan proposed by Japan appears to be too radical, and the IMF's "aid" and the AMF's stranding are the direct cause of redevelopment of currency swap agreements. In the CMI mechanism, the foreign exchange reserve bank is a multilateral mechanism, and the currency swap arrangements between ASEAN countries and the currency swap arrangements between China, Japan and South Korea and ASEAN are all bilateral mechanisms. If the reserve bank has developed significantly, then whether or not bilateral currency swaps will face marginalization becomes a question which is worth discussing.[97] Zheng believes that bilateral currency swaps cannot be

[95]Ogawa, Yoshihide and Yao Zhizhong, "On the Exchange Rate System for Pegging a Basket of Currency," *World Economy* 6 (2004): 3–10.
[96]Zhang, Bin and He Fan, "The Impact of Asian Currency Units on East Asian Monetary Cooperation and RMB Exchange Rate Reform," *Managing the World* 4 (2006): 11–18.
[97]Chen, Wenbin, "The Progress and Prospects of the East Asian Currency Swap Mechanism," *Southeast Asia* 3 (2003): 1–4.

replaced by multilateral mechanisms. The reason is that bilateral and multilateral mechanisms are both potential effective countermeasures, and to some extent, bilateral mechanisms are more rapid and effective than multilateral mechanisms. However, it should be pointed out that different bilateral agreements under the CMI have different arrangements and there is no standard sample. This means that if a country wants to obtain sufficient funds from multiple agreements, it must negotiate swap agreements with different exchange agreement partners separately, which considerably increases the transaction costs of financing arrangements.[98]

In order to prevent the spread of the global financial crisis, the Fed has provided liquidity facilities by signing bilateral currency swap agreements with central banks of other countries. From 12 December 2007 to 17 September 2008, before the US subprime mortgage crisis fully erupted, the US Federal Reserve Bank signed bilateral US dollar swaps with the European Central Bank and the Swiss Central Bank, and expanded the size of the swaps three times; from 18 September 2008 to 29 October 2008, with the bankruptcy of Lehman Brothers leading to the outbreak of the subprime mortgage crisis, the Fed added new bilateral US dollar exchange agreements with central banks of major developed countries such as Japan, England, Canada, Australia, Denmark, Sweden and Norway, which also significantly expanded the scale of swap agreements; on the other hand, it added bilateral swap agreements of the US dollars with emerging markets such as Brazil, Mexico, South Korea and Singapore. In this context, various levels of liquidity rescue mechanisms such as foreign exchange reserve banks, bilateral currency swap agreement networks, and bilateral currency exchange agreements in East Asia have also been strengthened to varying degrees. Yang pointed out that in the context of global financial turmoil, some countries in the East Asia

[98]Zheng, Liansheng, "Reservoir, Chiang Mai Initiative and East Asian Finance and Cooperation, Progress, Prospects and China's Policy," http://www.iwep.org.cn/info/content.asp?infoId=3908/, 2009-05- 07.

region began to transcend the regional financial cooperation framework and adopted a bilateral agreement signed by their central banks to provide liquidity to each other in the form of local currency in exchange for foreign currency. Bilateral exchange of local currency can not only lock in existing bilateral trade but also promote the further development of bilateral trade.[99] Li and Ding concluded that the currency swap agreement signed by the People's Bank of China has two distinct features: first, it focuses on the implementation of the strategy of RMB regionalization, and follows the path of "start with rim, then global"; second, there are distinctive roles of swap agreements with different countries. The exchange agreements with South Korea, Malaysia and Indonesia are mainly to facilitate mutual investment and trade settlement. The exchange agreement with Argentina is mainly to realize the role of using RMB as a trade payment settlement currency. The swap agreement with Belarus is mainly to use the RMB as a reserve currency.[100]

After the bilateral currency swap agreement under CMI and the global financial crisis, the bilateral currency swap agreements signed by China and other countries and regions all use the RMB as the currency of contract. Domestic scholars generally acknowledge the positive significance of currency swaps in responding to crises, so more research has been conducted on currency swaps from the perspective of RMB internationalization. He suggested that the bilateral currency swap agreements signed between China and East Asia and its neighboring countries should be transformed from the rescue model in emergency times to the ordinary model, that is, by the bilateral currency swap agreement between the monetary authorities of the two countries, they can promote the use of RMB in the

[99]Yang, Quan, "Development of Bilateral Currency Swap in East Asia under the Background of Global Financial Turmoil," *International Finance Research* 6 (2010): 30–40.

[100]Xiao, Li and Ding Yibing, "Change Trend of RMB Exchange Rate and Its Impact on Regional Monetary Cooperation," *International Finance Research* 3 (2009): 8–17.

private sector. For example, an RMB loan is provided to a foreign commercial bank with a shortage of capital.[101]

On 31 October 2013, the Fed, the European Central Bank, the Bank of England, the Bank of Japan, the Bank of Canada and the Swiss Central Bank, the world's six major central banks, converted their existing temporary liquidity swap agreements into long-term currency agreements. This was described by the American economist Pistor as the Six-Country Central Bank Club.[102] The Fed's actions meant that at the moment of crisis, the Fed only acted as the lender of last resort for some developed countries, while other emerging market-oriented countries were excluded. At the currency level, the currencies of these countries were further marginalized. Therefore, emerging market countries need to conduct further alliances to improve collective security capabilities. Regarding the relationship between Asian currency swaps and the internationalization of the RMB, Ma and Zhou believe that the expansion of bilateral currency swap countries and the increase in the amount of agreements have created opportunities for the internationalization of the RMB. China should utilize bilateral currency swaps as an important means of participating in international financial rescue.[103]

3.5.4 *Regional Cooperation in Asian Financial Supervision*

The development of monetary and financial cooperation in East Asia has promoted the financial supervision of East Asian countries to gradually move from individual to regional.

[101]He, Fan, "The Real Choice of RMB Internationalization," *International Economic Review* 4 (2009): 8–14.

[102]Pistor, Katharina, *The Legal Theory of Finance* (August 2013). https://www.ineteconomics.org/perspectives/blog/katharina-pistor-the-legal-theory-of-finance.

[103]Ma, Renqi and Yongkun Zhou, "Currency Swap: An Effective Tool for Participating in International Financial Assistance and Promoting Internationalization of RMB," *China Finance* 4 (2009): 20–21.

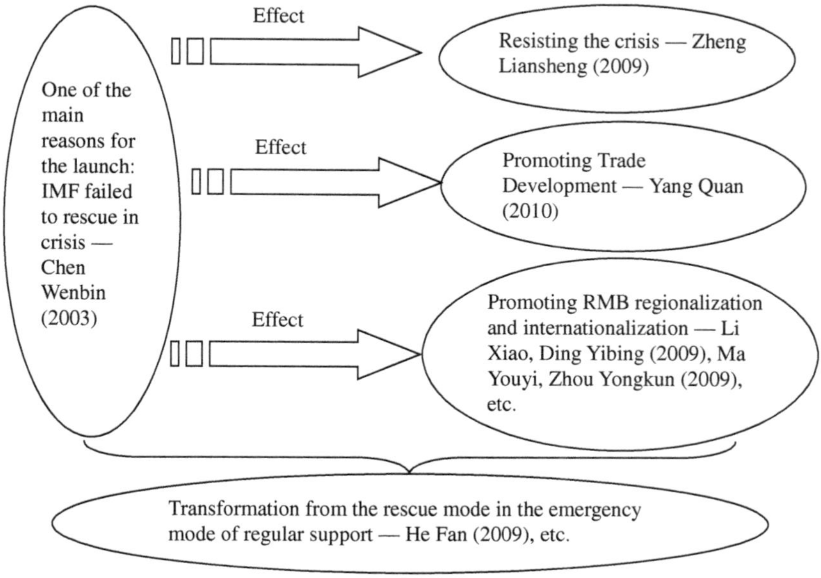

Figure 3.2. Domestic Scholars' Discussion on Currency Swap in Asia

Based on an analysis of the Asian financial crisis, Huang believes that in the future, East Asian countries will need to learn lessons and strengthen regional financial supervision and cooperation.[104] Cai in the article "Financial Supervision in ASEAN Countries: Unbalanced Development Trends and Path Selection for Regional Cooperation" suggested that ASEAN countries can strengthen regional cooperation in financial supervision from four aspects: (1) strengthen different levels of development within the region; (2) strengthen and improve information sharing and monitoring in the regional economic and financial fields; (3) accelerate the construction of regional financial infrastructure; (4) pay attention to the exchange, interaction and sharing of professionals in regional financial supervision.[105]

[104]Huang, Fanzhang, "Globalization of the Economy and Internationalization of Financial Supervision," *Macroeconomic Research* 12 (1998): 22–26.
[105]Cai, Xing, "Financial Supervision in ASEAN Countries: The Unbalanced Development Trend and Path Selection for Regional Cooperation," *Guangxi Social Sciences* 6 (2010): 39–43.

Considering that regional cooperation in East Asian financial supervision will be a long-term process, it is more practical to step up the construction of a monitoring mechanism at the regional level. With the development of the bilateral exchange of local currency swap agreements in East Asia and the use of East Asian foreign exchange reserve banks, it is imperative to establish an effective regional supervision mechanism in order to ensure the funds of the capital-supplying countries. At present, the Economic Review and Policy Dialogue (ERPD) under the ASEAN 10+3 framework bears the task of economic supervision in East Asia. However, the function of ERPD is still only at the level of information sharing. Yang pointed out that ERPD has obvious defects as a monitoring mechanism, compared with the three regional supervision methods of peer review, peer pressure and due diligence, which greatly limits the effectiveness of ERPD monitoring. Putting the ERPD under the CMI framework can facilitate its transition from information exchange to peer-reviewed surveillance.[106]

Cooperative supervision can effectively prevent the "contagious effects" of the financial crisis and curb the speculation generated by the asymmetry of the regulatory principles, and create favorable conditions and prerequisites for the development of the regional financial markets in East Asia. In theory, unified, transparent and accurate information is the basis for an efficient financial market and effective supervision. It can reflect the dynamics of the financial market in a timely and effective manner and promote the strengthening of regional supervision. Therefore, it is necessary to establish a unified principle of information disclosure and sharing in the region, and give regulators of various countries the ability to quickly grasp the dynamics of international investment, short-term capital flows, exchange rates and interest rates and coordinate their regulatory actions to maintain the stability of the international financial market. At the

[106] Yang, Quan, "Development of Bilateral Currency Swap in East Asia under the Background of Global Financial Turmoil," *International Finance Research* 6 (2010): 30–40.

same time, the establishment of a unified regional accounting standards will help control system risks and cross-border capital flows, help the market and regulators to effectively monitor, avoid arbitrage of accounting standards among countries in the region and create favorable conditions for regional cooperation in financial supervision. However, due to the complexity of relations among East Asian countries, political and economic interests, social, economic and legal institutions are different, so East Asian financial regulatory cooperation is bound to face many obstacles. Therefore, in the short term, East Asia's regulatory cooperation will have difficulty achieving the same regulatory standards and accounting standards. In the process of future financial supervision and cooperation, it is very likely that problems would appear, such as the competition for leadership of regional financial cooperation among countries, conflicts of regulatory laws and regulations, and the conflicts between the supervision of extraterritorial jurisdiction and national sovereignty. In addition, the establishment of the East Asian financial supervision system, such as the establishment of the objectives and principles of regional cooperation in financial supervision, the establishment of a regional early warning mechanism, the blocking of transmission routes after a financial crisis, the coordination of legal conflicts between countries in the regional financial supervision process, has not yet been completed. If these issues are not resolved, cooperation in East Asian financial supervision will be difficult to develop in depth.

Finally, it should be pointed out that although the regional cooperation in financial supervision in East Asia is continuously developing, the research results in this field by Chinese financial and legal scholars are rare.

From the progress of monetary and financial cooperation and cooperation in East Asia, it can be summarized that the cooperation in this region is mainly driven by the crisis, with Japan and China playing a key role. However, due to the fragile political relationship between China and Japan, the currency and financial cooperation in the region has always faced various contradictions and even shocks, and even suffered setbacks. The CMI multilateralization is a landmark system for East Asian monetary and financial cooperation, but this system will also be affected by the political relations among large countries. On 12 December 2013, before the special summit between Japan and ASEAN, the Bank of Japan and the Central Bank of Indonesia signed a third currency swap agreement, increasing the exchange quota from US$12 billion to US$22.76 billion. The agreement also added new crisis prevention mechanisms to deal with potential or actual liquidity needs. Japan and the Philippines have also basically reached an agreement on the scale of currency swaps from US$6 billion to US$12 billion. In addition, Japan will restart a $3 billion swap agreement with Singapore that expired two years ago. Japan also announced the resumption of the currency swap agreement with Thailand and Malaysia. The currency swap mechanism between Japan and ASEAN countries is mainly used as a safety net during market fluctuations to help governments deal with the outflow of international capital. With the withdrawal of the quantitative easing (QE) policy of the Federal Reserve, the East Asian emerging economies such as Indonesia have been severely influenced and the exchange rate has undergone major fluctuations. The incentives for countries to construct liquidity support mechanisms such as currency swaps are increasing.

Japan's expansion of bilateral currency swaps with the main ASEAN countries of Indonesia and the Philippines, and the resumption of bilateral currency swaps with Singapore, Thailand and Malaysia showed that Japan abandoned the CMI multilateralization process launched in 2008 and abandoned the regional cooperation mechanism of the East Asian foreign exchange reserve bank, returning to the unilateral route of monetary finance.

On 31 October 2013, Japan successfully joined the long-term currency swap network built by the Fed, which also included the United States, Europe, Japan, the United Kingdom, Canada and Switzerland. This means that the Bank of Japan will be able to receive US dollar support from the Federal Reserve. The People's Bank of China lacks this ability. Japan's actions will prompt China to rethink the currency–finance relationship between the RMB and the US dollar, and thus between China and the United States.[107]

After the crisis, the Fed's actions at the global level and Japan's actions at the regional level seem to indicate that the original international monetary system structure with the characteristics of "inequality, asymmetry, and unsustainability" has been strengthened. If a crisis comes, developed countries will be better protected, while other countries, especially developing countries, will not receive sufficient assistance from the developed countries. If these countries cannot organize collective support, they will face a more volatile external environment.

3.6 Plan for Reconstruction of Balance of Payment Coordination Mechanism

The evolution of the international currency system from the gold standard to the gold exchange standard, then to the Bretton Woods system and the Jamaican system, is accompanied by changes in the reserve currency and exchange rate system; the coordination mechanism for the balance of payments also shows different characteristics. Under the gold standard system, gold is used as an international standard currency. All currencies are linked to gold and a fixed exchange rate system is established. Under this system, the balance of payments has a mechanism of automatic adjustment: the gold reserve of each country determines the supply of money. When the country experiences a surplus in international payments, gold reserves increase, money supply increases and prices rise, thereby weakening the international competitiveness of the country's commodities and reducing the surplus, and vice versa. Under the gold exchange standard system, the United States and the United Kingdom restored the gold standard, while other countries use gold, the US dollar, the pound sterling as their foreign exchange reserves, and countries still

---

[107] Xu, Yisheng, *From the 'Jamaica System' to the 'Atlantic System'* (*First Financial Daily*, December 2, 2013).

adopt a fixed exchange rate system. The balance of payments coordination mechanism under this system is similar, and has a mechanism for automatic adjustment. Under the Bretton Woods system, the US dollar is linked to gold, and other currencies are linked to the US dollar. At this time, the exchange rate system adopts an adjustable pegging exchange rate, and the balance of payments adjustment is based on the original gold standard adjustment mode, which has intensified the supervision and institutional arrangements of the IMF. When a country suffers from a balance of international payments deficit, the IMF can increase the country's international solvency by providing loans to ease these deficits. In the Jamaican system, gold was non-monetized and the international reserve currency presented a diversified pattern. The exchange rate system of various countries was not consistent. In addition to the fixed exchange rate system and the floating exchange rate system, a series of intermediate exchange rate systems emerged and the means of international exchange management were diversified, mainly the policy of the adjustment of the exchange rate of the IMF. The adjustment mechanism of the exchange rate policy to the balance of payments is mainly reflected in that when a country has a balance of payments deficit, the foreign exchange demand exceeds the foreign exchange supply, and the exchange rate rises. The relative prices of domestic exports have dropped, and the relative prices of imported goods have risen, thereby increasing exports, reducing imports, and mitigating the balance of international payments deficit and vice versa.

The balance of international payments is a core part of the global economic imbalance. Since the 1990s, global imbalances have become more and more serious, mainly in the United States and China, Japan and oil-exporting countries. This is reflected in the continued expansion of the current account deficit in the United States and the continued expansion of current account surpluses in China, Japan and oil-exporting countries. Europe's overall external accounts are basically balanced, while there are huge imbalances within Europe between Germany, Finland, Norway and Greece, Italy, Spain and Portugal, which are represented by the current account surpluses of Germany, Finland, and Norway, and current account deficits in countries such as Greece, Italy, Spain and Portugal. During this period of time, surplus countries represented by China, Japan and oil-exporting countries represented the accumulation of foreign exchange reserve assets. These foreign exchange reserve assets were returned to the United States in the form of US Treasury bonds and other US assets, and then global economic imbalances and growth occurred. This type of global economic cycle is known as Bretton Woods II. When exploring the reason why the surplus countries want to accumulate large-scale foreign exchange reserves, a widely accepted theory that emerged is "self-insurance." For emerging market countries like China, because the local currency is not an international reserve currency, in order to respond to unexpected needs and prevent speculative shocks, it is necessary to accumulate international reserve currencies. However, taking China as an example, the level of foreign exchange reserves accumulated by China is far from being explained by the theory of "self-insurance." More than 20 years ago, many economists predicted that the US current account deficit was unsustainable. Since the 1990s, the relationship between the surplus countries and the deficit countries seems to be voluntary. The imbalance between China and the United States after 2000 has become more and more serious, and the two countries have repeatedly experienced trade frictions. After 2005, China and the United States launched the Strategic Economy Dialogue (SED), in which both parties held talks on the development of strategic, long-term and comprehensive bilateral relations. In 2009, the two countries developed the "Strategy and Economy Dialogue" (S&ED) mechanism, which has carried out five rounds till now. The two sides have promoted trade and investment cooperation, improved the financial system, strengthened financial dialogues, advanced structural adjustments, promoted strong, sustainable and balanced economic growth, and maintained the economic balance between China and the United States. S&ED has become an important platform for economic dialogue and economic adjustment between China and the United States and the rebalance of the Sino-US economy. In the Sino-US trade friction and multi-round economic dialogues so far, the exchange rate has been one of the important topics. The United States believes that the adjustment of the RMB exchange rate can correct the trade imbalance between China and the United States. However, it turns out that since 2005, the RMB has appreciated against the US dollar. Afterwards the trade imbalance between China and the United States has not been corrected. The role of exchange rates as a way of regulating the balance of payments is no longer as effective as economic theory envisages.

After the outbreak of the international financial crisis in 2008, the scale of external imbalances of almost all unbalanced countries has declined. However, this is the result of passive and destructive adjustments.[108] In the context of shrinking global trade, the scale of global imbalances is also shrinking. When the world economy recovers and trade growth rate rises upward, the adjustment of global economic imbalances will be restored. It will also inhibit the recovery of the economy and trade, and it will abolish the global economic and trade recovery.

After the crisis, various unbalanced countries have implemented macroeconomic policy assistance in varying degrees. The result of the US proactive fiscal policy and loose monetary policy was the expansion of US debt, which actually further aggravated the US economic imbalance. China's post-crisis adjustment of current account surpluses has been carried on, especially as it is committed to economic restructuring and efforts to adjust and reform export-oriented economic development models by promoting consumption and investment to expand domestic demand.

Although the situation of global economic imbalances before and after the crisis is not the same, from the perspective of balance of payments coordination mechanism, Dai's research shows that under the current international currency system, many exchange rate adjustment measures are not effective. Actual exchange rate fluctuations

---

[108]Dai, Jinping, "Global Imbalance Adjustment after the Crisis: Trends and Power," *Financial Markets* 1 (2013): 72–84.

do not promote international balance of payment adjustment as theoretically conceived. Instead, excessive floating increases the instability of the market and even worsens the balance of payments of many countries. In the absence of proper exchange rate adjustments, the lack of institutional arrangement is also an important reason why imbalances in international payments cannot be corrected.[109] Huang believes that after the dissolution of the Bretton Woods system, countries have lost their currency issuance constraints in the balance of international payments coordination and they have not established the necessary systems or norms in a timely manner. All countries have arranged and selected their own currency arrangements based on their own national interests. Theoretically, under the current international monetary system, although imbalances can persist for a certain period of time and to some extent, it is difficult for the balance of international payments to persist for a long time.[110]

In the event of failure of the traditional adjustment mechanism of the balance of payments, not only is the long-term development of the world economy difficult to maintain, but the interests of different countries also have different degrees of losses. Therefore, all countries should strengthen consultations and work hard to rebuild the balance of payments coordination mechanism and ease global economic imbalances. This requires the coordination of domestic reforms and related international cooperation. Driven by the crisis, the IMF and G20 provided a platform for relevant dialogues. Since 2006, the IMF has initiated many multilateral consultations to discuss the internal problems and solutions to global economic imbalances. At present, the G20 is gradually becoming an important promoter of the restructuring of the balance of payments mechanism. The G20 was established in 1999, but before the international financial crisis in

[109]Dai, Jinping and Aizong Xiong, Tan Shushi, *International Monetary System: Where to Go?* Xiamen: Xiamen University Press, 2012.
[110]Huang, Wei, "Reform of the International Reserve Currency System for Global Economic Governance," *International Finance Research* 12 (2012): 12–27.

2008, developed countries had monopoly rights in international financial governance. The G8 held the international financial governance mechanism. After the financial crisis, the first G20 summit was held in Washington DC in November 2008. It marked the beginning of the transformation of the international financial governance mechanism, from G8 to G20. After the Pittsburgh summit in 2009, the G20 mechanism officially became an important platform for discussing global economic issues. The G20 mechanism provided an important stage for developing countries to participate in international affairs, and gradually became the main platform for the reform of the current international monetary system (Table 3.7).

With the promotion of the G20, macroeconomic policy cooperation among countries in the world has gradually strengthened, and the G20 finance ministers and central bank governors' meetings and the G20 summit have gradually become regularized and institutionalized. Its main achievements in global economic governance are:

(1) IMF-led institutional reforms were promoted. Zhang summarized the progress of the IMF reform within the framework of G20: first, the Fourth Amendment approved by the IMF Board of Directors in 1997 took effect in August 2009.[111] This amendment has enabled all IMF members to participate in the SDR system. Equitable access to the financing facilities of the IMF were ensured. Second, the IMF's "income model" (Fifth Amendment) was amended, while some countries injected capital into the IMF; and third, the reform program that approved voting rights and quotas (Sixth Amendment) increased the voice of developing countries.
(2) In the area of financial regulation, a financial stability committee (Financial Stability Board, FSB) was established, and officially began operation on 27 June 2009. The FSB's member institutions include central banks, finance ministries, and regulatory

[111]Zhang, Ming, "RMB Internationalization: Policies, Progress, Problems and Prospects," *Financial Review* 5, no. 2 (2013).

Table 3.7. Progress of the G20 Leaders' Summit in International Finance

	Time	Location	Major Progress
1st summit	2008.11	Washington, DC, United States	Include emerging economies to join the financial stability forum, strengthen the IMF's functions, integrate the international financial supervision mechanism, increase the access of emerging economies and developing countries credit. The medium-term goal is to comprehensively enforce the reform of WB and the IMF.
2nd summit	2009.04	London, United Kingdom	Increase the IMF's available funds to US$750 billion, support the latest SDRs quota of US$250 billion, support multilateral development banks with at least US$100 billion in additional loans, and secure US$250 billion in support for trade financing.
3rd summit	2009.09	Pittsburgh, United States	Commitment to increasing the share of the IMF in emerging markets and developing countries to at least 5%; determine that developing countries and economies in transition will increase their voting rights by at least 3% in the WB; promise that all parties will inject capital in excess of US$500 billion. Expand the IMF's "new loan arrangement" mechanism.
4th Summit	2010.06	Toronto, Canada	Raise the proportion of officials and scholars in emerging market countries as senior officials of the IMF, the WB and other international financial institutions, and complete the IMF quota reform before the Seoul Summit.

(*Continued*)

Table 3.7. (*Continued*)

	Time	Location	Major Progress
5th Summit	2010.11	Seoul, Korea	Improve the reform problems that the WB and the IMF have not been able to completely resolve, establish a more stable and resilient international currency system, and further consolidate the global financial safety net.
6th Summit	2011.11	Cannes, France	The SDRs' currency composition will be reassessed in 2015 and perhaps earlier, better integration of bilateral and multilateral supervision; build a market-determined exchange rate system to increase exchange rate flexibility; support the IMF in launching new ones. Prevent liquidity quotas and a single tool to meet the urgent assistance needs of its member states and quickly implement the IMF's 2010 quota and management reforms.
7th Summit	2012.06	Los Cabos, Mexico	Commitment to continue to work to reduce economic imbalances, strengthen public finance stability in deficit countries, strengthen domestic demand in countries with a large current account surplus, and adopt more flexible exchange rate policies; many emerging economies make decisions to increase capital to the IMF.
8th Summit	2013.09	Saint Petersburg, Russia	Commitment to complete the 15th IMF general inspection by the end of January 2014 and implement the IMF quota and governance reform plan as soon as possible.

Source: Supplemented by Li (2012).
Xiao, Li, and Yongqi Feng, "Collective Actions in the Reform of the International Monetary System and the Role of the G20," *World Economy and Politics* 2 (2012).

agencies and major international financial institutions and professional committees in more than 20 countries. As mentioned earlier, as a global financial regulatory system, its main responsibilities include: assessing the fragility of the global financial system, supervising countries to improve their actions, promoting cooperation and exchange of information among national regulatory agencies and providing advice on national regulatory policies and regulatory standards; coordinating the work of international standard-setting agencies; formulating contingency plans for cross-border risk management.

(3) Agreement was reached on a quantitative approach to measuring imbalances and an operation to reverse the imbalances in the global economy was adopted. Huang summarized the major progress of the global economic rebalancing issue on the G20 platform: first, the quantitative indicators of imbalances gradually evolved into a set of imbalance indicators that span the three dimensions of the foreign sector, the public sector, and the private sector, such as debt to GDP, fiscal surplus to GDP, private saving to GDP, private debt to GDP, trade surplus to GDP, net investment income and transfer payments to GDP. Second, the concept of systemically important countries was introduced for the first time. Third, China, France, Germany, India, Japan, the United Kingdom and the United States were identified as seven systemically unbalanced countries. Finally, through the MAP mutual evaluation of macroeconomic policies, these countries have defined imbalanced distortion policies, adopted in the resolution of the "Cannes Action Resolution," and then proposed rectification options.[112]

In view of the relationship between international balance of payments imbalances and balance of payments coordination mechanisms, some domestic scholars have conducted distinctive analysis

[112]Huang, Wei, "Reform of the International Reserve Currency System for Global Economic Governance," *International Finance Research* 12 (2012): 12–27.

on the topic of the G20. Zhang[113] believes that the adjustment path of imbalances in the balance of payments is mainly mediated by the policy coordination and the financial market coordination, which is highly destructive. Countries take the initiative to implement domestic policy adjustments and achieve substantial adjustments to their costs. The sharing mechanism is optimal for both the Chinese economy and the world economy. Zhao put forward the strategy of international monetary policy coordination under the G20 mechanism, that is, strengthen the level of the central bank's information exchange and crisis management; improve the mutual evaluation mechanism under the G20 framework and improve the effectiveness of decision-making; establish a multi-level international monetary policy coordination framework under the G20 mechanism; build a global financial governance structure centered on the G20.[114] Li and Feng believe that the objective of the collective action for the current reform of the international monetary system in the near future is to "control the imbalance" and "suppress the risk of the US dollar." To "control the imbalance" by the cooperation of the balance of payments mechanism and to "suppresses the risk of the US dollar" by the exchange rate cooperation will provide a favorable external environment for the stable development of the world economy through the reform of the international reserve currency, international financial institutions and international financial supervision. In order to achieve this goal, the G20 mechanism should fully expand the common interests of G20 members and promote the reform of the international monetary system through international economic policy coordination and the reform of traditional

[113]Zhang, Ming, "Reform of the International Monetary System: Background, Reasons, Measures and China's Participation," *International Economic Review* 1 (2010).

[114]Zhao, Qingsong, "International Monetary Policy Coordination Practices and Strategic Choices under the G20 Mechanism," *Asia Pacific Economics* 5 (2011): 1–7.

international economic organizations.[115] Dai and Xiong believe that the solution to global economic imbalances is either to change the situation in which sovereign currency is used as an international currency, or to re-establish strict rules and regulations for sovereign currencies, or to establish effective mechanism of international economic coordination. From the actual situation, the first two solutions are difficult to implement at present, but the latter one is easy to implement. At present, the G20 has launched a "strong and sustainable framework with balanced growth." The core of this framework is the establishment of a mutual assessment process, whose main purpose is to supervise and evaluate policy adjustments by countries, including solutions to global economic imbalances, thus ultimately promoting strong and sustained global economic growth.[116]

The supervision of the exchange rate is an important way to ensure global financial stability and maintain the normal operation of the international currency system. In the mid-1990s, the IMF established the Consultative Group on Exchange Rate Issues (CGER) and began conducting multilateral assessments of developed countries as an important method for the IMF to monitor exchange rates. In 2012, the IMF launched a new exchange rate assessment method — the External Balance Assessment (EBA). Liu[117] obtained several conclusions through the analysis of the IMF's reforms of exchange rate supervision and assessment methods. First, research on the IMF's exchange rate focused on the theoretical analysis of the mid-term exchange rate imbalance, and it has relatively limited guidance on the exchange rate policy practice in various countries. Second, errors in domestic and foreign economic policies may lead to misalignment

[115] Xiao, Li, and Yongqi Feng, "The Collective Action of International Monetary System Reform and the Role of the G20," *World Economy and Politics* 2 (2012): 119–145.
[116] Dai, Jinping, Aizong Xiong and Shushi Tan, *International Monetary System: Where to Go?* Xiamen: Xiamen University Press, 2012.
[117] Liu, Bin, "An Empirical Study on the Relationship between Money Supply, Output and Price in China," *Financial Research* 07 (2002).

of exchange rates. Exchange rate policies should not bear full responsibility for imbalances in international payments. Third, there is no "universal" exchange rate model, and the process and mechanism construction of exchange rate adjustment is the key.[118] Zhang compared and commented on the CGER method and EBA method for evaluating the exchange rate imbalance of the IMF. The main advantage of the EBA method compared to the CGER method is that the EBA method introduces more independent variables and separates the policy factors from other dependent variables, and the structural factors are separated from the cyclical factors, increasing the number of economies covered by panel regression and extending the time dimension.[119]

Cui believes that although the G20 has replaced the G7 as the core institutional platform to govern the global economy and has reached many concrete measures for international cooperation, there are still some important international economic goals that have not been achieved because of differences among member states. For example, the commitment of the fifth summit to counter protectionism has not become a reality. The United States has not given up its veto power in the IMF. The international financial governance structure has not been fundamentally improved, and the new "Bretton Woods System" has not been completely established. He also believes that one of the drawbacks of the G20 is that it does not establish punitive measures against countries that do not comply with the agreement, which increases the inefficiency of the organization.[120]

In short, the reform of the balance of payments coordination mechanism is an important part of the reform of the international

---

[118]Liu, Bin, "An Empirical Study on the Relationship between Money Supply, Output and Price in China," *Financial Research* 07 (2002).

[119]Zhang, Ming, "Global Currency Swap: Status Quo, Functions, and Potential Directions for the Reform of the International Monetary System," *International Economic Review* 6 (2012): 65–88.

[120]Cui, Zhinan and Yue Xing, "From 'G7 Era' to 'G20 Era' — Changes in International Financial Governance Mechanisms," *World Economy and Politics* 1 (2011): 134–154.

monetary system. In the post-Bretton Woods period, although the floating exchange rate system had the effect of regulating the balance of payments, the "Triffin puzzle" under the leadership of the US dollar was still difficult to avoid. Since the outbreak of the global financial crisis, both the IMF and the G20 are committed to solving the problem of global economic imbalances, especially as the G20 becomes a new platform for global economic governance and international financial governance. In the long run, the reform of the balance of payments mechanism will rely heavily on the in-depth development of the G20 mechanism, so cooperation and communication among major countries around the world will become crucial.

Chapter 4

The Necessity for China to Actively Participate in International Monetary System Reform

4.1 Active Participation in International Monetary System Reform: From China's Perspective

4.1.1 *The Global Financial Crisis Exposes China to the Risks of the "Dollar System"*

4.1.1.1 *The "Dollar Trap" and the Dilemma of China's Foreign Exchange Reserve Management*

Since its World Trade Organization (WTO) entry in 2001, China's foreign trade surplus has been continually accumulating, with the foreign exchange reserves rapidly expanding in scale. From 2001 to 2012, China's foreign exchange reserves increased by 14 times (see Figure 4.1). By March 2013, the total amount reached nearly US$3.5 trillion, accounting for about one-third of total foreign exchange reserves worldwide. About 70% of China's foreign exchange reserves are denominated in the dollar, and the vast majority of China's US dollar-denominated reserves are the US Treasury Bonds. According to statistics of Treasury International Capital (TIC) of the US Treasury, the number of US Treasury Bonds held by China has increased by 15 times between 2001 and 2012. By July 2013, China held US$1.3 trillion worth of US Treasury Bonds (accounting for 22.8% of the

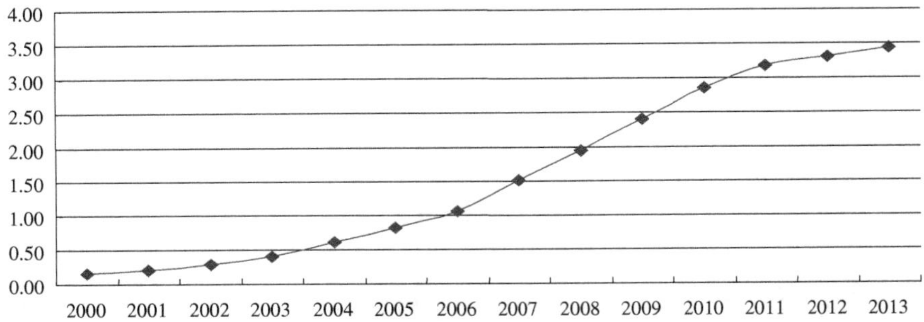

Figure 4.1. Changes in China's Foreign Exchange Reserves since 2000 (in Trillion USD)

Note: Data for 2013 is through 30 March 2013.

Source: China's State Administration of Foreign Exchange (www.safe.gov.cn).

total US Treasury Bonds held by foreign countries)[1] and became the largest creditor of the US in the world (see Figure 4.2). However, such a large and concentrated holding of dollar-denominated reserves has dragged China's foreign exchange reserves management into a "dollar trap."

In April 2009, the famous American Economist Paul R. Krugman published a signed article titled "China's Dollar Trap" in the New York Times, in which he claimed: China acquired its US$2 trillion stash — turning the People's Republic into the T-bills Republic — the same way Britain acquired its empire. And just the other day, it seems, China's leaders woke up and realized that they had a problem. The low yield does not seem to bother them much, even now. But they are, apparently, worried about the fact that around 70% of those assets are dollar-denominated, so any future fall in the dollar would mean a huge capital loss for China. There is nothing to keep

[1]In September 2008, the amount of US Treasury Bonds held by China (US$618.2 billion) surpassed that of Japan (US$617.5 billion) for the first time, making China the largest creditor of the United States. In 2010, the proportion of US Treasury Bonds held by China in total foreign-held US Treasury Bonds reached as high as 26.2%. Since then, despite some declines in the share, China has maintained its position as the US's largest creditor.

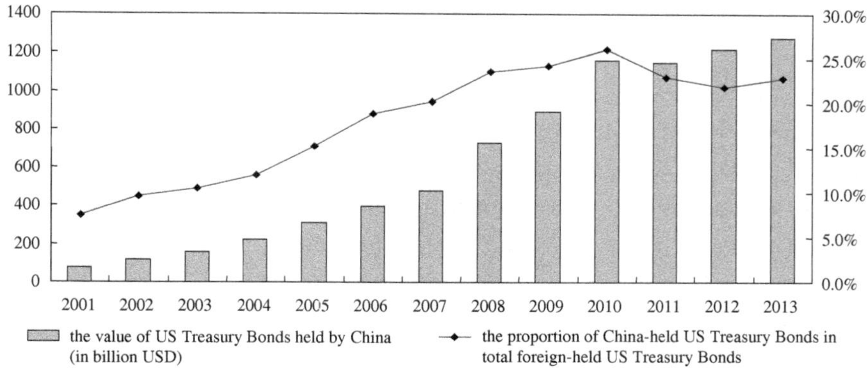

Figure 4.2. China-held US Treasury Bonds since 2001
Note: Data for 2013 is through July 2013.
Source: Database of the US TIC.

China from diversifying its reserves away from the dollar, indeed from holding a reserve basket matching the composition of the special drawing rights (SDRs) — nothing, that is, except for the fact that China now owns so many dollars that it cannot sell them off without driving the dollar down and triggering the huge capital loss that its leaders fear.[2]

The dilemma of China's foreign exchange reserves management aforementioned by Krugman has become a classic case of the "dollar trap." China's domestic scholars have also analyzed the "dollar trap" from different perspectives. Yu pointed out that under the current circumstances, China will risk a huge loss of capital if it continues to hold or even further increase its holdings of U.S. treasury Bonds.[3] If China diversifies the foreign exchange reserves immediately, the capital loss will be realized at once. This dilemma is what Krugman calls "China's Dollar Trap". Song argued that the "dollar trap" mainly points to a worrying unstable situation for China, in that the

[2]Yu, Yongding, "Witness Imbalance — Twin Surpluses, Renminbi Exchange Rate and the Dollar Trap," *International Economic Review* 3 (2010) (in Chinese). Krugman, Paul, *China's Dollar Trap* (*New York Times*, April 2, 2009): 7–44.
[3]*Ibid.*

US dollar assets held by it will be seriously damaged or threatened by the de facto special status of the US dollar and the US's use of this status.[4] In fact, the concept of "dollar trap" contains three interrelated core elements: first, China is holding and accumulating a huge sum of dollar-denominated assets; second, the US dollar maintains a special status in the current international monetary system and the US is taking advantage of this status; and third is the possibility of huge losses of China's dollar-denominated assets.

First, as mentioned earlier, since joining the WTO in 2001, China has accumulated huge amounts of foreign exchange reserves. Although the accurate data on the share of the US dollar in China's huge foreign exchange reserves is not accessible, it is reckoned in many research studies and estimations that a majority of China's foreign exchange reserves are in the form of dollar-denominated assets, of which the highly liquid and relatively secure U.S. Treasury Bonds take the largest proportion.[5] This constitutes the first cause for the "dollar trap"of China's foreign exchange reserve asset management.

Second, regarding the special status of the US's dollar in the current international monetary system and the US use of this special status, the US remains the only core country in the current international monetary system while the rest of the system becomes peripheral. This "center–periphery" structure determines that the current international monetary system is a replica of the Bretton Woods system, which is known as the Revived Bretton Woods System.[6] Under the current "dollar system", the US dollar is the most

---

[4]Song, Guoyou, "Dollar Trap, Debt Weapon, and Financial Dilemma between China and the U.S.," *International Review* 4 (2010): 72–79 (in Chinese).

[5]According to Setser and Pandey (2009), about 83% (or more than US$1.25 trillion) of China's US$1.5 trillion worth of U.S. assets exist in the form of US treasuries and federal agency bonds, and the remaining 17% are in the form of corporate bonds and stocks. See Setser, B. and Pandey, A., "China's $1.5 Trillion Bet: Understanding China's External Portfolio," Working Paper of Center for Geoeconomic Studies, Council on Foreign Relations (May 2009).

[6]Dooley, Michael P., Folkerts-Landau, David and Garber, Peter, "An Essay on the Revived Bretton Woods System," *NBER Working Papers* 9971, National Bureau of Economic Research, Inc. (2003).

important currency for foreign reserves around the world, exercising the functions as a global value measurement, exchange media and storage of value. Although the currencies of other developed countries such as the euro, the pound and the yen also play more or less the role of international currencies, their importance pale by comparison with the dollar. Therefore, the current "dollar system" is in fact a unipolar reserve currency system,[7] in which the central state's currency, the US dollar, becomes the de facto world currency. However, the intrinsic value of this currency rests with the US government. It is precisely this particular existence that allows the US government to use the special status of the US dollar as the world currency to serve the strategic interests of the United States. Since the "Plaza Accord" in 1985, the devaluation of the dollar against the Japanese yen, the "strong dollar" policy adopted in the late Clinton administration, and the devaluation of the dollar by the George W. Bush administration, are all typical cases of the US's achieving specific economic or diplomatic objectives through the dollar's special status and exchange rate policies.

Finally, from the perspective of China's serious asset losses, China's real gains from its huge dollar-denominated reserves have been seriously affected by the global financial crisis. The change in the exchange rate of the US dollar, especially the depreciation, would directly shrink China's dollar-denominated reserves (in the form of declines in the storage value of physical commodities). Thus, under the continued quantitative easing policies of the US, the falling dollar has decreased the actual value of China's dollar-denominated reserves. In March 2009, Wen Jiabao, then China's Premier, publicly stated that "the United States should maintain its credibility, keep its promises and ensure the safety of its assets in China."[8] Although the

[7]Zhang Ming, "The Impact of the Subprime Mortgage Crisis on the Current International Monetary System," *World Economy and Politics* 7 (2009): 74–80 (in Chinese).

[8]The Record of Premier Wen Jiabao's answers to questions raised by correspondents. See Xinhuanet (http://news.xinhuanet.com/misc/2009-03/13/content_11005906.htm).

US government has always declared that it will protect the interests of all foreign creditors, including China, in fact, its guarantee relates only to the nominal value of dollar-denominated assets and their interest income. From the specific market perspective, China-held US dollar assets have already been damaged by a series of factors such as the devaluation of the US dollar.[9] According to Song, the effective exchange rate index of the dollar decreased by 5.4% during the first eight months of 2009, causing China's dollar-denominated assets to shrink by US$42 billion.[10] Taking into account the devaluation of the dollar against RMB since 2005, the loss will be theoretically larger. Yu also pointed out that the effective exchange rate index of the dollar decreased by 41% from April 2002 to the end of 2009, directly causing the depreciation of the dollar-denominated assets held by China.[11] In addition, the US's inflation is expected to erode the value of China's foreign exchange reserves. The regular inflation rate of the US is about 2–3%, which can offset the interest income of China's foreign reserves and even reduce the principle. Not to mention that after the US economy recovers, the additional currency issued during the crisis will return to financial markets and the real economy; thus, inflation may go out of control.

Obviously, China, which is deeply trapped by the "dollar trap," lacks effective control over the value erosion of its own dollar-denominated reserves caused by changes in the dollar's exchange rate and the inflation rate in the US. In terms of the exchange rate of the US dollar, despite the nominal free-floating regime, it is directly affected by the US government's public position, intervention, and monetary policies, in particular. It is in this sense that the US government can influence the return and real value of China's

[9]Song, Guoyou, "China's Purchase of American Securities: Source, Profit and Impact," *Fudan Journal* 3 (2008): 31–38 (in Chinese).
[10]Song, Guoyou, "Dollar Trap, Debt Weapon, and Financial Dilemma between China and the U.S.," *International Review* 4 (2010): 72–79 (in Chinese).
[11]Yu, Yongding, "Witness Imbalance — Twin Surpluses, Renminbi Exchange Rate and the Dollar Trap," *International Economic Review* 3 (2010): 7–4 (in Chinese).

dollar-denominated reserves by changing the dollar's exchange rate. In addition, the "dollar trap" also holds political and strategic significances at a higher level. Under extreme circumstances (for example, if America thinks that China's internal affairs or diplomatic policies are not in line with their own, or even seriously infringe upon their interests), the US government will most likely hold China's huge holdings of dollar-denominated assets as a "hostage" to coerce China into making adjustments on policies.[12] Considering that the US government will be less likely to ignore the serious challenges from China's rise on its interests and international status, it will surely adopt a corresponding strategy to address and prevent the potential problems. The US government will take into account China's dollar assets and their strategic significance when formulating its strategies toward China. Thus, it is a must for the Chinese government to examine and respond to the "dollar trap" from the perspectives of economy, politics, as well as national security.

4.1.1.2 *The Impact on China's Real Economy*

The outbreak of the global financial crisis has promoted the desire and momentum of East Asian economies including China to drive economic growth by export surplus. Experience has shown that increasing export has been a preferred path for East Asian economies to resume or promote economic growth, since America has always been the most important market for East Asian economies, irrespective of changes in its domestic savings rate and consumption

[12] In history, the US government has set a precedent for using other countries' financial assets as a diplomatic tool. In 1956, the United Kingdom allied with France to launch the Suez Canal War in order to safeguard its interests in the Suez Canal. Then the United States thought that this move had seriously damaged its interests. To this end, the Eisenhower administration issued a warning to Britain that if Britain did not withdraw its troops, it would prevent it from retrieving its assets deposited in the IMF. This move succeeded in forcing Britain to cease fire and withdraw its troops from the Canal. The failure of the war hastened Britain's decline, and made its influences and interests dependent on the US. See Kunz, Diane B., *The Economic Diplomacy of the Suez Crisis*. Chapel Hill: University of North Carolina Press, 1991.

patterns amidst or after the crisis. However, the US's position as the final product market of East Asia has changed since the crisis. And China's final product export markets are becoming decentralized. This requires that China transform its foreign-demand-oriented pattern in a radical way. And its export-oriented economy, with sustainable growth, is to be greatly challenged and constrained.

Under the current international monetary system, the impact from the crisis on China's real economy can be analyzed from the perspectives of aggregate demand (AD) and aggregate supply. The AD shock has become a more common and normal phenomenon in modern economic conditions. In the "center-periphery" structure of the current international monetary system, there are many differences and asymmetries in both the "centre countries" and the "peripheral countries." Consequently, facing the global impact of AD, the coordination and monetary policy games among different countries and groups have become the core elements for the stability of the current systems.

In order to make the research as simplified and close to reality as possible, we assume the current international monetary system to be as follows: The world economy consists of N + 1 countries. The first N countries are divided into two parts: N1 countries adopt an exchange rate system where their own currencies are floating against the core country's currency and the remaining N2 countries have their currencies pegged to it. These N countries ($\mathrm{N} = \mathrm{N1} + \mathrm{N2}$) constitute the periphery of the current international monetary system, while the last country is the core country. The real AD of the core country depends on the AD demand shock λ, its effective exchange rate z, and its real interest rate r_c as $y_c = \beta_c\lambda - \delta_c z - vr_c$, where $\beta_c(0 \leqq \beta_c \leqq 1)$, known as the AD impact, indicates the degree of impact of the AD shock on the core country. δ_c indicates the degree to which the real AD of the core country depends on the effective exchange rate z. The total supply y_c of the core country is determined by employment n_c and in accordance with the law of decreasing returns to scale as: $y_c = (1 - \alpha)n_c$, $0 < \alpha < 1$.

The peripheral country i with floating exchange rate has a similar economic structure with the core country, and thus has its AD identically affected by the effective interest rate. The aggregate supply of i can be calculated by: $y_{fi} = (1-\alpha)n_{fi}$. And its AD is affected by the impact of global AD λ, its real effective exchange rate z_{fi} and its real interest rate as: $r_{fi} : y_{fi} = \beta_f\lambda - \delta_f z_{fi} - vr_{fi}$. The sign of the exchange rate z_{fi} is "+", since the AD would increase as the rise in bilateral exchange rate z_{fi} would result in depreciation of i's currency.

The currency-pegged peripheral countries have identical economic structures with the currency-floating ones but cannot use bilateral exchange rates as a strategic tool to withstand shocks. They have to peg their currencies to the core country currency at a fixed level. The aggregate supply and aggregate demand of the peripheral countries j can be expressed as: $y_{pi} = (1-\alpha)n_{pi}$; $y_{pi} = \beta_p\lambda - \delta_p z - vr_{pi}$.

Set $\bar{n}$ as the employment level in full employment status, and assume that policymakers of both core and periphery countries are pursing full employment, in other words, minimizing the absolute value of the deviation between the actual employment level n from the target employment level $\bar{n}$, that is, $n-\bar{n}$, or min $\frac{1}{2}(n-\bar{n})^2$ known as the loss function of certain countries.

Assuming all countries' unemployment equals to 0 in full employment, $\bar{n} = 0$, then the concrete formulas of actual employment level and loss function will be as follows:

For the core country, the actual employment level: $n_c = \frac{1}{1-\alpha}(\beta_c\lambda - \delta_c z - vr_c)$.

The loss function is: $l_c = \frac{1}{2}(n-\bar{n})^2 = \frac{1}{2}\ n_c^2 : \frac{1}{2}\frac{1}{(1-\alpha)^2}(\beta_c\lambda - \delta_c z - vr_c)^2$.

If it wants to achieve min (l_c), for $\frac{\partial l_c}{\partial r_c} = 0$, its reaction function would be $r_c = -\frac{\delta_c}{v}z + \frac{\beta_c}{v}\lambda$.

For i, the periphery countries with floating exchange rates.

the actual employment level is: $n_{fi} = \frac{1}{1-\alpha}(\beta_f\lambda - \delta_{fi}z_{fi} - vr_{fi})$.

The loss function is: $l_{fi} = \frac{1}{2}(n_{fi} - \bar{n}_{fi})^2 = \frac{1}{2}n_{fi}^2 : \frac{1}{2}\frac{1}{(1-\alpha)^2}$ $(\beta_f\lambda - \delta_f z_{fi} - vr_{fi})^2$.

If it wants to achieve $\min(l_{fi})$, for $\frac{\overline{\partial l_{fi}}}{\partial r_{fi}} = 0$, its reaction function would be $r_f = -\frac{\delta_f}{v} z_f + \frac{\beta_f}{v}\lambda$.

For j, the periphery countries with pegged exchange rates, the actual employment level is: $n_p i = \frac{1}{1-\alpha}(\beta_p\lambda - \delta_p z_{pi} - v r_{pi})$

The loss function is: $l_{pi} = \frac{1}{2}(n_{pi} - \bar{n}_{pi})^2 = \frac{1}{2}n_{pi}^2 : \frac{1}{2}\frac{1}{(1-\alpha)^2}(\beta_p\lambda - \delta_p z_{pi} - v r_{pi})^2$

If it wants to achieve $\min(l_{pi})$, for $\frac{\overline{\partial \mathrm{l}_{pi}}}{\partial \mathrm{r}_{pi}} = 0$, its reaction function would be $r_p = -\frac{\delta_p}{v} z + \frac{\beta_p}{v}\lambda$.

When the global AD shock equals to λ, the impact on the core countries is $\beta_c\lambda$: the impact on each currency-floating peripheral country is $\beta_f\lambda$; on each currency-pegged peripheral country is $\beta_p\lambda$. Assume that the impact on each currency-floating peripheral country and currency-pegged peripheral country is the same, then $\beta_c + \beta_f + \beta_p = 1$. Since China is a currency-pegged peripheral country, it can be stated based on the policy game model that under the AD shock, as long as it pegs its currency to that of the core country, its interest rate policy must change according to the interest rate of the core country. In other words, its monetary policy will inevitably lose independence. On this basis, we can also estimate the requirements for currency–pegged peripheral countries to unpeg when they are hit by demand shocks again, and the cost for peripheral countries to maintain full employment. Similarly, based on the current "center–periphery" international monetary system, we can also analyze the risks for China from the perspective of supply shocks. For example, money supply will have a significant impact on the real economy. And in an economic crisis, peripheral countries will increase foreign exchange reserves to resist external risks, but the increase can easily lead to a rise in the money supply. Shocks from irregular money supply are the main cause of China's short-term economic fluctuations.[13]

[13]Wu Zhiwen, "Anomalous Relationship between Money Supply and Prices: Theories and Empirical Analyzes Based on China," *Management World* 12 (2002): 15–26 (in Chinese).

Since money supply shock is in line with the Autoregressive model (AR): (1) process, it can be calculated through the following formula:

$$u_t = vu_{t-1} + e_t^u \sim N(0, \sigma_z^2).$$

In this formula, u_t is the deviation of the monetary growth rate during the period from its unconditional mean, and e_t^u is the random disturbance of the currency shock. In the short term, the money supply, no matter expected or unanticipated, has a significant impact on production (Lu and Shu, 2002).[14] The shock of narrow money (M1) has a relatively stable influence on economic fluctuations, while that of broad money (M2) has a more significant impact, reflected by sharposcillation.[15] In addition, the shocks of price supply and exchange rate supply also greatly influence the real economy.

A large number of empirical studies also confirm the analysis of theoretical models. Pei *et al.* conducted an empirical test on China's real economy based on the data of the global financial crisis in the early period.[16] The results show that the crisis had a serious negative impact on economic growth, financial markets and employment of China's largest 10 exporters represented by the United States, and has caused a sharp fluctuation in China's exchange rate. It thus has hit the confidence of investors and consumers in these countries (regions), reducing China's overseas import demand. China's exports to the sample countries mentioned earlier account for nearly 70% of its total annual export volume. Therefore, declines of these countries' real economies, especially declines in import demand, will have a serious negative impact on China's exporting.[17] Studies of

[14]Lu, Jun, and Yuan Shu, "Long-term Currency Neutrality: Theory and Its Empirical Evidence in China," *Financial Research* 06 (2002): 32–40.

[15]Liu, Bin, "An Empirical Study on the Relationship between Money Supply, Output and Price in China," *Financial Research* 07 (2002).

[16]Pei, Ping, Qian, Zhang and Zhifeng, Hu, "Impact of the International Financial Crisis on China's Export Trade: An Empirical Study Based on Monthly Data from 2007 to 2008," *Financial Research* 8 (2009): 103–113.

[17]Pei, Ping, Qian, Zhang and Zhifeng, Hu, "The Impact of International Financial Crisis on China's Export: An Empirical Study Based on the 2007–2008 Monthly Data," *Journal of Financial Research* 8 (2009): 103–113 (in Chinese).

Zeng *et al.* (2012) show that during the global financial crisis, the US economic recession had a clear "price effect" on China, namely, a serious negative impact on the price level and quantity level of China's import and export.[18] In addition, the quantitative easing monetary policy adopted by America's financial authority in crises, has exacerbated the dollar's depreciation, gaining a price advantage on export commodity over China, and then boosted China's import of US goods. At the same time, the depreciation of the dollar has also speeded up the rising in international energy and resource prices, further increasing the costs to Chinese exporters. This would weaken international competitiveness of Chinese products and suppress its export, thereby exacerbating the negative effects of the export-oriented strategies on its economy.[19] The empirical research by Chen and Liu also supports the forementioned conclusion.[20] Its result shows that America's financial crisis has significant price effect and income effect on China's import and export. Before the global financial crisis, the world economy was booming, the increase in income of trading partners and rapid growth of overseas demand were driving China's import and export to grow steadily. While after the crisis broke out, America's economic recession reduced the income of China's trading partners and thus decreased China's

[18]Zeng, Zhongdong, Zhichao Xie and Wei Ding, "An Analysis of Price Spillovers of Effects of the U.S. Financial Crisis on China's Trade," *Studies of International Finance* 2 (2012): 24–31 (in Chinese).

[19]Zeng, Zhongdong *et al.* (2012) argue that the trade spillovers in the financial crisis are mainly achieved through income and price effects. The price effect refers to the continued currency devaluation in the crisis countries. Imported goods prices in the local markets increased in local currency, while prices of export goods denominated in foreign currencies declined in foreign countries. Price competitiveness of crisis countries is thus strengthened, leading to an increase in imports and decrease in exports of trade partners and competitors. The income effect refers to the economic growth slowdown and drop in residents' real income which led to declines in crisis countries' overall spending power and demand for imports, which in turn decreased the export of their trading partners. The income and price effects will put trade-affiliated countries under the pressure of payment balance deterioration and even sacrifice.

[20]Chen, Shoudong and Liu, Linlin, "The Impact of the U.S. Financial Crisis on China's Trade," *Contemporary Economic Research* 6 (2013): 50–54 (in Chinese).

import and export trade drastically. At the same time, the currency crisis triggered by the financial crisis caused a substantial increase in the RMB's effective exchange rate, weakening Chinese products' price competitiveness in international markets. Thereby, China's imports and exports have been dropping significantly under negative income effects and price effects. Facts have proved that following America's financial crisis, the world economic pattern has undergone profound changes. Accordingly, the international environment for China's import and export also tremendously changed. Its export-oriented growth pattern has proven unsustainable.[21]

4.1.1.3 *Risks and Challenges Faced by China's Financial Sector*

After examining the systematic and regional natures of the financial crisis, Kaminsky and Reinhart pointed out that in a crisis the "central state" would shift the problems to the "peripheral countries" immediately.[22] The reality is a very good evidence of their assertion. He Fan and Zhang Ming demonstrate that the "center–periphery" structure dominated by dollar hegemony and the operation of having a national currency acting as a world currency are intrinsically unstable.[23] From the perspective of the conduction mechanism, the United States sells reserves to emerging countries to obtain resources and commodities and sells financial assets to Europe, Japan and the oil-exporting countries for capital. Due to the rapid response of financial markets, the "peripheral countries" inevitably suffered heavy losses during the initial period of the crisis. The massive capital flows especially the short-term ones triggered by the subprime crisis in the United States have had a huge impact on the money supply of the

---

[21] *Ibid.*

[22] Kaminsky, Graciela and Reinhart, Carmen M., "The Center and the Periphery: The Globalization of Financial Turmoil," *NBER Working Paper*, no. w9479 (November 2001).

[23] He, Fan, and Ming, Zhang, "Factors of Dollar Hegemony in the Instability of the International Monetary System," *Research on Financial and Economic Issues* 7 (2005): 89–99.

"peripheral countries", putting the effectiveness and independence of peripheral countries' monetary policies under grave pressure. Li and Fu argue that this effect is mainly due to the fact that the capital flow makes domestic currency hard to control for monetary authorities.[24] The correlation between the aggregate monetary index and actual economic activities proved to be worse in the later empirical studies.[25] More specifically, Cao pointed out that capital flows affect China's money supply by affecting diverse foreign exchange reserves, RMB matching funds and so on.[26] In this way, fewer and fewer financial variables are directly controllable by the central bank.[27]

Facts showed that the pattern of international capital flows has undergone significant changes after the global financial crisis broke out. The financial sector of "peripheral countries", including that of China, has been significantly influenced, so China's monetary policy has encountered unprecedented challenges. Before the outbreak of the global financial crisis, the international capital flow showed a rather obvious "two-way flow" tendency. That is, emerging market countries, while absorbing a large amount of private capital from developed countries, were also returning capital to developed countries by various means (mainly purchasing U.S. Treasury Bonds), which has made the United States the world's largest capital-importing country.[28] According to Debtor Reporting System of the World Bank, net capital inflows of emerging markets and developing countries' private department increased from US$181.6 billion to US$1.1105 trillion from 2001 to 2007, an increase of 3.2–8% in proportion to national

[24] Li Xindan and Hao Fu, "The Influences of Open Economy on Monetary Policies and the Adjustment of China's Monetary Policy," *Journal of Nanjing University* 2 (1998): 157–165 (in Chinese).

[25] *Ibid.*

[26] Cao, Yong, "International Reserve Currency Competition: Market Data Analysis Based on Classification of Monetary Functions," *Review of Investment Studies* 3 (2010): 2–9 (in Chinese).

[27] *Ibid.*

[28] Zong, Liang and Shuping, Liao, "Capital Flows in Emerging Markets in Global Economic Rebalancing," *The Banker* 6 (2010): 78–81 (in Chinese).

income[29]; at the same time, the total amount of securities investment inflows to the United States increased from US$3.10088 trillion to US$73.3208 trillion (twice the amount of the UK, which is in the second place).[30] However, this pattern has obviously changed since the global financial crisis, with net capital inflows for emerging market countries' private departments rapidly declining from September 2008 to the end of 2009. The total capital amount dropped from US$1.1105 trillion in 2007 to US$716.1 billion in 2008, and further went down to US$521.4 billion in 2009, a decrease of 53.04% from 2007 to 2009. The net foreign direct investment (hereafter referred to as FDI) to emerging markets, net long-term and medium-term debt, net and short-term debt increased from US$508.1 billion, US$283.1 billion and US$184.2 billion in 2007 to US$354.1 billion, US$52.7 billion and US$6.4 billion in 2009, respectively, representing decrease rates of 30.3%, 81.4% and 96.5%.[31] However, since 2010, the net capital inflows to emerging market countries have rapidly increased influenced by a series of factors including the continued quantitative easing policy in major developed countries. According to the International Monetary Fund (IMF) statistics, the total net capital inflow to emerging market countries' private sectors increased 98.7% over 2009, while their proportion on GDP rose from −0.4% in the first quarter of 2009 to 3.1% in the third quarter of 2010. Thus, influenced by the crisis, emerging countries markets experienced large-scale capital outflows and inflows in 2009 and 2010, with net capital inflows fluctuating as high as 150% in this period. In addition, it is noteworthy that Portfolio Investment accounts for a record 48% of total capital inflows. As the volatility and changeability

[29]World Bank, Global Development Finance 2011: External Debt of Developing Countries. http://data.worldbank.org/data-catalog/global-development-finance, March, 2011.

[30]The data is quoted from the International Monetary Fund CPIS database (www.imf.org/external/np/sta/pi/global).

[31]World Bank. Global Development Finance 2011: External Debt of Developing Countries. http://data.worldbank.org/data-catalog/global-development-finance, March, 2011.

of security investments are greater than direct investment and debt investment, emerging market countries are faced with greater volatility in capital inflows and higher risk of capital-flow reversals. The massive outflows and inflows of international capital (especially in cross-border loans and short-term debts) have a strong impact on economic and financial stability of "peripheral countries" in the current international monetary system, especially the great number of emerging economies, represented by China.[32] The impacts are shown by intensified shocks and worsening macroeconomic conditions amidst the crisis[33] and aggravated asset price rises and inflation during economic recovery period.[34] The specific situation in China is as follows:

First, during the early stages of the crisis, foreign-funded financial institutions represented by Bank of America have massively cut their holding of shares of Chinese banks, which has had a certain effect on China's financial stability. Since 2005, Chinese-funded financial institutions represented by state-owned commercial banks have sold part of their shares to foreign-funded financial institutions to attract so-called "strategic foreign investors." However, these "strategic foreign investors" represented by Bank of America began to cut down or even liquidate their stock holdings of Chinese-owned banks from the end of 2008. On 7 January 2009, Bank of America sold 5.62 billion H shares of China Construction Bank and cashed out approximately

---

[32] Cardarelli, R., Elekdag, S., and Kose, M. A., "Capital Inflows: Macroeconomic Implications and Policy Responses," *IMF Working Paper*, No. 09/04, 2009; IMF, Sovereigns, Funding, and Systemic Liquidity. Global Financial Stability Report (October 2010).

[33] Ozkan, F. G. and Unsal, D. F., "External Finance, Sudden Stops, and Financial Crisis: What is Different This Time?" *IMF Working Paper*, No. 10/158, 2010; Rai, K and Kamil, H., "The Global Credit Crunch and Foreign Banks' Lending to Emerging Markets: Why Did Latin America Fare Better?" *IMF Working Paper*, No. 10/102, 2010.

[34] IMF, Tensions from the Two-Speed Recovery Unemployment, Commodities, and Capital Flows (*World Economic Outlook*, April, 2011); Zhang, Ming, "How Emerging Market Countries Deal with Capital Inflows: A Case of China," *International Economic Review* 2 (2011): 89–99 (in Chinese).

HK$19.4 billion, accounting for some 2.4% of the bank's equity. On 28 April 2009, American Express sold its 638 million H shares of ICBC through private equity (hereafter referred to as PE) placement and cashed out approximately HK$2.463 billion. On 12 May 2009, Bank of America again unloaded 13.5 billion H shares of China Construction Bank at a phasic high point of the stock market. The Goldman Sachs group cut its holding of 3.03 billion H shares of Industrial and Commercial Bank of China on 1 June 2009 to cash out HK $14.86 billion. In 2010, Bank of America held three major drastic reductions in its shares of China Construction Bank at a total value of about US$16 billion. The "strategic foreign investors" such as Goldman Sachs and JP Morgan Chase also continued to reduce their holdings of shares in Chinese state-controlled Commercial banks. The total amount cut has exceeded US$10 billion (see Table 4.1).

The "strategic foreign investors" represented by the US financial institutions drastically reduced or sold their shares of China's state-owned commercial banks, seriously affecting China's capital

Table 4.1. 2010–2011 Strategic US Investors' Reduced Share-holdings in Chinese Banks

Date	State-owned Commercial Banks	Strategic US Investors	Number of Shares Reduced (US$)	Value of Shares Reduced (US$)
2011.11		Goldman Sachs	1.752 billion	1.099 billion
2011.01	Industrial and commercial bank of China	JP Morgan Chase	125 million	96.65 million
2010.10		Goldman Sachs	3.041 billion	2.25 billion
2011.10	Agricultural Bank of China	JP Morgan Chase	50.4152 million	17.99 million
2011.11		Bank of America	10.4 billion	6.6 billion
2011.08	China construction bank	Bank of America	13.1 billion	8.3 billion
2010.11		Bank of America	transfer the allotment right for US$1 billion cash	

Source: The statistical analysis report "Chinese banks are baffled by shares unloading of its strategic foreign investors and their positions" from China Venture's website (www.chinaventuregroup.com.cn/research/DetailFree.aspx?id=453), 24 November 2011.

market. Hong Kong's stock market in particular has experienced big shocks and panic. For instance, on 7 January 2009, the day Bank of America sold its shares of China Construction Bank, the Hang Seng China H-Financials Index fell by 5.23%. The share prices of China Construction Bank (00939.HK), China CITIC Bank (00998.HK), Industrial and Commercial Bank of China (01398.HK) and China Merchants Bank (03968.HK) dropped by 8.76%, 7.33%, 7.26% and 6.11% respectively.[35] In addition, statistics show from 5 to 14 January 2009, the Hong Kong Hang Seng Index dropped as much as 12.18% while the Hang Seng China H-Financials Index dropped by 16.88%. Declines in related stocks were even more dramatic — Bank of China, China Construction Bank and Industrial and Commercial Bank of China fell by 14.03%, 18.28% and 22.35%, respectively. Under these influences, the H share prices of three joint-stock commercial banks, namely Bank of Communications, China CITIC Bank and China Merchants Bank, also fell 15.46%, 8.47% and 21.75%, respectively. Moreover, such a massive divestment of "strategic foreign investors" represented by the US financial institutions has seriously dampened investors' confidence in China's financial markets and has exerted a strong negative impact on the subsequent reforms of China's state-owned commercial banks.[36] However, these divestments have made substantial speculative profits for US financial institutions through withdrawing liquid assets (see Table 4.2).

Second, following the outbreak of the global financial crisis, the United States continuously implemented the policy of reducing holding shares for its own interests, which led to a drastic increase in the liquidity of global financial markets. Influenced by this, the excess

---

[35]The data are quoted from various bank websites and Yuan, Zhaohui and Cheng, Zhiyun, "Chinese Banks: The Dominoes to be Sold," *Economic Observer* (January 12, 2009) (in Chinese).

[36]Xiang, Weixing and Da, Wang, *A Study on the Corporate Structure of State-owned Commercial Banks after the Restructuring — How China Draws Lessons from Central and Eastern European Transition Countries.* Beijing: Economic Science Press, 2012 (in Chinese).

Table 4.2. The Costs and Profits of Strategic US Investors' Holding Equity in Chinese State-owned Banks

Strategic Foreign Investor	Purchase Time	Cost of per Share (HK$)	Purchase Amount (billions)	Sell Time	Sell Price of per Share (HK$)	Sell Amount (billions)	Profits (billion HK$)
Bank of America	2005.10	1	19.133	2009.1	3.92	5.62	
	2008.5	2.42	6	2009.5	4.2	13.509	59.6329
	2008.11	2.8	19.58				
American express	2006.1	1.21	1.276	2009.4	3.86	0.638	1.6907
Goldman sachs	2006.1	1.21	16.477	2009.6	4.88	3.03	11.1201

Source: Xiang Weixing, Wang Da, *A Study on the Corporate Structure of State-owned Commercial Banks after the Restructuring — How China Draws Lessons from Central and Eastern European Transition Countries.* Beijing: Economic Science Press, 2012.

liquidity in developed countries rushed into emerging market countries represented by China during the global economic recovery in 2010, especially when the latter's economies were booming. In this way, net capital inflow, foreign exchange reserves and asset prices in these emerging markets were rapidly driven higher. According to China's State Administration of Foreign Exchange, the total amount of hot money inflow into China during 2001–2010 was about US$300 billion. Indeed, the amount in 2010 alone was as high as US$75.5 billion, accounting for 25.2% of the total hot money inflow. In addition, China's foreign exchange reserves increased by about 200 billion USD in the first quarter of 2011, of which about half could not be explained by the valuation effect caused by trade surpluses, FDI and major currency exchange rate movements.[37] The massive hot money inflow has intensified the expectation of a unilateral appreciation of

[37]The data are quoted from the "Monitoring Report on Cross-border Fund Flows in 2011" by the State Administration of Foreign Exchange of China. Zhang, Ming and Zheng, Ying (2011) argued that the actual hot money inflow may be significantly higher than the figure showed because the report did not estimate the hot money flowing through transfer pricing in trades.

For more details, please refer to Zhang, Ming and Zheng, Ying, A New Wave of Capital Control: Causes, Tools and Enlightenment to China, *Proceedings of*

the RMB, which has increased the pressure of rising domestic asset prices and imported inflation on China. From October 2010 to April 2011, China's consumer price index (CPI) rose by more than 4.4%, with CPI up 5% in the first quarter of 2011.[38] China has experienced the worst inflation since the East Asian financial crisis in 1997, during the period 2010–2011.

The massive inflow of hot money causes severe challenges to China's macro-control policies. Although the IMF has offered policy instruments for emerging market countries to respond to capital inflows, namely, the flexibility of the exchange rate regime, interest rate cuts and austerity measures, management of capital outflows, and prudential regulation and capital control measures,[39] the policy portfolios currently available for China are very limited.[40] Both the exchange rate policy and the monetary policy of China have fallen into a dilemma (see Table 4.3). From the perspective of exchange rate policies, maintaining the stability of the exchange rate of RMB against the US dollar will inevitably encounter pressures of America's request for RMB appreciation and bilateral trade frictions.[41] Opening the path to appreciating RMB is not expected to alleviate the pressure of China's external imbalances (RMB appreciated against the US dollar by 21% from 21 July 2005 to 30 June 2008, but China's trade surplus over the United States still increased by 32.1%[42]).

---

the Research Center of International Finance, Institute of World Economics and Politics, Chinese Academy of Social Sciences, No. 2011.023, 2011 (in Chinese).

[38]The data are quoted from the website of the National Bureau of Statistics of China (www.stats.gov.cn).

[39]IMF, *Meeting New Challenges to Stability and Building a Safer System.* Global Financial Stability Report, April, 2010.

[40]Zhang, Ming, "How Emerging Market Countries Deal with Capital Inflows: A Case of China," *International Economic Review* 2 (2011): 89–99 (in Chinese).

[41]Since 2010, the United States has been strongly urging an appreciation of RMB and putting pressure on the Chinese government by politicizing this issue. For details, please refer to Wang, Da, Weixing, Xiang and Xiaoxin Liu, "Imbalance and Adjustment of Sino-U.S. Economic Relations under the Global Financial Crisis," *Northeast Asia Forum* 1 (2011): 19–26 (in Chinese).

[42]The data are quoted from the country report website of China's Ministry of Commerce.

Table 4.3. Portfolios and Their Effects on China's Monetary and Exchange Rate Policies

Monetary Policy / Exchange Rate Policy	Tight (Raising Interest Rates)	Loose (Maintaining Interest Rates)
Appreciating RMB	Advantages: easing the political pressure, inhibiting imported inflation.	Advantages: easing political pressure and inhibiting imported inflation.
	Disadvantages: accelerating hot money inflow, rising asset prices.	Disadvantages: domestic inflation may go out of control.
Not Appreciating RMB	Advantages: stabilizing exports, restraining domestic inflation.	Advantages: stabilizing exports
	Disadvantages: exacerbating trade frictions with the US, accelerating hot money inflow.	Disadvantages: exacerbating trade frictions with the US, and domestic inflation may go out of control.

Source: Xiang, Weixing and Wang, Da, "On the Asymmetry of Sino-US Financial Interdependence" *World Economy Study* 7 (2011): 10–16 (in Chinese).

Instead, it will continue to intensify the expectation of RMB appreciation. In this way, China's macroeconomic control will become more difficult. And even the "bubble economy" faced by Japan after the appreciation of the yen in the 1980s will be repeated in China. If we continue to implement loose monetary policy, domestic inflation may go out of control; and if the monetary policy is tight and China enters its rate-increase cycle before the US, there would be an inevitable influx of hot money (mainly excess dollars liquidity) and a rise in asset prices. Thus, China as a "peripheral country" in the current international monetary system has always been in a passive position in its financial interdependence with the "central country", the US. In the face of America's continual quantitative easing currency policy and weak dollar policy, the policy portfolios for Chinese monetary authorities are very limited.[43] China's macroeconomic stability is thus faced with great challenges.

4.1.2 *China's Responsibility to Promote International Monetary System Reforms as OneParty of the Global Economic Imbalance*

4.1.2.1 *China Plays an Important Role in Global Economic Imbalance*

The broad reflection of global economic imbalance is global financial and trade imbalances that emerged from economic growth imbalances, while the narrow reflections are the current account deficit of the United States and the huge current account surplus of other countries, mainly Asian countries, including China. In general, two distinct characteristics of global economic imbalance in recent years have emerged, which are as follows:

First, the US's deficit has become large in scale and diverse in product structure, making the United States an important party in the global economic imbalance. It is estimated that as a major deficit party, the US's deficit products have evolved from primary products and resource-intensive products (such as Category 3 products of SITC) in early times, to labor-intensive consumer goods (e.g. SITC Class 8 products) after the 1980s, and to more capital-intensive

[43]Under such circumstances, the only option for the Chinese monetary authorities was to raise the interest rate and appreciate the RMB. Also, it had to bear the pressure of rising domestic property prices caused by the massive inflow of "dual hot money" (the capital for forex and interest arbitrage). In June 2010, China, under pressure from the United States, restarted the reform of the RMB exchange rate formation mechanism and the RMB then started to appreciate against the US dollar. In October 2010, China was forced to enter the rate-rise cycle ahead of the US in order to curb inflation. According to Zhang's (2011) estimate, from January to September 2010 alone, the short-term international capital inflow into China was valued as high as US$101 billion. For more details, please refer to Zhang, Ming, "Short-term International Capital Flows into China: Scaled Estimating by Different Means and Standards," *World Economy* 2 (2011): 39–56 (in Chinese).

products (e.g. SITC Class 7 products) after the 1990s. At present, the United States has deficits in almost all product categories.

Second, the surplus party, or the source of the deficits, has become more diversified. In 1980, the world surplus parties were mainly oil exporters; in the 1980s and early 1990s, Japan began to hold the lion's share of the global surplus; after the mid-1990s, the surplus parties increased significantly. China, other East Asian economies, and oil exporters' surpluses grew substantially, with the geographical structure of global surpluses remarkably changing.

A notable issue is that in recent years, China has played an increasingly important role in the global economic imbalance. At present, China, as the most important source for America's trade deficits, has become the most important party in the imbalance,apart from the United States. In other words, the Sino-US trade imbalance has become a representative of global economic imbalance. According to China's statistics, China's trade with the United States showed the first surplus of US$6.27 billion in 1993, accounting for only 1.02% of China's GDP for that year. Since then, China has been maintaining a steadily expanding surplus in trade with the United States, accounting for an increasing proportion of its GDP. In 2001, the surplus reached US$28.08 billion, almost 4.5 times that of 1993, accounting for 2.12% of China's GDP. In 2008, the trade surplus reached the highest value of US$170.86 billion, 5 times higher than in 2001. During the period of 2001–2008, the average annual growth rate of China's trade surplus with the US was as high as 29%, an increase of 1.8 percentage points in its share of GDP. Affected by the financial crisis, China's surplus with the US dropped 16.1% in 2009 compared with that of 2008, but still reached US$143.38 billion. However, according to the United States, as early as 1983, its trade with China began to show a deficit of US$320 million, yet accounting for only 0.01% of the US GDP in that year. Since then, the deficit has been rapidly expanding. In 2000, the US's trade deficit with China reached US$83.83 billion. It was the first time China surpassed Japan to become the largest trade deficit source of the United States. From 2001 to 2008, the US's trade deficit with China increased from

US$83.1 billion to US$268.84 billion, an average annual increase rate of 18%. The deficit decreased to US$226.83 billion in 2009. It is easy to conclude that the US deficits are much higher than those of China (the maximum difference was as high as US$97.1 billion in 2008).[44] Nevertheless, the data from both sides show that the Sino-US trade imbalance has been constantly aggravated before the financial crisis (see Table 4.4).

Due to differences in China and the United States' resources, economic scale and economic development, the imbalance between China and the United States in trade is not only reflected by economic aggregate but also by the asymmetry in their trade interdependent relations, namely, China's dependence on the United States is greater than the reverse. Specifically, since the 1990s, the proportion of Sino-US trade in China's total trade volume has steadily increased from 10.2% in 1990 to 13.03% in 2008. China's trade has been more and more dependent on the United States. However, the share of Sino-US trade in the total US foreign trade rose from 2.26% in 1990 to 12.02% in 2008, i.e. Sino-US Trade accounts for more of China's total foreign trade than that of the United States'. It needs to be further pointed out that China's exports to the United States accounts for a larger share of its total exports than China's import from the US for China's total imports. Thereby China's dependence on the United States is mainly manifested in exports. On the other hand, the United States' dependence on China is mainly through imports. More importantly, since 1990, China's exports to the United States have accounted for about 20% of its total exports, much higher than the proportion of the US's import from China to the total US imports (about 11%). Therefore, China's export dependence on

[44]On 19 March, the Joint Research Team of China and the United States Published "Research Report on Differences in the Statistics of Sino-U.S. Trade Goods." The report shows that the main causes of the statistical discrepancies include that the US would count the import goods as China-exported when they were actually transferred through a third country; the recorded prices of China and America were different and distinctive methods were used for customs statistics processing and so on.

Table 4.4. Year-on-Year Increase in China Trade Surplus with the US: 1979–2009

	China Data			US Data		
Year	Trade Surplus (US$100 million	Increase (%)	Proportion of China's GDP (%)	Trade Surplus (US$100 million	Increase (%)	Proportion of China's GDP (%)
1979	−12.7	—	—	10.7	—	−0.04
1981	−28.7	—	−0.98	15.4	—	−0.05
1982	−21	−26.8	−0.75	4.1	−73.4	−0.01
1983	−6.1	−71.0	−0.20	−3.2	−178.0	0.01
1984	−14.5	137.7	−0.47	−3.8	18.8	0.01
1985	−17.5	20.7	−0.57	−0.6	−84.2	0.00
1986	−20.9	19.4	−0.70	−16.6	2666.7	0.04
1987	−18	−13.9	−0.56	−27.9	68.1	0.06
1988	−32.5	80.6	−0.80	−34.7	24.4	0.07
1989	−38.5	18.5	−0.85	−61.8	78.1	0.11
1990	−14.1	−63.4	−0.36	−104.2	68.5	0.18
1991	−18.5	31.2	−0.45	−126.9	21.8	0.21
1992	−3.1	−83.2	−0.06	−183.1	44.3	0.29
1993	62.7	−2122.6	1.02	−227.8	24.4	0.34
1994	74.9	19.5	1.34	−295.0	29.5	0.42
1995	85.9	14.7	1.18	−337.9	14.5	0.46
1996	105.3	22.6	1.23	−395.2	17.0	0.50
1997	164	55.7	1.72	−497.0	25.7	0.60
1998	210.2	28.2	2.06	−569.3	14.6	0.65
1999	224.7	6.9	2.07	−686.8	20.6	0.73
2000	297.4	32.4	2.48	−838.3	22.1	0.84
2001	280.8	−5.6	2.12	−831.0	−0.9	0.81
2002	427.2	52.1	2.94	−1030.6	24.0	0.97
2003	586.1	37.2	3.57	−1240.7	20.4	1.11
2004	802.7	37.0	4.16	−1622.5	30.8	1.37
2005	1141.7	42.2	5.11	−2022.8	24.7	1.60
2006	1442.6	26.4	5.43	−2341.0	15.7	1.75
2007	1633	13.2	4.83	−2585.1	10.4	1.84
2008	1708.6	4.6	3.88	−2680.4	3.7	1.86
2009	1433.8	−16.1	2.92	−2268.3	−15.4	1.59

Source: Based on data from China's customs and US Commerce Department. http://www.customs.gov.cn/customs/302249/zfxxgk/gknb/index.htmlhttps://www.commerce.gov/data-and-reports/reports

the United States is far greater than the US's import dependence on China. That is, the United States is one of the major destinations of China's exports (China's export relies heavily on the US); while China is only one of the many US importing partners (the US imports does not obviously depend on China). At the same time, China's import to the US accounts for a slightly higher share of its total imports than the share of US's exports to China in its total exports. Therefore, China's import dependence on US is greater than US's export dependence on China. There is a significant asymmetry in the trade relations between China and the US. A study by Cooper[45] shows that the dependence between the two countries is to some extent determined by the economic costs of interrupting their economic interactions, while the degree of substitutability of import goods is the key factor to determine the costs. The higher the degree of substitutability of import goods from one country to another country, the smaller the loss of national income caused by the interruption of economic interactions between them, and the less dependence of the importer on the exporter. From the commodities composition of Sino-US trade, China exports mainly labor-intensive products to the US while the US exports mainly resource-intensive and capital-intensive products to China. As the demand-price elasticity of labor-intensive products is higher than that of resources and capital-intensive products, the degree of substitutability of the former is greater than that of the latter. It indicates that when interrupting trade exchanges, China's national income losses are relatively larger than those of the US. That is, the United States has a lower degree of dependence on China than the reverse. Therefore, the commodity composition of Sino-US trade proves the analysis on both sides' advantage comparison, and further indicates that China relies more on American goods than America depends on Chinese goods.[46]

---

[45]Cooper, R. N., "Financial Aspects of Economic Cooperation around the Pacific," *Pacific Trade and Development I*, Papers and Proceedings of a Conference Held by the Japan Economic Research Center in January, 1968.

[46]Lei, Da and Yong, Zhao, "Asymmetry and Symmetry in the Economic Interdependence between China and the United States," *International Economic Review* 2 (2008): 29–33 (in Chinese).

It is significant and crucial to view China's important role in the global economic imbalance in a rational way. First, it should be noted that although China has now become the most important source of current account deficits for the United States, the deficit composition of China to its trade partners including the US and China's positions in global economic imbalance are very different from Japan's in previous times. China, like Japan in the mid-1990s, needed to import primary products for domestic production. At that time, Japan directly obtained favorable surpluses from the US through its manufacturing industry's advantages. Its major exports in the mid-1990s were capital goods including spare parts and semi-finished products. However at present, China is importing capital goods, especially from East Asian countries such as Japan and South Korea, processing them domestically, and then exporting final consumer goods to developed countries like the US, and other emerging industrialized countries. Processing trade has become a major trade mode of China's foreign trade and basic source for trade surpluses. Thus, China is at the lower third level of the aforesaid global labor division system at present. Its status is higher than that of resource-exporting countries but lower than that of other emerging industrialized countries. It is still a manufacturing base of final consumer goods.

Second, China also plays a crucial role as a producing hub in global labor division. On the one hand, China's great advantage in labor costs has attracted many export-to-America final products' last processing that are originally completed from emerging countries to China. As a result, China has, to a certain extent, replaced other East Asian economies to export the final products to the United States. However, the more strengthened China's processing and export capacity is, the greater its demand for capital goods such as spare parts and intermediate goods. The scale of China's import of capital goods from developed countries and other East Asian economies has been constantly expanding, generating the most important capital goods market in this region. The regional labor division of East Asia promoted the formation of the "New Triangle Trade Model" in which East Asian emerging economies (including some developed countries) export capital goods (mainly spare parts, intermediate products and some raw materials) to China, and China processes and then exports the final products to developed countries such as the United States.

Overall, China's position in the global and regional labor division system has had a significant impact on global economic imbalance at this stage. First, China has become the largest final product processing base and the core of the regional labor division system. It acts as a production hub in the global trade cycle. As a result, China's trade surplus with the United States to a large extent reflects the production and export capacity of the entire East Asian region, which serves as an important background for China to rapidly expand its surplus in the trade with America in recent years and become the focus of global economic imbalance. Second, China's entry into the East Asian labor division system has promoted the structural adjustment and trade pattern changes of other economies in its region, gradually shifting their pattern from export-to-America to export-to-China, and from consumer-goods-oriented to capital-goods-oriented. Influenced by this, these countries have gradually extricated themselves from the "Deficit System"[47] and have started to gain trade surplus. In fact, China's trade balance at the current stage has formed a pattern by which it makes up for the deficit with East Asian economies by the surplus with the United States. Third, the new East Asian regional production system with China as its core or hub will further increase its overall production capacity. An increase in import demand resulting from the US's further industrial structure

[47]The so-called "deficit system" originally refers to trade status of increasing import and export in East Asian economies such as South Korea and Taiwan, caused by the processing-trade pattern, in which economies import capital goods and intermediate products from Japan and export the processed goods to the US. See Xiao, Li, and Ding Yibing, *Asia's Surpassing — Building an East Asian Monetary System and "Asianizing the RMB"*. Beijing: Contemporary China Press, 2006, 51 (in Chinese).

upgrade will become an important factor influencing future global economic imbalance.[48]

4.1.2.2 *China's Efforts and Effects for Rebalancing the Global Economy*

As an important party in the global economic imbalance, China has been working toward rebalancing the global economy since 2005, by reforming the RMB exchange rate system and allowing its appreciation against the dollar. In fact, since 2000, the underestimated RMB exchange rate as pegged to the dollar, the constant current account surpluses and the influx of various investment and speculative capital backed by RMB appreciation expectation have all caused great pressure for RMB to appreciate under the "double surplus" pattern. In addition, maintaining a fixed exchange rate under the foreign exchange-selling system caused a rapid expansion of foreign exchange reserves and growth in position for foreign exchange purchase (hereafter referred as Position for Forex Purchase). In this context, the RMB has been under a great pressure of appreciation. In addition, the United States has constantly pressed China to speed up the appreciation against the dollar and thus to cure its trade deficit. Therefore, on 21 July, 2005, the Chinese government officially announced that in order to improve China's socialist market economic system and give full play to the market's fundamental role in resource allocation, China would begin to establish and improve a managed floating exchange rate based on the market. It marked the end of the RMB's peg to the dollar which had lasted for nearly a decade. Since then, China has started to implement the new exchange rate system based on the market with reference to a basket of currencies (floating band of RMB against the dollar is limited to 3% of the last closing price, and 1.5% against other currency). On the day

[48]Xiao, Li, and Ding Yibing, "Global Economic Imbalances at Present and the Role of China," *Journal of Jilin University-Social Sciences Edition* 1 (2007): 17–27 (in Chinese).

of launching the exchange rate system reform, the RMB appreciated sharply by 2% against the USD. The following are the two important reasons for China to start the reform:

First, America's pressure on China to appreciate RMB is getting intensified in the Sino-US trade imbalances. The reasons for the appeal for rebalancing through appreciating RMB are that it has been hard for China to attract enough foreign investment to make up for the current account deficit, and its major trading partners can only withstand the crisis impact by appreciation against the dollar. The impact of trade partners' currency values on the dollar's value, as reflected by the Fed's trade-weighted dollar index, is the Canadian dollar, the euro, the Japanese yen, the Mexican peso and the Chinese yuan in descending order. In an analysis, the National Bureau of Economic Analysis (NBER) pointed out that as the euro has greatly appreciated against the dollar in the past few years and there was little scope for it to absorb the pressure of the dollar's depreciation, the UK was faced with a bubble economy, and Germany and France's economies were close to a recession. However, the Canadian dollar was also unlikely to withstand the US dollar's depreciation because Canada is an important industrial raw materials source for the US, with an economic cycle highly synchronized with the latter's. As for the Mexican peso, its crisis, lasting for several decades, and the resulting serious financial turmoil, have made it infeasible for the US to make it act as an engine for the dollar's depreciation. Only two currencies remained: the Japanese yen and the Chinese yuan. The potential pressure on the RMB to appreciate as a tool to release a dollar bubble is much greater than that on the yen. After all, the yen has nominally adopted a floating exchange rate system and has made a big compromise — the 1985 Plaza Accord and the long-term economic downturn it caused. On the other hand, China's "double surplus" has been constantly expanding and its economy has kept increasing rapidly. The RMB then inevitably became America's target. In fact, since 2003, the United States has repeatedly asked China to abandon RMB's peg to the dollar (the so-called "substantive fixed exchange rate system"), and required RMB should not continue to depreciate as had the dollar. The Japanese government then followed the United States to advocate the ideas that "China is a threat," "China's exporting deflation", and "RMB is appreciating." These moves were aimed at shifting the accusation that the yen was weakened by the low-interest-rate policy in the long term. In this context, the RMB was facing increasing pressure of appreciation.

Second, based on China's domestic macroeconomic situation and the "double surplus", the excess liquidity brought by the "Position for Forex Purchase" is hard to be dealt with by sterilizing monetary policies. The central bank's monetary policies are made more difficult to formulate. Pressure of maintaining the fixed exchange rate system has affected the main target of regulating and controlling the domestic price level. Specifically, due to the high external dependence of China's economy, exports and FDI have become two engines of promoting employment and boosting rapid economic growth. To this end, the Chinese government has provided a competitive low-cost investment environment. The obligatory foreign exchange-selling system and a fixed exchange rate system are among the most typical cases. In order to ensure that the limited foreign exchange resources can be used for importing scarce resources and technologies, and to encourage export for foreign exchange earnings, the Chinese government has long assumed the risk of corporate foreign exchange settlement and exchange rate fluctuations. As a result, the better the export performance and the more the foreign investors, the faster the foreign exchange reserves grow under "double surpluses", and at the same time the faster the expansion of China's money supply. In this way, the problem of excess liquidity will become more serious. In the context of unbalanced domestic and international economic development, unbalanced money supply and demand, and less open financial markets, the expected appreciation of RMB has been gradually formed and continuously strengthened, and illegal hot money to China continues to grow. In order to ensure the healthy development of China's real economy and alleviate the negative impact of excess liquidity, China's central bank continuously intensified its macro-control efforts by raising the deposit reserve ratio, raising interest rates, issuing central bank bills and increasing window guidance on banks. However, the results were not satisfactory and the issue of foreign exchange payment became more prominent. In this context, RMB appreciation has been recognized by the market as an effective means or an inevitable choice to redress the Chinese economy's structural imbalance and restrain excess liquidity.[49]

In all, under such internal and external situations, China initiated the RMB exchange rate system reform in 2005 and implemented a managed floating exchange rate system to rectify Sino-US economic imbalance. Since then, the yuan had begun to slow down its appreciation until the global financial crisis broke out in September 2008. Statistics show that the RMB rose by about 23% against the dollar from July 2005 to August 2008. However, the exchange rate, as a price factor, was proved to be an obscure impact on China's trade after the exchange rate system reform in July 2005. The rise in effective exchange even turned out to improve trade balance, which was not theoretically normal. In fact, during the 22-month period of RMB's unilateral appreciation against the US dollar since the reform, both China's imports and exports maintained a relatively fast growth rate. China's net exports showed a rise rather than a decline during this period. The annual data showed that China's trade surplus against the US had grown rapidly during 2005–2008.

The actual effect of the RMB exchange rate formation mechanism reform since 2005 proves that China's unilateral adjustment of rate is not helpful to correct the global economic imbalance. The rebalancing of the global economy must start with a deeper and broader institutional arrangement. After the global financial crisis, reforming the existing international monetary system has become an important

---

[49]Shao, Yu, The Trail of RMB (1949–2009): "The Internal Logic of the Evolution of China's Exchange Rate," Southwest Securities Research Report (February 2010) (in Chinese).

direction. Dooley *et al.* view the global economic imbalance as a "new Bretton Woods System," in which economic development is driven by the net saving flows from poor to affluent countries and the current global imbalance is a conscious and stable arrangement between surplus countries and deficit countries.[50] The current account deficit of the US is an inevitable result of restoring the Bretton Woods System.[51] Li and Yu further claimed that the root cause of the global economic imbalance lies in the central countries' dominance over the global labor division and the growth mode in the current international monetary system.[52] Therefore, simply relying on the exchange rate to redress economic imbalance cannot fundamentally solve the problem,even through the joint efforts of stakeholders.[53] The starting point for alleviating the imbalance is to prevent large growth losses of any party. The core of the current international monetary system, the United States, should assume the primary responsibility of controlling the sprawl of dollar credit, as it's the basis for rebalancing the global economy. Both China and the United States should start by resolving domestic economic structural issues. Facts have proved that although China plays an important role in the current imbalance, the core of redress is not Sino-US economic and trade relations, but maintaining East Asian regional production network, the "dollar system" and the global circulating mechanism of trades and funds. China's unilateral adjustment cannot fundamentally solve America's current account deficit which requires coordination and cooperation among the entire East Asian region and America. In particular, a large number of theoretical studies and RMB exchange

---

[50]Dooley, Michael P., David Folkerts-Landau and Peter Garber, "An Essay on the Revived Bretton Woods System," *NBER Working Papers* 9971, National Bureau of Economic Research, Inc. (2003).

[51]*Ibid.*

[52]Li, Yang and Yu, Weibin, "Global Economic Imbalances and Challenges Faced by China," *Studies of International Finance* 2 (2006): 12–18 (in Chinese).

[53]*Ibid.*

rate system reform since 2005 have proved that the exchange rate factor is not decisive in the imbalance. Solely relying on the adjustment of RMB exchange rate is not helpful to fundamentally solve the problem; instead, it might harm the environment for China's economic restructuring.

4.1.2.3 *China has the Responsibility to Redress Global Economic Imbalance by Promoting International Monetary System Reform*

An obvious fact is that the global imbalances, typified by China–US trade imbalances, cannot be sustained in the long run. First, as the foreign exchange reserves of "peripheral countries" accumulate, their costs of controlling inflationary pressures through sterilizing Position for Forex Purchase are increasingly high under the current "dollar system." If the sterilization is not complete, there will be risks of inflation and an asset price bubble caused by excess liquidity. Second, as foreign exchange reserves of "peripheral countries" grow in scale, they will find it increasingly difficult to withstand the impact of the drastic depreciation of the US dollar on their real purchasing power of forex reserves, with its tolerable ratio of US net debt to GDP gradually declining.[54] Finally, the valuation effect to constrain the rise of the US's net foreign debt can hardly be maintained. On the one hand, there is no credible evidence that the long-term interest rate on US financial assets will remain low; on the other hand, gains of property valuation would disappear once the dollar's exchange rate is stabilized or even strengthened.[55] Therefore, in a sense, the rebalancing is a necessary condition for the sustainable development of the global economy. However, the current dollar-oriented international

[54]Zhang, Ming, "International Monetary Reform: Background, Causes, Measures and China's Participation," *International Economic Review* 1 (2010): 114–137 (in Chinese).

[55]Milesi-Ferretti, G. M., "Fundamentals at Odds? The U.S. Current Account Deficit and the Dollar," *IMF Working Paper*, WP/08/260 (November 2008).

monetary system is not equipped with an "automatic mechanism"for redressing global economic imbalance; instead, it may even exacerbate the imbalance to a considerable degree.

Specifically, in the "center-periphery" structure of the "dollar system", since the "periphery countries" cannot use their national currencies for international payments, they must obtain the US dollar by exporting goods and services to or attracting investment from America. On the other hand, America exports the US dollar by purchasing goods and services (that is, by current account deficits) or by investing directly in the "periphery countries" (capital account deficits). However, since the US financial market is the largest and most developed in the world, it has the function of a capital intermediary for underdeveloped countries in the global financial markets. This means that America will have a constant capital account surplus rather than a deficit. Therefore, under the "dollar system", the United States exports dollars mainly through the current account deficit, which is an institutional cause of the global economic imbalance. In addition, the current international monetary system, with the dollar as its core, lacks the capacity to regulate international payments balance. The absence of a regulatory mechanism has further aggravated the global economic imbalance. In fact, under the monopolar credit international currency system, "peripheral countries" do not have their national currency internationalized, so they need to accumulate international currency reserves to obtain international credit and resist financial shocks. Their growing demand for global currency reserves can only be achieved through trade. Correspondingly, as one of the important ends of the global economic imbalance, China thrives on the stress of economic restructuring. While the United States, with its developed, open and extensive financial market, can utilize monetary policies toward economic goals without worrying about payment balances or exchange rate, as well as exporting the pressure to the other side of the imbalance.

Therefore, China has the responsibility to establish a bilateral coordination mechanism with the United States and formulate a specific timetable for action. It should also formulate a clear direction for policies and adjustments to solve the imbalances. By reforming the international monetary system, China intends to gradually adjust the capital inflows to the United States, narrow the US's structural trade deficits, set up a mechanism to coordinate payment balances and negotiate policies between major economies. It is worth mentioning that despite the alleviation on structural imbalances of the US's trade after the crisis, it is still hard to judge whether the rise in household saving rates are long-term trends.[56] Therefore, rebalancing the global economy still calls for a reform of the international monetary system promoted by China, as a major stakeholder.

[56] According to the statistics of the Bureau of Economic Analysis (BEA), US household savings rate quickly rose from 1.2% to 5% during the first quarter of 2008 and the second quarter of 2009, while the ratio of its current account deficit to GDP dropped from 6% in 2006 to 4.9% in 2008. One view is that up to now, the increase in the savings rate of US residents is mainly due to the tax rebate policies by the Bush and Obama administrations. It is a precautionary saving during the crisis. However, non-US residents have in real terms changed the credit-consumption pattern. The US current account deficit will be widened again as oil prices and commodity prices rebound. The expansion of the US budget deficit implies a further decline in government saving rate, which will also lead to an increase in the current account deficit. Dooley *et al.* (2009) further argued that the payments balance crisis caused by the "revived Bretton Woods System" (the current dollar-standard system) has not yet broken out. The subprime mortgage crisis may even strengthen the system and allow more countries to join it, extending its duration. Another view is that the subprime mortgage crisis may permanently change the demand distribution worldwide. US residents will dramatically change the pre-crisis overconsumption pattern, with a resident saving rate rising sustainably. And once clean energy and biomedicine become the new engines for the US economy, the improvement in exports will ease current account deficits. The deficits can also be eased by America's revitalization of high-end manufacturing or increases in exports of hi-tech products. In this way, reforms of the international monetary system are not necessarily required for global economic rebalancing. For more details, please refer to Zhang, Ming. "International Monetary Reform: Background, Causes, Measures and China's Participation," *International Economic Review* 1 (2010): 114–137 (in Chinese) and Dooley, Michael P., Folkerts-Landau, D. and Peter M. Garber, "Breton Woods II Still Defines the International Monetary System," *NBER Working Paper* No. 14731 (February 2009).

4.2 The Necessity of China's Active Participation in the Reform of the International Monetary System: From the Global Perspective

4.2.1 *China's Growing Economic Strength and Influence*

4.2.1.1 *The Increasing Influence of China in the Global Economy*

In the past three decades or so, China has taken advantage of the tendency of economic globalization that was prevalent in the late and post-Cold-War periods. It has greatly developed in its reform and opening-up to the world during the period of strategic opportunities.[57] The entry to the WTO embarked China's journey in developing an export-oriented economy. It gradually became the most dynamic economy in the world with foreign investment and exports as its engines. Statistics show that China's average annual GDP growth rate reached 9.9%, with an increase of 20.6 times in its total volume during the period 1979–2010. Based on such a huge population and poor conditions, China's sustainable economic growth for such a long period of time was seen as a miracle in modern history. The result of the constant and rapid economic growth after the outbreak of the global financial crisis in 2008 has been a stable mainstay for the global economy. China's economy has, to some extent, offset the negative influences in the world by developed countries' recession and subsequent slow rally. China has become a major engine for global economic resurgence. In 2010, China's contribution to global

[57]The concept of "the period of strategic opportunities" prevailed after the report of the 16th National Congress of the Communist Party of China. It is a term put forth on a comprehensive judgment by the Chinese leadership on the relationship between China's reforms and their internal and external environments. At the time of domestic reforms in the 1990s, China was also making great efforts to integrate into the international community and the economic globalization process, which has laid a sound institutional foundation for the rapid economic growth of the past decade or so. At the beginning of the new century, China formally proposed the concept of "the 20 years of strategic opportunities."

GDP growth was ranked No.1, bringing an increase of US$638 billion to the world's nominal GDP (compared with the US's contribution of US$497 billion).[58] According to calculations with temporal market exchange rates, China's economy surpassed France in 2005, outpaced Britain in 2006, outperformed Germany in 2007 and finally replaced Japan's position as the world's second-largest economy in 2010[59] (see Table 4.5). The sustained and rapid economic growth has lifted millions of Chinese people out of poverty and quickly moved China out of the list of poor countries. China has been recognized by the United Nations as an "upper middle-income country." The country with one-fifth of the world's population has witnessed a 16-fold increase in the national income only within one generation. This was an unprecedented success. As a large developing country and now the world's largest emerging economy, "China's economic development serves as a unique example of successful development and provides valuable lessons for those countries that are trying to catch up."[60] It should also be noted that in its rapid economic growth and opening-up, China has smoothly transited from a planned economy to a market economy without the violent economic and political fluctuations of other transition countries.[61] China has successfully completed the transition from a closed economy to an open economy.

Of course, in an era of economic globalization, a country's global economic position should be measured by not only its economic size

[58]Quoted from a joint project by the World Bank and China's State Council Development Research Center, *China in 2030: Building a Modern, Harmonious and Creative Society, Preface*. Beijing: China Financial and Economic Publishing House, 2013: 414 (in Chinese).

[59]In 2011, calculated with a market exchange rate, China's GDP totaled US$7.2981 trillion. The per capita GDP amounted to US$5,417, ranking 90th in the world.

[60]Quoted from the joint research group of the World Bank and the Development Research Center of China's State Council, *2030 China: Building a Modern, Harmonious and Creative Society, Preface*. Beijing: China Financial and Economic Publishing House, 2013 (in Chinese).

[61]See Yao, Yang, "The World Significance of China's Trails," *International Economic Review* 1 (2010): 7 (in Chinese).

Table 4.5. China's Economic Growth from 2001 to 2012 (US$100 million)

Year	GDP	Real Growth Rate (%)	Global Rank
2001	13248	8.3	6
2002	14538	9.1	6
2003	16410	10.0	6
2004	19316	10.1	6
2005	22569	11.3	5
2006	27130	12.7	4
2007	34941	14.2	3
2008	45218	9.6	3
2009	49913	9.2	3
2010	59305	10.4	2
2011	73185	9.3	2
2012	82271	7.8	2

Source: Database of the World Bank.

but also by its growth rate and its integration with the global economy. Seen from the perspective of foreign trade development, the proportion of China's foreign trade in global trade has reached 9.7%, an increase of nearly 10 times over the past three decades.[62] Especially after its WTO entry, China has stepped into a period of export prosperity. During the period 2002–2007, China's exports grew at an average annual rate of nearly 30%. Its export volume surpassed Japan's in 2004, ranking it at the third place in the world, and it overtook Germany and the United States in 2009 to become first. China's import surpassed Germany in 2009, making it the world's second largest importer. In 2011, China's total trade volume exceeded US$4.2944 trillion, accounting for 58.7% of its GDP, making it one of the most open countries in the world. In 2012, China's trade volume reached US$4.5514 trillion, surpassing the United States to be the world's largest trading nation (see Table 4.6). In the past decade, China's share in global industrial products trade has doubled. At present, China is one of the largest importers of all major global

[62]Based on the World Trade Report, 2011.

Table 4.6. Development of China's Foreign Trade in 2001–2012 (Unit: US$100 million)

Year	Total Exports of Goods and Services	Total Imports of Goods and Services	Total Imports and Exports of Goods and Services	The Degree of Foreign Trade Dependence (%)
2001	2994	2713	5707	43.1
2002	3654	3280	6934	47.7
2003	4850	4489	9339	56.9
2004	6558	6065	12624	65.4
2005	8369	7121	15490	68.6
2006	10617	8528	19145	70.6
2007	13422	10347	23769	68.0
2008	15817	12328	28146	62.2
2009	13333(1)	11132(2)	24465(2)	49.0
2010	18156	15834	33990	57.3
2011	22960(1)	19983(2)	42944(2)	58.7
2012	24198	21316	45514	55.3

Note: Bracketed numbers are the global rank of merchandise trade.
Source: The World Bank Country Database (data of 2012 are calculated on the data of the IMF's World Economic Outlook database).

markets (accounting for 35%, 30% and 25% of the total imports of manufactured goods of Japan, the EU and the United States respectively). The steady and rapid growth of trade has expanded China's impact on the global economy. It should be pointed out that the growth of China's trade is based on the trade in goods, which is based on the growth of the manufacturing industry. Therefore, the rapid growth of China's foreign trade is supported by its prosperous manufacturing industry. According to statistics, in 1990 China's manufacturing value added accounted for only 3% of global total. The proportion had risen to 6.64% in 2000 before China's accession to the WTO and rose to 9.79% by 2005.[63] In 2010, China's manufacturing output reached US$1.955 trillion (up 12.3% over 2009), accounting for 19.8% of the world's total manufacturing output, surpassing that

[63]Song, Hong, "An Analysis of the Opening-up and China's Economic Development Experience," *International Trade* 5 (2012): 19–27 (in Chinese).

of America for the first time and making China the world's largest manufacturer.

From the perspective of external financial strength, China's total foreign exchange reserves ranked second in the world in 2000; it exceeded US$1 trillion for the first time in 2006, reaching US$1.0685 trillion, surpassing Japan as the world's largest foreign exchange reserve; by the end of 2012, it reached US$3.3334 trillion, accounting for about 30% of the total global foreign exchange reserves and outnumbering the sum of global foreign exchange reserves of the early 21st century. Since 2006, China has been the world's second-largest creditor country after Japan.[64] (China's international investment net position was US$639.8 billion in 2006.) By 2011, China's net international investment position grew by 1.7748 trillion USD. The growing external financial strength increased China's share of the IMF from 3.72% to 6.39% in 2010, its voting rights rising from 3.65% to 6.07%; its voting rights in the World Bank went up from 2.77% to 4.42%, making it the third largest shareholder country, second only to the United States and Japan.

China began to implement the preferential policies of attracting FDI since 1980. By 2011, it has utilized a total of US$1.05 trillion of foreign investment. For the first time in 2010, China attracted more than US$100 billion of foreign investment, reaching US$114.7 billion, ranking second in the world, only after the US, and first among the developing countries. China is considered as one of the world's second most attractive investment options after the United States. In 2011, the size of foreign investment in China reached US$124 billion, representing 15.5% of global FDI inflows (13.9%), the highest level since 1994 (see Table 4.7). Indeed, 22% of China's tax revenue, 28% of the industrial added value, 55% of exports, 69% of the trade surplus and 50% of the technology imports all came from foreign-invested enterprises. FDI has allowed China to gradually integrate into the global

[64]In May 2005, the Chinese government released the China International Investment Position Sheet, which officially confirmed China's status as a creditor country.

Table 4.7. China's Introduction of Foreign Capital in 2001–2012 (Unit: US$100 million)

Year	Inflow FDI to China	Total Inflow of World FDI	Percentage (%)
2001	469	8176	5.7
2002	527	6788	7.8
2003	535	5596	9.6
2004	606	7421	8.2
2005	724(4)	9458	7.7
2006	695(4)	13059	5.3
2007	835	20027	4.2
2008	1083	18164	6.0
2009	950(2)	12165	7.8
2010	1147(2)	14085	8.1
2011	1240	16515	7.5
2012	1211	13509	9.0

Note: Bracketed number are the global rank of the year.
Source: United Nations Conference on Trade and Development, 1991–2003 Global Investment Reports Database.

production network and contribute to exports, employment, technological development and institutional reform. From the perspective of the development of China's FDI, since China's "going out" policy was implemented in the late 1990s, the level of China's FDI has rapidly risen from US$1 billion in 2000 to US$44 billion in 2009. During this period, China's FDI level was higher than all emerging market levels, except Russia and Hungary.[65] Even compared with several countries in East Asia that have seen a rapid growth in FDI, the annual growth rate of China's FDI was about the same as that of Japan and South Korea (starting from the year when the total amount of FDI exceeded US$1 billion. In 2010, China's FDI flow arrived at US$68.8 billion. In 2012, both the flow and the stocks of China's FDI hit a record high, reaching US$77.2 billion and US$443.2 billion, respectively. Although the stock of China's FDI accounted for only 2% of the

[65]Quoted from the joint research group of the World Bank and the Development Research Center of China's State Council, *2030 China: Building a Modern, Harmonious and Creative Society*. Beijing: China Financial and Economic Publishing House, 2013, 425 (in Chinese).

global stock of FDI in 2012, its share of global FDI flow has risen from 0.5% in 2003 to 6% in 2012. China has shifted from a one-way introduction of foreign investment in the past to an outward investment country. *The Economist* predicted that China's foreign investment would exceed the introduction of foreign capital.[66]

Over the past three decades, the rapid growth of China's economy and the rise of its international economic status have drawn wide attention from the international community. Calculated at the current price of USD, China's total GDP will reach US$22.69 trillion by 2020, more than 3% of the US's total GDP, making it the world's largest economy.[67] In short, as the world's second largest economy

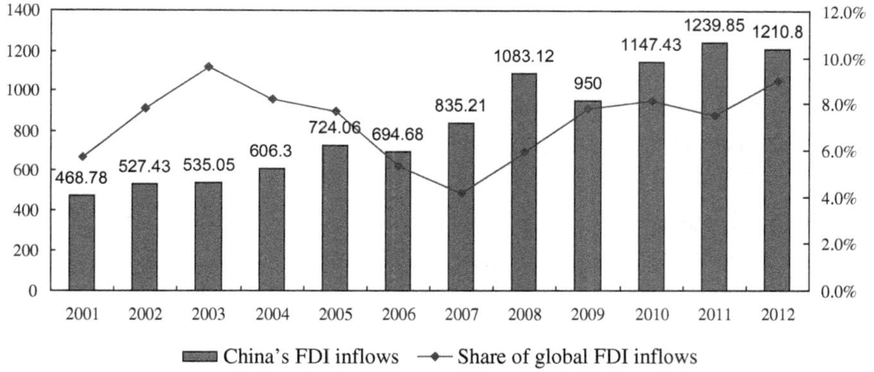

Figure 4.3. China's Utilization of Foreign Capital in 2001–2012 (Unit: US$100 million)

Source: See Table 4.7. United Nations Conference on Trade and Development, 1991–2003 Global Investment Reports Database.

[66]Ifeng Financial, Foreign Media: Attention: China's Foreign Investment to be More than the Introduction of Foreign Capital. http://finance.ifeng.com/a/2014 1107/13257764_0s.html.

[67]Morgan Stanley predicts that China would surpass the United States by 2016 if measuring by purchasing power parity. Robert Feenstra, a Professor from the University of California Davis, adjusted the World Bank's estimate, predicting that China would overtake the United States by 2014 in terms of purchasing power parities. Arvind Subramanian of the Peterson Institute for International Economics calculated that China surpassed the United States in 2010 in terms of purchasing power parity. See "China 2020" Research Group, "2020: China's Positioning in the World," *International Economic Review* 3 (2013): 12 (in Chinese).

currently, deeply integrated into the world, China is no longer an exogenous variable, acting negatively to the international economic environment, but an important endogenous variable that can influence the international economic environment.[68]

It should be noted that although China has become the second largest economy in the world in terms of total GDP, total volume of imports and exports, trade surpluses, scale of foreign exchange reserves and with the status of net foreign creditor, its economic status is merely measured by economic volume. The reasons are as follows: First, the total economic output is important, but GDP per capita is the most critical indicator that measures a country's economic development and maturity. China's GDP per capita had reached US$5,432 in 2012. However, it still lags far behind the global GDP per capita of US$8,000 (China's GDP per capita ranked 87th in the world in 2012). Judging from the history of economic development, many countries were able to raise their GDP per capita to US$5,000. However, only South Korea and Singapore have further increased their GDP per capita from US$5,000 to US$20,000 in the past 20 years.[69] Therefore, discovering how to cross the "middle income trap" is a major challenge for China. Second, in the era of economic globalization, as the global production networks powered by economic globalization and the development of transnational corporations have made intermediate goods (rather than raw materials and final products) the main targets of international trade, the profits created by a country's GDP and foreign trade are not completely credited to the country.[70] The trade among the transnational corporations has become the main form of international trade. Their

[68]Ye, He, "China Faces a Different Period of Strategic Opportunities," *International Economic Review* 5 (2012): 35 (in Chinese).

[69]Zhang, Ming, China Still has a Large Distance from Japan, Working Paper, International Financial Research Center of the Institute of World Economics and Politics, Chinese Academy of Social Sciences (May 2010) (in Chinese).

[70]Pascal Lamy is former Director General of the WTO. Lamy said: "The added value of Apple handsets produced in China is only about 4%, far less than what the United States, Japan, Germany and South Korea gained from their production." See Lamy, Pascal, Openness of Trade and Openness of Minds: Key to

profits are generated by more than one country. According to the statistics of China Customs, the exports of foreign-funded enterprises accounted for 55% of China's total exports. Third, the two financial indicators, the size of foreign exchange reserves and the size of net external debt, cannot prove the rising of China's international economic status, for the reason that China has accumulated only US$1.8 trillion of trade surplus within more than US$3.3 trillion of foreign exchange reserves while the remaining US$1.4 trillion goes to its FDI. The FDI is actually China's liability, and even its profits can be redeemed and withdrawn at any time. In a sense, the absolute size of foreign exchange reserves and the increase of its relative level suggest from another aspect that China's export-oriented economic growth model is facing a dilemma of external imbalance.[71] China's US$1.8 trillion of net foreign debt shows the trait of low yield. Therefore, China's position as a creditor is defensive for its currency structure. Fourth, China should have a sovereign currency that matches its economic status, as the second largest economy in the world, the major driving force for global economic growth, the world's largest foreign exchange reserve country, the largest manufacturing country and the top trading power in the world. However, among the six largest economies in the world, China is the only one that does not have its RMB as a reserve currency. In other words, the RMB is the only non-internationalized currency (it is neither freely convertible nor highly efficient in financial assets transactions).[72] All of these clearly demonstrate that China has not yet really become the

---

Meeting Challenges of the Future. http//www.wto.org/english/news-e/sppl-e/sppl250-e.htm.

[71]See "China 2020" Research Group, "2020: China's Positioning in the World," *International Economic Review* 3 (2013): 15 (in Chinese).

[72]Zhang Ming pointed out that "from a global economic history point of view, at least for the past 100 years or so, it is rare that the currency of the world's second-largest economy is not an international currency." See Zhang, Ming, "Internationalization of RMB: Policies, Progress, Problems and Prospects," *Financial Review* 2 (2013): 12 (in Chinese). Hua Min and Tian Suhua pointed out that "Simply comparing the aggregate size can easily overlook the most essential factor that

second largest economy in the world,[73] which should be the starting point and basis for the Chinese government to consider and formulate its current and future national development strategies. As for the rise of China's "soft power" (a country's influence and voice in the international system and its rule-making), it will undoubtedly take more time than the catching-up of economic volume.

The reform of the international monetary system is a major adjustment of the international monetary and financial relations in the world economy. The changes among countries' economic strengths are the driving force behind this reform and adjustment. The evolution and reform of the international monetary system over a hundred years indicate that it is a game involving the economic interests of all countries. Participating in this game requires a certain economic strength. In the past three decades, as the fastest growing economy and the largest emerging economy in the world, China has strengthened rapidly and has become an important endogenous variable in the international economic system, which determines that China must express its own appeals by participating in the reform of the international monetary system and indeed become the main force to promote the reform.

---

really determines whether a country's currency can become an international standard currency." See Huamin and Suhua Tian, "Reform of the International Monetary System is Imperative," Information Research Center of the State Council (23 June 2011) (in Chinese).

[73]Xia Bin said that China is "weak in finance" in 2007; Sun Lijian believed that China is a "small country" in finance in 2007; Xiang, Weixing and Wang, Da pointed out that the rapid economic growth in China was supported by underdeveloped financial system support. See Xia, Bin, "2020: The Main Considerations of China's Financial Strategy," *International Economic Review* 2 (2011): 29 (in Chinese); Sun, Lijian, "Conflicts in Dual Identities: Trade Power and Small Country in Finance," *World Economic Research* 1 (2007): 3–7 (in Chinese); Xiang, Weixing and Da, Wang, "Asymmetry in the Financial Interdependence of China and the United States," *World Economic Research* 7 (2011): 16 (in Chinese).

4.2.1.2 *The Rising Status of China's Economy in East Asia*

After the Asian financial crisis broke out in 1997, East Asian countries began to reflect on their export-oriented development strategy,[74] promoted for a long time. Although the "East Asian Miracle" may have lost its color after the financial crisis, the performance of China's economy remained impressive.[75] In particular, during the Asian financial crisis of 1997–1998, when many Asian countries carried out competitive currency devaluations, China maintained the stability of the RMB exchange rate and was therefore praised by the international community as a responsible country. That not only allows Asian countries to realize the external influence of China's economic policies but also shows that China is no longer an outsider in global and East Asian economic and financial activities. Japan, whose economy once had a chance to exceed the US in the 1980s, plunged into a bubble economy in the late 1980s. After the bubble economy collapsed in 1990, Japan's economy fell into a downturn for more than 20 years. In 2003, China surpassed Japan and became the largest importer in Asia. In 2004, China overtook Japan as the third largest exporter in the world. In 2008, China's manufacturing industry preceded Japan's and was ranking second in the world. Especially, driven by China's rapid economic growth after the global financial

---

[74] Zhang Ming believes that the key to the "East Asian Miracle" lies in building a huge production capacity through high input of factors and handling production surplus by exports supported by various preferential policies. The "Four Asian Dragons," the "Four Asian Tigers," including China, are inseparable from this "successful" set pattern. This model of development has been extremely successful in the early stages, but gradually it has faced two bottlenecks: the limited supply of factors and external demands limitation. See Zhang, Ming, *The Difficulties in the Transition of the Structure of Asian Countries.* Beijing: International Finance Research Center of Institute of World Economics and Politics, Chinese Academy of Social Sciences (in Chinese).

[75] Quoted from the joint research group of the World Bank and the Development Research Center of China's State Council, *2030 China: Building a Modern, Harmonious and Creative Society.* Beijing: China Financial and Economic Publishing House, 2013, 3 (in Chinese).

crisis, East Asian economies recovered in a relatively short period of time which outpaced the rest of the world. East Asia is still the most dynamic and fastest-growing region of the world. Accordingly, China's economic position is also on the rise in East Asia.

First, China has become the growth pole and stabilizer of East Asia's economy. Since the early 1990s, China has replaced Japan as a new economic engine in East Asia[76] and even in Southeast Asia. Since the end of 2008, China's ¥4 trillion fiscal stimulus plan and the huge credit of ¥9.5 trillion have brought a strong economic rebound and rapid growth in import. In 2009, China's GDP growth rate remained high, at 9.2%. The demand for imports from East Asia has brought China the total trade deficit of US$109.2 billion with South Korea, Japan, Thailand, Malaysia and Philippines, which has played an important role in stabilizing the economy in the region. On the whole, the economic growth rate of East Asia in 2010 was higher than 4%, the growth rate of the global economy in the same year, maintaining a relatively strong momentum (for example, Japan's annual GDP growth rate reached 4%). However, economic growth of other countries has slowed down in varying degrees. China's GDP growth rate has increased to 10.4% and its economic aggregate surpassed Japan's to be the world's second-largest economy. In 2011, due to the impact of the Great East Japan Earthquake, Japan's GDP showed negative growth while China's GDP growth rate remained high at 9.3%. In sum, since the global financial crisis, the strong demand from China has made up the gap left by insufficient demand in the Western countries. China's rapid economic growth not only plays an important role in the economic growth in East Asia, but also becomes the driving force in this region.

Second, China's supply of final products in East Asia is increasing. In the early 1980s, the United States and Japan were the major export markets of other East Asian economies. By the late 1980s, due to the substantial appreciation of the Japanese yen,

[76]East Asia includes a total of 10 economies including China, Japan, South Korea, Hong Kong, China Taiwan, Singapore, Malaysia, Thailand, the Philippines and Indonesia.

Japanese companies began to have direct investment in other East Asia economies, using them as a roundabout base of production for exports to the United States. This "triangular trade", in which capital goods were imported from Japan and manufactured goods were exported to the United States, was flourishing in 1990. Since the latter half of the 1990s, other East Asian economies' export to China has increased rapidly while their export to the United States and Japan has shown a downward trend. According to the statistics from Asian Development Bank, East Asian economies' export (mainly ASEAN countries) to Japan and the United States still accounted for a large share by 2007, but this share has dropped significantly in the previous decade while the share of China in the exports of East Asian economies has risen sharply. Besides some ASEAN countries, the percentage of other East Asian economies' exports to China was higher than that of Japan and the United States in 2007. More importantly, the United States gains more weight in China's export, while other East Asian economies' exports to the US have declined. As mentioned earlier, the original mode of regional trade in East Asia has undergone a major change, gradually transforming from the "old triangular trade" to "new triangular trade." The old mode refers to East Asian economies introducing capital and importing capital goods from Japan,and selling products to the United States to make up the trade deficit with Japan. The new one means that East Asian economies except Japan's, export capital goods to China, and after China's production and assembly, it exports the finished products to developed countries like the United States. This shift reflects the change in trade division of labor between China and Japan in East Asia's intra-regional trade. In other words, China's imported products from the region are increasing while Japan's are declining. China's position in the regional trade pattern of East Asia has determined that it has great potential to become the final goods provider in East Asia.[77]

[77]See Xiao, Li, and Fu, Jinghui, "Status Quo and Prospects of China as an East Asian Markets Provider," *Journal of Jilin University-Social Sciences* 2 (2010): 21 (in Chinese).

Third, the gap of overseas mergers and acquisitions (M&A) in terms of the size and the speed between China's enterprises and that of Japan's has been narrowed down. China's M&A, which started in the early 1980s, became active since the 1990s, with two peaks in 1992 and 1997 (US$1.05 billion and US$3.26 billion respectively). Since 2001, the number and amount of overseas M&A of Chinese enterprises have increased dramatically, rising from US$3.65 billion in 2005 to US$8.25 billion in 2007. After the global financial crisis broke out in 2008, Chinese enterprises accelerated their pace of overseas investment. The amount of their overseas M&A reached US$37.94 billion in 2008 and US$21.49 billion in 2009, respectively. While the overall scale was going up, the average size of Chinese enterprises' overseas M&A had also expanded, increasing from 40 million in 2002 to 550 million in 2008. Overseas M&A is one of the main characteristics of China's FDI in recent years. Its share of China's FDI was 44.1% in 2002, 55.8% in 2003, 57.1% in 2006 and 67.9% in 2008. The years of 2009 and 2010 are the peaks of its overseas M&A. Chinese enterprises realized US$29.7 billion of FDI in 2010 by means of M&A. In the meantime,after two consecutive years of decline in 2008 and 2009, Japanese companies' overseas M&A maintained strong growth in 2010 and 2011, reaching 66.5 billion USD in 2011. Although the scale of Chinese enterprises' overseas M & A dropped to US$22.2 billion in 2011, its gap with Japan has gradually narrowed down (the flow of China's FDI has overtaken Japan's in 2010).

Fourth, China has surpassed Japan as the US's largest creditor. As mentioned earlier, China's total foreign exchange reserves exceeded US$1 trillion for the first timein 2006, arriving at US$1.068 trillion and overtaking Japan as the largest foreign exchange reserve country in the world. In September 2008, at the outbreak of the global financial crisis, China replaced Japan as the US's largest Treasury securities holder overseas. By the end of June 2011, the amount of US Treasury securities held by China had reached US$1.318 trillion (at the end of June 2008, it was US$535 billion), accounting for 74% of the US financial assets held by China. Although the absolute size and relative size of China's investment in the US Treasury holdings decreased significantly from July 2011 to June 2012, there was a sharp rebound later. From July 2012 to June 2013, the amount of China's US treasury holdings increased by US$128.9 billion. By the end of July 2013, the amount of China's US treasury holdings reached US$1.28 trillion (the amount of Japan's was US$1.14 trillion).

In conclusion, with the continuous rise of China's economic status and strength in the East Asian region, China has become increasingly motivated to actively participate in the reform of the international monetary system, which is increasingly urgent and necessary.

4.2.2 *The Rise of Emerging Economies Represented by China and the Reform of the International Monetary System*

4.2.2.1 *The Rise of Emerging Economies Represented by China*

Since the 1980s, emerging economies have rapidly integrated into the world economy. After experiencing the crises in the 1980s and 1990s, the speed of the economic growth of emerging economies remained quickened. Since the 21st century in particular, the overall rise of emerging economies represented by China has become one of the basic characteristics of the drastic change in the global economic pattern. Since 2006, the growth rate of emerging economies has been much higher than that of the developed countries. According to statistics, from 2008 to 2009, emerging economies accounted for nearly 40% of global GDP while those in the developed countries dropped to 57%. In 2008 and 2009 when the global financial crisis broke out, emerging economies became the main engines of global economic growth. In particular, China's GDP surpassed other developed economies, except that of the United States, in 2010. Emerging economies were a great concern to the international community for more than a decade, but no clear definition of that concept has so far been given. As early as the early 1980s, the international community began to use the term "Newly Industrializing Economies" to describe several economies in East Asia and Latin America that experienced rapid growth and implemented many liberal policies. Later on, the International Financial Corporation (IFC), a member of the World Bank Group, came up with the concept of "Emerging Market", for the first time referring to a small number of middle-size and high-income economies in developing countries (they have a common characteristic, in that foreign investors can buy shares in their financial markets). Over time, the concept of "Emerging Markets" has gradually expanded, with some economists including all developing countries under that banner.[78] Concepts of "Newly Industrializing Economies" and "Emerging Markets" were replaced by a broader concept, "Emerging Economies."[79] In recent years, a new trend defined by the concept of "emerging economies" is categorizing a few countries into groups with specific titles such as the BRICS,[80] the "Next-11" ("N-11" for short)[81] and "BASIC."[82] According to Zhang and Tian, emerging economies refer to "developing economies with relatively rapid economic growth, large economic size and population, relatively low per capita income, relatively high degree of economic openness and broadly representative of developing economies after World War II." and they believe that "the natural differentiation between developed and developing members of the G20 provides us with a simple and readily available standard for defining

[78]Thorpe, Jodie and Kavita Prakash-Mani, "Developing Value: The Business Case for Sustainability in Emerging Markets," *Managing the Business Case for Sustainability: The Integration of Social Environment* 1, no. 62 (2006): 444–464.

[79]Hoskisson, Robert E., Lorraine Eden, Chung Ming Lau and Mike Wright *et al.*, "Strategy in Emerging Economies," *Academy of Management Journal* 3, no. 43 (2000): 249–267.

[80]The concept was originally proposed by Jim O'Neill, an Economist from Goldman Sachs, referring to Brazil, Russia, India and China, respectively; and later, South Africa was included into the BRICS. The common features of these countries are the rapid economic growth in development, higher incomes and greater potential for growth, with long-term investment value.

[81]This concept was also proposed by Goldman Sachs in 2005, referring to Bangladesh, Egypt, Indonesia, Iran, South Korea, Mexico, Pakistan, Nigeria, the Philippines, Turkey and Vietnam. In 2007, Japanese scholar Shimiku Takashi put forward the concept of "VISTA" in the *Journal of the Economist*, referring to Vietnam, Indonesia, South Africa, Turkey and Argentina.

[82]Refer to Brazil, South Africa, India and China.

emerging economies."[83] The 11 developing economies in the G20 are Argentina, Brazil, China, India, Indonesia, South Korea, Mexico, Russia, Saudi Arabia, South Africa and Turkey.[84] It is worth noting that since the advent of the term BRICS in 2001, it has evolved to encompass not only an academic concept, but also an essential platform for deepening cooperation and coordination between the major emerging economies in the world after a decade's development. Its position in the global economic landscape is also increasingly important, especially after South Africa's accession. The BRICS stretch across four continents, with 18% of the global GDP, 29% of the territory, 43% of the world's population, and 50% of contributions to the economic growth (based on purchasing power parities). BRICS countries have not only become a center of manufacturing products distribution and service outsourcing in the world but also the producer of bulk commodities, such as oil, iron ore, gold and so on. The rise of the "BRICS countries" not only changes the current geopolitical situation but also puts forward demands on changing the current international economic and financial order.

Since 2000, the overall rise of emerging economies represented by China is mainly manifested in the following three aspects:

First, in terms of economic growth, the emerging economies represented by China have grown much more rapidly than the developed economies and they have become engines to promote global economic growth. After the global financial crisis, the emerging economies have drawn much attention for their relatively rapid recovery and growth and have become the main driving force behind

---

[83]See Zhang, Yuyan and Feng, Tian, "The Definition of Emerging Economies and Their Position in the World Economic Structure," *International Economic Review* 4 (2010): 13 (in Chinese).

[84]In 2010, the Boao Forum for Asia put forward the concept of "Emerging 11 Countries" (E-11). Zhang Yuyan and Tian Feng consider the "E" here to have three meanings-including "Emerging", emphasizing "Economic" and representing "Economy." See Zhang, Yuyan and Feng, Tian, "The Definition of Emerging Economies and Their Position in the World Economic Structure," *International Economic Review* 4 (2010): 14 (in Chinese).

the global economic recovery. As a result, the global economic center has been further shifting to emerging economies. If measured by the economic growth rate and its stability,the performance of emerging economies in Asia is prominent. In particular, the economic growth rates of China, India and Indonesia remained at 9.2%, 6.8% and 4.6%, respectively, in 2009, even with the negative economic growth in the world. In 2010, their growth rates were 10.3%, 10.1% and 6.1%, respectively.[85] Although the economic growth rate of emerging economies slowed down a bit in 2011, they still maintained a rapid growth. Particularly, Brazil surpassed the United Kingdom as the sixth largest economy in the world in 2011, thereby diversifying the composition of today's global economic powers.

Second, the annual growth rate of the volume of imports and exports of emerging economies represented by China is significantly higher than that of developed economies and has become the main force of global trade growth. After the outbreak of the global financial crisis, global trade experienced the largest drop in 70 years: the actual global trade growth rate in 2009 dropped from 2.1% in 2008 to −12.2%. However, the strong rebound in the import and export of emerging economies represented by China is in stark contrast to the weak recovery in developed economies. From the regional trade figures, it is clear that Asia is still one of the fastest growing regions in terms of trade. It is worth noting that China surpassed Germany to become the world's largest exporter, under the condition that China's exports were going down by 15.9% (US$1.2 trillion in 2009 due to the impact of the global financial crisis). In 2012, China's total amount of foreign trade surpassed the United States and it became the world's largest trading nation. The rapid growth of China's import and export has made a double contribution to the global economy: the growth of exports has reduced the level of global inflation, which helped all countries, while the growth of imports has raised the prices of energy and raw materials in the international

[85]IMF, World Economic Outlook Database, November 2011.

market, which has helped the energy and raw materials exporters such as Russia, Brazil, Argentina and so on.[86]

Third, in the global capital flows, emerging economies represented by China have become the main body to attract international capital and major power to conduct FDI. Since the beginning of the 21st century, two large-scale changes in international capital flows that took place in 2004–2007 (before the global financial crisis) and in 2010–2012 (after the global financial crisis) have shown that the international capital flowing to emerging economies significantly exceeded the historical average.[87] According to the Institute of International Finance (IIF), private capital that flows to emerging economies averaged US$671.2 billion annually from 2001 to 2012. The direct equity investment (namely the difference between FDI and ODI) over the same period was US$223.7 billion. It is noteworthy that the average growth rate of FDI inflows of E-11 and BRICS countries is higher than that of the entire developing world. Its share of global FDI inflows rose from 18.2% in 2006 to 31.9% in 2011 (US$470.8 billion). Those countries are as significant as the G8 and European Union in G20. The inflows of FDI of BRICS are the fastest-growing among E-11. In 2011, FDI flows to these five countries reached US$388.2 billion. Meanwhile, the BRICS, represented by China, have also become important exporters of FDI. According to the World Investment Report 2010, China's FDI during the period of 2006–2009 was US$21.2 billion, US$22.5 billion, US$51.2 billion and US$48 billion, respectively. India's FDI was US$14.3 billion, US$17.3 billion, US$17.7 billion and US$14.9 billion respectively, during this period; Brazil's FDI was US$28.2 billion, US$7.1 billion, US$20.5 billion and US$100 billion USD respectively, and Russia's FDI was

[86]See Huang, Haizhou, "Dollars and RMB: Where To Go?" *International Economic Review* 2 (2010): 9 (in Chinese).

[87]See Zhang, Ming and Xiao Lisheng, *Variability Analysis of Short-term International Capital Flows in Emerging Market Economies, 2013 World Economic Situation Analysis and Prediction*. Beijing: Social Science Press, 2013, 314–315 (in Chinese).

US$23.2 billion, US$45.9 billion, US$52.4 billion and US$46.1 billion respectively.

4.2.2.2 *The Rise of Emerging Economies and the Development of the G20 Mechanism*

As the share of emerging economies in global GDP is increasing rapidly, their importance in the global economic landscape also levels up. For example, the voting power of the BRICS in the IMF and the World Bank has risen from 10.5% and 11.3%, respectively, in 2010 to 14.1% and 13.1% at the time of this writing. The good performance of emerging economies during the global financial crisis has also increased their weight in global economic governance. After the global financial crisis broke out in 2008, the G20 has gradually become the main platform[88] for governing the international financial order. The formation of the G20 mechanism has opened up a new round of collective action with a more inclusive and extensive reform of the international monetary system.[89]

The East Asian financial crisis that broke out in 1997 made the international community realize that the settlement of the international financial crisis requires not only the developed countries but also the participation of influential developing countries. At the Cologne Summit of the G7 (18–20, June 1999), the finance ministers of the seven countries said they would work together to establish a new informal mechanism to promote dialogue among countries that are systemically important within the Bretton Woods System. On September 25 of the same year, at the Washington meeting of the finance ministers and central bank governors of the seven

[88] G20 members include G7 members (the United States, the United Kingdom, Japan, France, Germany, Canada, Italy), E-11 (Russia, China, Brazil, Argentina, Mexico, South Korea, Indonesia, India, Saudi Arabia, South Africa and Turkey), EU and Australia. G20 members account for 2/3 of the world's population, 90% of the global GDP and 80% of the global trade.

[89] See Xiao, Li and Feng Yongqi, "Collective Action in the Reform of the International Monetary System and the Role of the G20," *World Economy and Politics* 2 (2012): 136 (in Chinese).

countries, the finance ministers of the seven countries proposed once again to establish a new informal dialogue mechanism within the framework of the Bretton Woods System, to broaden the scope of dialogue on core economic and financial policy issues among systemically important countries. On 16 December of the same year, the finance ministers and central bank governors of the seven countries put this proposal into effect, proclaiming the formal establishment of the G20 by inviting finance ministers and central bank governors of systemically important countries from all over the world to gather in Berlin, Germany.

Since the G20 included emerging economies for the first time in the structure of discussions on international financial governance, it is considered a crucial step[90] toward the reform of the global finance governance structure. However, in the following decade, the G20, as a cooperative mechanism, was dominated by the G7/G8 in discussion and operation, and became a puppet[91] for G7/G8 to enhance its legitimacy and influence in international finance governance, which showed its vulnerability. The global financial crisis that broke out in 2008 fully exposed the weak governance of the G7/G8, the traditional financial governance mechanism dominated by developed countries and its main implementing agency, namely the IMF. Therefore, the G20 was upgraded from the original ministerial meeting, to the summit and held its first summit in Washington in November of the same year, starting the global joint action and international coordination in response to the global financial crisis:

First, members adopted a Global Recovery and Reform Plan to cope with the financial crisis. In order to coordinate the actions of various countries, leaders of the participating countries agreed on the Global Recovery and Reform Plan at the G20 London Summit

[90]Germain, Randall, D., "Global Financial Governance and the Problem of Inclusion," *Global Governance* 7 (2001): 411.
[91]Porter, Tony, "The G-7, the Financial Studies Stability Forum, the G20, and the Politics of International Financial Regulation," Paper prepared for the International Association Annual Meeting, Los Angeles, California (15 March 2000). http://www.g20.utoronto.ca/biblio/porter-isa-2000.pdf.

in April 2009. One of the key contents of the plan is the approval of an "unprecedented" global economic recovery plan: expanding the amount of funds available to the IMF from its original level of US$250 billion to US$750 billion; supporting US$250 billion SDR distribution; providing at least US$100 billion additional loans to multilateral development banks; providing US$250 billion support for trade financing, and providing concessional loans to the poorest nations by selling a portion of the IMF's gold. Meanwhile, the plan also recommended that all countries jointly implemented the expansionary fiscal and monetary policies. In order to consolidate the global economic recovery, the G20 adopted the Growth and Employment Action Plan again at the Cannes Summit in November 2011.

Second, it was decided to strengthen global financial regulation. The outbreak of the global financial crisis indicated a lack of cross-border financial regulatory mechanisms around the world. To deal with this, the London Summit in April 2009 decided to establish a "Financial Stability Board" (FSB), to replace the previous "Financial Stability Forum" (FSF).[92] On 27 June, the board officially started operation. Since the membership of the board was expanded from the original G7 member states to all G20 member countries as well as to Spain and the European Commission, the financial stability of emerging economies was also included in the framework of global financial regulation. As a new cooperative organization outside the UN framework and an essential platform for implementing cross-border financial supervision in the future, the FSB was considered of great significance in enacting a series of measures for cross-border financial supervision in the future. The scope of its financial regulation has also been expanded to influential financial institutions, financial instruments and financial markets (hedge funds were also

[92]Its specific functions include assessing the vulnerability of the global financial system, overseeing the improvement of countries, promoting cooperation and information exchange among nations' regulatory agencies, advising on countries' regulatory policies and regulatory standards, coordinating the work of international standard setting bodies, and developing emergency plans for cross-border risk management.

put under regulation for the first time). The G20 London Summit stressed that the FSB should cooperate with the IMF to give early warning of the risks of the macroeconomic and financial crises and take action to resolve such crises.

Third, it was decided to reform the international financial institutions. The reform of the IMF has been one of the core issues of the G20. In February 2012, at the meeting of G20 finance ministers and central bank governors in Mexico, the member states' demands for reform of the IMF included: implementing the share reform in 2010 to effectively increase the position of developing countries in this organization; reforming the existing regulatory framework so as to enhance the fairness and effectiveness of the regulatory system; continuing to increase the size of available funds in this organization.

Fourth, it was necessary to reform the international monetary system. The "declaration of the summit" of the G20 Toronto Summit in June 2010 states that "our goal is to establish a more stable and resilient international monetary system"; we will "instruct the G20 finance ministers and central bank governors to put forward policy suggestions on securing a financial safety net and submit them to the Seoul Summit for discussion. "At the 2011 G20 Cannes Summit, France as the rotating presidency, put forward the reform of the international monetary system as a priority.[93] To achieve that goal, the meeting proposed greater coordination on five aspects: strengthening the management of capital flows in accordance with the agreed actions and principles; further clarifying the assessment criteria for the currency composition of SDRs and evaluating their currency composition to reflect global trade and financial conditions; further enhancing the monitoring capacity and effectiveness of the IMF and ensuring that the organization has sufficient

[93] As early as the period of the Bretton Woods System, France advocated the reform of the system. For Nicolas Sarkozy, the then President of France, there is an appeal to upgrade itself and its international influence through the reform of the international monetary system. See Dai, Jinping, Aizong, Xiong and Shushi, Tan, *International Monetary System: Where To Go?* Hainan: Xiamen University Press, 2012, 27 (in Chinese).

resources to facilitate the completion of its reform of the quota and voting rights for 2010; all countries committing themselves to implementing a more market-oriented exchange rate system, raising the exchange rate flexibility to reflect the basic economic conditions and avoid prolonged exchange rate misalignment, restricting the use of currency undervaluation to compete, and reducing foreign exchange reserves by exchange rate reform; strengthening the construction of the global financial safety net, and meeting the liquidity needs of member states under varying circumstances by the reform of IMF's rescue tool.

Fifth, members agreed to balance the global economy. In response to the increasing global economic imbalances in recent years, especially its impact during the global financial crisis, the "Strong, Sustainable and Steady Growth Framework" was proposed at the G20 Pittsburgh Summit in September 2009 and the relevant assessment procedures were initiated, to assess imbalances, develop guiding principles and put forward countermeasures for countries, with the help of the IMF. At the meeting of G20 finance ministers and central bank governors held in Paris in February 2011, countries agreed to quantify the main indicators of both external and internal imbalances, threatening mutual growth (such as public debt, fiscal deficits and external imbalances which include trade deficits and net investment income flows and transfers); in April of the same year, a consensus was reached on the guiding principles at the Finance Ministers' Meeting in Washington which also devised suggestions for addressing potential instability imbalances and policy remedies to support the G20's growth targets. When determining the unbalanced countries, the concept of "systematically important countries"[94] was introduced

[94] "Systematically important countries" refers to countries that not only have a larger weight in the global economy but also whose policies tend to have spillover effects. Judgments for such countries are based on nominal exchange rates or purchasing power parities (PPPs), which account for more than 5% of global GDP. See Huang, Wei and Dongmin, Liu, *G20 and Global Economy Rebalancing* in Wang Lulin and Zhang Yuyan, chief editors, *World Economic Situation Analysis and Forecast*. Beijing: Social Sciences Academic Press, 2012, 246 (in Chinese).

for the first time and countries including China, France, Germany, India, Japan, the United Kingdom and the United States were identified as unbalanced countries.

The common action and international coordination of the G20 countries in response to the global financial crisis have effectively deterred the further development of the crisis.[95] More importantly, they have marked the beginning of the transformation of the international financial governance mechanism, shifting from G7/G8 to G20. This shift is mainly reflected in the fact that the role of the G20 has further improved since the London Summit in April 2009 and has undergone significant changes in its charateristics. In particular, the G20 Pittsburgh Summit, which closed on 25 September 2009, formalized the G20 as the main platform for the discussion of global economic issues and the promotion of international economic cooperation.[96] The historic transformation of G20 replacing G7/G8 acknowledged the growing international influence of emerging economies such as China, Brazil, India and so on, manifesting the changes in the world economic landscape after the global economic center moves eastward. For the first time, emerging economies have come to the forefront of the conferences for global economic and financial policymaking.[97] At several subsequent G20 summits

[95]Lin Yifu believes that "due to the strong policy coordination of the G20 countries, the world has avoided another great depression." See Lin Yifu, *The Quest for Prosperity: How Developing Economies Can Take Off*. Beijing: Peking University Press, 2012, 3 (in Chinese). Zhao Jin said that "it is the common response of the G20 countries to the financial crisis that this international financial crisis did not lead to a crisis similar to the one of 1929–1933, and it was not as severe and long-lasting as the Great Depression in 1933." See Zhao, Jin, "G20: New Mechanisms, New Issues and China's Proposition and Action," *International Economic Review* 5 (2010): 15 (in Chinese).

[96]Zhang Hai Bing believes that the G20 Pittsburgh Summit marks the international economic governance system developing from "quantitative change" to "qualitative change." See Zhang, Haibing, "Trends and Impacts of the G20 institutionalization," *World Economic Research* 9 (2010): 8 (in Chinese).

[97]Li Wei said that "the centralization of the G20 and the marginalization of the G7 have led to the conclusion of a discussion on whether China should join the

and ministerial meetings, China, with joint efforts from other countries, successfully expanded the share of emerging economies in two major international financial institutions, the IMF and the World Bank. In addition, China has made significant progress in participating in the management of international financial institutions. After Chinese economist Yifu Lin was appointed as Chief Economist and Senior Vice Governor for development economics of the World Bank at the end of 2008 (expired in June 2012), Zhu Min, Deputy Governor of the People's Bank of China, took office in May 2010 as the IMF's "Special Adviser to the President," and was nominated as Vice President in July 2011. This shows that China's right to speak has been strengthened in the organization. In addition, Xiaozhun Yi, Vice Minister of China's Ministry of Commerce, took the post of Deputy Director-General of WTO since 1 November 2013.

As the main platform for collective action in the reform of the current international monetary system, the G20 mechanism has developed a series of progressive initiatives in the governance of international monetary financing. In particular, it has provided an important stage for emerging economies to participate in this governance.[98] It is precisely because the G20 mechanism recognizes the status and role of emerging economies in the international financial governance that the collective action on the reform of the international monetary system is likely to be deepened. The other reason is, on the one hand, that it has a relatively low cost of international transactions and satisfies the institutional preferences of most member states,[99]

G7 in the past decade or so." See Li, Wei, "The Rise of China's Financial Diplomacy," *World Economy and Politics* 2 (2013): 83 (in Chinese). For a discussion on whether China should join the G7, see He, Fan, "Does China Need to Join the G7?" *International Economic Review* 5 (2004): 13–16 (in Chinese).

[98]Zhang Haibing argues that the institutionalization of the G20 is an important symbol of the transformation of the international system and signals the beginning of a new international economic order promoted by the Group of 77. See Zhang, Haibing, "Trends and Implications of the G20 Institutionalization," *World Economic Research* 9 (2010): 9 (in Chinese).

[99]Cui, Zhinan and Yue, Xing, "From the Era of the G7 to the G20: Changes in the International Financial Governance Mechanism," *World Economy and Politics* 1 (2011): 134–154 (in Chinese).

creating preconditions for the achievement of significant results in related collective actions; and on the other hand, it not only implies the breakthrough of the traditional international economy and the old financial order, but also sprouted the birth of a new international economic and financial order. As for the role of the G20 mechanism in promoting the reform of the international monetary system, there are mainly three aspects: First, the principle of collective action is upheld. The disintegration of the Bretton Woods System proves that any country's currency that dominates in the international monetary system faces the "Triffin Dilemma," in that the establishment and operation of the international monetary system cannot be unduly dependent on any single sovereign currency,[100] and that no country can challenge the dollar hegemony by its own strength (as evidenced by the birth of the euro or the failure of the internationalization of the yen). Therefore, promoting the reform of the international monetary system requires collective efforts. Second, enhance the power of execution in decision-making through the construction of institutionalization. Although the informality of the G20 mechanism favors consensus among its members, this informality also diminishes the execution of its decisions. For this reason, it is extremely important to strengthen the institutionalization of the G20 mechanism. This institutionalization includes the upgrading of the G20 from informal dialogue to some institutional arrangement to create policy constraints on member states and enhance the implementation of policies; and at the same time, realize the transition from crisis management to long-term economic governance institutions.[101] Third, we should expand the common interest for the reform of the international monetary system through the coordination of international economic policies. Both the IMF and the World Bank established on the basis of the Bretton Woods System lack the function of coordinating the macroeconomic policies of all countries, while the G20 mechanism can exert

[100] Li, Ruogu, *International Monetary Reform and RMB Internationalization.* Beijing: China Financial Press, 2009, 30 (in Chinese).

[101] See Dai, Jinping, Aizong, Xiong and Shushi, Tan, *International Monetary System: Where To Go?* Hainan: Xiamen University Press, 2012, 271 (in Chinese).

its institutional advantages in this regard.[102] For example, the Summit under the G20 mechanism as well as the meeting of finance ministers and central bank governors can directly conduct broad policy coordination and reach consensus on such issues as expanding public investment, strengthening financial supervision, reforming international financial institutions and opposing trade protectionism in the light of the macroeconomic situations in various countries, so as to broaden the common interests among all members.[103]

It should be noted that since the G20 was originally launched by the G7, it is organized in a manner that follows the G7's operational framework. That is, the organization neither has the constitution and the agreement, nor does it formulate or implement the binding rules for its member states; it has neither an implementing agency nor statutory binding power and no jurisdiction or guidance over the existing international economic mechanism. All these have affected the organization's effect on global economic and financial governance.

As a member of the G20 group, China's role and influence in the G20 mechanism have become increasingly important. According to the IMF's prediction, the proportion of G20 in the global economy would rise from 87.8% in 2009 to 90.3% by 2015 and its contribution to global economic growth would reach 96.4%. The influence of emerging economies would be further enhanced, and its share of the total G20 economy would rise from 37.1% in 2009 to 46%; China's share would increase from 9.6% in 2009 to 12.8% (while the share of the developed countries would drop to 54%,that of the US would decrease from 28% to 24.7%, that of EU would drop from 32.3% to 26.37% and that of Japan would go down from 10% to 8.4%). From this perspective, we can see that the role and influence of China as a representative of emerging economies in the G20

[102]Huang, Fanzhang, "G20 and International Monetary System Reform," *Financial Research* 2 (2010): 44–51 (in Chinese).

[103]Xiao, Li and Feng Yongqi, "Collective Action in the Reform of the International Monetary System and the Role of the G20," *World Economy and Politics* 2 (2012): 119–145 (in Chinese).

will become increasingly important. To this end, this change in the global economic pattern requires China as an important endogenous variable in the international economic system and a representative of emerging economies, to actively participate in the reform of the international monetary system.

4.2.3 *The Virtuous Circle of the Global Economy Requires a Compatible International Monetary System*

4.2.3.1 *The Main Problems Facing the Global Economic Cycle*

From the perspective of the global economic cycle, the international division of labor determines the formation and development of the international monetary system. The differences between "financial countries" and "trading countries" determine their respective positions and roles in the international monetary system. As mentioned earlier, the dollar-dominated international monetary system is unequal and asymmetrical. It neither promotes the diversification of international reserves, provides a stable, super-sovereign international currency, nor does it have an automatic mechanism to adjust international balance of payments. It cannot even guarantee the normal flow of international capital.[104] Under this system, many non-reserve currency countries are extremely disadvantaged in the global economic cycle: on the one hand, these countries must transfer their resources cheaply to the US residents for necessary international reserves; on the other hand, they must hold international reserves in such a way as to hold dollar bonds or other dollar assets, namely, transferring the right of the funds to the United States, so that "the richest and most capitalized countries actually obtain financing from impoverished countries by creating an international reserve

[104]Ba, Shusong and Xianling, Yang, "Studying the Future Reform of the International Monetary System from the Perspective of Financial Crisis," *Contemporary Finance* 11 (2009): 51–56 (in Chinese).

currency."[105] In general, under the current international monetary system, there are mainly three major problems facing the global economic cycle, which are as follows:

First, the current international reserve currency system has weakened the ability of the global economy cycle, limiting the healthy development of this cycle. Under this circumstance, in order to prevent shortages of foreign exchange reserves caused by difficulties in the international balance of payments, non-reserve currency countries must obtain the necessary reserve assets through trade surpluses. If the reserve currency countries do not expect to see an equal amount of trade deficit, the total demand of the global economy will decrease. However, this unipolar credit reserve currency system forces the countries outside the system to accumulate foreign exchange reserves, but these foreign exchange reserves can neither be converted into consumption or investment in time nor be transformed into demand factors that promote the economic cycle. Therefore, to some extent, it affects the formation of global purchasing power and reduces the total demand of the global economy. This shows that such foreign exchange reserves accumulated by non-reserve currency countries have actually become a "leak" in the global economic cycle. Although the diversification of international reserves in the current international monetary system helps alleviate the "Triffin Dilemma," there will be no dollar confidence crisis under the Bretton Woods System and the normal operation of the international monetary system can be maintained. However, under the current system, there still exists the "New Triffin Dilemma" suggesting that the stability of the international monetary system depends on the stability of the US dollar and the stability of the US dollar depends on the US's international balance of payments. The supply of global liquidity depends on the US's international balance of payments deficit. The seigniorage of America has also constantly expanded its current account deficit.

[105]Teunissen, J. J., "The International Monetary Crunch: Crisis or Scandal?" *Alternatives* 12, no. 3 (1987): 359–395.

Second, the current international monetary system has brought asymmetrical benefits to different countries. As mentioned previously, the current international monetary system is unequal. This inequality is mainly manifested when the accumulation of foreign exchange reserves by non-reserve currency countries means that the richest states in the world can obtain cheap funds, while the poor countries not only lack access to cheap funds but also bear the risk of investment in currency countries.[106] It should also be noted that the United States, as a reserve currency country, has natural advantages in seigniorage revenue and risk avoidance. These advantages have exacerbated the asymmetries in returns of different countries under an international monetary system that lacks constraints and regulation.

Third, the current international monetary system has not adequately adjusted the global trade and capital flows, affecting the balanced development of global trade and the stability of capital flows. In the aspect of global trade, due to the difficulty in coordination of international balance of payments, reserve currency countries adopted measures to reduce their trade deficits, providing a reason for developing trade protectionism. From the aspect of international capital flow, due to the unipolar credit feature of the US dollar, the supply of the US dollar has become the fundamental factor that determines the global liquidity. The absence of the US dollar restriction and regulation has made the global liquidity either excessive or deficient. This is evidenced by the excess liquidity and liquidity shortfalls that have emerged around the world before and after the global financial crisis. For example, since the internet bubble broke in 2000, the Federal Reserve (FED) adopted an expansionary monetary policy to stimulate economic growth. By the two channels of trade and investment, the FED spread its excess liquidity to non-reserve currency countries. With the continuous devaluation of the US dollar, non-reserve currency countries had to resort to loose monetary policies, which led to excess liquidity. After the global financial crisis

[106] Namely, the so-called "Capital Doubtful Recycling."

broke out, there was a serious shortage of liquidity. In short, the regulatory role of the current international monetary system in issues such as the liquidity of international capital, the stability of capital flows and so on, appears to be very weak.

4.2.3.2 *The Reform of the International Monetary System is a Prerequisite for Achieving a Virtuous Circle of the Global Economy*

Because of the factors that hinder the healthy development of the global economic cycle in the current international monetary system in order to promote the balanced development of global trade, establish a free trade system, promote steady and orderly capital flows and achieve the goal of stable and sustainable global economic growth, it is necessary to adjust and reform the existing international monetary system. The establishment of an international monetary system conducive to the virtuous circle of the global economy requires not only "financial countries" but also the active participation of "trading countries." As an important "trading country", especially in East Asia, China has the responsibility to promote a virtuous circle in the global economy by promoting the reform of the existing international monetary system. The relationship is shown in Figure 4.4.

4.2.4 *The Mutual Promotion between the Reform of the International Monetary System and the Monetary and Financial Cooperation in East Asia*

4.2.4.1 *The Progress of Monetary and Financial Cooperation in East Asia*

The Asian financial crisis that broke out in 1997 not only interrupted Japan's economic integration in East Asia, which was spearheaded by the "Flying Geese" model for 20 years, but also ceased the internationalization of the yen, which had made some progress. In September 1997, Japan tried to promote the idea of an Asian Monetary Fund (AMF) (proposed to establish a fund of US$100 billion involving

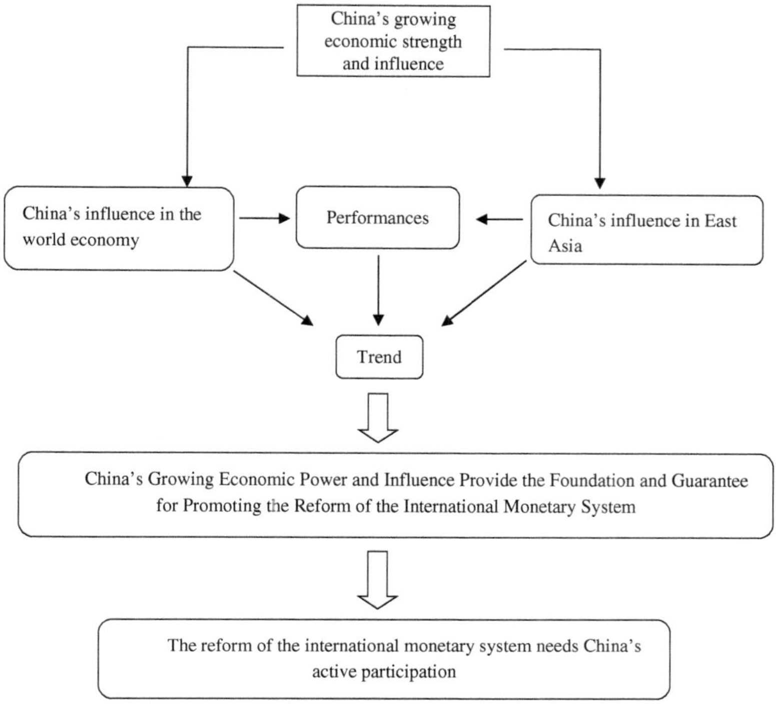

Figure 4.4. China's participation in the reform of international monetary reform and the virtuous circle of global economy

Japan, China, South Korea and other ASEAN countries, providing assistance for the countries that suffered from financial crisis to remedy the IMF's ineffective aid and its influence), which was completely rejected by the United States and the IMF (China did not support Japan's idea, which was obviously constrained by the international economic and political factors at that time). Nevertheless, in October 1998, Japan became the leader of monetary and financial cooperation in East Asia by adopting the New Miyazawa Initiative[107] aimed at assisting Southeast Asian countries and the

[107]The total amount of the program was US$30 billion, of which US$15 billion was used to meet the medium- and long-term funding needs of countries in crisis and US$15 billion to meet their short-term funding needs. The program has been

Chiang Mai Initiative (CMI) launched in 2000 aimed at a bilateral currency swap. Meanwhile, Japan was trying to enhance its international financial position by raising its voting power and holding higher posts in the IMF. At the "10 + 3" summit conference of ASEAN in October 2003, China's Premier Wen Jiabao first proposed integrating a bilateral currency swap network into a multilateral fund rescue mechanism. This proposal received a positive response from all participating summit leaders. In May 2006, the "10 + 3" finance ministers meeting of ASEAN decided to establish the Chiang Mai Initiative Multilateralization Working Group (CMIM) led by China and Thailand to conduct detailed research on the program. This marked China's participation in regional monetary and financial cooperation in a more positive way. Although multilateral currency swaps have many obvious advantages over bilateral currency swaps, China's proposal has not made substantial progress in the following four years or so. The main reason is that China and Japan started a fierce regional political rivalry around the system of the forthcoming East Asia Summit in 2005.[108] This competition weakened the political foundation of monetary and financial cooperation in East Asia greatly distracted the attention of East Asian countries in propelling monetary and financial cooperation, and greatly slowed down the

widely welcomed by all countries in East Asia, and the United States and the IMF have also expressed their support. According to the plan, on 2 February, 2000, Japan provided a total of US$21 billion in loans to Asian countries in crisis such as South Korea, Indonesia and Thailand (of which US$13.5 billion was for medium and long-term loans and US$7.5 billion was for short-term loans). In addition, the program also provided nearly US$2.26 billion in loans for Malaysia, Thailand and the Philippines.

[108]China hopes to carry out the construction of an East Asian Community within the framework of "10 + 3." For the sake of counterbalancing China, Japan hopes to include the countries outside the region into the cooperation framework in East Asia. Disagreements between the two parties have also led to differences in stand taken within the ASEAN countries. For a detailed analysis and discussion of this competition, see Li, Wei, "The End of East Asian Economies — The Dilemma of System Surplus and Economic Integration," *Contemporary Asia-Pacific* 4 (2011): 24–25 (in Chinese).

pace of multilateralization of CMI. The global financial crisis that erupted in September 2008 impacted the real economy and financial markets in East Asia. On 2 December of the same year, the People's Bank of China and the Bank of Korea announced the signing of a three-year bilateral currency swap agreement with a liquidity support of ¥180 billion/38 trillion. On 13 December, leaders of China, Japan and South Korea reached a consensus in Fukuoka, Japan, on accelerating the expansion of the regional currency swap system and increasing the Asian Development Bank's capital as early as possible. This was the first summit held by China, Japan and South Korea, having a symbolic significance. This shows that the global financial crisis has to some extent strengthened the will of East Asian countries to advance regional monetary and financial cooperation.[109] With the platform of the "10 + 3" Summit of ASEAN and the meeting of finance ministers and central bank governors, China has bridged the differences among parties through active financial diplomacy, so that the construction of the "East Asian Foreign Exchange Reserve Pool" was sped up. On 22 February 2009, the "10 + 3" special finance ministers meeting of ASEAN in Phuket, Thailand, jointly announced the "Asian Economic and Financial Stability Plan of Action." This is yet another critical step taken by the "10 + 3" member countries to strengthen the CMI following the US$80 billion Common Foreign Exchange Reserve Fund launched in May 2008, namely the "East Asian Foreign Exchange Reserve Pool." Under the plan, the "Chiang Mai Initiative Multilateral Mechanism" expanded the "East Asian Foreign Exchange Reserve Pool" from the original size of US$80 billion to US$120 billion. Three months later, countries reached a consensus on the issues including the distribution of investment shares, investment structures, loan quotas,

[109]Gao Haihong and Yu Yongding think that East Asian countries are passively united because of the financial tsunami, rather than acting out of mutual consensus. See Gao, Haihong and Yongding, Yu, "Implications and Conditions of RMB Internationalization," *International Economic Review* 1 (2010): 47 (in Chinese).

decision-making mechanisms, etc.[110] On 24 March 2010, the "East Asian Foreign Exchange Reserve Pool" came into force, a regional crisis rescue mechanism was formally established (at the 2012 finance ministers' meeting, all parties decided to double the scale of the reserve to US$240 billion and the proportion of funds decoupled from IMF's lending conditions, increasing from 20% to 30%). The launch of the "Asian Financial Stability Plan of Action" has provided the necessary preparations for the institutionalization of the "Chiang Mai Initiative Multilateral Mechanism" (in the medium and long term, it has also established a platform for higher-level policy coordination and monetary cooperation in the region). It should be noted that the building of "East Asian Foreign Exchange Reserve Pool" made Japan face up to China's financial strength and share the leadership of monetary and financial cooperation in East Asia with China.[111] In the initial funding plan for the reserve pool,the investment ratio of three parties, Japan, South Korea and China, was roughly 3: 2: 1 and China ranked third.[112] China and Japan each contributed US$38.4 billion (each accounting for 32% of the total funds) in the final fund-raising plan, as requested by China, with active diplomatic mediation among the parties; South Korea contributed US$19.2 billion (accounting for 16%); the other 10 ASEAN countries accounted for the remaining 20%, US$24 billion.[113] In addition, ASEAN 10+3 Macroeconomic Research Office (AMRO), which is responsible for monitoring the economic operation of East Asia, was

[110]Website of Chinese Ministry of Finance. http://www.mof.gov.cn/zhuantihuigu/12jiecaizhenhui/caijinhezuochangshi/200904/20090429-138271.html.

[111]See Li, Wei, "The Rise of Financial Diplomacy in China," *World Economy and Politics* 2 (2013): 87 (in Chinese).

[112]See Xu, Yisheng, Gradually Decoupling the IMF-East Asia Foreign Exchange Reserve will be Doubled (*First Financial Daily*, 22 March 2012) (in Chinese).

[113]In the US$24 billion invested by the ASEAN countries, there were US$20 billion loans provided by Japan (the channels are Official Development of Aid, ODA), while China's contribution consisted of US$4.2 billion from Hong Kong, China. Therefore, Japan's share was actually dominant in this organization. For related reports, see Sun, Tianren, Can Asian Foreign Exchange Reserve Pool Establish and Operate before the End of the Year? (*People's Daily*, 4 May 2009) (in Chinese).

established in Singapore in April 2011 to assist the operation of the "East Asian Foreign Exchange Reserve Pool" (the agency is essentially an "Asian Monetary Fund"). As for the question of the candidates for the appointment of the office's director, there have been different opinions between East Asian countries, especially between China and Japan. After diplomatic efforts, Wei Benhua, Deputy Director of China's State Administration of Foreign Exchange, was eventually appointed as the first director of the agency.[114] Following this path, AMRO would soon be upgraded to an exclusive regional international financial organization that would provide financial aid to East Asian economies during the outbreak of a financial crisis. This will undoubtedly weaken the influence of the current international monetary system led by the United States, especially its aid system.

It is worth noting that the monetary and financial cooperation in East Asia is characterized by "crisis-pushing", compared with the currency cooperation in European countries. European countries promote monetary cooperation mainly based on the economic interests of a unified market and a unified monetary zone. Since 1997, the initial purpose of monetary and financial cooperation in East Asia has been to deal with external shocks and prevent a financial crisis.[115] As for the monetary and financial cooperation among East Asian countries after the global financial crisis, they are "passively united by the financial tsunami rather than acting out of mutual consensus."[116] What's more, the promotion of monetary and financial cooperation

[114] But the term of office was only one year, and he has now retired. The incumbent director is the officer of the International Bureau of Japan's Finance Ministry, with a term of two years.

[115] After World War II, British Prime Minister Winston Churchill called for the establishment of a European Union. At that time, there was no such conception of the future of Europe. After that, this was actually established on a strong political will to promote European economic and financial cooperation. See Zhu, Dan Tao, *Global Financial Crisis Promotes East Asian Financial Cooperation*, Information Network of the Information Development Center of the State Council (in Chinese).

[116] See Gao, Haihong and Yongding, Yu, "Implications and Conditions of RMB Internationalization," *International Economic Review* 1 (2010): 47 (in Chinese).

in East Asia has always been constrained by some non-economic factors. In a sense, political consensus is the biggest obstacle to monetary and financial cooperation in East Asia.[117] This is because the regional monetary and financial cooperation first involves the partial abandonment of a country's currency sovereignty, which requires the government's political cooperation. In the monetary and financial cooperation in East Asia, it is bound to involve political compromise between China and Japan. Due to the current competition between China and Japan for regional leadership, there is neither a leader state nor a solid national alliance. In addition, since East Asian nationhood was formed in the late modern period, East Asian countries are generally in a "sovereign expansion period" in developing their nations. Nationalism and statism have become the targets rather than surmountable power of many political forces. Thus, historical grievances among countries within the region (such as Japan's inability to confront history), territorial disputes, contradictions and conflicts in the political system, values and even religious beliefs have all weakened the countries' participation in regional monetary and financial cooperation.[118] In this sense, the endogenous dynamics of monetary and financial cooperation in East Asia are not sufficient.[119] Therefore, the political commitment and compromise between China and Japan are the keys to the development of monetary and financial cooperation in East Asia.

---

[117] Li Yang said as far as various forms of regional integration are concerned, it is important to converge economic indicators toward a common goal, but political consensus is even more crucial. See Yang, Li, "Global Financial System Reform and Asia's Options: We Need to Think More," *International Finance Research* 10 (2010): 10 (in Chinese).

[118] See Xiao, Li, "Why does East Asian Monetary Cooperation Encounter Setback — The Internationalization of the Renminbi and Its Influence on the Future Monetary Cooperation in East Asia," International Economic Review 2 (2011): 118 (in Chinese).

[119] See Xiang, Weixing and Liu Xiaoxin, "The US Dollar Standard System and East Asian Regional Financial Cooperation," *International Finance* 8 (2009): 20 (in Chinese).

4.2.4.2 *The Promotion of the Monetary and Financial Cooperation in East Asia on the Reform of the International Monetary System*

The subprime mortgage crisis in the United States has exposed the flaws of an international monetary system that relies on a single sovereign currency, which acts as an international currency. Strengthening regional monetary and financial cooperation is an important step in promoting the reform of the international monetary system.[120] As an important supporter of the current international monetary system, the US dollar standard, the East Asian economies on the periphery or the outside of the existing international monetary system have decided that only by close regional monetary and financial cooperation can they become the main force for the reform of the international monetary system. The main reasons are as follows:

First, only by strengthening regional monetary and financial cooperation can East Asian economies reduce dependence on the US dollar standard. East Asia was the "loose dollar zone"[121] until the global financial crisis broke out. Although the status of the G8 was declining after the global financial crisis and that of the G20 was rising, East Asian economies greatly raised their voice in global economic governance,[122] but on the whole, East Asia is still a marginalized area in the current international monetary system. This is because in today's typical "center-sub-center-periphery" international monetary system, only Japan is in a "sub-center" position among East Asian

---

[120] Woo, Wing T., China and International Financial Reform, Part of the First Phase of the Project on China's New International Economic Responsibilities, 2010. http://epress.anu.edu.au/wpcontent/uploads/2011/06/ch025.pdf.

[121] See Kazuko, Shirono, Yen Area or RMB Area — An Analysis on Monetary Arrangements in East Asia http://www.imf.org/external/ft/wp/2009/wp0903.pdf.

[122] Among G8 countries, East Asian countries occupy only one seat (namely Japan); among the G20 countries, East Asian countries occupy four seats, namely China, Japan, South Korea and Indonesia. http://www.imf.org/external/ft/wp/2009/wp0903.pdf.

economies. The long-term economic downturn of Japan has caused a marked decline in its economic position and influence in the world and East Asia. As for China and other East Asian economies, they are located in the "periphery" of the system and act in a peripheral role.[123] Until 2007, before the outbreak of the global financial crisis, the US dollar dominated the Asian region, ahead of the euro. The GDP covered by both the US dollar and the euro reached 81.8% during 2005–2007, while the yen only covered 9.6%. In contrast, the sum of GDP in the United States and the Euro Area accounted for less than 50% of global GDP over the same period, while the one of Asia was as high as 35%.[124] Although the dependence of the demand for final products in East Asia on the markets outside the region is on a downward trend, the degree of dependence remains high. According to the database of the Institute of Industrial Economics of Japan, the index was 82.94% in 1986, 59.70% in 1996 and 65–70% in 1999. By 2010, it remained at 67.69%.[125] The high degree of dependence on external markets allowed East Asian economies to deeply embed the US dollar standard after the 1997 East Asian financial crisis, namely binding the US dollar, by reserving a large amount of US dollar

[123]See Li, Junjiu and Mozhu, Jiang, "Monetary-Financial Dependencies under the US Dollar Standard System," *World Economic Research* 6 (2011): 10–15 (in Chinese).

[124]Li Yang believes that the serious imbalance between these two proportions has caused the long-term serious "double mismatch" in Asian countries or regions (currency mismatch and term mismatch). This mismatch has not only made the Asian countries or regions inadvertently disturbed by the economic and financial turmoil in the United States and Europe but it has also made the former always face difficult choices in exchange rate arrangements and the management of foreign exchange reserves, making it the object of attack by developed countries. See Yang, Li, "Global Financial System Reform and Asia's Options: We Need to Think More," *International Finance Research* 10 (2010): 6 (in Chinese).

[125]Han Jinhong said that the two demands for the final product in the East Asian region should be each economy's demand for the final product produced by them, and the demand of each economy for the final product produced by other economies, represented by the import of final products from other economies. Here it refers to the second demand. See Jinhong, Han, "Analysis on the Determinants of Final Product Demand in East Asia," *World Economic Research* 2 (2013): 80 (in Chinese).

assets to prevent the possible recurrence of the financial crisis (at this point, the "de-dollarization" in Euro areas, "de-dollarization" of intra-euro trade settlement and the ultra-low dollar reserves in the region, began). An important way to get rid of or reduce dependence on the "dollar system" is to forge a market provider of final products in the region through the trade transformation in East Asia. However, as two major powers in East Asia, China and Japan do not have the capability to become final product market providers in the region in the short term because the scale of final product market provided by them is far from that of the US[126] Moreover, under the current "dollar system," both China and Japan do not have the capability to independently dominate the regional monetary and financial cooperation, for the reason that judging from Japan, although the yen is already an international currency, it has been very difficult for Japan to once again become the core of East Asia's most important trading partner and regional division of the labor system. The 20-year economic downturn, the structural problems of the industrial and financial institutions, the issues of opening up the market and the aging population have hindered Japan from becoming the major market provider in East Asia and thus impeded the yen in becoming the region's leading currency. From the perspective of China, due to the weaknesses of the RMB in terms of free convertibility, the fragility of the financial system and the opening up of financial markets, it is difficult for the RMB to assume the role of the dominant currency solely in the region at current stage.[127] For this reason, East Asian economies that have suffered from the pain of the international monetary system for a long time, which are on the periphery of the system, can only reduce dependence on the

[126]See Xiao, Li, and Fu Jinghui, "Status Quo and Prospects of China as an East Asian Markets Provider," *Journal of Jilin University-Social Sciences* 2 (2010): 17–28 (in Chinese).
[127]See Yibing, Ding, "Asian Monetary Cooperation and Sino-Japanese Coordination: China's Point of View and Conception," Li Xia and Hirokazu, Kagawa (Editor-in-Chief), *RMB, Yen and Asian Monetary Cooperation*. Tsinghua: Tsinghua University Press, 2010, 203 (in Chinese).

US dollar by strengthening regional monetary and financial cooperation. Such regional monetary and financial cooperation relies on the logic of regional collective action to promote the reform of the international monetary system.

Second, the development of monetary and financial cooperation in East Asia is conducive to propelling the reform of the international monetary system. From the international level, it is impossible for the current international monetary system, the "dollar system," to undergo radical structural changes in the short term. Therefore, the top priority of the reform of the international monetary system is to create a mechanism that can constrain the United States to arbitrarily increase the circulation of the US dollar, thereby reducing the global financial risk. The "reinvent the wheel" approach is irrational.[128] At this point, the development of the euro is the best example to prove this point. Before the birth of the euro, no European currency could compete with the US dollar. It is precisely this situation that has made way for the dollar hegemony,[129] so that the United States has obtained a large number of invisible seigniorages around the world. The European countries stepped on the path of regional monetary integration through regional monetary cooperation. By the joint efforts of all countries, the euro became the world's second largest international currency since its birth.[130] The

[128]See Hua, Min and Tian, Suhua, *Reform of the International Monetary System is Imperative*, Information Network of the Information Development Centre of the State Council, 23 June 2011 (in Chinese). Gao Haihong also believes that the reform of the international monetary system should follow "a gradual course," that is, the US dollar should be restrained by the diversification of international currency, but not be immediately abolished (of course, it also includes the mutual restraint of international currencies). See Dai, Jinping, Aizong, Xiong and Shushi, Tan, *International Monetary System: Where To Go?* Hainan: Xiamen University Press, 2012, 275 (in Chinese). See Zhang, Yuyan and Li, Zengang, *International Political Economics*. Shanghai: Shanghai People's Publishing House, 2008, 452 (in Chinese).

[129]See Zhang, Yuyan and Li, Zengang, *International Political Economics*. Shanghai: Shanghai People's Publishing House, 2008, 452 (in Chinese).

[130]The Euro, born in 1999, reshuffled the international monetary system. The share of the US dollar dropped from 71.01% in 1999 to 62.12% in 2011 in global

euro-zone countries thus started the "de-dollarization." The creation of the euro not only started the "de-dollarization" of trade settlement within the euro area, which greatly reduced the transaction costs in the euro area and allowed traders in all member countries to evade the exchange rate risk, but more importantly the euro is becoming an international currency standing against the dollar, and is beginning to weaken the dollar in areas such as its position as the international reserve currency and commodity transaction pricing and so on. Although the euro is still incapable of challenging the international monetary position of the US dollar, the former has apparently become a strong regional currency and is used as a currency anchor by countries in the Euro zone. It is a reference currency or media currency in financial transactions.[131] Its competitive substitution effect on the United States dollar has been very obvious. What is more, the euro area has overtaken the United States in terms of economic output, population, trade and manufacturing. In other words, the Euro-zone countries have constructed a "regional financialism" framework independent from the current international monetary system. This fact shows that with the multipolarization of the world economic pattern, the diversification of international currencies, namely the diversification of the international monetary system, is an inevitable development trend. This not only serves to constrain the US dollar and promote the stability of the international monetary system but also affects the development and changes of the global economic landscape. Therefore, only by further strengthening regional monetary and financial cooperation, that is, by means of "regional financialism" can East Asia economies raise East Asia's

foreign exchange reserves, down by 8.89%, while the share of the euro in global foreign exchange reserves rose from 17.90% in 1999 to 2011 Year 25.04%, increasing by 7.14%, which means the share of the US dollar is basically supplemented by the euro. See Dai, Jinping, Xiong Aizong and Tan Shushi, *International Monetary System: Where To Go?* Hainan: Xiamen University Press, 2012, 163 (in Chinese).

[131]See Peterson Institute for International Economics, *The Ten Years of Euro: Next International Currency*, Section 4 of Chapter 2, the Information Network of the Information Development Centre of the State Council (in Chinese).

voice in the existing international monetary system to balance the dollar hegemony with regional cooperation, and further promote the formation of a diversified international reserve currency. More importantly, as an important part of the remodeling of the international financial framework, monetary and financial cooperation in East Asia will become an effective supplement to the crisis rescue of international financial institutions. Strengthening this cooperation will help the smooth development of the international reserve currency diversification by the construction of a regional financial market with transactions conducted in the local currency, the expansion of the regional currency in regional trade settlements and calculations of the transaction value of financial capital.[132]

[132]See Gao, Haihong, "Roadmap for East Asian Monetary Cooperation in the Post-Crisis Period," *International Economic Review* 5 (2011): 132 (in Chinese).

Chapter 5

General Thoughts and Strategic Choice in China's Active Participation in the Reform of the International Monetary System

5.1 Opportunities and Challenges of China's Participation in the Reform of the International Monetary System

The outbreak of the US subprime mortgage crisis and its rapid spread on a global scale reflected the inherent flaws and systemic risks of the current international monetary system. The changes in the US economic structure and the increased risk of the US financial system indicate that the operating mode has been blocked within the international monetary system.

Not only that, after the outbreak of the subprime mortgage crisis, the US government introduced a large-scale stimulus plan to save the economy, leading to the surge of government debt and fiscal deficit. The US government stimulated the economy by printing money, and at the same time, it also transferred the risk of domestic inflation and recession to other countries relying on the international monetary advantage of the US dollar. In view of this, as early as October 2008, at the EU summit held in Brussels, Belgium, the leaders of the meeting put forward radical reform proposals for the current international monetary system from a global view. With the deepening of the crisis, leaders of emerging economies, such as China and Russia, have made it clear that the United States should have less control over the global economic order and put forward the idea of reshaping the international monetary system.[1]

Regardless of the direction of development taken by the reform of the international monetary system, the pattern of international monetary and financial relations is being reconstructed in the form of a mutually beneficial game. In the process of forging financial competitiveness and strengthening the financial system, China should make the necessary preparations for the establishment of a fair and reasonable international monetary system. Former President Hu Jintao said at the G20 summit in London in 2009: "We should make efforts to continue working for a fair, just, inclusive and well-managed international financial order. And we should do so in a comprehensive, balanced and incremental manner and lay emphasis on concrete results. We should improve the international monetary system and improve the regulatory mechanism of the issuance of reserve currencies, maintain the relative stability of the exchange rates of major reserve currencies and develop a more diverse and rational international monetary system. For the next stage, we should work out a practical timetable and road map on the basis of full consultations and make solid progress in various reforms, thus fostering an enabling institutional environment for the sound growth of the world economy."

China is the world's largest developing country, but also a highly open economy. After China's accession to the World Trade

[1]On 23 March 2009, Zhou Xiaochuan, Governor of the People's Bank of China, wrote that "the outbreak of the financial crisis and its rapid spread worldwide have reflected the inherent deficiencies and systemic risks of the current international monetary system." He suggested creating an international reserve currency that is decoupled from sovereign countries and can maintain long-term currency stability, thereby avoiding the inherent shortcomings of sovereign credit currencies as reserve currencies. Russia proposed setting up a conference of government representatives and experts to draft a global agreement on a new global monetary and financial architecture.

Organization (WTO) in 2001, its economy became closely integrated into the world economy. At the same time, China is also one of the countries that holds the largest proportion of reserve assets in US dollars, and has maintained close financial and economic ties with the United States. Therefore, both from the perspective of maintaining and promoting the steady and orderly development of China's economy and from the perspective of avoiding the adverse effects of the international monetary system on China and improving China's position in the international monetary system, China should actively participate in and promote the reform of the international monetary system, striving for a stable and favorable international monetary and financial environment for the countries' future economic development. As Guan concluded: "China should actively participate in and promote the reform of the international monetary system. It is not necessary to abolish or replace the US dollar, but to maintain and realize the national interests to the utmost *by* way of limited and feasible reforms."[2]

In theory, the current reform of the international monetary system has five main objectives: first, to promote the development of the global economy and free trade; second, to promote the orderly and stable circulation of global capital; third, to deal with the impact of the crisis with more flexibility; fourth, to be conductive to the fair distribution of income; fifth, to provide more space for market choice.

As an important part of the global economy and one of the important driving forces of global economic growth, China is participating in the reform of the international monetary system in order to achieve stable and sustainable economic growth, which will make a necessary contribution to stable growth and a healthy cycle of the world economy.

China is now in a critical historical period of its economic rise, so a stable external market environment is of vital importance to China. As mentioned in previous chapters, there are many drawbacks to

[2]Guan, Tao, "International Financial Crisis and Reserve Currency Diversification," *International Economic Review* 3 (2009): 18–19.

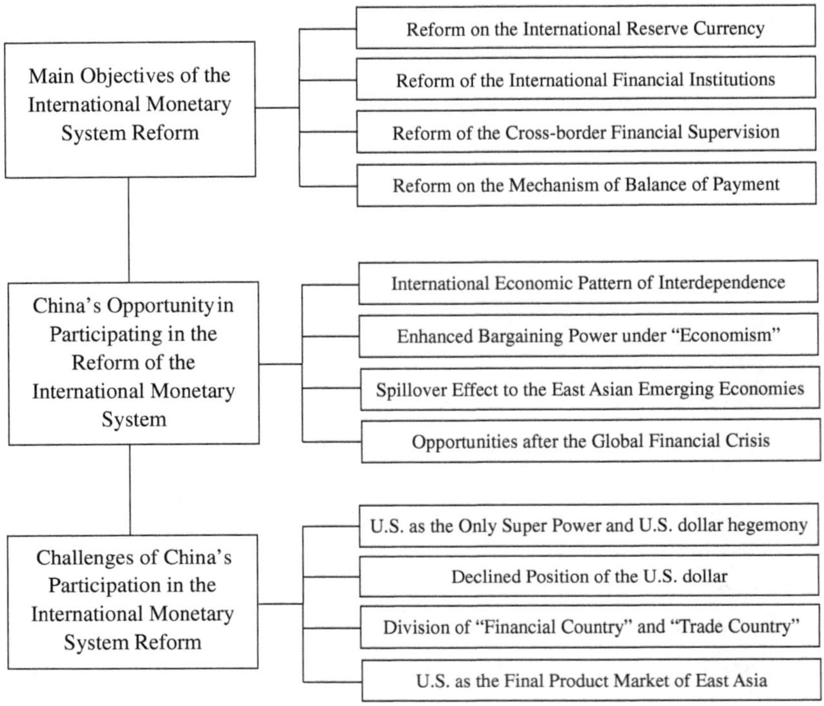

Figure 5.1. Opportunities and Challenges of China's Participation in International Monetary System Reform

the current reform of the international monetary system, which have caused a large negative impact on the stable and rapid development of the world economy. Therefore, China, as an important part of the global economic cycle, should take positive measures in the international monetary reform, to reduce the adverse effects of the current system on China's economic development, to take the initiative to create a favorable external environment for China's unprecedented rise and to maximize national interests.

5.1.1 *China's Opportunity to Participate in the Reform of the International Monetary System*

Former International Monetary Fund (IMF) Chief Executive Michel Camdessus once suggested that all the parties, including the United States, must first agree upon the importance of a more robust international monetary system and a generally accepted international reserve currency, in order to effectively establish a new international monetary order. The global financial crisis created an unprecedented and good opportunity for the reform of the international monetary system, with a bailout based on the cooperative efforts of many countries, and for avoiding a repeated crisis. As an existing important pillar for the "dollar system," East Asia, especially China, will become one of the important driving forces for the future reform of the international monetary system.

By virtue of sustained and high-speed economic growth, China has played an increasingly important role in the world economy, and has won the status of a world power (regional power). Therefore, China has the ability to shoulder the responsibility of actively promoting the reform of the international monetary system. In addition, while the development of a globalized world economy is changing the international economic and political situation, it also provides a historical opportunity for China.

First, at this stage, the international economic pattern has become one whole system which is complex and interdependent. The emerging market countries, represented by China, and the developed countries, represented by the United States, have become a community with common interests. With the intensified power of the emerging market countries and their greater willingness to change the existing system, the G20 has replaced the G8, and gradually become an important platform for discussion of international economic problems and adjustment of international economic relations. China, as an important component of the relations, has the responsibility to carry the voices of the developing countries.

Second, the development of international relations has entered the era of "Economism," so military force is no longer the main way to solve a problem in the relations between leading powers. Economic development has become the key factor in determining the status of a country.[3] Therefore, although the military strength of the United

[3]Xiao, Li, "Sino-Japanese Relation in the Age of 'Economicism'," *International Economic Review* 3–4 (2006): 19.

States is in an absolute dominant position, China and other developing countries can still express their views and take the initiative in international monetary system reform. In order to promote the development of the global free trade system and the steady flow of capital, China has the responsibility to actively promote the reform of the current international monetary system.

Third, at present, China has become an undeniable power in Asia, and the Chinese economy has strong homogeneous features with other emerging market economies in East Asia, which are all stuck in the "dollar trap." Therefore, the willingness and process of China's participation in the reform of the international monetary system have a positive spillover effect on the emerging economies of East Asia, which means that China's action will be supported by these countries and will contribute to gathering the multinational force necessary to jointly promote the reform process.

Fourth, the global financial crisis triggered by the US subprime mortgage crisis in 2008 led to a passive reduction in China's exports to the United States, providing a rare opportunity for China's economic restructuring and industrial transformation, as well as China's deep understanding of the risks in having huge foreign exchange reserves. It has provided an important historical opportunity for China's appeal for reform of the international monetary system.

5.1.2 *Challenges of China's Participation in the Reform of the International Monetary System*

It is important to note that China's participation in the reform of the international monetary system will also face many challenges. The Chinese government and academia are soberly aware that there are numerous constraints to the reform of the international monetary system with poor controllability, so that the relevant proposals and positive gestures are more strategic. China's participation in the reform of the international monetary system will face the following challenges:

First, the United States is the only superpower with political, economic, military and cultural strengths, thus the international relations pattern can be summed up as "Only Super Power and Multi-Great Power." However, in the short term, no great power has the possibility of replacing the United States as a hegemonic power, and the superpower status of the United States provides an important pillar for the "dollar system." In addition, under the present "dollar system," international capital flows have become one of the main forms of international economic relations. The results of competition among countries are often "positive" and highly connected to one another's costs and benefits. A prominent manifestation of the global financial crisis is that the world's major countries and regions will share the cost of the crisis. This shows that under the conditions of economic globalization, the external environment of the hegemonic position has undergone significant changes, and the changes may be more favorable for dollar hegemony in the long term.

Second, since the 1970s, the global financial crisis has shown that the dollar is still a strong currency during the period of crisis and the post-crisis period.[4] When the crisis broke out, regardless of the cause of the crisis and where the crisis broke out, the dollar was still the "straw" permitting the governments or investors to ensure their asset safety and avoid risk. The dollar's status has not only declined, but has risen (see Figure 5.2). This situation has not changed even with the birth of the euro. In fact, the economy of the Eurozone suffered even more than the United States itself after the global financial crisis. The outbreak of the debt crisis in Greece and other countries showed that there are a series of major issues with the economy of the Eurozone, which indicates that the international monetary system is still dominated by the dollar. The euro cannot replace the US dollar as a leading international currency in the current situation. This means that the "dollar system" itself still has strong sustainability, and it is difficult to completely overthrow or change the current situation.

[4]Xiao, Li, "Path Choice of East Asian Monetary and Financial Cooperation under the Global Financial Crisis," *Northeast Asia Forum* 5 (2009): 3–25.

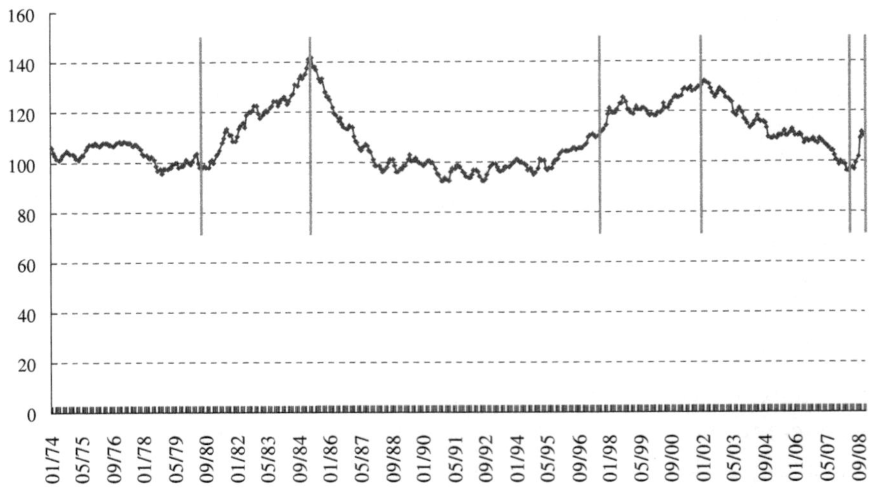

Figure 5.2. US Dollar Index (USDI) from January 1974 to December 2008

Third, after the Second World War, countries around the world formed a new model of industry division between the virtual economy and the real economy, based on their comparative advantage. The United States, is representative of a typically "financial country" with financial hegemony, based on the comparative advantage of the development of the financial sector. In contrast, some countries, including Japan and China, have become well-developed "trade countries." The economic imbalance between "financial country" and "trade country" is essentially a structural problem caused by the long-term industry division of the financial industry and the manufacturing industry. The export-oriented industrialization of East Asian economies is the result of international division of labor, which has resulted from endogenous factors, so changes in the economic growth model of certain countries cannot solve the problem of global economic imbalances, and a change in the current "dollar system" will be arduous. As the former US Treasury Secretary Lawrence Somers said, there is a so-called "financial and terrorist balance" between East Asian economies and the United States. In reality, this terror is very unbalanced; thus, the United States has a complete hold on the initiative, and the East Asian economies are caught in the dilemma of the dollar trap.[5]

Fourth, the East Asian economies, especially China, will be an important supporting force of the current "dollar system" in the future, with the distinctive feature of dependence on the US market, the final product market for East Asia.[6] Since the 1990s, although intraregional trade in East Asia has increased remarkably, most of its trade products are intermediate products, spare parts and capital goods which have arisen from the decentralization of the production process. The final product market is still dependent on other external countries and regions, such as the United States. Moreover, as the adjustment of economic structure is long term, it is difficult for East Asia to replace the United States as final product market providers, and neither Japan nor China really has the possibility to play a similar role. Therefore, East Asian countries' dependence on the "dollar system" is inevitable.

Despite the outbreak and deepening of the financial crisis, the Chinese government has recognized the inevitability and urgency of reforming the irrational global financial order, which has brought a series of opportunities for China to reform the international monetary system. It is difficult to make substantial adjustments to the international financial order in the short term, and the current reform of the international monetary system will face many challenges, so gradual reform can only start in a limited fashion. In establishing the objectives of the future reform of the international monetary system, China must recognize its own position and the opportunities and challenges it faces. It is difficult to fundamentally change the "dollar system" in the near future. This is the most important contemporary realistic basis of China's thinking concerning the boosting of reform of the international monetary system, and it also shows the

[5]Jiang, Yong, "'International Financial Terror Imbalance' and the Financial Trap of the United States," *Modern International Relations* 7 (2005): 54–60.

[6]Xiao, Li, and Fu Jinghui, "China's Status and Prospect as an East Asian Market Provider," *Journal of Social Science of Jilin University* 2 (2010): 17–28.

complexity and gradual nature of the future of RMB internationalization and monetary cooperation in East Asia.

5.2 General Thoughts on China's Active Participation in the Reform of the International Monetary System

Based on the aforementioned objectives and opportunities for China's participation in the reform of the international monetary system, the general idea concerning China's active participation in the reform of the international monetary system can be summed up based on background analysis and rational national orientation.

5.2.1 *China's Economic Rise within the Special Background of the Times*

Compared to the rise of previous great powers, China's economic rise has a distinctive background. After reform and opening-up, China joined an unprecedented open world market and this has brought about many benefits for China together with contradictions. A strong interdependence has been formed between China's economy and the world economy, especially the Asian regional economy, so China's economic rise is unlikely to transfer into a political or strategic advantage quickly, which has led to other countries taking advantage of the rise of China's economy and tending to contain the rise of China's economy in accordance with their own interests.[7] When any foreign economic strategy is formulated in this context, on the one hand, China should take into account the fact that China's economy is closely linked with the world economy, especially the Asian economy, but on the other hand, it is also necessary for China to make sufficient preparations when facing external pressure resulting from implementing or adjusting the strategy.

[7] Xiao, Li, and Fu Jinghui, "The Current Reform of the International Monetary System: The Dilemma and Strategic Choices of East Asia," *World Economics and Politics Forum* 4 (2010): 62–75.

Specific to the reform of the international monetary system, China is not qualified to directly challenge the "dollar system" at this stage, so it should be dependent on international coordination and cooperation to promote the reform. The internationalization of the RMB should learn the lessons from the internationalization of the Japanese yen. It remains unlikely that the RMB can take a direct pathway to complete internationalization under the "dollar system," but collective action in the form of regional monetary cooperation can help reduce various international pressures and reduce the cost of internationalization of the RMB. Therefore, the internationalization of the RMB should be achieved through regional monetary and financial cooperation, that is, promotion of the internationalization of the RMB should be based on the regionalization of the RMB. To a large extent, the process of monetary cooperation in East Asia will also determine the future prospects of the reform of the international monetary system.

5.2.2 *General Thoughts on China's Active Participation in the Reform of International Monetary System*

The anxieties about the imbalance and vulnerability of the "dollar system" have led the international community to reach a consensus on the necessity to reform the international monetary system. The continued low interest rates in the United States, the downgrade of the US Treasury rating and the volatility of the US dollar are the financial risks that China has to be confronted with in its future economic development. Therefore, it is necessary to rationally judge the objectives of the reform of the international monetary system, and China should put forward an objective analysis based on the country's interests. As matters stand, China's academia has two completely different opinions on the reform of the international monetary system: First, the current global economic imbalances and the "dollar system" are unsustainable, and a new international monetary order should be established to replace the existing one completely in a radical way. Second, despite the drawbacks in the existing international monetary system, maintaining the current international monetary system is conducive to stabilizing world economic development. Obviously, the former view can only serve as the long-term goal of the reform of the international monetary system, and the second view should be adopted as the recent reform target.

5.2.2.1 *Operational Problems with the Complete Replacement of the US Dollar*

There are three main types of alternative scheme in the reform of the international monetary system: the return from a credit-based currency to a physical currency, the establishment of a certain world currency, and the construction of "tripartite confrontation" in the international monetary system.

First of all, restoring the gold standard or the establishment of a commodity reserve currency system has no solid footing. Although the "anchor" effect of gold contributes to the stability of prices and its automatic adjustment mechanism also contributes to the global economic equilibrium, production volume of gold lags behind the tightening effect caused by the development of the world economy, so that the gold standard system is bound to collapse owing to "gold handcuffs."

Second, the establishment of a super-sovereign currency is not operable and practical in the short term. In reality, special drawing rights (SDRs) can only be applied to the settlement between governments and the IMF, and it can neither be the tool to intervene in the foreign exchange market nor can it be used for market participants for transactions, which makes it difficult to become an attractive form of reserves. Also, the creation of any new super-sovereign currency means the reallocation or adjustment of the interests of different countries and regions, which will incur a significant cost in negotiations.

Finally, only the US dollar meets the three requirements of an international reserve currency — stable currency value, low transaction costs and high transparency — whereas the conditions are not satisfied for the euro, Japanese yen or RMB. The "ternary" pattern of the US dollar, euro and RMB will take at least 30 years to be achieved. In the medium term (10 years), the global economy will be shown in an asymmetric dual-center pattern: the coexistence of Asia as a world manufacturing center and the US/Europe as a world financial center. Therefore, even if a "ternary" international reserve monetary system is achievable, it will certainly be a long process.

5.2.2.2 *The Recent Goal of China's Participation in the Reform of the International Monetary System: "Managing the Structural Imbalance" and "Preventing Risk against the Dollar"*

The recent goal of China's participation in the reform of the international monetary system should be "to manage the imbalance" and "to prevent risk against the dollar." The current reform of the international monetary system should fix the problems or restrain malpractice in the "dollar system" by international cooperation and coordination. China is trying to reduce the losses and risks in this system, rather than subvert or challenge it. The risk of global economic imbalances and volatility in dollar values is an inherent flaw in the current international monetary system.

As they form the relationship between the "dollar system" and global economic imbalances, "managing the structural imbalance" and "preventing risk against the dollar" are also two sides of a coin. Managing imbalance is mainly limiting the size or extent of imbalance within a certain range by structural adjustment and cooperation; preventing risk against the dollar is maintaining the stable value of the US dollar to a certain degree by global or regional cooperation.

It is gratifying to note that active cooperation has been made in countries around the world, both "to manage the structural imbalance" and "to prevent risk against the dollar." China has made a positive attempt to control imbalances. China and the United States have also proposed plans to adjust the economic structure in order to achieve goals of remodeling the economic growth pattern. The Chinese government plans to expand domestic demand and reduce the dependence on exports by "expanding domestic demand" and "urbanization." The US President Obama had proposed a national export initiative with the goal of "doubling exports within five years." It can be noted that the adjustment of economic structure between China and the United States is the fundamental way to manage the governance imbalance, but the transformation of the economic development mode is a painful and long process, so the two sides should seek long-term coordination and cooperation on the policies of science and technology development and industrial restructure. In terms of preventing risk against the dollar, exchange rate policy coordination and monetary cooperation between the central banks will help to stabilize the US dollar. The exchange rate cooperation program of Europe, America and Asia, proposed by some Chinese scholars, is an option.

In addition, as important parts of the international monetary system, international reserve currencies, international financial institutions and international financial regulation should also manage the imbalance and prevent risk against the dollar. The reform of the international reserve monetary system should continue to promote the trend of "diversification with one principal currency." The diversification of money avoids the imbalance caused by over-concentration and counterbalances the rights of the hegemonic country with a competitive pattern of diversified currencies, in order to avoid the spillover effect of monetary policy. The emerging market countries and developing countries should have more say in the reform of international financial institutions. The reform of international financial supervision should strengthen the construction of international financial regulatory coordination mechanisms to fill the regulatory gap and avoid regulatory arbitrage.

There is no perfect international monetary system in the world. Alternatives to the reform of the international monetary system are technically feasible, but they cannot be the operational target of the recent reform of the international monetary system. The current international monetary system is sustainable, has a catalytic role in global economic imbalances, but no decisive role. Overthrowing the current international monetary system will have little effect in solving the problems of global economic imbalances. Therefore, the recent goal of the reform of the international monetary system should be: "to manage the structural imbalance" combined with "to prevent risk against the dollar." We should exploit the coordination mechanism of international payments to control the structural imbalance, reduce the risk by joint efforts on exchange rate mechanisms and provide a better external environment for the stable development of the world economy through reform of international reserve currencies, international financial institutions and international financial supervisions.

As mentioned earlier, since the end of 2008, the Chinese monetary authorities have basically formed their own international financial strategy. They have taken three steps directly or indirectly: RMB internationalization, strengthening of regional monetary cooperation and reforming of the international monetary system. The following two points should be mentioned:

First, it will be difficult to make a substantial change in the "dollar system" in the near future. On the one hand, there can be no influence on "dollar hegemony" or "financial hegemony" in the short term. Even after the financial crisis, the global dollar-centric credit system will continue to be powerful, so the East Asian economies cannot escape dependency on the product market of the United States, with its firm support of the current system; on the other hand, while the dollar's position as an international currency, cannot be challenged by others, the emerging market countries appeal for less dependence on the dollar is making very slow progress. Despite one of the major financial policy orientations of China, Russia, Brazil and other emerging economies being the gradual international role of their local currencies, implementation takes time, as can be seen with the euro and its recent institutional problems, and the process may even experience repetition and frustration.

Second, China is still not equipped with the conditions and ability to independently challenge the US financial hegemony. The normal logic behind this problem is that China is one of the greatest beneficiaries of the current "dollar system" and has naturally become the most important supporter of the system and its potential victim. Moreover, the reality is that we still have to rely on the survival and development of this system for a long time in the future. Also, it should be pointed out that historical experience shows that the rise and fall of modern powers is not only the rise and fall of the so-called hegemonic countries but also largely depends on second-tier countries, whose actions and strategies determine the result of hegemony replacement. Therefore, for a long period of time, the goal of China's national strategy (economic strategy) should not be blind to the pursuit of the "first," but should lock in the goal of the "second," through the country's firm position as the world's second power. In fact, the promotion of China's international economic status at this stage has not affected the status of the United States, but rather "squeezed" the space of the EU and Japan, which is an important reason for "containment" of or "beating" China in various fields in recent years. Therefore, in order to grasp development opportunities, what China needs to do is to try to limit the loss or risk coming from this system, rather than to subvert or challenge it. We must formulate China's national strategy according to historical experience, China's national conditions and the basic situation of world economic and political development, aiming to maximize the safeguard of national interests.

China should be an active advocate of the reform of the international monetary system rather than a leader, which is the exact position of China's active role in its participation in the process.

Therefore, the formation or strategy formulation of China's reform of the international monetary system should follow the principle of "hide our capacities and bide our time" and have more say in the reform in the international economic system while ensuring the stable and rapid development of the domestic economy. Specifically, in the short term, we should steadily push forward some of the early stages of RMB internationalization, such as pilot schemes in RMB trade settlement, RMB-based currency exchange, RMB-denominated bond issuance, etc., and actively promote regional monetary cooperation in East Asia. In the medium term, we should promote the regionalization of RMB and East Asian regional monetary cooperation through exchange rate coordination and other high-level cooperation. In the long term, we should promote the reform of the international monetary system and the realization of RMB globalization. In the short, medium and long term, we should pay attention to China's domestic adjustment and change. Reforms in the financial sector and industrial structure should be strengthened, at the same time we should strengthen international coordination for a better international environment for RMB internationalization and international monetary system reform.

At this stage, China should pay attention to the following three aspects in participating in the reform of the international monetary system:

First, China should not take the initiative to become the challenger of the current international monetary system with the US dollar as the core, and also make greater use of the G20 as a platform.

Second, despite many unreasonable situations in procedure rules, voting rights and governance structure of the IMF, World Bank and other international institutions, China should not over-advocate the so-called "democratization reform" of these institutions, because it is neither in the interests of the world nor in the interests of China.

Thirdly, China should now expand the distribution area of the RMB in East Asia as a foothold, and the RMB should first seek the position of key regional currency. From RMB regionalization to RMB internationalization, China can combine its monetary strategy and the rise of the country's economy.

Fourth, based on the Belt and Road Initiative, that is, the construction of the "Silk Road Economic Zone" and the "21st Century Maritime Silk Road," China can build a cross-regional monetary strategy through regional cooperation of the European and Asian continents, involving China's participation in the reform of the

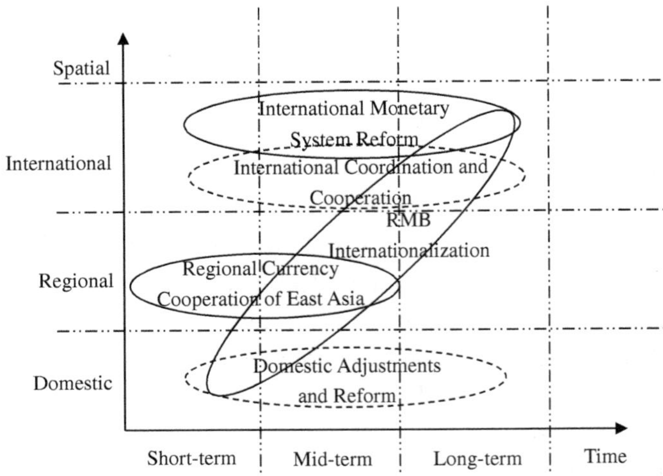

Figure 5.3. General Thoughts of China's Active Participation in the Reform of International Monetary System

international monetary system and China's overall diplomatic strategy in economic cooperation (refer to Figure 5.3).

5.3 Strategic Choice of China's Active Participation in the Reform of the International Monetary System

As mentioned earlier, China's strategy for the reform of the international monetary system adheres to the principle of "hide our capacities and bide our time." Therefore, China actively promotes the reform of the international monetary system that is in line with the interests of the country while ensuring stable and rapid domestic economic development. We believe that it will be difficult to achieve fundamental changes to the existing international monetary system in the short term, even though there are many contradictions within the system. From historical experience or realistic strategic needs, China, as a rising developing country, should not directly challenge the US as a financial hegemony or make fundamental changes to the international monetary system. It should pay more attention to its short-term goal in the process of actively participating in the reform

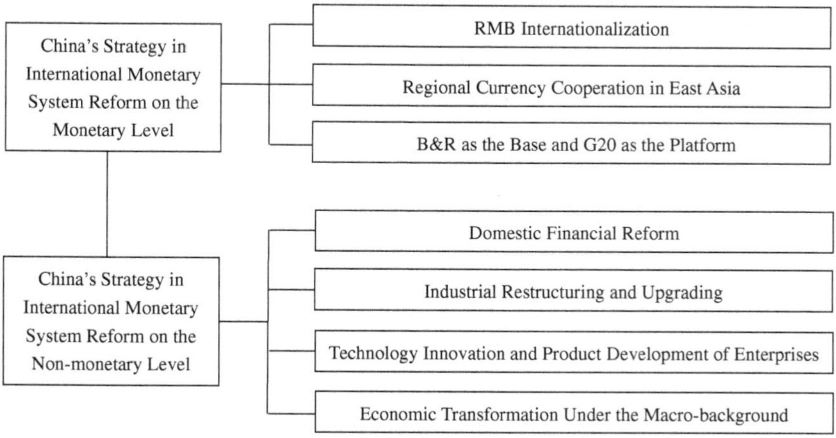

Figure 5.4. Strategy of China's Active Participation in the International Monetary System Reform

of the international monetary system, namely, "managing the structural imbalance" combined with "preventing risks against the dollar." Two specific strategic countermeasures should be mentioned. First, concerning the direct impact of international monetary system reform, the policy should be RMB internationalization, East Asian regional monetary cooperation and active participation in the reform of the international monetary system under the Belt and Road Initiative with the G20 as a platform. Second, concerning the necessary conditions for China's participation in the reform of the international monetary system, the policy should be reform of the relevant domestic financial sector, industrial restructuring and upgrading, technological innovation and product upgrades of enterprises and economic transformation in the following four areas on a macro level (refer to Figure 5.4).

5.3.1 *Strategic Choice of Participation in the Reform of the International Monetary System on the Monetary Level*

In choosing the strategy of reforming the international monetary system, the most direct choice is to meet the demands of China's interest by international financial strategic arrangements at the monetary level. Specifically, this can be achieved with the following steps: internationalization of the RMB, strengthening of regional monetary cooperation and active participation in the reform of the international monetary system under the Belt and Road Initiative with the G20 as a platform. Internationalization of the RMB can be undertaken in three steps. The first is to make the RMB an international trade settlement currency based on the convertibility of the RMB on current accounts. The second is to turn the RMB into an investment currency by allowing certified investors at home and abroad to jointly promote two-way flows of the RMB. The third is to achieve the internationalization of the RMB and turn the RMB into an international reserve currency.

5.3.1.1 *To Reduce the Risk of the "Dollar System" by the Internationalization of the RMB*

To achieve the goal of controlling the depreciation of the dollar within a certain range, to reduce China's dependence on the dollar in foreign trade, cross-border management of investment and foreign exchange reserves, active promotion of the internationalization of the RMB has become the most prominent strategic choice with the strongest controllability for the Chinese government.

At this stage, the stumbling block to promoting the internationalization of the RMB is that it is unlikely China can achieve the full liberalization of capital projects and complete convertibility of the RMB in the short term. China's capital market development is immature and financial institutions and enterprises lack the experience and ability in regulatory management to cope with risk control in capital flow, which makes capital account control in China the last line of defense to prevent financial risks. Therefore, internationalization of the RMB is doomed to be a long and gradual process and we can only objectively explore the strategic path to be taken at the initial stage of RMB internationalization.

Taking into account the economic, financial and political conditions of China and East Asia, regionalization of the RMB should work its way through our neighboring countries to the whole of East Asia. From the view of monetary function, it should evolve into means of exchange, then unit of account and value of storage. Specifically, the regionalization of the RMB should be promoted in the following stages:

Stage 1: China should promote steady progress in the circulation of the RMB in neighboring countries, then create conditions to promote the RMB as a trade settlement currency in transactions between China and neighboring countries and to improve market acceptance of the RMB in transactions between China and neighboring countries. At the same time, China should encourage the establishment of the RMB offshore financial market and the RMB international bond market, and develop offshore RMB-denominated financial products, so that the RMB takes on the role of investment currency within a certain range. If the capital account is not fully liberalized and the RMB is freely convertible, cross-border trade settlement in RMB requires places for offshore business and institutions to carry out RMB trading, investment and hedging, so the establishment of an offshore RMB market is inevitable. Since the beginning of 2010, the RMB offshore market in Hong Kong has made significant progress. In order to further promote the process of RMB internationalization, the Hong Kong RMB offshore market has to strengthen the following two functions in the future: first, improve the liquidity of the RMB by encouraging circulation of the RMB overseas; second, to provide more RMB-denominated financial products to foreign investors and to equip the RMB with the market function of trading and hedging in investment.

Stage 2: On the basis of the aforementioned work, China should promote RMB settlement in general trade with other economies in East Asia, by signing an official settlement agreement between China and neighboring countries, and encouraging the central banks of other East Asian economies to expand the official deal with China's central banks in the RMB, while making full use of currency swap agreements, etc., so that the RMB becomes the official reserve currency of other East Asian economies to some extent, and gradually achieve the convertibility of the RMB in official transactions. On the other hand, China should promote the gradual liberalization of domestic financial markets, relaxation of capital account control and improve the RMB reflow mechanism, so that the RMB can take on the complete functions of an investment currency in a wider range and at a higher level.

Stage 3: If there are gradual changes in domestic economic reform and the international trade model, East Asian economies will spontaneously take the RMB as a kind of "anchor" currency in exchange rate arrangements, and it will then become the major currency in operations on the foreign exchange markets of East Asian economies.

Stage 4: To promote regional monetary cooperation in East Asia, on the one hand, we should make use of regional financing arrangements to increase the attractiveness of the RMB as a reserve currency and intervention currency; on the other hand, achieve the monetary status of the RMB as an "anchor" on the institutionalized level by the gradual promotion of sub-regional cooperation arrangements of exchange rates, with better coordination with the yen, the dollar and other main currencies within the region, and ultimately make the RMB become the dominant currency or one of the region's major currencies.

Stage 5: With the gradual improvement in the status of the RMB in the surrounding areas and East Asia, we should actively promote the acceptance and use of the RMB in the countries along the Belt and Road, and promote the function of the RMB as an international monetary tool along the Belt and Road combined with economic cooperation among the countries along the Belt and Road with the creation of a mutually beneficial partnership.

5.3.1.2 *"Managing the Structural Imbalance" and "Preventing Risk against the Dollar" by Regional Monetary Cooperation*

In today's international monetary system, no currency of any country can challenge the hegemony of the US dollar. The classic cases of the birth of the euro and the failure of the "yen internationalization" show us that monetary regionalization is an important step in internationalization. If a country's currency is involved in international competition, it has to build on the platform of regional economic cooperation and regional institutional monetary cooperation.

There are two starting points for regional monetary cooperation in order to promote the reform of the international monetary system: First, the imbalanced regional monetary cooperation of East Asian countries must be controlled. As mentioned previously, after the Second World War, the international division of labor system has undergone a series of major changes; one of the most prominent changes is the international division of labor patterns between "financial countries" (such as the United States), with comparative advantage in the financial industry, and "trade countries" (such as Japan, China, etc.), with a different comparative advantages in international trade. As a result, on the one hand, more and more serious global economic imbalances have arisen, and the situation has become increasingly severe between the United States and China. Because of this, the adjustment of the imbalance is arduous, while radical adjustment goes against global economic growth. More importantly, this imbalance has little relationship with the current international monetary system, and it is difficult to change the pattern of imbalances in terms of adjustment to the international financial order. On the other hand, since the 1980s, the international division of labor in East Asia has undergone major changes. The Japanese-led "Flying-geese Model" has evolved into an intra-regional product (within the industry) with China's processing and assembly industry as the core or hub. China imports intermediate products from East Asia, and exports the final products to European and American markets after processing, resulting in China's trade surplus to Europe and the

United States offsetting the trade deficit to Japan and other East Asian countries. This division of labor within East Asia makes China the leading force in exports to Europe and the United States, thus trade frictions between China, the representative of Asian countries, and the United States have increased. On the other hand, this situation has greatly strengthened the industrial relations within the East Asia. Therefore, the structural imbalance can not only be managed within the Sino-US relationship but also requires closer cooperation among East Asian countries. To this end, we should strengthen the construction of the China–ASEAN Free Trade Area (FTA), and in particular, we should speed up the negotiations among China, Japan and South Korea free trade zones for its early realization.

Second, "preventing risk against dollar" requires regional monetary cooperation. Since the outbreak of the Asian financial crisis in 1997, East Asian countries have actively carried out and promoted the regional monetary cooperation process on the basis of CMI, and reached a series of achievements. In the face of the global financial crisis in 2008 and the risk of depreciation of the dollar resulting from the crisis, in particular, it is imperative for East Asia to prevent further risk against the dollar through monetary cooperation, leveraging their abundant dollar reserves and a large number of US Treasury bonds. At present, the progress of monetary and financial cooperation among China, South Korea and Japan is relatively smooth under the ASEAN $10 + 3$ framework, with substantial achievements in the rescue and prevention of regional financial crises, cooperation on foreign exchange reserves, bilateral currency swaps and other aspects. The scholars from China and South Korea have begun to explore and research the issues of local currency pricing and settlement in bilateral trade. With further development of the economic and trade ties between China and South Korea, there will be a breakthrough in RMB pricing and settlement problems. As two major powers in the region, China and Japan must aim at the stable and sustainable development of the regional economy and strengthen coordination and cooperation in related fields. For example, to increase the size of bilateral currency swap, to provide useful institutional advice and technical support for the RMB offshore financial center, to increase international financial market transactions among Hong Kong, Shanghai and Tokyo, strengthen bilateral policy coordination on exchange rate and information sharing, to jointly promote the stability of the exchange rate and maintain close exchange of exchange rate policy, to jointly promote the sustained and stable development of the East Asian economy, and to assist the issuance and transaction of international bonds.

According to the characteristics of economic development in East Asia and the progress of monetary and financial cooperation at the current stage, the regional coordination and cooperation on exchange rates will be the major task. The path of regional currency financial cooperation and development can be divided into four stages: crisis relief and prevention, coordination and cooperation on exchange rate policy, establishment of a common exchange rate linkage mechanism and implementation of a single currency (Figure 5.5). Specifically, first, it is imperative to establish a stable and safe system for crisis prevention, to strengthen coordination and communication on exchange rate policy and to maintain the region's stable bilateral exchange rate; second, on the basis of independent pegging, the exchange rate system of the pegged common currency basket, among certain regions, should be established; third, a common currency basket system in East Asia should be established to form a unified exchange rate linkage mechanism; fourth, a unified central bank should be established, thus achieving a single currency. Of course, this will be a rather long and arduous process, and its achievement depends on the joint efforts of the countries within East Asia.

5.3.1.3 *Participation in the Reform of the International Monetary System under the Belt and Road Initiative with G20 as a Platform*

A Silk Road Economic Belt and a 21st-Century Maritime Silk Road, together are now referred to as "The Belt and Road Initiative." The initiative attracted considerable attention from the international community and won a positive response from the countries involved.

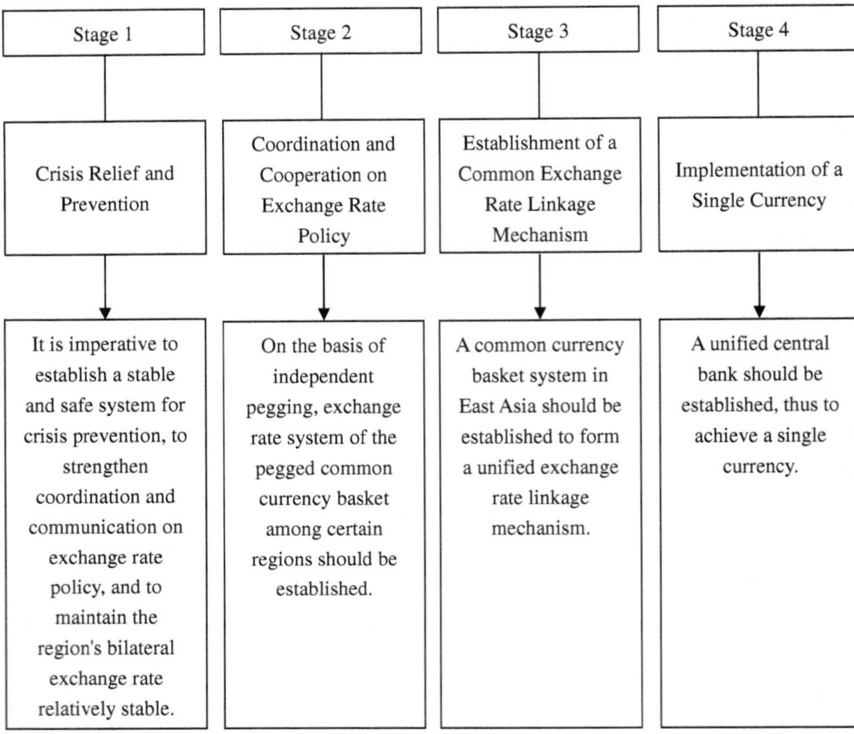

Figure 5.5. The Path Design of the Monetary and Financial Cooperation in East Asia

It integrates the historical symbolism of the ancient Silk Road with the new requirements of today. The initiative is a Chinese program with the goal of maintaining an open world economic system, and achieving diversified, independent, balanced and sustainable development, and also a Chinese initiative intended to advance regional cooperation, strengthen communications between civilizations, and safeguard world peace and stability. It showcases the fact that China, as the largest developing country and the world's second largest economy, shoulders its wider responsibilities in promoting international economic governance toward a fair, just and rational system.

"The Belt and Road" has a profound historical and cultural basis, and at the same time, it has advantages over other global or regional economic cooperation arrangements in terms of political trust, geopolitical strategy and economic complementarities. Whether in cooperation of industries, or in the area of monetary and financial cooperation, China can promote the reform of the international monetary system based on "The Belt and Road" initiative. Compared to other regional arrangements or global multilateral cooperation mechanisms led by the US, it is of great ease to operate and therefore more likely to succeed.

At the same time, "The Belt and Road" is an open economic cooperative initiative without any limitations on its member countries, and it is not an entity or a mechanism. Any country and economy is encouraged to be part of it and become supporters, builders and beneficiaries of "The Belt and Road." The properties of "The Belt and Road Initiative" provide higher flexibility in promoting economic and monetary cooperation, including the cooperation on the reform of the international monetary system. On the one hand, it can satisfy and embody the interests of all parties involved, thus is more in line with the principle of "fairness and justice" of the reform of the international monetary system. On the other hand, any country, including China, can make flexible efforts in monetary cooperation and the international monetary system reform with adjustments to the specific conditions, which are more realistic and feasible.

It is important to note that, on the one hand, "The Belt and Road" is the longest economic corridor in the world, through Central Asia, Southeast Asia, South Asia, West Asia and even some parts of Europe. If we can seek financial cooperation within such a broad range of countries, the joint force on the reform of the international monetary system will be tremendous. On the other hand, it should be noted that China should try to avoid a direct challenge to the core interests of the United States in the reform of the international monetary system, and therefore, we still need to make more use of G20 as an important platform.

First of all, G20 is a mechanism with a function and role for dealing with the financial crisis, which was established shortly after the Asian financial crisis in December 1999. After the 2009 London summit, its role and nature has been significantly improved from a general dialogue to encouraging a global consensus on stimulating the economy, expanding public spending, strengthening financial supervision, increasing IMF capital and other major issues. In particular, during the Pittsburgh meeting, leaders and ministers held in-depth discussions on whether to start the "exit" mechanism or continue to stimulate the economy, and finally after much debate reached a consensus to continue to stimulate the economy, to strengthen the confidence of the world, and to play a major role in the prevention of economic decline.

Second, the G20 is an important future platform for the world's macroeconomic coordination and cooperation. In the context of economic globalization, to prevent economic crises requires the macroeconomic policy cooperation among countries around the world, especially those with major economies. Except for the framework of the United Nations, G20 Finance Ministers and Central Bank Governors Meeting, is the new mechanism to achieve cross-border monitoring, prevention and response adapted to economic globalization. The GDP of the G20 countries accounts for 85% of the world's total and 2/3 of the world's population and impacts of its activities are globally significant.

Finally, the G20 has become an important stage for developing countries to participate in international affairs, especially the reform of the international financial system. While urging the developed countries to share the responsibility, the G20 has also pulled some important developing countries into the core stage of handling international affairs. The G20 is of great significance for the reform of the international monetary system: it not only means the breakthrough of the traditional world economic order but also breeds the seeds of the new international economic order. The three recent G20 meetings have offered a clear direction for the international monetary system reform. China should utilize the G20 platform to participate in the reform of the international monetary system in the future, to seek international coordination and cooperation with an image of "cooperative power," and achieve our own interests through joining forces with other countries.

5.3.1.4 *To Amend the Operating Rules of the International Monetary System by Promoting the Reform of International Financial Organizations*

The normal operation of a modern international monetary system is inseparable from the existence of international financial institutions or organizations. The IMF and the World Bank are undoubtedly the two most important international financial organizations that support the international monetary system after the Second World War. The reform of these two major international financial organizations will help to revise the rules of the operation of the international monetary system and restrict the negative externalities of the US economic policies in order to achieve the goal of "managing the structural imbalance" and "preventing risk against the dollar."

First of all, as an important member of international financial organizations, China should actively participate in the reform, so as to play its due role in the changing international environment.

First, China should actively participate in the reform of IMF's governance structure, call on the IMF to pay close attention to the major changes in the world economic structure, timely make the adjustment of share and voting rights of emerging market economies in the IMF, and increase their representation and voice in the organization.

Second, China should actively participate in strengthening the oversight function of the IMF, such as bilateral policy supervision and risk monitoring, keeping close cooperation with other counties in the G20, FSB, BIS, Basel Committee and other multilateral international institutions, and maintaining independence, authority and fairness in the implementation of the supervision.

Third, China should actively provide financial support to the IMF, by supporting the IMF to activate Substitution Accounts or to buy bonds issued by the IMF (especially bonds priced by SDRs). At the same time, China should provide advice to the IMF on simpler procedures of approval of loans to crisis countries and call for the elimination of the harsh conditions attached to the loans to crisis countries.

Fourth, exchanges and cooperation with the IMF should be increasingly frequent. We should send professionals to the IMF as technical assistance, and especially introduce experience in the policy design or improvement to the developing countries, to enhance the effectiveness of IMF technical assistance.

Next, as an important developing member of the World Bank, China's active participation in the reform of the World Bank is not only conducive to its own economic development, but also contributes to the economic growth of other developing economies.

Specifically, on the one hand, China, as the third largest shareholder of the World Bank, calls for the World Bank's attention to developing countries and adjustment of their shares and has more say due to the changes in the strength of the developing economies in the world economy. On the other hand, China advocates the repositioning of the loan function of the World Bank to enhance its role in stabilizing the international monetary and financial order. Specifically, consideration could be given to enhancing the functions of the World Bank Development Committee to increase its short-term emergency loans to countries undergoing crises and to partially mitigate the pressure placed on those countries, after a financial disaster.

It is of great importance to promote the reform of the two international financial institutions and promote their assistance to the countries facing crises in order to maintain the stability of the international financial order in the context of the current debt crisis in Europe. The stable operation of the euro will help promote the diversification of the international reserve currency, forming a containment of dollar hegemony. In order to solve the debt crisis in Europe, China should support the aid policy of the IMF to countries in crisis. Furthermore, China should purchase bonds issued by the European

Central Bank or the IMF, or provide support indirectly for European countries experiencing a debt crisis.

5.3.2 *Strategic Choice of Participation in the Reform of the International Monetary System on the Non-monetary Level (Basic Conditions)*

In the direct and gradual advance of the reform of the international monetary system, China needs to deepen reform in relevant areas to provide the appropriate basic conditions. Specifically, based on the relationship between the measures and the reform of the international monetary system, reform should be actively promoted both internally and externally. The measures should aim to deepen the reform of the relevant domestic financial fields, to adjust and upgrade the industrial structure, to promote independent innovation and product upgrading, and to promote economic restructuring on the macro level.

5.3.2.1 *Deepen the Reform of the Relevant Domestic Financial Fields*

The development of financial markets and the improvement of the financial system are not only necessary conditions for realizing the RMB internationalization but also a prerequisite for ensuring the smooth capital account liberalization. One of the important reasons that the US dollar has become the dominant currency of the international monetary system is that the United States has a more developed financial market with greater breadth and depth than Europe and Japan. Therefore, to provide conditions for the RMB regionalization and internationalization, we must first vigorously promote the relevant domestic financial reform. Specifically, the following five aspects require promotion and support:

First, we should vigorously promote financial reform, especially the reform of bond markets. China already has a rapidly expanding bond market that serves the needs of the government in two important ways: by financing a growing deficit and by providing long-term financing for much-needed infrastructure projects. Despite the growth in size, the government bond market is still in the very early stage of development. In addition, the corporate bond market remains extremely underdeveloped due to a variety of remaining restrictions. China has realized that there are powerful financial reasons to promote the expansion and deepening of the Chinese bond market. Among the most important are, first, that bonds would be desirable additions to the portfolios of Chinese insurance companies, banks, pension funds and the country's social security fund, and second, that bonds are preferred investments for international investors. The bond market is also where China's growing business sector could raise long-term capital for expansion. A fully functioning bond market would also provide liquidity to China's rapidly expanding economy. The features show that institutional investors who have relatively strong capability in identifying and undertaking market risks are ideal investors for corporate bonds. Therefore, efforts should be made to cultivate institutional investors including insurance companies, commercial banks, pension fund and investment fund companies to increase market liquidity and reduce market risks. Individual investors may indirectly invest in corporate bonds through collective investment instruments such as investment-insurance and fund products, etc. China should improve its credit rating system for corporate bonds and cultivate credit rating institutions. According to advanced international experience, a credit rating system with public credibility is the foundation for corporate bond market development, because credit ratings could provide important information for investors to make investment decisions.

The underdevelopment of direct financing was evident in the limited access to credit and low capability of the enterprises to directly raise funds in the market, which has resulted in a low proportion of direct financing in the economy. On the one hand, a great amount of idle funds lacks direct investment channels, and investors cannot make undistorted investment decisions according to their own risk preferences. On the other hand, enterprises cannot locate favorable strategies to lower the cost of financing and adjust the scale and structure of production according to the demand and supply of products and funds in the market. Steadily promoting the development of direct financing will provide incentives to market participants and enhance the efficiency of resource allocation.

In addition to the RMB internationalization and China-led regional monetary and financial cooperation, the development of financial markets, especially the bond market, will also improve the status and role of China's financial markets and the entire financial sector in global financial markets. China will have more say in the global financial system and the development of financial rules, which is the foundation of China's active involvement in the reform of the international monetary system.

Second, we should deepen the reform of financial sectors and promote interest rate liberalization. Interest rate liberalization can provide many benefits. By allowing for the better pricing of capital and risk, liberalization improves the allocation and efficiency of investment. A larger share of intermediation would be undertaken by more efficient banks and those better at assessing risk. More credit would also flow to sectors previously underserved. The range of financial products should also expand, allowing firms and households to better manage risk, and providing them with portfolio diversification opportunities. However, if attempted prematurely, interest rate liberalization may also expose weaknesses in the financial sector, inhibiting intermediation and creating economic volatility. China has already made substantial progress in liberalizing its financial markets, and its interest rates in particular. After years of reform, however, there still remains a floor on bank lending rates and a ceiling on deposit rates. The deposit rate ceiling, in particular, appears to bind, as deposit rates have remained clustered at their benchmark, and real deposit rates have on average been zero. As direct controls over interest rates and credit quantity are replaced by indirect controls, countries have benefited from strengthening their indirect policy tools. China has also made major advances in deepening its money markets, and removing the interest rate restrictions will catalyze further development of these markets. Nonetheless, there is a need to strengthen indirect monetary policy instruments, as the use of direct interest rate and credit controls becomes less effective after liberalization, especially as markets and new products develop.

Interest rate liberalization enhances the effectiveness of indirect monetary policy and interest rates as price signals. Although banks would like to respond to a higher interbank rate by attracting additional deposits, they cannot do this when the deposit rate is capped, and so the cost of funds, and ultimately the lending rate, is lower. The larger change in interest rates means, however, that the central bank will need to undertake larger intervention in the money market to achieve its target when the deposit rate is free. Consequently, quantity based monetary policy remains more effective in the regulated environment when deposits are unresponsive. Conversely, the impact of indirect monetary policy is greater when policy is loosened, either through a lower target IB rate or lower reserve requirement, if the deposit rate is able to fall. Macroeconomic and structural imbalances present important challenges. Inadequate regulatory and supervisory frameworks and poor governance in banks also have exacerbated problems in virtually all the aforementioned cases covered. The ideal time to remove a constraint is when the constraint is less binding. Interest rates have become considerably more flexible, with the ceiling on deposit interest rates the most prominent remaining restriction. Some recent steps include the expansion of the floating range of deposit and lending rates in mid-2012, and eliminating the floor on lending rates in July 2013. On 7 June 2012, the People's Bank of China (PBC) expanded the deposit and loan floating interest rate for the first time. While the development of non-traditional finance marks resulted in a shift to more market-based intermediation, the migration of activity to less regulated parts of the system poses risks to financial stability.

Concerning the increased competition in the financial industry, we must focus on the following aspects, on the basis of the pilot programs in Wenzhou and other places:

First is the deepening reform of the banking industry as the core of the financial sector. Proper regulation and supervision are the most important factors in the success or failure of interest rate liberalization. All banking crises after interest rate liberalization could be traced back to inadequate supervision or regulations not keeping up with the changing financial landscape. Removing interest rate constraints has led to more competition in almost all cases; but this competition became destructive rather than constructive when banks were allowed to enter overly risky businesses and support excess demand in the economy.

Next is the launch of the pilot programs developed by establishing private banks. The China Banking Regulatory Commission (CBRC) adheres to the principle of fairness and equal treatment to all forms of capital, including private capital, in their investment in the banking sector. There are no additional legal or regulatory barriers or preconditions inhibiting the flow of private capital into banking institutions. In terms of market entry, private capital flows to the banking sector result from participating in new entities establishment, new shares subscription, equity purchase, and mergers and acquisitions.

Finally, we will further improve the corporate governance of financial institutions, improve their business model and profit structure, optimize the capital restraint mechanism, strengthen the risk management and improve the quality of credit assets.

Third, China is well advanced in establishing the macroeconomic preconditions for capital account liberalization. Both the budget deficit and government debt are moderate in relation to GDP and inflationary pressures have been contained. The large current account and balance of payments surpluses have generated strains on domestic monetary policy and upward pressures on the exchange rate, but they are better addressed through greater exchange rate flexibility than through capital controls. External debt is moderate and the exceptionally large foreign exchange reserves provide a considerable cushion against even large sudden capital outflows. China's capital controls seem to have been effective enough to avoid major losses by domestic financial institutions and major businesses from unauthorized foreign currency transactions. The control regime has also given monetary authorities significant latitude to vary domestic interest rates independently of those abroad despite limited exchange rate flexibility.[8] The most important constraints on the pace of China's capital account liberalization are the incentives and capabilities of domestic financial institutions and non-financial businesses to prudently manage the risks of cross-border transactions and the ability of supervisory authorities to monitor external exposures sufficiently to contain systemic risk.[9]

First of all, China should continue to expand the breadth and depth of the foreign exchange market, enrich the foreign exchange market products, improve the trading mechanism and infrastructure construction of the foreign exchange market and promote the foreign exchange market opening to the world. This is the basis for financial liberalization and the convertibility of RMB in capital accounts.

Next, the international status of the RMB improved steadily as the RMB business in cross-border trade, investment and financing was in full swing, and the bilateral currency cooperation deepened.

Consideration should be given to accelerating capital account liberalization, especially with respect to controls on portfolio inflows. The rapid development of the Qualified Domestic Institutional Investor (QDII) program is a good step in this direction. The Qualified Foreign Institutional Investor (QFII) program could be expanded further in the near term, and restrictions on repatriation, investment options and the differential treatment of institutions eliminated or at least substantially relaxed with little if any cost to other objectives. Nevertheless, more rapid capital account liberalization would bring tangible benefits and could be achieved without serious risk to financial or macroeconomic stability. It would foster development of the foreign exchange market and make it easier to increase the flexibility of the exchange rate. Reduction in the extent of capital controls

---

[8] Yu, Yongding, "Reform of the International Monetary System and Preservation of China's Foreign Exchange Reserve Assets," *International Economic Review* 5–6 (2009).

[9] Xu, Jianwei and Yang Yao, "New International Division of Labor, Development of Financial Markets and Global Imbalances," *World Economy* 3 (2010).

would reduce incentives for evasion, helping reduce misreporting and potentially improving the ability of the authorities to enforce remaining limits and to monitor the exposure of the domestic economy to foreign exchange and other external risks. The QFII program could be expanded considerably by increasing the overall quota to as much as twice the present level. The current restrictions on repatriation and the discrimination among types of investors could also be ended without serious risk. Such steps could significantly improve the institutional investor support for capital market development and should not add more than modestly to the already large capital inflows China is now experiencing. QFII has been developing in China for 14 years, during when the RQFII, the Shanghai–Hong Kong Stock Connect Program, and the Shanghai–London Stock Connect Program further broadened the avenue for foreign capital to invest in the Chinese Security Market. As the FTA Financial Reform Program emerges, the RMB (CNY) Capital Project is likely to make the currency exchangeable. With the success in QFII, the RQFII and the Shanghai–Hong Kong Stock Connect Program, China's long-term advantage in interest rates, and the relatively low stock index value after the recent stock market crashes in mid-2015 and early 2016, foreign capitals' demand for the Chinese market to loosen its restrictions continually increases.

We should strengthen the statistical monitoring of cross-border capital flow, making it more timely, scientific and accurate. The emergency plan management should be further improved and the reserve of policy tools should be enriched. We could optimize the means of monitoring, strengthening the system data integration and information sharing, and establish the statistical monitoring system of cross-border capital flow, which provide technical support for the statistical monitoring and the foreign exchange inspection. The governments could severely crack down on the illegal activities which violate the rules of foreign exchange administration, and intensify the punishment on illegal activity such as the false transit trade and the illegal forward settlement of exchange.

It is noteworthy that, since the end of 2013, capital account liberalization has made significant progress in quantitative easing and system design, mainly in the following aspects.

First of all, the financial reform of the FTA and the construction of Shanghai's International Financial Center (IFC) created an opportunity for our country to transition from indirect foreign investments to direct foreign investments. The financial reform of the FTA, the convertibility of capital accounts under the FT account, the further liberalization of exchange rate and interest rate, and the construction of international financial assets trading platform of the FTA indicate that the current transition from indirect account opening to direct account opening is under a favorable time window. But before the opening the regulator should still pay attention to the orderly openings of the financial markets and the entry bars. However, China's current capital account is still not fully convertible, while exchange rate and interest rate liberalization has not yet been fully realized. Therefore, in the capital market globalization process, we must give full credit to the advantages of FTA's financial policies, and use the FTA trading platform as the channel to open up exchanges and overseas funds, and take the lead in opening accounts directly. To implement the general requirements of the Party Central Committee and the State Council on constructing China (Shanghai) Pilot Free Trade Zone, the PBC, together with the CBRC, the China Securities Regulatory Commission (CSRC) and the China Insurance Regulatory Commission (CIRC), has issued more than 10 policies and implementation rules and 51 proposals to support FTZ construction since 2013, thereby establishing the overall policy framework of FTZ financial reform. At present, with a number of innovative financial policies introduced for FTZ and risks controlled strictly, financial reform progressed smoothly, which effectively promoted real economic development and facilitated trade and investment. Firstly, capital account convertibility was promoted in an orderly manner as a response to the urgent demand of real economic development, and meanwhile, necessary macro-prudential supervision continued to be imposed on convertible accounts. Secondly, under the prerequisite of a basically stable interest rate level and deposit market, the interest rate ceiling was removed on small-value foreign currency deposits in the FTZ. Meanwhile, the interest rate monitoring and management mechanism was set up, and the Self-discipline Committee on Interest Rate Market was established, thereby leaving the market discipline mechanism to play an important role in the interest rate reform. Thirdly, work was done to deepen the reform of the foreign exchange management system, and to facilitate trade and investment.

Next, the connecting mechanism for trading in both the Shanghai and Hong Kong stock exchanges (Shanghai–Hong Kong Stock Connect) was officially launched, which would enable investors from both sides to trade through local securities companies (or brokers) the designated equity securities listed in each other's market with the RMB. The PBC and the CSRC published the Notice on Issues Concerning the Pilot Program of Shanghai–Hong Kong Stock Connect, spelling out stipulations on cross-border RMB flows in the pilot program. The pilot program adopts two-way cross-border investment mechanisms, under which domestic investors can make investments in overseas securities markets and overseas investors can invest in domestic securities markets. Since through the pilot program, funds shall be settled based on net offset balance, the amount of cross-border capital flows are far less than the amount of securities transactions; thus, reducing the scale of cross-border capital and stabilizing cross-border capital flows. Conforming to the international development trend of capital markets, the launch of the pilot program will help expand the two-way opening-up of China's capital market and promote its steady and healthy development. Meanwhile, it will help promote RMB capital account convertibility and the internationalization of RMB, cement Hong Kong as the IFC and promote the stable development of Hong Kong's financial market.[10]

Finally, the pilot reform was actively pushed forward by the State Administration of Foreign Exchange (SAFE) to accelerate the capital

---

[10]Xu, Jianwei and Yang Yao, "New International Division of Labor, Development of Financial Markets and Global Imbalances." *World Economy* 3 (2010): 3–30.

account convertibility. First, SAFE popularized the pilot program of multinational corporations' centralized operation of foreign exchange fund around the country, which realized the centralized receiving and payment, net settlement and sharing of external debt and overseas loans quota. Second, SAFE conducted the pilot program of voluntary settlement of foreign currency fund, which greatly simplified the settlement procedures of foreign currency fund and allowed enterprises to arrange the timing of exchange settlement according to their own need. Third, SAFE reformed the foreign exchange administration mechanism of cross-border investment and financing. It substantially simplified the foreign exchange administration concerning round-trip investment, cancelled all the prior approval procedures for the cross-border guarantee, unified the policy of credit secured by external guarantee for enterprises both at home and abroad, loosened the management of the upfront fee for the overseas direct investment, facilitated the overseas lending of domestic enterprises and enhanced the facilitation of cross-border investment and financing. The RQFII quota management was simplified and operation of relevant investment was facilitated.

Fourth, better coordination among regulators to guard against systemic financial risks and more policies improving the financial sector's efficiency to serve the real economy can be expected in the process of RMB internationalization, international cooperation in the financial sector and domestic financial development. The financial industry's expansion, coupled with credit easing to bolster growth, has led to rising systemic risks, capital speculation and a surge of shadow banking. The central bank will play a bigger role of containing financial risks. Its coordination with the three regulators of banking, securities and insurance will also be strengthened. Developing direct financing will be prioritized while the indirect financing structure should be optimized by accelerating strategic transformation of state-owned major banks and developing small and medium-sized banks and private financial institutions. Guarding against systemic financial risks is the eternal theme of financial work and the government should make a stronger effort to monitor, warn against and deal with risks in a timely manner. China should accelerate developing laws and regulations governing the financial sector, improve macro prudential management and emphasize functional as well as behavioral regulation. China should deepen financial reforms, including improving financial regulation coordination and shoring up weak links in supervision. We will strengthen the system of macro-prudential regulation for the financial sector, step up planning and coordination, reform and improvement the financial regulatory framework to see that it is better adapted to developments in modern financial markets, clarity regulatory function and responsibilities for guarding against and treating risks, and establish a financial management system that coordinates monetary policy and prudential regulation. China should also increase efforts to improve the legal framework, credit mechanisms and talent development for the financial sector, to help the Chinese economy expand steadily.

Fifth, the off-shore RMB markets maintained steady and sound development. The RMB has become a unit of account used in economic statistics, accounting and management related to foreign trade, cross-border investment and balance of payments, playing a bigger role in servicing the real economy. On 30 November 2015, the IMF decided to include the RMB in the basket of SDR reserve currencies, marking a milestone in the process of the RMB internationalization. This signified the international community's recognition of China's economic development as well as the reform and opening up achievements, especially of the RMB internationalization. The inclusion of the RMB in the SDR will bolster foreign investors' confidence in the RMB and boost their willingness to hold RMB assets as the domestic financial market continues to liberalize and RMB financial products on the international financial market continue to enrich. China will continue to deepen financial reforms toward the established objective, enhancing the openness of financial markets including bond market and stock market, supporting the healthy development of the offshore RMB market, further improving the convertibility and free use of the RMB and steadily promoting the convertibility of the RMB under capital account.

5.3.2.2 *Adjust and Upgrade the Industrial Structure*

To a certain extent, the current international monetary system is one of the necessary conditions for preventing the global economic imbalances. The "dollar system" embodies the relative comparative advantage of the United States and other countries in the international division of labor. The United States has a comparative advantage in financial sectors over the rest of the country (mainly in East Asia), while trade surplus countries have a comparative advantage in manufacturing. Therefore, if China wants to seek its own international status in the future reform of the international monetary system, it is necessary to adjust and upgrade the domestic industrial structure in order to take a more favorable position in the international division of labor. In addition, to achieving the regionalization of the RMB, China should replace the United States as the final product market of East Asia, which also requires China to adjust and upgrade its industrial structure.

At present, China has entered the middle stage of industrialization — there are controversial views on the direction of upgrading the future industrial structure in China[11]: First, the upgrading of industrial structure must rely on promoting the development of services; second, the direction of adjustment of the industrial structure should be based on the heavy chemical industry; third, in the process of industrialization, China should not emphasize the increased proportion of service industry in the national economy, as the major task is the development of the heavy chemical industry and traditional manufacturing industry. According to the actual development stage of China's economy and the constraints of resources and environment, the future direction and development goal of China's industrial structure should be to give high priority to developing production-oriented service industries, and carry out pilot and demonstration projects to

[11]He, Dexu and Zhanqi Yao, "The Effect of China's Industrial Restructuring, Optimization and Upgrading Goals, and Policy Measures," *China Industrial Economy* 5 (2008): 46–56.

advance the comprehensive reform of the service industry. We will integrate the development of cultural and creative industries as well as design services with related industries, and speed up the development of insurance, business, and science and technology services. We should speed up the creation of a new growth model and ensure that development is based on improved quality and performance. We should fire all types of market participants with new vigor for development, increase motivation for pursuing innovation-driven development, establish a new system for developing modern industries and create new favorable conditions for developing the open economy. This will ensure that economic development is driven more by domestic demand, especially consumer demand, by a modern service industry and strategic emerging industries, by scientific and technological progress, by a workforce of higher quality and innovation in management, by resource conservation and a circular economy, and by coordinated and mutually reinforcing urban–rural development and development between regions. Specifically, in order to achieve this goal, the following six measures should be implemented:

First, we should speed up making agricultural adjustments and improvements, raise our production capacity for agricultural products while also improving quality and safety, and see that a better structured, more effective supply of agricultural products takes shape. With the aim of raising agricultural productivity, we should improve systems for promoting innovation in and the application of modern agricultural science and technology, accelerate agricultural modernization, strengthen the integration of information technology into agriculture and develop intelligent agriculture. With an emphasis on strengthening the innovative capacity and basic capabilities of manufacturing, we will work to deepen the integration of information technology and manufacturing technology and promote the development of high-end, smart, green and service-orientated manufacturing so as to foster a new competitive edge in manufacturing. China's industrial layout is at a disadvantage in the international division of labor, so we can reposition China's status to the two ends of the "smile curve."

Second, we should accelerate the development of modern services, further open them to foreign competition, and improve their development environment, so as to help producer services move both toward specialization and higher up the value chain, and help consumer service become more refined, with increased quality. We will bring China's producer service standards more in line with international standards so as to increase their international competitiveness. In fostering new areas of economic growth, we will spur innovation and industrial application in emerging and cutting-edge fields.

Third, we should promote the development of strategic emerging industries. By targeting cutting-edge technologies, and optimizing the integration of policies, we will create space for the growth of emerging industries and see that they gain a competitive advantage in the future. We will support the development of next generation information technology, new-energy vehicles, biotechnology, green and low-carbon technology, and digital creative industries. The development of strategic emerging industries is the key to a new round of industrial and technological revolution. It is an important support for promoting the adjustment and upgrading of industrial structure and realization of low-carbon, green and intelligent industrial development. It is also an important support for China to change from "Produced in China" to "Created in China."

Fourth, the government's direct involvement in resource allocation and its direct interference in microeconomic activities should be reduced, so that the market plays a positive role in industrial restructuring and upgrading. The government should continue to streamline administration and delegate more powers, improve regulations, and provide services, so as to refine government performance and stimulate market vitality and social creativity. The development of a unified and open market system that ensures orderly competition, establishes a mechanism for ensuring fair competition, overcomes regional segmentation, breaks up industry monopolies and removes market barriers in order to promote the free and orderly flow and equitable exchange of goods and factors of production, must be a priority. We should reduce government intervention in pricing, and lift all pricing controls over goods and services in competitive industries. We will refine policies to promote competition, improve market competition regulations and implement a review system for fair competition. We should ensure that all parties have equal access to factors of production, participate in market competition on an equal footing. Based on the comparative advantages, we should press ahead with the coordinated development of different regions to avoid the low-level competition in the same industry.

Fifth, deepening reform is crucial for accelerating the change of the growth model. The underlying issue we face in economic structural reform is how to strike a balance between the role of the government and that of the market, and we should follow more closely the rules of the market and better play the role of the government. To address obstructions holding back development caused by certain systems and mechanisms, we should comprehensively deepen reform, invigorating the market to offset downward economic pressure. We should tackle many tough issues in industrial restructuring and carry out structural reforms in the economic, political, cultural, societal and ecological sectors.

We should formulate and implement a coordinated plan for deepening the reform of the fiscal and tax systems, the cultural sector, the management of social organizations, income distribution system, the policies for encouraging the flow of researchers and engineers and the systems for assessing their achievements. We will implement and improve preferential policies, such as extra tax deductions for research and development costs and policies that support new and high-technology enterprises, so as to encourage enterprises to increase their spending on innovation. Thus, the technological progress of enterprises will realize the industrial restructuring and upgrading.

Sixth, we will cultivate large-scale industrial capital groups by the optimization and reorganization of cross-regional elements. The experience of industrialization in the world proves that the rational allocation of space in the industry and the rational division of labor in the regional economy are mainly driven by the large-scale industrial capital groups rather than the government, but when government promotes the establishment of cross-regional large-scale industrial capital groups, it should also eliminate restrictions on cross-regional production, sales, procurement, personnel mobility, investment and others, creating a favorable policy and the legal environment for enterprises to reorganize the cross-regional factors.

5.3.2.3 *To Promote Industrial Restructuring and Product Upgrading*

In order to change China's position in the international division of labor, it is necessary to promote industrial restructuring and upgrading by promoting independent innovation and product upgrading. In particular, it is necessary to vigorously develop high and new technology industries and improve the independent R&D and innovation capabilities of enterprises in the microeconomic field. The 17th CPC National Congress promoted the strategy of "building an innovative nation," which explicitly put forward: "To speed up the establishment of a technological innovation system that takes enterprises as the main body, markets as the orientation, integrates production, education and research, supports the gathering of innovative elements to the enterprises and promotes the transformation of scientific and technological achievements into real productive forces."

To enhance China's competitiveness in the international market and to promote the steady and rapid development of China's economy, we must recognize that "innovation" is the only way for the development of Chinese enterprises.

Specifically, China should take positive policy measures from the following four aspects:

First, the capability of industrialization on independent innovation achievements of enterprises should be cultivated, a technological innovation system that takes enterprises as the main body, the market as the guide, and combines production, education and research should be established, the special project of industrialization of independent innovation achievements should be launched, and the government should earnestly implement tax support policies for the industrialization of promoting the achievements of independent innovation.

Second, the transfer of independent innovation achievements should be vigorously promoted. First of all, improve the releasing mechanism for independent innovation achievements; then, universities and research institutes should be encouraged to transfer independent innovation achievements to enterprises; next, researchers should be encouraged to carry out industrialization activities of independent innovation achievements.

Third, investing and financing support in industrialization of independent innovation should be increased. First of all, government should provide more support in the investment; then, the development of venture capital investment should be accelerated; next, the credit support of commercial banks and other financial institutions should be strengthened.

Fourth, a favorable environment conducive to the industrialization of independent innovation should be created. First of all, the transformation of the achievement of independent innovation into technical standards should be actively promoted; next, the market environment for the industrialization of independent innovation achievements should be accelerated; third, the service system for the industrialization of independent innovation should be established and improved.

5.3.2.4 *To Promote Economic Restructuring from a Macro Level and Create Conditions for the Reform of the International Monetary System*

In addition to the aforementioned specific conditions, China needs to create favorable conditions for the reform of the international monetary system at the macroeconomic level. This not only requires that China maintain a stable, rapid and sustainable economic growth but also the structural adjustment and reform at the macroeconomic level. We find that one of the very important reasons why the US dollar can be settled in East Asia is that the United States has played the role of market provider in East Asia. Therefore, to achieve regionalization of the RMB, China should be capable of replacing the United States, and gradually become the provider of final product markets in East Asia. This will involve the adjustment of China's trade structure, consumption structure and even economic structure and economic development model.

First, from the comparison of the trade structure between China and the United States, the analysis shows that the trade structure of the United States has been very stable: exports are dominated by processed products and parts, while imports are dominated by consumer goods; while China's trade structure is the same as previously analyzed: it is exactly the opposite of the United States. To a certain extent, it reflects that the huge trade surplus between China and the United States is a structural trade surplus. If we focus on the import of final products, we can see that China's imports of consumer goods accounted for only 4.5% (2007), which is roughly equivalent to 1/7 of the same category of the United States, and the gap is very clear. This trade structure of China is not conducive to providing markets for East Asian countries' final product exports. Therefore, it is necessary for China to adjust its own trade structure, change the mode of producing at the low-end of value chains and processing trade, and gradually shift to the trade mode of exporting intermediate products and importing final products, which requires China to make major adjustments to its economic structure.

Second, by comparing the consumption patterns of China, Japan and the United States, we can find out that the consumption rate in China is significantly lower than that in Japan and the United States. This is mainly reflected in the low level of household consumption. Therefore, in order to expand domestic demand, the consumption level and consumption of residents must be increased in the future. The dual economic structure in China has caused a huge disparity in disposable income per capita between urban and rural residents, and this gap has had the tendency of increasing since the 1990s. In 2006, the per capita consumption of rural residents was lower than 1/3 of the per capita consumption level of urban residents. Taking a closer look at the composition of China's consumer expenditure, it can be seen that the proportion of government consumer spending in final consumer spending has remained almost unchanged, while the proportion of urban and rural household consumer spending has shown a significant increase and a sharp decline since 1990, and the gap gradually widens. Obviously, this kind of domestic demand structure in China will seriously impede the growth of imports of consumer goods, and due to various institutional problems, the process of changing this structure will be very long. To some extent, it explains why the internationalization of RMB will be a long-term process.

At the macroeconomic level, China must make corresponding reforms and adjustments in the following three aspects: First, it is necessary to adjust the economic structure on the premise of maintaining sustained and stable economic development, and then gradually change the structure and pattern of trade, to achieve the mode of the export of intermediate products and imported end products; the second is to narrow the gap between urban and rural areas, regional disparities while the national income keep increasing. In particular, it should focus on making major or fundamental changes to agricultural policies and land systems. The reforms, at the same time, should also increase the national propensity to consume and expand domestic demand by reducing the monopoly of state-owned enterprises on the tertiary industry and reform the current social security system; third, gradually reduce China's foreign trade dependence and increase the contribution of domestic demand (final consumption) to GDP, thus change from external demand-led economic growth to domestic demand-led economic growth.

Mainly based on the analysis of China's actual international economic status, opportunities and challenges it faces, this chapter proposes the overall thinking and specific strategic options for China to actively participate in the reform of the international monetary system.

In view of the strong hard power and soft power of the United States, especially the fact that the United States has the most developed financial market in the world, the dollar's position as the dominant currency of the international currency system will not change in the short term. The "dollar standard system" has been in place for quite a long time, and it will continue to exist. Therefore, China does not have the ability to directly challenge the United States or the current international monetary system at this stage. The reform of the international monetary system will be a gradual and long-term process.

China's rational position in this process is a positive advocate rather than a leader. However, as a rising power, China needs to develop a reasonable currency strategy in the future international political and economic order. It is necessary to formulate a reasonable currency strategy, that is, to seize the opportunity to actively adjust its own strategy for an international financial system and strive to actively promote the reform of the international monetary system at the following two levels: at the monetary level, we implement our own international financial strategy from three perspectives, namely, through the internationalization of the RMB, regional currency cooperation, and actively promoting the "Belt and Road" monetary cooperation. We should actively participate in the G20 platform to promote the reform of the international currency system. At the non-monetary level, the internal and external reforms are implemented in accordance with the various measures and the reform of the international monetary system. In other words, reforms and upgrading of the domestic financial sector, industrial structure and enterprises are implemented. At the macro level, technological innovation and product upgrading, and economic transformation should be promoted, which will create the basic conditions for China to actively participate in the reform of the international monetary system.

Chapter 6

Steady Progress of the Internationalization of RMB

6.1 Theoretical Research on Currency Internationalization

6.1.1 *The Connotation of Currency Internationalization*

With regard to currency internationalization, researchers have given many different definitions. Xu and Liu explained the meaning of currency internationalization from the narrow and broad perspectives in a dynamic outlook: from the narrow perspective, currency internationalization refers to the expansion of some or all functions of a country's currency from domestic to foreign, so that its scope of usage can expand to the surrounding countries, a certain region and even the whole world, and it can finally turn into a common currency in the region and in the world; while in a broad sense, the internationalization of money breaks through the superficial phenomenon of the expansion of monetary functions, involving international capital credit and international investment, measured by the currency. That is, the dynamic process of money as a capital for profit expansion from the original applicable area to larger areas.[1]

[1]Xu, Qiyuan and Lizhen Liu, *The Study on the Changes in the Exchange Rate of RMB in the Process of Internationalization*. Beijing: Chinese Financial Press, 2009.

Zhou and Wen conducted a narrow and broad analysis of the meaning of currency internationalization from a static perspective: narrow meaning of internationalization of money refers to the use of currency issued by third countries. The term refers to the situation in which a country's currency plays the three functions of value scale, transaction medium and value storage outside the country.[2] The difference between these two definitions lies in the expansion of functions.

We believe that currency internationalization refers to the intensified dynamic process (stage) of a country's currency after it develops into an international currency or becomes an international currency, and the relative steady state formed by these dynamic stages. The internationalization of money is essentially a process that demonstrates the nature of competition among various currencies in different stages. The international currency is a state or result of the internationalization of money. It refers to the geographical scope and functional breadth of a country's currency circulating outside its issuing country. It also shows the international status of a country's currency at a certain point of time. At present, the currencies of many developed countries have achieved a certain degree of internationalization, and the degree of internationalization of various currencies has a relatively distinct level of characteristics. For example, the US dollar is the most important international currency widely used in pricing and official reserves worldwide. The euro, the yen and the pound are second. Other currencies such as the Swiss franc, the Canadian dollar and the Australian dollar only play the partial function of internationalized currencies in certain regions.[3] It can be concluded that the essence of currency internationalization is the internationalization of monetary functions.

The international function of a country's currency is an extension of its domestic functions. The external functions of a country's

[2]Zhou, Lin and Xiaozheng Wen, *The Currency Internationalization.* Shanghai: Shanghai University of Finance and Economics Press, 2001.

[3]Xu, Liang, "The Study on the Problem of RMB Internationalization," The doctoral dissertation of East China Normal University, 2009.

Table 6.1. Functions of International Currency

International Monetary Function	Private Sector	Government Department
Accounting unit	Valuation currency (denominated currency in trade and financial transactions)	Pegging currency (indicating exchange rate relationships and anchors as other currencies)
Trading medium, payment method	Tool currency (settlement currency for international trade and financial transactions)	Intervention currency (currency of foreign exchange intervention and currency for official international settlement)
Value storage	Wealth storage currency (currency substitution and foreign exchange asset currency)	Reserve currency (International Reserve of the Monetary Authority)

Source: Organized by Hartmann (1998) from Cohen (1971).
Hartmann P. "Do reuters spreads reflect currencies differences in global trading activity?" 17, no. 5, 1998: 0–784.
Cohen, Benjamin J., *Future of Sterling as an International Currency*. London: St. Martins Press, 1971.

currency are mainly reflected in several aspects: as a unit of account, a medium of exchange and means of payment, and a value storage currency. These functions can be divided into two sectors: the private sector and the official sector. International currencies are commonly used in the official sector as pegging currencies, intervening currencies and reserve currencies; in the private sector, they are used as denominated currencies, instrumental currencies and wealth storage currencies. The specific functions can be divided as shown in Table 6.1.

The functions of the international currency can be separated both vertically and horizontally. At the gold standard stage, the pound and gold were recognized in the private and official sectors, respectively. In the mid-1970s, currencies in many European countries were pegged to each other, and the dollar was used as an intervention and reserve currency. In some countries in the Gulf region, there is a phenomenon in which the functions of international currency pricing and trading media are separated. In the oil trade of these countries, the dollar is used as the currency of the valuation, but the pound is used as the payment currency. Under normal circumstances, considering the size of transaction costs, the number of international currencies used as trading media functions is decreasing. On the contrary, from the perspective of diversifying risks, the emergence of international currencies as value storage functions is more and more diversified. Historical experience tells us that it is often difficult for a single currency to enjoy all the functions of an international currency. Only a few major international currencies can play the multiple functions and regional competitive advantages, thus forming a relatively stable diversified international currency framework. Therefore, RMB can perform some functions of the international currency by expanding its international usage. One issue that needs special attention in this process is that sharing, not replacing the function of the incumbent international currency, which is a reasonable policy orientation for the internationalization of the RMB.

There is still an inherent mutual reinforcement mechanism among the three functions of the international currency. One of the three functions may predominate, and help other functions to be more fully utilized while reducing the associated costs of other functions. On the contrary, if one or several functions are in a weak state, it will inevitably have a greater negative impact on the internationalization process of the currency. In an official authority, if a country pegs its currency to another country's currency, the country prefers to use the currency as a foreign exchange reserve currency and use it as an intervention currency for the foreign exchange market. In the real world, the German mark and the Japanese yen are typical examples: because the German mark is in a weak position as a trading medium currency, its internationalization process is slow. The internationalization of the yen is partly hindered by the weakness of the yen as a function of pricing in international trade.

6.1.2 *Theoretical Analysis of the Influencing Factors of Currency Internationalization*

In the process of currency internationalization, what are the major functional factors and how these functions play a major role has always been the focus of the scholars. The traditional literature mainly depends on the economic scale of the currency issuer and the importance of the currency issuer in international trade, the level of financial development, the credibility of the currency, the stability of the currency, and the network externalities of currency use. The influence of currency internationalization was analyzed and a theoretical system with certain reference significance was formed.

6.1.2.1 *Analysis on Search Monetary Models*

The Search Monetary Models Monetary Models[4] were first proposed by Kiyotaki and Wright in the paper "On Money as a Medium of Exchange." They explored the motives and values of currency emergence, and an important premise that was followed in the process of theoretical analysis was the indivisibility of commodities and currencies. By the analysis, the result of the currency competition choice is that there is an equilibrium solution, that is, the money can be generated endogenously in the individual's transaction selection activities, and it also proves the value of the existence of legal currency. However, the currency search model at this time only discusses the emergence of currency in a relatively closed economic environment, and does not analyze the generation of international currency.[5]

Matsuyama *et al.* first used a currency search model to systematically analyze the generation of international currency. They mainly introduced the process of stochastic matching and related principles

---

[4]The Search Monetary Models mainly for the early to discuss the issue of unemployment and price; Kiyotaki and Wright (1989) for the first time through the establishment of a search model to analyze the behavior of individual trading decisions and characterize its transaction search process, this model is called monetary search model.

[5]Kiyotaki, Nobuhiro and Randall Wright, "A Search-theoretic Approach to Monetary Economics," *The American Economic Review* (1993): 63–77.

into theoretical research. By constructing a "two countries and two currencies" model, they analyzed the mechanism of mutual competition between two countries in the world. When certain conditions are met, sovereign currency can be used abroad beyond the borders.[6] Matsuyama *et al.* extended the models of Kiyotaki and Wright from two aspects: first, they mainly analyzed the competition process between sovereign currencies, not between commodity currencies, or between commodity currencies and fiat currencies, and assume that no other than the producer will store the raw product. Second, Kiyotaki and Wright established the premise for theoretical analysis: the process of random matching was assumed to be uniform, that is, the matching between the two sides of the transaction is symmetric with any other pair of individuals.[7] The study by Matsuyama *et al.* divides individuals into two types: domestic groups and foreign groups. It is also assumed that the probability of random matching between individuals in the same group is greater than the probability of random matching among different groups of individuals. Therefore, this assumption is closer to the reality, and the theoretical analysis based on this assumption is more credible.[8]

The model of Matsuyama *et al.* takes the size of the economic participants and the degree of economic integration in the two countries as the main parameters (Table 6.2). The values in the table represent the probability that different types of individuals will match each other. Among them,$n$is the number of economic participants in the country, $1 - n$ is the number of foreign economic participants, β can be seen as the level of economic integration between the two countries.

[6]Matsuyama, Kiminori, Nobuhiro Kiyotaki and Akihiko Matsui, "Toward a Theory of International Currency," *The Review of Economic Studies* 60, no. 2 (1993): 283–307.

[7]Kiyotaki, Nobuhiro and Randall Wright, "A Search-theoretic Approach to Monetary Economics" *The American Economic Review* (1993): 63–77.

[8]Matsuyama, Kiminori, Nobuhiro Kiyotaki and Akihiko Matsui, "Toward a Theory of International Currency," *The Review of Economic Studies* 60, no. 2 (1993): 283–307.

Table 6.2. Matching Probability Parameter Distribution

Country	Home Country	Foreign Country	Other
Home Country	n	$\beta(1-n)$	$(1-\beta)(1-n)$
Foreign Country	βn	$1-n$	$(1-\beta)n$

Source: According to Matsuyama, Kiminori, Nobuhiro Kiyotaki and Akihiko Matsui, "Toward a Theory of International Currency," *The Review of Economic Studies* 60, no. 2 (1993): 283–307.

Usually, the motivation of one country to accept another country's currency lies in its probability of encountering such currency in the country, and the probability is determined by the relative size and economic integration of the two economies. When the degree of economic integration between the two countries deepens, the use of the currency of a large country by an individual in a small country will increase its utility, because people prefer to use the currency that is considered to be held by other individuals in the future. By virtue of its competitive advantage, large country enables the local currency to circulate internationally and become an international currency. When the international economic integration reached a high level, the individual of the large country gradually accepted the currency of the small country. The final result was that both currencies became international currencies. However, when the overall size of the two countries vary greatly and under the conditions of highly integrated economy, the large country's currency might dominate the two markets and realize monetary integration. An analysis by Matsuyama *et al.* show that the externalities of currency use and the overall size of the currency issuer have an important impact on the internationalization of the currency.

The research by Matsuyama *et al.* can be divided into three parts, which are described as follows:

The basic assumptions of the model are as follows:

A general precondition for the model is to assume that economic participants in the country have an infinitely long life and live in both domestic and foreign countries. Other assumptions are:

(1) n and $(1-n)/n$ represent the relative amount of economic participants at home and abroad, respectively;
(2) inseparable $k(k \geq 3)$ kinds of goods. And within each country, k economic participants are responsible for three different divisions of production, consumption and storage. k also reflects the division of labor (diversity) of the economy. In addition, there is no "double consistency of demand" in countries;
(3) i economic participants can only get utility in a variety of goods i from consumption. After each individual (economic participant) consumes on i product you can produce 1 unit $i+1$ commodity without cost. Economic participants know how to store this unit of the product at no cost, but it should be noted that it cannot produce or store other types of products;
(4) β represents the degree of economic integration between the two countries; $u > 0$ expresses the instantaneous utility of economic participants' consumer products; $\delta > 0$ represents the discount rate of economic participants, whose value depends on the economic division of labor and nationality;
(5) $V_t = E\left[\sum_{s=0}^{\infty} \frac{u}{(1+\delta)^s} I_{t+s} \,|\Omega_t\right]$ indicates the utility at time t when the economic participants' expectations are discounted.
In the aforementioned formula, I_{t+s} is a random exponential function. If the economic participants consume products during the $t+s$ period, they make themselves reach the level of satisfaction, then $I_{t+s}=1$, otherwise $I_{t+s}=0; \Omega_t$ is the amount of effective information during the period t. If economic participants can successfully obtain these consumer goods, they will immediately produce one unit of products in the next period;
(6) there are two kinds of legal currencies in the economy that do not have intrinsic value, belonging to the country and the foreign country, respectively. The two currencies can be called local currency and foreign currency. If the economic participant does not store the products he produces, he can hold a currency at no cost. In other words, in any period of time, economic participants have and can only have one of the following items: local currency, foreign currency or products produced by themselves;

(7) $m_h(m_f)$ indicates the ratio of domestic (foreign) currency held by domestic economic participants. Therefore, the ratio of economic participants who own products is $1 - m_h - m_f$. This can be used as a row vector $(X = 1 - m_h - m_f \; m_h \; m_f)$ to reflect the inventory allocation of all economic participants in the country;
(8) $m \in (0, 1)$ indicates the amount of local currency owned by domestic economic participants;
(9) no participants can meet here or can conduct multi-party transactions of goods. Moreover, the economic participants can make a random match, and can decide whether to trade with the other party, and the other party has the autonomy to trade with it, and at the same time it can ensure that the trade is a one-to-one exchange.

Matsuyama *et al.* discussed the strategic choices of economic participants before conducting specific reasoning. They point out that given the trading strategies and inventory allocations of other individuals, economic participants will choose a trading strategy that maximizes their expected utility of discount. At the same time, the following inventory allocation matrix can be used to indicate the economic shareholder's inventory allocation:

$$\Pi = \begin{bmatrix} 1 - p_{gh} - p_{gf} & p_{gh} & p_{gf} \\ p_{hg} & 1 - p_{hg} - p_{hf} & p_{hf} \\ p_{fg} & p_{fh} & 1 - p_{fg} - p_{fh} \end{bmatrix}$$

p_{gh} is the possibility of economic participants converting from g to h.

The main principles for economic participants to choose include two aspects: one is that the principle of maximizing benefits should be satisfied. That is to say, given the choice of other individual strategies, each economic participant will choose a trading strategy that maximizes their expected utility. When the steady state is reached, the economic participants' stock allocation reaches the optimal value. The second is to follow the principle of rational expectations. That is to say, economic participants need to consider the transformation matrix, inventory allocation and steady state in the process of strategy selection.

In addition, Matsuyama *et al.* also gave a preliminary description of the model before further analysis.

They use V_g, V_h with V_f to indicate the equilibrium value of the expected discounted utility of the production item, the local currency and the foreign currency held by the economic participants. The following Bellman equation can be used to reflect the size of the aforementioned three equilibrium values:

$$V_g = [(1 - P_{gh} + P_{gf})V_g + P_{gh}V_h + P_{gf}V_f]/(1 + \delta),$$

$$V_h = [(P_{hg}(u + V_g) + (1 - P_{hg} - P_{hf})V_h + P_{hf}V_f]/(1 + \delta),$$

$$V_f = [(P_{fg}(u + V_g) + P_{fh}V_h + (1 - P_{fg} - P_{fh})V_f]/(1 + \delta).$$

The above mentioned equilibrium strategy (equation) must satisfy certain inherent constraints, that is, transactions can increase the utility of economic participants. The utility value of the economic participants in the two formulas following the equations is equal to the utility value of the consumer goods of $u + V_g$, and this value is equal to the sum of the utility obtained by direct consumption and the utility value obtained by holding the production item, because only the consumption can be satisfied to enable it to produce.

In any stable equilibrium, the following conditions are met:

(1) $0 \leq V_g, V_h, V_f < u + V_g$.
(2) $Max\{V_h, V_f\} > V_g > 0$, Or $V_g = V_h = V_f = 0$.
(3) $V_h \geq V_f$ If and only if $P_{hg} \geq P_{fg}$, $V_h \leq V_f$ If and only if $P_{hg} \leq P_{fg}$.
(4) $V_h \geq V_g$ If and only if $P_{hg}(\delta + P_{gf} + P_{fg} + P_{fh}) + P_{hf}P_{fg} \geq P_{gf}P_{fg}$, $V_h \leq V_g$ If and only if $P_{hg}(\delta + P_{gf} + P_{fg} + P_{fh}) + P_{hf}P_{fg} \leq P_{gf}P_{fg}$.
(5) $V_f \geq V_g$ If and only if $P_{fg}(\delta + P_{gh} + P_{hg} + P_{hf}) + P_{fh}P_{hg} \geq P_{gh}P_{hg}$, $V_f \leq V_g$ If and only if $P_{fg}(\delta + P_{gh} + P_{hg} + P_{hf}) + P_{fh}P_{hg} \leq P_{gh}P_{hg}$.
(6) $\delta[(1 - m_h - m_f)V_g + m_hV_h + m_fV_f] = [m_hP_{hg} + m_fP_{fg}]u$.

Based on the above-mentioned six conditions, a three-step algorithm for equalization should be formed: first, according to the constraints of 1 and 2, the utility function value of domestic economic participants is sorted as V_g, V_h, V_f. The equilibrium strategy that domestic economic participants will choose is that the outcome of the transaction will increase utility, and foreign economic participants will choose the same strategy. Second, according to the principle of equilibrium strategy, the steady conversion probability and inventory allocation are calculated. Then the formula should check if the ranking of utility function value and conversion possibilities in the first two steps do meet the constraints of conditions 3 and 5, and verify the situation of foreign economic participants. After calculation, a variety of equilibrium solutions are finally obtained, that is, there are multiple steady states. This is the equilibrium we have to analyze in the coexistence of local currency and foreign currency; the local currency and the foreign currency that eventually develops into an international currency, that is, the steady state of the international currency.[9]

In this equilibrium analysis, it is necessary to clarify that the domestic currency is only circulated in the country, and the foreign currency becomes an international currency and circulates internationally. And two conditions are specified:

(1) Domestic economic participants use local currency and international currency when conducting transactions ($u + V_g > V_h$, $V_f > V_g$).
(2) Foreign economic participants use only their own currency instead of other currencies when conducting transactions ($u + V_g^* > V_f^* > V_g^* \geq V_h^*$);

When residents follow these trading strategies, there are:

$$m_h = m, m_h^* = 0, m_f^* < m^*, m_f > 0.^{10}$$

[9]The equilibrium: $\beta < \min\{(1-m)^2 n/m(1-n)^2, m(1-n)^2/(1-m)^2 n\}$.
[10]$m_h(m_f)$ is their economic participation (outside) who holds the proportion of foreign currency; asterisk.

The stock allocation in this equilibrium is:

$$X = (1 - m - m_f, m, m_f).$$
$$X^* = (1 - m_f^*, 0, m_f^*).$$

Conditions to be satisfied when steady state is reached: "The ratio of foreign trade holders of commodity holders" in one country is equal to that of another country, namely: $m_f^*(1 - m - m_f) = (1 - m_f^*)m_f$ or $m_f = (1 - m)m_f^*$.

So there are:

$$X = ((1 - m)(1 - m_f^*), m, (1 - m)m_f^*),$$
$$X^* = (1 - m_f^*, 0, m_f^*).$$

The total supply of foreign currency and the conditions for its circulation in the other country are:

$$(1 - n)m^* = n(1 - m)m_f^* + (1 - n)m_f^* = (1 - nm)m_f^*.$$

In addition, the possibility of conversion is expressed as follows[11]:

$$P_{gh} = nm/k,$$
$$P_{gf} = [n(1 - m) + \beta(1 - n)]m_f^*/k,$$
$$P_{hg} = n(1 - m)(1 - m_f^*)/k,$$
$$P_{fg} = [n(1 - m) + \beta(1 - n)](1 - m_f^*)/k,$$
$$P_{fh} = P_{hf} = 0,$$
$$P_{gf}^* = [\beta n(1 - m) + (1 - n)]m_f^*/k,$$
$$P_{hg}^* = \beta n(1 - m)(1 - m_f^*)/k,$$
$$P_{fg}^* = [\beta n(1 - m) + (1 - n)](1 - m_f^*)/k,$$
$$P_{fh}^* = P_{hf}^* = P_{gh}^* = 0.$$

[11]Here, P_{ab} is the possibility of their inventory of residents will be converted from a to b.

m_f^* satisfies the conditions of the previous formula, the conversion probability equation indicates $P_{hg} < P_{fg}$. At the same time, according to the previous formula 3, $V_h < V_f$ can be derived, that is, for domestic economic participants, the value of foreign currency is higher than the local currency, because as an international trading instrument, foreign currency is more acceptable to the public. As a result, domestic economic participants are more willing to exchange their local currency for foreign currency, but this idea is often not easy to achieve because foreign economic participants also believe that their domestic currency is better.

Matsuyama *et al.* demonstrated the acceptance of two kinds of fiat currencies under different equilibrium states by constructing a "two-country, two-currency" economic model, and also analyzed the conditions needed to reach different equilibrium states. Under the condition that all countries use the legal currency, they analyze the random matching process of economic participants and calculate the size of the individual's expected discounted utility under different matching probabilities, and obtain the competition mechanism of the two currencies and the possibility of circulation as an international currency. It is pointed out that there may be multiple equilibria in the results of currency competition. According to the different currency circulation domains, the equilibrium state can be summarized into three types: first, when the economies of the countries are relatively independent, that is, the economic participants in each country are relatively closed, the currencies of the two countries are only circulated in their countries, so only the domestic economic participants are using their own currency. Second, when there is an phenomenon of international economic integration and the degree of such integration is deepening, countries with smaller scales or economies accept the currencies of the economies of larger scale (including economic size), and their currencies will increase their effectiveness (affected by externalities), so that large countries can rely on their competitive advantages to make their currencies international and become an international currency. That is to say, one of the currencies of the two countries has been internationalized and circulates abroad.

Third, when the economies of the countries are further integrated and reach a higher level, the large country will gradually accept the currency of the small country. The end result is that both currencies have been internationalized, that is, both currencies can be used internationally. However, in the context of economic integration, one extreme case is that when the overall size of the two countries differs significantly, the large country's currency rules the two markets and realizes monetary integration.

The search monetary model of Matsuyama *et al.* inevitably has some disadvantages. The first drawback is that in the search model, the factors of government department were not directly introduced to the model for analysis, which made it impossible to explore the impact of laws and monetary policies on currency internationalization. The second outstanding shortcoming is that in the analysis of the model, the assumptions of the indivisibility of the flat money, the constraints on the size of the flat money and the constraints of inventory make it impossible to measure the economic variables such as price and exchange rate and their effects. In addition, the model assumes that economic participants have high ability and complete knowledge, understand the entire game structure, can reasonably analyze and predict relevant situations and adopt effective strategies, that is, strategy choices are assumed to be common sense of these economic participants. In this way, each individual knows how to act to achieve a specific equilibrium state. Obviously, this assumption is too strict and oppressive, and it is quite different from reality.

Some economists conducted further analysis and discussion on the shortcomings of the search monetary model of Matsuyama *et al.* Trejos and Wright's research solved two shortcomings in the search monetary model of Matsuyama *et al.* On the one hand, they introduced bargaining analysis methods into the search monetary model to examine the determination and impact of nominal price levels; on the other hand, they introduced government departments into the model, and the government's monetary policy was also introduced into the model, assuming the actions of one government will be influenced by other countries' strategies, and the government can choose from a variety of monetary policies. Trejos and Wright listed three different types of equilibrium, confirming the possibility of multiple equilibria and the possible time lag of monetary policy that may occur with government involvement. In the end, they came to the conclusion that countries with larger economies are more likely to promote the internationalization of their currencies and become a universally accepted international currency. This also supports the conclusions of the study by Matsuyama *et al.*[12]

6.1.2.2 *Analysis Based on Exchange Structure Theory*

Although Matsuyama *et al.*'s search monetary model has some disadvantages, its theoretical analysis framework has laid a microanalytical basis for the follow-up study of international currencies, gradually making the research on international currency issues mature. Models developed on the basis of the search monetary model are increasingly receiving attention from the academic community, and the theory on analyzing the internationalization of money by establishing such models is collectively referred to as the Search Theory of International Currency and it has become a major research direction of monetary economics.

As for why some currencies can become international currencies and other currencies are difficult to obtain a wide range of foreign demand, some scholars have conducted theoretical and empirical research based on microscopic entities. Krugman first analyzed the influencing factors of international money demand with a simple exchange structure matrix as a tool. He proposed three basic assumptions when constructing the theoretical framework: (1) There are n countries in the world; (2) each country has only one foreign

[12]Trejos, Alberto and Randall Wright, "Search, Bargaining, Money, and Prices," *Journal of Political Economy* (1995): 118–141.

exchange market and one currency; (3) variable description: a_{ijkt} indicates the currency trading volume; i, j represents the currency type (currency i and currency j), currency i and currency j are exchanged, k represents the market name, and t represents time. i, j, k will produce a three-dimensional matrix.[13]

Under this framework, when the total amount of money is neglected ($a_{ijkt} = 0$), a small part of the foreign exchange market and currency will play a role. Krugman assumes that there is only one market for a pair of currencies exchanged, so $k = \bar{k}$ and $a_{ij\bar{k}} = a_{ji\bar{k}}$, If you have three countries, you can obtain one 3×3 two-dimensional matrix, expressed as follows:

$$[\mathrm{I}] = \begin{pmatrix} \otimes & a_{12} & a_{13} \\ & \otimes & a_{23} \\ & & \otimes \end{pmatrix}.$$

Flandreau and Jobst have extended the study of Krugman's theory of exchange structure. The currency exchange structure matrix established is comprehensive, because the amount of information is sufficient. It is also theoretically advanced than Krugman's model, and can study two different trading markets at the same time.[14] Obviously, if there are four countries in the economic system, you can build one 4×4 two-dimensional exchange structure matrix. When there is an economic system n in a country, we can construct an exchange structure matrix Ω of currency choices. In this matrix, the elements in the matrix can be divided into two types, namely, the transaction of internationalized currency and common currency. The element of switch fabric matrix Ω has a value of 1 or 0, 0 means no transaction is made; 1 means transactions are conducted. In the trading market i, $x_{iji} = x_{jii} = x_{ij}$, so k can be ignored, and

[13] Krugman, Paul, "Vehicle Currencies and the Structure of International Exchange," *Journal of Money, Credit and Banking* 12, no. 3 (1980): 513–526.

[14] Flandreau, Marc and Clemens Jobst, "The Empirics of International Currencies: Network Externalities, History and Persistence," *The Economic Journal* 119, no. 537 (2009): 643–664.

the three-dimensional matrix becomes a two-dimensional matrix.

$$\Omega = \begin{pmatrix} * & x_{12} & x_{13} & \cdots & x_{1n} \\ x_{21} & * & \cdots & \cdots & \cdots \\ x_{31} & \cdots & * & \cdots & \cdots \\ \cdots & \cdots & \cdots & * & x_{n-1n} \\ x_{n1} & \cdots & \cdots & \cdots & * \end{pmatrix}.$$

The first line indicates the exchange of all currencies in currency 1 of market 1, the second line indicates the exchange of all currencies in currency 2 of market 2, and so on, the nth line indicates the exchange of all currencies in currency n of market n. Element 1 represents the international currency and element 0 represents the non-international currency. The form of the data structure studied by this problem has been constructed.[15]

Based on the aforementioned exchange structure matrix, Flandreau and Jobst have empirically tested the influencing factors of currency internationalization by constructing an empirical model (logit model). They equate the availability of an exchange rate with a value and name this value u_{ij}. u_{ij} represents the value of currency j in market i. x_{ij} can be expressed as follows:

$$x_{ij} = \begin{cases} 1 & u_{ij} > 0 \\ 0 & u_{ij} \leq 0 \end{cases}.$$

u_{ij} is affected by multi-variates and Y_{ij} is introduced to express influence u_{ij}, the vector of this variable. Y_{ij} is a linear function, this function contains parameters β with η_{ij} (β is a vector of these parameters, η_{ij} is a random disturbance item, F is the cumulative distribution of η_{ij}). From the relevant principles of probability theory, the equation can be further derived as follows:

$$\Pr(x_{ij} = 1) = \Pr(y_{ij}\beta + \eta_{ij} \geq 0) = F(-y_{ij}\beta) = F(y_{ij}\beta) = \frac{1}{1 + e^{-y_{ij}\beta}}.$$

[15] *Ibid.*

6.1.2.3 *Theoretical Analysis Based on Cost and Benefit Theory*

By estimating the aforementioned models, it can be concluded that if a country has low short-term interest rates or a large trade scale, the country's currency is more likely to circulate internationally; on the contrary, if a country has higher short-term interest rates or trade on a smaller scale, the possibility of the country's currency circulation in the international arena is small. In addition, if the geographical distance between a country and another country is greater, the foreign demand for the country's currency will be lower; and *vice versa.* At the same time, their evidence supports the view of modern search theory on the currency matching dimension.

Based on the study of the direct influencing factors of currency internationalization, Flandreau and Jobst further analyzed the impact of holding costs and benefits on currency internationalization. Then they introduce the strategic externalities and persistence characteristics of currency internationalization.[16]

The large amount of overseas valuation of a currency affects the liquidity of the domestic currency market, and the externality of currency internationalization is achieved through this influence. This kind of inference is also consistent with the views of the predecessors. In order to control the risk of exchange rate fluctuations, the interest rate of the currency should be adjusted according to the interest rate parity condition, but the value of the interest rate cannot exceed the liquidity premium. In a less liquid market, the liquidity premium is generally higher and the assets that can be traded in a developed market are more expensive (or the same argument is that the sale of the asset has a low return).

Some scholars also provide reasons for the externalization of currency internationalization: the low interest rate of international currency is because many financial institutions are using this currency, the decline in interest rates has led to an increase in the amount of

[16] *Ibid.*

money held by foreign countries and the increase in currency holdings has prompted liquidity. The premium is lowered until the liquidity premium reach almost zero, so the country's currency is more likely to play a valuation role abroad, allowing foreign countries to hold the largest possible amount of this currency, which further strengthens its currency leadership (hegemony) status. In addition, there are no other factors that influence this trend.

Flandreau and Jobst also pointed out that the large amount of data available can prove that when a currency is widely used abroad, it has a low interest rate, and there is a causal relationship between a higher degree of currency internationalization and a lower liquidity premium. They constructed the model with two effects: the reduction of domestic short-term interest rates has led to an increase in the amount of foreign currency held by foreign countries; the increase in the amount of foreign currency held by foreign countries has led to a decline in domestic short-term interest rates. The result of the international monetary mechanism is derived from the Nash equilibrium. The important conclusion that transaction cost affects holding behavior and holding behavior affects transaction cost is derived from two-way causality, which is an important feature of the modern international monetary model. As stated in some theoretical literature, the externalities of international currency still exist.[17]

6.1.2.4 *Basic Conditions for Currency Internationalization*

Based on the aforementioned theoretical analysis and related research, it can be argued that the gradual evolution of a country's currency into an international currency requires the following conditions:

The first is the size of the country's economy. Econometrics shows that the size of a country's economy is important for the internationalization of the country's currency in the research of the size of the country in which the currency is issued and the potential use of

---

[17] *Ibid.*

the country's currency in the international market. The importance of this research is directly related to the size of its financial market, which in turn determines the potential use of the country's currency in the international market. Eichengreen and Frankel show that the percentage of major currency issuers in the world's total output increased by 1% (converted by the purchasing power parity index), which would cause the currency to rise 1.33% in the central bank's currency reserves.[18] Based on the data from 1971 to 1995, Eichengreen conducted the regression analysis of the share of the US dollar, the Japanese yen and the British pound in the foreign exchange reserves and the share of these countries' GDP in the global GDP, and the conclusion is: for every 1% increase in the share of a country's GDP in the global GDP, the country's share of global foreign exchange reserves will increase by 5%. When the lagged dependent variable and the export share variable are added to multi-variate linear regression, the conclusion is: the impact of the size of the national economy has declined significantly. After adding the variables of the export share, a more general model has been obtained, and the results show that the proportion of a country's GDP in the global share increased by 1%, and the country's currency increased by 0.8% in the foreign exchange reserves of countries.[19]

However, Japan's experience shows that the size of the economy is not a necessary condition for the internationalization of the currency. From the perspective of the size of the national economy, Japan is the world's second largest economic power, but the international status of the yen is not in line with it. This is the so-called "Japanese yen paradox." Another manifestation is that Japan's exports are denominated in yen, which is lower than other developed countries. This is worthy of our serious consideration.

---

[18]Eichengreen, Barry, and Frankel, J. A. *On the SDR: Reserve Currencies and the Future of the International Monetary System.* Berkeley: University of California at Berkeley, 1996.

[19]Eichengreen, Barry, "The Euro as a Reserve Currency," *Journal of the Japanese and International Economies* 12 (1998): 483–506.

The second is the international trade status of the currency issuer. The scale of international trade has an important influence on the internationalization of a country's currency, because the process of internationalization of a country's currency is the process of external supply of its own currency, and this process is inseparable from foreign trade. In general, the scale of international trade is positively related to the degree of currency internationalization. From a historical perspective, the development of money in the early and the late Middle Ages showed that an important feature of international currency is that it is issued by economic powers engaged in active international trade. Dwyer and Lothian conducted a historical review of the history of international currency before the Middle Ages and the 13th century, and analyzed the international currency, common currency and monetary union after the 17th century. The conclusions indicate that the development of a country's international trade is of great significance for its currency to become an international currency.[20]

The international trade status of a country clearly has a major impact on the internationalization of the currency. From the perspective of trade volume, "world currency theory" of Shams believes that the currency of the country with the largest share of world trade has a better chance of taking on the role of international currency. In addition, the internationalization process of a country's currency is inevitably accompanied by the outflow of money. From this perspective, the trade deficit is more conducive to the internationalization of a country's currency.[21]

The third is the maturity of the financial market of the currency issuer. In recent years, some scholars believe that whether a country's financial market is mature or not has an important impact on the internationalization of a country's currency. In the past, in discussing

---

[20]Dwyer Jr., Gerald P. and James R. Lothian, "The Economics of International Monies," *CRIF Working Paper Series* (2003): 10.

[21]Shams, Rasul, "Is It Time for a World Currency?" *HWWA Discussion Paper*, no. 167 (2002).

the issue of currency internationalization, the importance of product trade and the real economy was often emphasized. Recently more and more research has focused on the role of financial markets, international portfolio investment and international financing. The degree of development of a country's financial market is reflected in the size, liquidity and degree of development of financial markets. A mature financial market is a potential guarantee and institutional support for a currency to come into play. In general, the improvement of financial market quality and efficiency can reduce market friction, reduce the transaction costs of financial assets such as money, increase the liquidity of money and stimulate the use of money in a wider range. Moreover, developed financial markets can provide central banks and investors with low-cost, high-security and liquid financial instruments that help importers and exporters manage foreign exchange risk in international trade activities.[22]

It can be said that the larger the financial market of a country, the stronger its liquidity, the higher the degree of development, the more the country's currency will be used in international financial transactions. From experience, the world's three most important international currencies — the Dutch guilder, the British pound and the US dollar — are all produced in countries with mature financial markets. In response to this feature, Cohen discussed the two perspectives of "exchange convenience" and "capital certainty."[23] Tavlas put forward a similar point, pointing out that the international currency "issuing countries should have stable unregulated financial markets, and financial markets must have breadth (with a large number of financial instruments) and depth (with developed secondary market)."[24]

---

[22]Huang, Meibo, "Analysis on the Possibility of the Optimal Currency Area Theory and Monetary Cooperation in East Asia," *World Economy* 10 (2001): 41–46.

[23]Cohen, Benjamin J., *The Geography of Money*. Cornell: Cornell University Press, 1998, 55–201.

[24]Tavlas, George S., "The International Use of Currencies," *Finance and Development* 35, no. 2 (1998): 46–49.

The fourth is the convertibility and credibility of money. Currency convertibility refers to the abolition of foreign exchange controls on current and capital projects, and the free exchange of currency on current and capital projects. The internationalization of a country's currency is closely related to its degree of convertibility, but they are not the same. The free exchange of money is a stage of currency internationalization. The internationalization of a country's currency must be freely convertible, but it does not have to be fully convertible at a particular stage.

The credibility of money comes from the stability of monetary value and the confidence of expecting future stability. The instability of currency value tends to cause people's disorder of currency confidence, which is not conducive to the internationalization process of a country's currency. Therefore, price stability is an important prerequisite for the development of a country's currency and the maintenance of its international status.[25] Huang believes that people with stable currency values often have a basically stable understanding of their value, and they will have sufficient confidence.[26] The use of this currency in international transactions can reduce the time and expense of people obtaining and transmitting information. A currency must play a role in all areas of the international monetary function and occupy a favorable position, all of which require the currency to be stable. In addition, the expectation of a currency's continuous appreciation will bring confidence in the future of the currency and help promote and maintain the international status of the currency.

The stability and continuity of the issuing country policy supports the credibility of the currency, among which hegemony and government reputation play an important role. Hegemony can enhance the continuity of policies among countries in a complex monetary system.

---

[25] *Ibid.*

[26] Huang, Meibo, "Analysis on the Possibility of the Optimal Currency Area Theory and Monetary Cooperation in East Asia," *World Economy* 10 (2001): 41–46.

The leadership role of hegemony can enhance the convenience of cooperation between countries and is also conducive to strengthening macroeconomic coordination. Barro argues that government reputation is a viable solution to policy time inconsistencies. When the government establishes a good reputation for strict compliance with its commitments, continuing to maintain a good reputation is an important motivation to prevent the government from deceiving the public. This motivation will achieve optimal results.[27]

The fifth is historical inertia. The rise and fall of a country's currency also has the cause of "inertia." Inertia plays an important role in the process of currency internationalization, especially in the maintenance of the international status of money. An empirical analysis of the US dollar by Ogawa and Sasaki shows that even if the dollar is depreciated at a moderate level, the international status of the dollar will not decrease — this is the cause of inertia.[28] For example, in the early 20th century, the United States became the world's number one economic power. Its position was further consolidated in World War II, but the US dollar replaced the British pound by 50 years. This is a typical example of inertia.

The three factors of transaction cost, economies of scale and network effects explain the causes of inertia, which are related and integrated with each other. Early research by Swoboda emphasized the role of transaction costs in different currency exchanges, indicating that the currency used for trading medium should be those associated with low transaction costs.[29] Cohen believes that the currency internationalization originated from the economies of scale or reduce the transaction cost.[30] This is similar to the situation of barter: when

[27]Barro, Robert J., "Reputation in a Model of Monetary Policy with Incomplete Information," *Journal of Monetary Economics* 17, no. 1 (1986): 3–20.

[28]Ogawa, Eiji and Yuri Nagataki Sasaki, "Inertia in the Key Currency," *Japan and the World Economy* 10, no. 4 (1998): 421–439.

[29]Swoboda, Alexander K., *The Euro-Dollar Market: An Interpretation*, no. 64, International Finance Section, (Department of Economics, Princeton University, 1968).

[30]Cohen, Benjamin J., *The Geography of Money*. Cornell: Cornell University Press, 1998, 12–55.

different currencies exist, there will be higher search costs and low efficiency. When countries use one or a few currencies, the transaction cost will be significantly reduced. Some scholars believe that the currency internationalization is a collaborative process, which is facilitated by saving transaction costs. The research also shows that the currency internationalization will be widely traded network cross-border activity form — network externality effect. Any person holding on a currency depends on the other people's willingness to pay in this currency. The scope of a currency is more widely accepted, the higher the currency's value is. Using the terminology of economics, money is creating a positive network externality.[31]

Based on the aforementioned theoretical analysis, some important influencing factors of the internationalization of currency can be summarized as follows:

First of all, the impact of transaction costs. Due to the inevitable international economic transaction costs and the problem of "lack of dual consistency," the requirement of public financial media was generated, and international currency came into being. If the public medium of international monetary has formed, the transaction costs of both parties will be reduced. Cohen pointed out that the transaction cost reduction and the effect of economies of scale is an important impetus of currency internationalization.[32] If countries use their own currency in trade or other kinds of currencies, this will increase the cost of trading time, and it is then difficult to improve the efficiency. But if you use one or several public media effects of monetary transactions, the transaction cost among countries will be greatly reduced. At the same time, the higher the trading volume using the currency, the more cost of traders will be reduced.

Secondly, the financial market and cost-benefit factors of holding currency. The more developed financial market and the stronger the

---

[31]Dwyer Jr., Gerald P. and James R. Lothian, "The Economics of International Monies," *CRIF Working Paper Series* (2003): 10.

[32]Cohen, Benjamin J., *The Geography of Money*. Cornell: Cornell University Press, 1998, 12–55.

liquidity is, the lower short-term interest rate liquidity premium and the domestic market of its currency is, then the cost of money owner is reduced, and the revenue increased. More people are willing to accept this money, further expanding its internationalization, and then lead to a further decline in the liquidity premium and short-term interest rates and so forth; the currency's influence gradually increased, and gradually formed a certain scale of the transaction network.

Finally, the influence of network externality. On the one hand, if the issuing country can establish close trade links with many countries, it will form a huge network of trade, and expansion and development of the network will prompt the country currency in the international market, thus forming a network effect of currency, and thereby reducing the costs and risks. This kind of network effect will encourage more people to use the money, finally to promoting the role of currency internationalization. On the other hand, as trading volume of the currency in the international financial market increased, the currency traders will spontaneously form a network. On the influence of network externality, people are willing to hold the currency, and the accepted scope will be gradually expanded.

6.2 The Progress of RMB Internationalization and the Main Problems

6.2.1 *The Proposal of the Internationalization of RMB*

The internationalization of the RMB is that RMB plays a monetary function in international private and official trading transactions. International trade and financial transactions using RMB as carrier currency, currency and monetary investment function in private transactions. RMB used as the foreign exchange market intervention currency, currency anchor and reserve currency function in official trading. To define and analyze the internationalization of the RMB from the monetary function level is actually the theoretical definition of RMB internationalization.

The working definition of RMB internationalization, refers to the opening of the domestic and foreign credit, guarantee, implement foreign guarantee in RMB and issuing the international bills of companies and banks in RMB, and these are not refused in financing, investment, foreign direct investment (FDI), securities investment, in the international market, interbank debt, currency and settlement currency, the RMB offshore. A very important sign is that RMB exchange in foreign countries is not rejected.

The general currency, the domestic money market is the final single supply or is a "last resort" leading, is called supply-dominated. In general, the implementation of the national sovereignty region dominates the formation of the "Westphalia pattern," which is characterized as "one country, one currency." But in many cases, if a currency market transaction network influence extended to overseas, there is an important impact on the economic system of other countries; therefore, the domestic currency functions to achieve international expansion. Under this situation, the currency acts as an international currency. The influence mechanism generally depends on the advantage of the status of the international division of labor, allowing other countries to induce the demand for domestic goods, which causes the request of foreign residents for local currency. The expansion and accumulation of money demand can upgrade the status of the currency in the international financial market, promote its development as a vehicle currency in foreign exchange markets, and even become a reserve currency. Therefore, the range and degree of international currency is fundamentally the competitive advantage in the world division of labor, and there is no single dominant country in current supply. Therefore, the international monetary market is demand dominated, and the change of international monetary pattern is the result of competition, and the internationalization process is more competitive.

For a long time, China implemented an RMB non-internationalization strategy, which mainly comes from the three concerns about internationalization of currency: the first worry is that once the non-residents can obtain the local currency, the currency is vulnerable to the impact of speculation; the second worry is there is a challenge for the government's ability to control the money supply; the third worry is the domestic financial management system may be affected.

The outbreak of the Asian financial crisis in 1997 made China realize that if RMB is not held by non-residents, the currency will suffer no speculative risk. If capital account is closed, non-residents will not hold RMB, so this is the main reason why China survived the crisis. Then, the crisis has changed China's plan on the opening of capital projects and realize the full convertibility of the RMB in 2000. After crisis, China decided to strengthen its foreign exchange management and focused on the macro financial regulation.

However, After China's entry to World Trade Organization (WTO) in 2001, the foreign exchange management system of China was shocked by this impact. According to the agreement, China needs to open the financial and insurance business. The WTO is the catalyst of China to open the capital account and capital controls in the original framework, then China conducted a series of innovations, such as introduction of qualified foreign investment system and the system of qualified domestic institutional investors. The two innovations are the "amount" restriction to the progressive realization of two-way cross-border capital flows. Ten years after the entry to WTO, the main problem facing the external economy of China is double surplus, associated with the problem of the pressure of RMB appreciation. The major concern of the international community to China's economy is the level of RMB exchange rate. Although early at the end of 1990s, the circulation of RMB has been quite common in the neighboring countries. Mainland China and the Hong Kong special administrative region signed a memorandum of RMB business in Hong Kong in 2003 on the legalization of RMB business in Hong Kong. But this did not cause the attention of the international community, in essence, legalization of RMB in Hong Kong business is a major change in the currency policy in China. At the time, China did not notice the problems with a massive surplus and foreign exchange reserve to the real economy on the currencies policy of non-internationalization, and its negative effect on the national wealth preservation and currency appreciation. The most mainstream thinking of the RMB internationalization is that the RMB should obtain the status in scale commensurate with that of China's economy. The proposition of "RMB internationalization" does not receive much attention from domestic policymakers and academics in China.

The outbreak of international financial crisis in 2008 made China understand that a profound impact of the fluctuation of the US dollar on the economic cycle of China, and the US economic recession will affect the safety of the China holdings of the US dollar assets. Policymakers and economists, including the general public are aware that there is a direct relationship between this situation and the international currency status of the dollar. The internationalization of the RMB can overcome the dollar as the international currency constraints of export-oriented enterprises to reduce business risk, which is "self-help" actions of China in the crisis. At the end of 2008, China government explicitly proposed three international financial strategies: active promotion in the East Asian regional monetary and financial cooperation, reform of the international monetary system and the internationalization of the RMB.

Since 2009, the Chinese government has taken economic measures to promote cross-border RMB trade settlement between the pilot and the central bank currency swap agreement and Hong Kong offshore financial market development. In major international conferences, China actively promoted the reform of the international monetary system, got rid of the dependence on a single international reserve currency and called for developing countries to obtain more rights to speak. At the same time, China still maintained a high growth rate in crisis, while the developed countries are in a long economic recession; therefore, the global economy experienced recovery in an unbalanced way. In this context, the RMB internationalization has aroused widespread concern in the international community.

6.2.2 *The Progress of RMB Internationalization*

The internationalization of the RMB has close relations with the global financial crisis. During the financial crisis, the Chinese government and enterprises became deeply aware of the huge risk of the non-internationalization of RMB. For the government, even though there is an increase in foreign exchange reserves, the depreciated dollar will reduce foreign exchange reserve assets, while export-oriented enterprises will face the risk of exchange rate fluctuations. Therefore, the Chinese began to actively promote the internationalization of RMB by promoting cross-border RMB in trade and investment, and promote the development of offshore RMB market.

6.2.2.1 *The Initial Development of the Internationalization of RMB, the Logical Frame and Main Features*

From the trade settlement in private sector, "underground border banks" promote the RMB going global in an informal way. Since 1980s, with the achievements of reform and opening-up, China's economic strength has further increased, and the economic exchanges between the neighboring countries and regions have also escalated, and the scale of informal cross-border use of RMB surged, especially the rapid development in the southwest border areas. Along the borders of Laos, Burma and Vietnam, the RMB became the *de facto* anchor currency. "Underground border banks" is a special manifestation of this relationship, and it is the model by the spontaneous formation in different border regions with distinctive organizational characteristics and business practices, but they are not included in the formal financial system, while with a rapid development trend.

From the use of cross-border arrangements, the arrangement of "free independent travel" to Hong Kong and Macao and related economic and trade cooperation arrangements to promote the use of the RMB in offshore market, which is a pathfinder of RMB internationalization. Hong Kong and Macao is the main channel and distribution center of RMB flowing out of mainland in informal way. In order to cope with the economic downturn after the Asian financial crisis, especially because of the SARS epidemics, the Chinese central government and Hong Kong, Macao signed the "Closer Economic Partnership Arrangement" (CEPA) in June and October 2003, respectively. In the same year the Chinese government introduced "free independent travel" program that allowed the residents in certain areas in Mainland China to travel to Hong Kong and Macao with special permits, to promote the use of RMB in current account in Hong Kong and Macao from informal to formal. After November 2003, Hong Kong and Macao commercial banks could operate a specific range of RMB business by Bank of China (Hong Kong) as the clearing bank for RMB, with the settlement of the People's Bank of China, and expanded to capital account. After June 2007, financial institutions of the Mainland China issued RMB bonds in Hong Kong, and financial institutions of Hong Kong with mainland business also began to issue RMB bonds in Hong Kong.

From the official currency reserves to swap arrangements, in order to promote bilateral trade and reduce the risk of using the third currency settlement, at the beginning of 21st century, the People's Bank of China signed border trade currency settlement agreement with Russia, Vietnam and Nepal, and then extended to the formal trade and investment projects. The agreements allowed both trade and investment entities to use their own currencies in payment and settlement, and then lend to the central bank by its commercial bank funds, and the central bank through currency swaps to settle in other monetary funds. Since the end of 2008, the People's Bank of China further strengthened the currency swap exchanges with the neighboring countries, and the neighboring countries also took the initiative to promote the influence of the RMB in their foreign exchange reserves and the reference rate basket.

In July 2009, after the announcement of "the implementation rules on RMB cross-border trade settlement," the logical framework of the development of the internationalization of RMB is gradually clear. In short, the logical framework of RMB internationalization is the two cycles in two major markets — domestic and overseas and its six parts (Figure 6.1). The first cycle is cross-border circulation, and it can be divided into current account, capital account, the cooperation among banks and the cooperation among governments; the second cycle is overseas circulation mainly and RMB offshore market in Hong Kong and overseas RMB market. As the formulation of

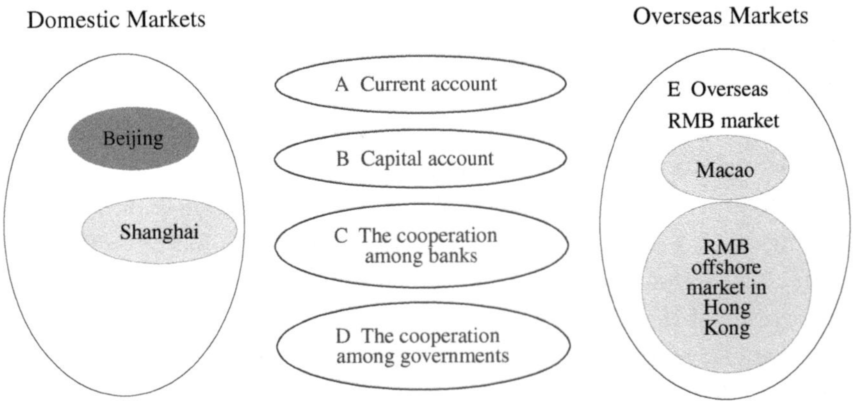

Figure 6.1. The Framework of the Internationalization of RMB

monetary policy center, Beijing is the designer and controller of the whole process; and as a target to be the offshore financial center, Shanghai will face great opportunities and challenges. The overseas RMB market was developed from Hong Kong as the starting point, and gradually extended to other offshore markets.

At present, cross-border RMB operations show the following characteristics:

(1) The rapid growth of the scale of cross-border RMB trade settlement. The cross-border RMB trade settlement of first three quarters of 2014 amounted to ¥4.28 trillion, far more than the size of the full year 2013. The direct investment in RMB clearing business amounted to ¥720.8 billion, twice more than the level of the year 2013.
(2) The offshore RMB market continues to grow. Preliminary statistics showed that the stock of overseas RMB has reached ¥2.6 trillion, among which RMB deposit balance in Hong Kong has exceeded ¥1 trillion, accounted for more than 8% of deposits in local financial institutions. The offshore RMB operations in Taiwan (China), Macao (China) and London (UK) have also made rapid development.

Table 6.3. The Scale of Operations in Major Offshore RMB Market (2011–2013)

Unit: Million Yuan (except specified)	2011	2012	2013	Remarks on 2013
Hong Kong, China				
The amount of cross-border RMB settlement	19,145	26,325	22,849	Before August
RMB foreign exchange trading volume	—	—	491	The daily average (in billions USD)
RMB deposit balance	5,885	6,030	7,095	End of August
The balance of RMB loans	308	790	887	End of March
Dim sum bonds outstanding balance	1,467	2,372	2,584	End of March
Taiwan				
RMB deposit balance	—	—	984	End of September
Total loans of RMB	—	—	1,044	Before September
RMB remittance balance	—	—	90	End of September
Macao, China				
RMB deposit balance	418	416	584	End of August
The amount of cross-border RMB settlement	628	973	910	First 8 months
Luxembourg				
RMB deposit balance	—	209	399	End of June
RMB bond issuance	—	320	423	The first half of the year
RMB loan balance	—	293	619	End of June
RMB trade financing	—	342	518	The first half of the year
RMB investment fund	—	—	2,141	The first half of the year
London				
RMB deposit balance	69	51	—	
RMB trade financing balance	168	336	—	
RMB foreign exchange trading volume	106	168	—	The daily average (in billions USD)

Source: Based on the study of Institute of International Financial Research, Bank of China. https://www.boc.cn/fimarkets/summarize/2013-5-6.

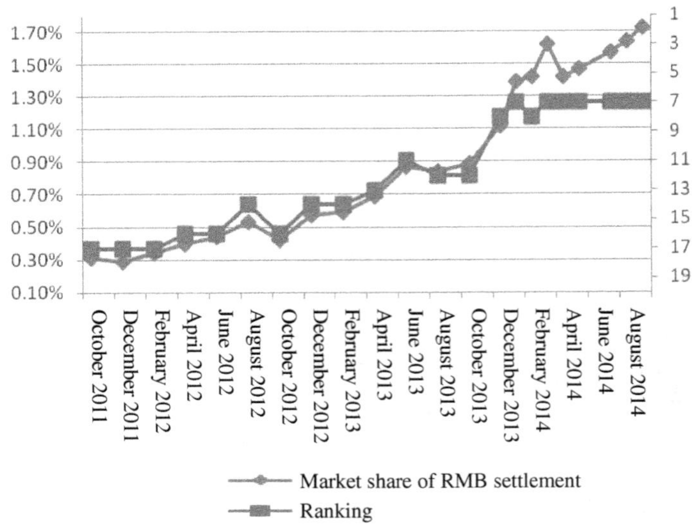

Figure 6.2. Market Share and Ranking in RMB Payment Settlement Based on the SWIFT Indicator System
Source: SWIFT "RMB Tracker" statistical report, obtained by the author. https://www.swift.com/our-solutions/global-financial-messaging/messaging-solutions-for-fx-and-treasury/swift-and-cls 2014-9-28.

(3) The international status of the RMB has risen remarkably. According to SWIFT statistics, RMB market share was only 0.25% in January 2012, ranking 20th among the major currencies. Subsequently, the amount of RMB payments continued to increase. In September 2014, the market share reached 1.72%, the highest level ever; on the other hand, the RMB replaced the Swiss franc and became the seventh largest payment currency in the world in 2014, fully demonstrating that the recognition and acceptance of the RMB in the international market is constantly improving.
(4) Cooperation between China and relevant countries and regions has been accelerated. China has just signed a bilateral currency swap agreement with European countries. So far, the mainland has signed currency swap agreements with 23 countries and regions, with a total scale of more than ¥2.5 trillion. The signing of these agreements not only provides RMB liquidity for the

global market but also facilitates the foreign trade and investment and promotes the use of the RMB in the overseas markets.

6.2.2.2 *Measurement of the Degree of Internationalization of the RMB*

The functions of international currency mainly include three major factors: pricing, transactions and reserve currency. Generally speaking, international trade has a huge impact on the process of currency internationalization. The function of international currency begins with cross-border currency settlement in international trade. With the continuous expansion of cross-border settlement, the currency was gradually recognized by the world, and the currency's transactions in the financial market are becoming more and more active. The function of the currency gradually expanded into the financial market and eventually became an international reserve currency. In view of this, we will measure the current degree of internationalization of the RMB from four aspects: trade settlement, cross-border investment, financial market transactions and foreign exchange reserves.

(1) The development of RMB settlement in cross-border trade[33]:

In December 2008, the Chinese government proposed to initiate the pilot use of RMB as a trade settlement currency in certain regions of China to specific surrounding countries and regions. On 8 April 2009, the State Council held a standing meeting to conduct pilot projects for RMB settlement of cross-border trade in Shanghai, Guangzhou, Shenzhen, Zhuhai and Dongguan. On 2 July 2009, the People's Bank of China, the Ministry of Finance, the Ministry of Commerce,

[33]Because there is no disclosure of the data, so the cross-border settlement of major currencies in the world is not a continuous record, which hinders the use of accurate estimates of the degree of internationalization of the currency. Our data are collected from the Research Report of SWIFT mainly in 2011 and 2012. Because RMB cross-border trade began to grow rapidly since 2010, so the data can still well reflect the use and change of RMB in cross-border trade.

the General Administration of Customs, the State Administration of Taxation and the China Banking Regulatory Commission issued Announcement No. 10 of [2009], promulgating the pilot management of RMB settlement of cross-border trade. From the perspective of trade facilitation, the management method provides a detailed explanation of the settlement method, supervision mode and export tax rebate method for RMB settlement of cross-border trade. The introduction of this rule is a milestone and is the institutional support for China to promote the function of the RMB as carrier currency in international trade.

Since June 2009, RMB settlement in cross-border trade has grown from scratch and has developed rapidly. In particular, in June 2012, the People's Bank of China and other six ministries and commissions jointly issued a list of key regulated enterprises for export goods trade in RMB settlement. The cross-border trade RMB settlement operations were fully promoted, and all import and export enterprises could choose to calculate and settle the receipt and payment in RMB, so the RMB settlement of cross-border trade has developed rapidly. In 2010, cross-border trade RMB settlement accounted for about 2% of the total foreign trade settlement. Although the growth rate of RMB settlement amount of cross-border trade in the fourth quarter of 2011 fell for the first time, the scale of RMB settlement in the cross-border trade reached ¥208 billion in 2011, accounting for 9.2% of the country's total trade volume, which was 7 percentage points higher than that in 2010. In 2012, the amount of RMB settlement of cross-border trade maintained a relatively fast growth rate. The bank handled a total of ¥2.94 trillion of cross-border trade RMB settlement operations, with an increase of 41% on year-on-year base. In 2012, the proportion of RMB cross-border trade settlement in total foreign trade settlement has increased to about 16%. The amount of RMB settlement of goods trade accounted for the proportion of customs goods trade, increased from 2.2% in 2012 to 11.7% at the end of 2013, and further increased to 18.4% in the first quarter of 2014. HSBC forecasts that more than half of China's foreign trade volume will be settled in RMB by 2015, which will reach US$2 trillion.

Table 6.4. Quarterly Data of RMB Settlement of Cross-Border Trade from 2009 to 2014

Time	Cross-border Trade Settlement in RMB (¥100 million)	
	Amount of Current Quarter	Cumulative Amount since the Pilot
Fourth quarter of 2009	—	35.8
First quarter of 2010	183.5	219.4
Second quarter of 2010	486.6	706.0
Third quarter of 2010	1, 264.8	1, 970.8
Fourth quarter of 2010	3, 128.5	5, 099.2
First quarter of 2011	3, 603.2	8, 702.4
Second quarter of 2011	5, 972.5	14, 674.9
Third quarter of 2011	5, 834.1	20, 509.0
Fourth quarter of 2011	5, 390.2	25, 899.2
First quarter of 2012	5, 826.6	31, 988.0
Second quarter of 2012	6, 715.5	38, 703.0
Third quarter of 2012	7, 989.6	46, 650.0
Fourth quarter of 2012	8, 933.0	55, 288.0
First quarter of 2013	10, 039.0	65, 328.0
Second quarter of 2013	10, 399.0	75, 826.0
Third quarter of 2013	11, 062.0	86, 888.0
Fourth quarter of 2013	14798.0	101686.0
First quarter of 2014	About 16,000	About 118,000

Source: CEIC database, http://www.ceicdata.com/; Wind information, http://www.wind.com.cn/.

Cross-border trade RMB settlement has not only developed very rapidly in terms of speed but also greatly improved in the trade settlement structure. Before 2012, the RMB settlement of cross-border trade was mainly based on trade in goods. After 2012, the settlement of RMB in service trade and other current account has developed faster, as shown in Figure 6.3. In 2012, amount of goods trade settled in RMB was ¥2.06 trillion, the amount of service trade and other current account settled in RMB was ¥876.45 billion. From 2013 to 2014, the amount of service trade settled in RMB and other current account has exceeded half of the amount of goods trade settled in RMB, so its proportion is also on the rise.

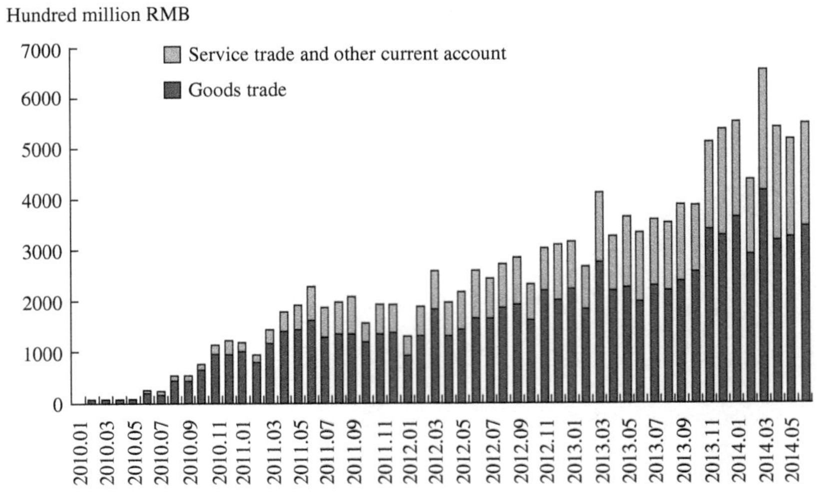

Figure 6.3. China's Cross-Border Trade Settlement in RMB from January 2010 to May 2014
Source: People's Bank of China Monetary Policy Analysis Group, *China Monetary Policy Implementation Report, Third Quarter of 2014* (2014).

The data showed that from October 2010 to January 2013, offshore RMB payments increased by 29.75 times. Among the world's major payment currencies, the ranking of the RMB jumped from the 35th in October 2010 to the 13th in 2013, which is a rapid growth. In addition, the international acceptance of RMB at this stage has also increased significantly. From June 2011 to June 2012, the number of countries and regions dealing with RMB payment operations increased from 65 to 91, and the number of institutions increased from 617 to 983. The number of RMB customers of the top five banks in RMB payment increased from 91 to 153 (Figure 6.4).

Although the cross-border trade settlement of the RMB has achieved good results since its inception, the absolute level of cross-border trade settlement of the RMB is still insufficient.

The data in Table 6.5 show the cross-border trade settlement of the world's major currencies from 2011 to 2014. The table shows that the euro, the US dollar, the British pound, the Japanese yen, the Australian dollar and the Canadian dollar are major currencies of cross-border trade settlement. Among them, the euro and the US dollar

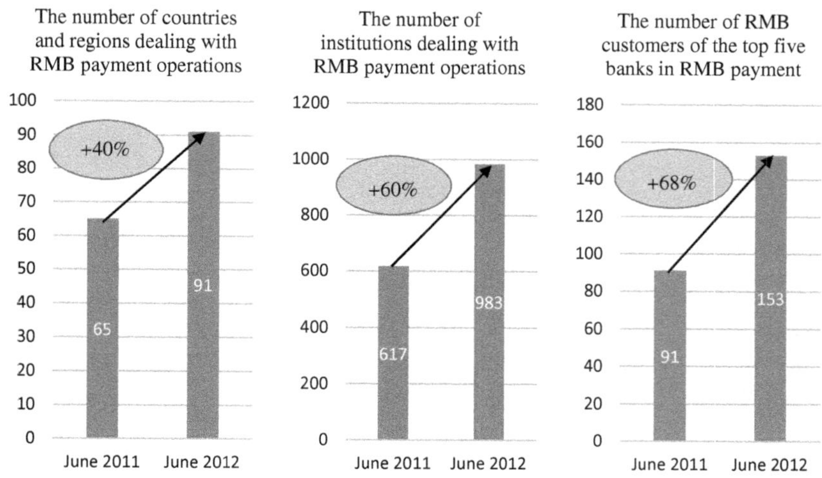

Figure 6.4. International Acceptance of RMB

Source: SWIFT "RMB Tracker" statistical report, obtained by the author.

are the most important currencies for cross-border trade, and they account for about 70% of cross-border trade settlement. Although the proportion of RMB cross-border trade settlement has experienced rapid growth from 0.24% in 2011 to 1.72% in 2014, surpassing the Russian ruble, South African rand and even Swiss franc, approaching the Australian dollar, Canadian dollar and even the Japanese yen, however, the overall share of RMB is still low.

Of course, Table 6.5 does not take into account the international trade situation of each country, but only the proportion of cross-border trade settlement. Since the driving force for cross-border trade settlement comes from international trade, to consider the cross-border trade settlement based on the international trade volume can reveal the international acceptance of a country's currency, and thus reflect the degree of internationalization of the currency. Table 6.6 builds a new indicator based on the proportion of international trade in each country: the proportion of a country's currency in cross-border trade settlement/the proportion of the country's trade volume in the total world trade. This new indicator shows a more accurate measurement of the degree of currency internationalization.

Table 6.5. Use of Currency in Cross-Border Trade Settlement (%)

Currency	2011.10	2012.1	2012.10	2013.1	2013.10	2014.1	2014.9
Euro	32.56	44.04	42.49	40.17	34.69	33.51	29.43
USD	29.32	29.73	31.18	33.48	38.12	38.75	42.93
GBP	7.04	9.00	8.84	8.55	9.92	9.38	8.59
JPY	2.12	2.48	2.34	2.56	2.56	2.49	2.74
Australian dollar	1.76	2.08	2.12	1.85	1.91	1.75	2.02
Canadian dollar	1.64	1.81	1.91	1.80	1.89	1.80	1.78
Swiss franc	1.04	1.36	1.86	1.83	1.72	1.38	1.40
Russian ruble	0.32	0.52	0.63	0.56	0.51	0.40	0.38
RMB	0.24	0.25	0.42	0.63	0.84	1.39	1.72
South African rand	0.40	0.48	0.42	0.42	0.44	0.41	0.46

Source: SWIFT "RMB Tracker" statistical report, obtained by the author.

It can be concluded from the data in Table 6.6 that, after taking into account the trade situation of various countries, the degree of internationalization of the currency has changed significantly. The US dollar ranked first in the index over 400%, reflecting the dollar's well-deserved world core currency status. The pound also ranked second with 200%, indicating that the pound remained strong in trade settlement and the euro fell to third place. Compared with the world's five major currencies and the BRICS currencies, the overall level of cross-border trade settlement in RMB has risen, but the trade ratio is still the lowest. Both the South African rand and the Russian ruble still exceed the RMB.

(2) The development of cross-border investment settlement in RMB:

Cross-border investment settlement in RMB can be divided into two types: RMB settlement of FDI and RMB settlement of FDI.

In recent years, the FDI of the RMB has developed very rapidly. This is mainly because the rapid development of China's FDI has laid the foundation for the development of overseas direct investment in RMB settlement. Under the guidance of the Chinese government's

Table 6.6. Percentage of Currency Use in Cross-Border Trade Settlement/Country Trade as a Percentage of Total World Trade (%)[1]

Currency	2011.10	2012.1	2012.8	2012.9	2012.10	2012.11	2012.12	2013.1	2013.2
Dollar	383.34	388.70	426.74	406.87	407.65	406.35	435.89	437.72	443.08
GBP	202.51	258.89	256.88	258.31	254.29	247.10	249.68	245.95	241.34
EUR	137.90	186.52	174.16	178.22	179.96	173.18	168.40	170.13	166.53
Australian dollar	126.50	149.50	148.78	156.69	152.38	168.91	151.66	132.97	141.60
Swiss franc	79.84	104.40	134.34	140.48	142.79	135.88	146.62	140.48	157.37
Canadian dollar	67.58	74.59	76.24	77.47	78.71	77.47	81.18	74.18	85.72
South African rand	71.43	85.71	78.57	76.79%	75.00	75.00	71.43	75.00	75.00
JPY	47.94	56.08	54.28	55.63	52.92	55.18	55.41	57.89	59.25
Russian ruble	14.55	23.65	28.65	27.74	28.65	29.11	30.47	25.47	30.93
RMB	2.66	2.77	5.87	5.65	4.65	6.21	6.32	6.98	6.54

Note: [1]The proportion of trade in countries in the world trade is 2011 data.

Source: SWIFT "RMB Tracker" statistical report, WTO World Trade Database, obtained by authors.

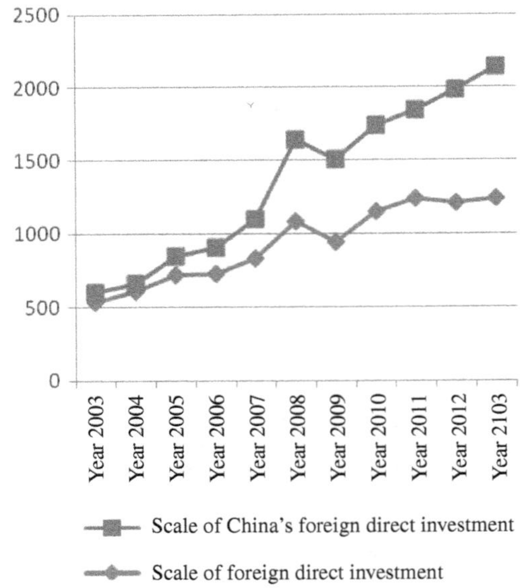

Figure 6.5. Scale of China's FDI and FDI from 2003 to 2013

Note: Units of billions of dollars.

Source: The author has compiled the data according to the data released by the Ministry of Commerce of China.

"going out" policy, China's FDI has developed rapidly. At present, China's FDI has reached an all-time high in both quantity of flow and stocks, as shown in Figure 6.5. In 2010, China's foreign investment flow reached 5.2% of the global current flow, surpassing Japan and the United Kingdom for the first time, ranking fifth in the world. At the same time, the cumulative stock of China's foreign investment has reached US$317.21 billion, moving up to the 17th spot in the world, and the proportion of China's foreign investment in mergers and acquisitions has significantly increased, reaching US$29.7 billion. In 2012, China's foreign investment flows further rose to US$87.8 billion. China's foreign direct investment majorly flows to Southeast Asia and developing countries. These regions are relatively easy to carry out overseas direct investment in RMB settlement business. The rapid development of China's FDI has laid the foundation for the development of overseas direct investment in RMB settlement business.

With the rapid development of China's FDI, the use of RMB for FDU has also developed rapidly. On 13 January 2011, the central bank issued the "Measures for the Administration of Pilot Settlement of Foreign Direct Investment in RMB," and the overseas settlement of RMB direct investment was fully launched. In the second quarter of 2011, direct investment in RMB amounted to ¥5.4 billion, rising to ¥10.85 billion in the third quarter. The introduction of the specific policy of RMB direct investment in October 2011 has further promoted the comprehensive development of overseas direct investment settlement in RMB. Since the policy was issued, there have been 74 cross-border RMB direct investment projects approved by the Ministry of Commerce, involving ¥15.53 billion. In December 2011, the cumulative amount of FDI in RMB was ¥20.15 billion. In November 2013, the cumulative amount of FDI in RMB was ¥95.4 billion. At present, in China's overseas investment flows, the average current profit reinvestment ratio has reached 34.9%, and this high reinvestment flow ratio has contributed to the growth of overseas stocks in RMB. Therefore, FDI in RMB has also become an important source of offshore deposits in RMB.

In China's FDI, outward foreign direct investment (OFDI) in RMB has also developed rapidly. Compared with RMB FDI, OFDI in RMB is larger. In the first 11 months of 2012, OFDI in RMB amounted to ¥195.3 billion. In the first 11 months of 2013, the amount of OFDI in RMB was ¥349.7 billion, with an increase of 79% on year-on-year base. OFDI in RMB accounted for 3.4% of China's absorption of all FDI. Therefore, FDI in RMB has also become an important channel for the reverse flow of offshore RMB.

Cross-border use of the RMB has developed rapidly through trade settlement and investment settlement. According to the latest report released by SWIFT, the proportion of RMB as a financing currency in global credit-related credit agreements has risen from 1.89% in January 2012 to 8.66% in October 2013. The RMB has surpassed the euro and the yen to become the world's second largest international trade financing currency after the dollar. The US dollar remains the dominant currency for global trade financing, accounting for 81.08% of global trade finance. The share of the euro in global trade finance fell from 7.87% in January 2012 to 6.64% in October 2013, currently the third largest trade financing currency in the world. The yen is the world's fourth largest trade finance currency, accounting for 1.36% of global trade finance.[34]

(3) The degree of internationalization of RMB in financial market transactions:

Data displays (Table 6.7)[35] that the US dollar accounted for 86.8% of the foreign exchange market transactions in 1998, and reached a peak of 89.9% in 2001. Although it has gradually decreased since then, it still accounts for 85–87% of the total, ranking first in the world, indicating that the international status of the US dollar cannot be shaken. After the birth of the euro, it inherited the German mark and French franc share, accounting for 37–39%, however, due to the negative impact of the European debt crisis, the share fell to 33.4% by 2013. The yen and the pound currently account for 23% and 11.8%, respectively. The RMB has experienced a process from scratch in foreign exchange trading. Currently, it accounts for 2.2% of the foreign exchange market transactions. The progress is very rapid, but the gap with the world's major currencies is still obvious.

The data in Table 6.7 basically reflect the international status of a country's currency, but because it does not consider the size of a country's economy, it does not accurately reflect the degree of internationalization of the currency. By combining the currency issuing economy's share of the world economy with the share of different currencies in the international foreign exchange market, we have

[34]SWIFT "RMB Tracker" Statistics Report.

[35]According to the statistics of the bank for International Settlements, the global foreign exchange trading can best reflect the degree of financial market in the currency, so we use this part of the global foreign exchange market trading simulation currency in financial market.

Table 6.7. Percentage of Major Currencies Trading in the Foreign Exchange Market

Currency	1998	2001	2004	2007	2010	2013
Dollar	86.8	89.9	88.0	85.6	84.9	87.0
EUR	—	37.9	37.4	37.0	39.1	33.4
Deutsche mark	30.5	—	—	—	—	—
French franc	5.0	—	—	—	—	—
JPY	21.7	23.5	20.8	17.2	19.0	23.0
GBP	11.0	13.0	16.5	14.9	12.9	11.8
Australian dollar	3.0	4.3	6.0	6.6	7.6	8.6
Swiss franc	7.1	6.0	6.0	6.8	6.4	5.2
Canadian dollar	3.5	4.5	4.2	4.3	5.3	4.6
Hong Kong dollar	1.0	2.2	1.8	2.7	2.4	1.4
Swedish krona	0.3	2.5	2.2	2.7	2.2	1.8
South Korean Won	0.2	0.8	1.1	1.2	1.5	1.2
Singapore dollar	1.1	1.1	0.9	1.2	1.4	1.4
Indian rupee	0.1	0.2	0.3	0.7	0.9	1.0
Russian ruble	0.3	0.3	0.6	0.7	0.9	1.6
RMB	0.0	0.0	0.1	0.5	0.9	2.2
South African rand	0.4	0.9	0.7	0.9	0.7	1.1
Brazilian riyal	0.2	0.5	0.3	0.4	0.7	1.1
Danish krone	0.3	1.2	0.9	0.8	0.6	0.8
New Taiwan dollar	0.1	0.3	0.4	0.4	0.5	0.5
Thai baht	0.1	0.2	0.2	0.2	0.2	0.3
Indonesian rupee	0.1	0.0	0.1	0.1	0.2	0.2
Other currency	8.9	6.5	6.6	7.6	4.8	1.6
All currencies	**200.0**	**200.0**	**200.0**	**200.0**	**200.0**	**200.0**

Source: BIS Triennual reports.

calculated a new set of data that better reflects the degree of internationalization of a country's currency.[36] Table 6.8 is the relevant data for the major currencies in 2007. It can be seen that the Swiss franc has the highest proportion of foreign exchange transactions/GDP ratio of 436%, which fully demonstrates the degree of internationalization of the Swiss franc after the impact of economic scale. The ratio of the four international currencies, the US dollar, British pound, Japanese yen and Euro, are 169.50%, 147.6%, 109.4% and 83.3%,

[36]Refer to the SWIFT published in 2012, calculation method in "RMB internationalization: Implications for the global financial industry."

Table 6.8. Foreign Exchange Transactions in Major Currencies/the GDP of Currency Issuing Country 2007 (%)

Currency	Foreign Exchange Trading Volume of the World in 2007	GDP Share of the World in 2007	Foreign Exchange/ GDP
Swiss franc	3.40	0.80	436.30
Hong Kong dollar	1.40	0.40	363.10
Australian dollar	3.30	1.70	192.80
Dollar	42.80	25.20	169.50
GBP	7.50	5.00	147.60
JPY	8.60	7.90	109.40
South African rand	0.50	0.50	87.70
Canadian dollar	2.20	2.60	84.10
EUR	18.50	22.20	83.30
South Korean won	0.60	1.90	31.90
New Taiwan dollar	0.20	0.70	28.30
Indian rupee	0.40	2.10	16.90
Russian ruble	0.40	2.30	15.00
Brazilian real	0.20	2.50	8.10
RMB	0.24	6.30	3.70

Source: BIS Triennual reports, IMF World Economic Outlook Database.

respectively, which is consistent with the international status of these four currencies.

Among the BRICS countries, except for South Africa, which has a high proportion of 87.7%, the proportions of the other four countries are relatively low. It shows that the currencies of the BRICS countries are less internationalized compared to their large economic scale. It is particularly noteworthy that the proportion of foreign exchange transactions in RMB/GDP is only 3.7%, showing not only the gap with the five major currencies but also that it is the lowest among the BRICS countries, indicating that the proportion of RMB used in financial markets is still low.

Table 6.9 recalculates the indicator using the data of 2013. Compared with the data of 2007, the ranking of each currency is basically the same as that of 2007, but there are also some discrepancies.

Table 6.9. Foreign Exchange Transactions in Major Currencies/the GDP of Currency Issuing Country 2013 (%).

Currency	Foreign Exchange Trading Volume of the World in 2013	GDP Share of the World in 2013	Foreign Exchange/ GDP
Swiss franc	2.60	0.87	298.85
Australian dollar	4.30	2.08	206.73
Dollar	43.50	22.43	193.94
Hong Kong dollar	0.70	0.37	189.19
JPY	11.50	6.54	175.84
GBP	5.90	3.37	175.07
Singapore dollar	0.70	0.40	175.00
South African rand	0.55	0.47	117.02
EUR	16.70	17.02	98.12
Canadian dollar	2.30	2.44	94.26
New Taiwan dollar	0.25	0.65	38.46
South Korean won	0.60	1.74	34.48
Russian ruble	0.80	2.80	28.57
Indian rupee	0.50	2.51	19.92
Brazilian real	0.55	3.00	18.33
RMB	1.10	12.34	8.91

Source: BIS Triennual reports, IMF World Economic Outlook Database.

The Swiss franc still holds the first place, but the Hong Kong dollar has dropped from the second place to the fourth place, while the proportion of the Swiss franc has fallen sharply. The proportions of the four major currencies, the US dollar, the British pound, the Japanese yen and the euro, have risen to varying degrees, indicating that their degree of internationalization is still rising. The proportion of currencies in the BRICS countries has risen in varying degrees, indicating that their degree of internationalization has increased. The proportion of RMB is 8.91%, which is the most obvious increase from the rate of increase, but its internationalization is still the lowest. This shows that from a holistic perspective, the degree of internationalization of the RMB is not comparable to that of developed countries, even if there is still a huge gap compared with other BRICS countries.

(4) The internationalization of the RMB in the reserve currency:

It is generally believed that a country's currency can only achieve full internationalization if it becomes the foreign exchange reserve of other countries. Therefore, the ratio of a country's currency to the world's reserves is the core measure of the degree of currency internationalization.

As can be seen from Table 6.10, the US dollar and the euro are the world's most important reserve currencies, accounting for nearly 90% of the world's reserve currency. The pound, the yen and the Swiss franc are ranked second, third and fourth, respectively. Together, they constitute the world's five largest reserve currencies. Except for 2007, the percentage rates of the five major currencies to the world's reserve currency are close to, or even exceed, 95%.

So far, there are still no data on the RMB as the world's reserve currency, but there are reports that the Nigerian central bank has used the RMB as a reserve currency, accounting for 5–10% of its US$33 billion foreign exchange reserve. On 13 March 2012, Japanese Finance Minister Azumi Aya also revealed that the Chinese government had agreed that the Japanese government would purchase up to ¥65 billion (equivalent to US$10.3 billion) of Chinese government bonds on 8 March and Japan would implement the purchase plan in batches. In addition, the Bank of Korea began to purchase Chinese bonds in the China's interbank market with a previously obtained

Table 6.10. Percentage of World Major Reserve Currencies (%)

Currency	2000	2002	2004	2006	2007	2008	2009	2010	2011
Dollar	71.1	67.1	65.9	65.5	64.1	64.1	62.0	61.8	62.1
EUR	18.3	23.8	24.8	25.1	26.3	26.4	27.7	26.0	24.9
GBP	2.8	2.8	3.4	4.4	4.7	4.0	4.2	3.9	3.8
JPY	6.1	4.4	3.8	3.1	2.9	3.1	2.9	3.7	3.6
Swiss franc	0.3	0.4	0.2	0.2	0.2	4.4	0.2	3.5	0.3
Other	1.5	1.6	1.9	1.8	7.0	2.2	3.1	4.4	5.3

Source: IMF, Foreign Reserve Composition Database.

trading quota of ¥20 billion (US$3.2 billion) in April 2012, and began to use the Qualified Foreign Institutional Investor (QFII) quota of US$300 million obtained in July 2012 to purchase Chinese stocks. According to the latest news, Philip Lowe, Deputy Governor of the Reserve Bank of Australia, said on 23 April 2013 that the Australian central bank will invest up to 5% of its foreign exchange reserves in Chinese government bonds and has obtained approval from the People's Bank of China. According to the *Wall Street Journal*, Australia's foreign exchange reserves are currently about A$38.2 billion, and 5% of foreign exchange reserves are about A$1.91 billion, or about ¥12.4 billion (about US$2 billion). Even if these reports are true, the total amount is only US$19 billion, which is still negligible compared to the world's total reserves of more than US$5.6 trillion.

In summary, although the internationalization of the RMB has achieved many results since the launch of the RMB internationalization process in 2008, from the four indicators of cross-border trade settlement, cross-border investment settlement, foreign exchange transactions and foreign exchange reserves, the degree of reconciliation is still low. Not only it is far from the major currencies of the world but it also lags behind other BRICS currencies. In the future, we still need to continue to advance the internationalization of the RMB from various aspects.

6.2.2.3 *Establishment and Development of the Offshore RMB Market in Hong Kong*

The establishment process of the offshore RMB market in Hong Kong can be divided into three stages, namely, the budding stage (end of 2003 to the end of 2008), the formation stage (early 2009 to mid-2011) and the comprehensive construction stage (since August 2011). The emergence of offshore RMB personal business in Hong Kong is considered to be the beginning of the development of offshore RMB business in Hong Kong. Following the offshore RMB deposit business in Hong Kong, the offshore RMB bond business is an important measure for the Chinese government to promote the development of offshore RMB in Hong Kong. On 10 January 2007, the Chinese government agreed to issue RMB-denominated financial bonds in Hong Kong. The People's Bank of China formulated the Interim Measures for the Administration of the Issuance of RMB Bonds by Domestic Financial Institutions to the Hong Kong Special Administrative Region. In July 2007, the China Development Bank issued the first RMB bond in Hong Kong. In order to support the development of offshore RMB business, Hong Kong launched the RMB Real-Time Payment and Settlement System (RTGS) in July 2007, which enables real-time settlement of RMB, Hong Kong dollar, US dollar and euro. Since the launch of RTGS, it has operated smoothly and the average daily transaction volume has increased significantly. From ¥5 billion in 2010 to ¥121 billion in 2011, it reached RMB ¥214 billion in 2012.

From July to August 2010, due to the revision of the clearing agreement and the construction of the offshore RMB return mechanism, the offshore RMB business in Hong Kong developed rapidly, and the offshore RMB product innovation was very rapid (Table 6.11). RMB offshore certificates such as RMB deposit certificates, structured deposits, RMB insurance policies, RMB investment funds and RMB syndicated loans came into being in Hong Kong, and the offshore RMB product system was improved. On 11 April 2011, Hong Kong's first RMB IPO offer, Huixian Real Estate Trust Investment Fund (REIT) sold for ¥5.24 – 5.58 per unit, with a total capital of ¥104.8 – 111.6 billion. So far, Hong Kong's RMB products have covered three aspects of "fixed-rate products, fund products, and IPO products." The product system framework of the offshore RMB market in Hong Kong has basically taken shape. The construction of the offshore RMB return mechanism and the formation of the offshore RMB product system mark the formation of the offshore RMB market in Hong Kong.

The National 12th 5-Year Plan clearly proposes to support Hong Kong's development as an offshore RMB business center and asset management center, which has become the policy basis for the comprehensive construction of the offshore RMB market in Hong Kong. On 17 August 2011, at the "National 'Twelfth Five-Year Plan'

Table 6.11. Innovation of Offshore RMB products in Hong Kong from July 2010 to July 2012

Category	Name of Innovative Product	Time of Appearance	Innovative Institution
Deposit and loan class	RMB deposit certificate	July 2010	CITIC Bank International
	RMB structured deposit	19 July 2010	HSBC and Standard Chartered Bank
	RMB syndicated loan	November 2010	Hang Seng Bank
Bond class	Offshore RMB corporate bonds	27 June 2010	Hopewell Highway Infrastructure
	Synthetic RMB bond	December 2010	Shui On Land
	RMB offshore bond index	31 December 2010	BOC Hong Kong
	RMB IPO	11 April 2011	Huixian Real Estate Trust
	Offshore RMB Qualified Foreign Investor (RQFII) products	March 2012	
Capital transaction	RMB foreign exchange swap transaction	20 July 2010	CITIC Bank International and ICBC Asia
	Deliverable RMB interest rate swap	22 October 2010	HSBC and Deutsche Bank
	Dividable RMB interest rate swap option	12 November 2010	HSBC Holdings and BNP Paribas
	Deliverable RMB options	Early October 2010	HSBC Holdings
	USD/RMB spot fixing price	27 June 2011	Hong Kong Financial Markets Association
	Double currency stock	October 2012	Hong Kong Stock Exchange
	RMB currency futures	17 September 2012	Hong Kong Stock Exchange
Asset management	RMB public fund	11 August 2010	Haitong Asset Management (Hong Kong)
	RMB life insurance	20 July 2010	HSBC, BOC Hong Kong, China Life, etc.
	Real estate investment trust	April 2011	Huixian Real Estate
	RMB gold ETF	14 February 2012	Hong Kong Stock Exchange
	A-share ETF	29 June 2012	Hong Kong Stock Exchange

Source: The author collected relevant information.

and the Economic and Financial Cooperation Development Forum between the two places" held in Hong Kong, Vice Premier Li Keqiang announced eight measures to actively develop offshore RMB business in Hong Kong (Table 6.12). The central government's strong support for Hong Kong's development of offshore RMB business is regarded as the beginning of a comprehensive construction of the offshore RMB market in Hong Kong.

These eight policy measures to build the offshore RMB market in Hong Kong include the improvement of the offshore RMB reverse flow mechanism, the offshore RMB bond market and the offshore RMB product market, which are the key elements to promote the maturity of the offshore RMB market in Hong Kong.

The comprehensive construction phase is an important step and process for establishing a mature offshore market after the initial formation of the offshore RMB market in Hong Kong. At present, the offshore financial business of RMB in Hong Kong has already had a certain foundation, but there is still a big gap compared with the mature offshore market. The pace of strengthening the construction of the offshore RMB market cannot be stopped. Since the capital account of RMB is not fully open, the construction of the offshore RMB market in Hong Kong must be gradual. Although comprehensive construction will lead to greater development of the offshore RMB business in Hong Kong, it is difficult to establish a mature offshore RMB market in Hong Kong in the short term. The establishment of a mature offshore RMB market needs to overcome more difficulties. The comprehensive construction of the RMB offshore market in Hong Kong will be a long-term and an arduous process.

Since its construction, the offshore RMB market in Hong Kong has developed rapidly. This can be reflected in the development of the offshore RMB currency market, securities market, foreign exchange market and product market.

The offshore RMB currency market in Hong Kong is a short-term capital market. The financial instruments in this market are mainly short-term credit instruments issued by the government, financial institutions and industrial and commercial enterprises. They have

Table 6.12. Eight Policy Measures for the Full Construction of the RMB Offshore Market in Hong Kong in August 2011

	Measure	Date of Implementation	Policy Release Department	Related Implementation Policy	Result Achieved
1	Cross-border RMB direct investment	12 October 2011	Ministry of Commerce and People's Bank	Notice on Issues Related to Direct Investment in Cross-border RMB	74 projects have been reviewed, involving funds of ¥16.53 billion, and investment from Hong Kong is about 70%
2	Expanding the pilot scope of cross-border trade RMB settlement to the whole country	24 August 2011	People's Bank of China, Ministry of Finance, Ministry of Commerce, General Administration of Customs, State Administration of Taxation, China Banking Regulatory Commission	Notice on Expanding the RMB settlement area for cross-border trade	In 2011, the cross-border trade RMB settlement business accumulated ¥2.08 trillion, accounting for 63.7% through Hong Kong
3	Continue to promote the pilot work of investment in inter-bank bond markets by three types of overseas institutions, including overseas central banks, Hong Kong and Macau clearing banks, and overseas participating banks	16 August 2010	People's Bank of China	Notice on the Relevant Matters Concerning the Use of RMB Investment in the Inter-bank Bond Market by Three Types of Institutions Such as the Overseas RMB Clearing Bank	At the end of 2011, about 40 overseas institutions have been allowed to enter the inter-bank bond market. On 10 November 2011, the People's Bank of China and the Austrian Central Bank signed an agency agreement to enter their inter-bank bond market. The Southeast Asian Central Bank is expected to follow up

(*Continued*)

Table 6.12. (*Continued*)

	Measure	Date of Implementation	Policy Release Department	Related Implementation Policy	Result Achieved
4	Increase the main body of domestic financial institutions that issue RMB bonds to Hong Kong.	11 January 2012	National Development and Reform Commission.	Development and Reform Commission announced on 11 January 2012.	The National Development and Reform Commission approved the approval of 10 banks including the National Development Bank to issue bonds worth 25 billion yuan in Hong Kong
5	Piloting foreign-funded banks to increase capital by RMB.	11 November 2011	—	—	HSBC Bank (China) increased its capital by ¥2.8 billion, the first foreign bank to complete the RMB capital increase since the pilot was launched, and became the largest foreign bank with the largest registered capital in China

6	Allow investment in domestic securities market in the form of qualified foreign institutional investors	4 January 2012	People's Bank of China	Notice on Relevant Matters Concerning the Implementation of the Pilot Measures for the Domestic Securities Investment of the Qualified Foreign Institutional Investors of the Fund Management Companies and Securities Companies	The starting capital of RMB qualified foreign institutional investors to invest in the domestic securities market is ¥20 billion
7	The issuance of RMB government bonds in Hong Kong as a long-term institutional arrangement, gradually expanding the scale	Long-term work continues to push	—	—	—
8	Encourage Hong Kong to innovate and develop offshore RMB products	Long-term work continues to push	—	—	—

Note: On 11 January 2012, the National Development and Reform Commission approved 10 banks that agreed to issue RMB bonds to Hong Kong for the China Development Bank, China Exim Bank, China Agricultural Development Bank, Industrial and Commercial Bank of China, Agricultural Bank of China, Bank of China, China Construction Bank, Bank of Communications, Bank of East Asia (China), HSBC Bank (China).

Source: The author collated according to relevant information.

the characteristics of short term, strong liquidity and low risk. The offshore RMB currency market mainly includes the interbank borrowing market, the discounted bill market and the short-term bond market. Until the end of 2012, the balance of RMB deposits and certificates of deposits were ¥603 billion and ¥117.3 billion, respectively, which was ¥720.2 billion in total, increased 9% from the end of 2011 of ¥661.6 billion. As of the end of 2012, the balance of RMB loans rose by 1.57 times to ¥790 billion on year-on-year base, and the figure at the end of 2011 was only RMB 30.8 billion. As of the end of October 2013, offshore RMB deposits in Hong Kong had reached ¥781.6 billion, an increase of 41% from October 2012 (Figure 6.6). Interbank lending rates are an important reference rate in financial markets and a standard for many financial products. Internationally important interbank interest rates are formed through the quotation system, which is obtained by calculating the quotations of many quotation banks in a certain way. In June 2013, the world's first offshore RMB interbank interest rate pricing mechanism was launched by the Hong Kong Treasury Market Association. Hong Kong RMB

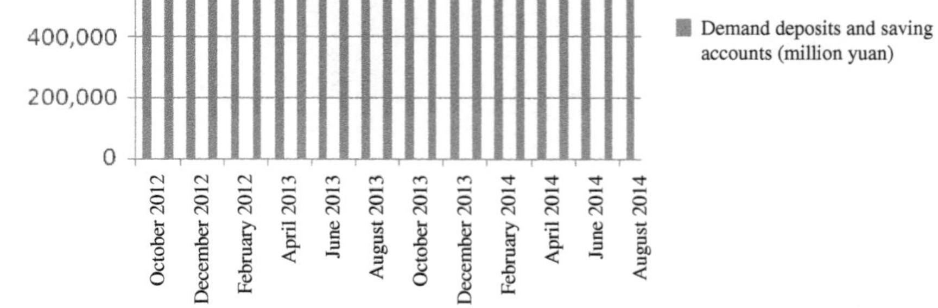

Figure 6.6. Scale of Offshore RMB deposits in Hong Kong from January 2012 to October 2013

Source: Hong Kong Monetary Authority, http://www.hkma.gov.hk/.

Interbank Offered Rate (HIBOR CNY) was formed by 18 banks set up by the Hong Kong Monetary Authority, including overnight, 1 week, 2 weeks, 1 month, 2 months, 3 months, 6 months and 12-month period. The RMB interbank interest rate in Hong Kong can promote the lending of RMB loans and financial developments related to interest rates. It will also help manage interest rate risk and promote the consolidation of the offshore center of Hong Kong.

The offshore RMB securities market in Hong Kong mainly includes the offshore RMB bond market and the offshore RMB stock market. The offshore RMB bond market is the focus of the offshore RMB market construction in Hong Kong. In 2012, the issuance of new RMB bonds for offshore RMB bonds market, commonly known as "dim sum debts," was ¥111.1 billion, up only 4% from ¥109.5 billion in 2011. The balance of outstanding bonds as of the end of 2012 was RMB 237.2 billion, an increase of 62% from the end of 2011 (Table 6.13). HSBC's Hong Kong President Feng Xiaomei expected that the size of RMB bond issuance in Hong Kong in 2013 would be ¥280 – 360 billion, and the overall size of the RMB bond market in Hong Kong would reach ¥460 – 540 billion by the end of 2013.

The offshore RMB foreign exchange market in Hong Kong is an important part of the offshore RMB market in Hong Kong and the basis for the formation of offshore RMB exchange rates.

Table 6.13. Issuance of Offshore RMB Bonds of Different Types of Issuers from 2007 to 2012

	Financial Debt	Corporate Debt	Government Agency	International Organizations	Total
2007	100	0	0	0	100
2008	120	0	0	0	120
2009	100	0	60	0	160
2010	165	132	80	12	389
2011	54	836	200	5	1095
2012	465	436	210	0	1,111
Total	1,004	1,404	550	17	2,975

Note: RMB 100 million.

Source: Wind Info, http://www.wind.com.cn/.

On 27 June 2011, the Hong Kong Treasury Market Association launched the USD/RMB spot exchange rate fixing price (hereinafter referred to as CNH spot) formed by the designated 15 banks. The offshore RMB foreign exchange market in Hong Kong has formed a unified market benchmark spot exchange rate. The emergence of CNH on the spot has a greater impact on the linkage between domestic and overseas forward markets, and generally reduces the linkage relationship between the domestic forward market and the overseas NDF market. Moreover, the emergence of the CNH spot exchange rate strengthens the price discovery ability of the CNY forward market, but weakens the price discovery function of the NDF market.

The offshore RMB product market in Hong Kong refers mainly to the market for RMB financial instruments and financial products in Hong Kong. Offshore RMB products include not only financial derivatives of offshore RMB but also other investment and financing products of offshore RMB. First, Hong Kong's first offshore RMB deposit certificate was launched by CITIC Bank International in July 2010. In 2011, the offshore RMB deposit certificate business in Hong Kong developed rapidly. In January 2011, the issuance scale of offshore RMB deposit certificates in Hong Kong was ¥2.5 billion. In December 2011, the total amount of offshore RMB deposit certificates issued in Hong Kong was ¥56.42 billion, and further increased to ¥117.3 billion in December 2012. Secondly, the first offshore RMB syndicated loan appeared in early December 2010, signed by 10 banks including China Automation Group and Hang Seng Bank, with an equivalent value of US$50 million and a term of 3.5 years. After that, there were several offshore RMB syndicated loans. Among them, in September 2012, Hengxin Leasing won an offshore RMB 1.145 billion term loan, which was the first offshore RMB syndicated loan completed by a non-bank financial institution in China. Third, Hong Kong's first offshore RMB fund was issued by Haitong Asset Management (Hong Kong) in August 2010. After that, offshore RMB fund products also developed rapidly, especially the development of private equity funds. At the end of 2011, there were 5 cemetery RMB bond funds in the Hong Kong market, and more than 40 private equity funds denominated in RMB. As of the end of 2012, Hong Kong has issued more than 200 offshore RMB funds.

6.2.2.4 *Assessment on the Outlook of RMB Internationalization*

From the current point of view, China has begun to try to promote capital project opening and RMB internationalization in a step-by-step manner. It has already opened up RMB foreign direct investment and allowed foreign capital to invest in the mainland capital market in the RMB situation. At the same time, it encourages domestic and foreign-funded enterprises to invest in each other in the form of RMB. Foreign companies are allowed to list and issue bonds in the form of RMB in China. The RMB, the Japanese yen and Australian dollar can be directly exchanged. The road map for the full convertibility of RMB is becoming clearer and its schedule is predictable, paving the way for further internationalization of the RMB.

In order to clearly present the future path of RMB internationalization, under the assumption that the RMB is fully convertible, according to the future development trend of China's economy and the current development conditions of the world economy, the prospect of RMB internationalization can be simulated theoretically. From a quantitative perspective, using the basic model of Chinn and Frankel[37] and based on the historical data of major international currencies to establish a mixed data model of panel data, and use relevant variables to explain the changing rules of international reserves:

$$Y_j = \sum \beta_i \times X_{ij} + \varepsilon.$$

Among them, Y is to explain the degree of internationalization of the currency, such as the reserve ratio, X is to explain variables

[37]Chinn, Menzie and Jeffrey A. Frankel, *Will the Euro Eventually Surpass the Dollar as Leading International Reserve Currency? G7 Current Account Imbalances: Sustainability and Adjustment.* Chicago: University of Chicago Press, 2007, 283–338.

such as economic aggregates, currency stability, etc. i marks the different explanatory variables, j marks the different currency types, but they only have one common interpretation coefficient in the regression equation β_i, ε is the error term.

In the choice of explanatory variables, we adopt a more cautious attitude and compare the relative optimal models by multiple standards, considering economic strength (including GDP/GNP ratio, import and export ratio, FDI stock and flow ratio), inflation stability (annual difference and monthly difference) and exchange rate stability (coefficient of variation, real effective exchange rate change rate). Based on the explanatory variables such as inertia (the ratio of the lag phase of the reserve) and the transaction (payment and settlement ratio), multiple regression models are established on different combinations of variables, and the choice between the explanatory force and the model parameters is relatively optimal. The model finally chose the following prediction model:

International reserve ratio = $-0.2743 + 0.967 *$ inertia $+ 0.068 *$ GDP ratio $- 69.80 *$ exchange rate change rate.

$$(0.0126) \quad (0.0319) \quad (18.9955)$$
$$[F = 14181.2, \mathit{Adj}\ R^2 = 0.9986].$$

Based on the aforementioned model, we make a medium-term forecast for the RMB international reserve and try to extrapolate to other cases. First, the initial value of the independent variable is selected, in which the GDP ratio is predicted by the IMF, the exchange rate change is extrapolated using the 5-year moving average, and the initial value of the RMB international reserve is based on the known international settlement amount of the RMB, using the US dollar reserve and transaction clearing. Based on the calculation of the relationship ratio, the international reserve forecast and extrapolation value of the RMB under the general conditions of the international currency are obtained. Judging from the forecast results, if the RMB launches all-round internationalization, the proportion of international reserves will reach 3% in 5 years, and it

Table 6.14. Forecast Ratio of RMB and Major International Currency Reserves (%)

Year	USD	EUR	JPY	RMB
2013	59.74	26.65	4.87	1.45
2014	59.25	26.65	5.21	1.91
2015	58.79	26.62	5.55	2.43
2016	58.27	26.62	5.91	2.93
2017	57.78	26.57	6.30	3.15
2020	56.38	26.29	7.27	5.15
2025	54.06	25.76	8.29	8.32
2030	51.85	24.97	8.99	11.87

will reach 10% or more in 2030, becoming the third largest international currency.

It should be emphasized that this forecast is based on the assumption that the RMB is fully convertible and the capital account is fully open, based on the current major international currency experience. It is intended to suggest that if the policy layer is about to fully promote internationalization, what the future direction is.

On this basis, the international clearing use of the RMB can be estimated. With the dollar as an example, the dollar accounted for a very stable ratio in international settlements and international reserves in the past 10 years, and the ratio maintain the range of 1.45–1.59 between 2001 and 2010, with an average of 1.52. If RMB clearing and reserve ratio has the same proportion, it can be calculated that the amount of RMB international settlement will reach US$2.5 trillion in 2016.

There are many factors that influence the international bond, which make forecast more complex. We use trend extrapolation to conduct conservative estimates, predicting the trend of RMB bonds based on the existing data of the BIS reports. From Figure 6.7, the RMB international bond issuance growth trend linear stable since 2005, and the conservative estimates of annual international bond issuance of RMB will reach ¥5000 billion in five years.

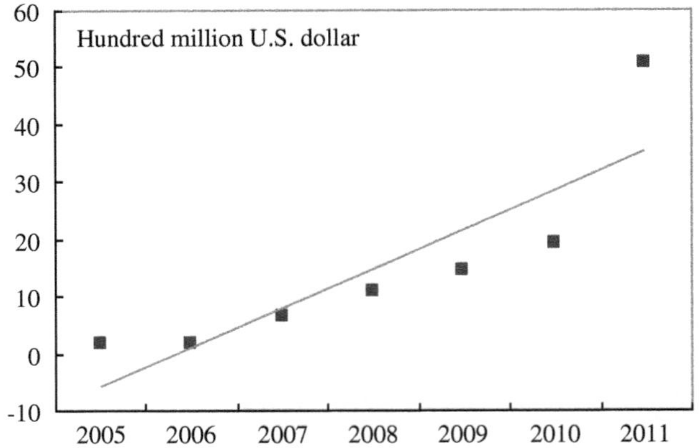

Figure 6.7. RMB International Bond Issuance Amount of Change
Source: www.bis.org.

From more intuitive point of view, the internationalization of the RMB will be promoted in a certain order: the current account trade settlement, capital account investment transactions and the international reserve of sovereign economies. The first step is to promote RMB as settlement currency in international trade, aiming at the rapid development in the next 5 years, to establish solid foundations of the real economy for the global use of RMB, and to provide ample pool of funds overseas. With the expansion of the RMB settlement of international trade and financing in the financial market, there will be a greater variety of RMB-denominated products. When the RMB investment transactions initiate, it will accelerate in the next 10 years, then keep an appropriate proportion and trade with steady development. When the application of the RMB in international trade and financial markets are increasingly expanding, many countries and regions will add RMB into its international reserves. To deal with the problem of RMB balance in international payments, the proportion of the RMB in international reserve is increased gradually and tends to be stable.

The analysis and prediction depict the current situation and broad prospects of RMB internationalization. On the one hand, since

RMB is used in the cross-border trade in international settlement, it experienced a rapid development both in the quantity and the settlement channel; on the other hand, the current international use of RMB is still very limited in breadth and depth. From the perspective of prediction and speculation, the future of international use of RMB will be very bright, with trillions of RMB as international reserves, trade settlement and liquidation valuation, etc.

Under the condition of the international monetary system and the development of the international financial crisis, RMB internationalization is not only the actual needs of the surrounding area but also the specific requirements of China's further reform and opening up. The development of RMB internationalization needs overseas demand and market, and also requires the reform of domestic financial market. This internationalization process is not only necessary to constantly promote the use of the RMB and the project in depth and breadth, but also to deeply reform the domestic market. We are looking forward to steadily push forward the process, and also deal with related risks and side effects.

Domestic and foreign experts and scholars generally believe that, from the development trend, China's economic scale is expected to reach the first in the world after 2030. Based on the progress of science and technology, geopolitical stability, harmonious cultural exchange, RMB may enter widely into the foreign non-resident balance sheet with households and enterprises involved, and become the third international currency with the same function as the dollar and euro.

From the specific perspective, with the continuous growth of China's economy, the internationalization of the RMB is facing a precious historical opportunity. The RMB is expected to become the world's main settlement, trading and reserve currency of payment in the next 15–20 years. We believe that the internationalization of the RMB will achieve new progress in the following three aspects.

First, the proportion of RMB in trade, investment and settlement will be significantly improved. The future of China's foreign trade and financial cooperation will be more diversified, especially with the neighboring countries. When the trade and investment exchanges among these countries become increasingly frequent, the RMB will be more and more functional as a settlement currency. It is expected that RMB will account for about 15% in foreign trade and investment in China in 2015, and is expected to exceed 30% in 2025.

Second, the onshore and offshore RMB market will continue to expand in scale. Shanghai will gradually form a mature mechanism for RMB product innovation, trading, pricing and settlement, build cross-border RMB financing center, RMB benchmark products price formation center, commodity pricing center and financial information service center, and it is expected to become an important onshore RMB market. Hong Kong's position of an offshore RMB market will be further highlighted. China will strengthen cooperation with major international financial centers and promote the coordination development in London, Singapore, Luxemburg and other offshore RMB markets.

Third, the international status of RMB will increase steadily. With the global settlement, clearing, trading network continues to improve, the future of the RMB may become the world's major trading currencies and the RMB in cross-border settlement, financing and hedging and other fields will be more widely used. In addition, according to the forecast of the World Bank, the proportion of RMB in the global official foreign exchange reserves is expected to exceed 5% in 2025.

By the aforementioned analysis, with cross-border use of RMB as well as the development of the offshore RMB market, the internationalization of the RMB has achieved remarkable results in recent years. Nevertheless, we still cannot say that the RMB is an international currency at present. Compared with the dollar, the euro and other major international currencies, whether the functions in the invoicing and settlement in a private transaction, or anchor currency function and reserve currency function in the official transaction, the RMB has played a very limited role. Therefore, the tactics of RMB internationalization should focus on finding and overcoming the major problems in the process, to continue steadily promoting the process.

6.2.3 *The Problems of the Internationalization of the RMB*

Since the promotion of cross-border RMB trade settlement, it has made substantial progress in the development of the internationalization of the RMB offshore market. At the same time, the promotion of cross-border RMB in the current economic and financial system is also facing some difficulties and inconsistency in practice, which needs to continue to accumulate experience and explore for the characteristics of the road of the further reform of the RMB internationalization.

6.2.3.1 *The Predicament of RMB Internationalization*

From the general theory of currency internationalization, two difficulties of the internationalization of RMB reflected in that the trade surplus and capital account is not completely open.

The first is the plight of trade surplus. After the collapse of the Bretton Woods system, the relationship between the credit currency and gold was completely cut off, and the international monetary system has entered an era led by credit currency. In an international currency system led by the credit currency, the issue of international currency must be able to form a long-term deficit mechanism, to provide sufficient liquidity to the international financial market. As we have analyzed previously, under the condition of open economy, there are two kinds of international currency flow: the currency flows behind the real economy and the currency flow directly from capital flows. The international currency outflow can transfer the real resources of "peripheral" countries to the "center" countries or the "center" countries make capital investment to "peripheral" countries. From the point of view of "center" countries, to provide the international monetary supply by way of a current account deficit or capital account deficit. That is to say, the international monetary supply can only be achieved by the deficit mechanism of the "center" countries. Of course, there is no essential difference between the capital account and current account. For example, the international supply of the US dollar in different periods is achieved by the capital account deficit and current account deficit, respectively.

In recent years, with the rapid development of foreign trade, China has become the world's largest exporter and second-largest importer of import and export in 2010. Its large trade surplus remains high over the years, and the amount of trade surplus has kept increasing in recent years. Trade surplus means of domestic foreign currency net payment in dollars, so China's foreign exchange experienced the rapid growth of reserves under the current international monetary payment conditions. In RMB payment conditions, you need to have enough foreign RMB to be able to pay for our deficit, while the cumulative offshore RMB also needs China to pay in the form of foreign trade deficit, the two conditions are a contradiction. How to promote the internationalization of RMB in condition of trade surplus has become a current dilemma.

The second predicament is that the capital project is not completely open. Capital account convertibility is an important condition for a country's currency to be an international currency, because whether a currency is exchangeable or not is an important deciding factor for the currency users. If a currency is not convertible, the transaction costs of the currency holder will rise. The asymmetry of the risk and return of a currency will significantly reduce the enthusiasm of using the currency, then the currency will be at a disadvantage in the competition, so the convertibility of capital projects will affect the progress of the internationalization of the RMB, and with the degree of internationalization is gradually increasing, the constraints will be more obvious.

Liberalization of RMB capital account is not only an inevitable result of the deepening reform of the market economy in China but also an important manifestation of the process of RMB internationalization. After the convertibility of RMB current account is realized in China in 1996, capital account convertibility has been an important goal of China's financial reform. According to the classification of IMF standard on capital account transactions in 2010 — "The Annual Report on Exchange Arrangements and

Exchange Restrictions," although the RMB capital projects achieved partial exchange accounted for 75% of all transactions, projects that achieved fully convertible accounted for only 12%, and non-convertible projects still accounted for 25%. In the future, the RMB capital account still need to further improve the process of internationalization of the RMB convertibility, otherwise the advance will be hindered, mainly reflected in the following aspects:

First, it hinders the construction of RMB back flow mechanism. To become an international currency, it is a prerequisite to establish a "two-way interaction mechanisms" for domestic currency inflow and foreign currency outflow. But in the capital account convertibility under limited circumstances, offshore RMB is lack of a stable back-flow mechanism. If the foreign settlement of RMB cannot return to the territory and involve in the investment, the investment channels are blocked, and the lack of liquidity of RMB will greatly weaken the RMB demand by the international financial market currency holders.

Only by transforming "one-way currency flow" to "two-way interaction mechanism," can RMB change the unilateral expectation in the international market, thus contributing to the formation of the two-way fluctuation mechanism of RMB exchange market. The capital account convertibility can facilitate the mechanism of backflow of the offshore RMB, and ultimately to expand RMB investment channels and benefit margin, enhance the enthusiasm of foreign investors to hold the RMB, provide a broader market space for the internationalization of RMB.

Second, it constraints the continuous expansion of the scale of RMB offshore market. The development of foreign currency market plays an important role on the currency internationalization of the country. In view of the special geographical and political advantages, Hong Kong has become the offshore RMB financial center. Although the RMB market in Hong Kong has a certain development, because China's capital account is not fully convertible, the functions of settlement and investment with overseas RMB is limited, such as offshore RMB loans, financial derivatives and securities investment business are still subject to a certain limit, which hinders the further development of the offshore RMB market. From the view of long-term development, the offshore RMB market is limited and will restrict the process of internationalization of the RMB in the future. Historically, in the process of internationalization of the dollar, if not supported by such a large euro–dollar market, it would be difficult for the dollar to be the dominant currency in the international trade and investment.

Third, it will restrict the depth of the financial markets. To become an international currency, there must be a highly developed financial market to provide a corresponding "monetary asset pool" for the currency demand, so that foreign investors can obtain and hold RMB with less cost. The higher the degree of free convertibility of the RMB, the lower the risk of currency holdings is; thus, RMB will have a competitive advantage in the competition of foreign currencies. If the convertibility of RMB capital account cannot be achieved, it will hinder the formation of a highly developed and open financial market. If the financial market is insufficient and is lacking of financial tools and financial products, it will not be able to meet the needs of investors in financial assets in safety, liquidity and profitability, which will significantly affect the willingness to hold RMB in the international market.

The depth and breadth of the market is a measure of a currency with economies of scale and scope. The larger the circulation area, the stronger is the ability to deal with the impact of the currency. Therefore, the extension of financial market depth will provide the matching conditions for the supply and demand of international RMB, and promote the process of internationalization of the RMB. Under the conditions of limited convertibility of capital account, this aim is obviously difficult to achieve. From the international experience, the development of New York, London, Tokyo and other developed financial markets has played an important role in promoting the internationalization of the dollar, pound and yen.

With the accelerating process of internationalization of the RMB, all speculative risk caused by the RMB capital control will increase. The cost of risk control will become increasingly higher, while the efficiency is declining. Therefore, in the process of internationalization of the RMB, convertibility in capital account should be orderly and steadily promoted. The convertibility of the capital account is not only a necessary technical condition for RMB internationalization but also an important manifestation of the process of internationalization of RMB. How to gradually open the capital projects and actively promote the development of RMB internationalization at the same time is also a dilemma.

In sum, the conditions of trade surplus and the partial openness of the capital account is the characteristics of economic and financial development in China, and it has important significance to keep the healthy and steady economic development in the short term. The dilemma cannot be completely resolved in the short term, and therefore it requires different development road of internationalization of the RMB. Through the different ways we can learn from the development experience of the major international currencies, different development roads can be designed to meet the characteristics of China.

6.2.3.2 *The Main Problems of Cross-Border RMB Trade Settlement*

The direct purpose of promoting RMB settlement of cross-border trade is to facilitate international trade, thereby enhancing and expanding the payment function of the RMB. The further expansion of the current RMB settlement of cross-border trade also faces a series of problems, which directly or indirectly affect the acceptance of the RMB abroad.

First, cross-border trade in RMB settlement has a serious uneven distribution of foreign business. Most of the business of cross-border trade settlement in RMB is in Hong Kong. In 2009, the RMB settlement amount of cross-border trade in Hong Kong totaled ¥1.9 billion, accounting for 53% of the total RMB settlement of cross-border trade in China. In 2010, the cross-border trade settlement of RMB through Hong Kong totaled ¥369.2 billion, and the proportion of total RMB settlements in the cross-border trade rose

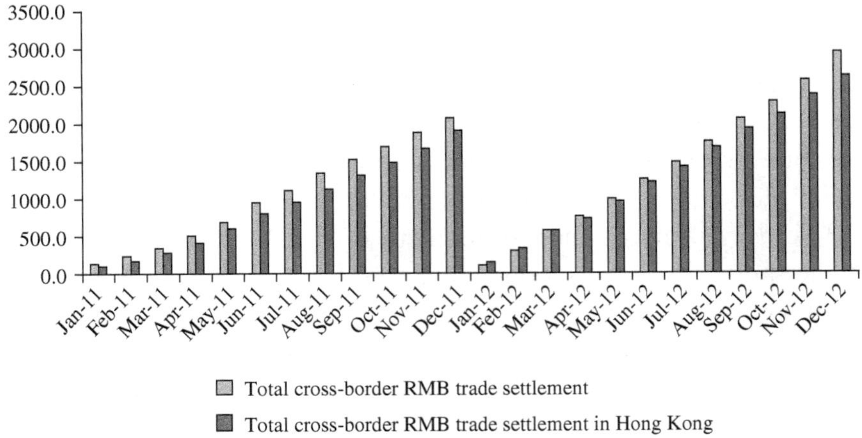

Figure 6.8. Total Amount of Cross-Border Trade RMB Settlement and the Amount in Hong Kong

Source: China Merchants Securities (Hong Kong) Co., Ltd., http://www.newone.com.hk/.

to 73%. In the first half of 2010, the monthly average RMB settlement of cross-border trade in Hong Kong was RMB 4.5 billion, and the monthly average in the second half of the year rose to RMB 57 billion. The amount of RMB settlement of cross-border trade through Hong Kong accounts for more than 80% of the total, as is the case from 2011 to 2012 (see Figure 6.8). This has determined that cross-border trade RMB settlement has become an important source of offshore RMB deposits in Hong Kong.

Second, the structure of cross-border trade RMB settlement of import and export is unbalanced. The unbalanced structure of cross-border trade RMB settlement, that is, the import is far greater than the export, so the RMB settlement is more used in Mainland China's overseas import business, and it is less used in the export. For example, in the first quarter of 2011, the total volume of goods imported from cross-border trade in RMB was ¥285.37 billion, while the total export was ¥20.23 billion. The import of goods accounted for 93.4% of the total amount of import and export, accounting for 79% of total value of goods and services. This can also be reflected in the cross-border ratio of cross-border trade in RMB settlement.

Table 6.15. Changes in the Settlement Ratio of RMB Settlement in Cross-Border Trade

Period	Payout Ratio
Full year of 2010	1:5.5
First quarter of 2011	1:5
Second quarter of 2011	1:2.9
Third quarter of 2011	1:1.67
Year 2011	1:1.7
First quarter of 2012	1:1.4
Second quarter of 2012	1:1.4
Third quarter of 2012	1:1.2
Year 2012	1:1.2
First quarter of 2013	1:1.4
Second quarter of 2013	1:1.3
Third quarter of 2013	1:1.5
Full year of 2013	1:1.46
First quarter of 2014	1:2
Second quarter of 2014	1:1.66

Source: The Monetary Policy Report of the People's Bank of China and the various periods from 2010 to 2014.

The asymmetry in the use of the RMB in import and export trade has caused the RMB settlement and payment ratio to deviate significantly from Table 6.15. The result of this practice and the original intention of promoting the internationalization of the RMB have deviated.

The structure of cross-border trade in RMB settlement of import and export is unbalanced, indicating that overseas exporters are more willing to accept the RMB, while mainland exporters mainly receive US dollars. Therefore, this settlement result is reflected in the balance of payments, that is, China's foreign exchange reserves have not decreased due to the settlement of the RMB, and on the contrary, they have increased. All these have not achieved the purpose of reducing the increase in foreign exchange reserves and preventing the risk of the US dollar reserve assets. For enterprises, this has led to a large number of domestic RMB exchanges through the cross-border trade settlement of RMB, and overseas export enterprises have benefited from the appreciation of the RMB.

Third, there is a large number of arbitrage financing activities of affiliated companies in the RMB settlement of cross-border trade. Hong Kong is the main concentration of RMB settlement for cross-border trade. Due to the division of financial markets between the two places and the restrictions on investment channels, the offshore RMB market interest rate in Hong Kong has been lower than that in the Mainland. In recent years, there has been a widespread expectation of RMB appreciation both at home and abroad, and the expectation of overseas RMB appreciation has become more intense, resulting in the exchange rate of offshore RMB against the US dollar in Hong Kong being higher than that in the Mainland. If there is no RMB settlement cross-border trade, since the overseas loan interest rate is lower than the domestic one, there is a model of utilizing the spread arbitrage between the two places. However, after the settlement of the RMB, the existence of the exchange rate difference between the Mainland and Hong Kong further increased the space for enterprise arbitrage financing. The imbalance business structure of cross-border trade in RMB settlement of import and export indicates that the overseas exporters are mostly affiliates of domestic import business, or the operating platform specially established outside the country. Currently, they are mostly located in Hong Kong and Singapore. The import settlements are mainly the financing behavior of arbitrage. The specific mode is that domestic companies generally apply to a domestic bank for a one-year forward letter of credit or a bank credit guarantee such as a guarantee payment. After the affiliate company exports to the country, it will use the domestic receivable claims in RMB, especially the bank guarantee and credit, to apply for low-interest dollar discounts overseas, and then use the non-deliverable forward (NDF) exchange rate to sell RMB to pay US dollar loans, and obtain double arbitrage of exchange rate and interest rate. This arbitrage financing behavior has deviated from the original intention of the RMB settlement of cross-border trade, which will lead to the accelerated inflow of RMB into Hong Kong. In the future, if this funds flow into the Mainland out of order, it will distort the implementation effect of domestic monetary policy and trigger financial turmoil. By then, the offshore financial market will no longer be a firewall, but a trigger for financial turmoil.

Fourth, the expansion of the RMB settlement operations is subject to the dual constraints of institutional and technical supply. At present, some trading companies hope to expand the scope of settlement to the payment of wages for overseas employees, trade credit and countries that have obstacles to pay in RMB. Apart from Hong Kong, overseas commercial banking institutions are generally unclear about how to enter specific operations, and lack of confidence in the technical investment in the transformation system. It is difficult to play the role of promoting RMB settlement only at the enterprise level. For example, some overseas customers of Chinese companies are willing to accept the RMB, especially under the condition of the stability of the RMB and the characteristics of a good appreciation prospect, but the other party's banking system does not know how to operate in the business, and the central bank has not provided a policy for this operation. Therefore, it is impossible to use RMB as the settlement currency for business transactions of this kind. The scale and geographical scope of RMB settlement of cross-border trade will be greatly restricted. (Although according to the policy issued by China, the geographical scope of overseas settlement is not restricted.)

6.2.3.3 *Main Problems Facing the Development of Offshore RMB Market*

First, the long-term of arbitrage possibility exists in the offshore RMB market. The financial institutions engaged in offshore RMB operations are mainly banks. The main starting point of RMB operations is to obtain RMB spot and forward exchange differences, as well as RMB and USD spreads. In the context of the expected appreciation of the RMB, financial institutions in the offshore market make the transactions of borrowing dollars in the spot market and buying RMB, while selling RMB and buying dollars in the forward market.

The profitability of financial institutions comes from two aspects, one is the difference between the spot and forward RMB exchange rates, and the other is the difference between the interest rate of the RMB and the US dollar. If many financial institutions conduct similar transactions, it will inevitably raise the spot RMB price of the offshore market, lower the price of the forward RMB, and the arbitrage opportunities will disappear.

In the CNH market, the aforementioned transactions can continue to be profitable for a long time. Due to the existence of RMB trade settlement, the Mainland RMB can continue to enter Hong Kong, and the offshore financial institutions will not significantly increase the spot RMB price. Although the sale of forward RMB by financial institutions will lower the price of forward RMB, if the revaluation of the RMB is lower than the market expectation of the future RMB exchange rate, it will still attract a large number of investors to purchase forward RMB. It can be concluded that the coexistence of the following three factors can enable the aforementioned arbitrage behavior of offshore financial institutions to continue: first, the RMB trade settlement has injected a large amount of RMB into Hong Kong; second, the development of the CNH market allows financial institutions to buy RMB; third, a large amount of foreign exchange market intervention in the Mainland market has enabled the market to maintain a unilateral RMB appreciation expectation, and financial institutions can sell forward RMB at a price higher than the spot exchange rate.

The main initiative of the use of RMB settlement by import and export trading companies in the Mainland and Hong Kong is to seek the exchange rate difference between the CNH and the CNY market. Since the establishment of the CNH market, RMB in Hong Kong market has been more expensive than the Mainland RMB for most of the time, and importers using RMB trade settlement can take advantage of the exchange rate difference between the two markets. By observing the linkage between the exchange rate difference of CNH–CNY and the payment and collection ratio of RMB cross-border trade settlement, evidence can be found for the aforementioned statement. In the context of the appreciation of the RMB, there are also good opportunities for hedge funds, and with the role of leverage, hedge funds are profitable.

In the offshore RMB market in Hong Kong, foreign trade enterprises, financial institutions and hedge funds have formed a complex and interdependent trading chain, each of which has its portion of profits. The foreign currency market intervention of the Mainland monetary authorities and the unilateral appreciation of the RMB are the basis for the maintenance of the aforementioned series of arbitrage transactions.

After September 2011, affected by the turmoil in the international financial market, the offshore RMB price reversed, and the offshore RMB was cheaper than the Mainland RMB. From the previous analysis, the offshore spot and forward RMB prices are the result of joint transactions between foreign trade companies, financial institutions and hedge funds. After September 2011, the analysis of offshore RMB spot and forward RMB prices should also be within this framework. The only difference is that the arbitrage conditions have completely reversed. The specific arbitrage mechanism is: the expectation of RMB appreciation is reversed → the hedge fund's forward RMB net demand is reversed → the financial institution sells the forward RMB at a forward depreciation price (the exchange rate difference is no longer beneficial, but constitutes a loss), and the US dollar loan interest increases. (The spread is also narrowing) → financial institutions reduce spot RMB net position, demand for spot RMB decline → RMB depreciation in the CNH market → import RMB trade settlement decline, export RMB trade settlement rises, RMB in Hong Kong outflow.

Therefore, under the condition that the exchange rate formation mechanism is not mature, the development of the offshore RMB market will inevitably lead to the difference between the offshore and onshore RMB exchange rates, which will directly promote the long-term existence of the offshore RMB market arbitrage space. The cross-border arbitrage will bring many unfavorable factors to China's economic development. It may cause the inflated trade volume of

China and the overestimation of output statistics, which will weaken the effect of monetary policy and will promote the excessive fluctuation of overseas RMB funds, thus inhibiting the process of RMB internationalization.[38]

Second, the final constraints on the development of the offshore market of the RMB are difficult to break through. At present, the RMB is still not fully convertible, which is bound to the development of offshore RMB finance, but this constraint is limited. First, the RMB is in the process of striving to achieve full convertibility goals, and the process is accelerating. Second, the complete free convertibility of money is not a necessary condition for the offshore financial development of the currency. When the offshore financial market in Tokyo was established, Japan also had foreign exchange controls on the yen. By the same token, the complete opening of capital account is not a necessary condition for offshore financial development. The development of the offshore market of RMB does not require capital account to be completely open.

The ultimate constraint on the development of the offshore RMB market in Hong Kong should be the process of reforming the financial system in the Mainland. For example, in the development of offshore financial markets in Tokyo, the lag in the development of Japan's domestic financial market is an important factor limiting the development of its offshore market. Due to the serious differences in the level of development of domestic and foreign financial markets, the offshore financial market in Tokyo has only taken the development model of "internal and external separation," which led to the ultimate failure of the internationalization of the yen. At present, in the development of the offshore RMB market in Hong Kong, the strict isolation of offshore and onshore markets is not possible, and the offshore RMB market cannot be developed. However, under the influence of initiatives such as offshore RMB reflow, the penetration

[38]He, Ping, and Zhong Hong, "The Economic Development Effect of RMB Internationalization and Its Problems," *International Economic Review* 5 (2014): 89–102.

between the two markets will be strengthened. With the strengthening of offshore finance's impact on onshore finance, the operation of onshore finance will inevitably be greatly affected. As a policy-driven offshore market, the policy orientation that limits the development of offshore markets will emerge due to its impact on onshore finance.

The root cause of this contradiction is the backwardness of the development of the onshore financial market. Only by advancing the reform of the Mainland financial system and financial system, and narrowing the differences in the price system and financial system between the offshore and onshore markets, can we resolve or alleviate these contradictions. Therefore, the ultimate constraint on the development of the offshore market in Hong Kong should be the process of financial reform in the Mainland. The financial reform in the Mainland involves many aspects such as interest rate liberalization, exchange rate formation mechanism and financial supervision. These financial reforms are not achieved overnight and will face various kinds of difficulties. Therefore, the development level of the financial market is also difficult to increase rapidly in a short period of time, which will restrict the in-depth development of the offshore market of the RMB.

Third, whether the RMB offshore market can avoid "re-lending games" remains to be discussed. The rapid growth of the offshore RMB market in Hong Kong has triggered a sharp increase in the concentration of loans from Mainland banks in the Mainland. In 2010, Hong Kong banks' loans to non-bank customers in the Mainland rose to HK$444 billion, on a year-on-year increase of 47%, while the long-term average growth rate was only 12%. According to estimates of S&P, loans from Mainland companies and their affiliates in Hong Kong account for 30% of all loans in Hong Kong. Under the influence of the expected appreciation of the RMB, most of the loans are still settled in US dollars, but the demand for loan financing in the Mainland is very strong. Especially when the offshore RMB is cheaper than the onshore RMB, most of the loans will be converted into RMB, and then the RMB "re-lending game" will be clearly reflected.

The "re-lending Game," in which domestic funds flow from onshore to offshore, and then from offshore back to onshore, has also become a "back-to-back trap." Such a capital cycle will not achieve true internationalization of the currency. The "re-lending game" between the offshore market and the onshore market of yen is called "self-playing their own money" by Japanese scholars, and the Japanese banking industry is the protagonist of this game. Between 1984 and 1989, the yen's offshore market developed rapidly, and the average annual growth rate of assets and liabilities exceeded 60%. The offshore yen in the offshore financial market of Tokyo has grown in size and returned to Japan through interbank lending and FDI, fueling the domestic economic bubble. The offshore financial centers of London and Hong Kong constitute an important channel for Japan's "re-lending games." In Hong Kong, for example, Hong Kong's claims on non-bank institutions in Japan are highly synergistic with liabilities to Japanese banking institutions. This clearly reflects the outflow of funds of Japanese yen from the Japanese banking industry and the return to the Japanese corporate sector through Hong Kong. With the bursting of Japan's domestic asset bubble and the concentration of various market risks, Japan's "re-lending game" scale shrank rapidly after the Asian financial crisis in 1997. But what is certain is that the "re-lending game" has promoted the return of funds from Japan to its domestic stock and real estate market, and has become an important reason for Japan's 1990 economic bubble burst and long-term depression.

At present, the development policy of the offshore RMB market is mainly based on the development of offshore RMB bond business and the unblocking of return channels of RMB. Although such policy choices are conducive to the development of offshore RMB business in Hong Kong, it is also likely to cause the RMB to flow out of the border and stay in Hong Kong, and then return to the territory in the form of RMB trade settlement of RMB FDI and RQFII. In this process, the role of pushing the RMB more widely accepted by the international community is not significant. If the establishment of channel for RMB return is the only way to develop the RMB offshore market, it will easily lead to the development of the RMB offshore market in Hong Kong, which will not be conducive to the realization of the internationalization goal of the RMB. It will even have adverse impacts and significant risks on the macroeconomic development of the Mainland.

6.2.3.4 *Other Issues of the Internationalization of the RMB*

First, the trial of RMB internationalization has worsened the country's external balance sheet. Based on the aforementioned changes in the ratio of receipts and payments, many researchers believe that the result of the internationalization of the RMB has worsened China's external balance sheet, that is, China has reduced its dollar debt, increased its RMB debt (written to Hong Kong) and increased the dollar assets, so that the interests of the country will be damaged in the short term.

From the perspective of the nature of the enterprise, the company must be profitable in the short term. This needs to be guided and constrained by national policies and regulations to overcome market failures. The problems that arise in the trail of RMB internationalization can be adjusted by continuous adjustment, and must not be squandered. The formation process of a mature market may experience speculative chaos, which is difficult to avoid in the early stage of market formation. Of course, policymakers should try to shorten this stage. If they are placed in a future time, the problems arising from cross-border trade settlement should not be a problem at all. In this process, the national interests will not been damaged, but a larger strategy has been realized. Taking the export tax rebate policy as an example, when it was just launched, there were some enterprises that shipped stones from Shenzhen to Hong Kong to defraud tax rebates. This was an individual phenomenon that caused losses to the country. At that time, it caused a lot of controversy, but the policy did not stop, and there are countless companies that benefit from it. Of course, we must severely punish malicious violations and purify the market.

As shown in Table 6.5, the collection and payment ratio of RMB cross-border settlement has been greatly reduced. This shows that with the increase in the two-way fluctuation of the RMB against the US dollar, the exchange gap between Hong Kong and the Mainland has narrowed, and the arbitrage behavior in the market has naturally decreased. However, the spread between Hong Kong and the Mainland still exists, and there will still be some arbitrage in the market. This shows that China can also narrow the gap between domestic asset prices and foreign asset prices by relaxing interest rate controls, enabling enterprises to achieve investment and financing in a more competitive market, and improving the efficiency of resource allocation.

Second, the pricing power of RMB is limited, and it still needs to be priced in dollars. The pricing power of RMB in international trade is influenced by the pricing power of enterprises and the structure of China's foreign trade. In terms of system, Chinese foreign trade enterprises can choose RMB pricing but it also depends on its ability to use RMB in pricing. Generally speaking, the pricing power of Chinese-funded enterprises in the international market is relatively weak. Although China has become the world's largest trader at the national level, China is still in a weak position in the production division and income distribution in global and Asian production networks, so its pricing power is relatively weak. In large-scale products, Chinese-funded enterprises simply do not have pricing power. According to the investigation of RMB settlement of cross-border trade between enterprises within Sinopec Group, when the RMB settlement is involved, the two companies within the group first sign a trade contract denominated in US dollars. When the payment is made at the exchange rate within the company, the domestic enterprise exchanges the equivalent value of RMB, and then remits it to Hong Kong, which can be paid to the RMB account opened by the enterprise in the group company. After receiving the RMB payment, the overseas enterprise often converts it into US dollars at the current market exchange rate and holds the US dollar in order to pay the overseas customers who do not accept the RMB. When a Chinese-funded enterprise and a foreign merchant conduct a contract pricing currency negotiation, the other party refers to the dollar price in the international market, and they can convert it into RMB at the market exchange rate, and settles it in RMB. In theory, the pricing and settlement in RMB can completely avoid exchange rate risk. Therefore, subject to the pricing power of the RMB, the US dollar is still an important intermediary currency, and the RMB cannot independently play the role of international currency. Enterprises still face exchange costs and bear certain exchange rate risks.

The function of the pricing in RMB is also subject to China's import and export commodity structure. In China's import trade structure, the proportion of international bulk commodities is relatively high, and international bulk products are basically priced in US dollars. Therefore, it is difficult for the RMB to shake the dominating position of the US dollar. The pricing power of Chinese export foreign trade enterprises are also very limited. "Both ends of the production process on the world market" and "low added value" are the major characteristics of processing trade, which accounts for a large proportion of China's foreign trade, and the proportion of imports and exports, and reaches about 40% and 50%, respectively. For foreign producers, both export and import are valued in the same foreign currency, which helps them avoid exchange rate risk and cost accounting. Therefore, for the nearly half of the trade volume, the pricing power of Chinese companies is quite weak.

In short, the problems exposed by the RMB internationalization experiment show the lack of China's financial development and financial openness, as well as the lack of pricing power. This means that further internationalization of the RMB needs to improve the level of financial development and the competitiveness of enterprises. The internationalization of the RMB is in line with the demands of enterprises to prevent exchange rate risks and gradually become internationalized, which is in line with the long-term interests of the country. In the future, China needs to consolidate the achievements of the internationalization of the RMB and create conditions for the internationalization of the RMB by further deepening domestic financial reforms.

6.3 Path Selection of RMB Internationalization

6.3.1 *Main Points about the Realization Path of RMB Internationalization*

Regarding the study of the internationalization path of the RMB, there are basically two kinds of propositions in the domestic academic circles. One is to advocate the RMB to follow the path of internationalization of the sterling or the dollar. The reason is mainly due to various obstacles in regional financial cooperation, which hinder the coordination of regional currency and exchange rate mechanism, and it is likely to slow down the process of RMB internationalization. Therefore, some scholars believe that the internationalization of RMB should be realized directly or independently by the stage of regionalization. For example, Zhao believes that because the regional currency is different from the world currency, the objectives and the contradictions that need to be resolved are different. They are not a relationship of ladder, and they do not have to be regional currency before they can become the world currency. On the contrary, it is much easier for the RMB to become a world currency than to become a regional currency. Therefore, we cannot deny the possibility that the RMB becomes one of the world's currencies only because the RMB is not the unified Asian currency of circulation.[39] Liu[40] also believes that there is no possibility of establishing a unified currency in the Asian region for a long period of time. Compared with the development of the RMB into the Asian currency, the possibility of the RMB becoming a world currency is even more objective and practical. As long as the RMB is strong, it can become a world currency, rather than follow the path of being an Asian currency first and then become a world currency.

The other advocates internationalization by way of the regionalization of the RMB. At present, this argument dominates. After the

[39] Zhao, Haikuan, "The RMB could become One of the World Currencies," *Economic Research* 3 (2003): 54.

[40] Liu, Qun, "Regional Currency and World Currency: Judgment and Choice Analysis of RMB Prospects," *Academic Journal* 9 (2006): 56–64.

outbreak of the Asian financial crisis, especially with the emergence of the euro and the discussion and progress of the "dollarization" in Latin America, many scholars have noticed the importance of RMB regionalization for the realization of RMB internationalization. They believe that the regionalization of RMB will gradually expand the influence of the RMB and ultimately promote the internationalization of the RMB (Pan Liquan, 2000; Li Wei, 2002).[41] Ba Shusong pointed out that before the RMB is completely freely convertible, the promotion of the internationalization of the RMB should adopt a pragmatic strategy, starting from the RMB regionalization strategy promoted by border trade, and gradually promoting the RMB under the rapid development of China's foreign trade.[42] The convenience of settlement currency in international trade increases the scale of using RMB. Li *et al.* pointed out that in the existing international monetary system, a country's currency must achieve full internationalization in the way of the "collective action" of regional institutional cooperation. The direct internationalization strategy of the RMB may bring huge risks and losses to China's economic development. China should combine the formulation of economic policies with the objectives of regional monetary and financial cooperation, and promote the Asianization of the RMB through multidimensional and multi-level efforts, which fosters the economic foundation of the internationalization of the RMB. It is not correct to emphasize the "direct" internationalization of the RMB or the spontaneous circulation of the RMB in neighboring countries and regions as "regionalization of the RMB."[43] Cao believes that China should focus on the internationalization of the RMB on a regional level.[44] Through the practical steps of regionalization, optimal currency zone should

[41]Pan, Liquan, "Reform of International Monetary System and RMB Internationalization," *East China Economic Management* 4 (2000): 36–45.

[42]Li, Chong, "On the Regionalization of RMB," *Hebei Academic Journal* 5 (2002): 24–35.

[43]Xiao, Li, Junjiu Li and Ding Yibing, "On the Asian RMB," *World Economy* 2 (2004): 21–34.

[44]Ba, Shusong, "How China's Financial Reform Adapts to Internationalization," *Financial Economy* 2 (2006): 45–48.

eventually be established with the RMB as the key currency in the entire region of Asia, and it will enhance Asia's Financial stability and break the deadlock in the reform of the global monetary system and open up new ways of currency internationalization other than the US dollar and the euro. Yan and Zhang believe that with the signing of the China–ASEAN Free Trade Framework Agreement, the economic and trade cooperation between China and ASEAN and the deepening of economic development will inevitably require exchanges and cooperation in the financial sector of China–ASEAN countries.[45] The trade zone will also build a better platform for the regionalization of the RMB.

Although most scholars have reached a consensus on the basic strategy for the RMB to achieve internationalization by Asianization, there are three different perspectives on the specific path of implementation: first, by participating in regional cooperation — the first stage of regionalization of RMB in Asia will be realized before the internationalization of RMB, which is called "The Support Theory of Regional Cooperation"; the second is the "The Rival Theory of Regional Cooperation" that support the independent regionalization of the RMB in Asia, and then realize the internationalization; the third is to realize the RMB in different stages with the relative intermediate standpoint, which is called "The Theory of Various Phases of Regional Cooperation."

Scholars who hold the view of "The Support Theory of Regional Cooperation" believe that China should realize the Asianization of the RMB by participating in the East Asian regional currency cooperation at this stage, that is, to achieve a certain degree of regionalization through the institutionalized cooperation form, and then realize the globalization. However, there are two starting points for regional cooperation:

First, East Asian countries and regions should directly carry out cooperation at the regional level and promote the Asianization of the RMB by pinning the Asian Currency Unit (ACU, or Asian Monetary

[45]Zhang, Ying, "Research on Sino-ASEAN Free Trade Area and Regional Development of RMB," 8th ed. 2006.

Unit, AMU). The launch of ACU is an important opportunity for China, which not only greatly increases the RMB's voice in Asian currencies but also enables the RMB to evade the risks generated by the world's major currencies in the ACU in international financial markets (Xie Luoqi, Huang Minghua, 2006).[46] Therefore, China can use the power of the international financial market to help the RMB exchange rate move closer to the equilibrium exchange rate with ACU (Zhang Bin, 2004).[47] In addition to the AMU approach, there is also the idea of jointly playing the role of the "money anchor" between the RMB and the yen in the East Asian region, in order to realize monetary cooperation at the regional level in East Asia. By establishing an East Asian exchange rate coordination mechanism with RMB and Yen as the joint currency anchor, the exchange rate volatility will be maintained at a reasonable level that is conducive to the stable economic development of each economy and the promotion of regional economic integration in a certain period of time. The future of the monetary cooperation in Asia will develop from this lower level, loose monetary cooperation mechanism to a more advanced stage.[48] Therefore, we should realize the "competition in cooperation" between China and Japan, and strive to seek sincere cooperation between the two regional strong currencies in exchange rate arrangements, liquidity support and even the future common currency (Chen Yulu, 2003; Luo Junyi, Zhou Wei, 2008).[49][50] On the one hand, it can maintain the stability of the exchange rate between the RMB and the Japanese yen and the US dollar at this stage. On the other hand, it can build a special dual system framework with

---

[46]Luoqi, Xie, and Minghua Huang, "Reflections on Asian Currency Units and Opportunities for China," *Jinan Finance* 3 (2006): 15–18.

[47]Bin, Zhang, "East Asian Regional Exchange Rate Cooperation: A Chinese Perspective," *World Economy* 10 (2004): 56–62.

[48]Li, Ping and Peizhi Liu, "The Basic Concept of East Asia Monetary Cooperation during the Transitional Period: the Exchange Rate Coordination Mechanism in East Asia," *World Economics and Politics* 12 (2003): 70–74.

[49]Yulu, Chen, "Currency Competition in East Asian Currency Cooperation," *International Finance Research* 3 (2003): 35–45.

[50]Luo, Junzheng, and Zhou Wei, "Games and Competition between China and Japan in the Field of East Asian Currency," *Modern Japanese Economy* 1 (2008).

RMB and JPY as the common currency anchor, forming a joint floating exchange rate system in the East Asia region with RMB and JPY as dual center.[51]

Second, the regional monetary cooperation in East Asia should first carry out the cooperation at the sub-regional level and then at the regional level. First of all, some scholars advocate the promotion of RMB Asianization by means of currency integration. East Asian currency cooperation should first build two sub-regional currency zones — the ASEAN currency zone and the RMB currency zone. In comparison, the conditions for establishing the RMB currency zone are more mature (Zhu Fang, 2003).[52] The realization of the RMB Asianization strategy has two paths to choose from, namely, building a "Euro model" with the "One China" framework of Mainland China, Hong Kong, Macao and Taiwan, and building a "yen model" with a larger scope in Southeast Asia and East Asia. Some scholars believe that the Asianization of the RMB should take the establishment of a complete "China Economic Circle" as the first step (Liu Zhenlin, 2006),[53] first integrating the RMB, the Hong Kong dollar and the Australian dollar, and achieving monetary integration in the sub-region, but the process integrating was initially difficult to include in Taiwan at the first stage. On this basis, China can strengthen cooperation with ASEAN, gradually establish the "China–ASEAN Economic and Monetary Union," conduct partial East Asian currency integration attempts (Liu Zhenlin, 2006),[54] and finally peg the RMB as the core sub-regional currency area, and then gradually converge on the economic platform centered on Japan and South Korea, realize the symmetry cooperation between the RMB

[51]Zheng, Haiqing, "The Asian Currency Cooperation Process: China Perspective," *Economics of Asia Pacific* 4 (2003): 32–35.
[52]Fang, Zhu, "Analysis of the Conditions for Establishing Currency in East Asia Subregion," *Contemporary Asia-Pacific* 12 (2003): 35–38.
[53]Zhenlin, Liu, Research on East Asian Currency Cooperation and the Choice of RMB Exchange Rate System. China Economic Publishing House, 2006.
[54]*Ibid.*

and the Japanese Yen, and realize the Asianization of the RMB.[55] Second, many scholars in China's economics circles pay more attention to the study of the common currency basket system, and then put forward some different views on regional exchange rate cooperation in East Asia. For example, Ding Yibing believes that East Asian countries should be pegged by regional currency basket such as ACU.[56] At the same time, ACU should maintain a stable exchange rate for major currencies outside the region. In fact, this is a "double" currency basket system. Xu Qiyuan and Liu Lizhen (2006) believe that East Asia should implement a common "hybrid anchor" type, which means that the currency basket is pegged to a currency basket consisting of currency within and outside the region.[57] Although scholars have different opinions on the structure of the currency basket, these scholars generally believe that the process of promoting regional exchange rate cooperation by virtue of China's significant influence in Asian economic development is the process of gradually evolving the RMB into one of the Asian central currencies. The specific steps of pinning the currency basket are divided into three stages: the first stage, based on the economic development of the country, is the independent construction of the currency basket system; the second stage, the economic development level and economic structure are similar, and the economic exchange is relatively close. The region establishes a sub-regional peg to the common currency basket system, and determines the central exchange rate system in these regions; in the third phase, a common currency basket system is established throughout the East Asian region to form a unified exchange rate linkage mechanism (Li Xiao, Ding Yibing, 2003).[58]

---

[55]Xiao, Li, Junjiu Li and Yibing Ding, "On the Asian RMB," *World Economy* 2 (2004): 21–34.

[56]Ding, Yibing, "New Progress in East Asian Currency Cooperation," *World Economy* 3 (2006): 82–90.

[57]Xu, Qiyuan, and Lizhen Liu, "Estimation of Hong Kong's RMB Stock: An Investigation of M1 Caliber," *World Economy* 9 (2006): 51–59.

[58]Xiao, Li, and Yibing Ding, "The Construction of East Asian Regional Monetary System: Necessity, Feasibility and Path Selection," *Frontier in Social Science* 4 (2003): 72–85.

There are a few scholars who hold "The Rival Theory of Regional Cooperation." They believe that the RMB can achieve Asianization with its own competitive advantages and strategies without participating in regional currency cooperation in East Asia. Since other countries in Asia have higher exchange rate stability requirements for the RMB than China's exchange rate stability requirements for other Asian currencies, China is in a very favorable position in Asian exchange rate coordination, so there is no need to participate in regional currency cooperation (Yao Zhizhong, 2004).[59]

Scholars who hold "The Theory of Various Phases of Regional Cooperation" point out that the RMB acceptance will be improved by the spontaneous flow of the RMB and the role of the market, and then the internationalization of the RMB will be realized. Thereupon, the regionalization of the RMB will be promoted by means of staged cooperation arrangements. The internationalization of RMB should follow the gradual path of "internationalization of RMB in neighboring countries → Asianization of RMB → internationalization of RMB." The internationalization of RMB must be synchronized with the opening of RMB capital projects and the flexibility of exchange rate regimes.[60] Since the internationalization of the RMB is a dynamic process, a phased strategy and a corresponding policy mix should be adopted. The internationalization of the RMB can be carried out in four stages: the first stage is the international circulation of RMB around the border trade and tourism consumption. The second stage is that the RMB gradually becomes an overseas borrowing asset, which is also the initial stage of the offshore RMB market. The third stage is that with the increase in the number of RMB held by overseas non-residents, the RMB will become an Asian investment asset, which is the real offshore RMB market. The fourth stage is the advanced stage of RMB internationalization, which means that

---

[59] Zhizhong, Yao, "Asymmetric Competition and the Asian Strategy of RMB," *World Economy and Politics* 7 (2004): 62–66.

[60] He, Huigang, "The Path and Mode Choice of Monetary Cooperation in East Asia," *Studies on Economics and Management* 17 (2007): 89–94.

the RMB has become the main reserve asset of Asian countries and has become a regionalized currency (Jia Huiyan, 2005).[61] Scholars who hold this view generally argue that the specific steps of the Asianization of the RMB do not have to be achieved via the liberalization of capital projects. As the largest "market provider" in the region, China should realize Asianization of the RMB by performing its functions of the regional settlement currency. At the same time, they advocate the construction of the offshore market for RMB in Hong Kong. This in fact means that the RMB capital account is basically open by way of the construction of the RMB offshore market. By this path selection, the RMB will be able to overcome the shortcomings of non-liberalization of capital account and enjoy the benefits of achieving the goal of Asianization.

There are two differences between "The Theory of Various Phases of Regional Cooperation" and "The Support Theory of Regional Cooperation." First, the peripheral internationalization of the RMB is the starting point for the Asianization and internationalization of the RMB. Second, whether the institutionalization of regional monetary cooperation is divided into different stages. It differs from "the Rival Theory of Regional Cooperation" in that it advocates the realization of the internationalization and the Asianization of the RMB by participating in regional monetary and financial cooperation.

Foreign researchers generally believe that there are two paths for the internationalization of the RMB, the global approach or the regional approach. Park believes that the ultimate goal of the global path of RMB internationalization is to make the RMB gain international currency status like the euro and the dollar.[62] Eichengreen pointed out that China may not need to participate in any regional

---

[61]Huiyan, Jia, "Offshore RMB Market and RMB Internationalization Process," *Journal of Beijing Institute of Economic Management* 3 (2005): 32–36.

[62]Park, Yung Chul, "The RMB Internationalization and Its Implications for Financial and Monetary Cooperation in East Asia," *China & World Economy* 18, no. 2 (2010): 1–21.

monetary union to obtain economic and financial status, thus, meeting the preconditions for the internationalization of sovereign currency. China is not trying to emulate the European Approach to achieve regional monetary union. What China needs to do is wait. The longer the waiting period, the greater the economic position in the region, and the RMB will eventually become the dominant currency in Asia.[63] This view actually advocates the regionalization of the RMB through natural evolution. The policymakers of China may also adopt a global path, which will make it easier to motivate and use political support to accelerate domestic financial reforms to achieve internationalization of the RMB. But for China this wait is long term, because according to the index published by the World Economic Forum, China has the lowest index of capital account liberalization and domestic financial liberalization in East Asian countries (World Economic Forum, 2009).[64] If Chinese can guarantee the current economic growth rates, GDP can double within 10 years, but this may challenge the status of dollar and the euro. Even if the absolute amount of economic growth is compatible to these two economies, the trade structure characteristics will also play a role in limiting the function of RMB as a trade currency.

The global path of RMB internationalization is restricted by its trade structure. Athukorala study shows that China purchases parts from Japan and other Asian economies, and then assembles them to export to the US and European markets. The more China imports from Asia, the more it exports to the United States.[65] Park thinks, although trade within Asian region is growing rapidly, it is very difficult to change the trade structure with China, reduce export to

[63]Eichengreen, Barry, "Dollar Dilemma-The World's Top Currency Faces Competition," *Foreign Affairs* 88, (2009): 53.

[64]https://www.weforum.org/reports?platform=shaping-the-future-of-financial-and-monetary-systems&year=2009#filter.

[65]Athukorala, Prema-Chandra, "The Rise of China and East Asian Export Performance: Is the Crowding-out Fear Warranted?" *The World Economy* 32, no. 2 (2009): 234–266.

Europe and the United States market, and these exports are denominated in dollar and euro. As long as the export is still with the two kinds of currency, its imports will take most of the two currencies.[66] The imports of China are mainly imports of oil and raw materials denominated by dollar. Most of the East Asian countries imported from other countries and regions, but they have trade surplus to China, therefore, unless they can enter financial products market denominated by RMB, they are not willing to choose RMB as a currency for import and export.

The global path of RMB internationalization is still further restricted by the development of financial factors. Park opined that the closed Chinese financial system and strict control will likely take the current "pilot" plan of RMB internationalization backwards.[67] "The pilot plan" could be the catalyst for a broader and faster domestic financial market reform but it is very difficult to give up the financial tools of China to achieve its goals of the industrial policy. In the absence of domestic and international pressure, China may not determine the target and speed of financial liberalization. Lee believes that China's bank dominated financial system under the guidance and control of the government, and the efficiency and transparency of the financial system fall behind the major international financial center.[68]

The global path of RMB internationalization has a spillover effect on the dollar. It is also equivalent to China's comprehensive capital account liberalization, which will have an important impact on the scale and structure of China's investment in the United States. So far, the main channel of capital flows to the United States is the increase in official reserves, and this flow pattern has brought great risks to the asset side of the balance sheet of China. In order to realize the full

[66]Park, Yung Chul, "The RMB Internationalization and Its Implications for Financial and Monetary Cooperation in East Asia," *China & World Economy* 18, no. 2 (2010): 1–21.
[67]*Ibid.*
[68]Lee, Jong-Wha, "Will the RMB Emerge as an International Reserve Currency?" *The World Economy* 37, no. 1 (2014): 42–62.

liberalization of the capital account, China is bound to implement a more flexible exchange rate, wider and deeper financial reform to hedge currency risk, reduce the accumulation of reserves and reduce "the fear of floating." Then, the policy of gradual increase of foreign exchange reserve will change foreign investment structure of China and affect the demand for dollars. In addition, China's broader and deeper financial reform will increase the price of RMB assets to make it more attractive, this will also affect the current position of the dollar.

Therefore, the efficiency of the global path of the RMB internationalization is not only subject to the trade structure and financial system of China, it also faces the risk of weakening leadership of China in Asia. China's image is likely to become indifferent toward the regional economic integration, and would no longer be interested in the regional cooperative arrangements of ASEAN 10+3. In short, the global path to realize the internationalization of RMB is not very realistic.

The regional path of RMB internationalization refers to developing RMB's international monetary function, taking advantage of the China's trade and financial foundation with neighboring countries, or some countries tending to peg their currency with RMB, or putting RMB in these countries' currency basket, with RMB accounting for a large weight. China has two options for the regional approach, the first is to establish a circle of RMB. And the second is leading the monetary cooperation under the economic integration of ASEAN 10+3.

The first option of regional path is to establish RMB circle in the ASEAN, Mainland China, Hong Kong and Taiwan. The advantage is: these countries and regions are geographically close, and China only needs to provide the transaction of RMB financial products for non-residents with financial deregulation and financial reform. But this path is also facing challenges: first, the size in the area is limited; second, China may not have any motives of domestic financial liberalization, which may delay the domestic financial reform, and it is unfavorable to the RMB internationalization; last, Chinese face the dilemma of RMB exchange rate stability and flexibility. In the short term, China needs a stable RMB exchange rate against the dollar and the euro to enhance confidence in the RMB in ASEAN countries. However, if the RMB has a trend of appreciation against the US dollar and the euro, pegging to RMB is likely to weaken the export of member countries to the European and American market. China is finding it increasingly difficult to implement the rigid exchange rate, which is inconsistent with the long-term goal of the exchange rate system and the internationalization of the RMB. But the flexible exchange rate needs enough financial products to hedge the investment risk, which the Chinese are not currently equipped with, thus this situation may affect the regional demand for RMB. Other challenges include: Japan and South Korea are against the establishment of the RMB circle and the establishment of the RMB circle will lose part of monetary sovereignty.

The second selection of regional path refers to wide monetary cooperation and economic integration within ASEAN 10+3 (China, Japan and South Korea). The advantage of this path is China can take the control effectively and accelerate the domestic financial reform. This path has a solid foundation: China and ASEAN countries have a lot in common, for example, external shocks have great impact on the region; there are many foreign exchange reserves; East Asia lacks the lender of last resort; East Asia needs to build a liquidity security network; all have the need to overcome the currency mismatch and maturity mismatch. The regional approach has many advantages: first, the advantage of scale, in which the GDP of ASEAN 10+3 countries accounted for nearly 20% of global GDP. If ASEAN 10+3 agreed to establish Free Trade Area led by China, the size of its economy can support the internationalization of RMB. Second, after the Asian financial crisis, Asian financial cooperation and the financial market have made some profound progress, such as the Chiang Mai accord and expansion of the Asian bond market. In addition, China can expand and strengthen the existing ASEAN 10+3 framework, and in the framework of a better deal with the relationship between China and US, China and EU countries can mutually hold foreign exchange reserves and improve asset size. In terms of the real economy, China has become the East Asian economic network anchor, so when experiencing external economic shocks in East Asia, China becomes a stable power smoothing the impact. The East Asian monetary cooperation mainly relies on cooperation efforts of China and Japan, without which currency cooperation of ASEAN 10+3 is difficult to make progress.

There is a close relationship between the prospect of regional path and the division advantage of China in the region. In fact, whether it is a small range of RMB circle or a larger range of "Asian monetary cooperation and economic integration," it is directly related to the division of labor in the region. "The Greater China Economic Circle" formed an important economic foundation of RMB circle. Asian countries can seek for the advantages of closer trade and financial links with China, and strengthen monetary linkages based on trade and financial linkages (China–Japan monetary agreement), which is of great practical significance for the stability of financial integration of the Asian market. As a believer of "One market, one currency," China is an important fund provider and demander in the Asian market, which will bring broad prospects for the status of the RMB as an international currency. Compared with the global path, the regional path has more advantages for China, less pressure of domestic financial reform and opening-up, and in keeping with China's thought of "active, gradual and controllable" financial openness.

The regional path of RMB internationalization has a wider geopolitical influence. The regional approach is conducive to the establishment of the status of the RMB in the Asian market, to control the cost of dollar fluctuations and even undermine the status of dollar. It is also conducive to the establishment of Asian financial order and financial stability mechanism, crisis rescue mechanism and overcomes the defects in crisis management of international capital flows and IMF. The action of RMB internationalization in Asia will promote the reform of international monetary system.

Based on the aforementioned studies, we believe that it is not feasible to follow the path directly to carry out institutional cooperation or to comprehensively promote the internationalization of the RMB under the existing conditions. Only from the regional perspective, to gradually promote regionalization in stages, can we realize the internationalization of RMB.

6.3.2 *The "Stage Choice" and "Regional Choice" of "the Regional Path" for the Internationalization of the RMB*

6.3.2.1 *Stage Choice of RMB Internationalization*

As an international currency it offers to function as a store of value, medium of exchange and unit of account.[69] For private purposes, it can play the role of currency substitution, foreign exchange market trading, and also functions as trade and financial transactions invoicing and settlement. For official purposes, the international monetary reserve currency can be used as the official foreign exchange intervention currency and monetary anchor. In short, in order to realize the internationalization of RMB, it has to become an international pricing currency, international currency of settlement and international reserve currency.

In these three functions, the international reserve currency is the most difficult to achieve. If a currency cannot play a role as reserve currency, even if it is has good invoicing and settlement functions, this currency cannot be regarded as the truly international currency. The yen is a true portrayal of this situation as a weak international reserve currency.[70] So, to achieve the goal of a reserve currency for RMB is a long-term aim of RMB internationalization.

In contrast, the function of valuation and international settlement currency internationalization is relatively easy to achieve. In view that China has become increasingly important in East Asia and even the world economy, it has the basic conditions to carry out

[69]Chinn, Menzie and Jeffrey A. Frankel, *Will the Euro Eventually Surpass the Dollar as Leading International Reserve Currency? G7 Current Account Imbalances: Sustainability and Adjustment.* Chicago: University of Chicago Press, 2007, 283–338.

[70]Yu, Yongding, "Witness Imbalance: Double Surplus, the RMB Exchange Rate and Dollar Trap," *International Economic Review* 3 (2010): 7–44.

foreign trade on a global scale in RMB as an international pricing currency and international settlement currency. RMB should first aim to become the current transaction method in the East Asia region, and then become a medium of the international financial activities and the international financial assets.[71] So, these two kinds of monetary functions can be realized in the recent stage of RMB internationalization.

To realize the function of international settlement and pricing in RMB also requires some basic conditions. For example, the increasing importance of China to world economy (export competitiveness, market providers); the establishment of offshore RMB market; promotion of financial transactions in foreign currency; the development of the domestic financial market and improving the degree of financial liberalization, and the full convertibility of the currency among others.

Therefore, the internationalization of the RMB should take feasible measures to promote the implementation of international pricing and settlement in RMB, which will also lay the foundation for RMB to become an international reserve currency. The positive measures include: encouraging enterprises in the Mainland to issue RMB bonds (government bonds and corporate bonds) for domestic and foreign investors; encouraging foreign lenders to issue RMB bonds in China; encouraging free trade zone (FTA) partners of China to use RMB as a trading currency; signing currency swap agreements (bilateral and multilateral) using RMB as the currency of payment; increasing the use of RMB in the regional regulatory system.

The analysis of the framework of RMB internationalization is shown in Figure 6.9.

6.3.2.2 *The Regional Choice of RMB Internationalization*

It can be concluded from the economic development of the developed countries that the currency internationalization is an inevitable topic when a country's economic development reaches a certain stage.

[71] Xu, Mingqi, "On the Reform of International Financial System and the Bretton Woods Institutions Remodeling," *International Finance Research* 1 (2006): 54–60.

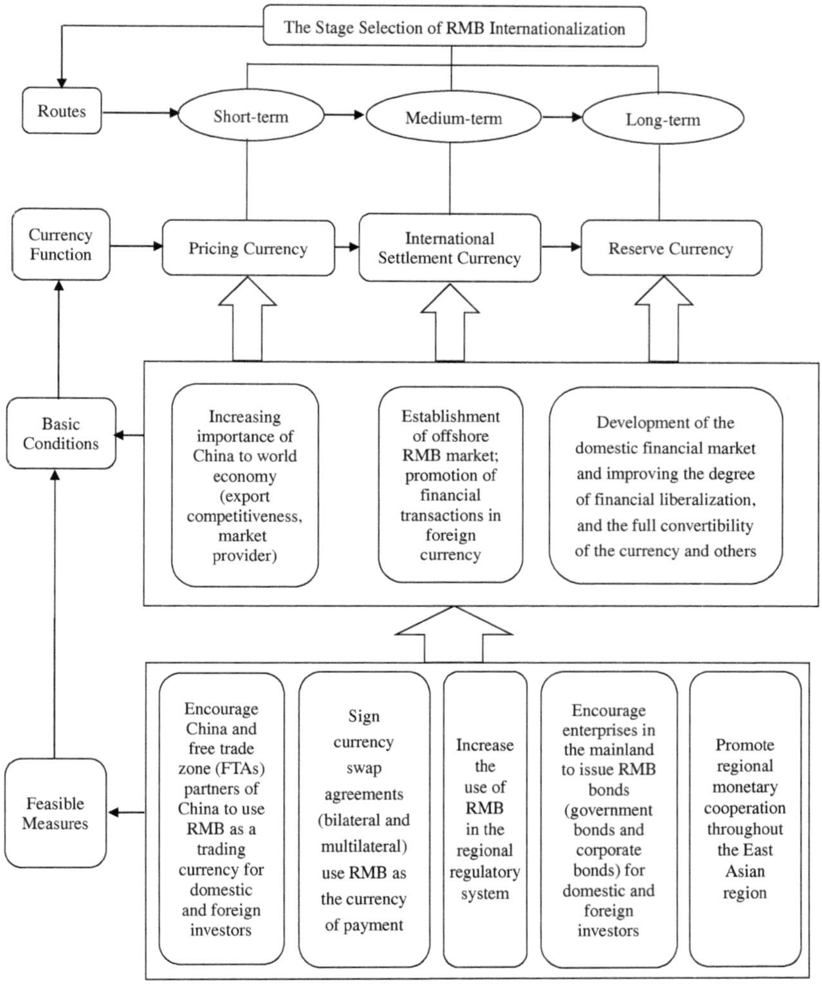

Figure 6.9. Diagram Analysis on the Framework of RMB Internationalization

With China's growing economic strength, China's economy is closely related to the global economy, and the internationalization of RMB will inevitably become the trend and the goal of China's economic development. The present condition and status are meant to realize the direct conditions of the internationalization of the RMB, that is, realizing the internationalization of RMB through regionalization of RMB.

In the current international monetary system, it is very difficult for any country's currency to rely on its own strength to successfully challenge the current monetary hegemony. A classic case of the birth of the euro and the failure of "internationalization of yen" can tell us that currency regionalization is an important step in the internationalization of the currency of a country to participate in international competition, which is inseparable from the overall framework of the platform and the system of regional monetary cooperation. A basic starting point of the strategy of RMB internationalization should be based on China's status as Asia's regional power. At the same time, in view of the present economic and financial conditions of China, it should not support the RMB internationalization directly. While the correlation degree in East Asia continues to increase, East Asian countries also agreed to carry out regional monetary and financial cooperation with "consensus" of East Asia. Therefore, RMB regionalization is the only necessary way of RMB internationalization.

Fundamentally, the RMB regionalization not only needs the natural result of market power but it also needs corresponding policy support and active promotion from the government of China, so as to find the logic of RMB regionalization system and the necessity and feasibility of the arrangement of "collective action." If we can combine the RMB regionalization process with domestic reform and necessary policy adjustments, it can bring the benefits of RMB regionalization, and then realize the internationalization of RMB.

Most scholars tend to support RMB regionalization to realize the ultimate internationalization of RMB. However, a brief analysis of how to realize regionalization as the path selection of RMB internationalization is insufficient. We will conduct an in-depth analysis on this issue.

The region involved for RMB internationalization has an order: Greater China, ASEAN Free Trade Area, Region of China, South Korea and Japan, and the whole East Asian region. The smaller the area is, the more difficult it is to promote the internationalization of the RMB, but there is no absolute sequence for promotion in these regions, and we even can simultaneously promote the internationalization of RMB in these regions.

First of all, in the Greater China region, composed of the Mainland, Hong Kong and Macao, close economic ties in this region provide inherent advantages for RMB regionalization. The internationalization of the RMB can be gradually realized relying on the growth of the comprehensive national strength and international status of China. With the development of "One China" policy, the Mainland China, Hong Kong, Macao and Taiwan will form a strong economy, so four currencies can fuse for the single currency (Li Jianjun and Tian Guangning, 2003).[72] In 29 June 2010, Cross-Strait Economic Cooperation Framework Agreement (ECFA) was signed. Also, the RMB and TWD can be exchanged in Hong Kong. The establishment of the RMB offshore market in Hong Kong will provide the conditions for the free circulation RMB in the region as a common currency.

Second, in the region of China and the ASEAN FTA, we must actively promote the scale of RMB settlement in the internal trade between China and the ASEAN FTA. In November 2002, China and ASEAN signed the China–ASEAN Free Trade Area Agreement, which was officially launched in 2010. This is an FTA with a population of 1.9 billion, a total GDP of US$6 trillion, and the regional trade accounts for 15% of the world's total. At present, China has allowed foreign trade enterprises in 20 provinces, municipalities and autonomous regions to use RMB for pricing and settlement. China should actively promote the official agreements with ASEAN countries on the basis of the smooth implementation of cross-border trade settlement of RMB. The signing of relevant agreements will promote the further development of the regionalization of the RMB.

Third, we must actively carry out monetary and financial cooperation with South Korea and Japan. At present, China's monetary and financial cooperation with South Korea and Japan under the ASEAN 10+3 frameworks has developed relatively smoothly,

---

[72]Li, Jianjun, and Guangning Tian, "Comparison and Enlightenment of the Paths of Three Major Currency Internationalizations," *Shanghai Finance* 9 (2003): 35–38.

and progress has been made in regional crisis rescue, risk prevention, foreign exchange reserve and bilateral currency swaps. Scholars have begun to explore and study the use of local currency pricing and settlement in bilateral trade. They believe that with the further development of economic and trade links between China and South Korea, the issue of RMB pricing and settlement in bilateral trade will likely create breakthroughs. As two major countries in the region, China and Japan must aim at a stable and sustainable development of the regional economy and strengthen coordination and cooperation in related fields, for example, increase the scale of bilateral currency swaps, provide useful institutional advice and technical support for the construction of offshore financial centers, and enhance the trading links between Hong Kong and Shanghai international financial markets and Tokyo's international financial markets.

Finally, the regionalization of the RMB should be promoted through regional monetary and financial cooperation throughout the East Asian region, for example, promote the institutionalization of CMIM, promote the construction and development of AMF, strengthen the regional financial supervision; strengthen the communication and coordination of exchange rate policies and information in East Asian economies, jointly promote exchange rate stability, maintain close communication on exchange rate policies; jointly promote a stable and sustainable development of East Asia's economy; develop and improve regional financial markets; jointly promote the establishment and development of ACIF; assist in the issuance and trading of international bonds.

The analysis framework for RMB internationalization with "regional path" is shown in Figure 6.10.

The internationalization of the RMB is a process in which the RMB participates in international currency competition. It is an important way for China to actively participate in the global economic division of labor, which has a very important economic and practical significance for the global monetary system. Different internationalization methods have different ways to affect the

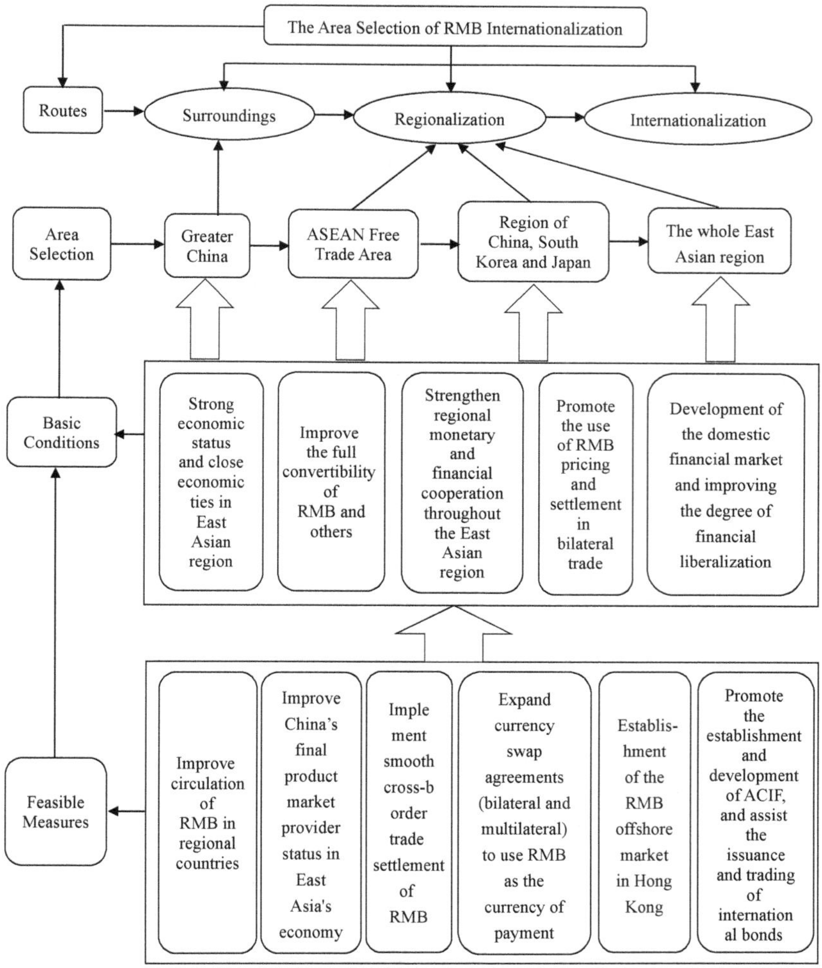

Figure 6.10. Analysis on the Area Selection of RMB Internationalization

international monetary system. The global path will directly affect the monetary and financial relations between China and the United States; the regional path is more realistic, and China has an advantage that can effectively overcome the shortcomings of the international monetary system. Moreover, at this stage, China is unable to challenge the hegemonic status of the US dollar. The introduction and implementation of the RMB internationalization strategy is largely due to the purpose of coping with international financial risks and is a passive, gradual and a long-term process. Therefore, the regional path of RMB internationalization should be from its usage in neighboring countries to regionalization, and then to internationalization; its functional path should be from the denomination currency to the settlement currency, and then to the reserve currency.

6.3.3 *Recent Strategies for RMB Internationalization*

In theory, an international currency must have the functions of settlement, investment and reserve. From the perspective of the relationship among these three functions, only when the currency can be widely used in international economic and trade exchanges, and various financial transactions can be carried out in the capital market to achieve hedging or investment profit with this currency, can it be accepted by the international community and be recognized as an international reserve currency. Therefore, if the RMB wants to become an international currency, it must be widely used in the transactions of trade and investment. In order to achieve this goal, we believe that we must grasp several key links: first, we must promote the coordinated development of offshore financial centers; second, we must expand the scale and scope of RMB exchanges; third, we must strengthen financial cooperation in East Asia; the fourth is to promote the pricing of commodities using RMB. In addition, the construction of RMB clearing channels and the promotion of China's position in the IMF are also indispensable components in the process of promoting the internationalization of RMB.

(1) Promote the Coordinated Development of Offshore Financial Centers:

The construction of the offshore RMB center is the basis for expanding the scale of RMB cross-border trade settlement, and it is also the best breakthrough to form an overseas RMB market under the situation that RMB is fully convertible. The essence of RMB internationalization is the continuous improvement of its recognition and acceptance in other countries. However, to achieve this goal, it is necessary to open up investment channels for the RMB and increase the willingness of the overseas market to hold RMB. However, taking into account the current situation in China, capital controls cannot be canceled in the short term, and the flow back of RMB is restricted, hindering the advancement of the internationalization of the RMB. Under the premise that the RMB capital cannot be exchanged, the convertibility under the RMB current account and the large output resulted from this will inevitably lead to conflict. To solve with this problem, the use of offshore financial markets has a special significance.

In view of the strong desires of the financial centers in the world to build the RMB market, the advantages of each center will be used to launch corresponding RMB products, and the offshore market will be gradually deployed. In these areas, the establishment of an RMB offshore market system with Hong Kong as the central center and other financial centers as regional centers will help the internationalization of the RMB.

First, we should encourage different RMB offshore markets to differentiate their positions, conduct policy coordination from the financial supervision level of each region and rationally plan the development path of each RMB offshore center to provide clear expectations for the financial institution's offshore RMB business layout.

The second is to maintain healthy competition between the offshore RMB markets and attract RMB-related businesses of residents, enterprises and financial institutions through superior infrastructure and a good policy environment, and continuously expand the scale and impact of the offshore RMB market.

The third is to establish a communication mechanism between the offshore markets of the RMB, pay close attention to the cross-regional flow of offshore RMB funds, promote mutual cooperation in the construction and supervision of the offshore market of the RMB, and promote the cooperative approach of the offshore RMB centers.

The fourth is to promote the integration of offshore RMB markets, seize the major opportunities of the China (Shanghai) Pilot FTA, accelerate the construction of the domestic offshore RMB market, and gradually explore the stability mechanism for the flow of RMB inside and outside the country.

Fifth, after the RMB is freely convertible, overseas RMB financial assets can be fully allocated according to market demand, and each center is encouraged to compete and cooperate with each other. At the same time, we must pay attention to the links between domestic and overseas markets, learn from the experience of construction international banking facilities of the US, accelerate the construction of financial centers in Shanghai, and ensure the effective connection between domestic and overseas markets.

(2) Expand the Scale and Scope of Currency Exchange in RMB:

Currency swap is an important way to promote internationalization under the conditions of free exchange under the situation that the capital account of RMB is not fully convertible. How to expand the use of the RMB in the trade sector, thereby promoting the RMB's borrowing and investment in the financial market, and promoting the RMB to become a reserve currency by mutual promotion of trade and finance is a problem that needs to be addressed at this stage. At present, more than 60% of China's foreign trade is carried out in the Asian region, and about 52% of them are carried out in Hong Kong, Macao and Taiwan. Moreover, these economies have a large trade surplus with China, so they vigorously promote the currency of the RMB and neighboring countries and regions. Based on the aforementioned considerations, China's central bank has established currency swap relationships with many countries. During 2013, it signed the currency swap agreement with the central banks and monetary authorities of Singapore, Brazil, Britain, Hungary, Albania, Iceland, Indonesia and other countries and regions. While prioritizing the expansion of the RMB swaps with neighboring countries and regions, it is also crucial to gradually expand the relationship to other developed countries and regions. Under certain conditions, China can also explore the possibility of signing a "Sino-US currency swap agreement." As of September 2013, the United States imported goods with a total of US$280.8 billion from China, accounting for 15.4% of US foreign imports. If China and the United States can sign a currency swap agreement, even if half of it is settled in RMB, its size will reach US$140.4 billion. This will not only reduce the demand for financial institutions and enterprises in the field of trade finance but also play a role in maintaining the stability of the US dollar exchange rate, ensuring the security of China's foreign exchange assets and appropriately reducing the scale of China's foreign exchange reserves.

At the same time, we also need to consider the use of currency swaps from the mode of current emergency rescue to the mode of daily trading to promote the use of the RMB in international trade and investment. In the future, we may also consider the possibility of RMB and special drawing right (SDR) swaps within the IMF framework to enhance the function of the RMB as an international reserve currency, so that the RMB can hold similar function as other fully convertible currencies under the IMF framework.

(3) Strengthening Financial Cooperation in East Asia:

Historical experience shows that monetary cooperation plays a crucial role in the internationalization of money. The current condition can support RMB as the trade settlement and financial investment in East Asia. However, if we want to push the RMB into a real "anchor currency" in the region and turn the tide of the dollar standard, we need regional monetary and financial cooperation. From the current point of view, the RMB is crucial in the financial cooperation of neighboring countries and regions. It is not only reflected in the bilateral and multilateral currency swaps but also in the subscription of the reserve bank and more initiatives in the Asian bond funds and the Asian bond market. To further strengthen the cooperation, China should first actively promote the development of the Chiang Mai Agreement to institutionalization, improve the regional economic monitoring and policy dialogue mechanism, and introduce local currency to establish regional monetary funds, which will help the RMB become the main intervention currency and reserve currency in the region. The second is to speed up the overcoming of the shortcomings of regional financial markets and infrastructure construction; to accelerate the development of regional capital markets; to enhance the role of local currency in the regional bond market; to design joint bond issuance plans; to design corporate bond issuance plans; to establish regional credit rating agencies. Coupled with trade settlement and the construction of offshore financial centers in Hong Kong, RMB may become an important financial investment transaction currency in the region in the future.

(4) Promote the Pricing of Commodities in RMB:

According to statistics, China's dependence on foreign energy will rise from 8.8% in 2008 to 15% in 2015. The dependence on oil and natural gas will increase from 51.2% and 5.8% in 2008 to 60% and 30%, respectively, in 2015. In the year 2030, the external dependence of China's energy, oil and natural gas will further increase to 25%, 70% and 50%. It is necessary for China to establish a new commodity pricing system priced in RMB, which will be a key step in the internationalization of the RMB. We can consider breakthroughs in the following two aspects: first, China's annual import of iron ore exceeds half of the world's total imports, and is the largest importer of iron ore; second, the annual export of rare earths accounts for 90% of the world's total supply of rare earths and China is the world's largest exporter. At present, the pricing power of these two commodities has not been monopolized by the US dollar, so we can make a breakthrough to explore the pricing of iron ore and rare earth in the RMB and promote the internationalization of the RMB.

(5) Expand Cross-Border Clearing Channels:

The cross-border liquidation arrangement of RMB is not only an important pillar for the realization of the internationalization goal of the RMB but also the basis for enhancing China's financial strength and ensuring financial security. As the scale of RMB cross-border funds continues to expand, the difficulty of management and monitoring will continue to increase, which will have a greater impact on domestic macroeconomic stability and financial security. With the payment clearing system, it is more convenient to collect the information of cross-border capital, monitor the flow of hot money and illegal funds, prompt relevant risks and provide early warning more effectively to prevent the impact of short-term large-scale cross-border capital to maintain financial security. Therefore, in the construction and layout of the RMB clearing system, it is necessary to proceed from the national interest and the overall situation to design a forward-looking layout.

(6) To Build a Global RMB Center in Shanghai:

The establishment of the Shanghai FTA provides a test field for the opening of China's financial industry. It is necessary to give play to the pioneering role of the Shanghai FTA, promote the diversification of the RMB return channel, enhance the openness of the financial market, expand the use of the RMB in capital allocation and financial markets, thereby accelerating the construction of the Shanghai International Financial Center and supporting the establishment of the global RMB center in Shanghai.

(7) Combine with the Construction of "Belt and Road" to Strive for Wider Acceptance and Use of RMB in Countries along the "Belt and Road":

First of all, judging from the current advancement of RMB internationalization, China and some countries along the "Belt and Road" have already formed some related arrangements in the use of RMB, such as the currency swap arrangements of Russia and Belarus along the "Silk Road Economic Belt," direct exchange arrangements with the Russian ruble, currency swap arrangements in Southeast Asia and other countries along the 21st Century Maritime Silk Road, and the construction of the offshore RMB market in Singapore, and even the relevant arrangements for transactions and settlement of the RMB in European countries, all of which have laid a good condition for further promoting the acceptance and use of the RMB within the scope of "Belt and Road." Therefore, there are corresponding basic conditions for promoting the internationalization of the RMB under the initiative of "Belt and Road."

Second, because of its relatively wide scope, the "Belt and Road" has greater flexibility in promoting the acceptance and use of the RMB within its scope. Different from promoting the internationalization of the RMB in East Asia, China can promote the use of RMB in a certain region or a specific country, and then turn to other countries along the "Belt and Road," so that the internationalization of the RMB will not be stalled due to certain restrictions or difficulties.

As mentioned earlier, an important part of promoting the internationalization of the RMB is to try to promote the pricing of some bulk commodity transactions in RMB, while the "Belt and Road" region has many resource-based countries that produce and export large quantities of commodities. Using economic cooperation with these countries to promote the pricing in RMB in bilateral transactions of China and these countries in resource-based products or commodities will obviously have a positive effect on the internationalization of the RMB.

Finally, in the face of the strong dominance of the US dollar in the current international monetary system, the geographical choice of the promotion of the internationalization of the RMB should clearly give priority to those regions where the dominant position of the US dollar is relatively weak. In the countries along the "Belt and Road," the dominance of the US dollar has not been very prominent in many countries and regions, which provides a possible breakthrough for the use and acceptance of the RMB.

(8) Strive to Gradually Improve China's Position in the IMF:

First, we should appropriately improve the voting rights in the IMF and carry out international cooperation. As an institution that maintains the world financial order, the IMF has major problems in its voting rights and structural design. According to the IMF rules, important proposals need to be approved by majority of 85%, which gives the United States with about 17% of voting rights a "one-vote veto" on IMF's major issues, making it impossible for the IMF to pass any resolution that is not in the interests of the US. There is no ability to supervise and restrain the dollar under the current IMF framework. Relatively speaking, China's voting rights in the IMF are only 3.81%, which not only cannot promote the substantive reform of multi-polarization of international currency but also cannot be related to the internationalization of the power of a country's currency in global trade settlement and commodity pricing. The right to speak on the key issues is not conducive to China's promotion of the internationalization of the RMB. Although as early as the Pittsburgh Global Leaders' Summit agreed to increase the voting power of developing countries in the IMF by 5%, considering the current status of China in the international political economy, we should strive to increase voting rights to at least 5–6%. In this way, although the ratio is still low, at least it can be combined with other emerging economies such as India, Brazil or Russia to jointly promote the multi-polarization of the international monetary system.

Second, strive to improve the soft power in the IMF. Since the establishment of the IMF, its leadership positions have been monopolized by the developed countries, so the developing countries do not have the right to speak in areas such as internal conference discussions, formulation of relevant issues and related decision-making procedures. While endeavoring to the right to vote, China should also strive to change the situation that senior managers of international institutions such as the IMF are basically monopolized by developed countries, and strive to hold key positions in the institution, while strengthening exchanges with relevant experts in the organization to improve soft power.

Third, we should strive to make the RMB the basket currency of the SDR. The government of China needs to actively strive to add the RMB to the SDR basket when the IMF initiates the reform. Considering China's influence in the international political economy, we should propose that the RMB accounts for about 10% of the SDR, which is also an important measure to improve the international status of the RMB.

Under the background of the reform and development of the international monetary system, the internationalization of RMB is a new topic facing China's economic and financial fields. At present, the internationalization of the RMB has achieved good results; however, it also faces certain problems, which cannot be comparable with the internationalization of the currencies of the developed countries. While continuing to promote various financial reforms, we should optimize the strategy of RMB internationalization, combine the actual situation at home and abroad, select the optimal path of internationalization, and continue to expand the international scope of the RMB so that it can become an international currency as soon as possible.

6.3.4 *Institutional Arrangement and Risk Prevention in the Process of RMB Internationalization*

6.3.4.1 *Top-level Design of RMB Internationalization*

(1) Coordinating interest rate and exchange rate reform, opening of capital account and RMB internationalization:

With the acceleration of the internationalization of RMB, the domestic financial system will be more connected with the international financial system, and the degree of interaction between the two will become stronger and stronger. Therefore, it is necessary to carry out comprehensive reforms of the financial system with the internationalization of RMB as the core. Based on China's national conditions, in the process of building the internationalization system of RMB, the supporting reform of relevant systems requires top-level design. In the process of China's RMB internationalization, it is necessary to consider and coordinate the adjustment of interest rate and exchange rate marketization and opening of capital account. In general, the relationship needs to follow the path of adhering to market-oriented reforms. The full marketization of financial assets such as interest rates and exchange rates is conducive to maximizing the fundamental role of market mechanisms in arranging financial resources. Cautious promotion of opening the capital account is conducive to preventing the transmission of international financial risks, and can also strive for the necessary reform of the supporting system.

In the process of RMB internationalization, the market-oriented reform of interest rates is the foundation. The domestic value of money is the basis of external value. As the domestic price of currency, only when interest rate fully realizes marketization, it is possible to realize the marketization of the international price of the currency, that is, the exchange rate. More importantly, the marketization of interest rates is a necessary condition for a country's financial products to greatly enrich and meet the investment needs of foreign institutions holding local currency. The market-oriented interest rate level will play a role in the allocation of interest rates to funds, which will help promote financial innovation, thereby promoting the richness of domestic financial market products and meeting the investment needs of overseas institutions with different risk preferences. If foreign investors can conveniently maintain and increase their value in the domestic financial market, the acceptance of RMB in the international financial market will be greatly enhanced.

Accelerating the reform of the exchange rate system is the guarantee for deepening the internationalization of the RMB. The increase in the degree of internationalization of the RMB will inevitably lead to an increase in the size of offshore RMB, which will gradually form a mature offshore RMB market. The marketization of the exchange rate is conducive to enhancing the independence of the central bank's monetary policy and laying the foundation for the orderly opening of capital projects. The fixed exchange rate system is the paralysis of capital project liberalization. If RMB is internationalized and the exchange rate is still stable, it will stimulate a large inflow of short-term speculative capital, because the stable exchange rate provides a potential guarantee for foreign speculators and domestic borrowers, so that they do not need to consider the risk of exchange rate fluctuations. This will increase the likelihood of a financial crisis, so the internationalization of the RMB must match the flexible exchange rate arrangement. In China, a managed floating exchange rate system should be implemented to maintain the stability of the value of the RMB.

The internationalization of the RMB requires an orderly and modest opening of capital account. The opening of capital account will greatly increase the liquidity of RMB assets and reduce the risk of holding; it will help promote Chinese enterprises to go global, develop FDI, ease the pressure on foreign exchange reserves, raise the international status of the RMB, and realize the domestic and foreign circulating flow of RMB.

The combination of institutional guarantee and market-oriented reform will make the internationalization of the RMB an inevitable historical process. There is no strict sequence between RMB internationalization and interest rate liberalization, exchange rate reform and opening of capital account. From the practice of national currency internationalization, interest rate liberalization, flexible exchange rate arrangements and opening of capital account can cooperate and coordinate with each other.

(2) Accelerate the development of interest rate marketization:

In 1996, the central bank launched the reform of interest rate marketization. In February 2003, the central bank announced in "China Monetary Policy Implementation Report 2002," which presented the general idea of the reform of China's interest rate marketization, that is, "first foreign currency, then domestic currency; first loan, then deposit; first long-term and wholesale, then short-term and micro-savings." In fact, China's interest rate marketization process can be divided into marketization of interest rates in money market, marketization of interest rate in capital markets and marketization of deposit interest rates of financial institutions. At present, except for the interest rate of deposits and loans in the local currency, most of the other interest rates have realized marketization.

The benchmark interest rate for deposits and loans in China is based on the principle of "lower limit of loan and upper limit of deposit." With the large-scale reform of China's financial institutions and the development of financial markets, the timing of further interest rate marketization has matured. In accordance with the principle of "first loan, then deposit," the floating range of loan interest rate should be gradually expanded to some simplified grades, and some financial institutions that meet the standards should be allowed to try the market-based pricing of interest rates. The impact of interest rate policies on financial markets at different stages should be carefully considered. The degree of openness of interest rates should be consistent with the tolerance of microeconomic entities.

On the basis of the pilot, the loans for interest rates can be gradually floated (market-based pricing). Since the loan interest rate involves the capital cost of the enterprise, the excessive rise in interest rates will have a major disadvantage to the business operation. Therefore, the marketization of the loan interest rate should be steadily implemented. As far as the marketization of deposit interest

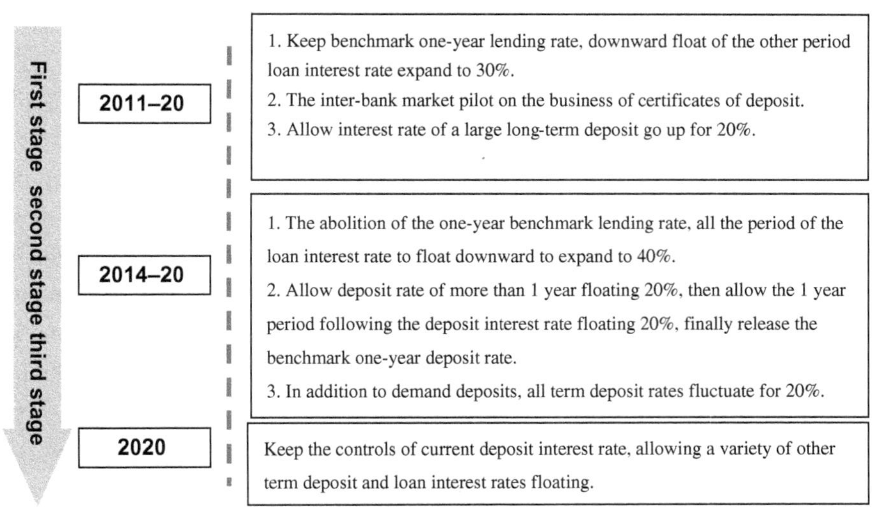

Figure 6.11. The Marketization of Interest Rate of RMB Deposit in China

rates is concerned, the central bank should maintain certain powers of market intervention. The purpose of this is to prevent financial institutions from raising interest rates and vicious competition in the deposit market, thereby pushing up loan interest rates and adversely affecting economic operations. The marketization of deposit interest rates is an important link and the ultimate goal of China's entire interest rate marketization reform. Specifically, it can be considered in three stages, and promoted in an orderly manner.

(3) Promote the reform of the RMB exchange rate:

In general, the purpose of the RMB exchange rate reform is to establish a more flexible exchange rate determination mechanism. China's current implementation of a "managed floating exchange rate system" means that the exchange rate will be determined by the market, but it is also regulated by the government. The internationalization of the RMB requires an exchange rate system that is largely determined by the market. Therefore, the next step in the reform of the RMB exchange rate is to increase the market's impact on the exchange rate and reduce government intervention.

Specifically, first, we must expand the floating range of the RMB exchange rate, establish a wider band-shaped floating range around the target exchange rate or the central exchange rate, and expand the floating range to about 10% of the central exchange rate. Second, the foreign exchange market should increase foreign exchange trading entities and trading varieties, enrich transaction types, and make the RMB exchange rate more based on the balance of supply and demand in the foreign exchange market. Third, we must reform the foreign exchange management system, expand the investment scale of the qualified domestic institutional investors (QDII) and qualified foreign institutional investors (QFII), and then further open up the capital account. Through the aforementioned reforms, the internal and external circulation mechanism of the RMB will be gradually established, and the exchange rate will be mainly determined by market supply and demand.

(4) Open capital account:

RMB capital account convertibility is an important condition for realizing the internationalization of the RMB. It is also conducive to a more balanced capital flow, reducing cross-border capital arbitrage motives, promoting effective operation of onshore offshore markets and ensuring the healthy development of RMB internationalization. China is a large-scale transition economy, so the opening of capital account should be "orderly and moderately open under control." The basic principles of "autonomous, gradual, and controllable" should be followed, and the benefits of the opening of capital project account should be maximized to reduce the risk.

According to domestic and international experience, the opening of capital account should follow the following sequence: first long-term capital outflows, then short-term capital outflows; first securities investment, then bank credit; first bond instruments, then equity and derivatives tools; first regulation on the primary market, then regulation on the secondary market; first foreign financing, then non-residents domestic financing; first financial institutions, then non-financial institutions and individuals. From the aforementioned sequence, the opening of capital account is not carried out in isolation, but should be coordinated with the reform of interest rate marketization and exchange rate formation mechanism. The opening of capital account should be carried out on the premise that the domestic financial market has been fully developed and matured and the supporting financial supervision system has been established. According to the SNA, the opening under the capital account should include the contents listed in Table 6.16.

Although there is no clear timetable for RMB capital account convertibility, according to the needs of China's economic transformation and RMB internationalization process, China should actively and steadily continue to promote the RMB capital account convertibility process under the control of risks. The important tasks include the liberalization of FDI in RMB settlement, the full implementation

Table 6.16. The Content of Opening the Capital Account

Direct investment	1. Cancellation of restrictions on direct investment capital outflows of domestic institutions and individuals 2. Relax the restrictions on the flow of funds by domestic institutions in operating overseas enterprises 3. Relax restrictions on capital inflows from overseas institutions and individuals
Stock investment	4. Relax domestic companies to issue shares and other equity securities to overseas 5. Lifting restrictions on prohibiting foreign investors from engaging in domestic stock trading 6. Relax the restrictions on domestic investment institutions and individuals investing in overseas stock markets and the corresponding foreign exchange restrictions 7. Relax the restrictions on the issuance of stocks or equity securities in China by overseas institutions 8. Relax restrictions on the issuance of corporate bonds and other debt securities by domestic operating institutions to overseas countries 9. Relax restrictions on foreign investors engaging in corporate bonds and other debt securities transactions in China 10. Relax the restrictions on domestic investment institutions and individuals engaged in investing in overseas bonds and other debt securities markets 11. Relax the restrictions on the issuance of bonds and other debt securities in China by overseas operating institutions
Other investment	12. Cancellation of the approval system for foreign borrowing by domestic operating institutions 13. Cancellation of the approval system for loans issued by domestic financial institutions 14. Cancellation of restrictions on obtaining foreign trade loans from domestic operating institutions

Source: The relevant information collected by the author.

of cross-border trade in RMB settlement, the expansion of domestic institutions to issue RMB bonds in Hong Kong, and the entry of RQFII into the domestic securities market.

In the process, the following points deserve the attention: first, the opening of capital account should be carried out within the framework of a comprehensive reform plan. The coordination of capital account liberalization and other policies must be based on a comprehensive examination of national conditions, and thus requires the choice of timing and certain flexibility to make capital account liberalization part of a comprehensive package of reforms in the process of RMB internationalization. Second, the opening of China's capital account should choose a gradual but positive model. The acceleration of the internationalization of the RMB has already created a mechanism for the opening of capital account. The speed of capital account opening itself includes considerations of political economy: although slow pace of liberalization can reduce the cost of making mistakes in the reform, it may also have the expectation of policy reversal, reduce the credibility of reform and weaken the role of reform measures. Third, we must balance the relationship between exchange rate reform and capital account opening. It is impossible for a country to achieve all the three objectives of currency independence, exchange rate stability and free capital flow at the same time. According to China's national conditions, economic development and economic fluctuations are more endogenous, so they need to be adjusted through monetary policy to iron out economic fluctuations. Therefore, the freer the capital flows are, the more flexible the exchange rate system should be in place. The fluctuation of a country's exchange rate should be a prerequisite for the opening of a capital account, and reforms should be avoided. Fourth, capital control measures should be moderate.

From the specific measures, it is recommended to first liberalize long-term capital flows, then liberalize short-term capital flows; first liberalize direct investment, then liberalize indirect investment; first liberalize the inflows, then release the outflows, and promote commercial credit and bonds. The relevant reforms in stock-based securities transactions will basically realize the convertibility of RMB capital account in about five years. At the same time, it is still necessary to take certain measures, such as strengthening anti-monopoly review, improving financing policies of anti-money laundering and anti-terrorism, clearing and abolishing super-national treatment, establishing a blacklist system, increasing the reserve requirements for non-resident deposits, and levying Tobin tax for short-term capital flows, etc. These measures will effectively control systemic risks, prevent cross-border capital flows (especially speculative capital flows) from impacting China's financial market and maintain market stability.

6.3.4.2 *Prevent Risks in the Process of RMB Internationalization*

At present, the internationalization of RMB is facing various risks: the current foreign exchange reserves are still increasing rapidly; the imbalance in the global economic recovery has led to inconsistent prices of internal and external funds of the RMB, and cross-border short-term capital flows remain fierce. Under the background of monetary policy, capital arbitrage in the process of RMB return may trigger the rise of domestic money supply, exacerbate the risk of domestic inflation and asset bubbles, and increase the difficulty of monetary policy regulation. This is the risk and cost that the RMB has to face in the process of internationalization. Therefore, various means should be adopted to prevent various risks in the process of RMB internationalization.

First, a diversified foreign exchange management system should be built to avoid further accumulation of risks in foreign exchange reserves. In recent years, in the context of the appreciation of the RMB, overseas companies are more willing to accept the RMB than to pay in RMB. Therefore, domestic enterprises will pay more in RMB when they import goods, and have to receive dollars when they export, which causes importers to reduce purchases. The demand for foreign exchange and the decline in foreign exchange demand further magnified the oversupply. The monetary authorities had to buy more foreign exchange for the purpose of stabilizing the exchange rate. Therefore, the faster the development of RMB trade settlement, the more likely it is to impact the balance of assets and liabilities of the central bank, resulting in an increase in foreign exchange reserves. In order to avoid further accumulation of risks in foreign exchange reserves, China must build a diversified foreign exchange management system from the three levels of formation, retention and structure of the foreign exchange reserve.

From the perspective of the formation of foreign exchange reserves, the current rapid growth of foreign exchange reserves is due to the expectation of RMB appreciation, and the realization of arbitrage through the difference in the form of return in RMB. In the future, due to the continued weakness of the European and American economies, the appreciation of the RMB will continue. Therefore, the current focus is to improve the ability to discriminate against the "hot money" of the RMB return process and prevent the impact of the abnormal return of the RMB on foreign exchange reserves. First, it strictly controls the number of clearing banks, so that the return of overseas funds is in a measurable and controllable state. In the future, we will continue to promote the role of BOC Hong Kong in the overall return of RMB deposits, carefully open the number of other offshore central clearing banks, and build a "firewall" between the offshore market and the onshore market. Second, it strictly examines the entry and scale of investment in the RMB bond market by overseas institutions, so that its impact on the domestic financial market is within the controllable range. Furthermore, the review of the use of FDI funds in RMB will be further strengthened. In way of the authenticity review of FDI investment transactions, the FDI funds in RMB will eventually be prevented from flowing to the asset market.

From the perspective of the retention of foreign exchange reserves, it is necessary to avoid excessive growth of the central bank's foreign exchange reserves by "hiding the wealth in the public." First, the existing policy restrictions on the holding and use of foreign exchange should be gradually relaxed, so that the private sector can hold more foreign exchange; second, the foreign exchange investment channels and varieties should be further improved, so that enterprises and residents are willing to hold foreign exchange, in order to creating conditions to achieve "hidden wealth in the public." In addition, in order to speed up the implementation of the "going out" strategy, the government should support Chinese companies to step up the acquisition of strategic assets or high-tech products. The types of assets acquired include not only rare metals but also high-tech products, equipment or purchases medical equipment that are related to people's livelihood, etc.

From the structure of foreign exchange reserves, China must adjust the current structure of the foreign exchange reserve to build a diversified foreign exchange reserve with stronger anti-risk ability. First, it should stop increasing the holdings and gradually reduce US Treasury bonds, and build a diversified structure of foreign exchange reserve including Australian dollar, Swiss franc, euro and Japanese yen. Second, it should increase the holding of physical resources such as gold and oil, and gradually become a large gold reserve country, which is commensurate with its economic strength. While relying on the status of a major consumer of commodities such as oil and iron ore, it can increase its voice in these markets.

Second, it should strengthen the monitoring of RMB cross-border funds and reduce the impact of liquid capital on financial markets. At present, the imbalance in the global economic recovery has led to inconsistent prices of internal and external funds in the RMB, and domestic asset prices have been affected.

First of all, from the perspective of interest rates, developed countries such as Europe and the United States continue to implement quantitative easing monetary policy. Therefore, the excessive liquidity causes the overseas interest rate of RMB to be significantly lower than the domestic RMB interest rate (for example, in October 2010, the interest rate of one-year RMB deposits in Hong Kong was about 0.6%, and the interest rate of the same deposit was 3.5%). On the other hand, due to the continued expectation of RMB appreciation, foreign investors are willing to accept lower RMB interest rates, which make the yield of RMB bonds issued in Hong Kong 50–200 basis points lower than the yield of similar domestic bonds. In addition, since the domestic RMB has not yet achieved market pricing of interest rate, the structure of domestic and foreign spreads has led to arbitrage in the currency. For example, a large number of Mainland enterprises in Hong Kong can borrow RMB loans and bonds, and then return to Mainland by the pathway of FDI in RMB with the formation of arbitrage.

Secondly, from the perspective of exchange rate, the continuous expectation of RMB appreciation results that the exchange rate of RMB to USD in the Hong Kong offshore market (CNH) is generally higher than domestic RMB exchange rate against the dollar (CNY), and the premium will induce the sales of RMB against USD to transfer into Hong Kong foreign exchange market to enjoy a more favorable exchange rate, so the RMB is likely to flow to overseas in a large scale. It should be noted that the outward flow of the current risk of RMB capital is still in a controllable state, however, the cross-border flow is conducive to the development of the RMB offshore market in the long run. At present, the difference between the offshore RMB dollar exchange rate CNH and onshore RMB dollar exchange rate CNY is relatively small, and trading volume of CNH per day is about US$300 million, only taking 1/10 of the RMB NDF market, therefore, the liquidity risk resulted from the rate spread is controllable. On the other hand, maintaining a small premium of offshore CNH/CHY can make the continuous inflow of RMB to Hong Kong, with an estimate volume of tens of billions of dollars for each month, and this is a healthy rate, which is conducive to support the development of the offshore market.

In the future, in order to avoid the two-way flow of capital to form a significant impact on the financial market, we must strengthen the monitoring of cross-border RMB funds and make the capital flow be measured in a controllable state from the following aspects. First, the government should strictly control the approval of overseas RMB bonds, RMB loans and IPO funds, strict monitoring of cross-border capital of RMB, total return in excessive, short-term impact on domestic market, due to slow pace of approval; second, it should control the size of foreign exchange of the Bank of China in Hong Kong, the size of foreign exchange swap of the Hong Kong monetary authority, and the growth of scale of RMB in Hong Kong; third, it can raise RMB deposit liquidity ratio requirement of the Hong Kong Monetary Authority (25%) when necessary, control the speed of derived deposit rate of RMB and the development of Hong Kong offshore market; finally, the government can also levy a special tax on the inflow of RMB funds under unusual circumstances, with the convergence of the domestic and foreign real financing cost, so as to reduce the excessive return of RMB funds in Hong Kong.

Third, the RMB return process should be controlled to prevent a significant impact on domestic monetary policy. At present, as the overseas RMB interest rate is lower than domestic one, this may lead to a large number of enterprises in Hong Kong issuing loans and bonds in RMB, resulting RMB backflow to Mainland, and leading to a significant increase in the domestic money supply (M2), thereby increasing the risk of domestic inflation and asset bubbles. Different ways of using the RMB will cause various influence on the domestic money supply. First, if the RMB deposits in Hong Kong market are used for local products and services in Hong Kong, and financial transactions and foreign importers to buy domestic products, these types of cases will not affect the domestic money supply. Because the former is mainly using RMB overseas, not flowing back to the Mainland, and directly using it at the time of purchase, which will reduce the pressure on the growth of foreign exchange reserves. Second, the FDI in RMB does not necessarily lead to the increase in domestic money supply. Only when the Mainland enterprises issue loans and bonds by RMB in Hong Kong and at the same time to return the domestic market of FDI in RMB, it will increase the pressure on the domestic money supply and domestic inflation. The use of RMB funds overseas and their return in other channels (replace USD with RMB on domestic FDI in real investment demand, foreign institutions obtain RMB in form of loans and bonds, then return to the Mainland in the form of FDI, etc.) do not form new money supply.

The following suggestions are put forward to control the risk of backflow of RMB: first, we should encourage more foreign enterprises to use the RMB to make domestic direct investment in RMB, use

RMB under the export trade settlement, encourage foreign companies to borrow RMB in Hong Kong and use the funds overseas, thus reducing the return motivation of RMB; second, the People's Bank of China or Hong Kong financial administration can intervene in the offshore RMB exchange market, reduce the exchange rate difference and alleviate the pressure resulted from excessive RMB flow to Hong Kong; third, Shenzhen Branch of the People's Bank of China can adjust the RMB deposit interest rate of BOC Hong Kong, thus affecting the Hong Kong deposit and lending rates, tightening or loosening the aggregate money supply of RMB.

As mentioned previously, after the global financial crisis, the dollar-based international monetary system has exposed great defects. Other countries and international organizations have put forward the reform of the international monetary system and promoted the diversification of the international monetary. With the increasing of the overall economic strength, the acceptance of RMB in the international market has gradually increased. The internationalization of RMB is the background of the international monetary system reform and development and is a new task of China's economic and financial fields. At present, the internationalization of RMB has achieved good results: the cross-border trade settlement in RMB continues to expand: the scale of Hong Kong's offshore RMB market continues to mature; the use of direct investment of RMB has begun to increase; the monetary cooperation between governments is deepening. In the third Plenary Session of the 18th CPC Central Committee, deepening the reform of the financial system has become the future of China's economic reform, and it is an important part of the promotion of RMB to go global, which will play a positive role in promoting the goal of RMB internationalization.

As the world's second-largest economy and the largest trading nation, although China has the initial prerequisite to realize the internationalization of RMB, it is not currently in conformity with the basic requirement of currency internationalization in the short term. RMB is used as a reserve currency only in some countries and regions: Malaysia, Thailand, Philippines, Kampuchea, South Korea,

Chinese Taiwan, Nigeria in Africa, Bolivia in Latin America, Belarus and other European countries and regions, and the RMB in the international foreign exchange reserves is also very limited. In fact, the internationalization of the RMB is also facing some difficulties, mainly in the trade surplus and capital account, which is not completely open. We believe that China should choose the path of development in a variety of ways based on the characteristics of economic ties between different regions of the world, and constantly promote the scope of the international use of the RMB.

At the same time, the comprehensive reform of RMB internationalization needs the support of the domestic financial system, coordinating the relationship between it and the market interest rate, exchange rate reform, the opening of the capital account, to provide institutional guarantee for the internationalization of RMB. In addition, we should pay special attention to the risk problem in the process of promoting the internationalization of the RMB, especially caused by cross-border RMB liquidity and cumulative risk of asset bubbles. The government should actively take measures to make policy adjustments to changes in a timely manner, and to ensure the stability of the financial order.

Chapter 7

Actively Promote the Monetary Cooperation in East Asia

The global financial crisis has triggered the thinking of the countries around the world on the reform of the current international currency system. As the major supporting force of the dollar system, East Asia and the adjustment and changes in its trade development model will become an important force in promoting the reform of the international monetary system. Although each East Asian economy is a beneficiary under the current international currency system, it bears certain losses under the current international currency system and faces considerable risks. Therefore, East Asian economies, particularly China, as a center of the economic cycle in the region, naturally have a strong incentive to promote the reform of the international monetary system.

Considering that the current international monetary system still has certain sustainability, fundamental reform of the international monetary system at the global level faces great difficulties; at the same time, although China is the largest trading country in the region at the current stage, it still cannot be a region for the provider of the end-product market and the RMB is still not a key currency in the region. Therefore, East Asian regional currency cooperation has an irreplaceable important position in China's participation in the international monetary system reform. On the one hand,

China can further promote the internationalization of the RMB through regional cooperation; on the other hand, it can also supplement and revise the current international monetary system with regional cooperation arrangements and create conditions for further reform of the international monetary system.

In this context, the study of the process of monetary cooperation in East Asia and how China has taken the initiative to advance this process can theoretically make new and innovative contributions to regional monetary and financial cooperation theories and international monetary system theories, and proposes the "East Asia model" for regional monetary cooperation. In practice, it is of great significance in clarifying the prospects for the future reform of the international monetary system and the realization of China's interest claims in the process of participating in the reform of the international monetary system.

7.1 The Significance of Promoting Monetary Cooperation in East Asia for China's Participation in the International Monetary System Reform

From the current development level of domestic financial system in China and the international status and influence of the RMB, as a developing country, China will maximize its own interest claims in the current reform of the international currency system and draw on East Asian regional monetary cooperation. It is the only way to achieve this benefit requirement.

7.1.1 *East Asian Regional Currency Cooperation and RMB Internationalization*

As an important supporting force of the current US dollar system, East Asia determines that it will become one of the important driving forces for the reform of the international monetary system in the future. To a large extent, the current problems in the global economic cycle reflect the dilemmas faced by the East Asian region under the dollar system. An important way to get rid of these difficulties is to provide the final product market in the region by the transformation of East Asian regional trade, free off the long-term dependence on the US market. However, the two major powers in East Asia, China and Japan, do not have the capability to become end-product market providers in the short term. Therefore, at this stage, the promising path to overcome difficulties is to strengthen regional monetary and financial cooperation in East Asia, rely on the logic of regional collective action to gradually advance the reform of the international monetary system, and then establish regional benefits for the healthy international currency environment for the development of East Asian economies. In this process, the internationalization of the RMB can be used as a driving force.

7.1.1.1 *Importance of Currency Cooperation in East Asia*

In fact, currency competition is a phenomenon that has existed since the currency was created. The first is the competition between the metal currency and the physical currency, and then the competition between the legal currency and the metal currency. If the competition is still limited to a domestic sector, then with the continuous strengthening of the economic globalization trend, the international expansion of production, trade and financial activities has brought currency competition to the international stage.[1] Due to the large differences in the level of economic development among countries, the international status of each country's currency is also quite different. At present, the international monetary system is an unbalanced system. The single currency of a small currency country does not change the monopoly position of a country with dominant currency. The establishment of a single currency union is an effective way for small currency countries to seek a stable environment

[1]Chen, Yulu, and Weihong Bian, "Monetary Union Theory: Progress in the Measurement of Optimal Currency Areas," *International Finance Research* 2 (2004): 4–12.

for economic development under the current exchange rate system, because a common central bank in a region will be smaller than a single currency. The central bank can effectively exert the functions of the lender of last resort and maintain the stability of regional currency order. The close cooperation of regional currencies will promote more integrated regional capital markets with higher liquidity, lower transaction costs in the region and increase the currency competitiveness of small countries in the international monetary sector.[2]

The ideological origins of East Asian regional monetary cooperation came from the idea of establishment of "Pacific Currency Area" proposed by Kiyoshi Kojima in the 1970s.[3] This idea was based on the devaluation of the British pound on 18 November 1967 and the corresponding defensive measures for the US dollar (a two-tier gold price system that puts the pound sterling and the US dollar as an international currency), and re-arranged the European exchange rate. In the context of the system, the international monetary and financial cooperation mechanism under the framework of the International Monetary Fund (IMF) and the World Trade Organization (WTO) (the General Agreement on Tariffs and Trade (GATT)) is full of uncertainty, and the "Triffin puzzle" of the lack of international liquidity and the depreciation of the US dollar under the Bretton Woods system, therefore, there is the need to strengthen international currency integration. At the same time, it is pointed out that a good international monetary system should be based on mutual cooperation between countries with the same ideas in order to realize their respective political and economic goals.

Kojima believes that the Pacific currency area should have the following five characteristics: First, the initial Pacific currency area should include five developed countries in the Pacific, namely, the United States, Canada, Japan, Australia and New Zealand, but the

[2]Sachs, J., "International Economics: Unlocking the Mysteries of Globalization," *Foreign Policy* 110 (1998): 97–111.

[3]Kojima, K., "A Pacific Currency Area: A New Approach to International Monetary Reform," *Hitotsubashi Journal of Economics* 2, no. 10 (1970): 1–17.

currency area should be open to other countries that are interested in this; and the currency area should be established simultaneously with the Pacific Free Trade Zone. Second, all member countries of the Pacific currency area should join the pooling of gold and foreign exchange reserves. Third, in the currency area, after the initial necessary exchange rate adjustment, member states should maintain a fixed exchange rate between their respective currencies and the US dollar. In fact, the Pacific currency area is a Regional Dollar Area. Fourth, when adjusting the balance of payments between the currency area and the rest of the world, the dollar face value can be allowed to adjust within a relatively small range (for example, 5% of the face value). Fifth, balance of payments among member states is regulated by more free capital flows and countries' loans to reserve pools.[4]

The fundamental reason for East Asia's pursuit of monetary cooperation to form a stable economic development environment lies in the close trade relations that exist within East Asia.

An important purpose of regional monetary cooperation is to maintain the stability of relative price levels in various countries in the region and avoid the risk of frequent currency fluctuations. Close trade flows between countries in the region are an important prerequisite for stabilizing relative prices. Liu and Xie inspected the regional distribution of foreign trade in East Asian economies, and believed that the foreign economies of East Asia, both in terms of trade and the use of foreign capital, are characterized by "diversification," and East Asian countries maintain greater economic relevance with the United States, Europe and Japan.[5] Branson and Healy[6] and Liu and Xie believed that whether it is from the target market structure or the type of commodity, China's export structure is similar

---

[4] *Ibid.*

[5] Liu, Lizhen and Chaoyang Xie, "East Asian Monetary Cooperation and RMB Exchange Rate System Selection," *Management World* 3 (2003): 34–44.

[6] Branson, William H., and Conor N. Healy, "Monetary and Exchange Rate Policy Coordination in ASEAN," *National Bureau of Economic Research Working Paper*, no. w11713 (October, 2005).

to the export structure of other East Asian economies.[7] By regional monetary cooperation, it is possible to further divert some imports from outside the region to imports within the region and strengthen economic links within the region.[8]

For East Asia, the region has formed a close network of contacts in the fields of production and trade. Li and Ding[9] used the Trade Intensity Index (TII) to measure the bilateral trade situation in East Asia (see Table 7.1). It was found that East Asia as a whole has a high internal trade intensity. The TII uses relative trade scale indicators. On the one hand, it can clearly compare intraregional trade links with foreign trade links. On the other hand, it can eliminate the factors that influence the economic scale differences on trade links and make the indicators themselves more comparable.

We can examine the position of China in the foreign trade of East Asian economies and explain the trade links of East Asian countries. To this end, we have calculated the four-year rolling correlation coefficient between the total exports of the East Asian economies and the total exports from China. For comparison purposes, we also calculated the correlation coefficient between the total exports of East Asian economies and the total exports of the United States and Japan, respectively. The rolling correlation coefficient is usually used to calculate the dynamic change of the correlation coefficient between variables and measure the dynamic correlation between variables. The rolling correlation analysis method not only reflects the degree of correlation between the two variables, but more importantly, it can reflect the trend of the correlation coefficient between the two variables. The higher the correlation coefficient is, the stronger the synergy or coordination of economic indicators are. The rolling correlation coefficient is widely used in the study

---

[7]Liu, Lizhen and Chaoyang Xie, "East Asian Monetary Cooperation and RMB Exchange Rate System Selection," *Management World* 3 (2003): 34–44.

[8]*Ibid.*

[9]Xiao, Li, and Yibing Ding, *Transcendence in Asia: Building a Regional Currency System in East Asia and Asianization of RMB*. Beijing: Contemporary China Press, 2005.

Table 7.1. Index of Intra-Regional Trade Strength in East Asia (10 Economies)

	Indonesia	Malaysia	Philippines	Singapore	Thailand	Taiwan, China	Hong Kong, China	Korea	Mainland China
Malaysia	2.61								
Philippines	1.55	2.82							
Singapore	5.58	11.18	3.67						
Thailand	2.85	3.47	2.59	4.90					
Taiwan, China	2.07	2.21	3.78	2.12	2.01				
Hong Kong, China	0.92	1.19	1.73	2.03	1.46	4.59			
Korea	3.39	1.82	2.53	1.71	1.15	1.76	1.61		
Mainland China	1.77	0.83	0.84	1.20	1.06	0.90	9.12	2.67	
Japan	4.67	2.25	2.95	1.82	3.02	2.92	1.56	2.49	2.52
Average					2.71				
United States	0.78	1.20	1.59	1.15	1.11	1.46	1.10	1.35	1.02

Source: Cited from Xiao, Li, and Yibing Ding, *Transcendence in Asia: Building a Regional Currency System in East Asia and Asianization of RMB*. Beijing: Contemporary China Press, 2005.

of economic cycle issues. In Liu and Liu,[10] rolling correlation coefficients are used to analyze the dynamic patterns of actual output volatility. In Huang *et al.*,[11] rolling correlation coefficients are used to study the positive correlation between the coordination of fiscal policy and monetary policy between China and Japan and the economic cycle cooperation between the two countries.[12] In Shi *et al.*, a fixed sample length rolling correlation coefficient measure is used the synergy of the economic cycles between China and Japan.[13] Wang *et al.* uses rolling correlation coefficients to study the dynamic correlation between China and the United States, Japan, South Korea and European countries.[14] Pontines and Siregar, and Shi *et al.* conducts research on the rolling correlation between South Korea, the Philippines, Indonesia, Thailand, and other four East Asian countries, respectively, and the exports of China and the United States.[15] It was found that between 2000 and 2008, there is a close correlation between the exports of the four East Asian countries and these two countries, especially after 2004, this degree of correlation has increased.

Rolling Correlation Coefficients can be used to examine the dynamic relationship between the total export volume of ASEAN 10 Countries and South Korea and the total export volume of China,

[10]Liu, Jinquan, and Zhigang Liu, "Dynamic Patterns and Causes of Real Output Volatility in China's Business Cycle Fluctuations," *Economic Research* 3 (2005): 26–35.

[11]Huang, Hongmei, Zhuxian Shi, and Yumei Li, "Impact of Sino-Japan Economic Policy Coordination on Business Cycle Comovement," *Modern Japanese Economy* 2 (2009): 1–6.

[12]*Ibid.*

[13]Shi, Zhuxian, Hongmei Huang, and Chuang Deng, "Research on Impact of Trade on Sino-Japan-Korea Business Cycle Comovement," *Northeast Asia Forum* 4 (2009).

[14]Wang, Liyong, Jinhua Han, and Yan Zhao, "Research on the Dynamic Correlation between Chinese and Foreign Business Cycles and the Forecast of China's Economic Growth," *Economic Developments* 9 (2009): 15–20.

[15]Pontines, Victor, and Reza Y. Siregar, "Fear of Appreciation in East and Southeast Asia: The Role of the Chinese Renminbi," *Journal of Asian Economics* 23, no. 4 (August 2012): 324–334.

Japan and the United States[16] to measure the status of China, Japan and the United States in the foreign trade of the 11 East Asian countries, respectively. The higher correlation and increasing correlation between the two variables indicate that the similarities between the two types of variables are higher.

The data used in the analysis are the export data of the 10 countries of ASEAN, South Korea, China, Japan, and the United States from 1990 to 2011. The data are from the UNCTAD database and uses variable dollar price data. The sample interval is from 1990 to 2011. The reason why this time period was chosen is mainly because East Asian economic cooperation, especially monetary and financial cooperation, has only gradually attracted attention after the Asian financial crisis, and this time period covered the Asian financial crisis and the years before and after the global financial crisis.

Using the rolling correlation coefficient of a fixed sample length can examine the dynamic development trend of the total export of the two types of countries. The calculation method of rolling correlation coefficient is as follows: the export sequence of country i and country j is $\{EX_{it}\}$ with $\{EX_{jt}\}$, where i is the 10 ASEAN countries and South Korea, and j is China, Japan and the United States. $t = 1, \ldots, T$, that is, the sample observation interval is $\{1, \ldots, T\}$. Given the scroll time window length m, the scroll correlation coefficient at time p (where p is from m to T); ρ_p is defined as a form of $(p - m + 1)$. The correlation coefficients of two sequences of m samples from time to time p. Specifically:

$$\rho_p = \frac{\sum_{t=p-m+1}^{p}(EX_{it} - \overline{EX_i})(EX_{jt} - \overline{EX_j})}{\sqrt{\sum_{t=p-m+1}^{p}(EX_{it} - \overline{EX_i})^2(EX_{jt} - \overline{EX_j})^2}},$$

among them: $\overline{EX_i} = \frac{1}{m}\sum_{t=p-m+1}^{p} EX_{it}, \overline{EX_j} = \frac{1}{m}\sum_{t=p-m+1}^{p} EX_{jt}$.

[16] ASEAN is the Association of Southeast Asian Nations, formerly known as the Association of Southeast Asian Nations established in July 1961. It was expanded to the Association of Southeast Asian Nations in August 1967. The existing 10 member countries include Brunei, Cambodia, Indonesia, Laos, Malaysia, Myanmar, Philippines, Singapore, Thailand and Vietnam. In the following, ASEAN 10+3 refers to the 10 ASEAN countries, China, Japan and South Korea.

A key issue of rolling correlation coefficient is the determination of rolling time windows; we learn from the research method of Pontines and Siregar and Shi *et al.* and determine the rolling time window m is four years.[17] Figures 7.1–7.11 depict the rolling correlation coefficients of the total export value between the 10 ASEAN countries and South Korea and the three countries of China, Japan and the United States, respectively, to illustrate the relative importance of bilateral trade between East Asian countries and China, Japan, and the United States.

According to the trends in the correlation coefficient between ASEAN and South Korea and China's exports, we can divide the former 11 countries into three groups.

The countries in the first group are strongly related and the numbers have small fluctuations. Vietnam and South Korea belong to this group, indicating that the dynamic relationship between the two countries and China's exports is strong. During the year under review, the export rolling correlation coefficient between Vietnam–China and Korea–China remained at a relatively high level, and the average annual rolling correlation coefficient between China and Korea was 92.4%, and that between China and Korea was 93.6%. The fluctuation range of the two sets of rolling correlation coefficients is very small. The maximum value of the Sino-Korea rolling correlation coefficient is 100% in 2007 and the minimum value is 49.9% in 2002. The difference between the two is 50 percentage points. The maximum value of the China–Vietnam rolling correlation coefficient is 100%, and the minimum value is 71.3% in 1991, with the difference of 29%.

The second group is the type of trough. There are two cases: single wave trough and double wave trough. Cambodia and Laos are in the single wave valley, and Indonesia, Malaysia, Myanmar, the Philippines, Singapore and Thailand belong to the double trough valley.

[17]Pontines, Victor, and Ramkishen S. Rajan, "1 Fear of Appreciation in East and Southeast Asia: The Role of the Chinese Renminbi," *Journal of Asian Economics* 23, no. 4 (August 2012): 324–334.
Shi, Z., Hongmei Huang and Chuang Deng, "Research on Impact of Trade on Sino-Japan-Korea Business Cycle Comovement," *Northeast Asia Forum* 4 (2009). 35–38.

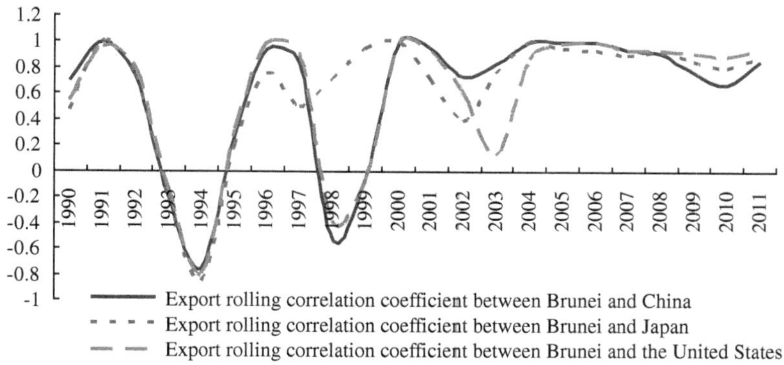

Figure 7.1. Export Rolling Correlation Coefficient between Brunei and China, Japan and the United States in 1990–2011

Source: According to UNCTAD DATABASE.

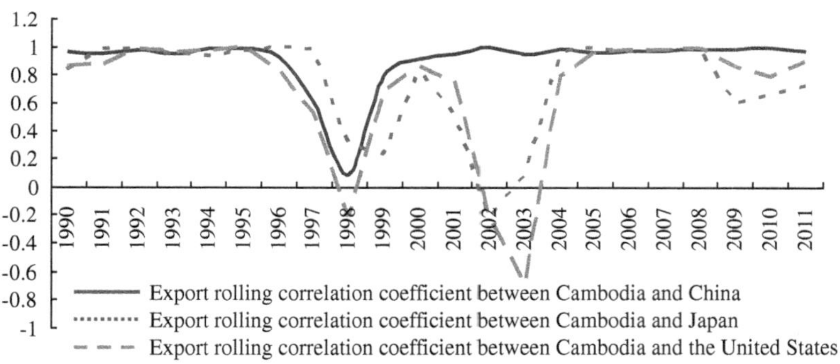

Figure 7.2. Export Rolling Correlation Coefficient between Cambodia and China, Japan and the United States from 1990 to 2011

Source: According to UNCTAD DATABASE.

In terms of the single-wave valley situation, Cambodia experienced a period of first decline after the correlation coefficient with China's export rolling in 1996–1999, among which, in 1998, it reached 8.4% of the trough. The Laos–China export rolling correlation coefficient fell from 98.3% in 1998 to −45.9% in 2000, and maintained a negative correlation between 2001 and 2002, reflecting the strong presence of the competitive relationship between Laos and China exports in the past three years. In the case of double troughs, the two trough phases of most countries' export rolling correlation coefficients with China

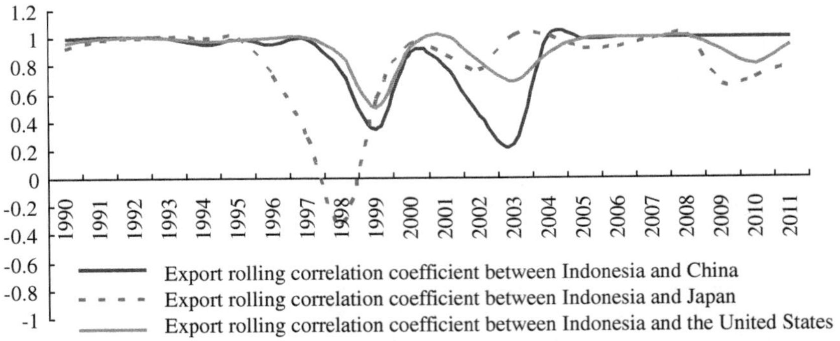

Figure 7.3. Export Rolling Correlation Coefficient between Indonesia and China, Japan and the United States from 1990 to 2011

Source: According to UNCTAD DATABASE.

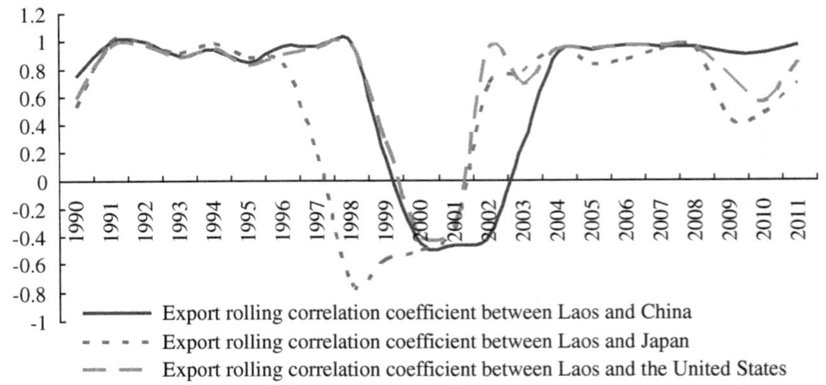

Figure 7.4. Export Rolling Correlation Coefficient between Laos and China, Japan and the United States from 1990 to 2011

Source: According to UNCTAD DATABASE.

appear before and after the 1997/98 Asian financial crisis and around 2003, such as Indonesia, Malaysia, Myanmar, Singapore and Thailand, but for the Philippines the troughs of China's export rolling correlation coefficient appeared in 2002 and 2009.

The third group is a wave type. Only Brunei belongs to this group. In the period under review, Brunei and China's export rolling correlation coefficient has a continuous lifting relationship, indicating that

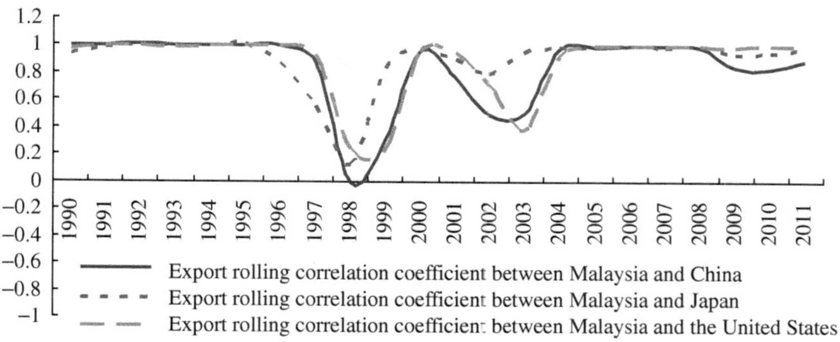

Figure 7.5. Export Rolling Correlation Coefficient between Malaysia and China, Japan and the United States in 1990–2011

Source: According to UNCTAD DATABASE.

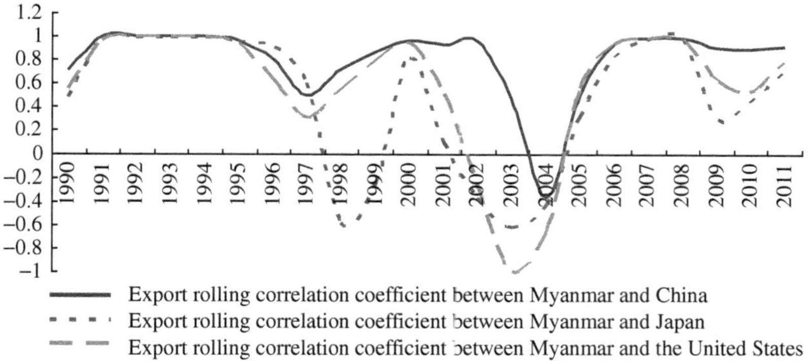

Figure 7.6. Export Rolling Correlation Coefficient between Myanmar and China, Japan and the United States from 1990 to 2011

Source: According to UNCTAD DATABASE.

the complementary and competitive relationship between Brunei's export trade and China's export trade are not stable.

Figures 7.1–7.11 also reflect the trend of the export rolling correlation coefficient between the 10 ASEAN countries and Korea, Japan and the United States. From a graphic point of view, other than Vietnam, the correlation coefficient between exports of other 10 countries before and after the Asian financial crisis and China's exports was not strong, but after the global financial crisis in 2008, the

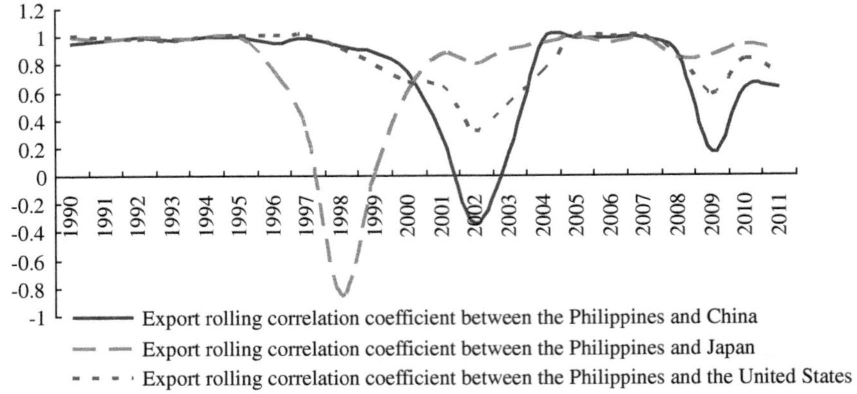

Figure 7.7. Export Rolling Correlation Coefficient between the Philippines and China, Japan and the United States from 1990 to 2011

Source: According to UNCTAD DATABASE.

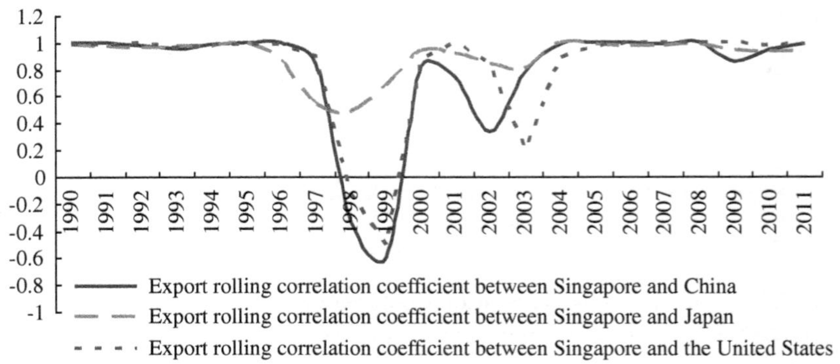

Figure 7.8. Export Rolling Correlation Coefficient between Singapore and China, Japan and the United States from 1990 to 2011

Source: According to UNCTAD DATABASE.

three-year average of the export-rolled correlation coefficient between countries of Cambodia, Indonesia, South Korea, Laos, Myanmar, Thailand, Vietnam, etc. and China for 2009–2011 exceeds the export-rolled correlation coefficient with that of Japan and the United States (see Table 7.2). This shows that after the global financial crisis,

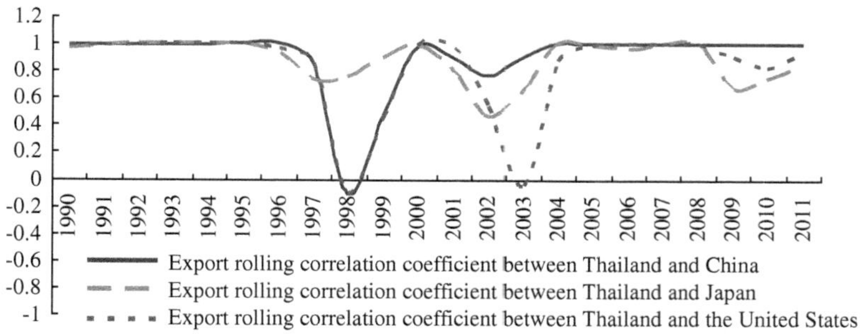

Figure 7.9. Export Rolling Correlation Coefficient between Thailand and China, Japan and the United States from 1990 to 2011

Source: According to UNCTAD DATABASE.

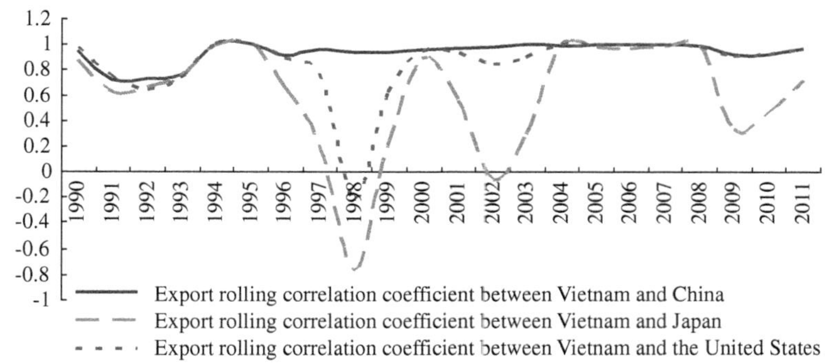

Figure 7.10. Export Rolling Correlation Coefficient between Vietnam and China, Japan, and the United States from 1990 to 2011

Source: According to UNCTAD DATABASE.

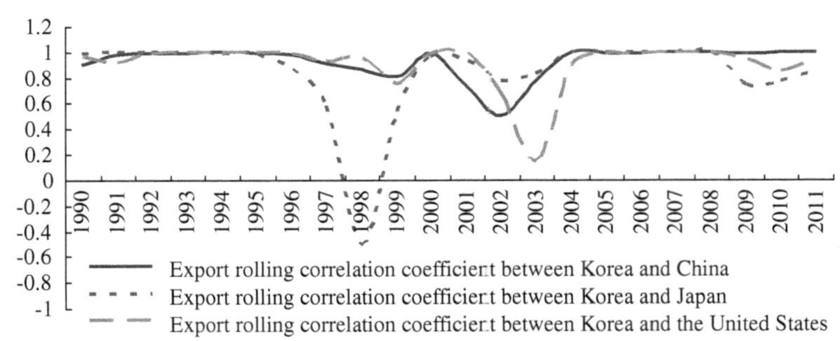

Figure 7.11. Export Rolling Correlation Coefficient between Korea and China, Japan and the United States from 1990 to 2011

Source: According to UNCTAD DATABASE.

Table 7.2. Average of Rolling Correlation Coefficients of ASEAN + China, Japan, Korea and the United States (unit: %)

		1990–1999 Annual Average	2000–2011 Annual Average	2009–2011 Annual Average	1990–2011 Annual Average
Brunei	China	28.9	88.0	76.1	61.1
	Japan	42.3	83.6	84.2	64.9
	United States	30.4	84.1	92.0	59.7
Cambodia	China	82.0	96.8	98.3	90.1
	Japan	81.8	67.5	66.8	74.0
	United States	74.6	66.4	85.2	70.1
Indonesia	China	89.1	85.6	99.3	87.2
	Japan	71.0	87.5	71.3	80.0
	United States	92.3	90.6	87.3	91.4
Korea	China	93.9	91.2	99.5	92.4
	Japan	74.1	90.3	78.3	82.9
	United States	94.8	86.6	91.4	90.3
Laos	China	84.2	53.0	92.0	67.2
	Japan	49.6	55.1	52.5	52.6
	United States	82.2	64.5	70.3	72.5
Malaysia	China	81.0	84.6	84.7	83.0
	Japan	82.4	94.8	95.2	89.2
	United States	82.9	90.0	98.7	86.8
Myanmar	China	85.6	76.0	90.9	80.4
	Japan	60.5	33.3	47.7	45.7
	United States	77.0	41.1	64.8	57.4
Philippines	China	95.8	58.4	46.7	75.4
	Japan	61.4	87.4	89.2	75.6
	United States	96.0	73.1	70.5	83.5
Singapore	China	68.2	86.7	92.4	78.3
	Japan	84.2	93.7	93.5	89.4
	United States	71.5	89.3	98.5	81.2
Thailand	China	81.5	96.1	99.9	89.5
	Japan	92.5	84.2	75.3	88.0
	United States	81.3	83.1	89.3	82.3
Vietnam	China	88.7	97.6	93.9	93.6
	Japan	51.8	67.4	50.1	60.3
	United States	71.6	95.1	93.5	84.4

Source: Calculated from UNCTAD Database data.

China's role within the East Asian region trade has been greatly improved.

The close trade links within East Asia require a relatively coordinated regional exchange rate system, but at present, the exchange rate systems of East Asian economies are quite different from each other, which is also one of the motives for promoting currency cooperation in East Asia.

According to the theory of the optimal currency area (OCA), the domestic commodity and factor markets of each member country in the currency area should achieve full competition and achieve equalization of prices, that is to say the common currency units have the same purchasing power in each member country, and eventually establish a common currency-fiscal authority to achieve consistency in monetary-fiscal policy within the currency area. This definition is too strict and too abstract. At the initial stage of the currency area, the same monetary system can be implemented in each member country, or a fixed exchange rate system can be implemented to ensure the convertibility of the currencies of various countries. Commodities and factors can flow freely among countries in the currency area. The degree of similarity between the price level of the countries in the region and the purchasing power of money is higher than that of the countries outside the region. Finally, the countries in the currency area implement the same policy in support of economic growth, full employment, low inflation and balance of international payments.[18]

The current exchange rate systems of Asian economies are quite different. According to the classification method of the exchange rate system in different periods of the IMF, each economy belongs to a different type of exchange rate system. Table 7.3 shows the classification of the exchange rate systems of East Asian economies according to the 1999 IMF exchange rate system, and Table 7.4 shows classification of the exchange rate systems of East Asian economies

[18]Kojima, Kiyoshi, "A Pacific Currency Area: A New Approach to International Monetary Reform," *Hitotsubashi Journal of Economics* 10, no. 2 (1970): 1–17.

Table 7.3. Foreign Exchange Rate System of East Asian Economies 2008–2009

Foreign Exchange Rate System	Country/Economy (the Exchange System Implemented by the Government is Showed in Brackets)
Fully free floating exchange rate system (free floating)	Japan (individual floating system)
Intermediate exchange rate system	N/A
Large fluctuations in managed floating	Cambodia, Indonesia, Laos, Thailand (managed floating system)
	South Korea, Philippines (individual floating system)
Small changes in managed floating	Malaysia, Singapore, Taiwan (China), China (managed floating system)
minimal changes in managed floating	Mainland China (crawling pegs since June 2005, June 2005)
	Vietnam (managed floating system)
Soft pegging system	Mainland China (after July 2008)
Hard pegging system	Brunei, Hong Kong (China) (currency board arrangements)

Notes:

1. The government's foreign exchange rate system is based on the IMF, Annual Report on Exchange Arrangements and Exchange Restrictions 1999.
2. On 1 April 2012, Myanmar began to implement a managed floating exchange rate system.

Source: Kawai Masahiro, "International Monetary System and East Asian Monetary and Financial Cooperation," In *East Asian Monetary and Financial Cooperation in the Post-crisis Era — Is the Coordination of RMB and Yen Possible*?" edited by Li Xiao, 27. Changchun: Jilin University Press, 2010.

according to the latest 2009 IMF exchange rate system. It should be noted that even if East Asian economies have adopted different exchange rate systems, East Asia is still a traditional US dollar zone. At the moment, East Asian economies are keeping their currencies in the US dollar, which is a "rejuvenation of the Bretton Woods system" (Dooley, Folkerts-Landau and Garber, 2004)[19] or constitute the

[19]Dooley, Michael P., David Folkerts-Landau, and Peter M. Garber, "The Revised Bretton Woods System," *International Journal of Finance and Economics* 9, no. 4 (October 2004): 307–313.

Table 7.4. Actual Foreign Exchange Rate System of East Asian Economies 2011–2012

Foreign Exchange Rate System	State/Economy (Monetary Policy System)
Hard pegging	
No separate legal tender	No
Currency board system	Brunei (another currency as anchor currency), Hong Kong, China (US dollar as the anchor currency)
Soft pegging	
Conventional peg	No
Stabilization arrangements	Cambodia (US dollar as the anchor currency), Laos (other#), Vietnam (with a currency basket as anchor currency#)
Crawling peg	No
Crawling-like arrangement	Mainland China (currency target system#)
Pegged exchange rate within horizontal band	No
Floating	
Floating	Indonesia (inflation targeting system), Philippines (inflation targeting system), Korea (inflation targeting system), Thailand (inflation targeting system)
Free float	Japan (other*)
Others	
Other managed arrangement	Malaysia (others*), Myanmar (others*), Singapore (pegging to a currency basket&)

Notes: *It includes countries that do not have an exact nominal anchor but control various indicators to monitor monetary policy.
#It actually uses the US dollar as the anchor currency.
&The exchange rate arrangements are reclassified based on the actual exchange rate regime of each economy.

Source: IMF, Annual Report on Exchange Arrangements and Exchange Restrictions 2012, Appendix Table II.9 *De facto* Classification of Exchange Rate Arrangements and Monetary Policy Frameworks, 30 April 2012.

"East Asian Dollar System" (McKinnon and Schnabl, 2004).[20] The exchange rate arrangement for pegging to the US dollar in the East Asia region is not an alternative to the US dollar, but rather reduces dependence on the US dollar as much as possible, and seeks to maximize the benefits within the region under the existing international monetary system.

In 2009, the IMF revised the classification criteria for the arrangement of the exchange rate system. According to the *de facto* implementation of the exchange rate system in each economy, the IMF's foreign exchange rate system arrangements in the 190 economies are divided into hard pegging, soft pegging, floating and the remaining categories. The hard pegging includes the exchange arrangement with no separate legal tender and the Currency Board Arrangements; the soft pegging includes the conventional peg, the stabilized arrangement, crawling peg, crawl-like arrangement and pegged exchange rate within horizontal band; the floating includes floating and free floating; other categories refer to other managed arrangements.

Table 7.4 shows that the actual foreign exchange rate system of East Asian economies in 2012 are distributed in all four major categories. The hard-pegging currencies are Brunei dollar and Hong Kong dollar. The economies that are soft-pegging are Cambodia and Laos. In Vietnam and Mainland China, countries namely Indonesia, the Philippines, Thailand, South Korea and Japan implement the floating exchange rate system, and Malaysia, Myanmar, and Singapore have implemented other systems of managing the floating exchange rate.

7.1.1.2 *Promoting the Relationship between Currency Cooperation in East Asia and RMB Internationalization*

Many scholars have studied the asymmetrical exchange rate intervention behavior in the exchange rate management of East Asian

---

[20]McKinnon, Ronald, and Gunther Schnabl, "The East Asian Dollar Standard, Fear of Floating, and Original Sin," *Review of Development Economics* 8, no. 3 (2004): 331–360.

monetary authorities.[21] Levy-Yeyati and Sturzenegger called it as "fear of floating in reverse" or "fear of appreciation." However, the aforementioned studies have emphasized the asymmetric management of the US dollar in domestic currency management and have not considered the impact of "third currency" on East Asian "floating phobia." The research results in Pontines and Siregar are an important supplement to the research field. Their research found that compared to the appreciation of the US dollar, East Asian currencies such as the Philippine peso and the Thai baht, are more reluctant to appreciate the RMB, that is to say, the asymmetric exchange rate of the East Asian monetary authorities. The intervention is more influenced by the RMB rather than the dollar, which reflects the significance of the RMB to East Asian currencies from another perspective.[22] The main reason why the RMB plays an important role in the formation of East Asian currency exchange rates is that China is gradually becoming a major trading partner of countries in the world, especially East Asian countries.

If China wants to gain greater voice in the current world economy stage under the "dollar system," reform of the current international monetary system cannot be separated from the support of economies in the East Asian region. Therefore, the internationalization of RMB must be rooted in the regional monetary and financial cooperation in East Asia, and the regionalization of RMB should drive the internationalization of RMB. It can be seen that there is an intrinsic link between regional financial and monetary cooperation in Asia and the internationalization of the RMB. The two can complement each other. Judging from the current development level of China's domestic financial system and the international status and influence of RMB, as a developing country, if China wants to maximize its own

[21]Asymmetric intervention refers to the behavior of the monetary authorities allowing the domestic currency to depreciate properly and strongly limiting the appreciation of the national currency.

[22]Pontines, Victor and Siregar, R. Y., "The Fear of Appreciation in East and Southeast Asia: The Role of RMB," *Journal of Asian Economics* 23, no. 4 (2012): 324–334.

interest claims in the current reform of the international monetary system, the East Asian regional currency cooperation is the only way to achieve this aim.

After the global financial crisis in 2008, the Chinese government proposed to construct a diversified international monetary system, and the pace of RMB internationalization and regionalization has been markedly accelerated. On the one hand, this reflects the continuous increase in the overall strength of China and the continuous deepening of its opening to the outside world. On the other hand, it is also an inevitable requirement to strengthen China's position and role in the monetary and financial cooperation of East Asian. The China–ASEAN Free Trade Agreement, which came into force on 1 January 2010, is considered to be the most powerful support for the internationalization of the RMB. According to the endogenous theory of the OCA standard, it can be inferred that as the degree of trade association between China and Asian countries is strengthened, the economic cycles among Asian countries will also tend to be the same, then the trade integration that will occur with the regionalization of RMB will insert symmetrical impact on other Asian countries, reducing the cost of macroeconomic adjustment.

In the current international monetary system, not only does RMB have an impact on the formation of currency exchange rates in East Asia but, at the same time, the East Asian currencies also have an impact on the fluctuation of RMB exchange rates.[23] Strengthening regional monetary and financial cooperation in East Asia can better realize the internationalization of RMB.

7.1.2 *Currency Cooperation and International Currency System Reform in East Asia*

As an important supporting force of the current US dollar system, East Asia determines that it will become one of the important driving

[23]Fratzscher, Marcel and Arnaud Mehl, "China's Dominance Hypothesis and the Emergence of a Tri-Polar Global Currency System," *ECB Working Paper Series*, No. 1392, 2011.

forces for the reform of the international monetary system in the future. The current problems in the global economic cycle reflect, to a large extent, the predicaments faced by the East Asian region under the "dollar system." An important way to get rid of these difficulties is to form the final product in the region through the transformation of East Asian regional trade to be the market providers, which will get rid of long-term reliance on the US market. However, the two major countries in East Asia, China and Japan, do not have the ability to become regional market final product providers in the short term. Therefore, at this stage, the path to overcome difficulties is to strengthen regional monetary and financial cooperation in East Asia, relying on the logic of regional collective action to gradually reform the international monetary system, and then establish regional benefits for the healthy development of East Asian economies in the international currency environment. In this process, the internationalization of RMB can be used as a driving force.

Through the analysis of the previous sub-topics, it can be concluded that under the current international economic and political environment, on the one hand, any foreign economic strategy formulated by China must take into account the fact that it is closely linked to the world, especially the Asian economy. It also requires China to prepare for the external pressures it may face in implementing or adjusting its strategy. On the one hand, under the current US dollar system, the RMB does not have the conditions and capabilities to go directly to the internationalization road. On the other hand, the collective action of regional currency cooperation will help reduce the internationalization of RMB and face various international pressures. As a result, regional monetary and financial cooperation is an important boost to the internationalization of the RMB. It will also largely determine the future prospects for the reform of the international currency system.

The initial form of East Asian monetary cooperation can begin with the Asian financial crisis. Although the Asian financial crisis has passed for many years, the lessons it has left for East Asian countries are profound. The rapid proliferation of the Asian financial crisis and the competitive devaluation of Asian currencies have aroused the attention of East Asian countries to regional financial cooperation. In fact, until the occurrence of the "subprime mortgage crisis" in the United States in 2008, the pace of financial cooperation in Asia has not stopped. As a major country in the region, China should actively participate in East Asian financial cooperation and play a corresponding role in the development of this cooperation.

The Asian financial crisis in 1997 revealed the impact of the "contagion effect" in the regional financial crisis. By statistical analysis, Qin Dou found that the key reason why South Korea was involved in the financial crisis at the time of the 1997 crisis was not the general overindulgence of companies but the contagion effects of other countries and regions.[24] The contagious nature of the financial crisis has made the financial crisis increasingly a regional phenomenon. Its prevention and resolution have increasingly become a regional issue that transcends national boundaries. Traditionally, when a country has a financial crisis, it can only resort to the International Monetary Fund (IMF). However, during the development of the global financial crisis caused by the Asian financial crisis and the US subprime crisis, the performance of the IMF made East Asian countries are disappointed. First of all, due to the miscalculation of the severity and possible consequences of the East Asian financial crisis, the rescue from the IMF came too late and the rescue effort was too small; secondly, the IMF's conditions were mainly to protect the benefits of the lenders (mainly from European and American developed countries), while ignoring the country's specific national conditions due to the conditions of the IMF have a strong ideological presence. So many of the reform measures imposed by the IMF not only did not ease the crisis but also made the crisis worse.

Although the idea of regional financial cooperation is a response to the Asian financial crisis in Asia, in other parts of the world, the idea of regional financial cooperation has a long history. The

[24]Duo, Qin, "To What Extent Did the Contagious Effects of Foreign Trade and Finance Caused Korea's Currency Crisis in 1997?" *World Economy* 023.008 (2000): 8–18.

development of regional financial cooperation, especially the idea of developing regional currency cooperation has a long history. For example, European currency cooperation is largely a challenge to the dollar hegemony status. For a long time, the United States has used the depreciated US dollar to pay its international trade deficit and received the seigniorage tax from the world, that is, it has occupied the resources of other countries through its unique currency issuance rights. Since the US dollar is the world's most important reserve currency, it can be used to pay the huge trade deficit, and the country has accumulated huge amounts of foreign debt in US dollars. Correspondingly, other countries have to hold large amounts of foreign exchange reserves in US dollars at the expense of their own actual resources. This shows the contradiction between the "financial country" of the United States in the center and the "trade country" in the periphery.

To some extent, the start of the euro challenged the hegemony of the US dollar. Mundell predicted that within the next 10 years, there will be three major currency areas, the euro area, the US dollar area and the Asian currency area.[25] Compared with the shape of the Eurozone and the dollar zone, Asian monetary cooperation is still in the stage of discussing and exchanging opinions. Under the influence of various constraints, Asian monetary cooperation has not made substantial breakthroughs. Even in the global financial crisis caused by the US "subprime mortgage crisis" in 2008, Asian financial cooperation not only failed to achieve substantive breakthroughs but also suffered certain setbacks.

Facing the unstable external financial environments that may have adverse effects on their own economies, East Asian economies must take measures to deal with them. Faced with the global financial turmoil, it is true that individual important countries have the possibility of making policy adjustments based on their own economic characteristics. However, taking into account the cost of unilateral

[25]Mundell, Robert, "Currency Areas, Exchange Rate Systems and International Monetary Reform," *Journal of Applied Economics* 3, no. 2 (2000): 217–256.

actions and the close economic relations within the region, the further promotion of regional cooperation, especially in the area of monetary and financial cooperation, should become an inevitable policy choice. From a realistic point of view, the proposal for the multilateralization of the Chiang Mai Initiative (CMI) and the "Asian Economic and Financial Stability Action Plan" put forward by the ASEAN 10+3 Special Finance Ministers' Conference in February 2009 have shown that the East Asian economies have a strong desire to further promote the integration of regional monetary cooperation to withstand the global financial crisis.

At the same time, from the perspective of China's economic development and RMB internationalization, Asian currency cooperation also has positive significance and necessity. Li and Ding proposed that the Asianization of RMB is a process of participating in the institutional cooperation of the East Asian regional monetary and financial sectors in order to become the key currency in the region.[26] It is an indispensable step in the internationalization of RMB. Li pointed out that Asian monetary and financial cooperation has achieved successes in common development and growth from scratch and achieved phase results, reflecting the confidence of Asian countries and economies in common interests and cooperation, but there are still significant limitations on the current cooperation mechanism in preventing crises. The demand for Asian currency and financial cooperation under the new economic environment still exists. China is the main demander and supplier of Asian currency and financial cooperation, so participating in cooperation will help China's economic and financial stability and security, and increase its economic impact in Asia. Through the expansion of the market, China's leading position in economic growth and the stability of the RMB exchange rate will promote the currency cooperation.[27] Zhang and Zhang believe that China

[26]Xiao, Li, and Yibing Ding, "East Asian Regional Monetary Cooperation in the New Century: China's Position and Role," *Journal of Jilin University-Social Science* 2 (2004): 79–87.

[27]Li, Jing, "China's Demand and Supply of Asian Monetary and Financial Cooperation," *Economics and Management Research* 2 (2005): 65–68.

urgently needs to establish the international status of the RMB in the international monetary system in order to safeguard its political and economic interests. China still does not have the conditions for direct internationalization of RMB, and it is more realistic to choose the route of regional currency cooperation that is in line with the common interests of Asia.[28]

On the other hand, the global financial crisis has triggered reflections on the hegemony of the US dollar, especially the reform of the international monetary system, and the Chinese government has also clearly expressed its position in the international community. However, we must also clearly understand that China currently has no condition or ability to independently challenge the US's financial hegemony. As one of the major beneficiaries of the dollar system, China still needs a long period of time to rely on this system for survival and development. What we need to do is to try our best to reduce the losses or risks of relying on this system. Therefore, the formation of China's thinking on the reform of the international monetary system or the formulation of strategies should first be based on enhancing the internationalization level of RMB. Based on this, the East Asian region should be the focus of financial cooperation and establish a stability system by the regional cooperation and be conducive to economic health. The growing regional currency order can create a more favorable external environment for the internationalization of the RMB. On the other hand, it also provides the basis and conditions for further reform of the international monetary system in a larger and deeper extent.

The dollar system is one of the necessary conditions for the current global economic imbalance, and the formation of the East Asian regional production network has made it an important supporting force of the system. East Asian economies have benefited from this, but also reflect the economic dependence and instability,

[28]Zhang, Yuyan and Jingchun Zhang, "The Nature of Money and the Future Choice of the RMB and Comments on Asian Monetary Cooperation," *Contemporary Asia Pacific* 2 (2008): 9–43.

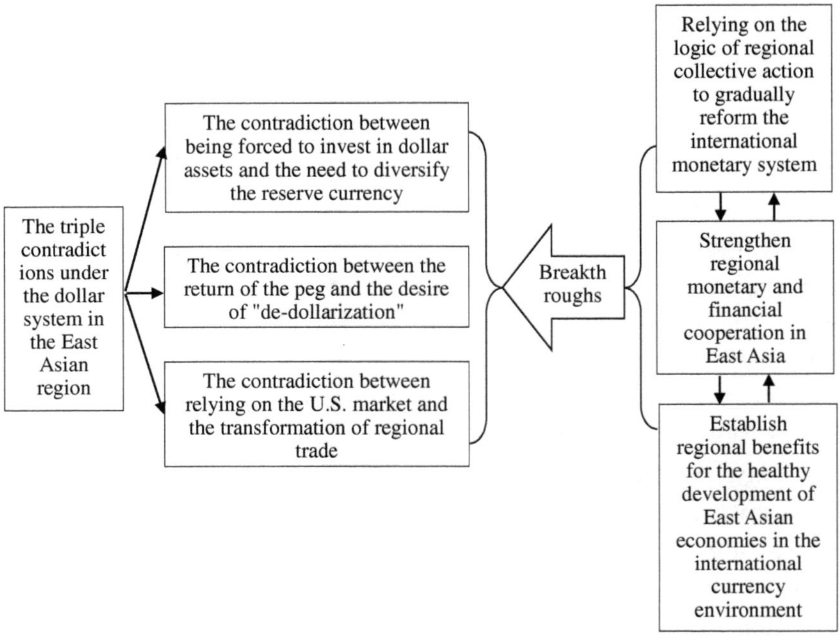

Figure 7.12. Triple Contradictions and Breakthroughs of the US Dollar System

especially the fragility of the financial system in the region. As shown in Figure 7.12, the impact of the global financial crisis has made the triple contradictions under the dollar system in the East Asian region even more prominent. If this dilemma is to be overcome, the strengthening of regional monetary cooperation and the gradual reform of the international monetary system should be promoted. In China's active participation in the reform of the international monetary system, it is the only way to promote the reform of the international monetary system by leveraging the overall strength of the East Asian region because of its high status in the East Asian production network and the economies formed by the regional production network. It is also a rational choice to actively promote and strengthen monetary and financial cooperation in the region in line with the vital interests of China.

From the in-depth study of the international regional currency cooperation model and the successful experience of the internationalization of euro and yen, we can recognize that the internationalization of a country's currency is an arduous system project that requires the efforts of decades. The internationalization of a country's currency requires the protection of both basic and internal conditions. On the one hand, it needs to establish a currency system with stable currency values and cultivate a developed financial market. On the other hand, it needs to establish a free trade system with its own core.

Judging from the experience of the internationalization of its own currency, China does not have the strength to rely on the power of one country to realize the internationalization of RMB. To increase the international influence of the national currency, it is necessary to strengthen cooperation with other countries and take the road to regionalization. To realize the path of RMB regionalization, we must first strengthen economic and financial cooperation with neighboring economies, with particular emphasis on close cooperation with regions of Hong Kong (China), Macao (China) and Taiwan (China), ASEAN regions, and Japan and South Korea, and gradually make full use of their respective advantages. Only on the basis of the free flow of goods, people, labor and capital in the region can a unified currency area be established in the East Asia region. From China's actual situation, it is rash to "directly" promote the internationalization of RMB. Not only are the objective conditions difficult to be fully equipped, but there are still great risks, which may even lead to failure and high costs.

Although great progress has been made in the cross-border circulation and use of RMB, the regionalization of RMB is still in its infancy stage of international development. There are many favorable conditions for the regionalization of RMB, and there are also many unfavorable factors. In recent years, the convenience of the RMB relative to the US dollar and the economies of scale brought about by the constant expansion of the China's economy have made the RMB attractive in Asia. However, the RMB is still a national currency of a transition country. The good development momentum of RMB regionalization is incompatible with the incomplete convertibility of the RMB and the underdevelopment of China's financial market. Therefore, we must adhere to the principle of gradual, coordinated, cooperative, and equal strength and opportunities in the regionalization of RMB, rationally plan the development path for RMB regionalization, formulate practical short-, medium- and long-term development goals, and build a platform for the development of RMB regionalization. The promotion mechanism is an important guarantee for realizing the RMB regionalization on the premise of gaining income and avoiding risks. The specific path of RMB internationalization consists of four dynamic convergence steps. The establishment of a currency system with stable currency values and the fostering of a developed domestic financial market are the guarantees for RMB regionalization. Under the condition that capital accounts are difficult to fully open for a short period of time, establishing an offshore market for the RMB is an effective way to increase the influence of the RMB region; actively promoting the RMB's progressive convertibility is the goal and basis for the RMB regionalization; and actively participate in the Asian currency cooperation is the only way for the internationalization of RMB.

The current international monetary system is still dominated by the US dollar. The RMB is still used for small-scale trade on the borders of surrounding areas of China. The regionalization of RMB is still a long road. However, China's economic strength and trade position in East Asia are sufficient to support the RMB regionalization because the status of regional currency is ultimately supported by economic strength and trade status. The United States has a long-standing Asian strategy and has established the core position of the US dollar in the international currency system in East Asia. However, the depreciation policy of the US dollar has made East Asian countries realize that US dollars are the core currency of the region. Since the yen has been pushed to be internationalized, the wrong strategy of internationalization of the yen and the downturn of the Japanese economy inhibited the process of internationalization of the yen. In the East Asian currency competition, China should treat the US dollar and the Japanese yen differently. With the close economic and trade exchanges between China and East Asian countries, RMB should expand its functions of pricing and settlement currency in economic and trade exchanges, and gradually become the dominant currency in the East Asian capital market.

7.2 Progress, Predicament and Challenges of Monetary Cooperation in East Asia

After the East Asian financial crisis in the 1990s, East Asian countries deeply realized the need to strengthen regional monetary cooperation and began to strengthen monetary and financial cooperation in the region in various ways. Fifteen years have passed since the CMI was put forward in 2000. What achievements have been made in the currency cooperation in the East Asia region? What is the *status quo*? What problems and difficulties have been encountered in the development process? Where will we go in the future? This is the main content to be discussed in this section.

The development of monetary cooperation in East Asia can be divided into three major stages: The first stage was before the outbreak of the Asian financial crisis in 1997. Although the region's relationship in the area of trade and investment has been quite close, as a whole, the region has not yet formed a substantial cooperation mechanism in the monetary and financial sector. The second phase was after the outbreak of the Asian financial crisis to 2000. The major countries in the region have proposed rescue plans or ideas, but there have been disputes and the economies have not yet reached a basic consensus on regional monetary cooperation. The third stage is the period after signing of the Chiang Mai Accord in 2000 as a symbol of the substantial advancement of monetary and financial cooperation in the region. In particular, after the international financial crisis in 2007, the willingness of monetary and financial cooperation among the economies of East Asia has rapidly risen. Therefore, the East Asian regional monetary cooperation is a relatively new financial and monetary phenomenon that gradually appeared after the Asian financial crisis of 1997–1998,[29] and the currency cooperation in the East Asian region is more affected by various crises.

So far, due to complicated historical, political, social, economic and cultural factors in East Asia, monetary cooperation in the region has failed to break through the CMI framework. It is still centered on the effective and safe use of foreign exchange reserves and attempts to establish a system to prevent financial crisis, as well as the rescue mechanism. The stability of the exchange rate in the region, which is more urgently needed, has failed to achieve a breakthrough. Therefore, on the whole, the progress of the monetary cooperation in the East Asian region at this stage is still passive — the consensus and progress in cooperation depend on the promotion of the outbreak of various crises, and whether the regional monetary cooperation can be further improved to a higher level. The exchange rate coordination and cooperation depend, to a large extent, on whether the various economies can reach a consensus in the face of new situations and challenges. In particular, this depends on whether the major countries in the region, especially between China and Japan, can take positive action together.

7.2.1 *Progress and Status Quo of Currency Cooperation in East Asia*

After experiencing the "fire-fighting phase" of the Asian financial crisis, especially after the concept of CMI was put forward and put into practice, the countries and regions in East Asia have jointly realized that in order to ensure the stable growth of the region's economy and strengthen policy dialogue and cooperation among themselves, a mutual assistance system that can fully coordinate regional economic, financial monitoring and financial self-support

[29] Hamanaka, Shintaro, "Asian Financial Cooperation in the 1990s: The Politics of Membership," *Journal of East Asian Studies* 11, no.1 (January-April 2011): 75–103.

should be established to avoid and prevent the impact of international financial speculation on the currency of the region and prevent the occurrence of the currency and financial crisis. As a result, the East Asian regional monetary cooperation has produced a series of relatively clear progress (see Table 7.5).

7.2.1.1 *Mechanism of Information Communication and Common Monitoring*

There is currently no unified and truly integrated framework for regional monetary and financial cooperation in Asia. Regional cooperation is conducted in multiple channels and in multiple ways under multiple organizational platforms and frameworks such as ASEAN, ASEAN 10+3, ASEAN 10+6 and APEC. However, cooperation in ASEAN 10+3 has been further strengthened in recent years. East Asian countries and regions are conducting preliminary discussions and studies on the establishment of regional monetary and financial supervision systems. The prevention of future financial crisis is the primary concern of East Asian economies. The prevention of crises must first effectively control and determine changes in the economic and financial situation.[30] The highly dependent economic relations between East Asian economies, the similarities in their economic structures, and the contagious and regional nature of the financial crisis have determined that it is difficult to prevent them from relying on economies to monitor and manage their own economic dynamics. Therefore, it is necessary to jointly share relevant economic information and jointly monitor the financial situation in every country.[31]

The relationship between monetary and financial cooperation in East Asia and trade and investment appears to be lagging behind. Before 1997/98, it not only didn't form a substantive cooperation

---

[30]Feng, Zhuo, "The Opportunities and Challenges Facing East Asian Cooperation," *Northeast Asia Forum* 15, no. 6 (2006): 17–20.

[31]Wang, Yonghui, "Issues on the Effectiveness of International Mechanisms in East Asian Monetary Cooperation," *Northeast Asia Forum* 17, no. 4 (2008): 15–19.

Table 7.5. The Monetary and Financial Cooperation in East Asia and the Asia Pacific Region

	ASEAN	ASEAN 10+3	APEC	Reference to the EC of the 1980s
Improve the capital market	AEC blueprint (strategic calendar)	ABMI	Policy initiatives (education and training)	European single market plan (completed in 1993)
Financial services liberalization	Same as above	Education training EWS	Same as above	Same as above
Capital trading liberalization	Same as above	Invention project	Same as above	Completed in 1990
Currency cooperation	Same as above	Crisis prevention and management	—	European monetary system
Credit supply	CMI	CMI	—	Short-term to mid-term
Auction monitoring	ASP	ERPD	—	Centered on the Central Bank
Exchange rate arrangements	Research in the ASEAN Central Bank Forum	—	—	Regional fixed exchange rate system (ERM)
Decision making agency	Prime Minister and Finance Ministers Meeting AFDM	Prime Minister and Finance Ministers Meeting AFDM+3	Prime Minister and Finance Ministers Meeting	Economic and Financial Governor's Council Currency Review
Secretariat	ASEAN Secretariat (Jakarta)	None (APT unit in ASEAN Secretariat)	APEC Secretariat (Singapore)	European commission (Brussels)
other	Action + CB	Action + CB	CB-centric	Action trends

Note: ASP, ASEAN Surveillance Process; AFDM, Finance Ministers' Agency Meeting; EWS: Early Warning System; ERM: Exchange Rate Mechanism; CB: Capacity Building; AEC, ASEAN Economic Community; ABMI, Asian Bond Markets Initiative; CMI, Chiang Mai Initiative; ERPD, Economic Review and Policy Dialogue; APT, ASEAN 10+3.

Source: Murakami, "East Asian Monetary and Financial Cooperation and the Role of China and Japan," In *East Asian Monetary and Financial Cooperation in the Post-Crisis Era-Is the Coordination of RMB and Yen Possible?*, edited by Li Xiao, 204–205. Changchun: Jilin University Society, 2010.

mechanism, but its contents and levels of regional financial cooperation were also relatively low (see Table 7.6). This is mainly due to the fact that prior to the Asian financial crisis, the region had never experienced a more serious regional currency crisis and lacked the need to cope with a common crisis, and there were disagreements between the various economies in the region in the areas of economy, politics and diplomacy. According to traditional theory, monetary and financial cooperation can only be achieved in the advanced stage of regional economic integration. For this reason, early East Asian monetary and financial cooperation has low-level, loose and informal characteristics.[32]

Among them, the Executives' Meeting of East Asia and Pacific Central Banks (EMEAP) was established in February 1991 and is the most important central bank cooperation organization in the region. The EMEAP-related mechanisms are divided into three levels: The first level is the governor-level meeting mechanism, which is dominated by the annual governors' meeting held in mid-year (since 1996), and includes the informal governors' meeting and the EMEAP-euro system, Central Bank Governor Forum.[33] The second level is the monetary and financial stability committee (MFSC) and the deputy-level meeting mechanism. The former is mainly responsible for financial stability cooperation in the financial stability monitoring and establishment of crisis management mechanism in the region. The latter focuses on promoting regional financial market development, the formulation and implementation of financial standards and guidelines, and financial infrastructure construction. The third level is the working group meeting mechanism, including the three working groups of the financial market, bank supervision, payment and settlement, and the Commissioner of Science and Technology. The main

---

[32]Shen, Hongfang, and Linglan Chen, "Research on East Asian Monetary and Financial Cooperation Mechanism and Its Characteristics," *Research on Nanyang Issues* 4 (2011): 38–42.

[33]Since 2004, the EMEAP-Eurosystem High Level Seminars have been held once a year to discuss the current economic issues between the two sides, aiming to increase cooperation and strengthen ties between the two sides.

Table 7.6. Regional Monetary Cooperation Arrangements before 1997

Names of Arrangements and Forum	The Starting Time	Number of Members	Purpose and Function
Central Banks of South East Asia, New Zealand and Australia (SEANZA)	1956	With 17 members including some countries in South East Asia and New Zealand, Australia	The Central Bank exchanges information and provides training opportunities for experts of central banks
ASEAN Currency Swap Arrangement and Repurchase Agreement (ASA)	1977	Five member countries of ASEAN: Singapore, Malaysia, Thailand, Indonesia, Philippines	Provide immediate short-term exchange facilities to members to resolve temporary liquidity difficulties (expanded to all members of ASEAN in 2000)
The South East Asian Central Banks (SEACEN)	1982	In addition to Laos, 9 ASEAN members, 13 central bankers and monetary authorities from Fiji, Mongolia, Nepal, and Sri Lanka (currently expanded to 16 members, including People's Bank of China, Chinese Taipei monetary authorities, and the Bank of Korea)	When ASEAN was established in 1966, it was an information exchange forum between the central banks. In 1972, training and research institutions were established. In 1982, they were transformed into independent legal organizations

Executives' Meeting of East Asia and Pacific Central Banks (EMEAP)	1991	Central banks and monetary authorities of 11 economies including Australia, China, Hong Kong (China), Indonesia, Japan, South Korea, Malaysia, New Zealand, Philippines, Singapore and Thailand	By cooperation and exchanges, it promotes the establishment of regional financial systems and deepen the relationship between central banks and monetary authorities
Six Economic Group (also known as G-6, or G-4 plus 2)	1994	The first four members were: Australia, Hong Kong (China), Japan and Singapore. Then China and the United States were also invited to attend the conference.	Stabilize regional finance and foreign exchange markets
APEC Finance Ministers Meeting	1994	21 APEC members	Provide members with proposals to promote regional financial development and propose financial cooperation projects to promote regional financial liberalization

Source: Shen, Hongfang and Lingxi Chen, "Research on East Asian Monetary and Financial Cooperation Mechanism and Its Characteristics," *Nanyang Studies* 4 (2011): 27–34.

function of the organization's early stage was to raise the level of regional financial supervision and exchange views and information on the financial market. The recent focus is the regional financial stability and monetary cooperation. Since its inception, EMEAP has achieved fruitful results in areas such as financial stability, financial markets, payment and settlement, and bank supervision. It is important to note that EMEAP still plays an important role in the current regional information communication in East Asia, mainly reflected in the launch of two Asian Bond Fund (ABF1 and ABF2), the macro-monitoring report on regional financial stability, initial layout of a crisis management framework, and establishment of a trading room network for financial markets.[34]

After the Asian financial crisis, the governments and theorists of East Asian economies gradually realized the importance of regional monetary and financial cooperation, and gradually established a number of information communication and monitoring channels, such as the Manila Framework Group (MFG), ASEAN 10+3 Surveillance Process, ASEAN 10+3 Early Warning System (EWS), etc.

(1) The MFG: In November 1997, the MFG proposed at the meeting of senior financial officials in the Asia-Pacific region in Manila, the capital of the Philippines, that the main contents of the framework include the establishment of regional early warning mechanisms to prevent financial crises and the strengthening of regional economic and technology cooperation and increase new financing methods. The MFG comprises 14 countries and regions including Australia, Brunei, Canada, China, Hong Kong (China), Indonesia, Japan, Korea, Malaysia, New Zealand, Philippines, Singapore, Thailand and the United States. The International Monetary Fund, the World Bank, and Asian Development Bank (ADB) and other international and regional organizations also participate in this group. The MFG is a regional financial forum

[34]Official website of the Executives' Meeting of East Asia and Pacific Central Banks: http://www.emeap.org/.

whose purpose is to strengthen regional cooperation, prevent financial crisis and promote regional stability.

(2) ASEAN 10+3 Surveillance Process: After the East Asian financial crisis occurred, the ASEAN 10+3 Group was formally established in November 1999. The original ASEAN Surveillance Process (ASP)[35] was expanded to the ASEAN 10+3 supervisory process. The first peer review meeting was held after the ADB's annual meeting in May 2000. The theme of the conference was to strengthen financial cooperation in East Asia and to promote the continued growth of the regional economy. The participants agreed to strengthen policy dialogue and regional cooperation, establish a regulatory, self-help and support mechanism for capital flows in the region and reform the international financial system. According to the framework agreement of the supervisory process, the finance ministers and the secretary-general of the 13 countries under the ASEAN 10+3 supervision process meet twice a year to exchange views on relevant economic issues and discuss policy coordination issues. The monitoring framework not only includes information exchange and policy dialogue but also includes supervision of exchange rates and macroeconomic trends in various countries. The ASEAN 10+3 supervisory process is a key issue in establishing the ASEAN 10+3 EWS in East Asia.

(3) ASEAN 10+3 EWS: In May 2001, the ASEAN 10+3 Finance Ministers' Meeting in Hawaii announced the establishment of the ASEAN 10+3 EWS to early identify the weaknesses of the macroeconomics, financial operations and corporate companies in East Asia, and prevent the occurrence of credit crisis at the micro level. ASEAN 10+3 conducted research on issues such as the supervision of capital flows and EWS under the auspices of

[35]At the ASEAN Finance Ministers' Meeting held in February 1998, 10 ASEAN countries decided to establish the ASEAN oversight process under the Manila framework, and formally established in October of the same year in order to strengthen regional policymaking capabilities.

the ADB. In November 2001, the Regional Cooperation Research Institute and the Asian Integration Center were established, mainly for governments of various countries. The relevant personnel provided a dialogue mechanism for the establishment of a regional supervision system. The parties to the ASEAN 10+3 finance ministers' meeting held in Phuket, Thailand, reached a number of important consensuses on strengthening regional financial cooperation and jointly coping with the crisis. The establishment of an independent regional economic monitoring agency and strengthening of regional economic monitoring capabilities are important contents.

(4) Other mechanisms: After the Asian financial crisis, the East Asian and Pacific Central Bank Governors Conference (EMEAP) began to develop in a substantive direction. It followed the establishment of the "Regional Foreign Exchange Market Supervision Conference" by the Bank of International Settlements (BIS) to discuss and formulate relevant standards of regional financial supervision and organize self-examination and implementation of standard.

In April 2000, the ADB and ASEAN jointly established the "Private Capital Flow Monitoring" working group to analyze and report on the flow of private capital in the region. At the ADB meeting held in May 2001, ASEAN 10+3 unanimously agreed to strengthen the monitoring of capital flows in the region and strengthen cooperation in the field of economic supervision and strengthen joint supervision of offshore financial centers and financial institutions with high leverage. On 10 December 2008, the Central Banks of China, Japan and the Republic of Korea issued a joint statement to establish a mechanism for the meetings of the governors of the three central banks and to strengthen the dialogue mechanism maintained by the three presidents over the years in order to promote monetary and financial stability in the region.

In general, the regional policy coordination and dialogue mechanism mainly include two aspects: one is to establish a monitoring mechanism, and the other is to establish a punishment mechanism related to breach of contract.[36] At present, there is only the coordination of regional policies in East Asia for the former, and the development of the latter lags behind.

7.2.1.2 *The Launch of CMI and Its Diversification*

To avoid the recurrence of the financial crisis, in May 2000, the ASEAN 10+3 finance ministers' meeting signed an agreement to establish a regional currency exchange network, the CMI, in which the currency swap mechanism was extended to the three countries of China, Japan and the ROK so that when the short-term financial difficulties of the countries arise, they will be able to exchange their currencies or the US dollar. As of April 2009, 8 countries have participated and 16 bilateral swap agreements have been signed, with a total value of US$90 billion. Since its establishment, CMI has held sway for more than 10 years. During this period, CMI has gone through roughly three stages of development.

First of all, the startup phase. The outbreak of the East Asian financial crisis has highlighted the necessity and urgency of regional monetary and financial cooperation. The governments and theorists of East Asian countries have put forward various kinds of ideas and discussions on improving regional monetary and financial cooperation. For example, in September 1997, the Japanese government proposed the idea of establishing the Asian Monetary Fund (AMF), forming an organization with the participation of ASEAN 10+3, and raising US$100 billion to provide assistance to countries suffering from the currency crisis. In October 1998, Japan also proposed the "New Miyazawa Initiative" in the name of Minister of Finance Miyazawa Kiichi, and also proposed the establishment of a total of US$30 billion of Asian funds, half of which were used to meet the medium and long-term funding needs of the countries affected by the crisis, and the other half used to meet its short-term funding needs.

---

[36]Xiao, Li, and Yibing Ding, *Monetary Cooperation in East Asia and the Reform of the RMB Exchange Rate System*. Beijing: Economic Science Press, 2010, 6.

In October 1999, Malaysian Prime Minister Mahathir put forward an initiative to establish the East Asian Monetary Fund to establish a fund entirely owned by East Asia. In 2000, Korean economists Tae-Jun Kim, Jai-Won Ryon, and Yun-Jong Wang proposed the plan to establish Asian Arrangements to Borrow (ABB), the operating mechanism of which is similar to the General Agreements to Borrow (GAB) of the IMF. It is a regional multilateral loan agreement. However, most of these ideas and discussions mentioned previously did not make substantial progress until the signing of the CMI in May 2000 made the monetary and financial cooperation in East Asia take a historic step forward.[37]

The predecessor of the CMI was a multilateral currency swap agreement signed by five ASEAN countries (Indonesia, Malaysia, the Philippines, Singapore and Thailand) in 1977. According to the agreement, each member country must provide hard currency funds when the balance of payments in other countries is difficult. As a support for liquidity, the agreement amounted to US$100 million, and in 1978, the amount of the exchange amounted to US$200 million. Based on this currency swap mechanism, East Asian countries further strengthened monetary and financial cooperation within the region after the 1997/1998 Asian financial crisis.

In November 1999, the ASEAN 10+3 summit held in Manila issued the "Joint Statement on East Asia Cooperation," which clarified the ASEAN 10+3 finance ministers' meeting as the main framework of this cooperation agenda. Subsequently, at the 33rd annual meeting of the ADB held in May 2000 in Chiang Mai, Thailand, ASEAN 10+3 finance ministers adopted the "Bilateral Swap Arrangement" (referred to as "Chiang Mai Initiative," CMI). CMI is a crisis relief mechanism and its main idea or principle is to prevent the financial crisis.

The "Chiang Mai Initiative" is one of the important results of Asian monetary and financial cooperation. Under the framework

[37]Liu, Lizhen, and Chaoyang Xie, "East Asian Currency Cooperation and the Choice of RMB Exchange Rate System," *Management World* 3 (2003): 34–44.

of this initiative, the scale of currency swaps between East Asian economies has continued to expand (see Table 7.7).

Second, development stage from bilateral to multilateral. In October 2003, Premier Wen Jiabao of the State Council of the People's Republic of China put forward the initiative to "promote multilateralization of the Chiang Mai Initiative" for the first time at the 7th ASEAN 10+3 Leaders' Meeting, and proposed to integrate the looser bilateral currency swap mechanism under the CMI to a multilateral fund relief mechanism.

During the ASEAN 10+3 finance ministers' meeting held during the period 2005–2008, countries and regions worked together and made some progress in strengthening the effectiveness and multilateralism of CMI. In May 2006, the ASEAN 10+3 Finance Ministers Conference in Hyderabad, India, established the Chiang Mai Initiative Multilateralization Working Group to study the form and content of the multilateralization of the CMI. On the basis of the continuous expansion of the total amount of bilateral swaps, ASEAN 10+3 countries have determined the collective decision-making mechanism of CMI and strengthened regional economic monitoring capabilities. All countries have agreed to establish a regional foreign exchange reserve pool that is managed by member states in principle under an overall contractual basis, which is a significant step forward on the technical level of the CMI multilateralization plan. In May 2008, at the ASEAN 10+3 finance ministers' meeting in Madrid, Spain, the finance ministers of various countries decided that the initial size of the regional foreign exchange reserve was US$80 billion, and determined that the proportion of China–Japan–Korean and ASEAN investment was 80% and 20%. The ASEAN 10+3 finance ministers' meeting held later discussed the key elements of the allocation of capital, the structure of capital contribution, the amount of loans and the decision-making mechanism of the reserve, and made great progress on these issues.

Third, the stage of multilateralization. Since 2006, East Asian countries have been discussing the issue of CMI multilateralism. The so-called multilateralization refers to the unification of past bilateral

Table 7.7. Currency Swap Arrangement for CMI

Credits	Debits	Exchange Currency	Scale (Unit: 1 Billion USD)	Interchange Direction
China	Indonesia	US dollar–Indonesian rupiah	4	Unidirectional
China	Thailand	US dollar–Thai baht	2	Unidirectional
China	Philippines	RMB–Philippine Peso	2	Unidirectional
China	Malaysia	US dollar–Malaysia ringgit	1.5	Unidirectional
China	Japan	Yen–RMB/RMB–Yen	3	Bidirectional
China	Korea	RMB–Korean won/Korean won–RMB	4	Bidirectional
Japan	Korea	Yen–Korean won/Korean won–Yen	3	Bidirectional
Japan	Thailand	USD/THB–Yen	6	Bidirectional
Thailand	Japan	USD/THB–Yen	3	Bidirectional
Japan	Indonesia	US dollar–Indonesian rupiah	12	Unidirectional
Japan	Philippines	US dollar/Philippine peso–yen	6	Bidirectional
Philippines	Japan	US dollar/Philippine peso–yen	0.5	Bidirectional
Japan	Malaysia	US dollar–Malaysian ringgit	1	Unidirectional
Japan	Singapore	US dollar/Singapore dollar–yen	3	Bidirectional
Singapore	Japan	US dollar/Singapore dollar–yen	1	Bidirectional
Japan	Korea	US dollar/Korean won–yen	10	Bidirectional
Korea	Japan	US dollar/Korean won–yen	5	Bidirectional
Korea	Thailand	US dollar/Korean won–Thai baht	1	Bidirectional
Korea	Philippines	US dollar/Korean won–Philippine peso	2	Bidirectional
Korea	Indonesia	US dollar/Korean won–Indonesian rupiah	2	Bidirectional
Korea	Malaysia	US dollar/Korean won–Malaysian ringgit	1.5	Bidirectional

Note: Total: US$90 billion.

Source: Zhang, L. and J. Li, "Regional Financial Cooperation in East Asia: Recent Developments and Prospects," Background Paper for "Regional Financial and Regulatory Cooperation, a Chinese-European Dialogue," Beijing, 2010, 23–24.

currency swap agreements and the signing of a new CMI multilateralization agreement. Multilateralization can enhance transparency in starting currency swaps and make decisions through majority voting in order to provide funds smoothly and quickly.[38] In response to the impact of the global financial crisis, the ASEAN 10+3 finance ministers meeting in 2008 decided to establish a joint foreign exchange reserve fund of US$80 billion, which was announced at the ASEAN 10+3 special finance ministers meeting in May 2009. The "Asia Economic and Financial Stability Action Plan" (the "Action Plan") raised the fund scale to US$120 billion. At the same time, it discussed and proposed the establishment of regional international institutions and monitoring entities. The creation of a common foreign exchange reserve fund enabled the "CMI Multiliteralization (CMIM)" or CMI multilateralization to be realized, and the launch of the "Action Plan" laid the foundation for the institutionalization of CMIM, and the start of a joint foreign exchange reserve fund. It has also become a new platform for East Asian currency and financial cooperation.

Through multilateralization, including ASEAN members who have not yet signed a bilateral currency swap agreement, all ASEAN 10+3 members have participated in the CMI. Around 80% of the total US$120 billion funds are financed by China, Japan and South Korea, and the rest are borne by 10 ASEAN countries. The burden on China, Japan and South Korea is 2:2:1. Specific burdens and ratios are as follows: China (including Hong Kong, China) invested US$38.4 billion, accounting for 32%; Japan contributed US$38.4 billion, accounting for 32%; South Korea contributed US$19.2 billion, accounting for 16%; and other 10 ASEAN countries contributed US$24 billion, accounting for 20%.

The participants of the Chiang Mai Initiative Multilateralization Agreement have the right to borrow funds in local currency equivalent to the US dollar amount of the sum of their capital contribution

---

[38]Kinkyo, Takuji, "East Asian Financial Cooperation: The Current Status and Challenges of the Chiang Mai Accord," *Translation Series of Nanyang Files* no. 2 (2011): 1–7.

and the specific borrowing multiplier in accordance with the procedures and conditions specified in the agreement.[39] The loan period is 90 days; it can be extended for 7 times and the maximum loan period is 2 years.

The CMI's multilateralism will strengthen East Asia's ability to prevent risks and its core objective is to resolve the international balance of payments and short-term liquidity difficulties in the region, and on the other hand, it complements existing international financing arrangements.

7.2.1.3 *Development of Regional Bond Market*

Under the current "dollar system," although East Asia has the world's highest savings rate and huge foreign exchange reserves, large amount of funds has flowed to the financial markets of developed countries headed by the United States. The funds required for their own economic development have to rely on the regional financial cooperation. The inflow of foreign short-term funds has led to dual currency mismatches and has become the main source of financial market turmoil and even financial crisis. After the outbreak of the Asian financial crisis, East Asian countries deeply understood the harm of the lack of regional capital markets, especially the bond market, so the development of regional bond markets became an important agenda for regional monetary and financial cooperation.

With the realization and expansion of the "Chiang Mai Initiative," the confidence of East Asian economies in strengthening regional monetary and financial cooperation has gradually increased. The discussion on the development of the bond market is also increasingly intense. The development of the Asian bond market is not only an important part of the regional monetary and financial cooperation in Asia but also an inevitable requirement for the development of real economy such as Asian East Asian trade and investment.

[39] Xinhuanet, Chiang Mai Proposed the Signing of a Multilateral Agreement with a Total Size of US$120 billion. http://news.xinhuanet.com/fortune/2009-12/28/content_12718026.htm, 2009-12- 28/2013-4-8.

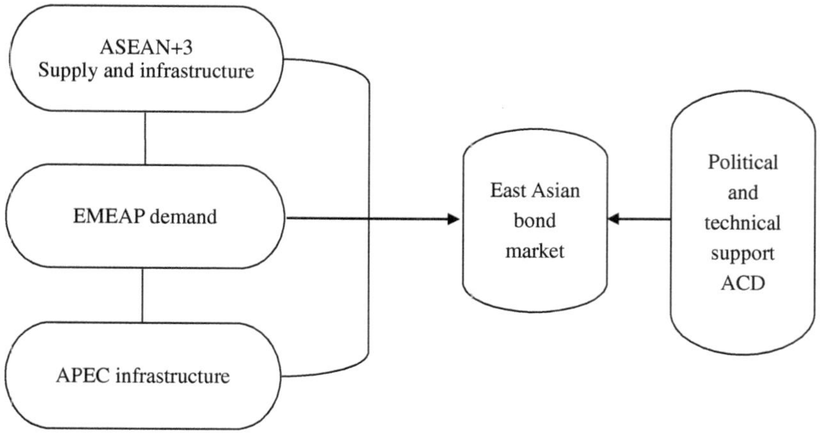

Figure 7.13. Role of Regional Organizations in Promoting East Asian Bond Development
Source: Adapted from Huang Meibo, and Lin Yang, *East Asian Emerging Bond Market Development Research: from Local Currency Bond Market to Asian Bond Market* (Beijing, Economic Science Press, 2008), 44.

The development of the Asian bond market is not only conducive to the adjustment of the East Asian financial structure and industrial structure and the elimination of the adverse effects of dollarization but also providing a new path for Asia to achieve regional financial stability through orderly opening up and gradual cooperation in finance.[40]

At present, at least four regional international organizations are actively promoting the development of the Asian bond market, namely the EMEAP, ASEAN 10+3, the Asia-Pacific Economic Cooperation (APEC) and Asia Cooperation Dialogue (ACD). The aforementioned four regional organizations have respectively promoted the development of the bond market in East Asia in different aspects (see Figure 7.13). Among them, EMEAP plays a role in demand promotion and is committed to enhancing the cognition and attraction of Asian bond products through the Asian Bond Fund (ABF).

[40]Cao, Honghui, and Yang Li, "Asian Bond Market: Strategic Conception and Preliminary Strategies," *Management World* 10 (2004): 3–11.

ASEAN 10+3 and APEC are mainly responsible for the innovation of new bond instruments (create supply), improvement of credit rating system, establishment and improvement of infrastructure and institutional framework, etc. ACD is mainly to provide political support and integrate all political resource to promote relevant countries to put efforts in the development of local currency and regional bond markets.[41]

The first is the creation and development of the ABF. Under the framework of the EMEAP, all parties in East Asia have proposed many influential programs for regional monetary and financial cooperation. The ABF is one of them.

At the World Economic Forum's annual East Asia Economic Summit held in Kuala Lumpur in October 2002, Thai Prime Minister Thaksin first proposed the idea of the ABF to take full advantage of East Asia's sufficient foreign exchange reserves to promote the development of the regional bond market. This idea was responded to by 10 countries and regions including Mainland China, Hong Kong (China), Japan, South Korea, Singapore, Malaysia, Indonesia, the Philippines, Australia and New Zealand. However, since it was only a rough plan, it did not specify the basics of the ABF, such as programs layout, participating members, regulatory agencies, types of investments and coordination mechanisms for different capital controls in the region.

After repeated demonstrations of the establishment of regional securities markets such as asset securitization, sovereign bond issuance, credit guarantees, credit rating and liquidation, EMEAP officially launched the Asian Bond Fund in June 2003 and determined that ABF will improve investment in reserves and promote two major functions of bond market development. According to the initial arrangement, the funds of the ABF are derived from the foreign exchange reserves of the countries concerned. The IBS is used as

[41]Huang, Meibo, Yang Lin, Research on the Development of Emerging Bond Market in East Asia: From Local Currency Bond Market to Asian Bond Market. Economic Science Press, 2008.

a fund manager to invest in bonds issued in East Asia. The related transactions and liquidations are completed in the regional financial markets. The ABF was first issued in US dollars, but when conditions mature, it can issue in the local currency of East Asia. The start of the East ABF marks the cooperation of East Asian economies in the development of the bond market into the specific implementation stage. It is another important achievement of the East Asian regional monetary and financial cooperation following the "Chiang Mai Initiative."

(1) ABF1: On 2 June 2003, the 11 central banks and monetary authorities of EMEAP announced the official launch of the ABF. The initial scale of the ABF1 was US$1 billion. It was funded by EMEAP economies from their official reserves and invested in eight members of EMEAP (except Japan, Australia and New Zealand), and issued a package of sovereign and quasi-sovereign bonds in US dollar. ABF1 is similar to an open-end fund with a minimum subscription of US$25 million. After notifying the BIS, subscribers can redeem funds. Central banks of EMEAP economies have invested in ABF1 to express their support for the fund.

The issuance of ABF1 has improved the stability of the East Asian financial system from both a policy level and an economic level. The issuance of ABF1 shows the determination of EMEAP economies to further promote and strengthen regional monetary and financial cooperation. At the same time, it contributes to the reduction of the excessive dependence on the East Asian region's banking system, and it is conducive to the decentralization of investment in foreign exchange reserves of various economies. However, the ABF1 has not yet realized the original intention of the ABF to reduce the dependence of the East Asian region on the US dollar, and has not yet realized the purpose of the East Asian economies to develop the local currency bond market and the regional bond market.

(2) ABF2: After the successful issuance of ABF1, EMEAP began to study the second, ABF2, an ABF that invests in the domestic currency bond market of its members. By the end of 2004, ABF2 had basically solved technical problems such as fund form, origination method, operation mode, and index compilation. On 12 May 2005, EMEAP announced that it officially launched the ABF2 with a total investment of US$2 billion.

Compared with the ABF1, the ABF2 has doubled in size and included sovereign and quasi-sovereign domestic currency bonds issued by eight other EMEAP members except Japan, Australia and New Zealand. ABF2 has greatly improved fund structure, including the Pan-Asian Bond Index Fund (PAIF) and eight single-market funds. The latter is also known as the Fund of Bond Fund (FoBF), the two capital injections are each worth US$1 billion. The PAIF is managed by the State Street Global Singapore Limited (SSgA) and invests in the combination of the sovereign and quasi-sovereign bonds denominated in the local currency of the eight members mentioned above and is quoted in unhedged dollars. Its purpose is to create a complete regional local currency bond index as a benchmark for investment instruments. Eight single-market funds or FoBFs are structured in a dual structure, with the parent fund investing in eight sub-funds, and the eight sub-funds investing in the corresponding local currency bond markets (see Figure 7.14). The purpose of setting up the FoBF is to meet the needs of the development of the member bond market, and to solve the problems that exist when members use the US dollar to enter the local currency bond market. The BIS is still the fund manager of ABF2.

(3) ABF3: ABF3 is being prepared. It is quite different from the previous two Asian bond funds. Its primary goal is to assist banks in the developing Asia-Pacific region to securitize their assets to a greater extent for the selection of investors within and outside the region. It will provide credit support to high rating East Asian bonds, especially non-sovereign bonds.

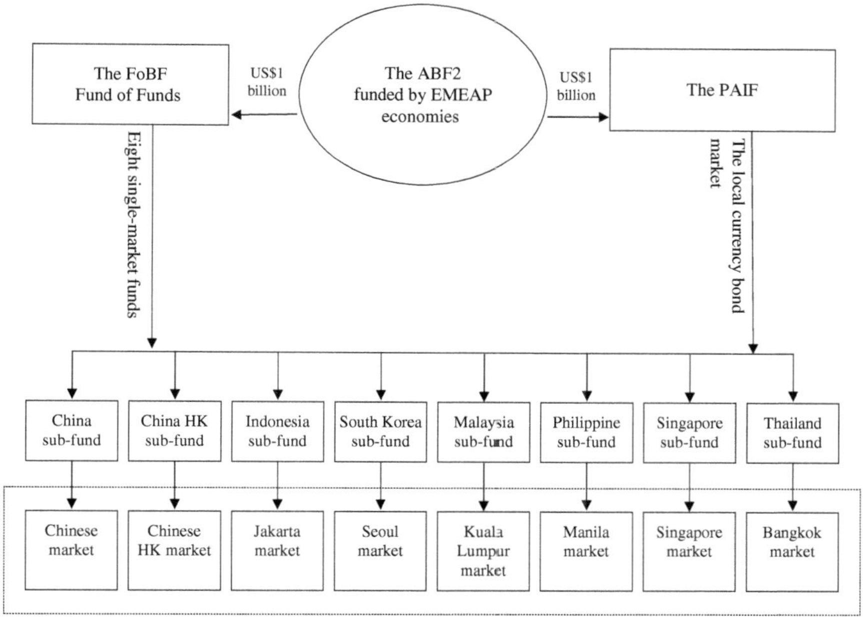

Figure 7.14. Structure of the ABF2
Source: Ma, G. and Eli. M. Remolona, "Opening Markets through a Regional Bond Fund: Lessons from ABF2," *BIS Quarterly Review* no. 6 (2005): 81–92.

It should be pointed out that the development of the regional bond market often encounters many complex technical problems. In the future, its development depends not only on the construction of relevant infrastructures in various countries and regions but also on how to attract more private investors. As the development of the regional bond market is a process of institutional change and innovation, as a public product, it cannot eliminate interest spillovers, and the private sector is difficult and unwilling to bear its costs. Therefore, the common aspirations and willingness of the governments of the countries in the region will, to a large extent, determine the direction and depth of the bond market in East Asia.

In addition to the ABF, there are other initiatives to promote the development of the regional bond market in Asia.

(1) The Asian Bond Market Initiative (ABMI): On 8 February 2003, the ABMI was presented at the ASEAN 10+3 informal meeting in Tokyo, and it was formally established on the 6th ASEAN 10+3 finance ministers' meeting in Manila, Philippines. ABMI is supported by the ADB and funded by the Japanese government. In order to implement the necessary measures to achieve the goals, ABMI has set up six working groups, such as the Thai-led Innovation Securitization Debt Tool Working Group, the China-Korea joint-led credit guarantee and investment mechanism group. At present, ABMI;s working groups have completed some of the predetermined goals, such as the realization of foreign institutions in East Asia to issue local currency bonds and so on. In order to complete other outstanding targets, the ASEAN 10+3 finance ministers' meeting held in May 2005 in Istanbul, Turkey, restructured the new framework for ABMI. The purpose of ABMI is to clarify the obstacles faced by the development of the domestic capital market of each member country and take effective measures to gradually eliminate these obstacles. At the same time, it improved the regional bond system and institution and promoted the development of regional bond market.[42]
(2) The Regional Bond Market Development Initiative (RBMDI): At the Ninth APEC Finance Ministers' Meeting held in Los Cabos, Mexico, in September 2002, Hong Kong (China) took the lead in proposing the "Development of Asset Securitization and Credit Guarantee Markets" to help members identify the obstacles of the development of assets, bonds, and credit market and seek for suitable solutions. After the continuous exploration of more than a year, the 10th APEC Finance Ministers' Meeting in Thailand in September 2003 officially approved the establishment of the RBMDI. There is a certain overlap between the work content of

[42]Huang, Meibo, Yang Lin, Research on the Development of Emerging Bond Market in East Asia: From Local Currency Bond Market to Asian Bond Market. Economic Science Press, 2008.

RBMDI and ABMI, but the former is to promote the development of the regional bond market in a larger region. In the two years of its existence, RBMDI has completed its mission and successfully promoted the development of asset securitization and credit guarantee markets in member countries, and promoted the development of the East Asian bond market from the supply side.

(3) The Asian Bond Market Development Initiative (ABMDI). At the time of the ASEAN Foreign Ministers Meeting held in July 2001, Thai Prime Minister Thaksin Shinawatra proposed the Asia Cooperation Dialogue (ACD).[43] The proposal aims to integrate the existing sub-regional cooperation mechanism in East Asia and promote dialogue and cooperation in the entire region. At the first ACD Ministerial Meeting held in June 2002, Thailand further introduced the ABMDI. The purpose of ABMDI is to seek for political consensus on the development of the regional bond market and raise public awareness of the development of the East Asian bond market. ABMDI did indeed play this role after the initiative was put into practice.

7.2.1.4 *Exchange Rate Cooperation and the Concept of "Asian Currency Unit"*

At the meeting of ASEAN 10+3 finance ministers held in Istanbul in May 2005, policy authorities of various countries and regions pointed out in the joint statement the need to strengthen the dialogue and coordination of economic policies (including exchange rate policies), followed by the meeting of the Central Bank Governors of China, Japan and Korea, who decided to renew the currency swap agreement. It also pointed out that maintaining exchange rate stability

[43] As of June 2012, ACD has 31 member countries, including 10 ASEAN countries (Brunei, Cambodia, Indonesia, Laos, Malaysia, Myanmar, Philippines, Singapore, Thailand, Vietnam), China, Japan, Korea, India, Pakistan, Bangladesh, Bahrain, Bhutan, Qatar, Kazakhstan, Sri Lanka, Oman, Kuwait, Iran, Mongolia, Russia, Saudi Arabia, United Arab Emirates, Kyrgyzstan, Tajikistan and Uzbekistan.

and strengthening policy coordination are the common needs of the three parties. It is in this context that some officials of ADB stated that it will be possible to compile and publish the weighted average of Asian currencies of the ACU. Although ADB does not disclose the specific form of ACU, it may be similar to the AMU discussed by Japanese scholars Ogawa and Shimizu, which is a currency consisting of 13 currencies of ASEAN 10+3 countries.[44] The weight of baskets and national currencies is determined by the weighted average ratio of the country's actual GDP to the total regional real GDP and the ratio of foreign trade to the total trade value in the area. Its exchange rate index is the weighted average exchange rate of the currency basket against the US dollar and the euro.

So far, domestic and foreign academics have mainly focused on the theoretical analysis on the exchange rate cooperation in the East Asia region. Although both theoretical analysis and practical experience have shown that East Asian economies have fallen into a dilemma of choice of exchange rate system and cannot be solved at the unilateral level, so a regional exchange rate cooperation and stabilization mechanism needs to be established, but due to the complexity of historical, political, economic and social factors in East Asia, regional currency cooperation has not been able to move forward further, and it has not entered the stage of exchange rate coordination or cooperation.

Stabilization of exchange rates in the region is a prerequisite for economic integration in East Asia. Under the current international and regional environment, striving for further regional economic development is an important regional strategy in the region. The current exchange rate cooperation in East Asia has important positive significance for the regional economic development.

Since the Asian financial crisis in 1997, monetary and financial cooperation among Asian economies has gradually accelerated, and

[44]Ogawa, Eiji, and Junko Shimizu, "A Deviation Measurement for Coordinated Exchange Rate Policies in East Asia," *RIETI Discussion Paper Series*, no. 05-E-017 (March 2005).

East Asian countries have gradually strengthened their mutual monetary and financial coordination. The starting point is to prevent the recurrence of the monetary and financial crisis. However, for the moment, East Asian currency cooperation is still in the stage of mutual financing, and regional exchange rate arrangements do not exist yet.

After the Asian financial crisis in 1997, the research on the East Asian exchange rate system focused on two directions. One was to try to use various methods to classify the real Asian exchange rate system.[45][46][47][48][49] Since 2000, the foreign exchange reserves of East Asian countries have continuously increased. After eliminating exchange rate changes, the main factors affecting this trend include safety motives (such as crisis prevention), economic motives (stimulating economic growth), and reducing exchange rate fluctuations.[50] A lot of research results show that the foreign exchange reserves accumulated by East Asian countries have provided these countries with a good barrier to financial arrangements. This also means that central banks of East Asian countries have a strong desire to avoid the appreciation of their currencies. East Asian currencies are subject to more interventions by their own central banks, and there are more obvious undervalued currencies to maintain their export competitiveness. The study of Calvo and Reinhart found that in the 1990s, a common phenomenon in many emerging economies was "the fear

---

[45]Frankel, J., E. Fajnzylber *et al.*, "Verifying Exchange Rate Regimes," *Journal of Development Economics* 66 (2001): 351–386.

[46]Calvo, G. and C. M. Reinhart, "Fear of Floating," *Quarterly Journal of Economics* 117 (2002): 379–408.

[47]Levy-Yeyati, E. L. and F. Sturzenegger, "Classifying Exchange Rate Regimes: Deeds vs. Words," *European Economic Review* 49 (2005): 1603–1635.

[48]Reinhart, C. M. and K. Rogoff, "The Modern History of Exchange Rate Reinterpretation," *Quarterly Journal of Economics* 199 (2004): 1–48.

[49]Shambaugh, J., "The Effect of Fixed Exchange Rates on Monetary Policy," *Quarterly Journal of Economics* 119, (2004): 301–352.

[50]Pontines, Victor, and Ramkishen S. Rajan, "Foreign Exchange Market Intervention and Reserve Accumulation in Emerging Asia: Is There Evidence of Fear of Appreciation?" *Economics Letters* 111, no. 3 (June 2011): 252–255.

of floating," which was a worry that the appreciation of the currency would affect the international competitiveness of domestic products and that the devaluation of the currency would affect its dollarization.[51] It is clear that the East Asian exchange rate system at the beginning of the 21st century can be described by the fear of appreciation, which was put forward by Levy-Yeyati and Sturzenegger.[52] The fear of appreciation of local currencies by East Asian economies has made the central banks (or monetary authorities) of these economies have distinctive policy responses to the appreciation and devaluation of their currencies. The East Asian Central Bank's response to the appreciation of the local currency is stronger, while it has a strong tolerance of the devaluation of the local currency. Pontines and Rajan constructed a simple central bank intervention reaction equation to test the response of the Central Bank of India, South Korea, the Philippines, Singapore, Thailand and Indonesia toward the devaluation and the appreciation of the local currency.[53] The empirical results confirm the asymmetric policy reaction of the central banks in these Asian countries. The conclusions of the two methods of nominal effective exchange rate and nominal bilateral exchange rate for the United States dollar are consistent. At the same time, it is shown that the use of nominal effective exchange rates in India, Thailand and Singapore has a larger asymmetric coefficient, indicating that these three countries are more concerned with trade-weighted exchange rate changes, or the local currency changes against a basket of currencies not US dollar.

The second is not only to test how much the region's currency has become more volatile, especially with respect to the dollar but also

[51]Calvo, G. and C. M. Reinhart,"Fear of floating," *Quarterly Journal of Economics* 117 (2002): 379–408.

[52]Levy-Yeyati, Eduardo, and Federico Sturzenegger, "Fear of Floating in Reverse: Exchange Rate Policy in the 2000s," unpublished: Washington, World Bank, (2007): 1–39.

[53]Pontines, Victor, and Ramkishen S. Rajan, "Foreign Exchange Market Intervention and Reserve Accumulation in Emerging Asia: Is There Evidence of Fear of Appreciation?" *Economics Letters* 111, no. 3 (June 2011): 252–255.

to consider the degree of fluctuations with other currencies (including trade-weighted exchange rates).[54] Due to the generally low level of economic development and the unsound development of financial markets, East Asian countries and regions have actually chosen a fixed exchange rate system that is pegged to the US dollar in order to obtain a more stable economic development environment. This has caused the East Asian region's exchange rate policy to adjust accordingly to the adjustment of the US's exchange rate policy, making it vulnerable to hot money attacks.

Discussion about whether East Asia meets the conditions of the OCA by statistical analysis, Goto and Hamada[55] found that there is a high correlation between major economic indicators such as the money supply, interest rates, consumer price index (CPI) and actual gross national product of Asian countries. Based on this, the actual impact on Asia is highly symmetric, so Asia meets the criteria for establishing an OCA. Bayoumi and Eichengreen[56] uses vector autoregressive (VAR) models to compare and analyze the symmetry of the impact of demand shocks and supply shocks on the rate of inflation and GDP growth in some Asian countries and regions, as well as the relevance, scale and the speed of adjustment of economic disturbances. The results show that from the criteria of external shock symmetry, Japan, South Korea and Taiwan (China), Thailand, Indonesia, Malaysia, Singapore and Hong Kong (China), China and South Korea are more likely to form the OCA. Kwan (1998) concludes that Asia is eligible to establish an OCA similar to the Eurozone based on similar inflation rates.[57]

---

[54]Cavoli, T. and R. S. Rajan, *Exchange Rate Regimes and Macroeconomic Management in Asia.* Hong Kong University Press, 2009.
[55]Goto, J. and K. Hamada, "Economic Preconditions for Asian Regional Integration," In *Macroeconomic Linkage: Savings, Exchange Rates, and Capital Flows*, edited by T. Ito and A. Krueger. IL: University of Chicago Press, 1994, 359–388.
[56]Bayoumi, Tamim, and Eichengreen, Barry, "Ever Closer to Heaven? An Optimum Currency Area Index for European Countries," *European Economic Review* 41, no. 3 (1997): 761–770.
[57]Kwan, C.H. The theory of optimum currency areas and the possibility of forming a Yen bloc in Asia Journal of Asian Economics, 9, no. 4 (1998): 555–580.

After the Asian financial crisis, ASEAN launched the Hanoi Plan of Action in 1998 to promote economic integration in the region. One of them is to establish a unified regional currency.[58] In May 2004, at the East Asian Single Currency Symposium organized by the ADB, Japanese scholar Haruhiko Kuroda pointed out the importance of the single currency in East Asia. In fact, by the end of 2005, East Asian countries have generally achieved a stable exchange rate against the US dollar and formed a stable exchange rate zone for East Asian currency swaps, including RMB. This can be seen as a stable exchange rate that has not been institutionalized circle.[59] In May 2006, the finance ministers of China, Japan, and Korea announced the attempt to establish a single currency in East Asia and eventually formed a common currency similar to the euro.

After the Asian financial crisis, there was a suggestion to establish an Asian currency unit (ACU or AMU) consisting of the currencies of 13 Asian countries. It is essentially a currency basket, but it has higher requirements for the level of regional cooperation.[60] If ACU can obtain the support of regional economies and develop smoothly, it will be beneficial to prevent competitive devaluation of currencies in neighboring East Asia, promote coordinated exchange rates in the region, maintain relatively stable monetary value in the region, and reduce East Asia's dependence on the US dollar. We will reduce large-scale regional monetary asset reserves, link global imbalances in international payments and promote economic integration in East Asia. For China, ACU contains very flexible exchange rate cooperation possibilities, which helps to promote the formation

---

[58] ASEAN, Hanoi Plan of Action, http://www.aseansec.org/8754.htm, 2013-1-10.

[59] Shi, Tianhou, "The Stability, Internationalization of the RMB, and the Future of the East Asian Monetary System," In *East Asian Monetary and Financial Cooperation in the Post-crisis Era-Is the Coordination of the RMB and the Yen Possible?*, edited by Li Xiao, 187.Jilin University Press, 2010, 187.

[60] Eiji, Yamashita, "The Necessity of Establishing the Asian Edition of EMS and Joint Leadership Mechanism between Japan and China," Post-Crisis East Asian Monetary and Financial Cooperation Ed. Li Xiao, Jilin University Press, 2010.

and development of the RMB exchange rate formation mechanism based on market supply and demand and with reference to a basket of currencies.[61]

7.2.2 *Predicament, Challenge and Reflection of the Monetary Cooperation in the East Asia Region at Current Stage*

Although there has been some progress in monetary cooperation in East Asia, the development will encounter many obstacles. On the one hand, there are still many shortcomings in East Asian financial cooperation at this stage. It cannot meet the requirements for stabilizing the monetary and financial environment and preventing financial risks. On the other hand, after the initial cooperation is achieved, the East Asian currency cooperation moves toward a higher level and faces great resistance.

7.2.2.1 *The Main Dilemma Faced by Currency Cooperation in East Asia*

First, there are major differences in the economic structure and macroeconomics of East Asia.

From the perspective of the economic structure of East Asian economies (see Table 7.8), each economy has a different level of economic development and different economic structures. There are major differences in per capita income, industrial structure, the degree of development of the financial market and the improvement of the legal system that supports the market economy system and government efficiency.

[61]Qi Junyan, "Global Financial Crisis and Asia: Impacts, Relevance, and Challenges," In *The RMB, Yen and Asian Monetary Cooperation-Dialogue between Chinese and Japanese Scholars*, edited by Li Xiao, and Kamikawa Takao, 41. Tsingshu: Tsinghua University Press, 2010.

Table 7.8. Economic Structural Indicators of East Asian Economies

	GDP/ POP	Inv/ GDP	Sav/ GDP	CA/ GDP	Industrial Structure*				Exp/ GDP*	Imp/ GDP*	FDI/ GDP*	Governance indicators			
	US$	%	%	%	Agriculture	Industry	Manufactures	Service Industry	%	%	%	Government Efficiency	Control Corruption	Control Quality	Legal Domination
Brunei	38801	13.9	—	49.1	0.6	71.7	11.8	27.7	81.3	29.1	7.4	77.3	77.3	8.48	77.9
Cambodia	934	23.5	13.8	−9.7	36.7	23.5	16.1	39.8	54.1	59.5	7.0	25.6	12.8	35.1	15.5
China Mainland	6094	47.8	50.1	2.3	10.0	46.6	29.6[a]	43.3	31.4	27.3	3.0	60.7	28.9	45.5	40.4
China Hong Kong, China	35961	23.3	27.4	4.1	0.1[a]	7.1[a]	1.8[a]	92.8[a]	225.5	221.5	36.3	94.3	94.3	99.1	90.6
Indonesia	3660	34.9	32.8	−2.1	14.7	47.2	24.3	38.1	26.3	24.9	2.1	46.9	27.5	41.7	31
Japan	46896	20.3	21.9	1.6	1.2[a]	27.4[a]	19.5[a]	71.5[a]	15.2	16.1	0.0	87.7	90.5	78.2	86.9
Korea	23021	29.0	31.0	1.9	2.7	39.2	31.2	58.1	56.2	54.1	0.4	86.3	70.1	79.1	80.8
Laos	1454	—	—	−21.9	30.8	34.7	7.6	34.5	37.7	43.9	3.6	17.1	13.7	19.4	18.3
Macao, China	—	—	—	—	0[a]	7.4[a]	0.9[a]	92.6[a]	112.4	53.6	12.6	87.2	70.6	87.7	70.0
Malaysia	10578	24.0	31.5	7.5	11.9	40.3	24.4	47.9	91.6	75.7	4.2	81.0	57.8	74.4	66.2
Myanmar	849	16.3	12.2	−4.4	48.4[b]	16.2[b]	11.6[b]	35.4[b]	0.2[b]	0.1[b]	1.6	2.4	0.5	1.4	4.2
Philippines	2462	21.1	24.1	3.0	12.8	31.4	21.0	55.8	31.0	36.0	0.8	55.9	22.7	43.6	34.7
Singapore	49936	22.9	43.9	21.0	0.0	26.6	20.9	73.4	209.0	182.3	26.7	99.1	96.2	97.2	93.4
Taiwan, China	19888	21.0	27.9	6.9	—	—	—	—	—	—	−0.4	83.4	77.7	84.4	82.6
Thailand	5848	31.3	31.1	−0.2	1.2.4	41.2	35.6[a]	46.5	76.9	72.4	2.3	59.7	44.5	56.4	48.4
Vietnam	1523	34.1	34.4	0.3	22.0	40.8	19.3	37.2	87.0	91.2	6.0	45	29.9	29.4	38.5

Notes: GDP/POP, per capita GDP (current US$), 2012; Inv/GDP, total investment, 2012; Sav/GDP, Gross national savings, 2012; CA/GDP, current account balance, 2012; Exp/GDP, total exports of goods and services; Imp/GDP, total imports of goods and services; FDI/GDP, net inflow of foreign direct investment ratio; *The data of 2011; [a]The data of 2010, [b]The data of 2004.

Source: World Bank, World Development Indicators Database, 2012; Worldwide Governance Indicators, 2012; IMF, International Financial Statistics, UNCTAD.

In terms of per capita income level,[62] there are both low-income countries or regions and high-income countries or regions, of which Cambodia and Myanmar belong to low-income countries, Indonesia, Laos, the Philippines, and Vietnam belong to low and middle-income countries. China, Malaysia and Thailand belong to middle- and high-income countries. However, Brunei, Hong Kong (China), Japan, South Korea, Singapore and Taiwan (China) are all high-income economies. The proportion of total investment and national savings in the GDP of each economy also differs significantly. China's total investment and national savings account for nearly half of the total, while Japan's total investment and national savings account for only one-fifth of GDP. In terms of the proportion of current accounts, Brunei, Singapore, and other countries are high surplus countries, while Laos, Cambodia, and other countries have a higher proportion of deficits. Japan, Thailand, and other countries basically maintain the balance of imports and exports. The importance of the three major industries of each economy in GDP is also quite different. The proportion of industries in Brunei, China, Indonesia, Malaysia, Thailand and Vietnam in the national economy exceeds 40%, especially in Brunei. The secondary industry accounted for the vast majority of the national economy. In 2011, it accounted for 71.7% of its GDP, while Hong Kong (China), Japan, South Korea and other economies were dominated by service industries. The proportion of the service industry in Hong Kong (China) accounted for 92.8% of its GDP in 2011. The difference between the volume of imports and exports and the amount of foreign direct investment inflows in the GDP still varies greatly among economies. At the same time, the various governance indicators that are closely linked to the development of the market economy are also quite different, reflecting the different levels of economic governance of each economy.

In addition to economic structural indicators, there are also large differences in the macroeconomic indicators of various economies. We

[62]According to the World Bank's 2013 latest income standard, countries or regions with per capita GNI is less than US$1035 is low income, between US$1035 and US$4085 is low-middle-income countries or regions, and between

Table 7.9. Macroeconomic Indicators of East Asian Economies (2013)

	Government Debt	General Government Revenues	Inflation Rate	Interest Rate	
	% of GDP (%)	Ratio of GDP (%)	Consumer Price Index (%)	12-Month Fixed Deposit Interest Rate (%)	Bank Loan Interest Rate (%)
Brunei	2.48	16.754	0.382	0.206	5.5
Cambodia	28.389	−2.693	2.955	1.343	—
Mainland China	39.364	−0.879	2.624	3	6
Hong Kong, China	6.66	0.755	4.329	0.01	5
Indonesia	26.105	−2.093	6.413	6.264	11.658
Japan	243.203	−8.198	0.357	0.542	1.304
Korea	33.903	0.65	1.302	2.891	4.643
Laos	107.117	61.326	6.371	—	—
Macao, China	—	—	5	0.045	5.25
Malaysia	57.707	−4.563	2.105	2.970	4.613
Myanmar	39.778	−1.649	5.711	8.000	13.000
Philippines	39.094	−0.133	2.933	1.662	5.767
Singapore	103.46	5.652	2.359	0.140	5.380
Taiwan, China	41.099	−3.14	0.793	—	—
Thailand	45.853	−0.201	2.185	2.883	6.958
Vietnam	51.628	−5.588	6.595	7.140	10.374

Notes: General government gross debt data is used for government sector debts; general government net lending/borrowing data are used for general government revenues.

Source: IMF, International Financial Statistics. World Economic Outlook.

look at several macroeconomic indicators as a convergence condition in the Maastricht Treaty (see Table 7.9). Each East Asian economy has not fully converged in terms of fiscal balance, inflation and interest rates. According to the "Maastricht Treaty," countries in the

US$4086 and US$12616 for medium-high income countries or regions, higher than US$12,616 is high-income countries or regions.

euro area must control their fiscal deficits below 3%, and reduce the fiscal deficit as a goal. At the same time, the proportion of treasury bonds in GDP is kept below 60%. The two important standards to be observed are also important standards that other EU countries must meet to join the Eurozone. Looking at various macroeconomic indicators of East Asian economies, the proportion of Japanese government bonds in GDP reached 243.2% in 2013, and Singapore and Laos also exceeded 100%, while Brunei and other countries have a lower proportion of this indicator. In 2013, Cambodia, Japan, Malaysia, Taiwan (China), Vietnam and other economies all exceeded 3% in their fiscal deficits. As far as the inflation rate is concerned, there are also large differences between East Asian economies. In 2013, the highest inflation rate was in Vietnam, which was 6.6%, while Japan still maintained a level close to zero inflation. The difference between interest rates and deposit and lending spreads of various economies is also very large. The 12-month fixed deposit interest rate in Hong Kong (China) is only 0.01%, while Vietnam's interest rate is 7.14%, and interest spreads of some economies' deposits and loans vary widely. For example, the interest rate for fixed-term deposits in December in Hong Kong (China) is only 0.01%, and the bank loan interest rate for the same period is 5%.

Second, the scale of existing monetary cooperation arrangements in East Asia is limited.

Compared with the current amount of foreign exchange reserves and savings funds in East Asia, the scale of East Asian monetary cooperation and the resources invested by countries are obviously insufficient. As far as the BSA framework is concerned, its amount is far less than the needs of East Asian countries and regions to cope with external shocks and currency crises. Take Thailand as an example. The bilateral swap agreement signed so far totaled US$9 billion, and the funding assistance that it sought from the IMF in the crisis in 1997 was as high as US$17.2 billion. In terms of the multilateral CMI framework (CMIM), although the projected scale of US$120 billion is significantly higher than in the past, it is still insufficient to meet the short-term funding needs of the region when liquidity is difficult. The existing scale of ABF is even more limited, and it is far from the requirements of the regional bond market.

Third, monetary cooperation in East Asia has not yet been able to achieve complete independent operation.

The start-up and operation of bilateral currency swaps before 2008 is still limited by the IMF assistance framework. Although the start of CMIM broke through the restrictions on the supply of funds under the framework of the IMF funded project, how to establish a strict regional supervision system and how to deal with the relationship with the IMF is still an open issue, which will inevitably have a certain adverse impact on the timeliness, flexibility and pertinence of the CMIM. Second, although the ABF2 breaks the limit of purchasing only the dollar-denominated assets, due to its size limit, it does not actually solve the problem of misallocation of financing currencies faced by East Asian countries and regions. It is also difficult to provide effective and larger-scale liquidity support when the currency crisis arrives. Finally, there is still a close connection between the actual exchange rate arrangements the East Asian economies and the US dollar. Therefore, as far as the progress of the current cooperation framework is concerned, it has largely failed to fully realize the effects of reducing the external economic disturbances such as the fluctuation of the exchange rate of the US dollar, solving the "double mismatch" problem and establishing prevention for external shocks and financial turmoil, which are all the original intention of East Asia monetary cooperation as mechanism.

Fourth, there is a lack of a mandatory coordinating institution.

Since CMI was put forward and implemented in 2000, it mainly focused on bilateral cooperation and loose cooperation. As far as the ASEAN 10+3 framework is concerned, it is actually the three countries of China, Japan and Korea that have bilateral cooperation with other ASEAN countries, and there is also a lack of multilateral institutional arrangements for financial cooperation among China, Japan and South Korea. In addition, formal institutional arrangements have not yet been established in areas such as East Asian supervisory processes and capital flow supervision mechanisms. Although from the beginning of 2008, East Asian monetary cooperation has moved from bilateral to multilateral, in order to ensure the effective management and use of the common reserve fund, CMIM has also proposed the establishment of an independent regional monitoring entity. However, its establishment and operation are still under discussion. How to establish an independent operation and a coercive supervision and policy coordination organization has become an urgent issue facing the regional monetary cooperation in East Asia. Taking into account the setbacks of the original AMF concept and the various complex relationships among East Asian countries and regions, the development of institutionalized multilateral cooperation mechanisms still faces many major issues that need to be resolved.

Fifth, exchange rate cooperation cannot be carried out.

From the Asian monetary and financial crisis in 1998 to the global financial crisis in 2008, the crisis experience of most East Asian countries was gradually diluted. Although the degree of interdependence among the economies in the region has gradually increased, the calls for stable exchange rates in various economies are not high. Faced with the complex historical, political, economic and social issues in East Asia, regional exchange rate cooperation has often been regarded as a long-term goal of East Asian currency cooperation and has not been included in the current cooperation agenda due to the difficulties involved in the transfer of sovereignty. However, it should be noted that, first of all, since East Asian economies have the similar economic development model, the stability of exchange rates in the region is crucial for the smooth development of their mutual trade and financial transactions, and even with regional economic and trade exchanges. It is an East Asian currency that is one of the most important goals of cooperation. At present, there is a diversified state of nominal exchange rate arrangements in East Asia. Under such circumstances, if there is no corresponding exchange rate cooperation and stabilization mechanism, it will be prone to "neighboring" exchange rate fluctuations, or each economy may be forced to face the pressure from the market, and the exchange rate arrangements may return to some form of "actual peg to the dollar system." Lessons from the Asian financial crisis show that the drastic fluctuations in the exchange rate between the US dollar and the Japanese yen will create preconditions for speculative activities and it becomes an important source of economic instability in East Asia. Moreover, if the stability of the exchange rate in the region cannot be effectively maintained, the implementation of various financing facilities and the construction of the regional bond market will also be hindered.

7.2.2.2 *The Roots of Barriers to Current Monetary Cooperation in Asia*

The differences in the level of economic structure and degree of openness among Asian economies and the degree of economic integration within the region may hinder the establishment of a higher level monetary and financial cooperation mechanism in the region. However, some relevant empirical analysis shows that East Asia still has the conditions to expand the scale and level of monetary cooperation on the existing basis, establish a more institutionalized cooperation mechanism, and conduct preliminary exchange rate cooperation. In fact, the more important roots of the challenges facing East Asian monetary cooperation lie in the following aspects[63]:

First, the dependence of East Asian economies on the dollar system. Since the collapse of the Bretton Woods system in the early 1970s, although the international currency system has shown a tendency of diversification of reserve currencies, the decoupling of the US dollar from gold has not really weakened the status of the US dollar. In fact, the US dollar still occupies a dominant position. As the world's key currency, it plays a central role in the international monetary system. The Bretton Woods system has been transformed into a hidden mechanism so-called "dollar system." As the United

[63]Xiao, Li, Yibing Ding, and Tingting Qin, "The Promotion of China's Status in the East Asian Economy: An Investigation Based on Trade Trends," *World Economy and Politics* 5 (2005): 57–61.

States further relaxed financial regulations and opened financial markets in the mid and late 1980s, and the successful transformation of the United States economy into a long-term sustained growth phase, a large amount of funds from other regions poured into the US market. As a result, although the current account deficit in the United States in the 1990s reached a historical record, the huge capital inflow not only made up for the current account deficit but also generated a large amount of surplus funds, and then invested from the United States to the rest of the world. A credit turnover system and circulation system with global core of US dollar has been formed. Since the establishment of the European Monetary System, especially since the 1980s, the emerging market economies, especially East Asian countries and regions, have gradually become the most important supporters of this "credit system" and thus the "dollar system." The US dollar funds they receive through their US export surplus are partially used for importing capital goods, and the other part is invested in US government Treasury bonds and stored in the United States as foreign exchange reserves. Since the 1990s, about 60% of the US capital account surplus has come from public sector funds. The expansion of these public goods is mostly supported by developing countries, mainly East Asian emerging countries, except Japan. So East Asian countries not only rely on the US commodity market but also rely more on the "dollar system" — the more East Asian countries want to ensure the export of the United States, we must strive to maintain the stability of the value of the dollar and peg the exchange rate. The more it is necessary to maintain the peg to the dollar, the more it wants to retain as much dollar reserves as possible. As a result, the external funds attracted by the United States continue to increase. The United States has not only solved the problem of financing the current account deficit but also has surplus funds available for export. With the attraction of high asset returns in various regions of East Asian countries, a large part of the export capital has returned to these countries and regions. They eventually become investments in the United States by converting their foreign exchange reserves into capital-importing countries. In this way, the scale of the US dollar credit circulation system has been continuously expanded worldwide, which has promoted the large-scale and frequent flow of funds globally. On the one hand, the United States provides an ever-expanding commodity export market, while on the other hand it provides increasing financial assets, thus maintaining the relative balance of supply and demand of the US dollar on the international market, and stabilizing the value of the currency, thus solving the "Triffin Puzzle" to some extent. On this basis, the dominant position of the US dollar can be maintained through economies of scale and network effects. In this sense, in today's world, the United States is a typical financial country that controls financial hegemony. Relatively speaking, Japan and other East Asian countries are trading countries. As the main market provider in the East Asia region, the United States has made it difficult for countries and regions in East Asia to exclude the US dollar from the choice of international settlement currency and exchange rate targeting target. The US dollar income obtained by the latter also needs to invest in US dollar assets. This makes it difficult for the East Asian region to establish a truly independent mechanism for financial and exchange rate cooperation. This is why it is still necessary to use the US dollar as the denomination currency in the construction of bilateral currency swaps and the Asian bond market. This is the root cause that the construction of the Asian bond market lacks of insufficient support from the private sector. Considering that the United States still has the most developed and open financial markets and the largest external product demand in the world today, combined with the economies of scale and network effects of the dollar system, the US dollar-based credit turnover system between Asia and the United States is very difficult to experience substantial changes in the short term. At the same time, given the long-term nature and arduous nature of the economic restructuring, it will be difficult for the East Asian region to replace the US as the provider of the final product market in the short term. At present, the final product market share provided by Japan and China in the region is far lower than that of the United States. Due to the narrow space in the domestic market and the aging society, Japan has made it difficult to play an important role in the status and role of end-product market providers. Although China has the potential to become the largest provider of final product markets in the region, facing the arduous and complex adjustment of industrial structure, economic structure, and economic growth model, the ability to expand domestic demand to stimulate economic growth in the short term is also limited. Under such circumstances, the US dollar system has remained a constraint factor in the Asian region's monetary and financial cooperation for a long time.

Second, at this stage, East Asia lacks the dominant currency that can replace the dollar at the regional level. An important reason why it is difficult to further develop the currency cooperation in the East Asian region at this stage is that the coordination of regional policies lacks suitable anchors in the region. To promote policy coordination, especially monetary policy coordination in a region, there must be a monetary policy goal as the core. The formulation of policies in all countries serves as a basic frame of reference-anchoring. For example, Germany's monetary policy is anchored at its core in Europe. Before and after the crisis, major economies have basically adopted the exchange rate system peg to the US dollar to introduce the US monetary policy as the core anchor. However, unlike Europe, the United States, as an economic power outside the region, formulates its monetary policy to adjust the cyclical fluctuations of its economy. The economic relations within the East Asia have little effect on its monetary policy, and there are huge differences between the economic cycles of the United States and East Asia. Therefore, anchoring the monetary policy of US as the core is obviously not suitable for the requirements of East Asian economies. In fact, although the United States has the inherent advantages of financial countries at the regional level, if there is a country that can play the role of the United States at the global level, it can provide an open and huge commodity market and it can also provide enough high flows. With stable financial assets, it is feasible to establish a relatively independent regional monetary and financial cooperation mechanism. Germany achieved this goal to a certain extent by liberalizing trade and actively opening up domestic financial markets in Europe. In Asia, Japan, which was supposed to have similar conditions, took the road of currency internationalization contrary to Germany, that is, on the one hand taking internal and external financial liberalization reform measures, making the domestic financial market relatively closed, and on the other hand it has taken direct challenges. The internationalization strategy of yen directly challenged the dollar hegemony and neglected the role of the yen as a regional key currency.[64] As a result, not only did the yen's internationalization process suffer but it also made Japan unable to lead regional financial cooperation. In the current East Asia region, except for Japan, only China has the potential to become a market provider in the region, but it is still unable to assume the responsibilities of financial asset providers. Therefore, under the existing conditions, there are certain difficulties in the exchange rate cooperation between the currency-denominated assets market in the construction area and the regional currency as the core.

Third, it is difficult for East Asian countries to grant national sovereignty at this stage. Whether it is the expansion or institutionalization of monetary cooperation or exchange rate cooperation and coordination, participants are required to give in to some economic sovereignty. However, it is difficult for East Asian countries to accept the transfer of sovereignty during the "sovereign expansion period" in the course of development of nations. In general, in the course of its development, nations will first experience a period of sovereignty expansion with the formation and consolidation of nations. Later, with the maturity of the state, the degree of international integration has deepened, and even after the contradictions between the countries and the huge damage caused by the war, it will gradually enter the period of convergence of sovereignty. Western European countries began their monetary cooperation process during

[64]Xiao, Li, Yibing Ding, and Tingting Qin, "The Promotion of China's Status in the East Asian Economy: An Investigation Based on Trade Trends," *World Economy and Politics* 5 (2005): 57–61.

the period of sovereignty convergence. The nations in East Asia gradually formed in the late modern period, and they are now in the period of sovereignty expansion. In addition, due to historical reasons, there are many contradictions between the great powers in the region such as China, Japan and South Korea. Unless powerful forces push it forward, or if major countries such as the willingness to cooperate between China and Japan and their relations have made breakthrough progress, cooperation involving economic sovereignty will be difficult to develop. This is also an important reason why trade cooperation that can take place in the form of bilateral FTA can take the lead in monetary and financial cooperation.

Specifically, the unfavorable impact of the strong sense of sovereignty prevailing in East Asian countries on monetary cooperation can be summarized as follows:

(1) The high degree of concern for economic sovereignty among countries has made it difficult to achieve multilateral institutional arrangements for regional monetary cooperation. Because an effective multilateral financing mechanism must not only act as a regional lender of last resort but also assume the responsibility of coordinating economic policies among countries, strengthening discipline, and monitoring the economic trends and balance of payments of each country. In other words, it requires member states to take more obligations and responsibilities.
(2) Part of the reason why it is difficult to make progress in regional exchange rate arrangements is that the preservation of economic sovereignty makes it possible for countries to maintain full autonomy in monetary policy, despite the fact that such monetary policy autonomy is notorious under the current international monetary system.
(3) The domestic financial reform caused by financial cooperation also involves sovereignty issues to varying degrees. For example, the main purpose of constructing the Asian bond market is to realize that through the regional capital market, East Asian economies will get rid of over-reliance on the financing structure

of domestic banks and foreign debt as much as possible to ease the problems of dual currency and maturity mismatches. The market obtains sufficient financial support and gains the trust of the private sector. It will inevitably require the content and procedures of financial reforms in various countries. This is a sensitive issue involving economic sovereignty.

(4) Most of the East Asian economies are in the developing stage. There are certain competitions between the current international trade pattern and the international currency system for growth competition and financial reform (enter the dollar-dominated international financial market). This also makes it difficult for them to make the necessary compromises in regional financial cooperation.

(5) The idea of regional monetary and financial cooperation with the core of crisis response needs to be reconsidered. The history of East Asian monetary and financial cooperation so far indicates that the role of crisis in promoting monetary and financial cooperation is enormous. After the outbreak of the Asian financial crisis, the main objective of the regional financial cooperation explored and pursued by the East Asian economies is to carry out crisis relief and strive to develop crisis prevention. All parties have been trying hard to explore how to develop a crisis management system such as CMI into a regional crisis prevention system and CMIM is such an effort. The history of the development of East Asian monetary cooperation so far shows that the financial crisis within and outside the region has a direct role in promoting cooperation. As compared with the development process of European economic and monetary integration, this is a prominent feature of East Asian regional monetary cooperation. The cooperation mechanism for dealing with crises established under the guidance of such a high degree of pragmatism philosophy is, to a large extent, an important reason for its difficulty in progress. Because the crisis is abnormal, common prosperity and stable development under the conditions of economic globalization should be the higher level goal of cooperation. Therefore,

the cooperation mechanism with the goal of directly responding to the crisis is an important cause of weak consensus in Asia and community awareness.

Therefore, the Asian Consensus and East Asian Community consciousness should establish longer-term goals, continue to explore the solution to the development difficulties of the new era and must seek for the common prosperity and development of East Asia. In this regard, the major countries in the region, especially China and Japan, should take due responsibility.

7.2.2.3 *Challenges and Reflections on the Monetary Cooperation in East Asia in the Background of Financial Crisis*

Since mid-2008, under the impact of the global financial crisis, the economic growth and financial development of East Asian countries and regions that have a high degree of dependence on the US economy are facing enormous difficulties. How to deal with challenges through regional monetary and financial cooperation has become an urgent issue. Triggered by the crisis, the outbreak of the "subprime mortgage crisis" and the global financial turmoil reflect the inherent risks and hidden dangers that cannot be ignored in the highly mature financial markets of developed countries and the rapidly developing global process, and may result in the formation of larger scale financial shocks. Because East Asian economies in a sense belong to the periphery of financial globalization, they are at the end of the subprime crisis. The current external financial turmoil has a collateral and indirect impact on its impact, and the dominant banking system in East Asia's financial sector has not been significantly affected. However, this does not mean that the East Asian region's economy has been decoupled from the developed markets such as the United States. The latter's changes in the economic and financial situation still have an impact on the East Asian region's economy that cannot be ignored.

The East Asian economies actually face two options: one is to choose unilateral actions centering on self-interest, and the other is to take collective actions and to resist possible external shocks by strengthening regional financial and monetary cooperation on the basis of the existing cooperation framework.

It needs to be pointed out that the choice of "unilateral actions" is not entirely incompatible with the needs of East Asian economies. Specifically:

First, for the risks and shocks from the financial markets of developed countries, East Asian economies with different financial market openness can adopt different responses. Considering the indirect nature of global financial turmoil on the financial sector in East Asia, countries that are less dependent on external financial markets can indirectly restrict the opening up of the financial sector by strengthening the control of capital flows in financial markets, which can isolate external financial risks to a certain extent and maintain macroeconomic stability of domestic financial sector.

Second, for important economies with large differences in economic structure characteristics, taking measures independently to respond to changes in the external economic environment may reduce the costs of policy adjustment. The current global financial turmoil does not have a specific impact on countries and East Asian countries. Those economies with high levels of dependence on foreign debt relatively slow the economic growth, and relatively small current account surpluses, and small foreign exchange reserves lead to the risks of overheating and a current account surplus. And economies with large foreign exchange reserves obviously need to take different adjustment measures.

Third, for some large countries in the region, the turmoil in the financial and economic situation of developed countries such as the United States and Europe may also increase the ease of economic and financial development of small countries within the region, or actively seek policy coordination with them, thus increasing the number of large countries to take a single initiative. In fact, some scholars, such as Yao Zhizhong, believe that at present, other East Asian economies have unilateral demands for maintaining the coordination of exchange rates with China. Therefore, China has to spontaneously take the initiative of leading position in the policy coordination through regional cooperation.[65]

In spite of this, Li Xiao and Ding Yibing pointed out that the choice of unilateral actions of Asian economies still faces relatively obvious difficulties and deficiencies[66]:

First, in today's rapid development of global financial markets and corresponding technological means, relying on the question of whether closed markets and regulations can effectively isolate external shocks, even if it can achieve isolation goals to a certain extent, it will prevail among post-development countries. In the case of competitive development, this kind of stability is likely to be at the expense of economic efficiency, market attractiveness and competitive advantage.

Second, unilateral actions are prone to inducing a paradoxical policy, and the proliferation and feedback effects that they cause will ultimately affect the stable development of the entire region.

Third, unilateral actions may also create "free rider" problems. For example, in the case of a slowdown in the US economy and a reduction in external demand, unilateral actions to increase domestic demand and guarantee growth may require a country to implement an expansionary fiscal policy. Since this kind of policy will bring about an expansionary effect spillover, which is conducive to countries with close trade with their own countries, in order to get the benefits of such a free rider, it is possible for each country to wait for each other to adopt policy adjustments and eventually fall into a prisoner's dilemma in order to avoid the occurrence of the above-mentioned situation; the East Asian economies obviously need close coordination in the policy coordination.

---

[65]Zhizhong, Yao. "China's High Investment Rate." *International Economic Review* 5 (2004): 39–43.

[66]Xiao, Li, and Yibing Ding, "East Asian Financial Cooperation in a Global Financial Turbulent Environment: Policy Options and Suggestions," *International Economic Review* 11–12 (2008).

Fourth, on the one hand, in the current situation of high degree of integration of the real economy of East Asian economies, the external financial turmoil will force East Asian economies to ensure the momentum of development, shift to the regional needs and further promote regional economic realities. Therefore, the policy adjustments of any country, especially the major countries in the region, will have a spillover effect, which will have a negligible impact on other economies in the region and will have a feedback effect on the country. On the other hand, facing the global financial turmoil, the huge liquidity accumulated in the East Asia region also needs to find new areas of activity in the region, which will inevitably strengthen the demand for regional financial cooperation.

In fact, from the recent upward movement of the East Asian economies, there are also the aforementioned two options. He's research reflects the fact that East Asian economies are still making preventive responses when faced with challenges.[67] There is an alternative relationship between regional growth in foreign exchange reserves and regional monetary cooperation. Therefore, after facing the global financial turmoil, individual East Asian countries are likely to adjust their policies according to their own economic characteristics. However, taking into account the cost of unilateral actions and the close economic relations within the region, further promoting regional cooperation in the field of currency and finance should become an inevitable policy choice. Just like this, the financial crisis inside and outside the region has a direct role in promoting cooperation. This reflects that the start-up and development of monetary cooperation in the region is driven to a large extent by common economic interests, not by common political will or common cultural background. The CMI system established to meet the regional monetary and financial crisis, prevent liquidity shortage and solve the payment dilemma is difficult to solve the new problems brought about by the "subprime crisis" and global financial turmoil in Asia. To a certain extent, Asian countries have faced new challenges after

[67]He, Liping, "Foreign Exchange Reserves of East Asian Economies and the International Financial Crisis," *Contemporary Asia-Pacific* 6 (2008): 11–18.

more than a decade of hard exploration of the CMI system that has just made progress. Or, the slow progress of regional monetary and financial cooperation in Asia cannot catch up with the pace of financial globalization and its effects.

Since the Asian financial crisis, the main objectives of the regional economies in East Asia in promoting regional monetary cooperation have been crisis relief and crisis prevention. Regional cooperation under the guidance of this pragmatic philosophy is an important reason for its own slow progress, and also leads to the weak consciousness of "Asian Consensus." Economic globalization should be based on common prosperity and stable development as the ultimate goal of cooperation. Obviously, the regional financial cooperation in East Asia has reached an important turning point. Under the circumstances where the political and economic patterns of contemporary "financial countries" and "trade countries" are increasingly clear, there are two aspects that need to be understood: First, the independent currency internationalization of any "trade country" is not feasible (this is a profound lesson of the "Yen internationalization"). Second, if there is no regional monetary and financial cooperation, the financial development or deepening of any "trade country" will be turbulent, or it will participate in the financial globalization. The cost will be greater than its revenue. Therefore, under the conditions of the new era, the "Asian consensus" or "community awareness" should not only be strengthened but also a more long-term goal should be established. It is necessary not only to explore the solution to the development difficulties of the new era but also to recognize historical trends and seek common prosperity. In this regard, the large countries in East Asia should shoulder their due responsibilities.

7.3 Path Choices and Prospects of China's Promotion of Monetary Cooperation in East Asia

Given the huge historical, cultural and political backgrounds and economic development gaps in East Asia, it is impossible to have the preconditions of OCA theory in the short term as a whole, and the regional monetary finance is only promoted with the CMI framework and the "ASEAN 10+3" mechanism. The deepening of cooperation is impractical; on the other hand, regional exchange rate coordination and cooperation have always been major difficulties in East Asian monetary and financial cooperation, but its necessity and its significance to regional monetary and financial cooperation are obvious. If breakthroughs or progress have not been made in this regard, there is no way to discuss the further development or further advancement of monetary and financial cooperation in East Asia.

So far, there are two problems in the existing research on the path choice of East Asian monetary and financial cooperation: First, trying to use the OC theory to verify the possibility and feasibility of monetary and financial cooperation across East Asia; Second, the discussion only focuses on monetary and financial cooperation on monetary and financial cooperation itself, and it lacks attention to the characteristics and development trends of real economic cooperation in regional industries and trade. The OCA theory has two important premises, namely the common cultural tradition and political will, the similar economic development structure and development level. In the foreseeable future, it is impossible for the East Asian region to have the prerequisites for OCA theory as a whole. Correspondingly, a higher-level issue of regional monetary and financial cooperation is the "anchor" in the region. This is not merely a matter of government's will, but rather the result of market search or selection. Therefore, how to form and what kind of regional end-product market are the key issues. One of the important reasons why the East Asian currency and financial cooperation can hardly enter the exchange rate cooperation stage is that it is difficult to form a market provider in the region that can partially or completely replace the final product of the United States. Therefore, each economy has to peg the currency to this external "residential anchor" of the US dollar in various ways.

Therefore, we should completely adjust or change the thinking of East Asian monetary and financial cooperation so far, and design or plan the future path of East Asian regional currency cooperation according to the following two principles: First, design must be based on a combination of overall coordination and local deepening. The second is to build regional exchange rate coordination and cooperation mechanisms as the main logic line.

7.3.1 *Overall Design of the Path of East Asian Monetary Cooperation*

Based on the characteristics of East Asian economic development at this stage and the progress of monetary cooperation, with regional exchange rate coordination and cooperation as the center, we divide the development path of regional currency cooperation into four phases: crisis relief and prevention, exchange rate policy coordination and cooperation, and the establishment of a common exchange rate linkage mechanism to achieve a single currency (see Figure 7.15).

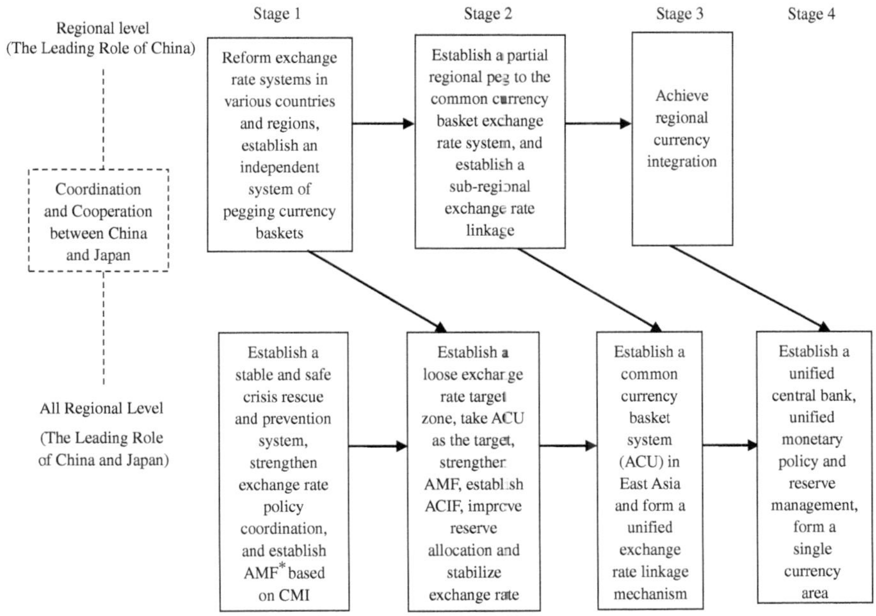

Figure 7.15. Overall Design of East Asian Monetary Cooperation Path

*The AMF has always existed in 1–3 stages, mainly undertaking the functions of monitoring economic indicators, coordinating policy measures, carrying out crisis relief, and providing and implementing restrictions on monetary cooperation.

7.3.1.1 *Crisis Assistance and Prevention*

The first phase of the East Asian monetary cooperation is mainly to establish a stable and safe crisis rescue and prevention system, and to strengthen exchange rate policy coordination and information exchange under the current exchange rate system of each economy and maintain the relative stability of bilateral exchange rates in the region.

At this stage, each economy continues to maintain its own exchange rate system, but measures should be gradually taken to weaken the actual peg of the local currency against the US dollar and expand the fluctuation range of the local currency against the US dollar so that the exchange rate of the local currency has certain independence and flexibility relative to the US dollar. Policy authorities of various economies should exert some intervention and guidance in actual operations to coordinate the level of bilateral exchange rates in the region. At the same time, CMIM should be used as the basis for the establishment of an institutionalized financial institution known as AMF, which will serve as a regional "quasi-lender of last resort," provide and manage regional emergency assistance funds, coordinate and manage crisis rescue operations, and establish early warning indicators. Early warning indicators, which supervise the macroeconomic trends and balance of payments of various countries and regions, coordinate the economic policies of various countries and regions to strengthen the discipline of policy coordination.

At a local level, each economy should establish an independent system of pegging currency baskets based on the specific characteristics of its own economic development. Given the pattern of foreign economic relations among East Asian economies, they need to maintain sufficient flexibility in the exchange rate of currencies outside the region. Therefore, at this stage, it is better to adopt a system of concealed pegging currency baskets that do not publish the central exchange rate, that is, the monetary authorities calculate the composition of the currency basket as a reference for the corresponding central exchange rate in the medium and long term and it will not be announced. The exchange rate of the center serves as a reference target to guide the medium and long-term trend of the exchange rate. However, in the short term, it is not necessary to stick to the aforementioned reference exchange rate and maintain certain exchange rate flexibility. At the same time, with the changes in economic fundamentals, it is allowed to gradually adjust the level of the central exchange rate.

7.3.1.2 *Coordination and Cooperation Exchange Rate System*

The second phase of the East Asian monetary and financial cooperation is mainly to establish a partial regional peg to the common currency basket exchange rate system based on independent pinning.

At the local level, some economies with similar economic development levels have the common requirement of stabilizing bilateral exchange rates, and they satisfy the conditions to adopt a system of pegging common currency baskets. Based on the similarity of the composition of the currency basket with the economic and trade structure, a common goal of currency baskets can be selected within the scope of a local region, the central exchange rate (open or closed) can be determined and the deviation of the value of each economy from the central exchange rate can be the degree of amplitude limit, which can establish a sub-regional exchange rate linkage mechanism. Considering that the economic size of the sub-region is relatively limited and that there will still be certain differences among various economies, larger extensive exchange rate volatility should be stipulated to prevent speculative attacks. The so-called basket-band-crawling (BBC) exchange rate system can be adopted, which can provide a certain degree of flexibility on the premise of ensuring the basic stability of the exchange rate.

At the regional level as a whole, sub-regional exchange rate cooperation should be used as an entry point, and regional exchange rate cooperation arrangements should be established gradually and hierarchically. In the sub-region, first of all, it should choose exchange rate cooperation with high degree of closeness in trade and investment linkages and economies that are greatly affected by the impact of exchange rate shocks, with a high degree of closeness but less impact from exchange rates. The level of contact is normal but it is again affected by the impact of the exchange rate.

Regarding the basic conception of East Asia exchange rate cooperation, Ogawa and Kawasaki (2001) believe that the current exchange rate system of East Asia pegging to the US dollar is a coordination failure because the countries that first turn to the currency basket may appear to maintain a single peg to the dollar exchange rate.[68] Because of the uncertainty in the trade relations between countries, all parties are reluctant to give up the dollar-pegged exchange rate system. Ohno also pointed out that if a country first adopts a currency exchange rate system that pegged a currency basket, and neighboring countries still pin their currencies to the US dollar, then the country that first adopts the exchange rate system that pegged the currency basket may experience the unstable balance of trade for some time.[69]

A preliminary East Asian Exchange Rate Mechanism (see Table 7.10) has been constructed in Liu and Xie.[70] Its main content includes the following three aspects: first, it is created on the basis of currency exchanges among the economies in the region. "East Asia Exchange Rate Cooperation Fund"; Second, the RMB cooperates with other currencies (excluding the yen temporarily) to implement a unified exchange rate system that is fixed on the currency basket; and third, it gradually forms the "10+3" model of the East Asian

[68]Ogawa, Eiji, and Junko Shimizu, "A Deviation Measurement for Coordinated Exchange Rate Policies in East Asia," *RIETI Discussion Paper Series*, no. 05-E-017 (March 2005).

[69]Ohno, Kenichi. "Exchange Rate Management in Developing Asia." Reassessment of the Pre-Crisis Soft Dollar Zone," *ADBI Working Paper* (1999): 35–40.

[70]Liu, Lizhen, and Chaoyang Xie, "East Asian Currency Cooperation and the Choice of RMB Exchange Rate System," *Management World* 3 (2003): 34–44.

Table 7.10. Exchange Rate Cooperation in East Asia

Currency Cooperation Process	East Asia Exchange Rate Cooperation	Participating Countries in East Asian Monetary Cooperation
The first stage	Establishing the East Asia Exchange Rate Cooperation Fund on the basis of currency swaps (providing financing services for exchange rate cooperation within the region and balance of payments deficits for member countries)	"10+3" (10 ASEAN plus China, Japan and South Korea)
The second stage	Establish a unified exchange rate cooperation mechanism for the peg to the currency basket (the currency basket includes the yen in the region and world currencies such as the US dollar and euro outside the region. Therefore, from the East Asian point of view, this is a basket of "mixed anchor" currency)	"10+2" (since it is difficult to build a currency basket within the region in the short term. The establishment of a joint exchange rate between the ASEAN 10 plus China and South Korea's peg to the hybrid currency basket is more realistic, more effective, more time efficient and lower in cost
The third stage	Create East Asia regional currency with China, Japan and Korea as the core?Asian Currency? Formation of a currency with the US dollar and the euro	"3+10" (China, Japan, South Korea, and 10 ASEAN countries, and further extended to Asia)

Source: Liu, Lizhen and Chaoyang Xie, The East Asian Monetary Cooperation and RMB Exchange Rate System Selection, *Management World* 3 (2003): 34–44.

currency alliance and finally launches. And ultimately the unified East Asian currency and even the “Asian dollar” are created in the region.

In general, East Asian monetary and financial cooperation cannot be separated from overall policy coordination in East Asia. While realizing monetary and financial cooperation, there is also a need for further cooperation in areas such as trade and investment resources and the formulation of rules. This overall policy coordination adjustment process is shown in Table 7.11.

In addition to direct exchange rate coordination, taking into consideration the specific conditions in East Asia, the Asian Cooperative Investment Fund (ACIF), which mainly invests in regional financial assets, should also be established with reference to the SWF model. Invest in sovereign or semi-sovereign bonds denominated in international currencies (such as US dollars) in the region. Compared with the CMIM and the “Forex Reserve Bank Plan,” ACIF can effectively achieve the goal of diversifying the risk of reserve assets in various countries, and allow more reserve assets to be deployed in the region. In particular, the combination of the cooperation of reserve resources and regional financial markets, especially bond market construction in East Asia can be achieved. For example, the use of ACIF to invest in international currency-denominated sovereign bonds and corporate bonds issued by countries in the region can increase the demand for bonds and facilitate the development of regional bond markets. On the other hand, it can ensure the liquidity of reserve assets and reduce the risk of asset reserves. In addition, another benefit of using ACIF to invest in financial assets such as local sovereign or semi-sovereign bonds is that when a member country has a payment crisis, it can directly obtain funds through the transfer of the aforementioned bonds, thereby avoiding the financing party’s risk of liquidation or exchange. On the other hand, ACIF can also be used as a preparation for the issuance of currency or currency basket-denominated assets in the issuing region. On the basis of the development of the international currency-denominated bond market in the region, issuing regional currency or currency

Table 7.11. East Asia Policy Coordination Steps

Steps of Policy Coordination	Policy of Foreign Exchange Rate	Financial System Coordination	Trade and Investment Coordination
Status Quo	Diverse and balanced coordination of foreign exchange rate system choice	CMI, ERPD, Asian Bond Market Conception	Coexistence Various FTA/EPA
Non-governmental sector foreign exchange rate coordination	Introduction of ACU with economic monitoring indicators, proficiency in foreign exchange rate system (SDR and even adoption of SDR+ basket currency system)	CMI Multilateralization, ASEAN 10+3 Finance Ministers and Central Bank Meetings, Independent Secretariat of CMIM and ERPD, Asian Financial Stability Council	Coordination and Adjustment between Various FTAs/EPAs (accumulation of principles of origin, etc.)
Slow foreign exchange rate coordination between government departments	Open SDR+ Basket Currency System and ACU System	The establishment of the AMF	East Asia's own trade agreements (ASEAN 10+3 and ASEAN 10+6)
Tight foreign exchange rate coordination	"Asian Serpentine System," "Asian ERM"	Ultra-short-term liquidity tools, regional financial supervision agencies	East Asian Customs Union
Complete foreign exchange rate coordination	East Asian currency alliance (single common currency)	East Asia Central Bank	East Asia Common Market

Source: He, Zhenghong, "International Monetary System and East Asian Monetary and Financial Cooperation," In *East Asian Monetary and Financial Cooperation in the Post-Crisis Era — Is the Coordination of RMB and Yen Possible?* edited by Li Xiao, 33–34. Changchun: Jilin University Press, 2010.

basket-denominated bonds can make better use of the large-scale reserves of East Asian economies and further promote the development of East Asian regional financial markets. European experience shows that only if the government provides guarantees for regional currency-denominated bonds, the private sector will be more likely to accept and issue similar bonds. ACIF can fully play the role of official issuance preparation and guarantee.

7.3.1.3 *Establish a Common Exchange Rate Linkage Mechanism*

The third stage of East Asian monetary and financial cooperation is mainly to establish a common currency basket system in East Asia and form a unified exchange rate linkage mechanism.

Although at present, there are no consensuses between the authorities on the ideal exchange rate system in East Asian countries, and all countries are making necessary adjustments to keep the stability of their exchange rates. In Kawai Masahiro,[71] it is believed that countries must first adopt a managed floating exchange rate system that refers to a basket of currencies. There are three types of currency baskets: the SDR consisting of the US dollar, the Japanese yen, the euro, and the British pound. The second is based on the SDR plus a basket of currencies of emerging Asian countries. The third is the ACU. In Yamashita (2010),[72] after the Asian financial crisis in 1998, had been advocating the establishment of an Asian regional monetary system through the following three steps: In the first phase, other Asian countries except Japan must establish a fixed exchange rate system anchored by a basket of currencies, including US dollar, Japanese yen and the euro as a basket currency;

[71]Kawai, Masahiro, "International Monetary System and East Asian Monetary and Financial Cooperation," See *The East Asian Monetary and Financial Cooperation in the Post-Crisis Era: The Coordination of RMB and Yen Is Possible?* Jilin: Jilin University Press, 2010, 34.

[72]Yamashita, Eisuke, "The Necessity of Establishing an Asian Edition of EMS and the Joint Leadership Mechanism between Japan and China," In *The East Asian Monetary and Financial Cooperation in the Post-Crisis Era: The Coordination of RMB and Yen Is Possible?* Jilin: Jilin University Press, 2010, 235–256.

the second phase is the establishment of East Asia common fixed exchange rate system, which is to create Asian version of ERM; in the third phase, China and Japan jointly establish ACU in financial cooperation.

At the local level, after the establishment of a system of pegging common currency baskets in various local regions, the establishment of a fixed exchange rate system in each local region is gradually established, and monetary integration within the sub-region is promoted, because the pegging currency basket system has unstable characteristics. Therefore, from a long-term point of view, if we must maintain the stability of the exchange rate and ensure the sustainability of the exchange rate system, we must replace the system of pegging the common currency basket with a relatively rigid fixed exchange rate system to achieve regional currency integration. According to the OCA theory, the smaller the scope or size of currency areas, the stronger the consistency of their economic development and the lower the cost of monetary integration, so the OCA is the most likely to form. Therefore, in the process of establishing a regional currency system in East Asia, local monetary integration attempts can be made on the basis of the sub-region's pegging of common currency baskets.

At the same time, at the regional level, a common currency basket system should be established in East Asia to form a unified exchange rate linkage mechanism and push the ACU concept into practical operation and application phases. The central exchange rate for the currency basket is determined, but the original pegging target for each local area continues to be maintained. In the sub-regional scope, the currencies of various economies maintain a relatively rigid fixed exchange rate. Then according to the relationship between the original pinning targets of each local area and the ACU, the fluctuation range of each local area pegged to ACU is determined, that is, ACU construct "snake hole" with different spread. On this basis, using the "self-pushing effect" of monetary integration, the "snake hole" in each local area gradually converges, and a unified exchange rate mechanism is formed in East Asia (similar to the European exchange rate mechanism of the 1980s — EMS).

7.3.1.4 *Implementing a Single Currency*

The fourth stage of East Asian monetary and financial cooperation is to realize a single currency and establish a unified central bank. This is the highest level of East Asian monetary and financial cooperation. There is no doubt that the realization of this goal will go through a long process. In terms of its realization path, it is possible to first establish a common currency between the defined economies that meet the conditions of the optimal currency zone, and then gradually add other East Asian economies that meet the conditions, and finally realize the unified currency in the East Asia region.

Zhao summarized the basic theories of regional monetary cooperation and believed that the Asian region only meets the basic conditions for constructing an OCA in certain aspects, but still lacks the conditions for monetary cooperation in some important aspects.[73] Therefore, Asia does not yet have the conditions to establish a monetary cooperation mechanism with a real sense, institutional guarantee and exchange rate target zone. The more realistic choice is for small open economies to choose the optimal partner based on their own differences, and then gradually promote sub-regional monetary cooperation. Yamashita Eisuke[74] considers that as an integration currency, the ACU, like ECUs and SDRs, would like to become an international currency and play an important role in the world, but that is impossible, though it can serve as a pricing currency when countries in the region issue bonds. That is, it can contribute to the issue of bonds from the region's foreign currency to regional currency transfer, and can promote the construction of ABMI. Nusair used the Generalized Purchasing Power Parity (G-PPP) proposed by Enders

[73]Zhao, Chunming, and Xiaoying Li, "Analysis of East-Asian Currency Cooperation and RMB Core Currency Status," *Contemporary Asia-Pacific* 2 (2007): 29–35.

[74]Yamashita, Eisuke, "The Necessity of Establishing an Asian Edition of EMS and the Joint Leadership Mechanism between Japan and China," In *The East Asian Monetary and Financial Cooperation in the Post-Crisis Era: The Coordination of RMB and Yen Is Possible?* Jilin: Jilin University Press, 2010, 235–256.

and Hurn to study the five countries of ASEAN (Indonesia, Malaysia, the Philippines, Singapore and Thailand) and the three countries of China, Japan and South Korea forming (OCA) possibility of the OCA.[75]

Some scholars have already made some studies on whether East Asia has the potential to become the OCA and have obtained some similar conclusions. Ogawa and Kawasaki used the G-PPP model to empirically analyze the possibility of the East Asian OCA (see Table 7.12).[76]

Other scholars have also conducted research on Asian sub-regional monetary cooperation issues. The results of their research are shown in Table 7.13.

In Ogawa, the corresponding proportion of East Asian currencies in the AMU is calculated (Tables 7.14 and 7.15).[77]

Since the relative balance of payments of the currency area is higher than that of a single country, the larger imbalance (surplus or deficit) of the currency area outside the area can be compensated by only a small exchange rate adjustment. The analysis of the foreign exchange reserves of each country establishes the basis of the currency area and calculates the foreign exchange reserves of the area as a whole. It is easier to establish a currency area if the foreign exchange reserves that are aggregated by various economies are large (see Table 7.16 for the foreign exchange reserves of each East Asian economy in 2013). The establishment of a reserve pool can reduce the amount of foreign exchange reserves that countries must hold because it can reduce the foreign exchange reserves that each member country must hold to pay for contingent liabilities. Research

[75]Nusair, Salah A, "Is East Asia an Optimum Currency Area? A Test of Generalized Purchasing Power Parity in the Presence of Structural Breaks," *Journal of the Asia Pacific Economy* 17, no. 3 (2012): 399–425.

[76]Enders, Walter, and S. Hum. "Theory and Tests of Generalized Purchasing-Power Parity: Common Trends and Real Exchange Rates In the Pacific Rim." *Review of International Economics* 2, no. 2 (1994): 179–190.

[77]

Table 7.12. Empirical Analysis of Ogawa and Kawasaki on East Asian Common Currency Area

Number of Countries in Currency Area	Currency Basket	USD
6	South Korea + Singapore + Indonesia + Malaysia + (Philippines) + Thailand	
5	South Korea + Singapore + Indonesia + Philippines + Thailand	South Korea + Singapore + Indonesia + Malaysia + (Thailand)
4	Indonesia + Singapore + (Philippines) + Thailand	(Korea) + Indonesia + Malaysia + Philippines (Korea) + Indonesia + Malaysia + Philippines + (Thailand) Indonesia + Malaysia + Philippines + (Thailand)
3	Indonesia + (Malaysia) + Philippines	(Indonesia) + Malaysia + Philippines Malaysia + Philippines + (Thailand)

Notes: The country in the brackets of the series is a weak exogenous sequence in the co-integration relationship.

Sources: Eiji, Ogawa, Takatoshi Ito and Yuri Naga, "The Costs, Gains, and Constraints of the East Asian Currency Basket System," In *Development Prospects of East Asian Monetary and Financial Integration*, 321. Beijing: Economic Science Press, 2005; Quoted from Xiao, Li and Yibing Ding *et al. East Asian Regional Monetary Cooperation and RMB Exchange Rate System Reform*. Beijing: Economic Science Press, 2010, 1st edn., 41.

of Kojima shows that this reduction can reach 41%, and the study result of Cooper[78] indicates 44%.[79]

[78]Cooper, Richard N., "Financial Aspects of Economic Cooperation around the Pacific," Pacific Trade and Development I: Papers and Proceedings of a Conference Held by the Japan Economic Research Center in January, 1968.

[79]Kojima, Kiyoshi, "A Pacific Currency Area: A New Approach to International Monetary Reform," *Hitotsubashi Journal of Economics* 10, no. 2 (February 1970): 1–17.

Table 7.13. Candidates for Asian Sub-regional Currency Cooperation

Researcher	Candidate List for Sub-regional Cooperation
Bayoumi and Eichengreen (1994)	Hong Kong (China), Indonesia, Malaysia, Singapore and Thailand
	Japan, Korea, and Taiwan (China)
Bayoumi and Mauro (1999)	Hong Kong (China), Indonesia, Malaysia and Singapore
	Hong Kong (China), Singapore, Indonesia, Malaysia
Yuen (2000)	Singapore and Malaysia
	Japan and Korea
	Taiwan (China) and Hong Kong (China)
Trivisvavet (2001)	Thailand, Singapore, Malaysia, Indonesia, Philippines and South Korea
Baek and Song (2002)	Japan, Korea, Hong Kong (China), Indonesia, Malaysia and Thailand
Zhang *et al.* (2003)	Singapore, Malaysia, Indonesia and Thailand
	Japan, South Korea, Hong Kong (China), Taiwan (China)
	China, Japan, Korea and ASEAN
	China, Japan and South Korea

Sources: Gao, Haihong, "Optimal Currency Area: Empirical Study of East Asian Countries," *World Economy* 6 (2007): 3–12.

Quah studies the performance in the OCA conditions of 10 East Asian Economies from 10 aspects,[80] and compares the results with the performance of these 10 aspects of the Eurozone. The main conclusions of this document are shown in Table 7.17. In the calculation of the first five indicators, the East Asian economies use the United States, Japan and China as the reference countries, and the Eurozone uses Germany as the reference country. Judging from the top five conclusions, the United States has more potential than Japan to become

[80]East Asian economies include Japan, South Korea, China, Taiwan (China), Hong Kong (China), Philippines, Thailand, Malaysia, Singapore and Indonesia. Quah C. H., "Is East Asia as Prepared as Eurozone for Monetary Union?" *Journal of Business Economics and Management* 13, no. 3 (2012): 471–488.

Table 7.14. Composition of Broad ACUs and Asian Currency Weights (Based year: 1999/2000)

	Trade Volume %	GDP–PPP %	Arithmetic Mean % (a)	Benchmark Exchange Rat % (b)	AMU Weights (a)/(b)
Australia	6.29	3.98	5.13	0.615285	0.0835
Brunei	0.30	0.11	0.20	0.587476	0.0035
Cambodia	0.13	0.13	0.13	0.000264	4.9517
China	23.40	35.70	29.55	0.121326	2.4355
India	3.35	16.01	9.68	0.022829	4.2399
Indonesia	4.71	4.45	4.58	0.000125	367.3403
Japan	20.79	23.63	22.21	0.009100	24.4015
Korea	11.56	6.44	9.00	0.000868	103.7352
Laos	0.09	0.07	0.08	0.000158	4.9820
Malaysia	6.67	1.91	4.29	0.264305	0.1622
Myanmar	0.30	0.23	0.27	0.161891	0.0165
New Zealand	1.05	0.63	0.84	0.494035	0.0170
Philippines	2.03	1.58	1.81	0.024204	0.7462
Singapore	11.43	1.19	6.31	0.587478	0.1074
Thailand	5.82	2.79	4.31	0.025777	1.6703
Vietnam	2.10	1.15	1.63	0.00071	227.4460

Sources: Ogawa, E., "Regional Monetary Coordination in Asia after the Global Financial Crisis: Comparison in Regional Monetary Stability between ASEAN 10+3 and ASEAN 10+3+3," *Public Policy Review* 6, no. 5 (2010): 837–858.

the monetary policy anchor of East Asian currencies, and Japan is stronger than China. The conclusions of the last five items show that the East Asian economies' preparations for a fixed exchange rate system or monetary cooperation have been very close to those of the EMU sponsoring countries at the time. Looking at the performance of all the indicators, the East Asian economies have already made economic preparations for monetary integration, especially in choosing the dollar as the anchor currency.

7.3.2 *The Leading Role of China and Japan in East Asian Monetary Cooperation*

Since the 1990s, a series of new changes have taken place in the economic and political landscape of East Asia. One of the important

Table 7.15. ACU Composition and East Asian Currency Weights Based on 2000/2001

	Trade Volume %	GDP PPP %	Arithmetic Mean % (a)	Benchmark Exchange Rate % (b)	AMU Weights (a)/(b)
Brunei	0.33	0.14	0.23	0.589114	0.0039
Cambodia	0.15	0.17	0.16	0.000270	5.8668
China	26.08	44.97	35.52	0.125109	2.8395
Indonesia	5.27	5.61	5.40	0.000113	477.8761
Japan	23.12	29.76	26.44	0.009065	29.1705
Korea	13.01	8.12	10.56	0.000859	122.9905
Laos	0.11	0.08	0.10	0.000136	7.0288
Malaysia	7.51	2.40	4.95	0.272534	0.1818
Myanmar	0.33	0.30	0.31	0.159215	0.0198
Philippines	2.37	1.99	2.18	0.021903	0.9964
Singapore	12.80	1.50	7.15	0.589160	0.1213
Thailand	6.59	3.51	5.05	0.024543	2.0580
Vietnam	2.33	1.45	1.89	0.000072	262.4862

Source: Ogawa, E., "Regional Monetary Coordination in Asia after the Global Financial Crisis: Comparison in Regional Monetary Stability between ASEAN 10+3 and ASEAN 10−3+3," *Public Policy Review* 6, no. 5 (2010): 837–858.

reasons for this change is the reversed change of economic status of China and Japan in the region. While Japan's economic growth has been sluggish and stagnating, China's economy has grown by leaps and bounds, and it has increasingly become the main force of economic growth of East Asia and the world. The absolute and relative changes in the economy of the two countries will inevitably have a significant impact on the status and role of the two countries in the process of East Asian monetary and financial cooperation, as well as the path and mode of cooperation, and thus affect the future prospects of East Asian monetary and financial cooperation. In view of this, this issue objectively evaluates the roles of the two countries in East Asian monetary and financial cooperation from the perspectives of the changes in the trade status of China and Japan in East Asia and the degree of integration with other economies.

Table 7.16. Foreign Exchange Reserves of East Asian Economies in 2013 Unit: Millions of SDRs

Country	Gold	IMF Position	SDR Holdings	Forex	Total International Reserves
Mainland China	33.9	4584	7255	2481373	2494399
Japan	24.6	9197	13071	781119	804249
Korea	3.4	1631	2266	217953	221968
Brunei	0.2	14	216	1976	2212
Cambodia	0.4	0	68	2864	2946
Hong Kong, China	0.1	44	—	201987	202034
Indonesia	2.5	145	1762	60666	62661
Laos	0.3	0	51	417.7	469
Malaysia	1.2	631	1286	84735	86693
Myanmar	—	0	1.13	—	—
Philippines	6.2	386	846	47916	49366
Singapore	4.1	672	873	175639	177184
Macao, China	—	—	—	10484	10484
Thailand	4.9	523	974	103261	104930
Vietnam	—	0.005	268	16545	16813

Source: IMF, International Financial Statistics Database.

At present, according to the development of East Asian currency cooperation and the policy choices of the major economies in the region, it is possible that some regions will use RMB regionalization as the core to promote cooperation. On the whole, China and Japan will jointly play a greater role. It is quite certain that since the political differences and economic disparities within the ASEAN countries are relatively large and their overall economic strength is not strong, the "10+3" mechanism that has previously played a role in promoting cooperation has more political significance and will promote the monetary cooperation of East Asian in the future. The role of in-depth development is limited. Whether or not East Asian currency cooperation can achieve deeper development in the future will depend, to a large extent, on the respective regional cooperation strategies adopted by China, Japan and South Korea, especially China and Japan, and whether they can develop corresponding cooperation.

Table 7.17. Main Conclusions of Quah (2012)

	Perspective	Findings
1	Bilateral trade intensity	Other East Asian economies have higher trade links with the United States and Japan and have higher homogeneity, but the overall level is lower than that of the Eurozone countries; Japan has very close trade links with the United States.
2	Business cycle synchronization	The synchronicity of the economic cycles of other East Asian economies with the United States and Japan is relatively high. This is similar to the situation in the Eurozone countries. The economic cycle between Japan and the United States is highly consistent.
3	Inflation convergence	Compared with China and Japan, other East Asian economies have the highest degree of convergence with US inflation, and their direction of change has greater homogeneity, but they are still lower than the convergence and homogeneity of inflation in the euro area countries.
4	Real exchange rate volatility	The real exchange rate volatility between the other East Asian economies against the US dollar and the yuan is low, but it is still higher than the real exchange rate volatility of the Eurozone.
5	Real interest rate symmetry	The consistency between the actual interest rate in other East Asian economies and the actual interest rate in the United States is higher than the consistency of the actual interest rates of these economies with Japan, and is higher than the consistency of these countries' real interest rates with China and the actual interest rates and German real interest rates in other countries in the Eurozone consistency.
6	Trade openness	East Asia's openness in trade in goods and services is comparable to that of the Eurozone.
7	Export commodity diversity	The diversity of East Asian exports is significantly lower than that of the Eurozone.
8	Labor market flexibility	East Asian labor market is more flexible than the Eurozone.
9	Financial restrictions	The budget deficit of the East Asian economies is slightly higher than that of the Eurozone, but the debt level of the East Asian economies is lower than that of the Eurozone.
10	Adequacy of foreign exchange reserves	Except for Japan, the level of foreign exchange reserves of other East Asian economies is higher than that of the Eurozone.

Source: Quah C. H., "Is East Asia as Prepared as Eurozone for Monetary Union?" *Journal of Business Economics and Management* 13, no. 3 (2012): 471–488.

Many scholars have studied the role and status of China and Japan (RMB and yen) in the regional currency cooperation in East Asia. From the perspective of currency competition, Chen examined the issue of currency cooperation in East Asia.[81] We believe that in the process of East Asian currency cooperation, it also involves competition among multiple currencies. However, due to the relatively small economies of the 10 ASEAN countries and South Korea, the competition between RMB and yen is particularly important.

In Li, a measure of the currency's internationalization was constructed to measure the degree of internationalization of the RMB, the US dollar, the euro and the yen.[82] The indicator consists of three parts: a country's currency external circulation scope index, the overseas circulation quantitative index and the proportion of the currency's share of the international official currency reserves. $I = \lambda_1 I_1 + \lambda_2 I_2 + \lambda_3 I_3$, among them I_1, I_2, I_3 represent the aforementioned three indices respectively; λ_1, λ_2, λ_3 are the coefficient; since it is difficult to determine the influence of three factors on the international degree of currency, the three coefficients all take a value of 1. The calculation results of this document show that the international degree of the RMB is 0.19, while the international degree of the yen is 1.17, and the international degrees of the dollar and the euro are 10.25 and 2.27, respectively. The results show that the degree of internationalization of the yen was higher than the degree of internationalization of the RMB before 2003. However, after more than a decade of development, China has surpassed Japan as the world's second largest economy. We expect that, as China's economic and trade exchanges with other countries, especially its neighboring countries, become more frequent, the scope of RMB's overseas circulation and there has been a substantial increase its volume of use in the international trade. In the past decade, the Japanese economy has not seen

[81] Chen, Yulu, and Weihong Bian, "Monetary Union Theory: Progress in the Measurement of Optimal Currency Areas," *International Finance Research* 2 (2004): 35–45.

[82] Li, Yao, "Non-international Currency, Currency Internationalization and Capital Account Convertibility," *Financial Research* 8 (2003): 104–111.

significant improvement. It has continued the situation of the "lost decade" at the end of the 20th century, that is, the degree of internationalization of the yen will not be greatly improved. However, in view of the current situation, the degree of internationalization of the yen is still higher than the RMB.

7.3.2.1 *The Role of RMB in East Asian Monetary Cooperation*

In the second quarter of 2010, China surpassed Japan to become the second largest economy in the world. According to the official data of China and Japan, in the second quarter of 2010, China's GDP was US$1.33 trillion, while Japan's GDP was US$1.28 trillion during the same period. Although the new Chinese leader has lowered his GDP growth forecast, China's GDP will maintain a relatively rapid growth rate in the coming years.

If the RMB is to become a regional key currency, it must have a stable and predictable exchange rate policy and establish the confidence of neighboring countries and regions in stabilizing the RMB. From a statistical view, the US dollar, instead of RMB, is the real "anchor" currency of other East Asian currencies. The potential "anchor" currency function of RMB can only be realized by maintaining a certain stable relationship with the US dollar.[83]

The results of the research of Song show that limited monetary cooperation arrangements cannot significantly increase the influence of RMB in regional currencies.[84] Therefore, for the Chinese government, it is necessary to further increase regional monetary and financial arrangements that are in line with the reality of East Asia and steadily and orderly promote the regionalization of RMB. The long-term impact of the RMB on the Hong Kong dollar, the Singapore

---

[83]Xiao, Li, and Yibing Ding, "Trend of RMB Exchange Rate Change and its Impact on Regional Currency Cooperation," *International Finance Research* 3 (2009): 8–15.

[84]Song, Yanan, "Research on the Influence of RMB Regionalization-An Analysis Based on Dynamic Distribution Lag Model," *International Trade Issues* 9 (2012): 169–176.

dollar and the Korean won indicates that strengthening the economic and trade exchanges with the East Asia region is of great significance for increasing the regionalization and even the internationalization of RMB.

Many scholars have studied the impact of the RMB on East Asian currencies and believe that the influence of the RMB in the East Asian region is gradually increasing. Therefore, the RMB should embody more of the functions of regional currencies. The influence of the RMB on other East Asian currencies has always been more controversial among policymakers and theorists. However, until recently, some documents have demonstrated the impact of the RMB on other East Asian countries from an empirical perspective.[85] Colavecchio and Funke studied the spillover effects of the RMB on other currencies in the onshore and offshore forward and future forward markets.[86] The study Ho and McCauley found that during the speculative appreciation of the RMB during 2003–2004, the RMB non-deliverable forward rates put pressure on the spot rates of other Asian currencies.[87] Using the research framework of Frankel and Wei, Shu[88] found that the exchange rate fluctuations of the RMB have become more independent of the fluctuation trend of the US dollar, since the RMB exchange rate reform in July 2005, but the exchange rate fluctuations of

[85] Pontines, Victor, and Reza Y. Siregar, "Fear of Appreciation in East and Southeast Asia: The Role of the Chinese Renminbi," *Journal of Asian Economics* 23, no. 4 (August 2012): 324–334.

[86] Colavecchio, Roberta, and Michael Funke, "Volatility Dependence across Asia-Pacific On-Shore and Off-Shore US Dollar Futures Markets," BOFIT Discussion Paper, no. 17/2007 (August 2007).

[87] Ho, Corrinne, Guonan Ma, and Robert N. McCauley, "Trading Asian Currencies," *BIS Quarterly Review* (March 2005): 49.

[88] Shu, Chang, "Impact of the Renminbi Exchange Rate on Asian Currencies," In Currency Internationalization: Global Experiences and Implications for the Renminbi, edited by Wensheng Peng, and Chang Shu, 221–235. London: Palgrave Macmillan, 2010.

other East Asian currencies have maintained the same direction as RMB.[89]

In Fratzscher and Mehl, the impact of RMB exchange rate changes on exchange rate fluctuations in emerging Asian economies was studied.[90] The results show that since the RMB exchange reform in 2005, especially after the financial crisis, the RMB has become the main driver of exchange rate fluctuations in emerging Asian economies. In the current international currency system, the dollar, the euro and RMB have formed a three-legged momentum. Although the dollar is still an international currency, the position and role of the euro and the RMB as regional currencies will become stronger.

Pontines and Siregar showed the research results on the important role of the RMB in the formation of the East Asian currency exchange rate.[91] Their research found that some East Asian currencies are more averse to the relative appreciation of the RMB relative to the US dollar, especially the Philippine peso and the Thai baht. This phenomenon shows that there is trade competition in the region, and the fear of RMB appreciation plays an important role in the exchange rate management of major East Asian currencies. China's rising trade position in East Asia and the world means that the RMB will play an increasingly important role in other East Asian currencies. They also studied the tendency of East Asian economies to fear the appreciation of their currencies and the role of the RMB in them, confirming that China's exchange rate policy

[89]Frankel, Jeffrey A., and Shang-Jin Wei, "Yen Bloc or Dollar Bloc? Exchange Rate Policies of the East Asian Economies," In Macroeconomic Linkage: Savings, Exchange Rates, and Capital Flows, edited by Takatoshi Ito and Anne O. Krueger, 295–333. Chicago: University of Chicago Press, 1994.

[90]Fratzscher, Marcel, and Arnaud Mehl, "China's Dominance Hypothesis and the Emergence of a Tri-polar Global Currency System," *ECB Working Paper Series*, no. 1392 (October 2011).

[91]Pontines, Victor, and Reza Y. Siregar, "Fear of Appreciation in East and Southeast Asia: The Role of the Chinese Renminbi," *Journal of Asian Economics* 23, no. 4 (August 2012): 324–334.

Table 7.18. Bilateral Coefficients of RMB and other East Asian Currencies

	5 January 1999–20 July 20 2005	21 July 2005–2 April 2007
Indonesian rupee	−0.436	0.625
Korean won	−0.040	0.764
Malaysia ringgit	−0.186	0.927
Philippine peso	−0.730	0.890
Singapore dollar	−0.083	0.893
Thai baht	−0.391	0.955

Source: Shu, C., N., Chow *et al.*, "Impact of the RMB exchange rate on the Chinese of Asian countries," *China Economic Issues* 3, 2007: 45–52.

is the main factor affecting the "appreciation phobia" of East Asian economies.

The study of Branson and Healy found that China's export structure is similar to the export structure of certain countries and regions in East Asia in terms of target markets and product types.[92] Therefore, East Asian countries and regions have the incentive to maintain the stability of the relative exchange rate between local currency and RMB to avoid the competition with China's export market, it suffered losses. The study of Shu *et al.* found that the importance of RMB in the currency basket of East Asian economies is continuously increasing.[93] This is mainly due to the fact that there is a greater competitive relationship between China and other East Asian economies in the global export market. In addition, the document also roughly calculated the bilateral relationship between RMB and other East Asian currencies (see Table 7.18).

[92]Branson, William H., and Conor N. Healy, "Monetary and Exchange Rate Policy Coordination in ASEAN," *National Bureau of Economic Research Working Paper*, no. w11713 (October, 2005).

[93]Shu, Chang, "Impact of the Renminbi Exchange Rate on Asian Currencies," In Currency Internationalization: Global Experiences and Implications for the Renminbi, edited by Wensheng Peng, and Chang Shu, 221–235. London: Palgrave Macmillan, 2010.

7.3.2.2 *The Role of Japanese Yen in East Asian Monetary Cooperation*

Japan's growing economic strength has prompted the issue of the internationalization of yen. Since the 1990s, many documents have studied the role of the yen in East Asia. According to an examination of exchange rate fluctuations in East Asian economies in Frankel and Wei, the East Asian economies are, to a greater extent, a dollar area than a yen area.[94] They examined the relative value changes of the nine East Asian currencies including the Korean won, Singapore dollar, Hong Kong dollar, New Taiwan dollar, Malaysian ringgit, Indonesian rupiah, Philippine peso, Thai baht and RMB, and found that the US dollar is still the anchor currency in East Asia, while the yen has played a role in the external value of some countries' currencies, it is far from replacing the dollar as the anchor currency of East Asia.

Reisen and van Trotsenburg explore the advantages and disadvantages of four Asian tigers' exchange rate pegging against the Japanese yen.[95] Park and Park studied the problems caused by the swinging of the exchange rate policies of these four economies around the yen/dollar.[96] Kwan discusses that the economies of four Asian tigers that compete with Japan for the third country's markets are best to keep their eyes on the yen, while ASEAN countries do not have to look at the yen because they import industrial goods from Japan and export to Japan of primary commodities.[97] Kwan further pointed out that there are inherent flaws in the exchange rate system of East

[94]Frankel, Jeffrey A., and Shang-Jin Wei, "Yen Bloc or Dollar Bloc? Exchange Rate Policies of the East Asian Economies," In *Macroeconomic Linkage: Savings, Exchange Rates, and Capital Flows*, edited by Takatoshi Ito and Anne O. Krueger, 295–333. Chicago: University of Chicago Press, 1994.

[95]Reisen, Helmut, and Axel Van Trotsenburg, "Should the Asian NICs Peg to the Yen?" *Intereconomics* 23, no. 4 (July 1988): 172–177.

[96]Haesik Park, ChiYoung Park. "Understanding the synchronisation of the movements of Korean won and Japanese yen from an FX Market Micro-structural Approach (in Korean)." *Economic Analysis* (1991).

[97]https://www.researchgate.net/publication/5033841_An_optimal_peg_for_the_Asian_currencies_and_an_Asian_perspective_of_a_yen_bloc.

Asian countries pegging to the US dollar.[98] Switching to a basket of currency exchange rate systems and increasing the proportion of the yen in the currency basket will help overcome this shortcoming and effectively avoid the dollarization in East Asia.

7.3.2.3 *Changes in the Status of China and Japan in the East Asian Regional Trade and Their Impact*

In the process of rapid development of trade in the East Asia region, the development of intraregional trade between China and Japan has different trends. At present, China is already the largest import and export economy in East Asian intraregional trade. China provides 30% of the export market for the East Asian region and occupies 1/4 of the export market share; while Japan provides less than 1/7 of the export market for the East Asia region and occupies less than one-fifth of the market.

First, China's scale in intraregional trade in East Asia has clearly surpassed that of Japan. In 1992, the scale of China and Japanese in the intraregional trade in East Asia was US$103.4 billion and US$182.3 billion, and China was 56.7% of Japan. By 2008, the scale of intraregional trade of China and Japan was US$1085.6 billion and US$654.8 billion respectively, China is already 1.66 times that of Japan.

Since 2000, China's intraregional trade has grown significantly faster than Japan, as shown in Figure 7.1. Before 1998, China's intraregional trade scale was far less than that of Japan. After 2002, China's scale in intraregional trade in East Asia began to catch up with Japan, and since 2002, China's intra-East Asian trade has grown even more rapidly. It can be analyzed by the changes in the proportion of the two countries' trade in the region, the growth rate of intraregional trade and the scale of trade with other economies in the region.

[98]Kwan, C.H. "Sayonara Dollar Peg: Asia in Search of a New Exchange Rate Regime." *Journal of Political Economy* 66 (2000).

Second, the proportion of China and Japan in the intraregional trade in East Asia has basically changed in the opposite direction. China's share of imports and exports in the region has increased significantly, while Japan's share has shown a significant decline. From 1992 to 2008, the proportion of China's import trade in the region rose from 15.72% to 30.0%, and the proportion of export trade in the region rose from 14.90% to 25.02%. The proportion of Japan's import trade in the region fell from 17.79% to 13.78%, and the proportion of export trade in the region dropped from 29.55% to 18.23%. China's share of imports in the region rose by 14.28 percentage points, while Japan's share fell by 4.01 percentage points. China's share in the region's export trade increased by 10.12 percentage points, while Japan's dropped by 11.12 percentage points. China has surpassed Japan by 6.79 percentage points. At the same time, the proportion of Taiwan (China), Hong Kong (China) and Singapore in the import trade in the region has dropped significantly, while the proportion of import and export trade in other economies has not changed significantly.

In terms of intraregional trade growth, China is higher than Japan. As shown in Table 7.19, the growth rate of China's intraregional export trade is higher than that of Japan from 2002. In addition to 2007 and 2008, China's intraregional export trade also has a higher growth rate than Japan's. In terms of the average growth rate of import and export trade in the region in 2002–2008, China was 1.86 times and 1.76 times that of Japan, respectively. From this we can conclude that China's scale advantage in intraregional trade in East Asia is obvious both in terms of scale and development trends.

Third, the scale of trade between China and Japan and other economies in the region has changed.

In terms of import trade in the region, Hong Kong (China), Taiwan (China), South Korea and Singapore are the main sources of the gap between China and Japan in the proportion of import trade in the region. In 2000, China's imports from South Korea and Singapore lagged behind Japan, but it was far more than Japan's import by 2008. While imports from Malaysia, Indonesia,

Table 7.19. Growth Rates of China and Japan in Import and Export Trade in East Asia 2001–2008 (%)

	2001	2002	2003	2004	2005	2006	2007	2008	02-08 Average
Exports (China)	−0.32	0.20	0.28	0.32	0.22	0.21	0.19	0.13	0.22
Imports (China)	−0.21	0.29	0.39	0.31	0.15	0.16	0.17	0.08	0.22
Exports (Japan)	−0.12	0.11	0.22	0.25	0.04	0.07	0.03	0.11	0.12
Imports (Japan)	−0.12	−0.01	0.16	0.20	0.10	0.10	0.20	0.13	0.13

Source: Calculated from data provided by ADB and UN Comtrade Database.

the Philippines and Thailand, Japan has always been higher than China, but this gap is continuously narrowing.

In terms of export trade within the region, the export of China and Japan to China's Hong Kong SAR is the reason for their disparity in the proportion of export trade in East Asia. For exports to Taiwan (China), the Philippines and Thailand, Japan is still larger than China, but the gap is continuously narrowing. In 2000, China's exports to South Korea, Singapore, Malaysia and Indonesia lag behind Japan's, and they have surpassed Japan by 2008.

It should be pointed out that as shown in Table 7.20, China surpasses Japan in the overall scale of regional trade, and Hong Kong (China) and Taiwan (China) play an important role. Excluding Hong Kong (China), Japan's export trade in the region will also slightly exceed China's, from Japan's 1.37 times that of China to Japan's 1.05 times that of China; if not including Hong Kong (China) and Taiwan (China), Japan's import trade in the region and China's, the gap is not so great. The import trade from China's region fell from 2.18 times that of Japan to 1.34 times. Therefore, considering the comprehensive trade scales of China and Japan with other economies in the region, China's influence in the regional trade in East Asia did not exceed that of Japan. For some ASEAN countries (such as the

Table 7.20. Flow Structure of Regional Trade in East Asia in 1992–2008 (%)

		Exporter										
Importer	Year	China	Japan	Korea	Singapore	Hong Kong, China	Taiwan, China	Malaysia	Indonesia	Philippines	Thailand	East Asia (10)
China	1992		3.14	0.70	0.29	9.34	1.55	0.20	0.37	0.03	0.10	15.72
	2000		3.86	2.34	0.68	8.87	3.24	0.38	0.35	0.08	0.36	20.16
	2008		6.22	5.59	1.55	8.90	5.15	0.94	0.58	0.27	0.80	30.00
Japan	1992	3.08		3.06	1.27	1.65	2.49	1.44	2.84	0.46	1.50	17.79
	2000	5.29		2.60	1.32	1.42	2.27	1.63	1.83	0.71	1.28	18.36
	2008	5.79		1.47	0.83	0.78	1.09	1.07	1.38	0.38	0.99	13.78
Korea	1992	0.63	4.69		0.38	0.51	0.35	0.37	0.55	0.05	0.14	7.66
	2000	1.43	3.90		0.62	0.47	0.60	0.42	0.55	0.15	0.16	8.30
	2008	3.68	2.96		0.61	0.35	0.50	0.39	0.45	0.13	0.18	9.26
Singapore	1992	0.54	3.42	0.85		0.83	0.82	2.47	0.87	0.07	0.74	10.60
	2000	0.73	2.64	0.72		0.60	0.76	2.29	0.83	0.40	0.76	9.73
	2008	1.61	1.33	0.90		0.36	0.86	1.46	0.64	0.13	0.50	7.78
Hong Kong, China	1992	9.89	5.46	1.56	1.31		2.96	0.41	0.23	0.12	0.40	22.34
	2000	5.65	3.45	1.36	1.38		2.02	0.56	0.20	0.24	0.44	15.31
	2008	9.50	2.01	0.78	1.75		1.23	0.42	0.09	0.25	0.50	16.53

(Continued)

Table 7.20. (*Continued*)

		Exporter										
Importer	Year	China	Japan	Korea	Singapore	Hong Kong, China	Taiwan, China	Malaysia	Indonesia	Philippines	Thailand	East Asia (10)
Taiwan, China	1992	0.18	5.57	0.60	0.82	1.12		0.33	0.34	0.08	0.16	9.20
	2000	0.64	4.56	1.02	1.04	0.67		0.47	0.30	0.36	0.30	9.38
	2008	1.29	2.30	0.65	0.48	0.36		0.24	0.16	0.09	0.13	5.70
Malaysia	1992	0.17	2.14	0.30	2.09	0.22	0.60		0.13	0.03	0.22	5.90
	2000	0.33	1.76	0.45	3.18	0.23	0.59		0.25	0.17	0.36	7.31
	2008	1.07	0.82	0.36	2.04	0.17	0.37		0.32	0.10	0.49	5.74
Indonesia	1992	0.12	1.47	0.51	0.44	0.19	0.34	0.13		0.01	0.07	3.30
	2000	0.39	0.96	0.44	1.25	0.12	0.16	0.22		0.02	0.17	3.74
	2008	0.86	0.63	0.35	1.78	0.11	0.14	0.31		0.00	0.31	4.48
Philippines	1992	0.06	0.93	0.20	0.21	0.29	0.26	0.13	0.05		0.04	2.16
	2000	0.19	1.30	0.43	0.43	0.25	0.31	0.22	0.10		0.14	3.37
	2008	0.45	0.50	0.16	0.36	0.14	0.20	0.15	0.10		0.17	2.23
Thailand	1992	0.24	2.73	0.40	1.04	0.28	0.13	0.39	0.09	0.03		5.33
	2000	0.28	1.73	0.26	0.74	0.23	0.37	0.45	0.13	0.15		4.35
	2008	0.77	1.47	0.34	0.66	0.23	0.31	0.47	0.18	0.08		4.51
East Asia	1992	14.90	29.55	8.17	7.86	14.43	9.50	5.88	5.47	0.87	3.38	100
	2000	14.93	24.17	9.61	10.65	12.87	10.31	6.64	4.55	2.30	3.97	100
	2008	25.02	18.23	10.58	10.05	11.41	9.85	5.46	3.91	1.43	4.07	100

Source: Calculated from UN Comtrade Database data.

Philippines, Thailand, and Indonesia), the degree of dependence on Japan's import and export trade exceeds that of China.

Analyzing only from the perspective of trade scale, it is difficult to fully reflect the overall status of China and Japan's position and changes in the intraregional trade in East Asia, and it is necessary to conduct in-depth discussions from the perspective of intraregional trade structure.

Trade products can be divided into primary products, intermediate products and final products. Intermediate products include semi-finished products and parts. The final products include capital goods and consumer goods. In the intraregional trade structure of East Asia, the proportion of primary products fell from 8.19% in 1990 to 4.26% in 2007, and the proportion of primary products has been very small. Therefore, we focus on a comparative analysis of the trade structures of China and Japan within the East Asian region from the perspective of intermediate products and final products.

For a long time, the trade in intermediate products was the main form of trade in East Asia. In 2007, trade in intermediate products accounted for 65.96% of total trade, and final product trade accounted for 29.77%. From 1990 to 2007, the fastest-growing component trade in intermediate products increased from 18.50% to 33.09% of total trade, and semi-finished products trade decreased from 35.91% to 32.87%. The most significant decline was in consumer goods in the final product. From 21.06% to 11.43%, capital goods only rose from 16.34% to 18.34%. The decline in the proportion of final product trade in the region indicates that East Asian economies are still highly dependent on the final product market outside the region at this stage.

Based on the overall trade structure in the East Asia region at this stage, we will conduct a comparative analysis of the status of China and Japan in the intraregional trade structure in East Asia for the final product trade and the intermediate product trade.

From the point of view of export trade, China has always been the largest exporter of consumer goods in the region, and its share in the export trade of consumer goods in the region has continued to rise, reaching 63.6% in 2007, while Japan accounts for only 9.8%. Japan and Hong Kong (China) are the main export market of Chinese consumer goods. At the same time, in the export of capital goods in the region, China has surpassed Japan and has become the largest exporter of capital goods in East Asia. In 2007, China's share of capital goods exports in the region reached 34.4%, 6.8 percentage points higher than that of Japan. Hong Kong (China) is China's major market for capital goods in the East Asian region, accounting for 36.7%, followed by Japan, accounting for 24.4%; Japan's largest export market for capital goods in East Asia is also China, accounting for 39.9% of capital goods of Japan's exports to East Asia. South Korea and Taiwan (China) accounted for 15.54% and 14.41%, respectively (Table 7.21).

Obviously, China has become the largest supplier of consumer goods and capital goods in East Asia. However, for China itself, the export trade of consumer goods and capital goods is more dependent on markets outside the region. In 2007, the intraregional trade of China's consumer goods and capital goods accounted for less than 28% of its total foreign trade, and showed a downward trend. The North American market has become China's largest market for consumer goods and capital goods exports. At the same time, the proportion of intraregional trade in capital goods and capital goods to foreign trade reached 44.4%, and its capital goods export market is mainly in the region. Although the export of Japanese consumer goods depends on the North American market, in absolute terms, Japan's exports of consumer goods to the United States are only 39.5% of China's. This also shows that under the new "triangle trade" model, China has become the main force for the export of East Asia. It can thus be observed that in the East Asian region and even outside the region, the final product export trade of China's consumer goods and capital goods has surpassed Japan, and Japan is more dependent on the regional market than China.

By 2007, China's exports of consumer goods and capital goods in the East Asian region were 6.51 and 1.25 times that of Japan, respectively. From the perspective of trade partners, as shown in Table 7.22,

Table 7.21. Export Direction and Change of End Products in China and Japan in 1992–2007 (%)

	China						Japan					
	Consumer Goods			Capital Goods			Consumer Goods			Capital Goods		
Direction	1992	2000	2007	1992	2000	2007	1992	2000	2007	1992	2000	2007
China							1.2	2.1	3.5	4.1	6.3	17.7
Japan	12.1	16.4	11.2	4.8	8.2	6.7						
Korea	0.5	1.3	2.2	0.9	2.5	3.0	0.8	1.2	1.6	5.3	5.8	6.9
Singapore	0.9	0.7	0.8	1.9	2.2	2.7	2.0	1.7	1.1	4.7	4.7	2.4
Hong Kong, China	35.9	24.0	10.1	38.5	22.5	10.4	5.2	2.7	1.8	5.5	3.6	4.3
Taiwan,China	0.1	0.4	0.6	0.0	1.4	1.8	2.0	2.2	1.8	5.4	10.7	6.4
Malaysia	0.3	0.3	0.5	0.9	0.9	1.1	1.2	1.4	0.9	2.7	2.3	2.4
Indonesia	0.1	0.2	0.3	1.3	0.2	0.6	0.2	0.1	0.3	1.9	0.8	1.0
Philippines	0.0	0.1	0.1	0.1	0.1	0.2	0.5	0.3	0.2	0.6	0.7	0.4
Thailand	0.1	0.2	0.4	1.1	0.8	1.1	1.3	0.9	0.9	2.7	2.2	3.1
East Asia	50.0	43.6	26.0	49.6	39.0	27.5	14.3	12.7	12.2	32.8	37.1	44.4
North America	27.4	33.2	35.3	25.3	34.6	31.3	41.7	51.6	42.5	30.4	31.9	21.5
EU	17.8	16.0	26.9	17.1	20.2	24.6	28.1	21.4	20.6	25.0	21.6	18.8
World	100	100	100	100	100	100	100	100	100	100	100	100
Proportion in Region	45.8	62.7	63.6	8.7	19.4	34.4	13.4	8.8	9.8	58.8	36.0	27.6

Source: Calculated from data provided by RIETI-TID 2008 (Japan Institute of Economic Research).

Table 7.22. Comparison of the Trade Volume of Final Products between China and Japan in 2007 and other Economies in the Region

Trade Object		Japan/ China	Korea	Singapore	Hong Kong, China	Taiwan, China	Malaysia	Indonesia	Philippine Bin	Thailand	East Asia (10)	East Asia (8)	World
Export	Consumer Goods	9.62	4.05	2.23	16.57	1.04	1.50	2.96	2.03	1.29	6.51	5.24	3.05
	Capital Goods	0.76	0.88	2.27	4.92	0.56	0.92	1.17	0.88	0.74	1.25	1.57	2.01
Import	Consumer Goods	0.10	0.99	1.13	4.20	0.44	0.27	0.23	0.22	0.27	0.19	0.52	0.28
	Capital Goods	1.32	5.32	2.47	12.78	5.65	1.27	1.20	2.35	2.23	2.15	3.55	2.14

Notes: The value of "Japan/China" indicates the ratio of China's export or import trade of Japan's related final products to the export or import trade of Japan's related final products to China; the remaining figures indicate that China and Japan are separate from the region. The ratio of the value of the export or import trade of the end product to the target of the domestic trade; East Asia (10) indicates the ten economies of East Asia, China, Japan, South Korea, Hong Kong (China), Taiwan(China), Singapore, Malaysia, Indonesia, Thailand and the Philippines. East Asia (8) represents eight economies after the removal of China and Japan from the East Asian region.

Source: Table 7.21.

China's export trade of consumer goods to other economies in the region exceeds that of Japan. In terms of export of capital goods in the region, China's capital goods exports to Hong Kong (China), Singapore and Indonesia surpass Japan's. Among them, China's capital goods exports to Hong Kong (China) are nearly five times that of Japan's exports, and the export of capital goods to Singapore is 2.27 times that of Japan; and for the export of capital goods from other economies, China is less than Japan. At the same time, China's capital goods exports to Japan are 76% of Japan's exports to China. It can be seen that China's position and influence in the export trade of consumer goods in East Asia is greater than that of Japan; while its status and influence in the regional capital goods export trade is still smaller than Japan, but Japan is in a downward trend, and China is on an upward trend.

From the perspective of import, as shown in Table 7.23, Japan's share of imports of consumer goods in the region exceeds one-third, while China's imports of consumer goods in the region are very small, less than one-fifth that of Japan. Specifically, China only imported more consumer goods from Singapore and Hong Kong (China) than Japan, and for other economies, Japan's consumer goods market for them was significantly higher than China's. Since Japan's consumer goods market for China is also very large, if we do not include China–Japan bilateral consumer goods import trade, from the perspective of the size of imports of consumer goods from other economies in the region, China's share of Japan's imports will increase to 51.6%. In 1992 and 2000, this ratio was only 10.3% and 16.0%. This shows that although China currently does not have a large consumer goods market for other economies in the region, it has experienced rapid development in recent years.

In the import of capital goods, Japan is the main source of China's capital goods imports. Around 38.6% of China's regional capital goods imports come from Japan, followed by South Korea and Taiwan (China); and China is also the main source of Japan's capital goods imports. About 62.8% of the import of capital goods in the region came from China; at the same time, the capital goods

Table 7.23. Sources and Changes of Imports of Final Products in China and Japan in 1992–2007 (%)

	China						Japan					
	Consumer Goods			Capital Goods			Consumer Goods			Capital Goods		
Import	1992	2000	2007	1992	2000	2007	1992	2000	2007	1992	2000	2007
China							35.5	65.0	78.1	13.3	23.9	62.8
Japan	34.6	41.6	41.8	58.4	57.2	38.6						
Korea	2.2	13.1	18.1	2.9	14.5	26.4	19.0	8.5	3.6	15.6	14.3	10.7
Singapore	1.5	3.0	3.0	1.1	7.1	3.7	1.2	1.2	0.5	16.8	8.4	3.2
Hong Kong, China	56.4	24.9	10.4	37.0	9.3	1.4	4.3	1.0	0.5	2.4	0.5	0.2
Taiwan,China	0.0	4.3	8.6	0.1	3.2	14.8	18.0	6.2	3.8	26.7	22.6	5.6
Malaysia	0.5	3.1	2.4	0.2	3.7	2.8	2.1	3.5	1.7	12.3	13.2	4.8
Indonesia	0.9	2.3	3.0	0.1	1.0	1.2	5.5	4.2	2.5	0.6	2.5	2.2
Philippines	0.4	1.8	2.2	0.0	1.7	3.4	3.5	2.3	1.9	2.1	6.7	3.2
Thailand	3.3	6.0	10.6	0.2	2.2	7.7	10.9	8.0	7.5	10.3	7.9	7.4
East Asia	100	100	100	100	100	100	100	100	100	100	100	100
Proportion in the Region	3.2	3.5	6.8	12.6	10.8	30.1	31.4	36.3	35.0	6.4	17.1	14.0
From East Asia/From the World	52.9	49.4	35.8	46.6	45.3	59.2	43.7	48.8	52.0	20.8	49.1	59.0

Source: Table 7.21.

import trade between China and other economies in the region surpassed Japan (Table 7.23). In 2007, the proportion of China's capital goods import trade in the region reached 30.1%. Obviously, China has provided the largest export market for capital goods in East Asia.

Therefore, there is a clear complementarity between China and Japan in the import of final products in the region, and Japan and China provide the largest capital goods market and consumer goods market for other economies in the East Asia region, respectively. Although the gap between China and Japan in the provision of consumer goods is continuously narrowing, there is still a large gap.

Judging from the export trade of intermediate products in the region, as shown in Table 7.24, Japan remained the largest supplier of intermediate products in the region in 2007, but its share in the trade in intermediate products in the region is continuously declining. The share of China in the intermediate product exports in the region is rising rapidly. At the same time, the trade in intermediate products between Japan and the region continues to increase compared with those outside the region, and the dependence on the intermediate product market in the region is increasing. On the contrary, for China, the proportion of trade within the region is declining, and the dependence on the regional market is decreasing.

As shown in Table 7.25, in terms of component exports, China only surpasses Japan in its exports to Hong Kong (China), Singapore and Malaysia. In semi-finished products, China exports more to Japan than Hong Kong (China), Singapore, Indonesia and the Philippines. For China, Hong Kong (China) is still the most important export market for parts and semi-finished products, but its status has been declining, especially for semi-finished products. Japan is China's second largest export market for intermediate products. China is also Japan's largest export market for parts and semi-finished products. Excluding China–Japan bilateral intermediate product export trade, China's exports of parts and components in the region have exceeded that of Japan, and exports of semi-finished products are almost the same.

Table 7.24. Export Direction and Change of Intermediate Products between China and Japan in 1992–2007 (%)

	China						Japan					
	Components			Semi-finished Products			Components			Semi-finished Products		
Direction	1992	2000	2007	1992	2000	2007	1992	2000	2007	1992	2000	2007
China							7.4	18.0	39.7	14.1	26.3	35.0
Japan	11.2	22.2	18.0	16.8	23.3	22.5						
Korea	2.2	7.8	11.8	10.9	12.5	22.5	17.0	14.2	10.9	17.8	18.3	20.6
Singapore	4.9	9.4	7.5	5.1	4.3	6.2	14.2	14.1	6.4	8.6	6.4	4.7
Hong Kong, China	75.6	45.8	42.1	56.3	45.2	25.4	12.6	13.3	13.2	17.2	12.1	6.9
Taiwan, China	0.1	6.6	7.6	2.0	5.9	8.1	20.1	14.3	10.2	17.8	16.5	15.4
Malaysia	1.9	3.7	7.7	1.8	2.0	3.9	10.2	10.8	6.1	7.2	6.5	4.8
Indonesia	1.6	0.5	0.9	1.8	2.3	3.7	4.8	2.7	1.8	5.3	3.3	1.9
Philippines	0.4	0.5	0.8	0.6	1.1	1.4	2.5	4.8	2.8	2.1	2.2	1.1
Thailand	2.2	3.5	3.5	4.6	3.5	6.2	11.2	7.9	8.9	9.8	8.4	9.6
East Asia	100	100	100	100	100	100	100	100	100	100	100	100
Proportion in the region	3.9	10.8	20.5	12.4	15.2	20.7	48.9	32.3	22.2	28.8	26.5	24.9
From East Asia/From the world	58.5	54.0	48.0	66.1	50.1	37.6	39.6	45.9	55.3	58.8	62.3	69.4

Source: Table 7.21.

Table 7.25. Comparison of Trade Size of Intermediate Products between China and Japan in 2007 and Other Economies in the Region

Trade Objects		Japan/ China	Korea	Singapore	Hong Kong, China	Taiwan, China	Malaysia	Indonesia	Philippines	Thailand	East Asia (10)	East Asia (8)	World
Export	components	0.42	1.00	1.08	2.96	0.69	1.18	0.48	0.26	0.37	0.93	1.26	1.07
	Semi-finished products	0.53	0.91	1.09	3.04	0.44	0.69	1.62	1.11	0.54	0.83	0.99	1.53
Import	Components	2.38	4.42	3.02	16.73	3.23	6.08	0.67	5.10	1.66	3.24	3.80	2.67
	Semi-finished products	1.87	3.68	2.76	14.84	6.05	0.77	0.36	0.73	1.54	1.99	2.05	1.47

Notes: The value of "Japan/China" indicates the ratio of China's exports or imports of Japan's relevant intermediate products to Japan's exports or imports of relevant intermediate products to China; the remaining figures indicate that the ratio of the export or import trade of intermediate economies in other economies with China and Japan, respectively; the economies represented by East Asia (10) and East Asia (8) are in Table 5, respectively.

Source: Table 7.21.

If we examine the scale of export trade of intermediate products between China and Japan and other economies in the region (Table 7.7), we can observe that in the export market of most intermediate products within the East Asia region, China's status and influence is still smaller than that of Japan. However, from the point of view of the trade development trend in the middle product area between the two countries, this gap is continuously narrowing, and China's status and influence in the export trade of intermediate products in the region will gradually exceed that of Japan.

From the point of view of the import trade of intermediate products in the region, China has become the largest recipient of intermediate products in the region. At the same time, China's share of the import trade of intermediate products in the region has continued to rise (Table 7.8). By 2007, China's import of parts and semi-finished products in the region was 3.24 times that of Japan and 1.99 times that of Japan, respectively (Table 7.7). Moreover, China's imports of intermediate products from most economies have exceeded that of Japan.

It is worth noting that the proportion of imported parts and components in China and the region has been continuously increasing, and the proportion of import trade with semi-finished products in the region is declining, while the proportion of import trade between Japan and regional intermediate products (parts and semi-finished products) is increasing (Table 7.26). However, from the point of view of the relations with import trade in the region, the import trade of Chinese intermediate products is more dependent on the regional market than Japan, and the proportion of China's imports of parts and semi-finished products imported from East Asia accounts for 75% and 56.8% of the total imports of the world, while two figures of Japan are 61.9% and 41.9%, respectively. At the same time, China has provided the largest export market for parts and semi-finished products in East Asia. Therefore, compared to Japan, China has a greater role in promoting the development of export trade in intermediate products of other economies in the region.

Table 7.26. Sources and Changes in Imports of Intermediate Products in China and Japan in 1992–2007 (%)

	China						Japan					
	Components			Semi-finished products			Components			Semi-finished products		
Sources of Import	1992	2000	2007	1992	2000	2007	1992	2000	2007	1992	2000	2007
China							6.0	19.9	39.7	13.2	22.4	34.5
Japan	39.6	47.5	29.1	25.5	34.9	32.4						
Korea	3.0	16.6	24.0	9.9	33.2	27.6	25.5	16.7	17.6	18.1	20.3	14.9
Singapore	1.1	5.7	3.7	4.5	4.4	4.5	10.6	7.5	4.0	6.3	3.2	3.2
Hong Kong, China	56.0	9.0	2.3	53.3	7.3	2.3	5.6	2.0	0.4	1.3	0.6	0.3
Taiwan,China	0.0	4.7	15.4	0.0	5.5	19.3	21.9	22.3	15.4	10.8	7.9	6.3
Malaysia	0.2	7.8	10.1	2.0	4.2	5.2	8.2	11.3	5.4	12.0	14.0	13.3
Indonesia	0.0	1.0	0.6	3.5	5.7	3.5	1.6	3.0	3.1	31.3	24.8	19.8
Philippines	0.0	3.4	10.9	0.5	0.6	0.7	6.5	11.0	6.9	1.8	1.6	1.8
Thailand	0.1	4.5	3.9	0.7	4.1	4.5	14.1	6.3	7.6	5.2	5.2	5.8
East Asia	100	100	100	100	100	100	100	100	100	100	100	100
Proportion in the region	9.2	12.3	30.2	15.9	20.0	26.9	7.2	12.0	9.3	15.8	15.8	13.5
From East Asia/ From the world	60.8	64.0	75.0	63.5	61.7	56.8	30.6	53.0	61.9	31.3	38.3	41.9

Source: Table 7.21.

To sum up, China has become the largest market provider of consumer goods and capital goods in the East Asian region, and will soon surpass Japan in the supply of parts and semi-finished products. Then, how does China and Japan compete with each other in intraregional trade in East Asia? Here, we use the trade competition pressure index for detailed analysis.

The trade competition pressure index is a kind of trade competition relationship reflected from the perspective of export. It can examine the competitive pressures of the two countries in the global market, and can also examine the competitive pressures of the two countries in a particular market. It can also be examined the pressure of competition between the two countries on certain specific commodities. It can be used to measure the degree of competitive pressure from the counterparty of trade competition to the domestic trade in order to reflect the competitiveness of the two countries in foreign trade.

As shown in Table 7.27, from 1992 to 2008, the changes in the competitive pressure index between China and Japan in the markets of various economies in the East Asia region varies greatly. Before 2000, Japan's performance on China's competitive advantage was very obvious, but since then China's competitive pressure on Japan has risen rapidly. After 2004, Japan's competitive pressure on China in markets other than Hong Kong (China) is greater than China's competitive pressure on Japan. As of 2008, China's competitive pressures on Japan in the markets of the three economies of the Philippines, Thailand and Taiwan (China) are less than Japan's pressure on China. If we look at the regional markets of the eight economies in East Asia, China's competitive pressure on Japan has already reached 0.64, which is a 0.42 increase compared with 0.22 in 1996, while Japan's competitive pressure on China has dropped to 0.40, compared with 0.64 in 1996. Compared with a decrease of 0.24, it shows that the asymmetry of trade pressures between China and Japan is undergoing a fundamental reversal.

Judging from the pressure of trade competition on all products in East Asia's regional markets, China has an advantage over Japan.

Table 7.27. Trade Competition Pressure Index between China and Japan in the Main East Asian Markets, 1992–2008

Export Market		Korea	Indonesia	Malaysia	Philippines	Singapore	Thailand	Taiwan, China	Hong Kong, China	East Asia (8)
China	1992	0.06	0.05	0.04	0.04	0.07	0.06	0.03	0.55	0.15
to Japan	1996	0.13	0.09	0.07	0.06	0.13	0.05	0.07	0.48	0.22
	2000	0.18	0.21	0.12	0.10	0.19	0.12	0.10	0.57	0.24
	2004	0.29	0.32	0.28	0.28	0.36	0.19	0.22	0.75	0.36
	2008	0.53	0.53	0.49	0.48	0.58	0.32	0.35	0.79	0.64
Japan	1992	0.47	0.57	0.47	0.69	0.45	0.68	0.80	0.32	0.36
to China	1996	0.49	0.59	0.76	0.53	0.69	0.77	0.69	0.37	0.64
	2000	0.49	0.51	0.66	0.68	0.69	0.70	0.70	0.35	0.49
	2004	0.47	0.47	0.43	0.64	0.51	0.66	0.69	0.26	0.36
	2008	0.43	0.39	0.38	0.52	0.47	0.60	0.63	0.17	0.40

Source: Calculated based on the annual trade data of 261 kinds of three-digit codes classified by UN Comtrade Database, SITC (Rev. 3).

In order to further analyze the changes in the pressures of trade competition between China and Japan in the regional markets and their trends, they can be examined from the perspective of capital-intensive products, labor-intensive products and primary products.

As shown in Table 7.28, in the trade of primary products of major economies in East Asia in 2008, China's trade pressure on Japan's trade is basically greater than Japan's competitive pressure on China. In the regional markets of eight economies in East Asia, China has an absolute competitive advantage over Japan in the trade of primary product. In labor-intensive product trade, only in the markets of Thailand and Taiwan (China), China's trade pressure on Japan is less than Japan's trade pressure on China. In general, in the regional markets of the eight economies of East Asia, China has a clear competitive advantage over Japan in the labor-intensive product trade. In the trade of capital-intensive products, China's trade pressure on Japan is greater than Japan's competition with China. At the same time, from the perspective of the markets of various economies, China's trade pressure on Japan's trade is greater than Japan's markets with China, mainly Hong Kong (China), Singapore, Malaysia, South Korea and Indonesia.

Obviously, China's competitive advantage over Japan in the primary product and labor-intensive products market in East Asia remains large, and its competitive advantage in the capital-intensive product market has also begun to emerge. Accordingly, Japan's competitive advantage of capital-intensive product market on China is weakening.

On the other hand, from the perspective of the changes in the competitive pressures of trade between China and Japan in major markets in East Asia since the early 1990s (Table 7.29), in terms of primary products, China and Japan are in the markets of various economies in East Asia. The pressure of trade competition showed a tendency to rise and fall interchangeably, but as can be seen from Table 7.28, China's trade pressure on Japan's trade still has an absolute advantage.

Table 7.28. Trade Competition Pressure Index of Various Products in Various East Asian Markets in 2008 in China and Japan

Category	Targeted Market	Malaysia	Korea	Singapore	Philippines	Thailand	Indonesia	Taiwan, China	Hong Kong, China	East Asia (8)
Primary	Japan to China	0.05	0.21	0.68	0.25	0.24	0.16	0.24	0.21	0.38
product	China to Japan	0.36	0.38	0.36	0.52	0.31	0.69	0.39	0.85	0.73
Capital	Japan to China	0.44	0.44	0.52	0.64	0.58	0.40	0.64	0.17	0.41
intensive	China to Japan	0.55	0.48	0.66	0.52	0.29	0.52	0.36	0.87	0.66
Labor	Japan to China	0.38	0.42	0.46	0.50	0.60	0.38	0.63	0.17	0.40
intensive	China to Japan	0.52	0.56	0.68	0.50	0.33	0.55	0.38	0.89	0.69

Source: Table 7.27.

Table 7.29. Changes in the Competitive Pressure Index of Various Products in Various Major Markets in East Asia between China and Japan

Category		Stage	Malaysia	Korea	Singapore	Philippines	Thailand	Indonesia	Taiwan, China	Hong Kong, China
Primary product	Japan to China	1992–2000	0.02	0.01	0.02	−0.19	−0.17	−0.03	−0.18	−0.03
		2000–2008	−0.04	0.03	0.50	0.12	0.05	0.08	0.02	0.07
	China to Japan	1992–2000	0.17	0.16	0.10	0.14	−0.06	0.14	0.08	0.04
		2000–2008	0.03	−0.05	−0.39	0.19	0.04	0.43	0.22	0.19
Capital intensive	Japan to China	1992–2000	0.13	−0.16	−0.01	−0.10	0.04	−0.22	−0.10	−0.11
		2000–2008	−0.50	−0.40	−0.41	−0.26	−0.29	−0.29	−0.26	−0.39
	China to Japan	1992–2000	0.10	0.14	0.16	0.06	0.09	0.14	0.08	0.08
		2000–2008	0.43	0.32	0.47	0.44	0.17	0.33	0.27	0.33
Labor intensive	Japan to China	1992–2000	−0.27	−0.34	−0.19	−0.14	−0.11	−0.16	−0.32	0.00
		2000–2008	−0.13	0.02	0.01	−0.16	−0.05	−0.18	0.03	−0.04
	China to Japan	1992–2000	0.06	0.08	0.06	0.11	0.02	0.23	0.07	−0.03
		2000–2008	0.39	0.34	0.45	0.31	0.21	0.27	0.25	0.18

Notes: A positive number indicates a rise, and a negative number indicates a decrease.

Source: Table 7.27.

In the regional market of capital-intensive products, Japan's competitive pressures on China have been declining, especially during the period 2000–2008. In the same period, China's competitive pressure on Japan has been rising, and the increase was even greater during 2008. Here, in the capital-intensive product markets of the Philippines, Thailand and Taiwan (China), Japan's trade pressure on China's trade is still greater than China's pressure on Japan's competition, but in these markets, the competitive pressures between China and Japan have relatively small changes. Therefore, in the capital-intensive product market in the East Asia region, the room for potential growth of China's competitive advantage over Japan remains large.

In terms of labor-intensive products, China's competitive pressure on Japan has increased to varying degrees, and Japan's competitive pressure on China has also declined to varying degrees, which indicates that in terms of intraregional trade in capital-intensive and technology-intensive products, the advantages of China's trade competitiveness to Japan have been rising.

7.3.2.4 *RMB and Japanese Yen in the Basket of East Asian Currency as Implied Currencies*

As far as the current exchange rate system of the East Asian countries is concerned, most countries adopt a floating exchange rate system that sticks to a basket of currencies, but few countries publish the currency composition of their currency baskets and the proportion of various currencies. East Asia is still the dollar area. Song uses the dynamic lag model to analyze the influence of RMB regionalization. He found that the US dollar's influence on major Asian currencies fell, the Australian dollar's influence increased significantly, and the yen's impact on Asian currencies gradually declined, while the RMB's impact on Asian currencies was more pronounced.[99] Song uses the time series data from January 1999 to March 2012. He uses

[99]Song, Yanan, "Research on the Influence of RMB Regionalization-An Analysis Based on Dynamic Distribution Lag Model," *International Trade Issues* 9 (2012).

a dynamic lag distribution model to study the long-term effects of the major currencies (US dollar, yen, Australian dollar, euro, RMB) against currencies in East Asia.[100] The study found that during the period from January 1999 to July 2005, the yen had an impact on the exchange rates of the 9 currencies other than Hong Kong dollar and the Vietnamese dong, while the effect of the RMB on the exchange rates of the 10 currencies was not significant. From July 2005 to December 2009, the impact of the yen on the exchange rate of Asian currencies declined, while the impact of the RMB on the exchange rate of Asian currencies increased. From January 2010 to March 2012, the impact of the Japanese yen on the exchange rate of Asian currencies fell further. The RMB basically sustained the impact of the previous period, and its long-term impact on the Hong Kong dollar, Korean won and Singapore dollar increased. In conclusion, the study found that the impact of the yen on Asian currencies has gradually declined, while the impact of the RMB on Asian currencies is still relatively limited.

To measure the role of the RMB and the Japanese yen in the exchange rate policies of other East Asian economies, we use the method of Frankel and Wei, implying a currency basket that has calculated the weights of the yen, the yuan, the won and the dollar in the basket of currencies implied by other East Asian economies.[101] The data are derived from the daily exchange rate of OANDA (www.oanda.com) in various currencies against the Swiss franc, that is, using Swiss francs to measure the currency changes of the research currency and using the OLS estimation method. There are three regression equations. It first separately measures the weight of the RMB and the yen in the implied currency basket of East Asian

[100]The major currencies in East Asia include 11 currencies: Hong Kong dollar, Indonesian rupiah, Indian rupee, Japanese yen, Korean won, Malaysian ringgit, Philippine peso, Singapore dollar, Thai baht, Taiwan dollar and Vietnamese dong.
[101]Frankel, Jeffrey A., and Shang-Jin Wei, "Yen Bloc or Dollar Bloc? Exchange Rate Policies of the East Asian Economies," In Macroeconomic Linkage: Savings, Exchange Rates, and Capital Flows, edited by Takatoshi Ito and Anne O. Krueger, 295–333. Chicago: University of Chicago Press, 1994.

currencies, and then measures the weights of currencies of the RMB, the yen and the US dollar in the basket of currencies of other East Asian currencies, respectively. And finally, euros, New Zealand dollars, Australian dollars[102] are added to the basket as the implied currencies.[103] The data period is from RMB exchange reform (21 July 2005) to 22 January 2013, and this sample period is divided into four biennial subsamples, i.e. 21 July 2005 to 20 July 2007, 21 July 2007 to 20 July 2009, 21 July 2009 to 20 July 2011, 21 July 2011 to 22 January 2013.

The Brunei dollar (BND), the Myanmar kyat (MMK), Malaysian ringgit (MYR), Philippine peso (PHP), Singapore dollar (SGD), Thai baht (THB), Hong Kong dollar (HKD), Taiwan dollar (TWD), Macau pataca (MOP), China yuan (CNY), Japanese yen (JPY), and Korean won (KRW),USD, EUR, NZD and AUD are used in the research. The midpoint data of the daily currency exchange rate for the currency Swiss Franc are taken as the logarithm of each series. All the first-order difference sequences are verified to be stable.

The results of a review of 12 East Asian currencies showed that the US dollar still plays an important role in the formation of exchange rates in East Asia (except for the yen), which is reflected in the fact that the coefficient of the US dollar is high in most countries' implied currency baskets. The RMB has a higher share of the basket of currencies implied in most countries in East Asia (excluding the yen), while the yen has a smaller impact on East Asian currencies

[102]In Bowman (2005), the Australian dollar is considered to play the same role in the East Asian region as the Japanese yen in the 1990s and it shows the link between the Australian dollar and East Asian currencies. See also Bowman, C., Yen Bloc or Koala Bloc? Currency Relationships after the East Asian Crisis, *Japan and the World Economy* 17 (2005): 83–96.

[103]Since the exchange rates of Indonesian rupiah (IDR), Cambodian riel (KHR), Lao kip (LAK) and Vietnamese dong (VND) on Swiss francs fluctuate little, they are basically maintained at a fixed ratio, so we only examined East Asian currencies including Brunei dollar (BND), Myanmar kyat (MMK), Malaysian ringgit (MYR), Philippine peso (PHP), Singapore dollar (SGD), Thai baht (THB), Hong Kong dollar (HKD), Taiwan dollar (TWD), Macau Pataca (MOP), China yuan (CNY), Japanese yen (JPY) and Korean won (KRW).

(Singapore and Hong Kong dollars rely on the yen to a certain extent).

(1) Brunei dollar:

In general, Brunei takes an exchange rate policy that sticks to a basket of currencies (see Table 7.30). The RMB played a major role in the exchange rate fluctuations of the Brunei Dollar, while the role of the Japanese yen in the Brunei Dollar exchange rate policy was not significant during the same period. In each sample interval examined, the impact of RMB on the exchange rate of Brunei was significant. From 2007 to 2009, the impact of the yen on Brunei's exchange rate was significantly different (it was significant at the 1% level). The US dollar, euro and Australian dollar have also had a significant impact on the Brunei exchange rate policy. It should be noted that the "Singapore–Brunei Exchange Equivalent Exchange Agreement of 1967" guarantees the equivalent exchange of Brunei dollars and Singapore dollars, and can be freely circulated in the other country.[104] This makes the exchange rate baskets of the two currencies very similar.

(2) Myanmar kyat:

The role of the RMB in the exchange rate policy of Myanmar in 2005–2011 was obvious. The role of the yen in the exchange rate policy of Myanmar only appeared in 2005–2007, but its share was only about 5%. In the US dollar regression equation, the US dollar has a stronger share than the RMB and the Japanese yen. It can be seen that the practice of Burma is still mainly to peg to the US dollar. However, the results of the 2011–2013 regression show that the role of various currencies in the Myanmar dollar exchange rate policy is not significant, reflecting the effective implementation of the managed floating exchange rate system implemented

[104]People's Bank of China International Division. Brunei's monetary and monetary policies [EB/OL]. http://www.pbc.gov.cn/publish/goujisi/3049/2010/2010 0324113408327311246/20100324113408327311246_e.html, 2009-8-14/2013-1-28.

Table 7.30. Composition of the Implied Currency Basket of Brunei Dollar (21 July 2005–22 January 2013)

	Constant	RMB	JPY	USD	EUR	SGD	AUD	R^2/D-W
2005–2007	0.0000	0.5737***	0.0322					0.13/2.83
	0.0002	0.0594	0.0470					
	0.0001	0.2151	0.0250	0.3828*				0.13/2.83
	0.0002	0.2258	0.0471	0.2326				
	0.0001	0.2369	0.0081	0.2432	0.5933***	−0.0888	0.1779*	0.15/2.85
	0.0002	0.2247	0.0470	0.2343	0.1773	0.0641	0.0941	
2007–2009	−0.0001	0.6291***	−0.1415***					0.44/2.21
	0.0001	0.0267	0.0205					
	−0.0001	0.2149#	−0.1462***	0.4090***				0.45/2.21
	0.0001	0.1481	0.0205	0.1439				
	0.0001	−0.0333	−0.0176	0.4691***	0.4464***	0.0305	0.0233	
	0.0001	0.1352	0.0225	0.1302	0.0531	0.0277	0.0284	
2009–2011	0.0001	0.6967***	−0.0189					0.42/2.36
	0.0001	0.0331	0.0237					
	0.0001	0.3393***	−0.0308	0.3710***				0.43/2.35
	0.0001	0.1235	0.0239	0.1236				
	0.0001	0.1650#	0.0341#	0.3379***	0.2150***	−0.0081	0.2446***	0.56/2.56
	0.0001	0.1096	0.0216	0.1090	0.0365	0.0331	0.0357	

(*Continued*)

Table 7.30. (*Continued*)

	Constant	RMB	JPY	USD	EUR	SGD	AUD	R^2/D-W
2011–2013	−0.0000	0.7556***	0.0245					0.65/1.94
	0.0001	0.0346	0.0279					
	0.0000	0.5760***	0.0143	0.1909*				0.66/1.89
	0.0001	0.1048	0.0284	0.1051				
	0.0000	0.1807*	0.0026	0.2964***	0.3075***	0.0265	0.1465***	0.74/2.24
	0.0001	0.0960	0.0247	0.0928	0.0450	0.0478	0.0520	
2005–2013	0.0001	0.6670***	−0.0398***					0.35/2.51
	0.0001	0.0191	0.0147					
	0.0000	0.3518***	−0.0479***	0.3231***				0.35/2.50
	0.0001	0.0780	0.0148	0.0776				
	0.0000	0.1560**	0.0166	0.3129***	0.3363***	−0.0023	0.1234***	0.43/2.62
	0.0001	0.0738	0.0145	0.0726	0.0305	0.0214	0.0228	

Notes: The numbers below the coefficients are standard errors, ***indicates it is significant at the 1% level, **indicates it is significant at the 5% level and *indicates it is significant at the 10% level, #indicates it is significant at the 15% level.

Source: The daily exchange rate of each currency to Swiss franc is retrieved from http://www.oanda.com, and the data in the table are calculated by the author.

by the Myanmar government on 1 April 2012 (see Table 7.31).[105] In the entire sample interval examined, Myanmar kyat was depreciated against the Swiss franc, the base currency, and fell from 1 kyat to 0.1408 Swiss franc on 4 April 2012, to 1 Kyat to 0.0011 Swiss francs. On 27 February 2015, the exchange rate is still at this level.

(3) Malaysia ringgit:

The exchange rate of Malaysian Ringgit is more like fixing a basket of currencies (see Table 7.32). Specifically, during the period 2005–2007, the RMB was largely weighted in the ringgit's implied currency basket, accounting for 83.6%, and it was not 0 at the 1% significance level. During the period of 2007–2011, the RMB, Japanese yen and the US dollar are important currencies that affect the exchange rate of ringgit. Compared with 2007–2009, the proportion of RMB in the sample interval 2009–2011 rose from 83.7% to 85.3%, an increase of 1.6 percentage points, while the proportion the US dollar dropped from 68.7% to 44.2%. In the sample period of 2011–2013, RMB still occupies a greater weight in the exchange rate basket of ringgit. At this time, the weight of the yen is no different from zero. It should be noted that China began to implement a managed floating exchange rate system based on market supply and demand, with reference to a basket of currencies on 21 July 2005. After the news was transmitted to Malaysia, Malaysian ringgit immediately disconnected from RMB and the US dollar. Instead, it used a managed floating exchange rate system instead.[106]

[105]Myanmar adopts a floating exchange rate system from 1 April, http://news.163.com/12/0329/03/7TO20I5J00011121M.html

[106]Quoted from Xiao, Li and Yibing Ding, *The East Asian Regional Monetary Cooperation and RMB Exchange Rate System Reform*. Beijing: Economic Science Press, 2010, 123.

Table 7.31. Composition of the Myanmar Kyat Implied Currency Basket (21 July 2007–22 January 2013)

	Constant	RMB	JPY	USD	EUR	SGD	AUD	R^2/D-W
2005–2007	−0.0001#	0.8343***	0.0637***					0.62/2.22
	0.0001	0.0266	0.0211					
	0.0000	−0.0677	0.0456**	0.9726***				0.66/2.24
	0.0001	0.0456	0.0199	0.0980				
	0.0000	−0.0495	0.0436**	0.9506***	0.1701**	−0.0365	−0.0095	0.67/2.26
	0.0001	0.0954	0.0200	0.0995	0.0754	0.0272	0.0399	
2007–2009	−0.0001	0.8115***	−0.0254					0.56/2.37
	0.0001	0.0291	0.0224					
	0.0000	−0.4238***	−0.0396*	1.2197***				0.60/2.42
	0.0001	0.1557	0.0215	0.1513				
	0.0001	−0.5230***	−0.0116	1.2561***	0.3651***	−0.0388	−0.0252	0.62/2.40
	0.0001	0.1536	0.0256	0.1479	0.0603	0.0315	0.0322	
2009–2011	−0.0001	0.7988***	0.0720**					0.33/2.76
	0.0002	0.0499	0.0358					
	−0.0000	−0.3777**	0.0331	1.2215***				0.37/2.76
	0.0002	0.1821	0.0353	0.1822				
	0.0000	−0.4341**	0.0508	1.2136***	0.1204**	−0.0283	0.0686	0.37/2.76
	0.0002	0.1827	0.0360	0.1817	0.0609	0.0552	0.0596	

2011–2013	−0.0079	−2.6948	0.2815					0.00/2.00
	0.0088	2.3318	1.8809					
	−0.0079	−1.2616	0.3634	−1.5227				0.00/2.00
	0.0088	7.0885	1.9210	7.1112				
	−0.0076	−5.2144	0.3407	−1.3582	5.2483#	−3.1350	3.9889	0.01/2.01
	0.0088	7.4861	1.9234	7.2383	3.5067	3.7244	4.0565	
2005–2013	−0.0019	0.0275	−0.0997					0.00/2.00
	0.0018	0.4216	0.3244					
	−0.0019	−0.3997	−0.1108	0.4381				0.00/2.00
	0.0018	1.7244	0.3273	1.7144				
	−0.0018	−0.6709	−0.0352	0.4023	0.7865	−0.2051	0.2343	0.00/2.00
	0.0018	1.7427	0.3431	1.7153	0.7194	0.5045	0.5379	

Notes: The numbers below the coefficients are standard errors, ***indicates it is significant at the 1% level, **indicates it is significant at the 5% level and *indicates it is significant at the 10% level, #indicates it is significant at the 15% level.

Source: The daily exchange rate of each currency pair Swiss franc is from http://www.oanda.com and the data in the table are calculated by the author.

Table 7.32. Composition of the Basket of Implied Currencies of Malaysia Ringgit (21 July 2005–22 January 2013)

	Constant	RMB	JPY	USD	EUR	SGD	AUD	R^2/D-W
2005–2007	0.0000	0.8364***	0.0326					0.24/2.92
	0.0002	0.0581	0.0460					
	0.0001	0.4300*	0.0246	0.4338*				0.25/2.92
	0.0002	0.2209	0.0461	0.2276				
	0.0000	0.4299	0.0096	0.3504	0.3409	−0.0831	0.1838	0.26/2.92
	0.0002	0.2210	0.0463	0.2305	0.1745	0.0631	0.0926	0.26/2.92
2007–2009	−0.0002	0.8365***	−0.1233***					0.53/2.25
	0.0002	0.0301	0.0231					
	−0.0001	0.1920	−0.1307***	0.6364***				0.54/2.24
	0.0002	0.1664	0.0230	0.1617				
	0.0000	0.0455	−0.0669**	0.6871***	0.1648***	0.1499***	−0.0880***	0.57/2.25
	0.0001	0.1639	0.0273	0.1577	0.0643	0.0336	0.0344	0.57/2.25
2009–2011	0.0001	0.8533***	−0.0974***					0.52/1.92
	0.0001	0.0316	0.0227					
	0.0001	0.3865***	−0.1128***	0.4846***				0.53/1.89
	0.0001	0.1175	0.0228	0.1175				
	0.0001	0.2103**	−0.0394**	0.4419***	0.1325***	0.0061	0.2994***	0.67/1.97
	0.0001	0.1000	0.0197	0.0995	0.0333	0.0302	0.0326	

2011–2013	0.0001	0.8352***	−0.0121					0.70/1.8
	0.0001	0.0333	0.0268					
	−0.0000	0.6493***	−0.0227	0.1975*				0.70/1.78
	0.0001	0.1008	0.0273	0.1011				
	−0.0000	0.2273**	−0.0393*	0.3452***	0.1911***	0.0496	0.2012***	0.78/1.80
	0.0001	0.0908	0.0233	0.0878	0.0425	0.0452	0.0492	
2005–2013	−0.0000	0.8426***	−0.0679***					0.46/2.47
	0.0001	0.0191	0.0147					
	0.0000	0.4412***	−0.0783***	0.4117***				0.46/2.46
	0.0001	0.0778	0.0148	0.0774				
	0.0000	0.2871***	−0.0240#	0.4101***	0.1757***	0.0586***	0.0748***	0.50/2.50
	0.0001	0.0759	0.0149	0.0746	0.0313	0.0220	0.0234	

Notes: The numbers below the coefficients are standard errors, ***indicates it is significant at the 1% level, **indicates it is significant at the 5% level and *indicates it is significant at the 10% level, # indicates it is significant at the 15% level.

Source: The daily exchange rate of each currency pair Swiss francs comes from http://www.oanda.com and the data in the table are calculated by the authors.

(4) Philippine peso:

In the two sample intervals of 2005–2007 and 2011–2013, RMB accounted for 85% (2005–2007) and 88% (2011–2013) of the Philippine peso's external value, while the proportion of the yen in the exchange rate basket is negligible for the same period. Within these two sample intervals, the effect of the exchange rate of the US dollar against Philippine peso accounted for more than half of the country's total. In the two sample intervals of 2007–2011, although the RMB still affects the foreign price of the pesos to a certain extent, the influence of the dollar is even greater. While the influence of the yen in the peso exchange rate basket is higher than that of the last two sample intervals, but its weight is still not positive (see Table 7.33).

(5) Singapore dollar:

The Singapore dollar exchange rate is related to a basket of currencies. From the regression results of all the samples, the weights of all currencies, including the RMB, the Japanese yen, the US dollar, the euro, the New Zealand dollar and the Australian dollar, are all significantly different, and not equal to zero at the significance level at 1%, the goodness of fit R^2 reached 0.86. This conclusion is consistent with the study of the IMF (2012)[107] on Singapore's actual foreign exchange rate system. During the period 2005–2007, if only the RMB and yen currencies were inspected, the impact of the RMB in the composition of the Singapore dollar exchange rate was higher than that of the yen, and when other currencies were added, especially after the US dollar was added, the impact of the RMB on the Singapore dollar could be ignored, while the yen's weight in the composition of the Singapore dollar exchange rate is still significant. This is mainly because when the regression equation does not include US

[107] IMF, *Annual Report on Exchange Arrangements and Exchange Restrictions 2012*, Appendix Table II.9 *De facto* Classification of Exchange Rate Arrangements and Monetary Policy Frameworks, 30 April 2012.

Table 7.33. Composition of Philippine Pesos Implied Currency Basket (21 July 2005–22 January 2013)

	Constant	RMB	JPY	USD	EUR	SGD	AUD	R^2/D-W
2005–2007	0.0002#	0.8502***	0.0135					0.54/2.24
	0.0001	0.0308	0.0243					
	0.0003	0.1633#	−0.0002	0.7333***				0.56/2.25
	0.0001	0.1141	0.0238	0.1176				
	0.0002**	0.1635#	0.0055	0.6803***	0.1639**	−0.0039	0.0728#	0.57/2.27
	0.0001	0.1143	0.0239	0.1191	0.0902	0.0326	0.0478	
2007–2009	−0.0002	1.0017***	−0.1677***					0.59/2.13
	0.0002	0.0317	0.0243					
	−0.0001	0.0013	−0.1792***	0.9879***				0.61/2.09
	0.0002	0.1728	0.0239	0.1679				
	0.0000	−0.2104	−0.0502*	1.0302***	0.2002***	0.0901***	0.0366	0.65/2.07
	0.0002	0.1662	0.0277	0.1600	0.0652	0.0340	0.0349	
2009–2011	0.0000	0.8533***	−0.0769***					0.46/2.30
	0.0001	0.0364	0.0261					
	0.0001	0.2202#	−0.0979***	0.6573***				0.47/2.28
	0.0001	0.1348	0.0261	0.1348				
	0.0001	0.0842	−0.0397#	0.6232***	0.0744*	0.0214	0.2336***	0.54/2.39
	0.0001	0.1265	0.0250	0.1258	0.0421	0.0382	0.0413	

(Continued)

Table 7.33. (*Continued*)

	Constant	RMB	JPY	USD	EUR	SGD	AUD	R^2/D-W
2011–2013	0.0001	0.8784***	0.0074					0.74/2.14
	0.0001	0.0324	0.0262					
	0.0001	0.4665***	−0.0161	0.4376***				0.75/2.08
	0.0001	0.0968	0.0262	0.0971				
	−0.0001	0.1821*	−0.0309	0.5684***	0.0166	0.0745#	0.1471***	0.78/2.13
	0.0001	0.0957	0.0246	0.0925	0.0448	0.0476	0.0518	
2005–2013	0.0000	0.9216***	−0.0796***					0.57/2.20
	0.0001	0.0164	0.0126					
	0.0001	0.2355***	−0.0974***	0.7035***				0.59/2.17
	0.0001	0.0658	0.0125	0.0654				
	0.0001	0.0841	−0.0372***	0.7022***	0.0945***	0.0522***	0.1170***	0.63/2.20
	0.0001	0.0632	0.0124	0.0622	0.0261	0.0183	0.0194	

Notes: The numbers below the coefficients are standard errors, ***indicates it is significant at the 1% level, **indicates it is significant at the 5% level and *indicates it is significant at the 10% level, #indicates it is significant at the 15% level.

Source: The daily exchange rate of each currency pair Swiss franc is from http://www.oanda.com and the data in the table are calculated by the author.

dollar, the Singapore dollar's dependence on the US dollar is mainly reflected by the dependence on RMB, which further explains that RMB still has a greater degree of dependence on the US dollar during this period. The effect of the yen on the Singapore dollar in 2005–2007 is independent and will not change because of the existence of the US dollar in the regression equation. However, after 2007, the yen's impact on Singapore's exchange rate basket was small, and in most cases it was negative. The euro and the Australian dollar also play a larger role in the Singapore exchange rate formation, and the role of the New Zealand dollar is relatively small (see Table 7.34).

(6) Thai baht:

The relationship between Thai baht and RMB is tight, and there is no close correlation with the yen. In the regression equation without the US dollar, the RMB can explain the 73–97% change in the value of Thai baht, and the goodness of fit R^2 continues to increase over time, rising from 0.38 in 2005 to 0.82 in 2013, which shows the important role of RMB in the formation of the exchange rate of Thai baht. In the US dollar regression equation, the US dollar is still the main factor affecting the exchange rate of the Thai baht. Except for 2005–2007, the coefficient of the yuan in the remaining sample ranges is still not zero, and the RMB and US dollar are equally divided during the 2011–2013 period. It shows that the RMB is occupying a more important position in the currency basket formed by the Thai baht exchange rate. However, the impact of the yen on the movement of the exchange rate of Thai baht is small (see Table 7.35).

(7) RMB:

The dollar is still an important factor in the exchange rate of the RMB. Within each sample interval, the US dollar explained 94.1–99.5% of the fluctuation of exchange rate of RMB, and the goodness of fit R^2 was between 0.94 and 0.97. The yen's impact on the fluctuation RMB exchange rate is relatively small. In addition,

Table 7.34. Composition of Singapore Dollar Implied Currency Basket (21 July 2005–22 January 2013)

	Constant	RMB	JPY	USD	EUR	SGD	AUD	R^2/D-W
2005–2007	0.0001	0.6489***	0.1164***					0.76/2.02
	0.0001	0.0153	0.0121					
	0.0001***	0.0095	0.1037***	0.6826***				0.80/1.67
	−0.0001	0.0530	0.0111	0.0546				
	0.0001**	0.0023	0.0963**	0.6000**	0.2012**	0.0198	0.1193**	0.84/1.65
	0.0000	0.0490	0.0103	0.0510	0.0386	0.0140	0.0205	
2007–2009	−0.0001	0.7739***	−0.1160***					0.77/1.76
	0.0001	0.0161	0.0124					
	−0.0000	0.4333***	−0.1199***	0.3363***				0.78/1.73
	0.0001	0.0888	0.0123	0.0863				
	0.0000	0.2455***	0.0109	0.3623***	0.1164***	0.0601***	0.0857***	0.85/1.66
	0.0001	0.0732	0.0122	0.0704	0.0287	0.0150	0.0153	
2009–2011	0.0001	0.7783***	−0.0375***					0.72/1.73
	0.0001	0.0196	0.0141					
	0.0001	0.3859***	−0.0505***	0.4073***				0.73/1.66
	0.0001	0.0722	0.0140	0.0722				
	0.0001***	0.2224***	0.0131#	0.3742***	0.1558***	0.0189	0.2350***	0.89/1.80
	0.0000	0.0462	0.0091	0.0459	0.0154	0.0139	0.0151	

2011–2013	0.0001	0.8784***	0.0074					0.74/2.14
	0.0001	0.0324	0.0262					
	0.0001	0.4665***	−0.0161	0.4376***				0.75/2.08
	0.0001	0.0968	0.0262	0.0971				
	0.0001	0.1821*	−0.0309	0.5684***	0.0166	0.0745#	0.1471***	0.78/2.13
	0.0001	0.0957	0.0246	0.0925	0.0448	0.0476	0.0476	
2005–2013	0.0000	0.7514	−0.0249					0.74/1.73
	0.0000	0.0096	0.0074					
	0.0000	0.4125***	−0.0337***	0.3475***				0.74/1.66
	0.0000	0.0386	0.0073	0.0384				
	0.0001**	0.2231***	0.0390***	0.3437***	0.1637***	0.0466***	0.1447***	0.86/1.65
	0.0000	0.0291	0.0057	0.0286	0.0120	0.0084	0.0090	

Notes: The numbers below the coefficients are standard errors, ***indicates it is significant at the 1% level, **indicates it is significant at the 5% level and *indicates it is significant at the 10% level, #indicates it is significant at the 15% level.

Source: The daily exchange rate of each currency pair Swiss francs is from http://www.oanda.com and the figures in the table are calculated by the authors.

Table 7.35. Composition of the Basket of Implicit Currency in Thai Baht (21 July 2005–22 January 2013)

	Constant	RMB	JPY	USD	EUR	SGD	AUD	R^2/D-W
2005–2007	0.0004***	0.7281***	0.0922***					0.38/1.57
	0.0001	0.0382	0.0302					
	0.0005	0.0465	0.0786	0.7276				0.40/1.5
	0.0001	0.1433	0.0299	0.1476				
	0.0004***	0.0511	0.0744*	0.6496***	0.2189*	0.0288	0.0596	0.41/1.52
	0.0001	0.1433	0.0300	0.1494	0.1121	0.0409	0.0601	
2007–2009	−0.0003#	0.9697***	−0.0875***					0.51/2.18
	0.0002	0.0372	0.0285					
	−0.0002	0.4579**	−0.0934***	0.5054***				0.52/2.17
	0.0002	0.2066	0.0285	0.2007				
	−0.0002	0.3699*	−0.0501#	0.5349***	0.0246	0.1289***	−0.0603	0.52/2.20
	0.0002	0.2074	0.0345	0.1997	0.0814	0.0425	0.0435	
2009–2011	0.0001	0.8865***	0.0141					0.76/2.97
	0.0001	0.0205	0.0147					
	0.0001	0.1831**	−0.0091	0.7302***				0.79/2.05
	0.0001	0.0720	0.0140	0.0721				
	0.0001*	0.1068#	0.0176	0.7197***	0.0844***	0.0303#	0.0741***	0.82/2.08
	0.0001	0.0684	0.0135	0.0680	0.0228	0.0206	0.0223	

2011–2013	0.0001	0.8403***	0.0310#					0.82/1.98
	0.0001	0.0252	0.0203					
	0.0000	0.5691***	0.0155	0.2881***				0.82/1.94
	0.0001	0.0757	0.0205	0.0759				
	0.0000	0.3052***	0.0057	0.3743***	0.1295***	−0.0034	0.1571***	0.86/0.85
	0.0001	0.0717	0.0184	0.0694	0.0336	0.0357	0.0389	
2005–2013	0.0000	0.8791***	−0.0065					0.58/1.98
	0.0001	0.0163	0.0128					
	0.0001	0.3113***	−0.0212*	0.5822***				0.59/1.95
	0.0001	0.0659	0.0125	0.0655				
	0.0001	0.2143***	0.0126	0.5847***	0.0882***	0.0729***	0.0191	0.60/1.97
	0.0001	0.0654	0.0129	0.0643	0.0270	0.0189	0.0202	

Notes: The numbers below the coefficients are standard errors, ***indicates it is significant at the 1% level, **indicates it is significant at the 5% level and *indicates it is significant at the 10% level, #indicates it is significant at the 15% level.

Source: The daily exchange rate of each currency pair Swiss francs is from http://www.oanda.com and the figures in the table are calculated by the authors.

the euro and the New Zealand dollar also have a certain influence on the fluctuation of RMB exchange rate (see Table 7.36).

(8) Japanese yen:

The fluctuation of the exchange rate of the Japanese yen is also affected by the value of the US dollar currency to a certain extent, but its degree of influence is much lower than that of the US dollar affected by the US dollar. The highest share of the dollar in the yen exchange rate is 84.9%, but its goodness of fit is only 0.20. At the same time, the yen is also affected by other currencies such as the euro, New Zealand dollar, Australian dollar, etc., and the goodness of fit is generally low (see Table 7.37), which fully reflects the free floating exchange rate system of Japan.

(9) Korean won:

South Korea operates a floating exchange rate system. By examining the changes in the exchange rate of Korean won for each year, it can be seen that the weights of various currencies in the Korean won currency basket are almost insignificant, and the level of significance is low, and the goodness of fit R^2 is less than 0.1 in most years. However, in the regression equation of RMB and JPY, the Korean won shows a closer relationship with the RMB, but there is no such relationship with the JPY. In 2011–2013, the proportion of the euro and the Australian dollar in the currency basket of the Korean won was also significant (see Table 7.38).

(10) Hong Kong dollar:

In the regression equation excluding the US dollar, the proportion of the RMB in the Hong Kong dollar currency basket is quite high. The minimum RMB share in the four sub-sample ranges is also 93.8% (2011–2013), and the goodness-of-fit R^2 is 0.95. To a large extent, it explained the changes in the exchange rate of the Hong Kong dollar. In each subsample interval, the coefficient of the yen is also

Table 7.36. Composition of the Implied Currency Basket of RMB (21 July 2005–22 January 2013)

	Constant	JPY	USD	EUR	SGD	AUD	R^2/D-W
2005–2007	0.0001***	−0.0026	0.9939***				0.94/2.07
	0.0000	0.0077	0.0100				
	−0.0001***	−0.0039	0.9946***	−0.0629**	−0.0066	0.0320**	0.94/2.08
	0.0000	0.0078	0.0116	0.0293	0.0106	0.0155	
2007-2009	0.0001***	−0.0003	0.9557***				0.97/2.01
	0.0000	0.0051	0.0065				
	0.0001***	0.0107*	0.9408***	0.0310**	0.0110#	−0.0033	0.97/2.03
	0.0000	0.0062	0.0076	0.0145	0.0076	0.0078	
2009–2011	0.0001#	−0.0091	0.9646***				0.94/2.43
	0.0000	0.0072	0.0099				
	0.0001*	−0.0049	0.9503***	0.0223*	0.0124	0.0014	0.94/2.44
	0.0000	0.0073	0.0109	0.0124	0.0112	0.0121	
2011–2013	0.0001	0.0117	0.9473***				0.95/2.10
	0.0001	0.0116	0.0141				
	0.0001	0.0052	0.8921***	0.0234	0.0399*	0.0348#	0.95/2.23
	0.0001	0.0110	0.0160	0.0200	0.0212	0.0232	
2005–2013	0.0001***	−0.0023	0.9640***				0.95/2.16
	0.0000	0.0036	0.0046				
	0.0001***	0.0048	0.9445***	0.0216***	0.0135**	0.0048	0.95/2.19
	0.0000	0.0038	0.0053	0.0079	0.0055	0.0059	

Notes: The numbers below the coefficients are standard errors, ***indicates it is significant at the 1% level, **indicates it is significant at the 5% level and *indicates it is significant at the 10% level, #indicates it is significant at the 15% level.

Source: The daily exchange rate of each currency pair Swiss francs is from http://www.oanda.com and the figures in the table are calculated by the authors.

Table 7.37. Composition of the Implied Currency Basket in Japanese Yen (21 July 2005–22 January 2013)

	Constant	RMB	USD	EUR	SGD	AUD	R^2/D-W
2005–2007	−0.0001	−0.0596	0.4545**				0.09/2.24
	0.0002	0.1778	0.1824				
	−0.0002	−0.0883	0.4447	0.0563	−0.1416	0.2433	0.11/2.25
	0.0002	0.1776	0.1844	0.1402	0.0504	0.0738	
2007–2009	0.0003	−0.0146	0.5744**				0.20/1.81
	0.0003	0.2684	0.2600				
	0.0001	0.3868	0.3672	−0.0417	−0.0798	−0.3366	0.45/1.91
	0.0002	0.2228	0.2145	0.0876	0.0456	0.0451	
2009–2011	0.0001	−0.2412	0.8492***				0.20/2.04
	0.0002	0.1913	0.1890				
	0.0002	−0.1269	0.8406***	−0.0134	−0.0051	−0.2240***	0.24/2.02
	0.0002	0.1885	0.1848	0.0628	0.0569	0.0609	
2011–2013	−0.0002	0.1587	0.7371***				0.53/2.04
	0.0002	0.1575	0.1550				
	−0.0002	0.0789	0.7940***	−0.0796	0.0738	0.0258	0.54/2.04
	0.0002	0.1667	0.1576	0.0780	0.0829	0.0903	
2005–2013	0.0000	−0.0634	0.6930***				0.24/1.98
	0.0001	0.1006	0.0992				
	0.0000	0.1243	0.6318***	0.0818**	−0.0528*	−0.2459***	0.31/2.01
	0.0001	0.0971	0.0948	0.0401	0.0281	0.0296	

Notes: The numbers below the coefficients are standard errors, ***indicates it is significant at the 1% level, **indicates it is significant at the 5% level and *indicates it is significant at the 10% level, #indicates it is significant at the 15% level.

Source: The daily exchange rate of each currency pair Swiss franc is from http://www.oanda.com and the data in the table are calculated by the author.

Table 7.38. Composition of the basket of implied currencies in Korean Won (21 July 2005–22 January 2013)

	Constant	RMB	JPY	USD	EUR	SGD	AUD	R^2/D-W
2005–2007	0.0001	0.6707***	0.0977					0.04/2.59
	0.0005	0.1304	0.1032					
	−0.0001	2.6309***	0.1368	−2.0926***				0.07/2.6
	0.0005	0.4912	0.1025	0.5059				
	−0.0002	2.6177***	0.1266	−2.1752***	0.2022	−0.0002	0.1602	0.07/2.60
	0.0005	0.4942	0.1035	0.5153	0.3901	0.1410	0.2069	
2007–2009	−0.0004	1.1672***	−0.3082*					0.04/2.46
	0.0011	0.2137	0.1642					
	−0.0002	−0.4608	−0.3269**	1.6076				0.04/2.46
	0.0011	1.1919	0.1647	1.1578				
	−0.0002	−0.7630	−0.0357	1.5856	0.0166	−0.1089	0.4583*	0.05/2.46
	0.0011	1.2018	0.2000	1.1568	0.4717	0.2461	0.2520	
2009–2011	0.0000	0.7098***	−0.2397#					0.02/2.40
	0.0008	0.2106	0.1513					
	0.0001	−0.4417	−0.2778*	1.1955#				0.02/2.40
	0.0008	0.7906	0.1532	0.7912				
	0.0001	−0.6618	−0.1766	1.1293	0.0820	−0.0028	0.4547*	0.03/2.41
	0.0008	0.7934	0.1565	0.7890	0.2644	0.2395	0.2588	

(Continued)

Table 7.38. (*Continued*)

	Constant	RMB	JPY	USD	EUR	SGD	AUD	R^2/D-W
2011–2013	0.0000	0.7258***	0.1176					0.08/2.28
	0.0007	0.1733	0.1398					
	0.0000	0.4245	0.1004	0.3202				0.08/2.28
	0.0006	0.5265	0.1427	0.5282				
	0.0000	0.1829	0.1137	0.1906	0.6633***	−0.7201***	0.6337**	0.11/2.28
	0.0006	0.5512	0.1416	0.5330	0.2582	0.2742	0.2987	
2005–2013	−0.0001	0.9015***	−0.1436*					0.03/2.43
	0.0004	0.0958	0.0737					
	−0.0001	0.4757	−0.1546**	0.4367				0.03/2.43
	0.0004	0.3919	0.0744	0.3896				
	−0.0000	0.2312	−0.0418	0.4136	0.1403	−0.1438	0.4417	0.04/2.44
	0.0004	0.3941	0.0776	0.3879	0.1627	0.1141	0.1216	

Notes: The numbers below the coefficients are standard errors, ***indicates it is significant at the 1% level, **indicates it is significant at the 5% level and *indicates it is significant at the 10% level, #indicates it is significant at the 15% level.

Source: The daily exchange rate of each currency pair Swiss franc is from http://www.oanda.com and the data in the table are calculated by the author.

significant, but its value is small. From 2005 to 2009, in the regression equation that includes the US dollar, the RMB coefficient is no longer significant, while the coefficient of Japanese yen is significant, although its value is still small. Between 2009 and 2013, in the regression equation that included the US dollar, the coefficient of RMB was significant, but its value was relatively small, while the yen coefficient was the same as zero during the same period. From the results of the regression, the Hong Kong dollar still uses the US dollar as the anchor currency, and the RMB and the Japanese yen also have a certain influence in the currency basket of the Hong Kong dollar, and the former is slightly higher than the latter (see Table 7.39).

(11) New Taiwan dollar:

In the sample interval of 2005–2007, the proportions of the four currencies of RMB, yen, US dollars, and euros in the TWD currency basket were significant. In particular, the RMB affected 57.1% of the exchange rate fluctuation of New Taiwan Dollar. In the sample interval of 2007–2009, the coefficients of RMB, USD, EUR and NZD were significant, and the goodness of fit R^2 at this time was 0.79. During the sample interval of 2009-2011, the Hong Kong dollar was mainly pegged to the US dollar and the euro. However, the goodness of fit R^2 of the three regression equations is low. In the sample interval of 2011–2013, the coefficients of RMB and US dollar were 0.235 and 0.700, respectively, and the goodness of fit R^2 was 0.84 (see Table 7.40).

(12) Macau pataca:

In the regression equation without the US dollar, the impact of the RMB on the Macau pataca is quite significant. During the four biennial sample intervals in 2005–2013, the RMB's share in the exchange rate fluctuation of the Macau pataca accounted for 80%. The influence of the yen on the Macau pataca is mainly reflected in the two subsample ranges 2009–2011 and 2011–2013, but the coefficient value is small. The US dollar is still the main factor affecting the exchange

Table 7.39. Composition of Hong Kong Dollar Implied Currency Basket (21 July 2005–22 January 2013)

	Constant	RMB	JPY	USD	EUR	SGD	AUD	R^2/D-W
2005–2007	−0.0001***	0.9211***	0.0300***					0.92/2.16
	0.0000	0.0103	0.0082					
	0.0000	−0.0005	0.0116***	0.9839***				0.99/2.66
	0.0000	0.0170	0.0035	0.0175				
	0.0000	−0.0016	0.0113***	0.9824***	0.0009	−0.0003	0.0065	0.99/2.66
	0.0000	0.0171	0.0036	0.0178	0.0135	0.0049	0.0071	
2007–2009	−0.0001***	1.0020***	0.0162***					0.97/2.07
	0.0000	0.0074	0.0057					
	0.0000	0.0117	0.0049**	0.9778***				0.99/2.31
	0.0000	0.0171	0.0024	0.0166				
	0.0000	0.0108	0.0052*	0.9783***	−0.0008	0.0027	−0.0017	0.99/2.31
	0.0000	0.0173	0.0029	0.0167	0.0068	0.0035	0.0036	
2009–2011	−0.0001**	0.9568***	0.0260***					0.94/2.36
	0.0000	0.0102	0.0073					
	−0.0000	0.0397***	−0.0044#	0.9521***				0.99/2.42
	0.0000	0.0152	0.0029	0.0152				
	−0.0000	0.0278*	0.0007	0.9495***	0.0022	0.0084*	0.0161***	0.99/2.51
	0.0000	0.0147	0.0029	0.0146	0.0049	0.0044	0.0048	

2011–2013	−0.0000	0.9377***	0.0509***					0.95/2.13
	0.0001	0.0142	0.0114					
	0.0001	0.0361***	−0.0006	0.9579***				0.99/2.49
	0.0000	0.0140	0.0038	0.0140				
	0.0001	0.0142	−0.0018	0.9678***	−0.0013	−0.0014	0.0200***	0.99/2.54
	0.0000	0.0145	0.0037	0.0140	0.0068	0.0072	0.0079	
2005–2013	−0.0001***	0.9656***	0.0274***					0.95/2.19
	0.0000	0.0049	0.0038					
	−0.0000	0.0241***	0.0030**	0.9653***				0.99/2.47
	0.0000	0.0078	0.0015	0.0078				
	−0.0000	0.0179**	0.0055***	0.9653***	0.0029	0.0031	0.0043*	0.99/2.48
	0.0000	0.0079	0.0015	0.0077	0.0032	0.0023	0.0024	

Notes: The numbers below the coefficients are standard errors, ***indicates it is significant at the 1% level, **indicates it is significant at the 5% level and *indicates it is significant at the 10% level, #indicates it is significant at the 15% level.

Source: The daily exchange rate of each currency pair Swiss franc is from http://www.oanda.com and the data in the table are calculated by the author.

Table 7.40. Composition of the Implied Currency Basket of New Taiwan Dollar (21 July 2005–22 January 2013)

	Constant	RMB	JPY	USD	EUR	SGD	AUD	R^2/D-W
2005–2007	−0.0001*	0.8030***	0.0766***					0.68/2.14
	0.0001	0.0223	0.0176					
	−0.0001	0.5701***	0.0720***	0.2486***				0.68/2.15
	0.0001	0.0844	0.0176	0.0869				
	−0.0001	0.5713***	0.0686***	0.1908**	0.1524**	0.0230	0.0513#	0.69/2.17
	0.0001	0.0840	0.0176	0.0875	0.0663	0.0240	0.0352	
2007–2009	−0.0001	0.9248***	−0.0805***					0.76/2.10
	0.0001	0.0205	0.0157					
	−0.0001	0.3796***	−0.0868***	0.5383***				0.77/2.10
	0.0001	0.1124	0.0155	0.1092				
	−0.0000	0.2477**	−0.0213	0.5750***	0.1909***	0.0661***	−0.0217	0.79/2.17
	0.0001	0.1090	0.0181	0.1049	0.0428	0.0223	0.0229	
2009–2011	0.0001	0.8727***	−0.0228					0.38/2.52
	0.0002	0.0455	0.0327					
	0.0001	0.0009	−0.0516#	0.9051***				0.40/2.48
	0.0002	0.1677	0.0325	0.1678				
	0.0002	−0.1046	−0.0201	0.8993***	0.1430***	0.0749#	0.0411	0.42/2.51
	0.0002	0.16609	0.0328	0.1652	0.0553	0.0501	0.0542	

2011–2013	−0.0000	0.8647***	0.0519**					0.81/2.35
	0.0001	0.0267	0.0215					
	0.0000	0.2346***	0.0159	0.6695***				0.84/2.31
	0.0001	0.0759	0.0206	0.0762				
	0.0000	0.0532	0.0089	0.7300***	0.0738**	−0.0241	0.1384***	0.85/2.41
	0.0001	0.0766	0.0197	0.0740	0.0359	0.0381	0.0415	
2005–2013	−0.0001	0.8820***	−0.0120					0.62/2.36
	0.0001	0.0148	0.0114					
	−0.0001	0.2762***	−0.0277**	0.6212***				0.64/2.34
	0.0001	0.0592	0.0112	0.0589				
	0.0000	0.1725***	0.0067	0.6209***	0.1362***	0.0496***	0.0306*	0.66/2.40
	0.0001	0.0582	0.0115	0.0573	0.0240	0.0169	0.0180	

Notes: The numbers below the coefficients are standard errors, ***indicates it is significant at the 1% level, **indicates it is significant at the 5% level and *indicates it is significant at the 10% level, #indicates it is significant at the 15% level.

Source: The daily exchange rate of each currency pair Swiss francs comes from http://www.oanda.com and the data in the table are calculated by the authors.

rate of the Macau pataca. Except for the sample interval of 2011–2013, the US dollar value remained at around 86.5%. In other years, the US dollar occupies an absolutely important position in the movement of the exchange rate of the Macau pataca. The euro also has a certain degree of influence on the exchange rate of the Macau pataca (see Table 7.41).

7.3.2.5 *Comparison of the Degree of Integration between China and Japan and other East Asian Economies*

We use the theoretical implications of economic cycle synchronicity for regional economic integration and measure the synchronization of the economic cycles of nine East Asian economies.[108] The nine economies include: China (CN), Japan (JP), South Korea (KR), Hong Kong (HK), Singapore (SG), Philippines (PH), Indonesia (ID), Thailand (TH) and Malaysia (MY). In addition, taking into account the outward-looking nature of East Asian economies and the fact that the United States is the main export market for East Asian economies, the United States (US) was included in the analysis of the economic cycle synchronicity.

To examine the dynamics of the synchronization of the economic cycles, this topic divides the sample interval into two parts: sub-interval 1 (1990Q1–2000Q4) and sub-interval 2 (2001Q1–2011Q3), and measures the synchrony of the economies within the two sub-intervals. The synchrony of the economic cycles is expected to reveal the changes in the roles of various economies, especially the roles of China and Japan in the process of regional economic integrations.

Multidimensional scaling technology is used here to visualize the multidimensional information of the economic cycle distance matrix of each economy on the same planar graph. The purpose of this method is to use low-dimensional coordinate systems to display multidimensional objects, and to generate the low-dimensional planar

[108]Yu Zhen, and Li Xiao. "China's Role Evolution and Strategic Choice in East Asian Economic Integration: An Empirical Study Based on the Synchronization of Business Cycles." *World Economic Research* 06 (2013): 79–86.

Table 7.41. Composition of the Basket of Implied Currencies of Macau Pataca (21 July 2005–22 January 2013)

	Constant	RMB	JPY	USD	EUR	SGD	AUD	R^2/D-W
2005–2007	−0.0001	0.8176***	0.0230#					0.62/2.4
	0.0001	0.0253	0.0200					
	0.0001	−0.1360#	0.0109	1.0181***				0.67/2.54
	0.0001	0.0891	0.0186	0.0918				
	0.0000	−0.1124	0.0113	0.9750***	0.2070***	0.0047	−0.0389	0.68/2.55
	0.0001	0.0892	0.0187	0.0930	0.0704	0.0255	0.0374	
2007–2009	−0.0001	0.7908***	−0.0181					0.54/2.29
	0.0002	0.0300	0.0230					
	0.0000	−0.4838***	−0.0328#	1.2586***				0.57/2.34
	0.0001	0.1604	0.0222	0.1559				
	0.0001	−0.5751***	−0.0041	1.2887***	0.3516***	−0.0611*	−0.0021	0.59/2.31
	0.0001	0.1586	0.0264	0.1526	0.0623	0.0325	0.0333	
2009–2011	−0.0001	0.7975***	0.0572**					0.54/2.37
	0.0001	0.0314	0.0225					
	−0.0000	−0.2794**	0.0216	1.1180***				0.60/2.34
	0.0001	0.1104	0.0214	0.1105				
	−0.0000	−0.3266***	0.0342#	1.1126***	0.1473***	−0.0560*	0.0584#	0.61/2.37
	0.0001	0.1097	0.0216	0.1091	0.0365	0.0331	0.0358	

(*Continued*)

Table 7.41. (*Continued*)

	Constant	RMB	JPY	USD	EUR	SGD	AUD	R^2/D-W
2011–2013	0.0000	0.8148***	0.0877***					0.75/2.17
	0.0001	0.0315	0.0254					
	0.0000	0.0016	0.0412*	0.8640***				0.79/2.18
	0.0001	0.0885	0.0240	0.0888				
	0.0001	−0.1501*	0.0415*	0.8658***	0.2874***	0.0254	−0.0427	0.81/2.19
	0.0001	0.0887	0.0228	0.0858	0.0416	0.0441	0.0481	
2005–2013	−0.0001*	0.8092***	0.0309***					
	0.0001	0.0147	0.0114					
	0.0000	−0.1979***	0.0048	1.0327***				0.64/2.36
	0.0001	0.0570	0.0108	0.0566				
	0.0000	−0.2603***	0.0170#	1.0255***	0.2315***	−0.0313*	0.0123	0.66/2.36
	0.0001	0.0563	0.0111	0.0554	0.0232	0.0163	0.0174	

Notes: The numbers below the coefficients are standard errors, ***indicates it is significant at the 1% level, **indicates it is significant at the 5% level and *indicates it is significant at the 10% level, #indicates it is significant at the 15% level.

Source: The daily exchange rate of each currency pair Swiss francs comes from http://www.oanda.com and the data in the table are calculated by the authors.

graph to give the approximate distance (Euclidean distance) between the targets, so that we can intuitively review the overall picture of the synchronization of the overall economic cycle.

In order to avoid the conclusion bias caused by single methodology and ensure the robustness of the conclusion, this chapter selects five representative measures of the synchronization of business cycles, namely: (1) HP filtering method. Among them, the value of the smoothing parameter is 1600; (2) BBQ method; (3) MS model. The mean-adjustment model with Markovian zone transfer is used, and the lag order is determined by the AIC criterion. Except for adopting the three-zone system for China and South Korea, all other economies are two-zone systems; (4) Time-domain methods based on VAR prediction errors. The degree of synchronization of the business cycle based on the forward 1.5-year and 4-year forecast errors is analyzed, and it represents the short-term and long-term synchronization, respectively; (5) Frequency-domain method based on spectral analysis. Using the standard Bartlett lag window value, the economic cycle synchronization between the two economies on the frequency bands $[0, \pi/3]$ and $[0, \pi/8]$ were analyzed, corresponding to 1.5 years and 4 years in the time domain method, respectively.

It can be easily seen from the figures (a)–(f) in the multidimensional scale chart that the economic cycles of China, the United States and the Philippines were relatively poorly synchronized with other economies during the entire period, and Japan and South Korea were relatively strong, and conclusions are not sensitive in methodology. However, comparing the trends in the two sub-intervals of Figure 7.16 (g) and (h), we can see that the synchronic distance between China and the United States and other economies has been significantly reduced. As a comprehensive indicator reflecting the depth and breadth of the economic fundamentals of each country, the dynamic information of the synchronization of the economic cycles will have a certain enlightening effect on the evolution of the East Asian cooperation pattern. At present, there are a large number of bilateral and multilateral free trade agreements in the East Asia region, but there is always no unified free trade zone. The

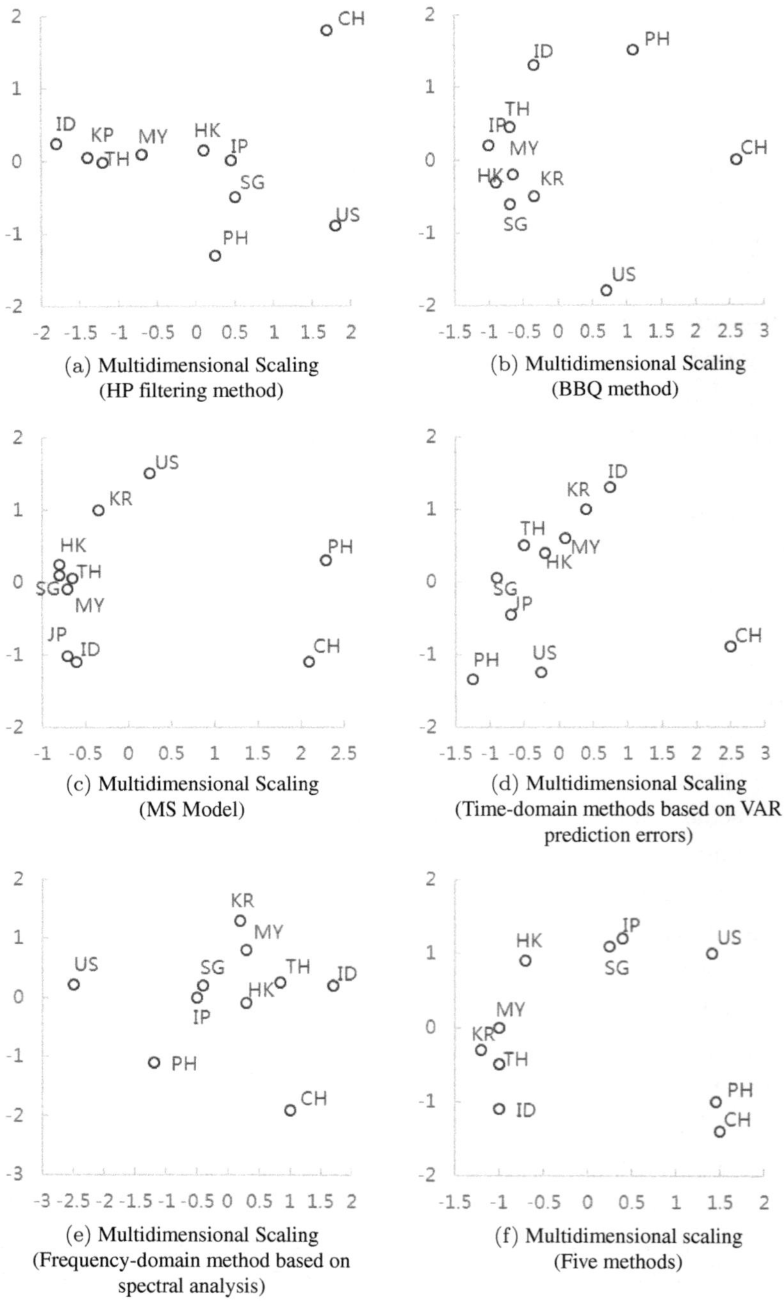

(a) Multidimensional Scaling (HP filtering method)

(b) Multidimensional Scaling (BBQ method)

(c) Multidimensional Scaling (MS Model)

(d) Multidimensional Scaling (Time-domain methods based on VAR prediction errors)

(e) Multidimensional Scaling (Frequency-domain method based on spectral analysis)

(f) Multidimensional scaling (Five methods)

Figure 7.16. Economic Cycle Synchronization of 9 East Asian Economies

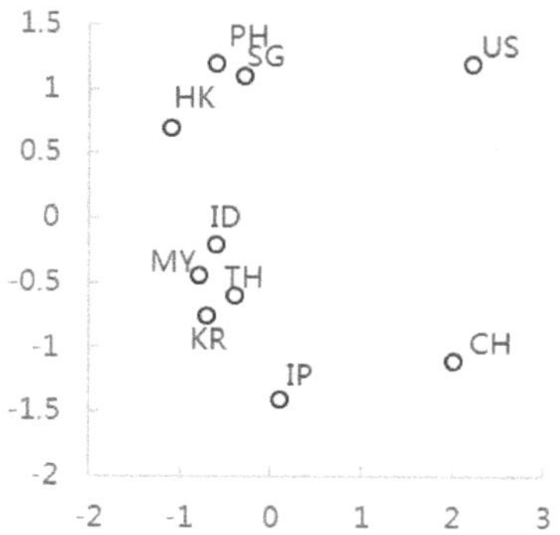

(g) Three methods (1990Q1–2000Q4)

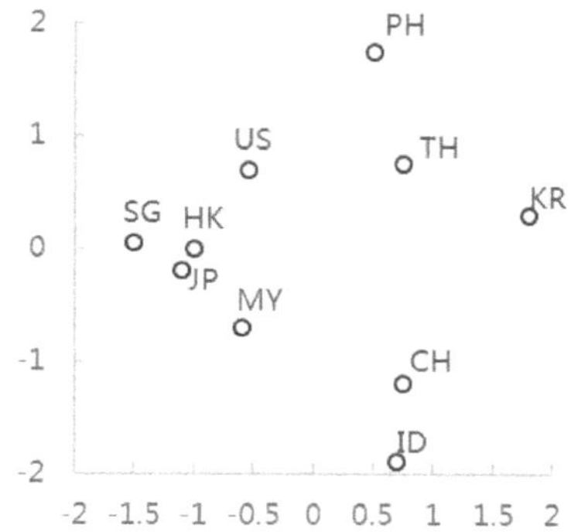

(h) Three methods (2001Q1–2011Q3)

Figure 7.16. (*Continued*)

"spaghetti bowl effect" resulting from the overlapping and conflicting of various cooperation mechanisms has been a potential threat to the sound development of the East Asian economy.[109] For the future of East Asia cooperation, it is a "multiple-choice question" before each economy: the East Asia Free Trade Agreement (EAFTA) of ASEAN 10+3, the East Asia Comprehensive Economic Partnership Agreement of ASEAN+6 (CEPEA), Asia-Pacific Free Trade Area (FTAAP), or the United States-led Trans-Pacific Partnership Agreement (TPP). Obviously, as the two major countries in the region and the core and dominant of East Asia integration, the attitude and strategy of China and Japan on this issue will inevitably determine the process and path of economic integration in East Asia.

Judging from the empirical results, China's degree of integration with various East Asian economies in the entire sample range is less than that of Japan. This will hinder China's leading role compatible to its economic strength in the process of regional cooperation and

[109] Kawai, Masahiro, and Shinji Takagi, "Towards Regional Monetary Cooperation in East Asia: Lessons from Other Parts of the World," *International Journal of Finance & Economics* 10, no. 2 (April 2005): 97–116.

economic integration. However, China's increasingly obvious advantages in its latecomer and its active participation in regional economic cooperation have resolved this unfavorable factor. According to the statistics of the previous topic, China's GDP surpassed Japan to become the world's second largest economy in 2010. As a market provider, China provides East Asia with the largest export market for final capital goods. It will also challenge Japan's position as the largest supplier of final consumer goods in the region through economic restructuring based on expanding domestic demand. In addition, with the full launch of the ASEAN+1 Free Trade Zone, China's trade competitiveness and influence in the ASEAN market are gradually catching up or even surpassing Japan. The significant increase in the synchronicity of the economic cycle between China and East Asian economies in sub-region 2 precisely reflects the above trend (Figure 7.16(h)). It also shows that the ability of China competing with Japan in the regional integration dominance is constantly improving.

Compared with China, Japan is more integrated with East Asian economies. As the "head geese" of the East Asian region's "flying geese model" division of labor system, Japan has a longer history of economic and trade cooperation with other economies, and the degree of integration between its own economy and the regional economy is bound to be relatively high. With the traditional vertical division of labor system gradually shifting to a new regional production division system in recent years, there is a trend of horizontal division of labor between Japan and Korea and other East Asian newly industrialized economies, which played a positive role in keeping with the high synchronization between Japan's economic cycle and other economies. Since 2002, Japan has gradually established a network of trade agreements with various economies in East Asia through the Economic Partnership Agreement (EPA), which has objectively further enhanced the close relationship between its real economy and other East Asian economies. This point has fully proved by our synchronicity results of the economic cycle. According to the findings of Shen, Japan's benefits from TPP and East Asia cooperation are almost equal.[110] In summary, even based on economic considerations, Japan's choices will have certain uncertainties. It is not surprising that Japan started the TPP negotiations.

As the main target market for the final products of East Asian economies, the United States, from the entire study interval (from (a) to (f) in Figure 7.16), is not in sync with the economic cycles of East Asian economies. Even synchronicity with the two major trading partners China and Japan is weak. This situation has a clear negative impact on East Asia including China, which currently relies on the "dollar system" and the US market. The lack of synchronization with the US economic cycle means that adjustment of US macroeconomic policies and economic fluctuations based on self-interest will have huge external interference with the East Asian economy, which is an important supporter of the "dollar system." A further comparison of (g) and (h) in Figure 7.16 shows that the synchronicity of the economic cycles between the United States and East Asian economies has been significantly enhanced in sub-region 2. However, combining the results of the two "turning point" economic cycle division methods, it can be found that after the "subprime mortgage crisis" occurred, the economic cycles of some East Asian economies appeared to be the turning point from prosperity to recession. In other words, this increase actually reflects that the United States has pulled part of the East Asian economies into recession, not only revealing the negative impact of the "dollar system" dependence on East Asian economic stability but also exposing the lack of regional currency cooperation and exchange rate coordination. The mechanism's ability to withstand external shocks in the East Asian economies is still weak. It is clear that there is a fundamental difference in the synchronicity between China and other economies. At the same time, under the background of the "return to Asia" strategy of United States, it also proves that the TPP has not objectively

[110]Shen, Hongfang, and Linglan Chen, "Research on East Asian Monetary and Financial Cooperation Mechanism and Its Characteristics," *Research on Nanyang Issues* 4 (2011): 35–40.

been supported by economic fundamentals. To a certain extent, it is not the fundamental purpose of promoting regional cooperation, especially with the upcoming negotiations between China, Japan and South Korea. This is especially true of FTA. According to the conclusion of Shen, the short-term US economic benefits from TPP are limited.[111]

In summary, faced with the potential threat of TPP to its own interests, China can, on the one hand, maintain and deepen the momentum of cooperation with East Asian economies, accelerate the integration with East Asian economies and continue to reduce the position of Japan's economy in the regional economy. Differences, on the other hand, will be handled in an orderly way to adjust the structure of economic growth, weakening its reliance on external markets and improving its position as a market provider in East Asia.

7.3.2.6 *Sino-Japanese Cooperation in East Asian Monetary Cooperation*

So far, the academic circles and governments of China and Japan have started to plan the path of expanding their currency's influence in East Asia from their favorable conditions and status. The government of China has tried to use its enormous potential for economic growth and market expansion to advance the peripheralization and regionalization of RMB by promoting the role of the RMB in the settlement of currencies with the surrounding economies. Japan has tried to utilize the existing international status of yen and the influence of its developed financial markets and related experience directly expanding the role and influence of the yen in the East Asian region with promotion of ACU.

In Xu and Li,[112] the Competitive Pressure Index was used to study the competitive pressures of China, Japan, South Korea,

---

[111] *Ibid.*

[112] Xu, Qiyuan, and Jing Li, "Currency Internationalization from the Perspective of International Division of Labor System: Typical Facts of the US Dollar and the Japanese Yen," *World Economy* 2 (2008).

Indonesia, Malaysia, the Philippines, Singapore and Thailand in the world market and the US market. The results show that, overall, China's competitive pressures on other Asian countries is comparatively large, but Japan is still a country with strong competitive pressures on China, and Japan's competitive pressure on other Asian countries is also large. This result means that the economic cooperation between China and Japan plays a vital role in keeping the stability of Asian exchange rate and the development of Asian economies.

The positions of China and Japan on monetary and financial cooperation in the East Asian region are not exactly the same. Table 7.42 gives a concise introduction.

About the possibility of coordination between the RMB and the yen, in Yamashita,[113] the following three points have been pointed out: first, the RMB should change its current currency regime that is similar to the crawl-like arrangement, and it should not turn to a floating exchange rate system. Instead, it should be pegged to the basket currency of dollar, euro and yen to avoid the exchange rate risk caused by excessive exchange rate fluctuations among the three major currencies; second, the important prerequisite for the coordination between the RMB and the Japanese yen is the convertibility of the RMB, which is also the first step for the RMB to become the international currency; third, China and Japan should strengthen cooperation and actively promote the establishment of ACU.

In fact, in advancing the future regional monetary and financial cooperation and designing its own monetary and financial strategy, China and Japan should attach importance to the following two important issues:

First, at this stage of the "dollar system," China and Japan do not have the ability to independently lead regional monetary and financial cooperation. In the near future, with regard to Japan's exchange

[113]Yamashita, Eisuke, "The Necessity of Establishing an Asian Edition of EMS and the Joint Leadership Mechanism between Japan and China," In *East Asian Monetary and Financial Cooperation in the Post-crisis Era-Is the Coordination of RMB and Yen Possible?* edited by Li Xiao, 247. Jilin: Jilin University Press 2010.

Table 7.42. China and Japan's Standpoint on Monetary Cooperation in East Asia

Items	China	Japan
The common interests of currency, financial, economic issues of China and Japan in East Asia	Economic stability and sustained development in the region, responding to global shocks	
Currency convertibility	Limited to current account transactions	Yes, international currency
Capital account transaction liberalization	At present, it is a restriction, complete liberalization as a long-term goal	Free
The proportion of fiscal deficit to GDP	2012: −1.3%*	2012: −10.0%*
Government debt balance as a percentage of GDP	28.5% at the end of 2012*	At the end of 2012, 236.6%*
Inflation rate (CPI)	3.0% of full year 2012*	0.0% of full year 2012*
System, system-related issues		
The political system	Fully concentrate on the Communist Party of China	Parliamentary Democracy, Separation of Powers
Basic political issues	To maintain social stability (regime base), economic growth and job creation are at the top of the list	Economic growth, job creation, price stability, external equilibrium, social security, etc.
Independence of the Central Bank	No	Yes
The perspective of international relations theory		
Regional leadership	With China's economic growth gradually expanding	Because the stagnation of the Japanese economy gradually receded

Worries about other countries in the region	Share basic values	Reliance on government and Japanese banks' policy capabilities
Relations with the United States	Sino-US Strategic and Economic Dialogue	Japan-US Alliance
Government and civilian attitudes toward regional currency cooperation (exchange rate mechanism)		
Government	Cautious (establish leadership within the region and wait for the RMB to achieve exchangeability)	Cautious (Shadow of leadership, loss of confidence in the future, lack of prospects)
Central Bank	Cautious	Cautious (concerns about the internationalization of the yen and self-discipline of financial policies)
Academia	Going positive (RMB circle theory)	Positive (Arguments around ACU, etc.)

Notes: *Updated the 2008 data in the original table.

Source: Murakami, "East Asian Monetary and Financial Cooperation and the Role of China and Japan," In *East Asian Monetary and Financial Cooperation in the Post-Crisis Era-Is the Coordination of RMB and Yen Possible?* Edited by Li Xiao, 218. Changchun: Jilin University Publishing Society, 2010.

rate system and its potential for market expansion, the conditions for the yen's direct participation in East Asia's exchange rate cooperation are not yet available. In contrast, China's strategy of promoting the use of RMB as a currency for trade settlement in some areas is likely to make greater progress. It is thus possible to take the lead in advancing exchange rate cooperation in some regions and to deepen monetary and financial cooperation in some regions. Of course, this also depends on the extent to which the RMB is freely convertible. In other words, some East Asian economies have the conditions to first establish a stable exchange rate that does not include the yen, and then to promote the exchange rate stability mechanism in the entire East Asian region, including yen. China and Japan should conduct in-depth studies on this issue and gradually reach a consensus, and on this basis, carry out close coordination and cooperation on the policy.

Second, the smooth progress of regional monetary cooperation requires Sino-Japanese cooperation and joint promotion. The experience of regional monetary integration shows that the monetary integration model is highly correlated with the economic aggregate of regional economies and their changes. The formation of the euro is based on the relative balance of economic power among the countries in the Eurozone. In the event that the currency of any country cannot solely dominate the process of monetary integration, a unified currency is eventually formed through mutual cooperation. The formation of "dollarization" in the Americas is based on the "US Dominance" pattern. In the game of strong currencies and weak currencies, it eventually leads to the dominance of the strong currencies and withdrawal of weak currencies. The reality in East Asia is that the proportion of Japan's GDP in East Asia accounted for about 70% in the 1980s, however, since 2000, the proportion of China's GDP has risen rapidly, while Japan's share has declined rapidly. According to the GDP growth trends of the 8 economies in East Asia from 1960 to 2007, their future economic scales can be predicted: by 2040, China's share of GDP in major East Asian economies will exceed 60%, and the proportion of Japan's GDP will fall to 23.5%. In this sense, over time, the East Asian region is likely to form an economic structure dominated by the Chinese economy that is similar to the "US Dominance" today. It must be pointed out, however, that unlike the Americas, the complex historical, political and cultural traditions of East Asia have determined that it is difficult for the region to adapt to the economic structure with "uni-pole." In the same way, with the different modes of economic ties between the United Kingdom and the European continent, Japan and the United States have obvious asynchrony in the economic cycle (commercial, investment, trade, etc.), while maintaining a highly consistent economic cycle with other East Asian economies. It is impossible for Japan to be independent of the process of regional monetary and financial cooperation like the pound sterling. Therefore, whether from the perspective of international politics or the international economy, the rapid increase in China's economic aggregate does not mean that China can dominate the process of East Asian monetary and financial cooperation, which, on the contrary, shows that cooperation between China and Japan is indispensable.

7.3.3 *Measures for Promoting East Asian Monetary Cooperation in the Near Future*

As mentioned earlier, East Asia, as the role of "trade account zone," is the main beneficiary, and therefore, is also an important dependent and supporter of the dollar-dominated international currency system. On the other hand, the experiences and lessons of the Asian financial crisis of 1997–1998 and the global financial crisis of 2008–2009 show that over-reliance on the dollar system is an external factor that poses a serious disturbance to the sustainable development of the East Asian economy. Therefore, deepening regional monetary and financial cooperation in East Asia is not only an important part of the future development process of the international monetary system reform but also an appeal for the interests of East Asian economies, who are trying to avoid or eliminate the dollar system and seeking the sustained and stable development of the regional economy. From the perspective of China, the key four areas for its recent participation in East Asian regional monetary and financial cooperation should be: the construction of financial market, reserve banks, currency swaps of central banks and regional cooperation in Asian financial supervision.

7.3.3.1 *The Construction of Financial Market in East Asian*

In theory, a highly efficient and effective regional financial market has two important implications for East Asian monetary and financial cooperation: first, the higher the level of development and integration of financial markets in the East Asian region, the closer it will meet the standard for the formation of an OCA[114]; second, the breadth and depth of regional financial markets helps to improve the efficient use of foreign exchange reserves and financial sector assets that have been rapidly accrued by East Asian economies.[115] However, from a realistic point of view, although East Asia has the world's highest savings rate and huge foreign exchange reserves, it lacks a unified and efficient financial market. This is true both within the economies and at the regional level as a whole. A large amount of money in East Asia has flowed into the financial markets of developed countries headed by the United States, and the funds needed for their own economic development have to rely on the inflow of funds from outside the region, especially the short-term ones, resulting in a "double mistake" in borrowing currency and loan maturity. This "original sin" has become the main source of turbulence and even financial crisis in East Asian financial markets.[116] Even after the Asian financial crisis, East Asia's financial integration was enhanced by the integration of

---

[114]Ingram, James C., "Comment: The Currency Area Problem," In Monetary problems of the International Economy, edited by Robert Mundell and Alexander Swoboda, 95–100. Chicago: University of Chicago Press, 1969.

[115]Ghosh, Swati R., East Asian Finance: The Road to Robust Markets. Washington, DC: World Bank Publications, 2006.

[116]Eichengreen, Barry, and Hausmann, Ricardo, "Exchange rates and financial fragility." *National Bureau of Economic Research Working Paper*, no. w7418 (November 1999).

various economies in the regional and international financial markets, and the region's financial integration was still in its infancy.[117]

However, at the same time, we should also note that East Asian economies have already deeply realized that the undeveloped regional capital markets, especially the bond market, have caused harm to the stable economic development of the region, and have made efforts to improve this situation. In terms of the integration of the stock market, East Asian economies have initiated cooperation based mainly on bilateral forms. The main bodies of cooperation are stock exchanges and the regulatory authorities of securities. With regard to the cooperation of the stock exchanges, on 1 October 2001, the Singapore Stock Exchange and the Tokyo Stock Exchange announced their intention to establish a strategic alliance, emphasizing that the two sides will cooperate on transaction and liquidation of the financial products, new product development, marketing information technology development, information sharing, etc. In 2002, the Tokyo Stock Exchange intends to unite with stock exchanges in 10 Asian cities such as Shanghai, Shenzhen, Hong Kong and Taipei to jointly study the concept of market integration to capitalize on the flow of funds within the region. On 31 August 2005, the Tokyo Stock Exchange and the Korea Stock Exchange signed a memorandum of cooperation, which intended to explore cross-border securities transactions between the two countries. On 7 July 2006, the two sides signed a memorandum of understanding on the market alliance project and announced that they will further deepen their cooperation. With regard to the cooperation of securities regulatory authorities, with the opening of the stock market and the increasing number of cross-border stock issuances and transactions, various economies in East Asia have also signed a series of bilateral memoranda of supervision.

[117]Zheng, Haiqing, "Research on the Design and Effect of East Asian Financial Cooperation System," Fudan University, 2007.
Yang, Quan, "Development of Bilateral Currency Swap in East Asia under the Background of Global Financial Turmoil," *International Finance Research* 6 (2010): 30–40.

Take China as an example, as of June 2007, the China Securities Regulatory Commission has signed 37 memoranda of cooperation with the securities regulatory authorities of 34 economies, including Hong Kong (China), Singapore, Japan, Malaysia, South Korea, Indonesia, Thailand and Vietnam.

Compared with the cooperative efforts in the regional stock market, the cooperation of East Asian economies in the bond market is even more significant. The Asian Bond Fund (ABF1 and ABF2) has been launched, and the Asian Bond Market Agreement (ABMI) (ASEAN+3, 2009) has been launched under the framework of ASEAN 10+3 and received technical assistance of ABMI (Figures 7.17 and 7.18) from the ADB.

The focus of East Asian economies on regional financial market construction is the bond market, mainly based on the following considerations. First, by cultivating the bond market in the region, changing the long-term reliance on economies to adapt to catch-up industrialization needs the bank-led financial system enhances the price signal discovery function of financial markets, and it overcomes the widespread fragility of the East Asian financial system, and second, it rationalizes the financing channels of East Asian economies by changing the bond market in the region and changes them. Holding large amounts of foreign exchange reserves relies mainly on the embarrassing situation of out-of-area financing, and effectively solves the "double mismatch" problem. Third, it overcomes the disadvantages of the over-concentration on a single channel in East Asian economies by fostering regional bond markets, and provides an alternative mechanism for efficiently converting high savings into productive investment for the governments and private sectors of East Asian economies. Fourth, by fostering bond markets in the region and the relative stability of exchange rates between the currencies of various economies, it can lay the foundation for the establishment of a regional coordination and cooperation mechanism for exchange rates in the medium term.

Although certain progress has been made in the construction of the bond market in East Asia, there are still many problems that

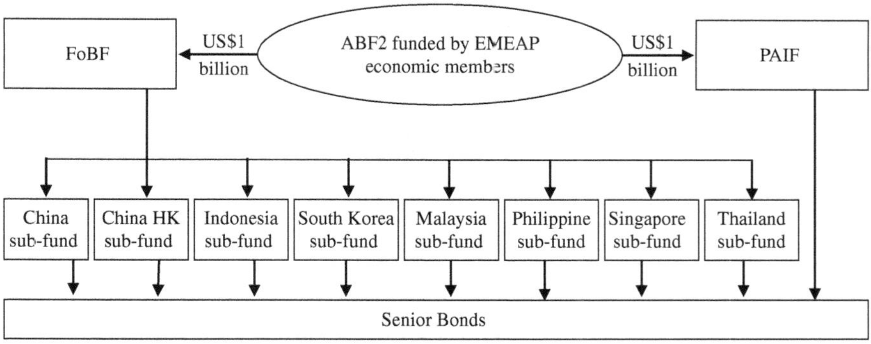

Figure 7.17. ABF2 Frame 1
Source: EMEAP, "Review of the Asian Bond Fund 2 Initiative", EMEAP Working Group on Financial Markets (June 2006).

need to be improved: first, government debt occupies a large proportion in the regional bond market. In addition to Hong Kong (China), South Korea, Malaysia and Singapore, the public sector is the main bond issuer, accounting for more than three-quarters of all debt securities outstanding in each of the other EMEAP member markets. The second is that the ABF3 that had been under preparation in 2005 has not shown signs of starting. The main goal of ABF3 is to provide credit support for those East Asian bonds, especially non-sovereign bonds, that cannot be rated well, and to help expand banks in developing Asia-Pacific countries. The securitization of a greater portion of its assets is offered to investors within and outside the region. Since it largely responds to the private sector's concerns about the credit quality of bond issuers, it will boost the East Asian regional bond market develop to a new stage. Although EMEAP members basically support the concept of ABF3, not all members are willing to use more foreign exchange reserves to subscribe for bonds issued by the regional issuers.

It can be seen that the future construction and development of the bond market in East Asia need to focus on solving two major problems: first, the depth of the market and liquidity issues. It is not only necessary to develop the government bond market but also

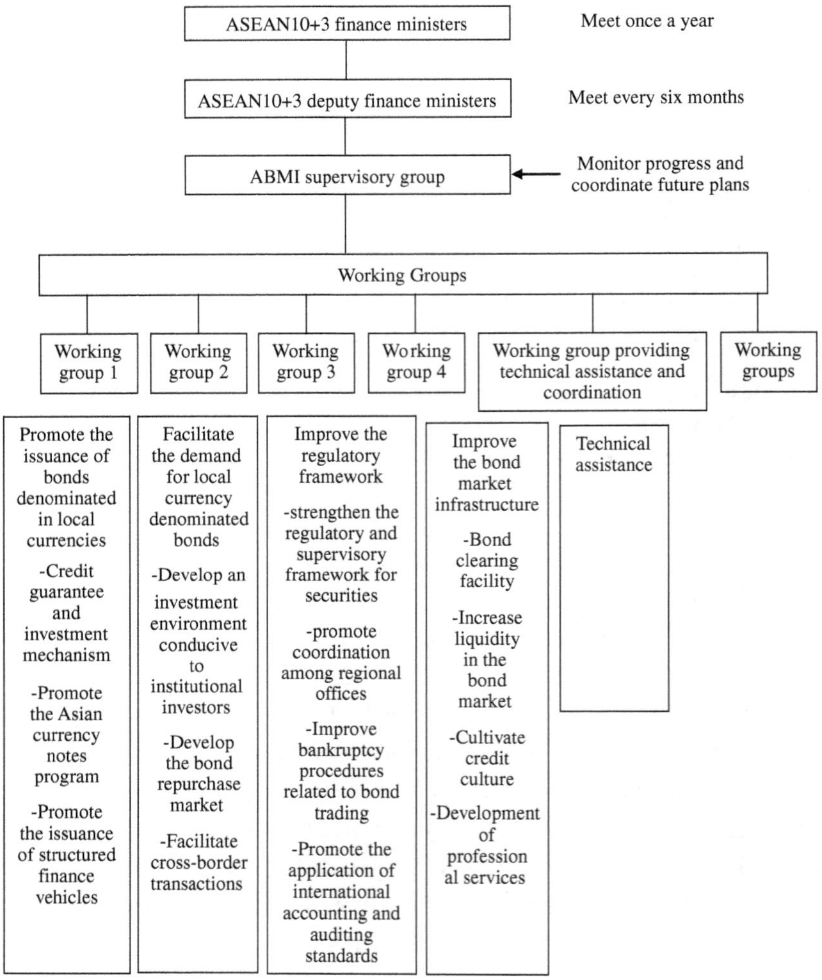

Figure 7.18. Organization Structure of ABMI

Source: www.adbi.org/files/2013.04.05.cpp.sess6.3.kawashima.asian.bond.markets.initiative.pdf.

to promote the market for corporate bonds (including bonds issued by non-residents); it is necessary to focus on the bond issuance and transactions. The second is the issue of incentives for foreign exchange reserves. Among the various portfolios, East Asian domestic currency bonds are only an option for foreign exchange reserves.

If such bonds have lower risks and higher returns than other investment types within and outside the region, then the support of foreign exchange reserve countries for the East Asia currency bond market will further promote its development. As an important member of East Asia region, China can make contributions to the development of the East Asian financial market in three aspects. First, it actively participates in the organization and institutional development of ABMI, and at the official level, it attaches great importance to the regular meetings of ASEAN 10+3 finance ministers and deputy finance ministers. At the think tank level, provide advice and suggestions for each work. The second is the formulation and introduction of innovative policy measures to stimulate the development of the RMB-denominated bond market and provide stable supply diversified portfolios of securities to both domestic and foreign official and private investors, and to promote the Asianization of the RMB. The third is to use part of foreign exchange reserves to invest in the region's relatively high-quality local currency-denominated bond assets, this aspect can reduce the cost of the excessive holding of foreign exchange reserves to some extent, on the other hand, it also plays a role as a "public goods provider" in stabilizing and developing regional financial markets.

7.3.3.2 *The East Asian Foreign Exchange Reserve Pool*

The East Asian Foreign Exchange Reserve Pool is a mechanism for the implementation of emergency financing and assistance to crisis countries in the East Asian region. It is an intraregional security financial network based on the lessons learned from the two financial crises in East Asian economies. Its origin was the AMF proposed by Japan in September 1997, which was based on the CMI signed by ASEAN 10+3 Finance Minister in May 2000. It started in May 2006 at the ASEAN 10+3 finance ministers meeting in Hyderabad, India, formed in December 2009 at the ASEAN 10+3 special meeting of finance ministers, and formally became effective on 24 March 2010. The establishment and development of the East Asian Reserve Bank has major political and economic implications: first, it represents important milestones in the monetary and financial cooperation in the East Asia region. It helps to lay a good institutional environment for the economic stability and financial development of the East Asia region; second, the Reserve Bank is trying to solve the short-term liquidity shortage problem of the relevant member countries in the region in order to increase the ability of East Asian countries to cope with the financial crisis; finally, the reserve bank is a reform and improvement of the existing international currency system. It has made up for the inadequacies of the international financial system or mechanism such as the IMF and the Financial Stability Forum in crisis warning, prevention and assistance in East Asia, and can partially alleviate the impact of institutional deficiencies in the existing international monetary system on the East Asian economy.

As a multilateral assistance mechanism, the East Asian Reserve Bank has the following features: first, in terms of composition and management methods, it is a liquidity reserve pool that is jointly funded in the form of US dollars. The central bank of member countries managed their own contributions in no-crisis period, but did not actually manage the dollar reserves to a common or centralized fund organization. In the "period of crisis," the reserve pool is jointly managed by member states, and the member countries that experience international payments or liquidity crises can exchange their currencies with the US dollar in the reserve pool.

Second, in nature, it is a "crisis-driven" regional financial safety net. The establishment and expansion of the reserve bank are the result of the impact or stimulation of the financial crisis inside and outside the region. As the prototype of CMIM, CMI is the collaborative effort of East Asian countries to reflect on the Asian financial crisis. Similarly, due to the impact of the global financial crisis, in an agreement reached at the Madrid meeting in May 2008, ASEAN 10+3 finance ministers agreed to set the initial reserve funds to US$80 billion. In the "Asian Economic and Financial Stability Action Plan" announced by the ASEAN 10+3 Special Finance Ministers Conference in February 2009, this scale has been expanded to US$120 billion. Stimulated by the unfavorable rescue of the European debt crisis, at the 15th meeting of the ASEAN 10+3 in May 2012, it passed a resolution to double the scale of the existing reserve pool to reach US$240 billion.

Third, in the form of capital contribution, voting power and borrowing multiplier, it is a system arrangement in which the interests of large countries play a game and the rights and obligations are obviously not equal. First of all, it is the product of the game of the interests of the great powers. In the initial plan, the ratio of Japan, South Korea and China to the three countries was roughly 3:2:1. China, the country with the largest foreign exchange reserves, ranked the third in funding. In the end, on 3 May 2009, the finance ministers of China, Japan and South Korea reached a final consensus on the proportion of capital contributions from the three countries. China nominally (Mainland China + Hong Kong, China) achieved the same dominant position as Japan, which continued to the post-expansion CMIM. However, in fact, if the factors of Hong Kong (China) are removed, China's actual share in the East Asian reserve is 28.5%, which is less than 32% of Japan's. If we take into consideration the fact that the ASEAN contribution is provided by Japanese loans, Japan has a clear dominant advantage in the reserve pool. This point is also reflected in the voting power. Second, it is an institutional arrangement that prioritizes the interests of small foreign exchange reserves. Specifically, the maximum exchangeable quota between China, Japan and South Korea is US$117.3 billion. Among them, the loan multiplier for China (excluding Hong Kong, China) is 0.5, and the maximum swap is US$34.2 billion; the Japanese borrowing multiplier is also 0.5, the maximum swap size is US$3.844 billion; Korea's borrowing multiplier is 1. The largest swap size is equivalent to Japan. In contrast, the total exchangeable size of ASEAN 10 is US$126.2 billion, which is higher than that of China, Japan and Korea. Among them, the borrowing multipliers of Indonesia, Thailand, Malaysia, Singapore and the Philippines are 2.5, respectively. The loan multipliers for weaker economies of Vietnam, Cambodia, Burma, Brunei and Laos are 5 (see Table 7.43 for details). It can be seen that this unequal design of rights and obligations is a priority for the interests of ASEAN foreign exchange reserve small countries. It is due to the reality that ASEAN countries cannot rely on self-help to effectively resist the impact of the financial crisis inside and outside the region.

Fourth, in terms of loan conditions and loan procedures, it is a repository of stringent conditions and procedures. In terms of loan conditions, in order to prevent moral hazard, the East Asian Reserve Bank adopts a link with the IMF. The specific operation method is that only 20% of the crisis loans that can be freely applied by East Asian member states are used. The remaining 80% are related to the loan conditions of the IMF. After the expansion of the scale in May 2012, the proportion of loans that Member States can use freely has been raised to 30%, and in 2014 it may be increased to 40%. In the loan procedure, before the voting member countries withdraw the fund's swap application, a comprehensive assessment of the economic and financial conditions of the member states needs to be conducted to examine the member states' compliance with the agreement, such as submitting regular supervision reports and participating in the Economic Review and Policy Dialogue (ERPD) process of ASEAN 10+3.

Fifth, in the decision-making mechanism, the East Asia foreign exchange reserve bank follows the principle of collective decision-making and the one-nation, one-vote system. Unlike bilateral decisions under the CMI framework, East Asian Reserve Banks implement collective decision-making under the CMIM framework, which are major changes to the Chiang Mai agreement.[118] The major issues related to regional currency and finance, such as the deliberation of the total size of the reserve pool, the amount of capital contribution by each party, the borrower multiplier, the re-admission of membership and loan conditions are determined by consensus of ASEAN 10+3. The 85% voting right of the IMF rule is very different, so as to avoid the possibility of one country's dominance and embody the East Asia cooperation model of a consensus and win–win

[118]Zheng, Haiqing, "Regional Response to the Financial Crisis: East Asian Foreign Exchange Reserve Bank," *World Economic Research* 12 (2009): 35–42.

Table 7.43. Contributions by Parties, Borrowing Multipliers and Voting Power in East Asian Reserve Bank

Country	Capital Contribution (US$1 billion)	Proportion	Borrowing Multiplier	Maximum Exchange (US$ 1 billion)	Basic Votes	Basis Number of Votes	Voting Rights: Number of Votes	Voting Rights: The Ratio of the Amount of Investment
Three countries	192	80		117.30	9.6	192.00	201.6	71.59
China	76.8	32.0						
China (excluding Hong Kong China)	68.4	28.5	0.5	34.2	3.2	68.4	71.6	25.43
Hong Kong (China)	8.4	3.5	2.5	6.3	0.0	8.4	8.4	2.98
Japan	76.80	32	0.5	38.40	3.20	76.80	80.00	28.41
Korea	38.40	16	1	38.40	3.20	38.40	41.60	14.77
ASEAN 10	48	20		126.20	32.00	48.000	80.00	28.41
Indonesia	9.104	3.793	2.5	22.76	3.20	9.104	12.304	4.369
Thailand	9.104	3.793	2.5	22.76	3.20	9.104	12.304	4.369
Malaysia	9.104	3.793	2.5	22.76	3.20	9.104	12.304	4.369
Singapore	9.104	3.793	2.5	22.76	3.20	9.104	12.304	4.369
Philippines	9.104	3.793	2.5	22.76	3.20	9.104	12.304	4.369
Vietnam	2.00	0.833	5	10	3.20	2.00	5.20	1.847
Cambodia	0.24	0.100	5	1.20	3.20	0.24	3.44	1.222
Myanmar	0.12	0.050	5	0.60	3.20	0.12	3.32	1.179
Brunei	0.06	0.025	5	0.30	3.20	0.06	3.26	1.158
Laos	0.06	0.025	5	0.30	3.20	0.06	3.26	1.158
Total	240.00	100.00		243.50	41.60	240.00	281.60	100.00

Source: The Joint Statement of the 15th ASEAN+3 Finance Ministers and Central Bank Governors Meeting, 3 May 2012, Manila, Philippines.

development based on equal participation, gradual progress and common ground seeking. On issues related to loans such as extensions and breaches of contract, the reserve bank has adopted a decision rule passed by a majority vote.

From the aforementioned analysis, at this stage, the East Asian reserve still has some key issues to be resolved: first, since the form of investment in reserve assets is US dollars, East Asia cannot continue to shake off the strong influence of US dollar exchange rate and US financial market in the short term. Second, compared with the huge contagiousness and destructive power of the contemporary financial crisis, the reserve bank's funding scale is obviously insufficient. Third, since the reserve bank is implemented by the member countries on their own during the "non-crisis period," the crisis countries apply for the exchange of US dollars in their own currency during the "crisis period," while the credit line is linked to the IMF's conditional loans. Therefore, during the crisis in East Asia, the intensity and efficiency of providing emergency liquidity support to member countries are questionable. Fourth, the existence and expansion of the reserve bank have typical "crisis-driven" features, and their crisis coping response is far more significant than crisis warning and prevention, and the normalization of the operation of the reserve bank has not yet been achieved. Fifth, due to the fact that China's capital contribution includes the factors of Hong Kong (China) and Japan's support for the foreign exchange reserves of ASEAN countries, China's actual representation in the reserve bank is insufficient, which is not commensurate with its status of the second largest economy and the largest foreign exchange reserve in the world.

Based on the aforementioned understanding, China needs to take the following countermeasures: first, further expansion of the scale of funds in the East Asian Reserve Bank and enhancing of its ability to rescue regional members from the impact of the financial crisis. Second, gradual introduction of regional currencies in the reserve pool to dilute the negative impact of the US dollar on the East Asian currency and financial markets. The policy measures are to vigorously develop the RMB-denominated East Asia regional bond market and enhance RMB-denominated bonds to attractive investors inside and outside the region. Third, share the dominance with Japan. Due to the absorption of China's Hong Kong membership, China cannot make marginal adjustments to the sharing of dominance in the proportion of existing contributions. The tasks that will need to be taken in the future are accelerating the reserve of talents, deepening institutional research and summing up international experience and shortening the gap with Japan in this regard by strengthening its own capacity building, and then strengthening its ability to share equal rights with Japan on a reserve basis. Fourth, actively participate in the construction of rules and regulations for the East Asian Reserve Bank. For example, China can provide constructive comments on issues such as strengthening regional financial supervision, risk management of reserve banks, member states and non-member countries.

7.3.3.3 *Central Bank's Currency Swap*

The central bank's currency swap means that the central banks of the countries exchange their currencies at the beginning of the period according to the conditions stipulated in advance. They exchange the foreign currency required by the counterparty with short-term loans, exchange their respective principals and pay interest to each other at the end of the period. The agreement signed on this basis of market transaction is called the bilateral currency swap agreement. Judging from the situation in East Asia, the currency swap between central banks is an important measure reflecting the progress of East Asian monetary and financial cooperation. As of the end of April 2009, the bilateral currency swap agreements signed between China, Japan and South Korea and ASEAN5 in the framework of CMI totaled US$90 billion. Among them, China provided local currency swap to Japan, South Korea and the Philippines with the RMB. Between the two countries, they involved the dual operations of US dollar swaps and local currency swaps. The vast majority of the remaining businesses are US dollar swaps. Judging from the scale of the agreement, Japan, South Korea and China are the largest lenders; South Korea,

Indonesia and Japan are the largest borrowing countries; Japan and China are the largest net lenders; Indonesia is the largest net borrowers (Table 7.44).

Since the official launch of the CMI in May 2000, the global financial crisis has erupted and no member countries have used swap funds. The reason is that the pre-crisis CMI consists of a series of bilateral swap agreements and lacks an intermediary coordination agency. Countries that need funds have to obtain sufficient financial support through multiple rounds of bilateral negotiations, and they may lose the best opportunity to deal with crises. Second, CMI has to rely on the IMF's monitoring mechanism because of the lack of independent monitoring agencies in the region. To prevent moral hazard, the specific approach is to link 90% of the financial support with the IMF's corresponding loans, lacking the necessary flexibility and promptness. Third, despite the fact that the total scale of CMI far exceeds the G-10 swap agreement, due to funding Aid is bilateral in nature, each member country can obtain limited funds.[119] In order to cope with the risk of liquidity shortage caused by the crisis, some major economies in East Asia have sought financial support from the United States outside the region. For example, Japan has signed a US$60 billion, US$120 billion and unlimited amount of short-term currency swap agreements with the United States in three separate installments (18 September, 29 September and 14 October 2008). Korea and Singapore also signed a US$30 billion currency swap agreement with the Federal Reserve on 29 October 2008.[120] This shows that the CMI mechanism has not played its intended role, and the East Asian monetary and financial cooperation has

[119]He, Fan, and Ming Zhang, "Factors of Dollar Hegemony in the Instability of the International Monetary System," *Research on Financial and Economic Issues* 7 (2005): 32–37.

[120]Allen, William A, and Richhild Moessner, "Central Bank Co-Operation and International Liquidity in the Financial Crisis of 2008-9," BIS Working Papers, no. 310 (June 2010).

Table 7.44. Bilateral Currency Swaps Signed under the CMI Framework (As of the end of April 2009) (Unit: US$1 billion)

From \ To	China	Japan	Korea	Indonesia	Malaysia	Philippines	Singapore	Thailand	Total
China		3.0[a]	4.0[a]	4.0	1.5	2.0[a]		2.0	16.5
Japan	3.0[a]		13.0[b]	12.0	1.0[c]	6.0	3.0	6.0	44.0
Korea	4.0[a]	8.0[b]		2.0	1.5	2.0		1.0	18.5
Indonesia			2.0						2.0
Malaysia			1.5						1.5
Philippines		0.5	2.0						2.5
Singapore		1.0							1.0
Thailand		3.0	1.0						4.0
Total	7.0	15.5	23.5	18.0	4.0	10.0	3.0	9.0	90.0

Notes: [a]It refers to the bilateral exchange of local currency, rather than exchange of US dollar currency.
[b]The bilateral currency swaps between Japan and South Korea include US dollar swap (from Japan to South Korea US$10 billion, from South Korea to Japan US$5 billion), including domestic currency swaps (two-way equivalent of US$3 billion). The exchange of yen against the Korean won was expanded from US$3 billion to US$20 billion in December 2008 and the amount is maintained until the end of October 2009.
[c]There is also a pledge of US$2.5 billion on 18 August 1999 under the framework of the New Miyazawa Initiative.

Source: Masahiro, Kawai, "From the Chiang Mai Initiative to an Asian Monetary Fund," *Asian Development Bank Institute Report* (April 2010).

encountered setbacks in strengthening regional crisis management and prevention capabilities.[121]

On the other hand, after the outbreak of the global financial crisis, major changes have also taken place in the regional monetary and financial cooperation within East Asia. After ASEAN 10+3 upgraded a series of bilateral currency swap agreements under the CMI framework to a multilateral self-managed reserve under the CMIM framework, the battle for the currencies influence has also begun quietly between Japan and China in the East Asian on bilateral exchange agreements. For Japan, "connecting with Korea in the North and cooperating with ASEAN in the South" is the consistent strategies for curbing China. However, due to diplomatic conflicts with the Republic of Korea regarding territorial and historical understanding, the currency swap agreement between the two countries reached the lowest point in July 2013. Following currency swap agreement that expired in July 2012 of the US$3 billion and the US$57 billion in October 2012, the currency swap between the two sides has dropped from US$70 billion in October 2011 to today's US$10 billion.[122] In this way, ASEAN countries will become the target of Japan's efforts to expand the influence of the yen in East Asia. On 12 December 2013, the Bank of Japan, as the agent of Japan's Ministry of Finance, signed the third bilateral currency swap agreement with Indonesia's Central Bank, expanding the swap size from US$12 billion to US$22.76 billion, and introducing a crisis prevention mechanism to support potential and/or realistic liquidity needs. At the same time, the Ministry of Finance of Japan, the Monetary Authority of Singapore and the Central Bank of the Philippines reached a tentative agreement, respectively. Among them, Japan and Singapore agreed to maintain the swap scale that had expired in 2011. That is, Singapore can borrow US$3 billion from Japan, and

[121]Xiao, Li, "Why did East Asian Currency Cooperation Suffer Setbacks?" *International Economic Review* 1 (2011): 111–130.

[122]Han, Intaek, "Currency Swaps Move South Korea Closer to China, Away from Japan," Last modified July 18, 2013. http://www.eastasiaforum.org/2013/07/18/currency-swaps-move-south-korea-closer-to-china-away-from-japan/.

Japan can borrow US$1 billion from Singapore. Japan and Philippines agreed to double the size of the swap from the previous US$6 billion to US$12 billion and introduce a crisis prevention mechanism.

Compared with Japan's "fragmentation" in ASEAN, the bilateral currency swap agreement launched by China is developed in an all-around and impressive way. It not only renewed with Korea in North-East Asia and expanded the scale of exchange of RMB and South Korean won, but also relied on Hong Kong (China) as an offshore RMB financial center to expand the overseas circulation of RMB, and have signed or renewed bilateral RMB swap agreements with the four major economies of ASEAN — Thailand, Malaysia, Indonesia and Singapore (see Table 7.45). This shows that the strong market demand caused by the rapid rise of the Chinese economy, the strength of the RMB and the prudent monetary policy of the People's Bank of China are clearly attracting other East Asian economies. The degree to which the RMB has been officially recognized and accepted by East Asia has gradually increased. What needs to be emphasized is that the use of these bilateral currency swap agreements is no longer limited to dealing with the possible liquidity shortage of members in the region, but is clearly regarded by the People's Bank of China as facilitating the widespread use of the RMB as the important means of activities of trade and investment with these economies.[123] In this sense, the currency swaps between central banks, especially the currency swaps between the central bank and other central banks of East Asian economies, are important ways to effectively promote regional monetary and financial cooperation in East Asia and gradually reduce the dependence of regional members on the dollar system.

7.3.3.4 *Regional Cooperation of Financial Supervision in Asia*

Regulatory cooperation is based on information sharing, adopts active policy coordination and technical assistance, adopts a

[123] People's Bank of China. "People's Bank of China Annual Report 2012." Http://www.pbc.gov.cn/image_public/UserFiles/chubanwu/upload/File /2012People'sBankofChinaAnnualReport.pdf

Table 7.45. Bilateral Currency Swap Agreement between China and East Asian Economies since the Global Financial Crisis

Country/Region	Scale	Signing date	Validity Period
Korea	180 billion yuan/38 trillion won	12 December 2008	3 years
	365 billion yuan/64 trillion won	26 October 2011	3 years
	365 billion yuan/64 trillion won (extension)	27 June 2013	3 years
	360 billion yuan/64 trillion won	11 October 2014	3 years
Hong Kong, China	200 billion yuan/22.7 billion HKD	20 January 2009	3 years
	400 billion yuan/490 billion HKD	22 November 2011	3 years
Malaysia	80 billion yuan/400 billion ringgit	8 February 2009	3 years
	180 billion yuan/90 billion ringgit	8 February 2012	3 years
Indonesia	100 billion yuan/175 trillion Indonesian rupiah	23 March 2009	3 years
	100 billion yuan/175 trillion Indonesian rupiah	2 October 2013	3 years
Singapore	150 billion yuan/30 billion Singapore dollars	23 July 2010	3 years
	300 billion yuan/$60 billion Singapore dollars	7 March 2013	3 years
Thailand	700 billion yuan/320 billion baht	22 December 2011	3 years

Source: Author according to the information published by the People's Bank of China.

consistent macroeconomic policy stance and fully considers domestic policy frameworks and regulatory measures in order to seek a unified policy integration process with regulatory objectives.[124] The motivation for regulatory cooperation lies in the fact that all parties have a realistic need to deal with the serious problems. Judging from the situation in East Asia, starting from the Asian financial crisis, people gradually realized the importance of regional cooperation in financial supervision for the economic development and financial stability of related parties. For example, in resolution 54/197 adopted on 22 December 1999, the United Nations General Assembly emphasized the role of regional and sub-regional financial institutions in preventing and managing international financial crisis in a timely and effective manner. When Rose analyzed the causes of the Asian currency crisis, he also pointed out that the currency crisis tends to spread among countries with international trade links.[125] Therefore, it is necessary for the Asian region to reduce costs and improve efficiency by establishing a financial safety net.Eichengreen advocates the establishment of an Asian Financial Institute (AFI) within the framework of ASEAN 10+3.[126] It has four tasks to undertake: first, coordinate the actions of member states to promote financial stability in the region; second, provide technical assistance to state agencies that seek to strengthen prudential supervision and control; third, carry out training programs for bank inspectors, securities trading commissioners and accountants, recruit students from all member states, and seek economies of scale and economies of scope, encourage the effective reserve of knowledge and professional skills; fourth, just as the BIS provides central bank services to its members, AFI needs to provide the central bank of member countries with services such

[124]Ba, Shusong, and Yuanqian Zhu, New Basel Capital Accords in the Financial Crisis: Challenges and Improvements. China Finance Press, 2010.
[125]Rose, Andrew, "Is There a Case for an Asian Monetary Fund?" *FRBSF Economic Letter*, no. 1999-37 (December 1999).
[126]Eichengreen, Barry, and Nathan Sussman, "The International Monetary System in the Long Run," *International Monetary Fund Working Paper*, no. 00/43 (March 2000).

as reserve management, clearing and settlement. In short, AFI can become a common agreement to negotiate the regulatory process on capital and liquidity needs and to promote the stability of the banking system, negotiating information disclosure standards, listing of securities, and corporate governance to promote the development of regional financial markets.

Judging from the progress in cooperation, East Asia's financial regulatory cooperation has gradually deepened after the Asian financial crisis. In October 1998, ASEAN finance ministers signed the "Treaty of Understanding," which marked the beginning of the establishment of the ASEAN's internal financial supervision mechanism. Under this mechanism, all parties will continue to strengthen their mutual supervision mechanism in accordance with the principle of mutual attention and equal consultation in order to strengthen the decision-making capabilities within ASEAN. In the Chiang Mai agreement reached in May 2000, an important part was that all parties agreed to fully mobilize and utilize related resources and strengths within the ASEAN 10+3 framework, strengthen cooperation in oversight of capital flows, and conduct extensive data exchange and information sharing. In May 2001, the ASEAN 10+3 Finance Ministers' Hawaii meeting achieved important results. All parties agreed to establish an EWS to early detect the weaknesses of the member countries' macroeconomic, financial systems and companies, and prevent the occurrence of potential financial crisis, actively use ASEAN 10+3 as a cooperation platform to enhance financial self-help capabilities of member countries, promote the exchange of data and information among countries, supervise the flow of international capital, especially short-term capital, and establish an open, interconnected cooperation network, and establish effective crisis warning mechanisms to prevent financial risks and maintain the stability of regional financial order. The ABF launched in June 2003 used BIS as the custodian of the fund, and at the same time it established a relevant supervisory committee in operation. The main purpose and goal is to improve the stability of the Asian financial system.

Affected by the global financial crisis, the ASEAN 10+3 Finance Minister Bali decided to establish an independent regional supervisory organization in May 2009. In May 2010, ASEAN 10+3 Finance Minister Tashkent reached consensus on the establishment of the ASEAN 10+3 Macroeconomic Research Office (AMRO). AMRO was established in Singapore in May 2011. The agency is governed by an Executive Committee (EC), which includes the deputy finance ministers and deputy governors of the member countries. It supervises AMRO, and it is responsible for providing guidance, setting a major policy direction for the management of AMRO, and appointing AMRO Director and Advisory Group members. At present, the operation of AMRO is carried out by 12 professionals under the leadership of the Director. Its number of members is planned to expand to 16 in the near future. The functions of AMRO are different in the "non-crisis period" and "crisis period." In the "non-crisis period," AMRO's main responsibility is to prepare a comprehensive quarterly report on the overall macroeconomic assessment of ASEAN 10+3 members and the entire region. In the "period of crisis," AMRO's role and responsibilities are diversified, including: (1) Providing analysis of economic and financial conditions of countries applying for currency swap under the CMIM framework; (2) Monitoring funds approved by the CMIM agreement; (3) Monitoring the compliance of CMIM exchange application countries with CMIM agreement.

In spite of this, regional cooperation in financial supervision in Asia still needs to be strengthened in two aspects: on the one hand, prudential supervision at the macro level in the region is progressing rapidly and prudential supervision at the micro level needs to be strengthened. Judging from the system of various economic entities, China and Hong Kong (China) implement the Institutional Approach. Under this model, the legal status of a company (such as banks, broker-dealers or insurance companies) determines which supervisor will be given the task of supervising the company's activities in terms of safety and soundness and business operations. Japan and Singapore are implementing the Integrated Approach, in which a single all-encompassing regulator performs the function of supervising the security and soundness of all financial services departments and regulates their business activities (Group of 30, 2008). Due to differences in the modes of supervision of micro-financial entities in different economies, different regulatory authorities in different economies will face the difficulties of function matching and information sharing to a certain extent when implementing micro-level prudential supervision and cooperation. On the other hand, despite the progress in the macro-prudential supervision among various economies, the monitoring organizations with clear functional positioning and complete organization are still in the process of construction and improvement. Judging from the development trend, AMRO has the potential to further develop into a leading financial regulatory institution in the region, but its credibility needs to be enhanced. It still lacks the research capacity, human resources, experience and institutional settings that are competent for the CMIM professional secretariat. It still plays a role mainly as a research office of CMIM and undertakes the task of providing macroeconomic and financial supervision and evaluation. Unless the member states promise to substantially increase the supply of AMRO resources to enhance and expand its functions, AMRO will be independent and credible and it is impossible for AMRO to realize its full function, not to mention that it functions fully as the secretariat of CMIM.[127]

In view of this, China can adopt the following countermeasures when participating in regional cooperation of financial supervision in Asia: first, improve the domestic legal basis for international cooperation in financial supervision. The relevant laws and regulations in the banking, securities, insurance and other industries are revised and updated to establish a procedural legal basis for participation in regional financial cooperation and coordination in Asia. Second, improve China's financial supervision rules and gradually bring its financial laws and financial supervision methods into line with international rules and practices. The international standards that can

[127]Menon, Jayant, and Hal Hill, "Does East Asia Have a Working Financial Safety Net?" *Asian Economic Journal* 28, no. 1 (March 2014): 1–17.

be referred to as financial supervision include the banking supervision standards set by the Basel Committee, and the establishment of foreign issuers in the host country by the International Securities Regulatory Commission in the "International Standards for Foreign Issuer Cross-border Raising and Initial Listing Information Disclosure." International standards for information disclosure at the time of securities raising and listing, and the International Insurance Regulators Association's "Applicable Principles for the Supervision of International Insurance Institutions and Insurance Groups and the Cross-border Businesses" established for international insurance institutions and insurance groups for cross-border business Regulatory standards, the standards of cooperation established in the "Group Regulatory Collaborative Standards' for the supervision of international financial groups engaged in insurance business. Third, pay attention to the exchange and interaction of regional financial supervisors. One feasible solution is to carry out training programs for multinational financial supervisory talents. In this way, not only can the regulatory level of domestic supervisory personnel be improved but also the platform can be used to familiarize each other with the regulatory model and regulatory rules of the other country, and to promote the communication, sharing and cooperation of regulatory information of all parties. Fourth, actively participate in the institutionalization of financial supervision and cooperation in the Asian region. For example, in view of the lack of credibility of AMRO, China may send management personnel with rich experience in foreign affairs to make up for the shortage of its human resources reserves, and select researchers with rich professional knowledge to enhance the research capability and monitoring capabilities of AMRO as the CMIM secretariat.

Chapter 8

China's Global Strategy to Participate in the International Monetary System Reform

On the basis of the comprehensive analysis in the previous chapters, this chapter first attempts to present an outlook on China's participation in the reform of the international monetary system, and China's role, guiding ideology, strategic objectives, principles of compliance, participation strategies, framework design and specific measures. Taking this as a starting point, we will analyze the main aspects involving the reform of the international monetary system.

First, the choice of reserve currency or reserve assets is the basis of the international monetary system. In view of the fact that the global financial crisis has revealed a major inherent flaw in the US dollar standard, China must first actively participate in the reform of the international reserve currency system.

Second, in the world economy of the ubiquitous sovereign credit currency, the determination of the exchange rate system also constitutes an important part of the international monetary system. Therefore, participation in the reform of the international exchange rate system is also an important requirement for China's participation in the reform of the international monetary system.

Third, in the open economy, the balance of payments and its adjustment are not only the policy objectives of the decision-making authorities of a country, but also an important deciding factor of the political and economic relations between countries. Therefore, participating in the reform of the balance of payments adjustment mechanism is another focus of China's active participation in the process of international monetary system reform.

As a result, the increase in the speed and scale of international speculative capital flows has become an important factor in inducing an international financial crisis. In particular, the rapid development of "shadow banking systems," such as pension funds that lack international supervision, money market mutual funds, and investment banks, pose a great threat to the economic and financial stability of the developing countries. In view of this, actively participating in the reform of the international financial regulatory system is also an important agenda for China to participate in the reform of the international monetary system.

Finally, unlike the gold standard in history, the international monetary system after the war included an important part of the international financial organization. Although international financial organizations dominated by the International Monetary Fund (IMF) and the World Bank (especially the IMF) have played an important role in stabilizing the post-war international monetary and financial order, every major international financial crisis has exposed its serious flaws. Therefore, the call for effective reform of major representative international financial organizations constitutes an important aspect of China's participation in the reform of the international monetary system.

The basic idea of China's active participation in the international monetary system reform at the global level is shown in Figure 8.1:

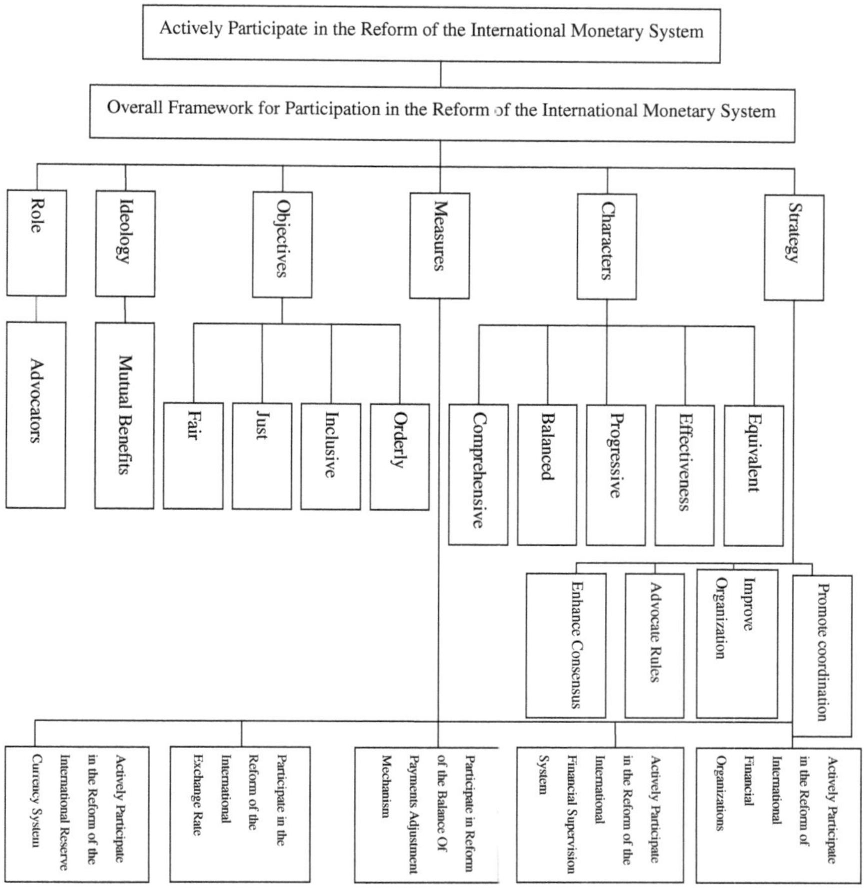

Figure 8.1. Global Participation in International Monetary System Reform

At present, the inherent defects and systemic risks of the international currency system have not been able to effectively promote the stable and orderly development of the global economic cycle, that is, the current international monetary system cannot effectively serve the global economic cycle. Under the current international monetary system, the problems faced by the global economic cycle are mainly manifested as the following:

First, the current international reserve currency system has reduced the circulatory capacity of the global economy and has restricted the sound development of the economic cycle. On the one hand, in order to obtain the necessary reserve assets and prevent the shortage of foreign exchange, non-reserve currency countries must obtain a corresponding trade surplus, and if the reserve currency country does not expect to hold the equal trade deficit, the total demand of the world economy will decrease. On the other hand, the reserve currency system of unilateral credit has forced countries in the periphery of the system to accumulate large amounts of foreign exchange reserves, and the accumulation of large amounts of foreign exchange reserves has actually become a "leakage" in the global economic cycle system. Because these foreign exchange reserve accumulations cannot be transformed into consumption or investment in a timely manner, they cannot be transformed into demand factors that promote the economic cycle. To a certain extent, this has reduced the formation of global purchasing power and reduced the total demand of the world economy.

Second, the current international monetary system brings asymmetric returns to different countries. For example, the current international monetary system is unequal. The accumulation of foreign exchange assets in non-reserve currency countries means that the United States, as the world's richest country, can receive cheap funds, while poor countries can not only obtain cheap funds but also take investment risks in reserve currency countries. The reserve currency countries also have inherent advantages in coin tax revenue gains and risk avoidance. These advantages make the returns of reserve currency countries even more pronounced under the international monetary system that lacks constraints and supervision.

Third, the inadequate regulation of the current international monetary system and global trade inhibits the balance of global trade and the stability of capital flows. Due to the difficulty in coordinating the balance of payments, the reserve currency countries have new reasons for the development of trade protectionism in order to reduce the trade deficit. In terms of international capital flows, due to the unilateral credit characteristics of the US dollar standard, the supply of the US dollar has become the fundamental factor in determining global liquidity, and the lack of constraints and supervision of dollar supply has caused global liquidity either to appear surplus or to be insufficient. With regard to the problems of international capital mobility and the stability of capital flows, the current role of the international monetary system is very weak.

It is precisely because there are factors in the current international monetary system that is not conducive to the healthy development of the global economic cycle. Therefore, to achieve sustainable and stable global economic growth, it is necessary to reform the international currency system so as to achieve the goal of promoting global trade balance, establishing a free trade system, and promoting the stable and orderly flow of capital.

The establishment of an international currency system conducive to the realization of the global economic cycle requires not only the "financial countries" (central countries) but also the "trade countries" (peripheral countries) to participate. Through the reform of the international currency system to promote the healthy operation of the global economic cycle, the relationship is shown in Figure 8.2. As an important "trade country," China should take the responsibility to promote a virtuous circle of the global economy. To this end, it is naturally responsible for actively participating in and advancing the reform and development of the international monetary system.

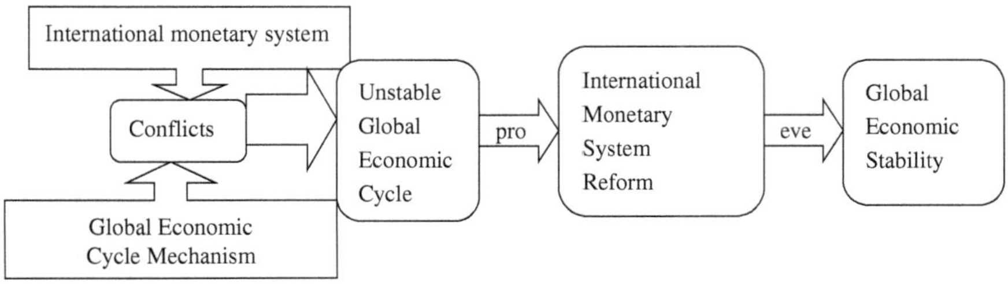

Figure 8.2. Operation of International Monetary System Reform and Global Economic Cycle

8.1 Prospects for China's Participation in International Monetary System Reform

The famous American economist Cooper once said: "From two perspectives, "the reform of the international monetary system" is a modern concept." Reform is a combination of the conscious behavior of willingness and coordination, which is different from the series of changes caused by the individual banks or commercial enterprises, and should call for the conscious reform of the government. The concept of an "international monetary system" reflects a different perspective, thus it is an overview of how all constituent components work together. It focuses on the ultimate result of collective actions of individuals or how the government will or should act in the international currency reform with some main features."[1] It can be concluded that the reform of the international monetary system includes two aspects: first, the international monetary system is an organic whole, and its reform needs to emphasize integrity and balance. It should not overemphasize the reform in one area and neglect other aspects. It is the wide range of interests involved in the reform process. There is not enough consensus and collective action based on consensus. The result is either that the reform is difficult to advance effectively or that the effectiveness of the reform will be greatly reduced. Based on the above aforementioned understanding, we believe that it is necessary for China to formulate a more systematic overall strategic framework for participating in the reform of the international monetary system, and make a more detailed strategic plan.

8.1.1 *Strategic Framework for China's Participation in International Monetary System Reform*

From President Hu Jintao's advocacy of the reform of the international financial system at the G20 Washington Summit, to the

[1]Cooper, R. N., "Is There a Need for Reform?" *The International Monetary System: Forty Years after Bretton Woods* (1984) 21, 45–51.

Governor of the People's Bank of China Zhou Xiaochuan's "Reflections on Reforming the International Monetary System", to the Finance Minister Xie Xuren's call for "speeding up the construction of a diversified international monetary system", to Vice Premier Wang Qishan's statement of "China is willing to contribute to the expansion of the IMF's fund pool", then to President Hu Jintao's speech at the G20 London Summit and the "BRICS" leaders' meeting, China actively participated in the international currency reform, with positive desire for the system reform. The goals, basic principles, and the direction of efforts for self-improvement are gradually clear. However, on the whole, these claims of the Chinese government have also been scattered on official occasions. They have neither been put together into a more systematic comprehensive strategic framework, nor have they made concrete strategic plans on how to participate in the reform. On the basis of the existing research, this research will present the comprehensive strategic framework for China's active participation in the reform of the international monetary system.

8.1.1.1 *China's Role*

China's role in the reform of the international monetary system should first be based on the basic national conditions of China. Although China today has grown into an important emerging economy in the world economy, it is still a developing country. Since the reform and opening up, the process of accelerating industrialization, urbanization, and modernization in China has also brought about many social issues such as structural imbalances within the economy. If no effective solution to the difficulties can be found, these problems will have a major impact on China's economic growth. Therefore, in participating in the reform of the international monetary system, China should proceed in a gradual and orderly manner in accordance with its own national conditions, and it is not easy to be too hasty.

In addition, judging from the diplomatic tradition, China has consistently adhered to the "Five Principles of Peaceful Coexistence." In order to create a favorable external environment conducive to its own stable development, China has long been working hard to improve its relations with neighboring countries and aims to establish the image of a large country. Therefore, in the process of reforming the international monetary system, China should also follow the external principle of "keep a low profile and never be a leader."

Finally, we look at the outside world's perception of China's international status and role. Since the founding of the P. R. China, especially after the reform and opening-up, China's economy has experienced rapid economic growth, a growing national strength and a significant increase in its international status. This series of changes has been regarded as "the most important geopolitical change in the world today." The rise of China has also been regarded as a major challenge by the relevant countries, and it has even been exaggerated as the "China threat" theory. Under such circumstances, in the process of China's participation in the reform of the international monetary system, it is also necessary for China to stay afloat and strive for the best interests that will benefit its own development.

Therefore, when participating in the games of interest in the reform of the international monetary system, China should combine its actual conditions with the outside world's perception of China and position itself as an "active advocator" of system reform rather than an "active leader" or the focus of the system's transformation game.

8.1.1.2 *Guiding Ideology*

The reform and opening up have brought China and the world together in close cooperation. China's economic growth cannot be separated from the world, and the world's economic development will inevitably lead to China's development. On the one hand, since the reform and opening up, especially after entering the 21st century, China's economy has developed rapidly and its international status has improved significantly. In 2013, China's contribution rate to world economic growth reached nearly 30%, the total GDP was second in the world only to the United States, and it was also the world's largest foreign exchange reserve country and the largest exporter. Its manufacturing base is known as the "world factory." These elements show that China has an irreplaceable position in the development and changes of the world economy, and plays a pivotal role in the reform of the international monetary system and the transformation of the international order.

On the other hand, the development and reform of the world economy have an immeasurable impact on China. From the reform and opening up in 1979 to the accession to the World Trade Organization (WTO) in 2001 and to the establishment of the Shanghai Free Trade Zone in the near future, China is gradually accelerating its pace with the world economy. However, opening up brings huge benefits to China as well as unpredictable risks. The huge amount of foreign exchange reserves, the increasing dependence on foreign trade and the gradual opening of the capital account all make the Chinese economy more vulnerable to changes in the global economic environment.

Based on these facts, the guiding ideology for China's active participation in the reform of the international monetary system is mutual benefit and win — win cooperation. It focuses on developing its own economy and ensuring financial stability and security. It also focuses on the stability and development of the world economy and finance.

8.1.1.3 *Strategic Objectives*

"Establishment of a fair, just, inclusive and orderly new international financial order" has become China's strategic goal of actively participating in the reform of the international monetary system.

The so-called "fairness" means that the ideal international monetary system should be able to guarantee both advanced industrialized countries and developing economies, that they can fairly express their own interest demands and enjoy the voting power commensurate with their strengths, safeguarding resources and benefits in both types of economies. The distribution is more equitable and the protection risk is more equitably shared between the two kinds of economies.

The so-called "justice" is related to many aspects of the reform of the international monetary system. It should be able to take into account "procedural fairness" in voting and decision-making and "substantial justice" in specific operations and implementation.

The so-called "inclusive" means that the ideal international monetary system must take the economic reality of developing economies into consideration and also consider the monetary and financial institutional arrangements that are compatible with these countries, and cannot blindly require that developing economies strictly abide by the "standard" of hegemonic countries in the system.

The so-called "orderly" means that the ideal international monetary system should be able to guarantee the stability and healthy development of the international monetary and financial order. Specifically, it must be able to guarantee the orderly supply of international reserve currency or assets, protect the reform process of the international exchange rate system, ensure the orderly adjustment of imbalances in international payments and safeguard the orderly flow of international capital.

8.1.1.4 *Principles*

Specifically, China's participation in the reform of the international currency system needs to follow five principles: comprehensiveness, balance, gradualism, effectiveness, and reciprocity.

The "comprehensiveness" means that the international monetary system is an integral whole system, so its reform cannot ignore the synergies between the various components. It is necessary to reform the international reserve currency system and international financial organizations and to improve international financial planning. The procedure should not only reflect the general laws and principles of international financial supervision but also fully consider the development stages and characteristics of different types of economies.

The "balance" means that the reform of the international monetary system is a process of institutional change involving multi-stakeholder coordination and adjustment. In this process, the balance of interests of all parties is related to the success of the system reform.

In the process of the interest games, it is necessary to take into account the interests of developed countries and their current status, as well as the interests and realities of emerging economies and developing countries.

The "progressiveness" means that the reform of the current international monetary system is not a "big bang" type, but should be implemented gradually. On the one hand, gradual and incremental reforms within the system help to maintain the stability of the international monetary and financial order, thus ultimately contributes to the stable development of the world economy. On the other hand, as with any other type of system reform, the formation and evolution of the international monetary system have the obvious features of "path dependence": First, the central country (the issuing country of dominant reserve currency) in the system still has the political, economic, technical and even military advantages to support its hegemony. Therefore, it has the ability to prevent radical changes in the system. Second, the peripheral countries in the system can obtain the benefits of development from the current international monetary system. Therefore, they do not have the will to make the radical changes. Third, the peripheral countries in the system are not yet equipped with sufficient capabilities in the economic growth, government capacity and financial markets to achieve radical changes in the international monetary system.

The so-called "effectiveness" means that reform programs and proposals should be feasible, operational and practical. The ultimate goal is to achieve mutual benefit and win — win results and to create a stable and orderly international monetary and financial order for China's economic development, which will also help promote the economic development of other economies.

The so-called "reciprocity" means that China actively participates in the reform of the international monetary system and must uphold the principle of reciprocity between rights and obligations. Under the background of growing interdependence with other economies in the world, on the one hand, China must clarify its own developing country status; on the other hand, it must also insist on reciprocity of enjoying rights and commitments, and avoid falling into the "trap" of other countries.

8.1.1.5 *Strategy of Participation*

Specifically, China needs to consider the participation strategies that enhance consensus, advocate regulations, improve organization and promote coordination.

The so-called "enhance consensus" seeks to increase the common interests of various economies in reforming the international monetary system. This is the basis for advocating rules, improving organization and promoting coordination. Since 2008, China has expressed its strong willingness to actively participate in the reform of the international monetary system on different occasions. The EU, BRICS and other developing economies have also adopted a positive attitude toward the reform, but the related parties do not have a broad consensus on the starting point of reform, the objectives and the direction of reform. To avoid the reform of the international monetary system to be the slogan, China needs to work hard to seek wider consensus in the countries or regions affected by the crisis. Otherwise, we will once again face the following dilemma: "On the one hand, the international monetary system is clearly unsatisfactory, so that an urgent effort for a cooperative reform is required. On the other hand, the willingness or ability of the government to cooperate at the international level looks unpleasant unless facing an immediate crisis, all proposals for reform face the risk of being quickly abandoned and deemed impractical."[2]

The so-called "advocate regulations" means that the direction of reform is to reform the international currency system committed to the rules. Specifically, it is committed to advocating the rules

[2]Witteveen, H. J., *Developing a New International Monetary System: A Long-Term View*. Washington DC: Per Jacobsson Foundation, 1983, 13.

for improving the transparency of information disclosure and financial activities; it is committed to advocating the strengthening of the rules for the financial supervision of the "shadow banking system"; it is committed to advocating allowing the crisis countries and regions to follow the principle of self-protection without damaging the premise of economic interests of other countries and regions; and it is committed to advocating the rules of unilateralism that restrict the abuse of monetary power by the issuing countries of leading reserve currency.

The so-called "organizational improvement" is to improve and strengthen the IMF's capabilities in monitoring, early warning, prevention and rescue of crises, and to improve and strengthen its ability to improve information disclosure in member states and restrict member countries" violation of regulations, thus improve their share allocation and voting and improve the mechanisms to enhance the representation and voice of developing members to reflect changes in the world economic landscape; to enhance the Bank's ability in crisis relief, increase short-term emergency loans, and stabilize the international monetary and financial order; to enhance the share and representation of development of member countries in the World Bank; to advance the institutionalization of the G20, as an important platform for enhancing consensus among members, advocating the establishment of rules, and facilitating coordination among members; and to strengthen the ability of IMF, the Bank for International Settlements (BIS), and the Financial Supervisory Commission (FSB) in the context of international financial supervision.

The so-called "improving coordination" is to promote the coordinated actions of all stakeholders while participating in the reform of the international monetary system. On the one hand, it is necessary to promote the policy coordination among China and other developing economies (especially the other members of the BRICS countries); on the other hand, it is necessary to promote policy coordination between China and the developed countries, such as the unanimous actions in reforming the international reserve currency system, reforming international financial organizations, and reforming the international financial regulatory system.

8.1.2 *Specific Strategic Plan of China's Participation in International Monetary System Reform*

After clarifying China's role, guiding ideology, strategic objectives, principles, and strategies in participating in the reform of the international currency system, this research believes that strategic plans needs to be made in the following areas in the specific implementation process:

First, participate in the reform of the international reserve currency system.

Second, participate in the reform of the international exchange rate system.

Third, participate in the reform of the balance of payments adjustment mechanism.

Fourth, participate in the reform of the international financial supervision system.

Fifth, participate in the reform of international financial organizations.

It is necessary to point out that: first, although the choice of the international reserve currency, the determination of the exchange rate system and the adjustment mechanism of the balance of payments constitute the three core elements of the international monetary system, the existence of international financial organizations and international financial supervision systems guarantee the normal operation of the system. Above five aspects affect each other and restrict each other, which constitute a comprehensive whole of the international monetary system. In the words of Boorman, "The parts that need reform are so closely interconnected that each piece can be dealt in a piecemeal approach that will not produce a coherent strategy."[3] Therefore, this research believes that the specific actions of China's participation in the reform of the international monetary system need to be carried out in these five areas at the same time. Second, in the reform of the above five areas, the focus of China's participation should be different. Since the international reserve currency system, the international financial supervision system, and the international financial organizations are of great concern to China and many other economies, there is a high possibility of enhancing consensus and promoting coordination. China needs to adopt a positive attitude and position. In terms of the reform of the international exchange rate system and the reform of the international balance of payments adjustment mechanism, the interests involved are far less extensive than the previous three. In most cases, the nature of bilateral consultations is the core. Therefore, the possibility of promoting consensus on reforms and promoting collective action is weak, which determines that China will have reservations in terms of participation in these two areas.

8.1.3 *The Interoperability of International Currency System Reform and Currency Cooperation in East Asia*

In order to effectively establish a new international currency system, all parties, including the United States, must first recognize the importance of a more stable international currency system and a universally accepted international reserve currency. In this global financial crisis, the multinational government's joint rescue of the market and their unprecedented cooperation to ensure that the crisis will not repeat itself have created a good opportunity for the reform of the international monetary system. As an important supporting force of the current "dollar system", East Asia determines

[3] Boorman, J., *An Agenda for Reform of the International Monetary Fund (IMF)*. New York: Friedrich-Ebert-Stiftung, 2008, 5.

that it will become one of the important driving forces for the reform of the international monetary system in the future. East Asia, which is on the periphery of the international monetary system, endures long-term suffering from the international monetary system and naturally should become an active promoter of this reform. Therefore, the East Asian region will become an important force in the reform of the international monetary system. The development of monetary and financial cooperation in the region and the exertion of regional collective forces will be particularly important.

Under the current "dollar system" the East Asia region faces many difficulties, and its important way to get rid of the predicament is to form the final product market provider in the region through the East Asian regional trade transition and to get rid of the long-term dependence on the US market. However, as two major countries in the East Asia region, Japan and China do not have the capability to become the final product market providers in the short term. The scale of the final product markets for East Asia is far from that of the United States (Li Xiao, Fu Jinghui, 2010).[4] Li Jin[5] pointed out that the monetary and financial cooperation in East Asia started from scratch, reflecting the confidence of Asian countries and economies in common interests and cooperation, and the demand for monetary and financial cooperation in the region is still strong at this stage.[6] Yamashita pointed out that in order to establish a system of stabilized exchange rate at the government level in East Asia, the SDR and even the SDR+ basket of monetary systems should be implemented first in a non-government form, followed by a clear policy of stabilizing exchange rates such as the SDR+ basket of currencies and even the basket of currencies in the East Asian region (ACU) at the

[4]Xiao, Li, and Fu Jinghui, "China's Status and Prospect as an East Asian Market Provider," *Journal of Jilin University-Social Science* 2, (2010), 68–79.

[5]Li, Jing, "China's Demand and Supply for Asian Monetary and Financial Cooperation," *Economic and Management Research* 2, (2005), 65–68.

[6]Eiji, Yamashita, "The Necessity of Establishing the Asian Edition of EMS and Joint Leadership Mechanism between Japan and China," Post-Crisis East Asian Monetary and Financial Cooperation Ed. Li Xiao, Jilin University Press, 2010.

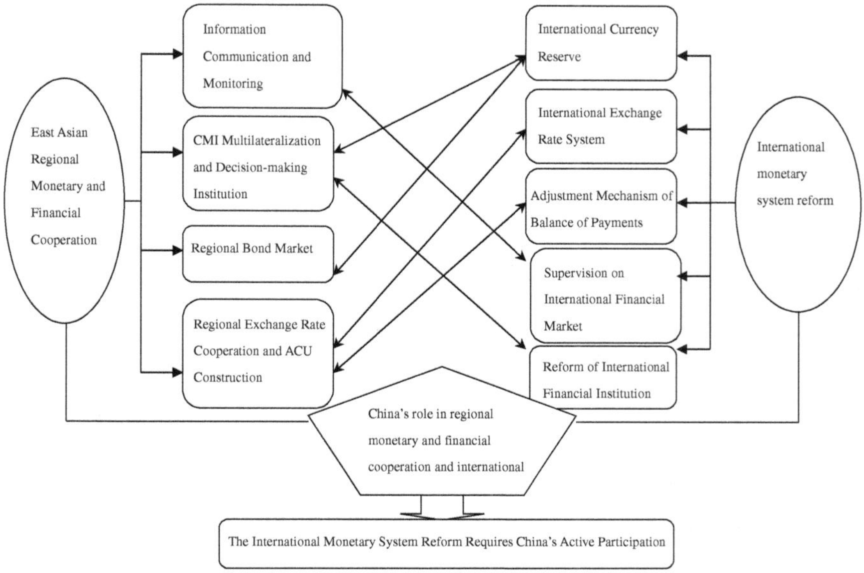

Figure 8.3. The Relationship between Currency Cooperation and International Currency System Reform in East Asia

government level, and then the strict currency stabilization coordination must be implemented by some countries and regions that are economically and institutionally convergent and close or consistent in political judgment. Therefore, the only way to get rid of the plight of the "dollar system" at this stage should be to strengthen regional monetary and financial cooperation in East Asia and rely on the collective action in the region to gradually promote the reform of the international monetary system.

The participation in East Asian regional monetary and financial cooperation and the reform of the international monetary system are mutually beneficial. The relationship between the monetary and financial cooperation in East Asia and the international monetary system reform is shown in Figure 8.3.

In the promotion of monetary and financial cooperation in East Asia and the reform of the international monetary system, China will play a pivotal role in East Asian regional monetary and financial coordination. Because of the economic homogeneity of emerging market countries in East Asia, China's participation in the international currency reform has a positive spillover effect on its neighboring countries. Therefore, from the perspective of monetary and financial cooperation and coordination in East Asia, China needs to actively participate in the reform of the international monetary system.

8.1.4 *The Promotion of the Reform of the International Monetary System and "the Belt and Road Initiative"*

As mentioned previously, "the Belt and Road" serves as a concept and initiative for China to promote cooperation and development at the cross-regional level. Its purpose is to build a common interest community, a destiny community, and a responsibility community for political mutual trust, economic integration, and cultural inclusion. During the construction process with the active efforts of China, the formation of a consensus on the reform of the international monetary system among the countries associated with the "Belt and Road Initiative" will not only contribute to the advancement of the reform of the international monetary system but will also in turn further promote the win — win cooperation in various countries around China and countries along the "Belt and Road."

For most countries along the "Belt and Road", whether it is the firm supporter of the US dollar-led international monetary system or the peripheral global power, they have to bear risks of the US dollar-led international monetary system to a certain degree. In fact, since the 1990s, the world's economic turmoil caused by monetary and financial issues, especially the US dollar system, has been dominated by countries along the "Belt and Road", with the exception of Latin American countries. From this point of view, most countries along the "Belt and Road" are motivated by the reform of the international monetary system.

On the other hand, unlike the situation in Latin America, many countries along the "Belt and Road" are relatively economically and politically dependent on the United States, or they have certain differences from the United States in the interest claims, which is the partial reason for their willingness to participate in reforming the current international monetary system dominated by the US dollar. If China can build cooperation through the "Belt and Road Initiative", it will actively promote consensus among relevant countries on a broader platform that is larger than the East Asia region and jointly promote the international monetary system reform.

Conversely, if countries along the "Belt and Road" can form a concerted effort to promote the reform of the international monetary system, not only will it have a positive impact on the reform of the international monetary system itself, but it will further increase mutual trust among countries along the "Belt and Road" and enhance the cooperation among countries. The identification of interests can thus have a positive impact on the "Belt and Road" economic cooperation and even political and diplomatic cooperation. Therefore, in addition to consistent promoting regional monetary cooperation in East Asia, strengthening the mutual promotion of the reform of the international monetary system and the "Belt and Road Initiative" should also be an important part of China's active participation in the international monetary system reform.

8.2 Actively Participate in the Reform of the International Reserve Currency System

The outbreak of the global financial crisis revealed that the current international reserve currency system has serious shortcomings. The current international reserve currency system is essentially the dollar standard system. In such an international reserve currency system, there is only one central country — the United States; there is only one central market — the Wall Street; there is only one central currency — the US dollar. While it has won huge economic benefits and financial power for the United States, and passed economic and financial crises to peripheral countries, it has plunged peripheral countries into monetary — financial attachment to the US dollar and US assets and the Wall Street financial markets. This is true for East Asia as a "trade account zone", and also in the form of a "financial account zone" of the EU and Latin America. For this reason, many economies including China have paid high attention to the reform of the US-led international reserve currency system.

From China's point of view, accumulated foreign exchange reserves of China have exceeded trillion US dollars. In the short term, although maintaining the dominant position of the US dollar is conducive to the stability of the value of China's purchases and investment in US dollar financial assets, this dependency situation is clearly not conducive to the independent development of China's economy and the sound development of financial markets in the medium to long term. Therefore, it is a rational choice for China to participate in the reform of the international monetary system by actively participating in the reform of the international reserve currency system, devoting itself to promoting the diversification of the international monetary system in the medium term, and seeking the possibility of creating a super-sovereign reserve currency in the long term. At the practical level, we must attach importance to the role of the G20's platform in order to promote the reform of the international reserve currency system (Figure 8.4).

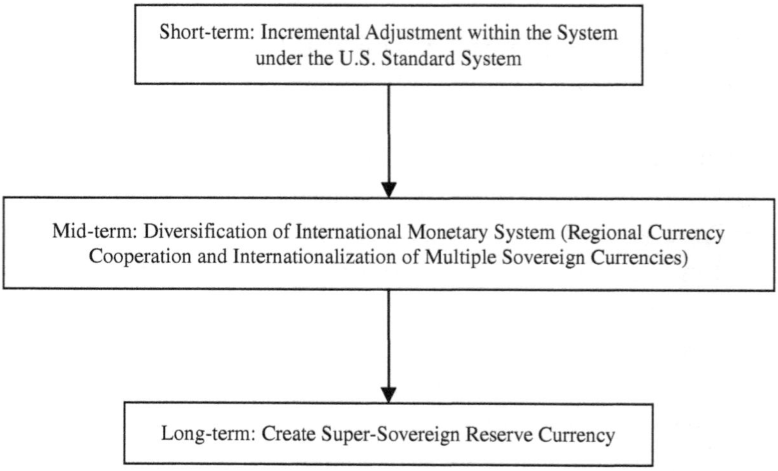

Figure 8.4. Phased Goal of China's Participation in International Reserve Currency System Reform

8.2.1 *Diversification of International Monetary System and Stability of International Monetary System*

Some foreign economists believe that in addition to increasing the volatility of the exchange rate from a single key currency system to a diversified monetary system, the international reserves expressed in any national currency will lead to the accumulation of reserves and the deficit of reserve currency countries. Therefore, it is inherently unsustainable (Greenwald and Stiglitz, 2008; Ocampo, 2007).[7,8] Despite of this, most economists prefer to diversify the international monetary system. For example, the famous international financial scientist Eichengreen thought that "a diversified reserve system" is approaching. We need to prepare for a system in which the US dollar, the euro and the RMB will be the international currency and the reserve currency.[9] Compared with its possible negative effects, the diversification of the international monetary system is more conducive to the stability of the international monetary system.

First, compared to a single key currency system — the dollar standard system — a diversified international currency system can spread the risk of exchange rate fluctuations of a single peg to the US dollar and the resulting loss of value of dollar assets. At the same time, it can also reduce the risks of mismatches. From the perspective of China, when the RMB has not yet grown into a member of a diversified international currency system and when it chooses to reserve assets or use foreign currency for investment and financing, China can make choices in international currencies such as the euro other than the US dollar. Once the RMB grows into a diversified

[7]Greenwald, Bruce, and Joseph E. Stiglitz, "A Modest Proposal for International Monetary Reform," In Time for a Visible Hand: Lessons from the 2008 World Financial Crisis, edited by S. Griffith-Jones, J. A. Ocampo, and J. E. Stiglitz, Oxford: Oxford University Press, 2010, 314–344.

[8]Ocampo, Jose Antonio, "The Instability and Inequities of the Global Reserve System," *International Journal of Political Economy* 36, no. 4 (2007): 71–96.

[9]Eichengreen, B., *Managing a Multiple Reserve Currency World.* Berkeley: University of California, 2010, 1.

international currency system, not only other economies can choose the RMB to decentralize and defuse risks, but the Chinese government, banks and enterprises can also rely on the advantages of the internationalization of local currency to minimize the risk of risk.

Second, compared to the single key currency system — the dollar standard system — the diversified international monetary system can provide alternative monetary policy constraints under the condition of the absence of global monetary policy anchor. Under the dollar standard system, the role of the Fed is not only the American central bank, but also to some extent the "central bank" of other countries in the world. However, the Fed's decision is based solely on the interests of the United States and ignores the interest needs of the countries. In this way, while there is a global currency, there is no global monetary policy anchor. In this monetary system, the Fed's monetary policy cannot serve as a stable anchor for other countries: When the US domestic economy is in recession, the Fed will adopt an expansionary monetary policy to export domestic inflation outside the US economy.; At the time, the Fed will use tight monetary policy to induce deflation in the peripheral countries of the currency. In contrast, the diversified international currency system provides a variety of money selection opportunities for the peripheral countries of the currency, thereby creating a "substitution effect" that can constrain the US monetary policy to a certain extent and counterbalance the US dollar currency issuance. This is a sign of China's pursuit of economic growth and stability.

Third, the diversified international monetary system will be an improvement over a single key monetary system — the "dollar system," — and no country will monopolize the seigniorage tax revenue. Spreading seigniorage tax among three, four, or five countries is not socially optimal, but it is an improvement over the state of being overly privileged by a country issuing reserve currency. And in such a world, there is not a reserve currency country like the United States in the year of crisis, which has the ability to freely finance for their current account deficits."[10] Therefore, the diversification of the

[10]Eichengreen. B., *Managing a Multiple Reserve Currency World.* Berkeley: University of California, 2010, 3.

international monetary system will, to a certain extent, weaken the seriousness of global trade imbalances and financial imbalances and ensure the stability of the international monetary system.

8.2.2 *Forms of Diversification of the International Monetary System*

How can we achieve the diversification of the international monetary system? In general, we can take two forms: to promote regional currency cooperation and equal emphasis on the internationalization of multiple currencies. Judging from the actual situation in China, efforts to promote the diversification of the international monetary system are both an established goal of China and a middle-term target. From a practical point of view, the dedication to developing the RMB as an international reserve currency has become a strategic orientation of the Chinese government and related functional departments. From the perspective of promoting regional monetary cooperation, the euro as a model in this area has inspired the enthusiasm of some peripheral regions to develop and deepen their monetary cooperation (East Asia, Gulf Cooperation Council, etc.). As an important member of East Asia, China has made a substantial progress in participating in the regional monetary cooperation of East Asia. Correspondingly, RMB has received certain breakthroughs in the East Asian region and has been accepted by some foreign governments. However, unlike the euro area, there are many differences in the history, political systems and economic development levels among the various economies in the East Asia region. Therefore, efforts to promote regional monetary cooperation as a whole under the "10+3" framework are facing many obstructions. The difficulty of the RMB to grow up as an international currency by the platform of East Asia's regional currency cooperation can be imagined, and trying to create an Asian currency similar to the Euro is nowhere in sight. In particular, the successful entry of the RMB into a diversified international monetary system in the form of regional currency cooperation not only depends on the smooth adjustment of China's own economic structure, but also enables China to successfully replace the United

States as a market provider of final products in East Asia, and rely on the coordination and cooperation of exchange rate policies between major countries of China and Japan.[11]

From the perspective of the internationalization of multiple currencies, the realization of the internationalization of sovereign credit currencies is also an important form of promoting the diversification of the international monetary system. Judging from the reality of China, the circulation and internationalization of the RMB in the periphery and even beyond the region is remarkable. At the official level, the People's Bank of China has successively signed currency exchange agreements with the central bank of South Korea, Hong Kong, Malaysia, Belarus, Indonesia and Argentina, thereby expanding the scope and scale of the use of RMB in other economies. From the perspective of private use, cross-border circulation of the considerable scale of RMB can be achieved by cross-border trade settlement, personal tourism and overseas savings, bonds issued overseas by the Chinese government and banking industry, and regional bonds issued by the regional financial organizations within the border of China.[12,13] In October 2013, in the global trade-related credit agreement, the proportion of using RMB as a financing currency has soared from 1.89% in January 2012 to 8.66%, making the RMB the second-largest international trade and financing currency after the US dollar (Figure 8.5).

8.2.3 *Diversification of the International Monetary System*

Whether it is through the form of regional currency cooperation or the means of internationalization of multiple currencies, we cannot

[11]Li Xiao, "The Path Choice of East Asian Monetary and Financial Cooperation under the Global Financial Crisis," *Northeast Asia Forum* 5, (2009): 3–25.
[12]He, Fan, "Realistic Choice of RMB Internationalization," *International Economic Review* 7–8, (2009), 9–11.
[13]Gao, Haihong, and Yongding Yu, "The Meaning and Conditions of RMB Internationalization," *International Economic Review* 1, (2010), 43–61.

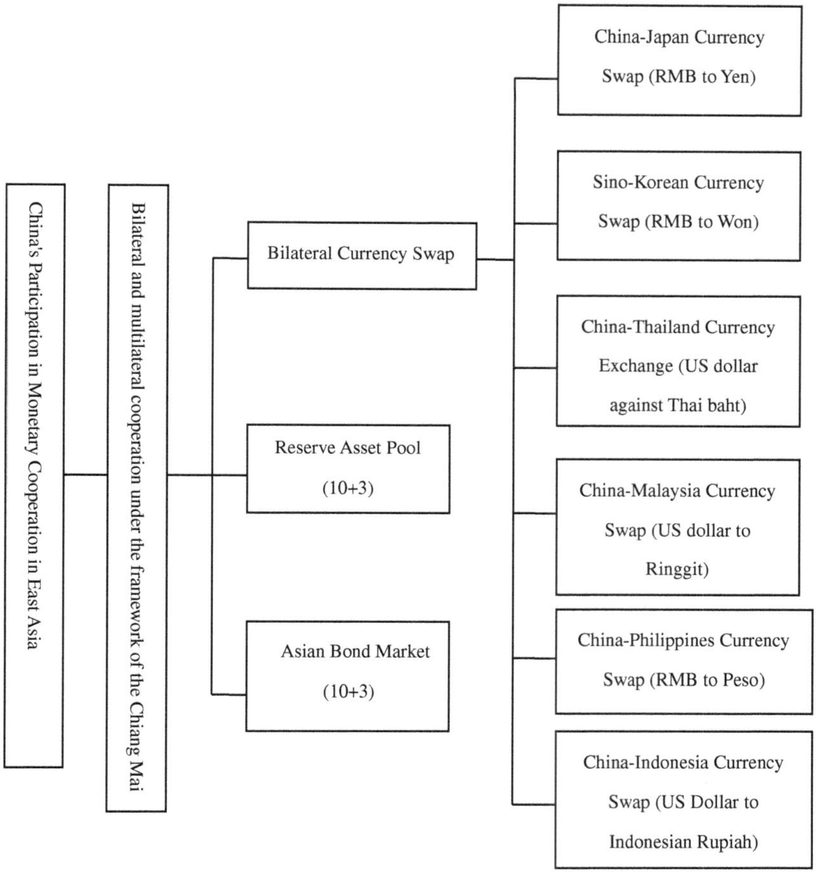

Figure 8.5. China's Participation in Monetary Cooperation in East Asia

avoid the diversification of the international monetary system. It is worth noting that in the increasingly fierce international currency competition, the realization of a diversified international monetary system is an endogenous and exogenous process. In terms of endogeneity, the diversification of the international monetary system is fundamentally a market-driven process. Whether a currency can become a diversified international currency system pattern depends fundamentally on the degree of acceptance of the market trading entity. From the perspective of exogeneity, today's sovereign credit currencies must be placed in a diversified international monetary system, facing the powerful "network effect" of incumbent international currencies and the high "entry threshold" erected by international currency issuing countries. It is determined that the money of latecomers needs to be promoted by the government forces to realize the advantage of later development and eventually grow into an international currency.

It should be pointed out that, as mentioned earlier, the degree of recognition and acceptance of RMB by the market is gradually increasing, that is, in addition to the swap arrangement of the local currency signed under the Chiang Mai agreement with the currencies of the three East Asian partner countries. With regard to the currency swap agreements signed by the central and foreign central banks that use RMB as the currency of payment, the acceptance of RMB by the official institutions of other economies is still low, so the RMB is far from the real international currency. Second, apart from private endorsement and acceptance of the market-driven endogenous nature of the RMB, China's idea of? promoting the diversification of the international monetary system has obvious exogeneity characteristics. From the end of 2008, the Chinese government has made significant progress in promoting the internationalization of the RMB in the following three aspects. First, China has begun to accelerate the pilot work of the RMB in cross-border trade settlement. Second, as mentioned above, China has successively signed bilateral swap agreements with South Korea, Hong Kong SAR, Malaysia, Belarus, Indonesia and Argentina with a total value of ¥650 billion for three years to promote the development of a pilot program for cross-border trade settlement of RMB. The third is to restart the exchange rate formation mechanism reform. On 19 June, 2010, the week before the G20 Toronto Summit, the People's Bank of China announced that it would restart the reform of the RMB exchange rate formation mechanism. The new exchange rate reform will continue the RMB exchange rate formation mechanism from July 2005 to June 2008. The Third Plenary Session of the 18th CPC Central Committee also explicitly proposed to promote the marketization of the RMB exchange rate formation mechanism, promote the liberalization of interest rates and the opening up of capital accounts. These policies are important supporting measures to promote the internationalization of the RMB. Third, China's efforts to promote the diversification of the international monetary system have clearly drawn lessons from Japan's failures, and this avoided the internationalization path that directly challenged the US dollar hegemony, and instead chose to follow an integrated "dual track" mode relying on East Asia's regional monetary cooperation with both market-driven and government-promoted characters. This is a correct rule that China still needs to stick to in the process of actively participating in the reform of the international reserve currency system and promoting the diversification of the international monetary system. Fourth, China's efforts to promote the internationalization of the RMB to promote the diversification of the international monetary system should be cautious. The liberalization of the RMB trade settlement policy and the development of the RMB offshore market in Hong Kong can be regarded as the relaxation of capital account controls. In an exchange rate formation mechanism that does not yet reflect market supply and demand fundamentals, loosening capital controls will only incur greater speculative capital shocks and threaten the domestic macroeconomic stability. China must take warnings from all recent lessons of the financial crises in Latin America, Southeast Asia and other countries. Under the dual control of exchange rates and capital controls, the above-mentioned process of internationalization of the RMB is largely the result of expected arbitrage of RMB appreciation under policy subsidies. The monetary authorities have paid heavy price for this purpose, but the process of internationalization of the RMB supported by this is not solid.

8.2.4 *International Reserve Currency Reform and Super Sovereign Reserve Currency*

The article "Reflections on Reforming the International Monetary System" published by Zhou Xiaochuan once again ignited people's enthusiasm for establishing a super-sovereign reserve currency. There are several points worth thinking about the super-sovereign reserve currency in this article. First, the dollar-led international currency system has internal defects and systemic risks. Second, rebuilding a new reserve currency that has a stable benchmarking value and is accepted by all countries may be a long-term goal. Therefore, the reform can only be a gradual progress, and a pursuit for common prosperity. Third, special drawing rights (SDRs) have the characteristics and potential of the super-sovereign reserve currency, for example, the currency value is stable, the supply is orderly and the total amount is adjustable. Fourth, the enlarged issuance of SDRs will help the International Monetary Fund to overcome the difficulties faced in the reform of funding, discourse power and representation. Fifth, to further improve the valuation method of the SDRs, it can expand a fixed basket currency range to the world's major economic powers, and consider GDP as one of the weighting factors.

Although the analysis of this article is justified, the creation of a super-sovereign reserve currency requires many necessary conditions. The SDRs as an alternative to the super-sovereign reserve currency have drawbacks and complexity of the reform.[14] In a nutshell, first, SDRs only exist as a bookkeeping unit and reserve assets and cannot be used for private transactions and settlements. Second, SDRs lack financial markets that can actually be traded, thus limiting the breadth and depth of its use. Third, the allocation of fixed currency, issue amount, and share of SDRs relate to the game of interests of all parties involved in the international monetary system. It is very difficult to promote it as a super-sovereign reserve currency. In the end, although the SDR has some advantages over the super-sovereign reserve currency, the "Triffin problem" between quantitative supply and price stability will not be completely eliminated. Therefore, although this idea is good, it does not have practical operability and

[14]Cao, Honghui, and Liping Zhou, "The Reform Direction of the International Monetary System and Its Related Mechanisms," *International Finance Research* 9, (2009), 8–14.

can only be regarded as a long-term appeal.[15] Based on these analyses and judgments, in the process of participating in the reform of the international reserve currency system, China's more realistic choice is to actively seek to promote the diversification of the international monetary system.

First, taking into account the political, economic, military, and cultural strengths that the United States possess at this stage, despite the emergence of international relations pattern of the so-called "one superpower and many powers," there is no possibility of replacing the United States as a hegemonic country in the short term. This status of the United States provides an important support for the "dollar system." In addition, under the current "dollar system", international capital flows have become one of the main means of realizing international economic relations at the current stage. The results of competition among countries are often "positive", and the costs and benefits of each other are highly correlated. One of the outstanding performances of this global financial crisis is that the major countries and regions in the world must share the cost and loss of the crisis. This shows that major changes have taken place in the environment and conditions for hegemonic entrenchment under the conditions of economic globalization, and this change may continue to be more favorable to the hegemony of US dollar for a long period of time.

Second, the global financial crisis after the 1970s indicates that during the crisis and the post-crisis period, the US dollar is still a strong currency.[16] Whenever a crisis erupts, regardless of the reason and place, the dollar remains a "life-saving straw" for governments and investors to ensure asset safety and risk aversion. The status of the US dollar has not only fallen but has risen. This situation has not changed even after the birth of the euro. In fact, after the

[15]Yu, Yongding, "Reform of the International Monetary System and Preservation of China's Foreign Exchange Reserve Assets," *International Economic Review* 5–6, (2009), 15–19.

[16]Xiao, Li, and Yongqi Feng, "Changes in the Status of China and Japan in Intra-Asian Trade and Its Enlightenment," *Contemporary Asia-Pacific* 6, (2009).

global financial crisis, the euro zone economy suffered even more than the United States itself. The outbreak of the debt crisis in Greece and other countries revealed a series of major issues concerning the economic connotation of the euro zone, which all indicate the current stage of the international currency. The system is still dominated by the US dollar, and the euro does not yet have the ability to replace the US dollar as the dominant international currency. This determines that the dollar system itself is still very sustainable, and the situation is difficult to completely overturn or change in the short term.

Third, after the Second World War, all countries in the world formed a new division of labor between virtual economy and real economy based on comparative advantage. Based on the comparative advantages of the development of the financial industry, United States has become a typical "financial country" that controls financial hegemony. However, countries such as Japan and China have developed into "trade country" focusing on manufacturing industries. Therefore, the economic imbalance between "financial countries" and "trade countries" is essentially a structural problem caused by the long-term division of labor between the financial industry and the manufacturing industry. The export-oriented industrialization of the East Asian economies is the result of international division of labor. It is an endogenous decision. Therefore, relying on changing the economic growth model of some countries in the short term cannot solve the problem of global economic imbalance. This also determines the arduous and long-term nature of changing the existing dollar system. Just as the former US Treasury Secretary Lawrence Summers said: there is a so-called "financial terror balance" between the East Asian economies and the United States. In fact, this type of horror is extremely unbalanced. The United States completely takes the initiative, and the East Asian economies, such as China, are trapped in the dollar trap and fall into a dilemma.[17]

[17] Jiang, Yong, "'International Financial Terror Imbalance' and the Financial Trap of the United States," *Modern International Relations* 7, (2005). 35–40.

Fourth, East Asian economies, especially China, as an important supporting force for the existing US dollar system, will not be able to escape the dependence on the US market in the near future. The US position as a provider of final product markets in East Asia will not be changed in the short term.[18] Since the 1990s, although the development of intraregional trade in East Asia has been very rapid, most of its trade products are intermediate products, parts and components and capital goods that accompany the decentralization of production processes in the region. The final product market is still dependent on the countries and regions such as the United States. Moreover, in view of the long-term nature of the economic restructuring, it will be difficult for the East Asian region to replace the US as the end product market provider in the short term. It is difficult for Japan and China to perform similar functions or roles. Therefore, it is difficult for East Asia to shake off its dependence on the "dollar system" in the short term.

Despite the outbreak and deepening of the financial crisis, the Chinese government recognized the necessity and urgency of reforming the unreasonable global financial order, and this also brought a series of opportunities for China to participate in the reform the international monetary system. However, from the perspective of global finance, it is difficult for the order to undergo substantive adjustment in the short term. This also determines that the current reform of the international monetary system will face many challenges and can only gradually promote local reforms on some levels. When establishing the goals of the future reform of the international monetary system, China must recognize its own position and the opportunities and challenges it faces. The "dollar system" cannot be fundamentally changed for a long time to come. This is the most important practical background for China to reflect on and promote the reform of the international monetary system at the current stage. It also indicates

[18]Xiao, Li, and Fu Jinghui, "China's Status and Prospect as an East Asian Market Provider," *Journal of Jilin University-Social Science* 2 (2010), 68–79.

the complexity and gradualness of the internationalization of RMB and East Asian monetary and financial cooperation in the future.

8.3 Actively Participate in the Reform of the International Exchange Rate System

8.3.1 *Changes and Dilemmas of International Exchange Rate Regime*

Since the formation of the world economic system, the international financial system has undergone three major exchange rate systems: the fixed exchange rate system under the gold standard system, the fixed exchange rate system under the Bretton Woods system, and the exchange rate system under the Jamaican system.

The fixed exchange rate system under the gold standard links the currency with gold, and its unique stability reduces the risk of exchange rate fluctuations and promotes the development of the world economy. However, limited world gold reserves cannot keep pace with the progress of the global economy. With the advancement of science and technology and the continuous economic growth, the trade between countries has been increasingly strengthened. The contradiction between the increase in demand for money and the shortage of supply has become increasingly prominent. The outbreak of war has increased the demand for gold in various countries and further shakes the foundation of the gold standard system. With the outbreak of the First World War, the international gold standard system will end up dying.

In order to build a new international economic order, the Bretton Woods system came into being. The system is an international gold exchange standard system that uses the United States dollar as a benchmark. Gold is no longer the only international currency. To a certain extent, this solved the problem of insufficient global gold production after World War II. At the same time, the supply of the US dollar also filled the shortage of the international reserve currency and eased the lack of international solvency. However, this kind of exchange rate system also links the exchange rates of various countries with the economic development of the United States and its domestic inflation, thus leading to the unbalanced of responsibility for balance of payments adjustments and making the implementation of exchange rate systems between countries full of contradictions. With the United States unilaterally announcing the termination of the exchange of dollars with gold in 1917, the Bretton Woods system finally terminated.

After the collapse of the Bretton Woods system, the international monetary system entered the era of the Jamaican system. Since the Jamaican meeting in 1976 formally confirmed the "exchange rate legalization", the strict disciplinary discipline under the classical Bretton Woods system — the fixed and adjustable pegged exchange rate system — has ceased to exist and has been replaced by the term "a system without a system" — the Jamaican system. Under this system, the currencies of the major industrialized countries exhibit a managed floating exchange rate relationship. However, both the IMF's annual report (IMF, 2005) and academic and empirical studies have revealed that there are still a number of developing economies that maintains a pegging relationship with major currencies.[19] The assumption that many some scholars envisaged that the developing economies by will choose the "corner solution" fails to become a reality. On the contrary, "abandon the two heads and take the middle" will become a true reflection of the choice of exchange rate system for most developing economies. It can be seen that no exchange rate system is suitable for all countries, and no exchange rate system is suitable for all periods of a same country.

It is worth noting that unlike the Bretton Woods system, under the Jamaican system, which is characterized by a floating exchange rate system, exchange rates have become an important means for countries to regulate their economic operations. Severe imbalances and instability in the exchange rate and exchange rate system

[19] Meissner, Christopher M., and Nienke Oomes, "Why Do Countries Peg the Way They Peg? The Determinants of Anchor Currency Choice," *Journal of International Money and Finance* 28, no. 3 (April 2009): 522–547.

constitute the typical features of the system. The "unbalanced" manifests that, although the Jamaican agreement nominally allows countries the right to freely choose their own type of exchange rate system, in fact, except for a few countries that are able to freely adopt a floating exchange rate system, most economies (developing economies in particular) still choose to continue to maintain a fixed exchange rate relationship with the major reserve currencies, because most of them are open economies and need to stabilize their own currencies with developed countries (especially countries that are export markets for the former). The price relationship between the currencies can stabilize foreign trade in the country and promote the country's economic growth. The "unstable" situation is reflected in the fact that major advanced economies adopting a floating exchange rate system did not take into account the spillover effects of exchange rate adjustments when adjusting their exchange rate policies, and their lack of coordinated exchange rate adjustments would induce great world economic and financial conditions. Based on the current plight of the international exchange rate system and the phenomenon of large fluctuations in the exchange rates of some countries during the financial crisis in 2008, two reform programs have emerged in the international community. One is the "devaluation of the exchange rate system", which is to reintroduce the concept of Keynesian super-sovereign currency and establish a new Bretton Woods system; the other is to return to a fixed exchange rate system and establish a new Bretton Woods system.[20] However, the aforementioned two reform programs have fundamentally changed the current international exchange rate system. The amount crisis and the European crisis are not enough to reshuffle the global economic structure. The existing international exchange rate system is also difficult to be fundamentally transformed.[21]

---

[20] Wang, Lirong, and Lizhen Liu, "China's Role in the Future Reform of the International Exchange Rate System," *Contemporary Economic Research* 12, (2012), 5–13.

[21] *Ibid.*

8.3.2 *China's Role in the Reform of International Exchange Rate System*

From the actual point of view of China, after two major reforms in 1994 and 2005, the RMB exchange rate formation mechanism has been continuously improved. While developing its own economy, it has also made contributions to stabilizing the region and the global economy. The major difference is that, the stability of the RMB exchange rate commitment was a unilateral action of the Chinese government during the Asian financial crisis in 1997. During the global financial crisis, the adjustment of the RMB exchange rate was inseparable from responsible international cooperation and coordination, especially through the bilateral coordination between the China — US Strategic and Economic Dialogue with the United States. It is not difficult to conclude that the coordination of the international exchange rate system based on rigid rules in the past is gradually transforming to the coordination of the institutionalized (China — US Strategic and Economic Dialogue, G20 Financial Summit) and contingent exchange rates.

For China, participating in the coordination of the international exchange rate system needs to grasp several key points. First, it emphasizes the coordination and stability of exchange rates among major global powers; second, it fully emphasizes and makes use of various mechanisms and platforms to enhance the international exchange rate system. The consensus of reform and coordination promotes the realization of collective concerted actions. Third, it emphasizes that the reform of the international exchange rate system cannot be implemented in one direction. It should take into account the different national conditions and development stages of different economies. Fourth, the equivalence of the reform of the international exchange rate system must be maintained. As an important oversight agency of the international exchange rate system, the IMF cannot blindly implement the will of the leading countries in the international monetary system. As the leading country in the international monetary system, the developed industrial countries cannot blindly impose pressure on the reform and adjustment of the exchange rate system over the developing countries. On this point, Eichengreen made it clear: "The key point is that the exchange rate system is a system and the countries involved are obliged to ensure the stability and smooth operation of the exchange rate. The actions of surplus countries and deficit countries are systematic. Their significance is that their actions are important to the stability and smooth functioning of the international system; in practice, they cannot assign all adjustment responsibilities to the deficit. This is the lesson that Keynes learned from the practice of the Great Depression."[22]

8.4 Actively Participate in the Reform of the Balance of Payments Adjustment Mechanism

8.4.1 *Defects in Current Balance of Payment Adjustment Mechanism*

The balance of payments adjustment mechanism is an important part of the international monetary system. Under the classical gold standard system, the adjustment mechanism of the balance of payments is relatively symmetrical for both the surplus countries and the deficit countries. The "price-coin flow mechanism" plays a self-regulating function. However, after the gold standard, the sovereign credit currency gradually pushed gold out of the international currency sphere. In the international monetary system where the hegemonic currency alone dominates (the status of gold has been lost), the adjustment mechanism of the international balance of payment is mainly embodied in exchange rate adjustment. The process of adjustment has also become increasingly asymmetric and unequal for both the surplus countries and the deficit countries. This asymmetry and inequality manifest itself as: when a hegemonic power is in a surplus, the developing economies that are in a position of deficit countries have to

[22]Eichengreen B., and Temin P., "Fetters of Gold and Paper," *Oxford Review of Economic Policy* 26, no. 3, (2010): 370–384.

endure the pain caused by adjusting the balance of payments imbalance. On the contrary, when a hegemonic country becomes a deficit country and its own economic interests are damaged, it often blames the rigidity of the exchange rate system of the developing economies and the manipulation of the exchange rate, and uses the "beating" of the latter to make necessary concessions. Responsibility for adjusting the balance of payments imbalances is borne by the peripheral countries or regions in the international monetary system.

This is particularly evident in East Asia, which is a "trade account area." Since the end of the war, as the first successful country in East Asia, Japan has increasingly accumulated a large current account surplus with the United States, which is the leading reserve currency issuing country. It has become the first country in East Asia to be beaten by the United States. To adjust the exchange rate system of the US dollar against the yen and open capital accounts, Japan has been dragged into a "lost decade." The same situation has gradually reappeared in China's current account surplus with the United States. The US's accusation against China's manipulation of the RMB exchange rate and its pressure on the appreciation of the RMB are measures taken by the United States to "hit" China on the issue of imbalances in international payments. Some scholars believe that in today's world economy, the United States is the main source of imbalances in the global economy. Even without the trade imbalance between China and the United States, the world economy will still lose its balance due to the imbalance of the US economy. Because after the collapse of the Bretton system, the institutional arrangement of the entire world monetary system is conducive to the United States' maintenance of its unbalanced economic system to excessively possess the wealth of resources, goods, and money of the world.[23] Further, as shown in Figure 8.4, the dominance of the US dollar in the international monetary system determines the dominant position of the US in the adjustment of global imbalances. Other subordinate economies, including China, find it difficult to make adjustments by

[23]Hua, Min, "Triggering Mechanism of Global Economic Imbalance and China's Choice," *International Economic Review* 2, (2006): 45–49.

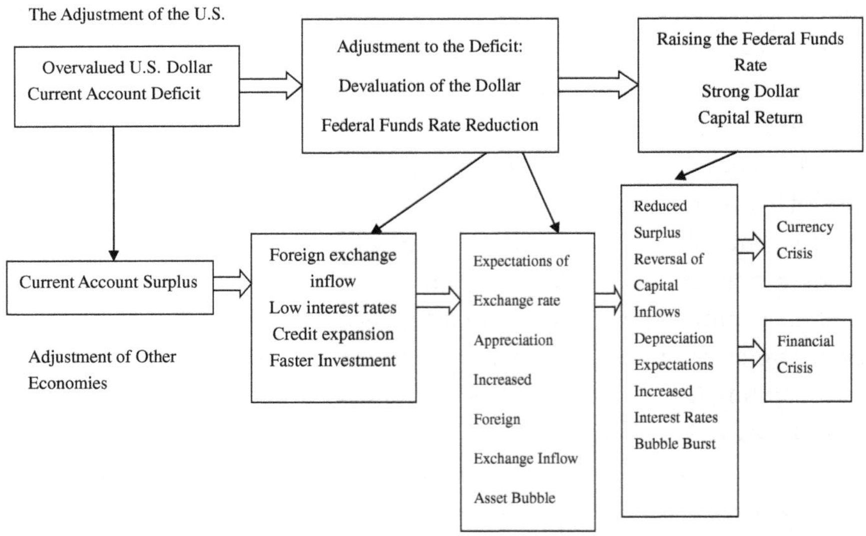

Figure 8.6. Adjustment of the United States and Other Economies under Global Imbalance

changes of the exchange rate and interest rates. The fundamental approach to achieve international economic balance lies in promoting the denuclearization of international currency and the further development of the international policy coordination mechanism, and establishing a balanced new international monetary system that can flexibly adjust international payments (Figure 8.6).[24]

8.4.2 *China's Participation in the Reform of the Adjustment Mechanism of International Payments*

One phenomenon that should not be overlooked is that today's balance of payments imbalances have exhibited huge trade imbalances

[24]Huang, Xiaolong, "Global Imbalances, Excess Liquidity and Currency Crisis: An Analytical Prospective Based on the Imbalanced International Monetary System," *Financial Research* 8 (2007).

and huge financial imbalances.[25] As an important emerging economy in the world economy, when China participates in the reform of the international balance of payments adjustment mechanism, it is necessary to clarify the following important issues: First, in what areas does China make the adjustment of international payments? On the balance of international payment, it is not difficult to find that China's balance of payments presents a double surplus pattern of current account and capital and financial accounts. Therefore, the adjustment of these two aspects is very important. Second, what means should we rely on to make the adjustment? From China itself, it is necessary to change the mode of economic growth, and gradually change the export-oriented growth model for the domestic demand-led growth, supplemented by external demand growth model. However, the accumulation of sustained surpluses is not an issue that China can independently solve. It also needs to make appropriate adjustments to the deficit countries (especially the United States, which is the leading reserve currency issuing country), and change the situation that the savings rate is too low. Third, at what pace does it adjust the international balance of payments? The huge balance of international payments imbalances does not accumulate in the short term. Therefore, the adjustment to it is also a non-immediate process and requires gradual adjustments. Fourth, what principles should be adopted to adjust the balance of payments? The international balance of payments imbalance corresponds to two different unbalanced countries, the surplus countries and the deficit countries. Both parties need to make efforts to correct imbalances, and their adjustment needs to be based on both sides on the principle of balance and reciprocity. Fifth, what kind of platform will be used to reform the adjustment mechanism of the international balance of payments? The adjustment of international balance of payments imbalances may involve two interest entities, or it may involve the situation of one

[25]Bracke, Thierry, Matthieu Bussière, Michael Fidora, and Roland Straub, "A Framework for Assessing Global Imbalances," *European Central Bank Occasional Paper*, no. 78 (2008).

region to one country, or even one country to most other economies. In terms of physical conditions, therefore, the institutional coordination of bilateral or multilateral efforts is very important. As far as China is concerned, the reforms that involve the adjustment mechanism of the international balance of payments mainly deal with the huge surplus of current account of the United States. In addition to the effective use of the Sino-US strategic and economic dialogue as the window of bilateral consultation and dialogue, we must also make full use of the G20 and other international organizations. The platform of the multilateral mechanism has made efforts to establish an international currency system that is balanced, flexible, and effective in adjusting international payments.

8.5 Actively Participate in the Reform of the International Financial Supervision System

8.5.1 *Directions of International Financial Supervision in the Future*

8.5.1.1 *The Logic and Attempt of the United States to Lead the Reform of International Financial Supervision after the Crisis*

First of all, since the implementation of Basel III from the early 1990s, the competitive landscape of the international banking industry has undergone tremendous changes. The US commercial banks have achieved an overwhelming advantage in international competition with Japanese, German and French commercial banks. Therefore, the United States has spared no effort to implement the strategic objectives of the Basel Accord in the early 1980s. Second, since the beginning of the new century, a series of major changes have taken place in the global economic and financial landscape. On the one hand, the establishment of the euro area and the acceleration of the process of European financial integration have enabled France and Germany to compete with the United States.[26] Major developed

[26]Damro's (2012) research shows that the acceleration of European economic integration has enabled the European Union to have the ability to externalize its

countries unfolding game around Basel II and Basel III has fully demonstrated that the European Union, led by France and Germany, has expanded its discourse power and influence in the framework of the Basel Accord. In other words, the US's influence and control over the Basel Accord regulatory framework are declining. On the other hand, the overall rise of the emerging market countries is an indisputable fact. At present, among the 27 members of the Basel Committee, 10 are emerging economies. In this context, the cost of the United States to coordinate and advance international financial regulatory reforms under the framework of the Basel Accord has continued to increase. Finally, the "Dodd–Frank Law" promulgated by the United States in July 2010 is generally regarded as the cornerstone of the US and global financial regulatory reforms in the coming period. However, the bill is not fully compatible with Basel III.[27] This also led to the slow move of the US authorities in implementing Basel III. The aforementioned three aspects constitute the basic logic of the United States restructuring the existing international financial regulatory framework, that is, the United States needs to reconstruct the current international financial regulatory framework and reshape the international financial regulatory rules (the same as the promotion of Basel I in the early 1980s) to better respond to the challenges posed by changes in the global financial landscape, and continue to consolidate its position as a global financial leader, and thus better safeguard its own financial interests.

As early as the beginning of 2010, the Obama administration tentatively put forward the regulatory reform plan of collecting "bank tax" from large-scale financial institutions. That is to say, during the period from 2010 to 2020, financial institutions with total assets of

---

economic and social policies, that is, its ability to adopt moderate or mandatory means and tools to influence international affairs.

[27]For example, Basel III stipulated that the supervisory authority may refer to the evaluation report of the credit rating agency when prudential supervision of a commercial bank is conducted, and Section 939A of the Dodd–Frank Act expressly prohibits such behavior. In addition, the latter emphasizes the protection of financial consumers, strengthens the collection and analysis of financial data, and the "Volcker Rule" in the absence of a clear expression in Basel III.

over US$50 billion in the US and the total liabilities of hedge funds with assets of more than US$10 billion are taxed at a tax rate of 0.15% and the estimated total taxation is US$90 billion. Its internal logic is: first, after the global financial crisis broke out, a large amount of financial resources was used to rescue stranded financial institutions. Among them, large-scale financial institutions with systemic importance were the biggest beneficiaries, and therefore they were obligated to repay them through tax payment. Second, large financial institutions are excessively engaged in complex derivative financial transactions as an important incentive for the financial crisis. Therefore, they should pay a "Financial Crisis Responsibility Fee" to share the cost of crisis relief and to ease the ongoing domestic political pressure of rising demands to "punish" Wall Street. Third, the promotion of this program on a global scale can ensure that the competitiveness of US financial institutions is not weakened, and eliminates the possibility of financial institutions making regulatory arbitrage.

This reform program, based entirely on the interests of the United States, has caused great uproar in the United States and in the international community. From the perspective of the United States, this reform program aimed at "liquidating" large financial institutions has not only caused strong opposition from the Wall Street interest groups but also caused fierce debate in the US Congress. The Republican Party believes that this reform program may not only cause financial institutions to tighten credit and further exacerbate the deterioration of the real economy but also induce financial institutions to pass the tax cost to consumers and SMEs, thereby increasing the cost of the latter's access to financial resources. The major US financial institutions generally believe that taxation can only further inhibit the competitiveness of US financial institutions and does not help prevent systemic risks. From an international perspective, although the reform plan proposed by the United States has quickly gained the support of Britain, France and Germany, which have been severely affected by the crisis, countries such as Canada, Australia and Japan that have not been severely affected by the financial crisis have taken a stand against the plan. As a result, within the G20, two large groups of countries represented by the above-mentioned two parties are represented again. At the G20 Toronto Summit held in June 2010, the United States tried to bridge the differences of the various parties, and then adopted the proposed reform of the "bank tax" on a global scale. However, this effort ended in failure and the United States itself had to abandon the plan.[28] The game among the parties' concern on the issue of whether to levy a "bank tax" once again shows that whether in a country or on an international level, changes in financial regulatory rules mean adjustments to the existing pattern of interests, which inevitably leads to the strong opposition from the side that has the erosion of interests. This also highlights the difficulties of the international financial regulatory reform process.

8.5.1.2 *The Latest Progress and Reform Direction of International Financial Regulatory Reform: Global Financial Market LEI System*

After the discussions between the United States and the international community over the reform of the "bank tax", the US financial authorities adjusted their reform strategies again. In November 2010, the US Department of the Treasury's Office of Financial Research put forward the idea of financial system called LEI (Legal Entity Identifier) in the United States, which is to assign a unique digital identification code to legal entities involved in financial transactions. The financial institution that obtains the identification code must submit or update its own information (especially the ownership structure information) according to the standardized data submission criteria. In addition, the financial regulatory authority and all financial institutions that have an identification code can query the relevant information of counterparty in the system (FSB, 2012).

[28]On 29 June 2010, the U.S. Congress removed from the financial regulatory reform bill the bank tax provisions for which the estimated total taxation has been reduced to US$19 billion. This marked the premature death of the program of US bank tax reform.

The US proposed this reform plan mainly based on the following three considerations: first, the main problem facing the major developed countries in monitoring and analyzing systemic risks is the lack of continuous and high-quality aggregated data. However, data collection and integration are prerequisites for risk analysis and management. As Bottega and Powell pointed out, the LEI system in the financial market, as a standardized data collection and sharing system, can provide a reliable data guarantee for the supervisory authority to monitor and analyze the overall risk of the financial market. Second, the fuse of the global financial crisis, the bankruptcy of Lehman Brothers in the United States, proves that in the highly globalized and complicated financial transactions, the counter party risk of SIFIs may become an important cause of systemic risk.[29] LEI system of the global financial market can not only provide financial support for financial institutions to analyze their own risk exposures and manage counterparty risk, but can also greatly improve the transparency of the entire financial system and financial transactions, avoid market failures and enhance the effectiveness of financial markets. Third, the LEI system in the financial market can cover all types of financial institutions involved in financial transactions, especially the large-scale shadow banking system that is divorced from the current regulatory framework, as well as hedge funds engaged in complex derivative financial transactions, which will undoubtedly greatly improve the effectiveness of macro-prudential supervision.

[29]Lehman Brothers had as many as 2,985 subsidiaries with independent legal status in more than 50 countries and regions in the world. However, because the company's financial derivative transactions are too secretive and complex, even after its application for bankruptcy protection, it is impossible to judge how much the "counter party risk" caused by its closure will be affected. It is estimated that it will take at least 20 years to clarify Lehman Brothers" entire trading party (Bowley, 2010). As a result, fear of the unknown has induced panic in the global financial market, which has led to a full-blown crisis. Gordy (2011) believes that the bankruptcy of Lehman Brothers is a direct cause of the US financial authorities" efforts to establish the LEI system in the financial market, thereby increasing the transparency of financial transactions.

US financial authorities took the lead in proposing the idea of building an LEI system for the financial sector. They also concealed a deeper strategic objective: first to complete the construction and trial operation of the LEI system in the United States, and then to rely on the US influence in the international financial system. By globalizing this system, the "US standards" will naturally become the blueprint for the formulation of "international standards"; while the US can lead the reform of the international financial regulatory framework and further strengthen its leadership position in the global financial system.[30] In fact, the US Department of the Treasury's Office of Financial Research has already foreshadowed this plan in its "statement." As clearly stated in the "statement," the planned US LEI system and its data collection guidelines should be developed and operated by a "voluntary and unanimously recognized international standards body" (such as the International Standards Organization (ISO)); furthermore, The system should be able to become the "only international standard" for identifying legal entities in the financial sector. The "declaration" was used as a draft for soliciting comments. After its release, it triggered widespread concern and heated discussions in the United States. In the first half of 2011, the US Department of Finance's Office of Financial Research received several dozen feedbacks from various agencies and international organizations. Surprisingly, after comprehensively considering various opinions, the office changed the previous "America First" strategy to promote the construction of LEI systems in August 2011, that is, first to strive for support of the international community to build a global financial market LEI system, and then on this basis, it seeks to establish a global financial market LEI system platform that is led by the United States and participated by major global countries to promote the globalization of LEI systems.[31] This subtle

[30]In fact, the 8% bank capital adequacy ratio prescribed in the Basel Accords passed in 1988 was proposed by the Fed.

[31]In a brief statement issued on 12 August, 2011, the U.S. Department of the Treasury's Office of Financial Research adjusted its plans for the initiation of the LEI system on 15 July, 2011, and clearly stated that the construction

change in the attitude of the US financial authorities is very intriguing. We believe that this is mainly due to the following two reasons: first, since the US financial market has been highly internationalized, the US-built LEI system will undoubtedly become a public product in the global financial market. Under this circumstance, the existence of regulatory arbitrage will make multinational financial institutions easily become free riders, thus enjoying the benefits of information disclosure brought about by the system and evading the responsibility of reporting data to the system and receiving supervision. In fact, in today's highly globalized financial trading and financial markets, no country has enough incentives to provide this global public product. Therefore, only the collective actions of all countries to build a truly global LEI system can eliminate the possibility of regulatory arbitrage and "free rider" from the institutional level in order to effectively solve this problem. Second, the extensiveness and diversity of the participants in the US financial market have determined that the construction of the LEI system in the financial market has gone far beyond the terms of reference of the financial regulators; in other words, it is difficult for the US Treasury Department's financial research office to organize and coordinate such a huge and complex system.[32] Therefore, only by starting from the national level, that is, by the coordination of federal government, can we maximize the integration of resources and reduce resistance. Once the proposal to construct the LEI system has been widely recognized internationally and a global governance platform has been formed (such as the G20),

---

should be strengthened for the "global initiative" and "international consensus" of the LEI system. For details, see the website of the US Department of Finance's Office of Financial Research (www.treasury.gov/press-center/press-releases/Pages/tg1275.aspx).

[32]On 14 July, 2011, the US Department of Commerce clearly stated: in the hearing to the subcommittee on oversight and investigations of the House of Representatives Financial Services Committee, the U.S. Department of Finance's Office of Financial Research proposed the idea of a LEI system in the financial market. The LEI system has overreached the authority granted to it by the Dodd–Frank Act and it recommended that the committee should review and evaluate the plan. For details, see the US House of Representatives Financial Services Commission website (http://financialservices.house.gov/UploadedFiles/071411uscc.pdf).

this will not only be beneficial to the construction of the LEI system in the US financial market, but also be able to break the collective action dilemma at the global level and be effective. Solve the problem of insufficient market incentives to promote the construction of the LEI system of global financial market.

Because this reform program proposed by the United States belongs to the scope of financial market infrastructure construction, it not only meets the needs of the current global reforms to strengthen macro-prudential supervision, but also does not involve major adjustments to the existing financial regulatory rules and existing interests. Therefore, the program not only received positive responses from all parties in the United States but also received support from most G20 members. The US Commodity Futures Trading Commission (CFTC) has explicitly requested that all participating swap transactions must be provided by the US Deposit Trust and Clearing Corporation (DTCC) and the Global Banking Finance and Telecommunications Association (SWIFT) starting from October 2012, from the temporary code to the final transition to the global financial market LEI. European Market Infrastructure Regulations (EMIR), which was passed by the European Union in March 2012, also explicitly stated that it supports the promotion of global corporate identity standards that comply with the International Payments and Settlement System Committee and the CPSS-IOSCO Principles. In June 2012, under the leadership of the United States, the G20 Los Cabos Summit officially passed a resolution to build a global financial market LEI system. In early 2013, the Global LEI Foundation and the Regulatory Oversight Committee (ROC) were formally established. The governance structure of the LEI system in the global financial market became clear gradually, and the formulation of various regulatory rules was also carried out in an orderly manner.

8.5.1.3 *Comparison of the Global Financial Market LEI System and the Basel Accord Regulatory Framework*

Obviously, both systems are the product of a crisis. As milestones in the international financial regulatory reform process, both systems have distinctive characteristics of the times and both reflect the profound changes in the international financial market and landscape in the specific era. In addition, both are under the leadership of the United States, established by major developed countries through game and negotiation. Therefore, its established international financial regulatory rules not only reflect the will of the United States but also represent the mainstream of international financial regulatory reform to some extent. However, there is a clear difference between the two in terms of regulatory philosophy. The Basel Accord is limited by the background of its time, and is mainly regulated from the perspective of micro-prudential, emphasizing the individual stability of financial institutions through the implementation of capital supervision, and indirectly maintaining the stability of the entire financial system. Although the supervisory concept of Basel III is combined micro-prudential supervision with macro-prudential supervision and its attempts were made to make up for the inadequacies of Basel II from strengthening countercyclical supervision and strengthening the supervision of systemically important financial institutions, it still maintain the stability of the financial system from the perspective of financial institutions (in particular, systemic-minded financial institutions have their own perspective). Obviously, it is still difficult to solve the systemic risk problem caused by information asymmetry. Starting from the perspective of macro-prudential supervision, the global financial market LEI system uses the "interconnectedness" between financial institutions as a breakthrough point to publicly disclose and follow-up research on the micro-data of risk exposures of financial institutions, thereby restraining the market failure and avoiding excessive accumulation of financial risks, and ultimately achieving the goal of effectively preventing systemic risks. The global financial market LEI system has two main advantages compared to the Basel Accord regulatory framework: first, the system not only provides data security for national financial authorities to monitor the systematic risks of their financial systems, but also makes it possible for the authorities to monitor the systemic risks (especially transnational transfers of financial risks) of the global financial system; second, the LEI system legally included all legal entities engaged in financial transactions, which in turn strengthened the supervision of shadow banking and OTC derivatives and covered "blind area" of Basel agreement supervision.[33]. Therefore, the LEI system in the global financial market can, to a certain extent, make up for the shortcomings of the current international financial regulatory framework. With the improvement of its various rules and the promulgation of the regulations, it will become the cornerstone of monitoring and responding to systemic risks in parallel with Basel III.

8.5.2 *Participate in the Reform of International Financial Regulatory Agencies and International Standards*

From the aforementioned analysis, the following conclusions can be drawn:

First, the solution to construct the global financial market LEI system is the result of the reflection of the global financial crisis by the major developed countries represented by the United States. Therefore, it is possible to reach a consensus among the developed countries. This is also the solution proposed by the United States to the world. One of the preconditions for the promotion of LEI system globally is that the developed countries are undoubtedly the main driving force of the construction of the system.[34]

Second, the construction of the global financial market LEI system represents, to a considerable extent, the main direction of international financial regulatory reform, namely, the collection and

---

[33]Of course, the construction of the global financial market LEI system is also facing a series of problems and challenges. This issue involves a lot of technical details, so we no longer specifically carry out. For details, please refer to Wang, Da, and Weixin Xiang, "On the Latest Progress of International Financial Regulatory Reform: The Construction of Global Financial Market LEI System," *World Economy Research* 1, (2013): 10–14.

[34]In other words, the global financial crisis broke the predicament of collective action that has long existed in the field of international financial regulatory reform.

integration of micro-financial information, the improvement of the transparency of the global financial system and the strengthening of international financial regulatory cooperation on the monitoring and response to systemic financial risks. For this reason, the system's central executive will most likely become the new international financial regulatory organization that is at par with the Basel Committee and will play a greater role in strengthening international financial regulatory cooperation and the harmonization of regulatory standards.

Third, the dominance of the international financial regulatory reform process has always been in the hands of developed countries. The construction of the US-led global financial market LEI system is no exception. This global information system, which is based on the development of financial markets in developed countries and the need for financial regulatory reforms, will have a complex impact on a large number of emerging markets and developing countries. Although it is difficult to make a systematic assessment of this effect, it is undoubtedly worthy of our sustained attention and in-depth study.

Finally, the construction of the LEI system in the global financial market is an complex system. At the current stage, it still faces a series of problems at the operational level. The solution to these problems will ultimately depend on the cooperation and support of financial authorities around the world.

We believe that China, as the world's second-largest economy and an important member of the Financial Stability Committee of G20, not only has the obligation to actively participate in the construction of the global financial market LEI system, but also plays an important role in this new international financial regulatory platform. In the long run, this is also a rational choice for safeguarding the vital interests of China. However, so far, China has been slow to participate in the construction of the international financial regulatory reform, especially the global financial market LEI system.[35]

[35]On 12 January, 2012, the Financial Stability Commission called for the establishment of an expert group composed of representatives of private sectors in various countries to assist the LEI system expert group established previously to

We believe that on the one hand, China's financial authorities should rely on the Financial Stability Board as a platform to comprehensively strengthen exchanges and cooperation with financial supervisory authorities of various countries, and then accumulate valuable experience for improving China's macro-prudential financial supervision framework, and continue to expand our country's influence in the international financial regulatory field; on the other hand, relevant domestic market entities such as commercial banks, financial industry associations, securities and futures exchanges, insurance companies, financial research institutes and related high-tech companies and networks companies should be encouraged to actively participate in advisory groups of the global private sector organized by the Financial Stability Board,[36] and then fully participate in the discussion and formulation of the details of the LEI system for the construction of a global financial market. This will help China's financial authorities to maintain and assert their own interest claims reasonably under the G20 framework;, thus, creating a favorable external environment for the deepening reform of China's financial sector. It will also help expand the international perspective of relevant domestic participants, and we have accumulated experience in international exchanges and cooperation for our financial institutions and market players at all levels. In short, the international financial regulatory reforms have a long way to go. Whether it is to ensure the stability

carry out relevant work. Emerging economies such as Brazil, Mexico, and South Korea have private sector or organization representatives, but they do not have representatives from China; in addition, the Emerging Markets and Developing Economies Assessment Team established in the first half of 2012 by the Financial Stability Board (in EMDEs Review Group, there is no representative of China other than a representative from Hong Kong, China). Representatives from emerging markets such as Brazil, Chile, India, Indonesia, South Korea, Malaysia, Russia, South Africa, and Turkey all participate in the board.

[36]On 3 July, 2012, the Financial Stability Commission publicly announced the establishment of the "Lead Sector Preparatory Group" of the LEI system and called for the active participation of experts from private sectors around the world. For details, see the Financial Stability Board website: (www.financialstabilityboard.org/publications/r_120703.pdf).

of the global financial system or to protect China's own interests, China, as the world's largest emerging economy, should be subject to the current international financial regulations. To play a greater role in the reform process, actively participation in the construction of the LEI system in the global financial market is undoubtedly the rational choice to achieve this goal.

In addition, what needs to be emphasized is that we should also pay close attention to the spillover effects that the financial regulatory reforms of major developed countries may have on China and take effective response measures in time. In July 2013, after the European Union's comprehensive strengthening of supervision measures for hedge funds took effect, it lead to the shift of global hedge funds to loosely regulated emerging economies. This undoubtedly had an impact on the latter's financial stability. In the context of the acceleration of China's financial opening process, China's financial authorities should bring forward and release relevant regulatory regulations in a timely manner, thus maximally eliminating the possibility of regulatory arbitrage. It should follow the trend to promote and deepen the reform of China's financial supervision system. After the crisis, major developed countries have established regulatory agencies that monitor and prevent systemic risks on the basis of systematically integrated regulatory resources (such as the US Financial Stability Regulatory Commission and the UK's Financial Stability Council), and have given the responsibilities to the central banks' participation in the system and supervision of the systematic risk. However, at present our country has not made any progress in this reform. The People's Bank of China, on behalf of the China's financial authorities, has participated in the discussion of the financial management reforms of the Basel Committee, the Financial Stability Committee and the G20, but has exercised its own monetary policy while exercising less regulatory functions. Obviously, this pattern of internal and external inconsistencies is not conducive to the implementation of macro-prudential supervision policies in China.

8.6 Actively Participate in the Reform of International Financial Organizations

8.6.1 *Actively Participate in the Reform of IMF*

As mentioned earlier, there are some factors in the current IMF decision-making mechanism that are not conducive to the developing countries, so the mechanism must be reformed. However, since the reform involves the readjustment of the interests of developed countries, the difficulties of reform are considerable. In promoting the reform of the IMF's decision-making mechanism, the developing countries, represented by China, must ensure that there are practical measures for pushing forward reforms in the short and medium-term as well as long-term economic development goals. In the short to medium term, China should negotiate with the vast number of developing countries to actively promote the reform of the IMF. Under the current circumstances, the developing countries represented by China must actively commit themselves to the IMF in order to increase their influence on the international monetary system reform and increase effective participation in the IMF.

First, we should actively use the IMF's consensus principle to safeguard our own legitimate rights and interests. At least, the IMF's consensus principle shows that large countries and small countries have equal rights to objections in the IMF. However, the consensus decision-making method depends on the game of interest groups. In the 60 years since the establishment of the IMF, there has been an internal power struggle between developed and developing countries. In the mid and late 1960s, with the rise of developing countries' power, developing countries began to actively seek power and status in the IMF, and developed the interests of developing countries in the IMF that correspond to the developed interest groups of G10 and G7. In 1972, the Group of Twenty Four — G24 and the G20 Committees — were established, and the Development Committee was established in 1974. The developing countries have gradually gained strength in the IMF and their influence has gradually increased.

At present, in order to promote the reform of the IMF and seek a greater say in the IMF, China should use the developing country groups in the IMF to strengthen unity and negotiate with the group of developing countries on the IMF's decision-making stance. In fact, if developing countries want to gain more say in the IMF, they need to seek common ground while reserving differences, coordinate internal conflicts and speak in the same voice before they can form a joint force and veto the initiatives of the developed countries that are not conducive to the developing countries.

Second, China should seek its own interests in cooperation with the developed countries. At present, one paradox of reforming the IMF's decision-making mechanism is that the reform of decision-making mechanism must also be determined by the current decision-making mechanism. Under any substantive reform under the IMF's existing governance framework, it is impossible to form a decision without the support of major developed countries. However, the developed countries cannot voluntarily give up their vested interests on issues such as voting rights. Therefore, in the near future, the reform of the IMF can only be the result of balanced forces between the parties. The acceptable scheme for the reform of the Board of Directors is to obtain the support of major creditor countries such as Europe and the United States; it may also be necessary to retain the interests of the creditor countries, such as retaining the veto power of the United States and Europe, and retaining the principle of permanent majority of creditor countries. Bringing the developed and developing countries in a roughly balanced position in the IMF's decision-making mechanism is the key to ensure that the IMF fulfills its development function in accordance with professional standards, and is also a prerequisite for substantial reform of the IMF. To fight for their own interests, developing countries such as China, must learn to cooperate with the developed countries and actively discuss, negotiate and fully express their opinions in the international economic organizations. Some international forums established since the end of the 20th century, such as the Financial Stability Forum

(FSF)[37] and the G20, also included some of the emerging market countries. These countries should fully participate in the FSF, G20 and other international organizations or forums, and jointly discuss the reform of the IMF with developed countries. Developing countries must rely on and strive for the support of some developed countries to increase their influence on the decision-making of the IMF and safeguard the common interests of the developing countries.

Finally, it needs to be pointed out that developing the economy and increasing the overall economic strength is a long-term plan for the developing countries to seek international status. The history of the international economic development proves that the majority of developing countries represented by China must seek the status in the international economic arena. Apart from actively participating in the reform process of the existing international economic order, it is more important to enhance national economic strength. The reason why developed countries can play a dominant role in the IMF is related to the IMF's decision-making mechanism, but the decision-making mechanism is only a manifestation and result. Its essence is the global political and economic strength of the developed countries. The WTO adopts the rules of one country one vote, a majority vote and consensus, but developed countries can still play a major role in the WTO. Therefore, it is very difficult to make substantive reforms to the international monetary system with the current political and economic strength of developing countries. Therefore, for China with the rapid economic development, the sustained development of the national economy and the continuous improvement of comprehensive national strength are the most effective ways to win the initiative for decision-making, and it is also the fundamental way for all developing countries to reform the international economic order.[38]

---

[37]The predecessor of the Financial Stability Board (FSB).

[38]Huang, Meibo, "International Monetary Fund's Internal Decision-Making Mechanism and its Reform," *International Forum* 1 (2006), 54–59.

8.6.2 *Specific Proposals for IMF Reform*

8.6.2.1 *Reform Share Allocation Mechanism*

The key to the reform of the quota allocation mechanism is to change the existing pattern of quotas and increase the relative share of developing countries so as to correct the imbalance in power between the developed countries and the developing countries within the current IMF, and to strengthen the democracy, legitimacy and participation within the IMF.

First, we must promote the expansion of fund shares.

The strength of the IMF's financial resources directly relates to the IMF's ability to rescue the crisis and is directly related to its goal of maintaining international financial stability. Therefore, with the expansion of the world's gross national product, world trade, and international capital flows, the capital base owned by the IMF should be increased. However, the financial strength of IMF is declining compared to the ever-increasing scale of the world economy, international capital flows and any comparable global liquidity indicators. The share of IMF to GDP fell from 1.4% to 0.8%, and the share of IMF to the foreign exchange reserves dropped from 33% to 9%, the proportion of global current account transactions from 8.5% to 1.8%, share to world imports from 9% to 4%. If taking the scale of the world's GDP and the share of the IMF fund as the standards, the current financial strength of IMF is only one-third of that in 1948. If the funds are paid according to the standards of the member countries at that time, the fund size of the current IMF should be expanded by five times, and the scale measure should be nine times the current share according to international trade. Increasing the IMF's funding scale has always been an important part of the IMF reform proposal. The overwhelming majority of recommendations are to increase and adjust the IMF's membership, and others have suggested that the IMF's funding should be increased from other sources. Former US Treasury Assistant Minister Edwin Truman had proposed to raise funds for the IMF by US$ 300 dollars by imposing a 0.5% international investment income tax (income tax on international investment). At the end of 2001, George Soros, an international financial speculator, also proposed plans for the IMF to assist developing countries in raising funds through the issuance of SDR. The distribution of SDR is still linked to the IMF's share of funds, but developed countries will allocate new funds to them. All SDRs were donated as special funds to assist the LDCs. At present, the appeal for increasing the IMF's share is still high, but due to the lack of enthusiasm of the major developed countries, the issue of increasing the share of funds of developing countries has not received effective attention.

Second, we must promote the revision of the share calculation formula.

The share is the basis of the rights and obligations of the member countries in the fund. In the 60 years after the war, the total number of member states of the IMF increased from 40 to 184, and the scale of the share expanded by 37 times. The formula used by the IMF to calculate the share of member states has also undergone several changes. Although the voice of modifying the share formula has always been loud, none of the programs received 85% of voting rights. In June 1999, the Executive Board hired external experts to evaluate the share formula. In February 2002, the Executive Board discussed the relevant proposals of the expert group, favored the simplification of the existing formula and updated the formula to consider the enhancement of the role of capital flows. However, more work needs to be done to reach a consensus. At the end of the 20th century, the share of developing countries such as China, Brazil and South Korea in the world's total output and trade has greatly increased. It is expected that the first half of the 21st century will continue to grow, reflecting fully the economic growth of these countries. Many countries believe that the IMF should complete the work of modifying the share formula as soon as possible. Some people have suggested that the share calculation should be based on GDP data, and that GDP should use data that has been converted by purchasing power parity (not using market exchange rates). Developing countries have also proposed to modify the quota allocation criteria and consider the population, develop capabilities, raw materials provision and other factors in the share calculation formula. However, the developed countries have used the statistics of the fund's data based on market exchange rates, and opposed the use of purchasing power parity data. Other proposals have not been recognized and supported by developed countries. From the IMF's point of view, it is very difficult to design a share formula that is reasonable in both financial sharing and equity. On the one hand, we need to ensure that the allocation of shares is fair and reasonable, increase the share of developing countries' holdings, and on the other hand, we must also ensure that the industrial countries continue to be majority shareholders in order to reflect their role as the major creditors in the IMF. This is because if the share of the developing countries is increased too much, it may significantly reduce the solvency that the IMF can provide. Since 75% of the share is paid in the member's own currency, if the majority of these currencies are non-convertible currencies of developing countries, the IMF's actual loan quota will be limited.

8.6.2.2 *Reform Voting Mechanism*

First, we must promote the increase in the proportion of basic votes in the total voting rights.

In the IMF voting mechanism, in addition to distributing voting rights according to the number of shares held by member states, each country is allocated the same amount of basic voting rights to reflect the principle of equal status of all countries. However, since the foundation of the IMF, the total number of voting rights of the Fund has increased by 37 times, but the number of basic votes has not changed so far, resulting in a decrease in the proportion of basic votes in the total voting rights from 11.3% in the initial year to 2.1% in 2008. The role of basic voting rights existed in name only and the influence of developing countries in the IMF's decision-making was further reduced. In order to protect their legitimate rights and interests in the IMF, many developing countries propose that the number of basic tickets and their proportion in total voting rights should be increased, and at least the proportion of basic votes should be returned to the level of year 1945.

Second, we must promote the development of voting rights of the developing countries.

The voting power of the IMF is basically dominated by the share system, which has led the developed countries to have an absolute advantage in the distribution of voting rights of the IMF. As a result, all major decisions of the IMF, including the final decision power of the size of funds, gold sales, exchange rate arrangements, and resource allocation, were concentrated in the hands of the developed countries represented by the United States and Europe. Developing countries were basically on the front lines of marginalization. The purpose of the reform of the voting mechanism is to rectify the current imbalance between the developed countries and the developing countries in the IMF and to increase the dialogue among the member states. Judging from the current situation of the world economic development, the voting rights of the European Union should fall. The voting rights of some emerging market countries in Asia and Latin America should increase. On the one hand, the total voting power of the current 25 EU member states is as high as 32%. This voting right was established at the early stage of the IMF. After the EU has achieved integration, it should deduct the EU's internal trade from the share calculation, which will reduce the total share of the EU's share and voting rights by about 9 percentage points. On the other hand, East Asian countries have become the undisputed engine of world economic growth in recent years. The proportion of the GDP of China, Japan, Korea, and the 10 ASEAN countries of the total world GDP was 9% in 1960 and rose to 19% in 2003. The apparent increase in the economic power of East Asian countries should be reflected in the redistribution of voting rights such as the IMF. The voting rights of other emerging market countries (such as Brazil and Mexico) are also seriously out of line with the growing strength of their economies. Therefore, the voting rights of the developing countries, especially the emerging market countries, should be adjusted according to their economic development level.

Third, we must work hard to abolish the *de facto* veto power of a few developed countries.

In order to improve the voting rights of the developing countries in the IMF, while adjusting the voting rights of each country, it is also possible to consider modifying the requirement for majority of the proportions for special voting rights. The provision of special voting rights conferred a one-vote veto power on the interest groups of a developed country or a developed country, forming the control of developed countries over the IMF. One way to change this situation is to reduce the majority of special voting rights for certain key policy issues (such as share capital increase and revision of the charter) from 85% to three-fourths (75%) or two-thirds (66%). In this way, no country will be able to reject the relevant decision by one vote. The influence of the developed countries on the IMF's decision-making will be reduced.

8.6.2.3 *Reform the IMF's Policy-Making Body*

The IMF's decision-making body includes the Council, the Executive Board, the International Monetary Finance Committee and the Development Committee. The top decision-making body of the IMF is the Board of Governors. The IMF Council is composed of the finance ministers and central bank governors of 184 member countries. It meets once a year to decide major issues of the IMF and the international monetary system, such as accepting new members and amending funds agreements, adjustment of fund shares, adjustment of currency parity in member countries, allocation of SDRs, and determination of withdrawal of member states. Other powers are given to its committees and executive boards, and the Council exercises the final power of oversight of the executive board. The executive board of directors is the permanent decision-making body of the IMF. It is responsible for handling day-to-day affairs within the scope of the Council's mandate and plays a central role in policy formulation and decision-making. The Executive Board is composed of the chairman and 24 executive directors. The chairman is also the president of the IMF and is elected every five years. The executive director is appointed by the member states or the constituency election, with a total number of 24. The distribution of the chairmanship of the Executive Board and the membership of the Executive Board is also based on the number of fund shares in each country. In addition to the voting rights system, the IMF's decision-making bodies also have problems. The decision-making mechanism for the reform of the IMF must be adjusted to the organizational system of the presidential election system, the distribution system of executive directors and the diversity of sources of IMF staff.

First of all, we must increase the transparency of the presidential elections and expand the voice of developing countries in the IMF presidential election.

The managing director of the IMF is both the highest executive head of the IMF and the chairman of the Board of Directors, and its selection largely determines the direction of the IMF. In principle, the IMF's president is elected by the Executive Board, but in fact, during the 60 years since the IMF and the World Bank were established, the United States and Europe have an unwritten "gentleman's agreement" on the issue of the leadership of these two major institutions. That is, Europeans are the presidents of the IMF and Americans are the presidents of the World Bank. Although the United States has the largest share in the IMF, the 15 EU countries have a share of about 30% in the IMF, which is higher than the total share of the United States and Japan, thus ensuring European dominance in the IMF's decision-making. However, because the United States has single-nation veto power over major decisions, no matter who gets the European Union's joint election, it cannot be elected without the support of the US. The electoral process for the president was opaque, making it a battleground for all kinds of political forces. In recent years, there has been a growing call for transparency in the election of the IMF's president. In 2001, a working group of the IMF submitted a special report recommending the establishment of clear criteria for the selection of presidential candidates: the establishment of an advisory board of directors to accept candidates for nominations and submit a list of qualified candidates to the Board of Directors. According to the list and other candidates nominated by the members of the Board of Directors, the Executive Board produces a list of formal candidates after consultation. Finally the Board of Directors votes or brainstorms to select the new president. Although the report was approved by the IMF Executive Board, the report did not form a final resolution. Obviously, Europe hopes to continue to enjoy the IMF's leadership, and the United States is also happy to use the IMF's presidential position as a political bargain with the Europeans. However, due to weak economic and political influence, other large countries are basically in the position of being arbitrarily placed in major decisions in the IMF, and have little influence on the presidential election. However, there have been some changes that are beneficial to the developing countries in the presidential election in recent years. Among the ninth presidential candidates, Mohamed El-Erian, born in Egypt, was also a very strong candidate. Moreover, part of the reason why Rodrigo de Rato from Spain was elected in 2004 was that he received support from many Latin American countries. Developing countries have a certain say in the election of the top leader of IMF.

Second, it is necessary to change the unbalanced status of the Executive Board representatives and expand the seats of developing countries in the Executive Board.

The Executive Board of Directors is the daily decision-making body of the IMF, and it is also the actual *de facto* body of the IMF. Therefore, the composition of the Executive Board members has a direct impact on their final decision. However, as the distribution of members of the Executive Board is also based on the number of funds in each country, it will inevitably lead to the composition of the Board of Directors to be tilted toward the developed countries. Of the 24 seats on the IMF's Executive Board, Europe has 10 seats (3 full seats and 7 seats of representatives), compared to 5 in Asia and 2 in Africa. Measured by purchasing power parity, Europe's share of global GDP is 29% and Asia is 32%. The uneven distribution of the membership of the Executive Board is evident. The uneven distribution of representations has made it impossible for member states, especially developing member states, to express their opinions, and their interests have not been valued and maintained. Developing countries' sense of identity with the IMF has declined, ultimately affecting the IMF's long-term decision-making efficiencies and legitimacy of the IMF. In addition, developing countries, as the main recipients of IMF loans, have insufficient ability to influence the IMF, which makes IMF's loan assistance plan unrealistic and difficult to meet their needs. The IMF's policy implementation effect has declined. Therefore, if the IMF wants to reflect the current reality, its management structure (mainly the number of executive board seats on the Executive Board) needs to be readjusted.

Third, we must increase the diversity of the regional and professional background of IMF staff.

The IMF's current loans are mainly targeted at developing countries and transition countries. Therefore, the dramatic increase in the number of IMF member states and changes in their functions require the IMF to increase the diversity of its staff sources. On the one hand, the IMF should recruit staff from a wider range of countries around the world and increase the regional diversity of IMF staff sources. According to statistics provided by "International Financial Statistics," up to 70–80% of senior employees within the IMF come from a small number of industrialized countries. If the IMF can assign more senior management positions to staff recruited from developing countries, it will help bring a new perspective to the IMF and find a development path that suits the economic development of each member country. On the other hand, the IMF should also pay attention to the diversity of background and expertise of its staff in dealing with structural issues so as to better deal with the issues encountered by new members in the process of integration into the world economy and the transition to a market economy in recent years.[39]

[39]Huang, Meibo, "International Monetary Fund's Internal Decision-Making Mechanism and its Reform," *International Forum* 1 (2006), 54–59.

8.6.3 *Proposals for SDR Reform*

The SDR is an international reserve asset created by the IMF in 1969. Its purpose is to make up for the shortage of US dollar assets. The most important role of the SDR is for member states to exchange foreign exchange with other member states designated by the IMF in the event of a balance of payments deficit, in order to pay back the balance of payments deficit or to repay IMF loans. It can also act as international reserve like gold and freely convertible currencies.

At the beginning of the establishment of the SDR, 1 unit of SDR equaled 0.888671 grams of gold (equivalent to 1 dollar at the time). After the decoupling of the US dollar from gold, the IMF decided to price the SDR in a basket of 16 currencies in July 1974, and reduced the currency in the currency basket from 16 species to 5 in 1981, including the US dollar, the Deutsche mark, and the French franc, Japanese yen and pound sterling. With the introduction of the euro, the euro replaced the mark and franc in 2001, and the SDR currency basket was further reduced to four types. In order to ensure that the currency in the basket is a representative currency in international trade payments and its weightings represent its importance, the IMF will review the fixed value of the SDR every five years (Table 8.1). The proportion of each currency in the SDR is mainly determined by two factors: the amount of exports of goods and services by member states or currency unions, and the number of reserve assets held by

Table 8.1. Adjustment and Changes of Various Currency Weights in SDR

Currency Name	1980 (%)	1986 (%)	1991 (%)	1996 (%)	2001 (%)	2006 (%)	2011 (%)
USD	42	42	40	39	45	44	41.9
Deutsche mark	19	19	21	21	—	—	—
JPY	13	15	17	18	15	11	9.4
French franc	13	12	11	11	—	—	—
GBP	13	12	11	11	11	11	11.3
EUR	—	—	—	—	29	34	37.4

Source: http://www.imf.org/external/fin.htm.

other member countries of the IMF. In 2010, the IMF conducted a routine five-year review of the SDR basket currency and determined that the value of the SDR will continue to be based on a weighted average of a basket of currencies consisting of the US dollar, the euro, the British pound, and the Japanese yen, and make adjustments to the weight of the currency basket.

After the creation of SDR, the total amount of SDR has not been effectively increased due to the obstruction of the United States. In 2009, the IMF took advantage of the US subprime mortgage crisis and increased the SDR of US$250 billion, which further increased the role and influence of SDR. Since the SDR is a basket of currencies, expanding the issuance and use of SDRs can help the international currency countries share their responsibility for regulating global currency supply to avoid major adjustments in the exchange rates of major international reserve currencies. This measure is not only beneficial to the economic stability of the world, but also beneficial to the stability of major international reserve currencies and it is a win — win solution. It can provide new investment channels for foreign exchange reserves of various countries, reduce the size and speed of the return of the US dollar and avoid large fluctuations in exchange rates between major currencies at the same time, which will play an important role in restraining US dollar surcharges and stabilizing the international financial order. In the future, SDR should play an increasingly important role in the international financial system.

Supporting SDR to play a greater role will not only help to break the monopoly position of the US dollar in the international monetary system, but also help safeguard the safety of global reserve assets and it is in the national interest of China. Whether a country's currency can become a basket currency of the SDR not only marks the international status of the currency but also shows the country's international financial status. We should take action to promote the RMB to be the basket currency of SDR as soon as possible. At present, the United States and some other developed countries have always used "free exchange" as one of the "thresholds" to prevent RMB to be a basket currency of the SDR. However, when the SDR currency basket was created by the IMF in 1974, several of the 16 currencies in the basket were not freely convertible. In addition, from the perspective of the current role of SDR, it is only the bookkeeping currency of the inter-governmental economic exchanges, so it is not necessary that the currency in the basket is fully convertible. Specifically, further strengthening cooperation with the IMF and promoting SDR to play a greater role is an important way for the RMB to play a greater role. We can provide the IMF with an RMB loan or purchase the bonds it sells, and actively encourage the IMF to issue RMB bonds to make the RMB more useful. In addition, it is possible to explore the signing of a currency swap agreement between the IMF and China for exchange of the RMB and the SDR to ensure that the RMB can perform its functions in the SDR framework in the same way as other convertible currencies, and gradually realize the goal of the RMB to be a basket currency of the SDR.

8.6.4 *Actively Participate in the Reform of World Bank*

The special national conditions of China determine that its participation in the reform of the World Bank's governance structure must be based on the special position as a developing, transitional, and emerging economy.

First of all, China must stand in the position of the developing countries. For a long time, China has been a major developing country. China is a representative of the developing countries in international economics and politics. Among various international organizations including the United Nations, it has always been advocating justice and striving for the rights and interests of the developing countries. Although China's economy has achieved considerable development since the implementation of reform and opening up, China remains a developing country. Therefore, in the adjustment of the voting power of the World Bank, China should naturally take the position of the developing countries to strive for more rights and interests for the developing countries, guarantee the voice of the developing countries, and make all developing countries a part in the overall real share. The proportion has increased significantly, and the voice of low-income countries in the World Bank has been strengthened. This is not only in line with the needs of developing countries, but also conducive to the development of China.

Second, China should also take the position of a transitional country. Although China is different from the former Soviet and East European transition countries in the full sense, it still shows the distinctive features of the transition economy in development. The World Bank has provided a great deal of assistance to countries in transition, but it has also attached many conditions, especially the political conditions attached to the neo-liberal "Washington Consensus." Practice has proven that these conditions have had many adverse effects or hindered the economic transition and development of the recipient countries. Therefore, China should work with other transition countries to require the World Bank to reduce or modify (rather than abandon) additional conditions when aid is provided so that aid can work better. Therefore, it is of utmost importance to enhance the voice of the transition countries in the World Bank's decision-making bodies, so it is clear that the increase of voting rights is a priority.

Finally, China should also take the position of an emerging market economy. Emerging market economies have the ability and responsibility to launch an impact on the traditional international economic order and work hard to establish a more rational new international economic order. China is one of the most important representatives of the emerging market economies. It shows many common features of the emerging market economies, such as rapid economic growth, increasing openness and increasingly important role in the world economy, unmatched position in the important international economic organizations including the World Bank. China's economic indicators, international trade volume, foreign exchange reserves and other major economic indicators have leapt to the top of the world. They are both important commodity suppliers and important demanders in the world market and are important influencers on the prices of many commodities in the world. China's international influence is increasingly rising and it is increasingly showing the image of a responsible world power. To this end, in the adjustment of the voting power of the World Bank, China should join with other emerging market economies to increase its share of the power structure of the World Bank and its voting rights, and strengthen its right of speech and influence for developing countries, making the development of the World Bank more conducive to its purpose.

In view of this, China should fully participate in the World Bank's reform process from the following aspects: First, the quota formula should be revised as soon as possible to expedite the progress of the quota review so as to bring it in line with changes in the economic strength of various countries and strengthen the organization's fund. Second, it should significantly increase the voting rights of emerging market countries and appropriately increase the voting rights of transition countries and African countries. Third, it should strive to increase the proportion of basic voting rights or implement a group voting system, and gradually change the mechanism of capital-led decision-making. Fourth, it should reduce the proportion of the majority voting power on major policy decisions. By reforming the decision-making mechanism and changing the situation in which a small number of major powers control the World Bank, it would become a fair and democratic organization that fully reflects the wishes of the overwhelming majority of countries and wins the trust of the overwhelming majority of countries in order to enable them to play a more important role in international economic cooperation in the future. In short, the adjustment of voting rights is the focus of the Bank's decision-making mechanism (and therefore institutional reforms). Developing countries, including China, have important responsibilities for guiding the direction of the World Bank's voting rights reforms (and thus institutional reforms), but it will be a long process. In the short term, although the progress of the voting rights reform of the World Bank can only be the result of balanced forces among all parties, its reform must be limited. However, the full expression of the claims of the developing countries will make the World Bank's development orientation closer to the common interests of global development. However, it must also be realized that the reform of voting rights of the World Bank is only an external factor for the development of the developing countries, and the reforms of the developing countries themselves are the internal causes of their development.

Bibliography

[1] Allen, W. A. and R. Moessner, "Central Bank Co-Operation and International Liquidity in the Financial Crisis of 2008-9," *BIS Working Papers*, no. 310 (June 2010).

[2] Aminian, N., "Economic Integration and Prospects for Regional Cooperation in East Asia," *Structural Change and Economic Dynamics* 16, no. 1 (March 2005): 91–110.

[3] Anderson, J., "Why Asia Can't Sell the Dollar," *UBS Investment Research* (January 2005).

[4] Angeloni, I., A. Benassy-Quere, B. Carton, Z. Darvas, C. Destais, L. Gauvin, J. Pisani-Ferry, A. Sapir, and S. Vallee, *Reforming the International Monetary System: Options and Implications.* Report submitted to the European Commission, 2011.

[5] Arnone, M. and A. Gambini, "Architecture of Supervisory Authorities and Banking Supervision," In *Designing Financial Supervision Institutions: Independence, Accountability and Governance*, edited by D. Masciandaro and M. Quintyn, 262–308. Cheltenham: Edward Elgar, 2007.

[6] ASEAN+3. "The Joint Media Statement of the 12th ASEAN plus Three Finance Ministers' Meeting," Bali, Indonesia, May 3, 2009. http://www.asean.org/communities/asean-economic-community/item/the-joint-media-statement-of-the-12th-asean-plus-three-finance-ministers-meeting-bali-indonesia-3-may-2009-2.

[7] ASEAN+3, "The Joint Statement of the 15th ASEAN+3 Finance Ministers and Central Bank Governors Meeting," Manila, Philippines, May 3, 2012.

[8] Baron, D. P., "Fluctuating Exchange Rates and the Pricing of Exports," *Economic Inquiry* 14, no. 3 (September 1976): 425–438.

[9] Barro, R. J., "Reputation in a Model of Monetary Policy with Incomplete Information," *Journal of Monetary Economics* 17, no. 1 (January 1986): 3–20.

[10] Bayoumi, T. and B. Eichengreen, "Shocking Aspects of European Monetary Integration," In *Adjustment and Growth in European Monetary Union*, edited by Torres G. and F. Giavazzi, 193–235. Cambridge: Cambridge University Press, 1993.

[11] Bayoumi, T. and B. Eichengreen, "One Money or Many? Analyzing the Prospects for Monetary Unification in Various Parts of the World," *Princeton Studies in International Finance*, no. 76 (September 1994): 1–52.

[12] Bayoumi, T. and B. Eichengreen, "Ever Closer to Heaven? An Optimum-Currency-Area Index for European Countries," *European Economic Review* 41, no. 3 (April 1997): 761–770.

[13] Bergsten, C. F., *Dilemmas of the Dollar: The Economics and Politics of United States International Monetary Policy.* New York: ME Sharpe, 1996.

[14] Bergsten, C. F., "The Dollar and the Global Imbalances," *CESifo Forum* 8, no. 4 (2007): 3–5.

[15] Bergsten, C. F., "The Chinese Exchange Rate and the US Economy," Housing and Urban Affairs, Washington, DC: US Congress, 2007.

[16] Bernanke, B. S., "Alternative Explanations of the Money-Income Correlation," *Carnegie-Rochester Conference Series on Public Policy* 25 (Autumn 1986): 49–99.

[17] Bernanke, B. S., "Central Banking and Bank Supervision in the United States," *Remarks given at the Allied Social Sciences Association*, January 5, 2007.

[18] Bernanke, B. S., Jean Boivin and Piotr Eliasz, "Measuring the Effects of Monetary Policy: A Factor-Augmented Vector Autoregressive (FAVAR) Approach," *The Quarterly Journal of Economics* 120, no. 1 (2005): 387–422.

[19] Bhattacharya, A., S. Ghosh and W. J. Jansen, "Has the Emergence of China Hurt Asian Exports?" *Applied Economics Letters* 8, no. 4 (2001): 217–221.

[20] Bini S., L., "Independence and Accountability in Supervision," In *Designing Financial Supervision Institutions: Independence, Accountability and Governance*, edited by D. Masciandaro and M. Quintyn, 41–62. Cheltenham: Edward Elgar, 2007.

[21] Blanchard, O. J. and D. Quah, "The Dynamic Effects of Aggregate Supply and Demand Disturbances," *American Economic Review* 79, no. 4 (September 1989): 655–673.

[22] Boorman, J., *An Agenda for Reform of the International Monetary Fund (IMF)*. New York: Friedrich-Ebert-Stiftung, 2008.

[23] Bowman, "Yen Bloc or Koala Bloc? Currency Relationships after the East Asian Crisis," *Japan and the World Economy* 17, no. 1 (January 2005): 83–96.

[24] Bracke, T., M. Bussiere, M. Fidora and R. Straub, "A Framework for Assessing Global Imbalances," *European Central Bank Occasional Paper*, no. 78 (2008).

[25] Branson, W. H. and C. N. Healy, "Monetary and Exchange Rate Policy Coordination in ASEAN," *National Bureau of Economic Research Working Paper*, no. w11713 (October, 2005).

[26] Brooks, R., K. Rogoff, A. Mody *et al.*, "Evolution and Performance of Exchange Rate Regimes," *International Monetary Fund*, 2004.

[27] Bryant, R. C., *Reform of Quota and Voting Shares in the International Monetary Fund: "Nothing" Is Temporarily Preferable to an Adequate "Something"*. Washington, DC: Brookings Institution, 2008.

[28] Calvo, E. and H. Peters, "Dynamics and Axiomatics of the Equal Area Bargaining Solution," *International Journal of Game Theory* 29, no. 1 (February 2000): 81–92.

[29] Calvo, G. A. and C. M. Reinhart, "Fixing for Your Life," *Brookings Trade Forum*, (2000): 1–38.

[30] Calvo, G. A. and C. M. Reinhart, "Fear of Floating," *The Quarterly Journal of Economics* 117, no. 2 (2002): 379–408.

[31] Cavoli, T. and R. S. Rajan, *Exchange Rate Regimes and Macroeconomic Management in Asia*. Hong Kong: Hong Kong University Press, 2009.

[32] Camdessus, M., "The Future of the IMF," *The World in Words*, February 12, 2000.

[33] Cardarelli, R., S. A. Elekdag and M. Ayhan Kose, "Capital Inflows: Macroeconomic Implications and Policy Responses," *IMF Working Paper*, no. 09/04 (March 2009).

[34] Carnicer, J. E and J. Penuelas, "The World at a Crossroads: Financial Scenarios for Sustainability," *Energy Policy* 48 (September 2012): 611–617.

[35] Chan, E., M. K. F. Chui, F. Packer and E. M. Remolona, "Local Currency Bond Markets and the Asian Bond Fund 2 Initiative," *BIS paper*, no. 63f (January 2012).

[36] Chinn, M. D., "A Note on Reserve Currencies with Special Reference to the G-20 Countries," written for the International Growth Centre (IGC), India Central Programme, 2012.

[37] Chinn, M. D. and Jeffrey A. Frankel, "Will the Euro Eventually Surpass the Dollar as Leading International Reserve Currency?" *NBER Working Paper*, no. 11510 (August 2005).

[38] Chinn, M. D. and Hiro Ito, "What Matters for Financial Development? Capital Controls, Institutions, and Interactions," *Journal of Development Economics* 81, no. 1 (October 2006): 163–192.

[39] Chinn, M. Da. and Jeffrey A. Frankel, "The Euro May over the Next 15 Years Surpass the Dollar as Leading International Currency," *National Bureau of Economic Research Working Paper*, no. w13909 (April 2008).

[40] Cihak, M. and J. Frankel, "Will the Euro Eventually Surpass the Dollar as Leading International Currency," *NBER Working Paper*, no. 11510 (2005).

[41] Cihak, M. and R. Podpiera, "Experience with Integrated Supervisors: Governance and Quality of Supervision," In *Designing Financial Supervision Institutions: Independence, Accountability and Governance*, edited by Masciandaro D. and M. Quintyn, 309–341. Cheltenham: Edward Elgar, 2007.

[42] Cihak, M. and A. F. Tieman, "Assessing Current Prudential Arrangements," In *Integrating Europe's Financial Markets*, edited by Decressin J., H. Faruqee and W. Fonteyne, 171–198. Washington, DC: International Monetary Fund, 2007.

[43] Cihak, M. and A. F. Tieman, "Quality of Financial Sector Regulation and Supervision Around the World," *International Monetary Fund Working Paper*, no. 08/190 (August 2008).

[44] Clark, P. B. and J. Polak, "International Liquidity and the Role of the SDR in the International Monetary System," *IMF Working Paper*, no. 02/217 (December 2002).

[45] Clarida, R. and J. Gali, "Sources of Real Exchange-Rate Fluctuations: How Important are Nominal Shocks?" *Carnegie-Rochester Conference Series on Public Policy* 41 (December 1994): 1–56.

[46] Cline, W. R., *The United States as a Debtor Nation.* Washington, DC: Peterson Institute, 2005.

[47] Cline, W. R., *Financial Globalization, Economic Growth, and the Crisis of 2007-09.* Washington, DC: Peterson Institute, 2010.

[48] Coffey, Peter and Robert J. Riley, *Reform of the International Institutions: the IMF, World Bank and the WTO.* Cheltenham: Edward Elgar Publishing, 2006.

[49] Cohen, B. J., *Future of Sterling as an International Currency.* London: St. Martins Press, 1971.

[50] Cohen, B. J., *The Geography of Money.* New York: Cornell University Press, 1998.

[51] Colavecchio, R. and M. Funke, "Volatility Dependence across Asia-Pacific On-Shore and Off-Shore US Dollar Futures Markets," *BOFIT Discussion Paper*, no. 17/2007 (August 2007).

[52] Commission of the European Communities. "Communication from the Commission. European Financial Supervision." COM (2009) 252 final (May 2009).

[53] Cooper, R. N., "Financial Aspects of Economic Cooperation around the Pacific," *Pacific Trade and Development I*, Papers and Proceedings of a Conference Held by the Japan Economic Research Center in January, 1968.

[54] Cooper, Ri. N., "Is There a Need for Reform?" *The International Monetary System: Forty Years after Bretton Woods* (1984): 21–39.

[55] Cooper, R. N., "The Future of the Dollar," *Policy Brief in International Economics*, no. PB09-21 (September 2009).

[56] Cooper, R. N. and Edwin M. Truman, "The IMF Quota Formula: Linchpin of Fund Reform," *Policy Briefs in International Economics*, no. PB07-1 (February 2007).

[57] Corsetti, G., L. Dedola and S. Leduc, "International Risk Sharing and the Transmission of Productivity Shocks," *CEPR Discussion Paper*, no. 4746 (November 2004).

[58] Corsetti, G. and P. Th. Konstantinou, "Current Account Theory and the Dynamics of US Net Foreign Liabilities," *CEPR Discussion Paper*, no. 4920 (February 2005).

[59] Council EU, "Council Conclusions on Strengthening EU Financial Supervision." *2948th Economic and Financial Affairs*, Luxembourg (June 9, 2009).

[60] Crockett, A., "Issues in Global Financial Supervision," Remarks at the 36th SEACEN Governors' Conference held in Singapore, 2001.

[61] Dalla Pellegrina, L. and D. Masciandaro, "Politicians, Central Banks, and the Shape of Financial Supervision Architectures," *Journal of Financial Regulation and Compliance* 16, no. 4 (November 2008): 290–317.

[62] De Larosiere Group, "Report of the High Level Group on Supervision," 2009.

[63] De Luna-Martinez, J. and T. A. Rose, *International Survey of Integrated Financial Sector Supervision*. Washington, DC: World Bank Publications, 2003.

[64] Deane, P. and H. J. Habakkuk, "The Take-Off in Britain," Conference on the Economics of "Take-Off" into Sustained Growth [of the] International Economic Association, 1960.

[65] Demertzis, M., A. H. Hallett and O. Rummel, "Is the European Union a Natural Currency Area, or Is it Held Together by Policy Makers?" *Weltwirtschaftliches Archiv* 136, no. 4 (2000): 657–679.

[66] Denters, E., "Regulation and Supervision of the Global Financial System: A Proposal for Institutional Reform," *Lecturer in International Economic Law*, VU University Amsterdam, 2009.

[67] Department of the Treasury, "Blueprint for a Modernized Financial Regulatory Structure," Washington, D.C., 2008.

[68] Department of the Treasury, "Financial Regulatory Reform: A New Foundation," Washington, D.C., 2009.

[69] Ding C., "Euro, Dollar, Yuan Uncertainties: Scenarios on the Future of the International Monetary System," *World Economic Forum*, 2012.

[70] Dobson, W. and P. R. Masson, "Will the Renminbi Become a World Currency?" *China Economic Review* 20, no. 1 (March 2009): 124–135.

[71] Dooley, M. P., D. Folkerts-Landau and P. M. Garber, "An Essay on the Revived Bretton Woods System," *NBER Working Paper*, no. 9971 (September 2003).

[72] Dooley, M. P., D. Folkerts-Landau and P. M. Garber, "The Revised Bretton Woods System," *International Journal of Finance and Economics* 9, no. 4 (October 2004): 307–313.

[73] Dooley, M. P., D. Folkerts-Landau and P. M. Garber, "Bretton Woods II still Defines the International Monetary System," *NBER Working Paper*, no. 10332 (2009).

[74] Duncan, R., *The Dollar Crisis: Causes, Consequences, Cures.* New Jersey: John Wiley & Sons, 2005.

[75] Dwyer Jr., G. P. and J. R. Lothian, "The Economics of International Monies," *CRIF Working Paper* (2003): 10.

[76] D'Arista, J., "Financial Regulation in a Liberalized Global Environment," In *International Capital Markets: Systems in Transition*, edited by J. Eatwell and L. Taylor, 75. Oxford: Oxford University Press, 2002.

[77] Eatwell, J. and L. Taylor, *International Capital Markets: Systems in Transition.* Oxford: Oxford University Press, 2002.

[78] Eichengreen, B., *International Monetary Arrangements for the 21st Century.* Washington, DC: Brookings Institution Press, 1994.

[79] Eichengreen, B., "The Euro as a Reserve Currency," *Journal of the Japanese and International Economies* 12, no. 4 (December 1998): 483–506.

[80] Eichengreen, B., "Whither Monetary and Financial Cooperation in Asia?" PECC Finance Forum Conference Issues and Prospects

for Regional Cooperation for Financial Stability and Development (2002): 11–13.

[81] Eichengreen, B., "Hanging Together? On Monetary and Financial Cooperation," In *Global Change and East Asian Policy Initiatives*, edited by Shahid Yusuf, M. Anjum Altaf and Kaoru Nabeshima, 25. Washington, DC: World Bank and Oxford University Press, 2004.

[82] Eichengreen, B., "The Dollar and the New Bretton Woods System," Thornton Lecture, Cass Business School, London, 2004.

[83] Eichengreen, B., "Sterling's Past, Dollar's Future: Historical Perspectives on Reserve Currency Competition," *National Bureau of Economic Research Working Paper*, no. 11336 (May 2005).

[84] Eichengreen, B., "A Blueprint for IMF Reform: More than just a Lender," *International Finance* 10, no. 2 (Summer 2007): 153–175.

[85] Eichengreen, B., "From the Asian Crisis to the Global Credit Crisis: Reforming the International Financial Architecture Redux," *International Economics and Economic Policy* 6, no. 1 (June 2009): 1–22.

[86] Eichengreen, B., "The Dollar Dilemma — The World's Top Currency Faces Competition," *Foreign Affairs* 88, no. 5 (September/October 2009): 53–68.

[87] Eichengreen, B., "Managing a Multiple Reserve Currency World," Berkeley: University of California, 2010.

[88] Eichengreen, B., *Exorbitant Privilege: The Rise and Fall of the Dollar and the Future of the International Monetary System*. Oxford: Oxford University Press, 2010.

[89] Eichengreen, B., "The Renminbi as an International Currency," *Journal of Policy Modeling* 33, no. 5 (September-October 2011): 723–730.

[90] Eichengreen, B. and Jeffrey A. Frankel, *On the SDR: Reserve Currencies and the Future of the International Monetary System*. Berkeley: University of California, 1996.

[91] Eichengreen, B. and Ricardo Hausmann, "Exchange Rates and Financial Fragility," *National Bureau of Economic Research Working Paper*, no. w7418 (November 1999).

[92] Eichengreen, B. and Donald J. Mathieson, "The Currency Composition of Foreign Exchange Reserves: Retrospect and Prospect," *International Monetary Fund Working Paper*, no. 00/131 (July 2000).

[93] Eichengreen, B., Yeongseop Rhee and Hui Tong, "China and the Exports of Other Asian Countries," *Review of World Economics* 143, no. 2 (July 2007): 201–226.

[94] Eichengreen, B. and Nathan Sussman, "The International Monetary System in the Long Run," *International Monetary Fund Working Paper*, no. 00/43 (March 2000).

[95] Eichengreen, B. and Peter Temin, "Fetters of Gold and Paper," *Oxford Review of Economic Policy* 26, no. 3 (Autumn 2010): 370–384.

[96] EMEAP, "Review of the Asian Bond Fund 2 Initiative." EMEAP Working Group on Financial Markets, June 2006.

[97] Fabella, R., "Monetary Cooperation in East Asia: A Survey," *ERD Working Paper Series*, no. 13 (2002).

[98] Fiorentini, R. and G. Montani, "Global Imbalances and the Transition to a Symmetric World Monetary System," *Perspectives on Federalism* 2, no. 1 (2010).

[99] Frankel, Je. A., "No Single Currency Regime Is Right for All Countries or at All Times," *National Bureau of Economic Research Working Paper*, no. w7338 (September 1999).

[100] Frankel, J., "On the Yuan: The Choice between Adjustment under a Fixed Exchange Rate and Adjustment under a Flexible Rate," *CESifo Economic Studies* 52, no. 2 (2006): 246–275.

[101] Frankel, J., "Historical Precedents for Internationalization of the RMB," Council on Foreign Relations/China Development Research Foundation Symposium, The Future of the International Monetary System and the Role of the Renminbi, Beijing, 2011.

[102] Frankel, J. A., E. Fajnzylber, S. L. Schmukler and L. Serven, "Verifying Exchange Rate Regimes," *Journal of Development Economics* 66, no. 2 (December 2001): 351–386.

[103] Frankel, J. A. and A. K. Rose, "The Endogenity of the Optimum Currency Area Criteria," *The Economic Journal* 108, no. 449 (1998): 1009–1025.

[104] Frankel, J. A. and Shang-Jin Wei, "Yen Bloc or Dollar Bloc? Exchange Rate Policies of the East Asian Economies," In *Macroeconomic Linkage: Savings, Exchange Rates, and Capital Flows*, edited by Takatoshi Ito and Anne O. Krueger, 295–333. Chicago: University of Chicago Press, 1994.

[105] Fratzscher, M. and A. Mehl, "China's Dominance Hypothesis and the Emergence of a Tri-polar Global Currency System," *ECB Working Paper Series*, no. 1392 (October 2011).

[106] Frenkel, J. A. and M. Goldstein, "The International Role of the Deutsche Mark," In *Fifty Years of the Deutsche Mark: Central Bank and the Currency in Germany since 1948*, edited by Deutsche Bundesbank, 685–792. Oxford: Oxford University Press, 1999.

[107] Freytag, A. and D. Masciandaro, "Financial Supervision Fragmentation and Central Bank Independence," In *Designing Financial Supervision Institutions: Independence, Accountability and*

Governance, edited by D. Masciandaro and M. Quintyn. Cheltenham: Edward Elgar, 2007.

[108] Friberg, R., "On the Role of Pricing Exports in a Third Currency," *SSE/EFI Working Paper Series in Economics and Finance*, no. 128 (September 1996).

[109] Fukuda, S., and M. Ono, "The Choice of Invoice Currency under Uncertainty: Theory and Evidence from Korea," *CIRJE Discussion Papers*, no. CIRJE-F-271 (2004).

[110] Funke, M., "The Nature of Shocks in Europe and in Germany," *Economica* 64, no. 255 (February 1997): 461–469.

[111] G20, "Declaration Summit on Financial Market and the World Economy." Last modified November 15, 2008. http://www.g20.org/Documents/g20_summit_declaration.pdf.

[112] Germain, R. D., "Global Financial Governance and the Problem of Inclusion," *Global Governance* 7, no. 4 (October 2001): 411–426.

[113] Ghosh, S. R., *East Asian Finance: The Road to Robust Markets.* Washington, DC: World Bank Publications, 2006.

[114] Gilpin, R., *US Power and the Multinational Corporation: The Political Economy of Foreign Direct Investment.* New York: Basic Books, 1975.

[115] Gilpin, R. and Jean M. Gilpin, *The Political Economy of International Relations.* Princeton: Princeton University Press, 1987.

[116] Giovannini, A., "Exchange Rates and Traded Goods Prices," *Journal of International Economics* 24, no. 1 (February 1988): 45–68.

[117] Goldberg, L. S., "Is the International Role of the Dollar Changing?" *Current Issues in Economics and Finance* 16, no. 1 (January 2010): 1–7.

[118] Goldberg, L. S., "The International Role of the Dollar: Does It Matter if This Changes?" *FRB of New York Staff Report*, no. 522 (October 2011).

[119] Goldstein, M., "China's Exchange Rate Regime," *Testimony before the Subcommittee on Domestic and International Monetary Policy, Trade, and Technology Committee on Financial Services*, 2003.

[120] Goodhart, C., "Introduction," In *Designing Financial Supervision Institutions: Independence, Accountability and Governance*, edited by D. Masciandaro D. and M. Quintyn, 12–26. Cheltenham: Edward Elgar, 2007.

[121] Goto, J., "Economic Preconditions for Monetary Cooperation in East Asia," *Discussion Paper Series from Research Institute for Economics & Business Administration, Kobe University*, no. 132 (2002).

[122] Goto, J. and K. Hamada, "Economic Preconditions for Asian Regional Integration," In *Macroeconomic Linkage: Savings, Exchange Rates, and Capital Flows*, edited by Takatoshi Ito and Anne O. Krueger, 359–388. Chicago: University of Chicago Press, 1994.

[123] Gourinchas, P.-O. and H. Rey, "From World Banker to World Venture Capitalist: US External Adjustment and the Exorbitant Privilege," *NBER Working Paper*, no. 11563, (August 2005).

[124] Gourinchas, P.-O. and H. Rey, "International Financial Adjustment," *Journal of Political Economy* 115, no. 4 (August 2007): 665–703.

[125] Grassman, S., "A Fundamental Symmetry in International Payment Patterns," *Journal of International Economics* 3, no. 2 (May 1973): 105–116.

[126] Greenwald, Br. and J. E. Stiglitz, "A Modest Proposal for International Monetary Reform," In *Time for a Visible Hand: Lessons from the 2008 World Financial Crisis*, edited by S. Griffith-Jones, J. A. Ocampo, and J. E. Stiglitz, 314–344. Oxford: Oxford University Press, 2010.

[127] Group of Thirty, *The Structure of Financial Supervision: Approaches and Challenges in a Global Marketplace.* Washington, DC: Group of Thirty, 2008.

[128] Harding, D. and A. Pagan, "Dissecting the Cycle: A Methodological Investigation," *Journal of Monetary Economics* 49, no. 2 (March 2002): 365–381.

[129] Hartmann, P.p and O.r Issing, "The International Role of the Euro," *Journal of Policy Modeling* 24, no. 4 (July 2002): 315–345.

[130] Hamanaka, S., "Asian Financial Cooperation in the 1990s: The Politics of Membership," *Journal of East Asian Studies* 11, no. 1 (January-April 2011): 75–103.

[131] Han, I., "Currency Swaps Move South Korea Closer to China, Away from Japan," Last modified July 18, 2013. http://www.eastasiaforum.org/2013/07/18/currency-swaps-move-south-korea-closer-to-china-away-from-japan/.

[132] Hefeker, Ca. and A. Nabor, "China's Role in East-Asian Monetary Integration," *International Journal of Finance & Economics* 10, no. 2 (April 2005): 157–166.

[133] Herring, R. J. and J. Carmassi, "The Structure of Cross-Sector Financial Supervision," *Financial Markets, Institutions & Instruments* 17, no. 1 (January 2008): 51–76.

[134] Heywood, A., *Political Ideas and Concepts: An Introduction.* London: Macmillan, 1994.

[135] Ho, C., G. Ma and R. N. McCauley, "Trading Asian Currencies," *BIS Quarterly Review*, (March 2005): 49.

[136] Holopainen, H., "Integration of Financial Supervision," *Bank of Finland Research Discussion Paper*, no. 12/2007 (2007).

[137] Ikenberry, G. J., "Future of the Liberal World Order: Internationalism after America," *Foreign Affairs* 90, no. 3 (May/June 2011): 56–62, 63–68.

[138] Hoskisson, R. E., L. Eden, Chung Ming Lau and M. Wright, "Strategy in Emerging Economies," *The Academy of Management Journal* 43, no. 3 (June 2000): 249–267.

[139] IMF, "Annual Report of the Executive Board for the Financial Year Ended April 30, 2005," Last modified September, 2005. http://www.imf.org/external/pubs/ft/ar/2005/eng/index.htm.

[140] IMF, "The Managing Director's Report on the Fund's Medium-Term Strategy," Last modified 2005. http://www.imf.org/external/np/omd/2005/eng/091505.pdf.

[141] IMF, "The IMF's Advice on Exchange Rate Policy," *Issues Paper for an Evaluation by The Independent Evaluation Office (IEO)* (April 2006).

[142] IMF, "Statement by IMF Managing Director Rodrigo de Rato on IMF Executive Board Decision to Approve New Framework for Surveillance," *International Monetary Fund*, Press Release no.07/137 (June 2007).

[143] IMF, "Lessons of the Financial Crisis for Future Regulation of Financial Institutions and Markets and for Liquidity Management," *International Monetary Fund, International Capital Markets Department*, 2009. http://www.imf.org/external/np/pp/eng/2009/020409.pdf.

[144] IMF, "The IMF's Advice on Exchange Rate Policy," *Issues Paper for an Evaluation by The Independent Evaluation Office (IEO)*, (2010).

[145] IMF, "Meeting New Challenges to Stability and Building a Safer System," *Global Financial Stability Report* (April 2010a).

[146] IMF, "Sovereigns, Funding, and Systemic Liquidity," *Global Financial Stability Report* (October 2010b).

[147] IMF, "Tensions from the Two-Speed Recovery Unemployment, Commodities, and Capital Flows," *World Economic Outlook* (April 2011).

[148] IMF, "World Economic Outlook Update Gradual Upturn in Global Growth During 2013," Last modified January 23, 2013. http://www.imf.org/external/pubs/ft/weo/2013/update/01/index.htm.

[149] Ingram, J. C., "Comment: The Currency Area Problem," In *Monetary Problems of the International Economy*, edited by Robert Mundell and Alexander Swoboda, 95–100. Chicago: University of Chicago Press, 1969.

[150] Isogai, Takashi and Shunichi Shibanuma, "East Asia's Intra-and Inter-Regional Economic Relations; Data Analyses on Trade, Direct Investments and Currency Transactions," *Bank of Japan Working Paper Series*, no. 00-E-4 (October 2000).

[151] Ito, Takatoshi, Eiji Ogawa and Yuri Nagataki Sasaki, "How Did the Dollar Peg Fail in Asia?" *Journal of the Japanese and International Economies* 12, no. 4 (December 1998): 256–304.

[152] James, H., "The Historical Development of the Principle of Surveillance," *Staff Papers-International Monetary Fund* 42, no. 4 (1995): 762–791.

[153] Kaminsky, G. and C. M. Reinhart, "The Center and the Periphery: The Globalization of Financial Turmoil," *NBER Working Paper*, no. w9479 (November 2001).

[154] Kawai, Masahiro and Shinji Takagi, "Towards Regional Monetary Cooperation in East Asia: Lessons from Other Parts of the World," *International Journal of Finance & Economics* 10, no. 2 (April 2005): 97–116.

[155] Kawai, Masahiro, "From the Chiang Mai Initiative to an Asian Monetary Fund," *Asian Development Bank Institute Report*, April 2010.

[156] Kenen, P. B., "Substitution Account as a First Step toward Reform of the International Monetary System," *Policy Brief*, no. PB10-6 (March 2010). Peterson Institute for International Economics.

[157] Kenen, P. B., "Beyond the Dollar," *Journal of Policy Modeling* 33, no. 5 (September-October 2011): 750–758.

[158] Keohane, R. O., "The Theory of Hegemonic Stability and Changes in International Economic Regimes, 1967–1977," In *Change in the International System*, edited by Ole R Holsti, Randolph M. Siverson and Alexander L. George, 132. Boulder: Westview Press, 1980.

[159] Keohane, Ro. O., *After Hegemony*. Princeton: Princeton University Press, 1984.

[160] Kim, Hak-Min, *Globalization of International Financial Markets: Causes and Consequences*. Hampshire: Ashgate, 1999.

[161] Kindleberger, C. P., *The World in Depression 1929–1939*. London: Penguin Press, 1973.

[162] Kindleberger, C. P., "Lessons of Floating Exchange Rates," *Carnegie-Rochester Conference Series on Public Policy* 3, no. 1 (February 1976): 51–77.

[163] King, M., "Reform of the International Monetary Fund," at the *Indian Council for Research on International Economic Relations (ICRIER)*, New Delhi, February 20, 2006.

[164] Kojima, Kiyoshi, "A Pacific Currency Area: A New Approach to International Monetary Reform," *Hitotsubashi Journal of Economics* 10, no. 2 (February 1970): 1–17.

[165] Kojima, Kiyoshi, "A Pacific Currency Area: Reply to Professor Arndt's Comment," *Hitotsubashi Journal of Economics* 11, no. 2 (February 1971): 73–76.

[166] Krugman, P. R., "The International Role of the Dollar: Theory and Prospect," In *Exchange Rate Theory and Practice*, edited by John F. O. Bilson and Richard C. Marston, 261–278. Chicago: University of Chicago press, 1984.

[167] Krugman, P. R., "Target Zones and Exchange Rate Dynamics," *The Quarterly Journal of Economics* 106, no. 3 (August 1991): 669–682.

[168] Krugman, P. R., "China's Dollar Trap," *New York Times*, April 3, 2009.

[169] Krugman, P. R. and Maurice Obstfeld, *International Economics: Theory and Policy (6th edition)*. New York: Pearson Education, Inc., 2003.

[170] Krugman, P., R. N. Cooper and T. N. Srinivasan, "Growing World Trade: Causes and Consequences," *Brookings Papers on Economic Activity* 1995, no. 1 (1995): 327–377.

[171] Kudoh, Noritaka, "A Search-Theoretic Model of Money as a Store of Value," 2003. www.ipcku.kansai-u.ac.jp/~kudoh/MyResearch/store.pdf.

[172] Kui, Ng Beoy, "The Economic Rise of China: Threats and Opportunities from the Perspective of Southeast Asia," *Copenhagen Journal of Asian Studies* 25, no. 1 (January 2007).

[173] Kunz, D. B., *Economic Diplomacy of the Suez Crisis*. Chapel Hill, NC: Univ. of North Carolina Press, 1991.

[174] Kwack, Sung Y., "Exchange Rate and Monetary Regime Options for Regional Cooperation in East Asia," *Journal of Asian Economics* 16, no. 1 (February 2005): 57–75.

[175] Lamy, P., "Openness of Trade and Openness of Minds: Key to Meeting Challenges of the Future," October, 2012. http//www.wto.org/english/news-e/sppl-e/sppl250-e.htm.

[176] Lannoo, K., "Concrete Steps towards More Integrated Financial Oversight: The EU's Policy Response to the Crisis," *CEPS Task Force Reports*, (December 2008).

[177] Lavigne, R. and L. L. Schembri, "Strengthening IMF Surveillance: An Assessment of Recent Reforms," *Bank of Canada Discussion Paper*, no. 2009–10 (July 2009).

[178] Leijonhufvud, A., "Curbing Instability: Policy and Regulation," *CEPR Policy Insight*, no. 36 (2009).

[179] Levy-Yeyati, E. and F. Sturzenegger, "Classifying Exchange Rate Regimes: Deeds vs. Words," *European Economic Review* 49, no. 6 (August 2005): 1603–1635.

[180] Levy-Yeyati, E. and F. Sturzenegger, "Fear of Floating in Reverse: Exchange Rate Policy in the 2000s," unpublished: Washington, World Bank, (2007): 1–39.

[181] Ma, G. and R. N. McCauley, "The Evolving Renminbi Regime and Implications for Asian Currency Stability," *BIS Working Paper*, no. 321 (September 2010).

[182] Ma, G. and E. M. Remolona, "Opening Markets Through a Regional Bond Fund: Lessons from ABF2," *BIS Quarterly Review*, no. 6 (June 2005): 81–92.

[183] Macdougall, G. D. A, "The Benefits and Costs of Private Investment from Abroad: A Theoretical Approach," *Economic Record* 36, no. 73 (March 1960): 13–35.

[184] Maehara, Yasuhiro, "The Internationalization of the Yen and its Role as a Key Currency," *Journal of Asian Economics* 4, no. 1 (Spring 1993): 153–170.

[185] Mann, C. L., "Breaking Up Is Hard to Do: Global Co-Dependency. Collective Action, and the Challenges of Global Adjustment," *Paper of CESITO Forum* 6, no. 1 (2005): 16–23.

[186] Marchesi, S. and J. P. Thomas, "IMF Conditionality as a Screening Device," *The Economic Journal* 109, no. 454 (March 1999): 111–125.

[187] Masciandaro, D., "Reforming Financial Supervision Institutions: An International Comparison," *The Journal of Financial Transformation* 18 (2005): 157.

[188] Maskin, E. S., "Mechanism Design: How to Implement Social Goals," *The American Economic Review* 98, no. 3 (June 2008): 567–576.

[189] Masson, P. R. and J. C. Pattison, "Financial Regulatory Reform: Using Models of Cooperation to Evaluate Current Prospects for International Agreement," *The Journal of Economic Asymmetries* 6, no. 3 (December 2009): 119–136.

[190] Matsuyama, Kiminori, Nobuhiro Kiyotaki and Akihiko Matsui, "Toward a Theory of International Currency," *The Review of Economic Studies* 60, no. 2 (April 1993): 283–307.

[191] McCauley, R., "Unifying Government Bond Markets in East Asia," *BIS Quarterly Review* (December 2003).

[192] McCauley, R., "The Internationalisation of the Renminbi," speech to the Second Annual International Conference on the Chinese Economy, Macroeconomic Management in China: Monetary and Financial Stability Issues, Hong Kong Institute for Monetary Research, Hong Kong SAR, 14 January 2011.

[193] McCauley, R., "Internationalizing the Renminbi and China's Financial Development Model," a Council on Foreign Relations/China Development Research Foundation Symposium, The Future of the International Monetary System and the Role of the Renminbi, Beijing, 2011, 1.

[194] McGuire, P. and G. v. Peter, "The Dollar Shortage in Global Banking and the International Policy Response," *International Finance* 15, no. 2 (2012): 155–178.

[195] McKinnon, R. and G. Schnabl, "China's Exchange Rate and International Adjustment in Wages, Prices and Interest Rates: Japan Deja Vu?" *CESifo Economic Studies* 52, no. 2 (2006): 276–303.

[196] McKinnon, R. I., "The International Dollar Standard and the Sustainability of the US Current Account Deficit," *Brookings Papers on Economic Activity* 2001, no. 1 (2001): 227–239.

[197] McKinnon, R. I, "Optimum Currency Areas," *The American Economic Review* 53, no. 4 (September 1963): 717–725.

[198] McKinnon, R. and G. Schnabl, "The East Asian Dollar Standard, Fear of Floating, and Original Sin," *Review of Development Economics* 8, no. 3 (2004): 331–360.

[199] Mead, W. R., "America's Sticky Power," *Foreign Policy*, no. 141 (March-April 2004): 46–53.

[200] Meissner, C. M. and N. Oomes, "Why Do Countries Peg the Way They Peg? The Determinants of Anchor Currency Choice," *Journal of International Money and Finance* 28, no. 3 (April 2009): 522–547.

[201] Menon, J. and H. Hill, "Does East Asia Have a Working Financial Safety Net?" *Asian Economic Journal* 28, no. 1 (March 2014): 1–17.

[202] Milesi-Ferretti, Gian Maria, "Fundamentals at Odds? The U.S. Current Account Deficit and the Dollar," *IMF Working Paper*, WP/08/260 (November 2008).

[203] Morck, R., "Behavioral Finance in Corporate Governance-Independent Directors and Non-Executive Chairs," *National Bureau of Economic Research Working Paper*, (2004).

[204] Muzaffar, C., "The Empire: What It Is and What It Means for All of Us," Global Research, Last modified December 30,

2005. http://www.globalresearch.ca/the-empire-what-it-is-and-what-it-means-for-all-of-us/1681.

[205] Mundell, Robert A., "EMU and the International Monetary System, A Transatlantic Perspective," *Oesterreichische Nationalbank (Austrian Central Bank) Working Papers*, no. 13 (1993).

[206] Mundell, R., "Currency Areas, Exchange Rate Systems and International Monetary Reform," *Journal of Applied Economics* 3, no. 2 (2000): 217–256.

[207] Mundell, R., "The Euro and the Stability of the International Monetary System," In *The Euro as a Stabilizer in the International Economic System*, edited by Robert Mundell, and Armand Clesse, 57–84. Boston: Springer, 2000.

[208] Naik, V., A. Arora, S. Balakrishnan and A. Jiltsov, "Global Savings-Investment Imbalances: A Look through the Life-Cycle Model," New York: Lehman Brothers, *Fixed Income Research* (September 2005).

[209] Nasution, A., "Monetary Cooperation in East Asia," *Journal of Asian Economics* 16, no. 3 (June 2005): 422–442.

[210] Ng, F. and A. Yeats, "Production Sharing in East Asia: Who Does What for Whom, and Why?" In *Global Production and Trade in East Asia*, edited by Leonard K. Cheng, and Henryk Kierzkowski, 63–109. Boston: Springer, 2001.

[211] Noyer, C., "The G20 and the Role of Emerging Markets in the New Financial Architecture," *BIS Review*, (2009). http://www.bis.org/review/r090902a.pdf.

[212] Nusair, S. A., "Is East Asia an Optimum Currency Area? A Test of Generalized Purchasing Power Parity in the Presence of Structural Breaks," *Journal of the Asia Pacific Economy* 17, no. 3 (2012): 399–425.

[213] Nye, J. S., "The Changing Nature of World Power," *Political Science Quarterly* 105, no. 2 (Summer 1990): 177–192.

[214] Oatley, T. and J. Yackee, "American Interests and IMF Lending," *International Politics* 41, no. 3 (September 2004): 415–429.

[215] Obstfeld, M., "The Logic of Currency Crises," In *Monetary and Fiscal Policy in an Integrated Europe*, edited by Barry Eichengreen, Jeffry Frieden and Jürgen von Hagen, 62–90. Berlin, Heidelberg: Springer, 1995.

[216] Obstfeld, M., "External Adjustment," *Review of World Economics* 140, no. 4 (December 2004): 541–568.

[217] Obstfeld, M., "The International Monetary System: Living with Asymmetry," *NBER Working Paper*, no. w17641, (December 2011).

[218] Obstfeld, M. and K. Rogoff, "The Mirage of Fixed Exchange Rates," *National Bureau of Economic Research Working Paper*, no. w5191 (July 1995).

[219] Ocampo, J. A., "The Instability and Inequities of the Global Reserve System," *International Journal of Political Economy* 36, no. 4 (2007): 71–96.

[220] Ocampo, J. A., "Special Drawing Rights and the Reform of the Global Reserve System," In *Reforming the International Financial System for Development*, edited by Jomo Kwame Sundaram, 314–342. New York: Columbia University Press, 2011.

[221] Ogawa, E., "Regional Monetary Cooperation in East Asia against Asymmetric Responses to the US Dollar Depreciation," *Journal of the Korean Economy* 5, no. 2 (2004): 43–72.

[222] Ogawa, E., "Regional Monetary Coordination in Asia after the Global Financial Crisis: Comparison in Regional Monetary Stability between ASEAN+3 and ASEAN+3+3," *Public Policy Review* 6, no. 5 (2010): 837–858.

[223] Ogawa, E. and J. Shimizu, "A Deviation Measurement for Coordinated Exchange Rate Policies in East Asia," *RIETI Discussion Paper Series*, no. 05-E-017 (March 2005).

[224] Oi, Hiroyuki, Akira Otani and Toyoichirou Shirota, "The Choice of Invoice Currency in International Trade: Implications for the Internationalization of the Yen," *IMES Discussion Paper Series*, no. 2003-E-13 (2003).

[225] Ozkan, F. G. and D. F. Unsal, "External Finance, Sudden Stops, and Financial Crisis: What Is Different This Time?" *IMF Working Paper*, no. 10/158 (July 2010).

[226] Padoa, S. T., "Financial Supervision: Inside or Outside the Central Banks?" In *Financial Supervision in Europe*, edited by J. Kremers, D. Schoenmaker and P. Wierts, 160–175. Cheltenham: Edward Elgar, 2003.

[227] Pontines, V. and R. S. Rajan, "Foreign Exchange Market Intervention and Reserve Accumulation in Emerging Asia: Is There Evidence of Fear of Appreciation?" *Economics Letters* 111, no. 3 (June 2011): 252–255.

[228] Pontines, V. and R. Y. Siregar, "Fear of Appreciation in East and Southeast Asia: The Role of the Chinese Renminbi," *Journal of Asian Economics* 23, no. 4 (August 2012): 324–334.

[229] Porter, T., "The G-7, the Financial Stability Forum, the G-20, and the Politics of International Financial Regulation," International Studies Association Annual Meeting, Los Angeles, California, March 15, 2000.

[230] Prasad, E. S., "Role Reversal in Global Finance," *National Bureau of Economic Research Working Paper*, no. 17497 (October 2011).

[231] Prasad, E. S. and Lei Sandy Ye, "The Renminbi's Role in the Global Monetary System," *IZA Discussion Paper*, no. 6335 (2012).

[232] Quah, Chee-Heong, "Is East Asia as Prepared as Eurozone for Monetary Union?" *Journal of Business Economics and Management* 13, no. 3 (2012): 471–488.

[233] Quintyn, M. and M. Taylor, "Building Supervisory Structures in Sub-Saharan Africa–An Analytical Framework," *International Monetary Fund Working Paper*, no. 07/18 (2007).

[234] Rai, K. and H. Kamil, "The Global Credit Crunch and Foreign Banks' Lending to Emerging Markets: Why Did Latin America Fare Better?" *IMF Working Paper*, no. 10/102 (2010).

[235] Rana, P. B., "Monetary and Financial Cooperation in East Asia: The Chiang Mai Initiative and Beyond," *ERD Working Paper Series*, no. 6 (February 2002).

[236] Reinhart, C. M. and K. S. Rogoff, "The Modern History of Exchange Rate Arrangements: A Reinterpretation," *Quarterly Journal of Economics* 119, no. 1 (2004): 1–48.

[237] Reisen, H.t and A. Van Trotsenburg, "Should the Asian NICs Peg to the Yen?" *Intereconomics* 23, no. 4 (July 1988): 172–177.

[238] Roland-Holst, D., J.-P. Verbiest and F. Zhai, "Growth and Trade Horizons for Asia: Long Term Forecasts for Regional Integration," *WIDER Working Paper Series*, no. 106 (2008).

[239] Rose, Andrew, "Is There a Case for an Asian Monetary Fund?" *FRBSF Economic Letter*, no. 1999-37 (December 1999).

[240] Rottier, S.e and N. Véron, "Not All Financial Regulation Is Global," Peterson Institute for International Economics, 2010.

[241] Roubini, N.l and B. Setser, "Will the Bretton Woods 2 Regime Unravel Soon? The Risk of a Hard Landing in 2005–2006," Unpublished manuscript, New York University and Oxford University, 2005, 6.

[242] Rupert, P., Martin Schindler, Andrei Shevchenko and Randall Wright, "The Search-Theoretic Approach to Monetary Economics: A Primer," *Economic Review-Federal Reserve Bank of Cleveland* 36, no. 4 (2000): 10–28.

[243] Ryan, J., "China and the Global Roles of Currencies," *International Network for Economic Research Working Paper* (2009).

[244] Ryou, Jai-Won and Yunjong Wang, "Monetary Cooperation in East Asia: Major Issues and Future Prospects," *Journal of International Economic Studies* 8, no. 1 (2004): 4–33.

[245] Sachs, Je., "International Economics: Unlocking the Mysteries of Globalization," *Foreign Policy*, no. 110 (Spring 1998): 97–111.

[246] Santor, E., "Governance and the IMF: Does the Fund Follow Corporate Best Practice?" *Bank of Canada Working Paper*, no. 2006–32 (2006).

[247] Sarr, A. and T. Lybek, "Measuring Liquidity in Financial Markets," *IMF Working Paper*, no. 02/232 (December 2002).

[248] Schlesinger, J. R., "Statement of James Schlesinger before the Committee on Foreign Relations United States Senate," November 16, 2005. http://planetforlife.com/oilcrisis/oilschlesinger.html.

[249] Scott, K. E., "The Dual Banking System: A Model of Competition in Regulation," *Stanford Law Review* 30, no. 1 (November 1977): 1–50.

[250] Seelig, S. A. and Alicia Novoa, "Governance Practices at Financial Regulatory and Supervisory Agencies," *International Monetary Fund Working Paper*, no. 09/135 (May 2009).

[251] Selgin, G., "World Monetary Policy after the Euro," *Cato Journal* 20, no. 1 (Spring 2000): 105–108.

[252] Setser, B. W. and Arpana Pandey, "China's $1.5 Trillion Bet: Understanding China's External Portfolio," *Working Paper* (Council on Foreign Relations, Center for Geoeconomic Studies) (May 2009).

[253] Shambaugh, J. C., "The Effect of Fixed Exchange Rates on Monetary Policy," *The Quarterly Journal of Economics* 119, no. 1 (February 2004): 301–352.

[254] Shams, R., "Why Do Countries Form Regions? The Political Economy of Regional Integration," *HWWA Discussion Paper*, no. 169 (2002).

[255] Shin, Kwanho and Yunjong Wang, "Trade Integration and Business Cycle Synchronization in East Asia," *Asian Economic Papers* 2, no. 3 (2003): 1–20.

[256] Shu, Chang, "Impact of the Renminbi Exchange Rate on Asian Currencies," In *Currency Internationalization: Global Experiences and Implications for the Renminbi*, edited by Wensheng Peng and Chang Shu, 221–235. London: Palgrave Macmillan, 2010.

[257] Srinivasan, N., V. Mahambare and M. Ramachandran, "Preference Asymmetry and International Reserve Accretion in India," *Applied Economics Letters* 16, no. 15 (October 2009): 1543–1546.

[258] Stigler, M., I. Patnaik and A. Shah, "Asymmetries in Central Bank Intervention," *Mimeo*, 2009.

[259] Stiglitz, J.h E. and Bruce Greenwald, "Towards a New Global Reserve System," *Journal of Globalization and Development* 1, no. 2 (2010): 1–26.

[260] Stone, R. W., *Lending Credibility: The International Monetary Fund and the Post-Communist Transition.* Princeton: Princeton University Press, 2002.

[261] Strand, J. R. and D. P. Rapkin, "Voting Power Implications of a Double Majority Voting Procedure in the IMF's Executive Board," In *Reforming the Governance of the IMF and the World Bank*, edited by Ariel Buira, 235–250. Chicago: Anthem Press, 2005.

[262] Strange, S. *States and Markets.* London: Pinter Publishers, 1988.

[263] Subacchi, P. and J. Driffill, *Beyond the Dollar: Rethinking the International Monetary System.* London: Chatham House, 2010.

[264] Subramanian, A., "Renminbi Rules: The Conditional Imminence of the Reserve Currency Transition," *Peterson Institute for International Economics Working Paper Series*, no. 11–14 (September 2011).

[265] Swoboda, A. K., *The Euro-Dollar Market: An Interpretation* . Princeton: International Finance Section, Department of Economics, Princeton University, 1968.

[266] Tavlas, G. S., "On the International Use of Currencies: The Case of the Deutsche Mark." *Essays in International Finance*, no. 181 (1990). International Finance Section, Department of Economics, Princeton University.

[267] Tavlas, G. S., "More on the Chicago Tradition," *Journal of Economic Studies* 25, no. 1 (February 1998): 17–21.

[268] Taylor, M., *"Twin Peaks": A Regulatory Structure for the New Century.* New York: Centre for the Study of Financial Innovation, 1995.

[269] Taylor, M. and A. Fleming, "Integrated Financial Supervision: Lessons from Northern European Experience," *World Bank Policy Research Working Paper*, no. 2223 (September 1999).

[270] Teunissen, J. J., "The International Monetary Crunch: Crisis or Scandal?" *Alternatives: Global, Local, Political* 12, no. 3 (1987): 359–395.

[271] Thorpe, J. and K. Prakash-Mani, "Developing Value: The Business Case for Sustainability in Emerging Markets," In *Managing the Business Case for Sustainability: The Integration of Social, Environmental and Economic Performance*, edited by Stefan Schaltegger and Marcus Wagner, 444–464. London: Routledge, 2006.

[272] Triffin, R.T., *Gold and the Dollar Crisis: The Future of Convertibility.* New Haven: Yale University Press, 1960.

[273] Turner, A., *The Turner Review: A Regulatory Response to the Global Banking Crisis.* London: Financial Services Authority, 2009.

[274] Verhoef, B. A., "The Asymmetry of Shocks in the EMU," *DNB Staff Reports*, no. 106 (2003).

[275] Véron, N., "Financial Reform after the Crisis: An Early Assessment," *Bruegel Working Paper*, no. 680 (2012).

[276] Wall, L. D. and Robert Allen Eisenbeis, "Financial Regulatory Structure and the Resolution of Conflicting Goals," *Journal of Financial Services Research* 16, no. 2–3 (December 1999): 223–245.

[277] Walter, A.w, *World Power and World Money: The Role of Hegemony and International Monetary Order*. New York: Harvester Wheatsheaf, 1993.

[278] Weimann, M.o, "OCA Theory and EMU Eastern Enlargement: An Empirical Application," *Research Notes Working Paper Series*, no. 8 (2003).

[279] Weiss, J., "People's Republic of China and Its Neighbors: Partners or Competitors for Trade and Investment?" *Asian Development Bank Institute Discussion Paper*, no. 13 (2004).

[280] Wellink, N., "A New Structure for European and Global Financial Supervision," 37th Economics Conference, Vienna (14 May 2009).

[281] Westrup, J., "Independence and Accountability: Why Politics Matters," In *Designing Financial Supervision Institutions: Independence, Accountability and Governance*, edited by D. Masciandaro and M. Quinty, 117–150. Cheltenham: Edward Elgar, 2007.

[282] Williamson, J., "Dollarization Does Not Make Sense Everywhere," In *Dolarizacion Oficial de la Economia: Un Debate en Once Actos*, edited by Jurgen Schuldt. Lima: Universidad del Pacífico, 1999.

[283] Wilson, P., "Prospects for Asian Monetary Cooperation after the Asian Financial Crisis: Pipedream or Possible Reality?" *National University of Singapore Working Paper*, no. 151 (2002).

[284] Witteveen, H. J., *Developing a New International Monetary System: A Long-Term View*. Washington, DC: Per Jacobsson Foundation, 1983.

[285] World Bank. *Medzinárodný Menový Fond. Financial Sector Assessment: A Handbook*. Washington, DC: World Bank, 2005.

[286] World Bank, "Global Development Finance 2011: External Debt of Developing Countries," March, 2011. http://data.worldbank.org/data-catalog/global-development-finance.

[287] World Federation of Exchanges, "2012 WFE Market Highlights," http://www.world-exchanges.org/files/statistics/2012%20WFE%20Market%20Highlights.pdf.

[288] Woo Wing Thye, China and International Financial Reform, Part of the First Phase of Project on China's New International Economic Responsibilities, 2010. http://epress.anu.edu.au/wpcontent/uploads/2011/06/ch025.pdf.

[289] Zebregs, H., "Intraregional Trade in Emerging Asia," *International Monetary Fund Policy Discussion Papers*, no. 04/1 (2004).

[290] Zhang, L. and J. Li, "Regional Financial Cooperation in East Asia: Recent Developments and Prospects." Background Paper for "Regional Financial and Regulatory Cooperation, a Chinese-European Dialogue," Beijing (2010): 23–24.

[291] Zhang, Z., K. Sato and M. McAleer, "Is East Asia an Optimum Currency Area," *Proceedings of iEMSs*, 2002.

[292] Ba, S., "How China's Financial Reform Adapts to Internationalization," *Financial Economy* 2 (2006).

[293] Ba, S., "Trends and Prospects of Global Financial Supervision under the Financial Crisis," *Southwestern Finance* 10 (2009).

[294] Ba, S., "Actively Promote Internationalization of RMB," February 13, 2013. http://finance.sina.com.cn/economist/jingjiguancha/20081112/05125495707.shtml.

[295] Ba, S., "Basel III Represents the General Trend of International Financial Regulatory Reform," *China Economic Times*, January 4, 2012.

[296] Ba, S., L. Jin and Y. Zhu, "Impact of Capital Supervision on Chinese Banking Industry under Basel III," *Rural Finance Research* 6 (2011).

[297] Ba, S., L. Jin and Y. Zhu, "Reform of the Market Risk Capital Framework under Basel III and the Application of Chinese Commercial Banks," *Research on Financial Development* 1 (2013).

[298] Ba, S. and X. Yang, "Future Financial System Reform from the Perspective of Financial Crisis," *Contemporary Finance and Economics* 11 (2009).

[299] Ba, S. and Y. Zhu, *New Basel Capital Accords in the Financial Crisis: Challenges and Improvements*. Beijing: China Finance Press, 2010.

[300] Cai, X., "Financial Supervision in ASEAN Countries: The Unbalanced Development Situation and the Choice of Regional Cooperation Path," *Social Sciences in Guangxi* 6 (2010).

[301] Cao, F., "Enlightenment of Global Financial Crisis on China," *International Finance Research* 5 (2009).

[302] Cao, H., "Regionalization of RMB in the Internationalization Strategy," *China Finance* 5 (2006).

[303] Cao, H. and Z. Hu, "Valuation Currency of Asian Bonds and Internationalization of RMB," *International Finance Research* 10 (2007).

[304] Cao, H. and Y. Li, "Asian Bond Market: Strategic Conception and Preliminary Strategies," *Management World* 10 (2004).

[305] Cao, H. and L. Zhou, "The Reform Direction of the International Monetary System and Its Related Mechanisms," *International Finance Research* 9 (2009).
[306] Cao, J., "Strengthen the Supervision Function of the International Monetary Fund," *Business Culture* 9 (2008).
[307] Cao, Y., "International Reserve Currency Competition: Analysis of Market Data Based on the Classification of Currency Functions," *Investment Research* 3 (2010).
[308] Chang, Z., "Global Economic Imbalances and Adjustments: Challenges in the New Century," *NTU Business Review* 13 (2007).
[309] Chen, H., "The Road to Internationalization of Japanese Yen," *World Economy and Politics* 5 (2004).
[310] Chen, H., "Foster Asian Bond Markets," *World Economy and Politics* 6 (2005).
[311] Chen, P. and X. Wang, "Non-equilibrium Analysis of RMB Exchange Rate and Macro Efficiency of Exchange Rate System," *Economic Research* 6 (2002).
[312] Chen, Q., "Competition or Cooperation: A Game Theory Analysis of International Financial Supervision," *Financial Research* 10 (2008).
[313] Chen, S., and L. Liu, "Impact of the US Financial Crisis on China's Import and Export Trade," *Contemporary Economic Research* 6 (2013).
[314] Chen, T. and Y. Tan, "Dilemma and Countermeasures of IMF Share and Voting Rights Reform," *Finance Teaching and Research* 3 (2013).
[315] Chen, W., "Advances and Prospects of East Asian Currency Swap Mechanisms," *Southeast Asia* 3 (2003).
[316] Chen, Y., "Currency Competition in East Asian Currency Cooperation," *International Finance Research* 3 (2003).
[317] Yulu, C. and W. Bian, "Monetary Union Theory: Progress in the Measurement of Optimal Currency Areas," *International Finance Research* 2 (2004).
[318] Yulu, C., F. Wang and M. Yang, "Currency Internationalization as a National Competitive Strategy: Empirical Evidence from the US Dollar-and on the Internationalization Issue of RMB," *Economic Research* 2 (2005).
[319] Yulu, C., "Major Defects of the International Monetary System, Reform Directions and China's Participation Strategies," *Inner Mongolia Finance Research* 5 (2010).
[320] Chen, Z., *Why Chinese are Hardworking but Not Rich*. Beijing: CITIC Publishing House, 2008.

[321] Shi, C., "Future Development of the International Monetary System: After the Subprime Crisis: Standard Choice, Direction and Path," *Economist* 7 (2009).

[322] Zhinan, C. and Y. Xing, "From 'G7 Era' to 'G20 Era': Changes in International Financial Governance Mechanism," *World Economy and Politics* 1 (2011).

[323] Dai, J. and X. Xiong, "Stage Determination and Shape Selection of East Asian Currency Cooperation," *Nankai Economic Research* 8 (2001).

[324] Dai, J., A. Xiong and S. Tan, *International Monetary System: Where to Go from Here?* Xiamen: Xiamen University Press, 2012.

[325] Dai, J. and Z. Wan, "Research on the Economic Basis of Monetary and Financial Cooperation in East Asia," *Journal of Yunnan University* 2 (2005).

[326] Ding, J., "Research on the Sustainability of the Current RMB Exchange Rate Mechanism," *International Finance Research* 5 (2003).

[327] Ding, J. and F. Yang, "Research on the Linkage of RMB Exchange Rate with Reference to Currency Basket and East Asian Currency," *International Finance Research* 7 (2007).

[328] Ding, D., *Research on Thoughts and Models of Financial Supervision at Home and Abroad after the Subprime Crisis*. Liaoning: Liaoning University, 2013.

[329] Ding, Y., "New Progress in East Asian Currency Cooperation," *World Economy* 3 (2006).

[330] Ding, Y., "Asian Monetary Cooperation and Sino-Japanese Coordination: China's Perspectives and Ideas," In *RMB, Japanese Yen and Asian Currency Cooperation*, edited by Xiao Li and Ugawa Takao. Tsinghua: Tsinghua University Press, 2010.

[331] Ding, Y. and X. Li, "Research on East Asian Regional Monetary Cooperation: A Literature Review," *Contemporary Asia Pacific* 6 (2004).

[332] Ding, Z., "New Rules of the IMF Exchange Rate Test the Reform of the International Monetary System," *China Foreign Exchange* 8 (2007).

[333] Fan, Y., "The Theory and Policies of Hegemonic Stability Theory," *Modern International Relations* 9 (2000).

[334] Fang, L. and L. Wang, "Monetary Reform in the Euro Area Is Imperative," *Guangzhou Daily*, June 27, 2010.

[335] Pei, P., Q. Zhang and Z. Hu, "Impact of the International Financial Crisis on China's Export Trade: An Empirical Study Based on Monthly Data from 2007 to 2008," *Financial Research* 8 (2009).

[336] Feng, Z., "The Opportunities and Challenges Facing East Asian Cooperation," *Northeast Asia Forum* 15, no. 6 (2006).
[337] Gao, H., "Common Foreign Exchange Reserve Funds of ASEAN, China, Japan, and South Korea: Important Steps towards the Asian Monetary Fund," *Working Paper of the International Financial Research Center of the Chinese Academy of Social Science Policy Brief No.* 08030 (2008). www.ricf.org .cn.
[338] Gao, B., "Analysis of Brazil's Recent Economic Situation and Prospect Forecast," *Institute of World Economy and Politics, Chinese Academy of Social Sciences* 11, *Policy Brief no.* 201341 (2013).
[339] Gao, H., "From Chiang Mai Initiative to Asian Bond Fund," *International Economic Review* 3 (2004).
[340] Gao, H., "Optimal Currency Area: An Empirical Study of East Asian Countries," *World Economy* 6 (2007).
[341] Gao, H., "The Role of China-Asia Regional Financial Cooperation," *International Economic Review* 5–6 (2009).
[342] Gao, H., "Roadmap for East Asian Monetary Cooperation in the Post-Crisis Period," *International Economic Review* 5 (2011).
[343] Gao, H. and Y. Yu, "The Meaning and Conditions of RMB Internationalization," *International Economic Review* 1 (2010).
[344] Guan, T., "International Financial Crisis and Reserve Currency Diversification," *International Economic Review* 3 (2009).
[345] Gong, G., "The Choice of Exchange Rates and Exchange Rate Regimes for Developing Countries under Non-international Currencies: On the Reform of the RMB Exchange Rate System and RMB Internationalization," June 24, 2010. http://www.cfrn.com.cn/get Paper.do?id=2593.
[346] Guo, C. and M. Zhu, "Strengthen International Coordination and Cooperation in Financial Supervision," *Shanghai Finance* 10 (2004).
[347] Han, J., "Analysis of Influential Factors of Demand for Final Products in East Asia Area: Study of Gravity Model Based on Panel Data," *World Economic Research* 2 (2013).
[348] Han, M. and X. Yuan, "Microeconomic Analysis of RMB 'Regionalization' from the Perspective of Trade," *International Trade Issues* 9 (2006).
[349] Han, M. and X. Yuan, "Research on RMB Regionalization from the Perspective of Trade," *Economics (Quarterly)* 6, no. 2 (2007).
[350] He, D. and Z. Yao, "The Effect of China's Industrial Restructuring, Optimization and Upgrading Goals, and Policy Measures," *China Industrial Economy* 5 (2008).
[351] He, F., "History and Enlightenment of Dollar Internationalization," *Doctor Coffee* (2004).

[352] He, F., "US Dollar and American Hegemony." *Doctor Coffee Website* 2004. http://doctor-cafe.com/detail1.asp?id=2856.
[353] He, F., "Does China Need to Join G7?" *International Economic Review* 5 (2004).
[354] He, F., "Realistic Choice of RMB Internationalization," *International Economic Review* 7–8 (2009).
[355] He, F., "International Financial Regulatory Cooperation Doing a Disservice," *International Economic Review* 3 (2010).
[356] He, F. and J. Li, "Path, Experience and Lessons of Dollar Internationalization," *Social Science Front* 1 (2005).
[357] He, H., "East Asian Monetary Cooperation and RMB Internationalization," *Finance and Investment* 8 (2005).
[358] He, H., "Comparative Analysis of Euro and US Dollar Model and Their Implications for East Asian Currency Cooperation," *Finance and Investment* 11 (2005).
[359] He, H., "Model and Path Choice of East Asian Regional Monetary Cooperation," *Economic Management Research* 7 (2007).
[360] He, H., "Comparative Analysis of Euro and US Dollar Model and Their Implications for East Asian Currency Cooperation," *Finance and Investment* 11 (2005).
[361] He, D., "On the Reform of the Decision-making Mechanism of the International Monetary Fund," *Hubei Rural Finance Research* 6 (2007).
[362] He, L., "Foreign Exchange Reserves of East Asian Economies and the International Financial Crisis," *Contemporary Asia-Pacific* 6 (2008).
[363] Hu, Y. and J. Hu, "Focus of Asian Financial Cooperation: Developing Asian Bond Markets," *International Financial Research* 5 (2004).
[364] Hua, M., "Triggering Mechanism of Global Economic Imbalance and China's Choice," *International Economic Review* 2 (2006).
[365] Hua, M., "Imbalance of World Economy: Concept, Causes and China's Choices," *Journal of Social Science of Jilin University* 1 (2007).
[366] Hua, M. and S. Tian, "Reform of the International Monetary System is Imperative," *Information Network of the Development Research Center of the State Council*, June 23, 2011.
[367] Huang, D., "Renminbi: Challenges and Opportunities," *Economic Research* 7 (2004).
[368] Huang, F., "Economic Globalization and Internationalization of Financial Supervision," *Macroeconomic Research* 12 (1998).

[369] Huang, F., "Thoughts on International Macroeconomic Policy Cooperation and the Reform of the World Monetary System," *International Finance Research* 7 (2009).

[370] Huang, F., "G20 and Reform of International Monetary System," *Financial Research* 2 (2010).

[371] Huang, F., "Economic Globalization, G20 and Reform of International Monetary System," *Journal of China Jinggangshan Institute of Leaders* 2 (2010).

[372] Huang, H., "US Dollar and Renminbi: Where to Go from Here?" *International Economic Review* 2 (2010).

[373] Huang, H., Z. Shi and Y. Li, "Impact of Sino-Japan Economic Policy Coordination on Business Cycle Comovement," *Modern Japanese Economy* 2 (2009).

[374] Huang, J. and D. Yin, "Changes in the International Monetary System: An Analytical Framework of New Institutional Economics," *Journal of East China Normal University* 7 (2000).

[375] Huang, M., "Currency Internationalization and Its Determinants-Comparison between Euro and US Dollar," *Journal of Xiamen University (Philosophy and Social Sciences)* 2 (2001).

[376] Huang, M., "International Monetary Fund's Internal Decision-making Mechanism and Its Reforms," *International Forum* 1 (2006).

[377] Huang, M. and Y. Lin, "Development of East Asian Emerging Bond Markets after the East Asian Financial Crisis," *World Economy* 4 (2007).

[378] Huang, M. and Y. Lin, *Research on the Development of Emerging Bond Market in East Asia: From Local Currency Bond Market to Asian Bond Market*. Beijing: Economic Science Press, 2008.

[379] Huang, M. and A. Xiong, "The Feasibility of the Development of the East Asian Regional Bond Market from the Perspective of Investors," *International Finance Research* 10 (2008).

[380] Huang, M. and A. Xiong, "On the Space and Opportunity of RMB Internationalization," *Journal of Shanghai University of Finance and Economics: Philosophy and Social Science Edition* 11, no. 2 (2009).

[381] Huang, H., "US Dollar and Renminbi: Where to Go from Here?" *International Economic Review* 2, no. 7 (2010).

[382] Huang, W. and D. Liu, "G20 and Global Economic Rebalance," In *Analysis and Forecast of World Economic Situation in 2012*, edited by Luolin Wang and Yuyan Zhang. Beijing: Social Science Literature Press, 2012.

[383] Huang, X., "Global Imbalances, Excess Liquidity and Currency Crisis: An Analytical Prospective Based on the Imbalanced International Monetary System," *Financial Research* 8 (2007).

[384] Huang, Y., "Changes in the International Monetary System and RMB Internationalization," *International Economic Review* 3 (2009).
[385] Jia, H., "Offshore RMB Market and RMB Internationalization Process," *Journal of Beijing Institute of Economic Management* 3 (2005).
[386] Jiao, J., *Research on RMB Internationalization.* Liaoning: Liaoning University, 2004.
[387] Jiang, Y., "'International Financial Terror Imbalance' and the Financial Trap of the United States," *Modern International Relations* 7 (2005).
[388] Jiang, D., "Improving Financial Supervision in Crisis," *CCISSR Forum,* 2009.
[389] Li, C., "On the Reform of the International Monetary System," *Economic Review* 4 (2000).
[390] Li, C., "On the Path and Prospect of Establishing a Super-sovereign International Currency," *Academic Research* 2 (2010).
[391] Li, C., "On the Regionalization of RMB," *Hebei Academic Journal* 5 (2002).
[392] Li, D., "Policy Analysis of China's Participation in the New Pattern of International Finance," *China Finance* 22 (2008).
[393] Li, D., "China Should Reject Asian Dollar," *Big Economy and Trade* 6 (2006).
[394] Li, D. and L. Liu, "Dual-track System Promotes RMB Internationalization," *China Finance* 10 (2008).
[395] Li, J. and G. Tian, "Comparison and Enlightenment of the Paths of Three Major Currency Internationalizations," *Shanghai Finance* 9 (2003).
[396] Li, J. and L. Zong, "Thoughts and Suggestions on Further Expanding RMB Cross-border Trade Settlement," *International Trade* 5 (2011).
[397] Li, J., F. Zhen and X. Cui, "Status Quo of RMB Internationalization Development, Degree Measurement and Prospect Evaluation," *International Finance Research* 10 (2013).
[398] Li, J., "China's Demand and Supply for Asian Monetary and Financial Cooperation," *Economic and Management Research* 2 (2005).
[399] Li, J., T. Guan and F. He, "The Status Quo of RMB Cross-border Circulation and Its Impact on Chinese Economy," *Management World* 9 (2004).
[400] Li, J. and M. Jiang, "Currency-financial Attachment under the Dollar Standard," *World Economic Research* 6 (2011).
[401] Li, P. and P. Liu, "Basic Conception of the Transitional Phase of East Asian Currency Cooperation — Economic Exchange Rate

Coordination Mechanism in East Asia," *World Economy and Politics* 12 (2003).
[402] Li, R., *Reform of the International Monetary System and RMB Internationalization.* Beijing: China Finance Press, 2009.
[403] Li, W., "End of East Asian Economic Regionalism?" *Contemporary Asia-Pacific* 4 (2011).
[404] Li, W., "The Rise of Financial Diplomacy in China," *World Economy and Politics* 2 (2013).
[405] Li, W., "Discussion on Counter-cyclical Policies under the Framework of Macro-prudential Supervision," *Financial Research* 7 (2009).
[406] Li, X., "The Dilemma of 'Japanese Yen Internationalization' and Its Strategic Adjustment," *World Economy* 6 (2005).
[407] Li, X., "Sino-Japanese Relation in the Age of 'Economicism'," *International Economic Review* 3–4 (2006).
[408] Li, X., "Path Choice of East Asian Monetary and Financial Cooperation under the Global Financial Crisis," *Northeast Asia Forum* 5 (2009).
[409] Li, X., "The Sustainability of 'Dollar System' and the Path Choice of East Asian Monetary and Financial Cooperation," *Academic Monthly* 6 (2010).
[410] Li, X., "Why did East Asian Currency Cooperation Suffer Setbacks?" *International Economic Review* 1 (2011).
[411] Li, X. and Y. Ding, "On the Specific Measures of East Asian Currency Cooperation," *World Economy* 11 (2002).
[412] Li, X. and Y. Ding, "The Construction of East Asian Regional Monetary System: Necessity, Feasibility and Path Selection," *Frontier in Social Science* 4 (2003).
[413] Li, X. and Y. Ding, "East Asian Regional Monetary Cooperation in the New Century: China's Position and Role," *Journal of Jilin University — Social Science* 2 (2004).
[414] Li, X. and Y. Ding, "Current East Asian Financial Cooperation: Challenges and Policy Suggestions," *International Economic Review* 3 (2005).
[415] Li, X. and Y. Ding, *Transcendence in Asia-Constructing East Asian Regional Monetary System and "Asianization of RMB."* Beijing: Contemporary China Publishing House, 2005.
[416] Li, X. and Y. Ding, "Global Economic Imbalances and China's Role at this Stage," *Journal of Social Science of Jilin University* 1 (2007).
[417] Li, X. and Y. Ding, "East Asian Financial Cooperation in a Global Financial Turbulent Environment: Policy Options and Suggestions," *International Economic Review* 11–12 (2008).

[418] Li, X. and Y. Ding, "Trend of RMB Exchange Rate Change and Its Impact on Regional Currency Cooperation," *International Finance Research* 3 (2009).

[419] Li, X. and Y. Ding, *East Asian Regional Monetary Cooperation and Reform of RMB Exchange Rate System.* 1st ed. Beijing: Economic Science Press, 2010.

[420] Li, X. and Y. Ding, *Research on RMB Regionalization.* 6th ed. Tsinghua: Tsinghua University Press, 2010.

[421] Li, X., Y. Ding and T. Qin, "The Promotion of China's Status in the East Asian Economy: An Investigation Based on Trade Trends," *World Economy and Politics* 5 (2005).

[422] Li, X. and Y. Feng, "Changes in the Status of China and Japan in Intra-Asian Trade and Its Enlightenment," *Contemporary Asia-Pacific* 6 (2009).

[423] Li, X. and Y. Feng, "Collective Actions in the Reform of the International Monetary System and the Role of the G20," *World Economy and Politics* 2 (2012).

[424] Li, X. and J. Fu, "China's Status and Prospect as an East Asian Market Provider," *Journal of Jilin University-Social Science* 2 (2010).

[425] Li, X. and J. Fu, "The Current Reform of the International Monetary System: The Dilemma and Strategic Choices of East Asia," *World Economics and Politics Forum* 4 (2010).

[426] Li, X., J. Li and Y. Ding, "On the Asianization of Renminbi," *World Economy* 2 (2004).

[427] Li, X. and T. Kamikawa, *RMB, Japanese Yen and Asian Currency Cooperation-Dialogue between Chinese and Japanese Scholars.* Tsinghua: Tsinghua University Press, 2010.

[428] Li, X. and J. Wang, "American Economic Hegemony and Global Economic Imbalances," *Northeast Asia Forum* 3 (2007).

[429] Li, X. and X. Zhang, "On the Integration of World Economy and Regional Grouping of World Economy," *World Economy* 4 (1994).

[430] Li, X. and W. Zheng, "Liquidity Analysis of Asian Bond Markets," *Foreign Affairs Review* 12 (2006).

[431] Li, X., "Comment on the Goals and Content of the Reform of the International Financial System," *International Economic Review* 3 (1999).

[432] Li, X. and H. Fu, "On the Influence of Open Economy on Monetary Policy and the Adjustment of China's Monetary Policy," *Journal of Nanjing University* 2 (1998).

[433] Li, Y., "Macro-prudential Supervision and Financial Stability," *Financial Research* 8 (2009).

[434] Yang, L., "Bond Market Development: Challenges Facing Asia," *International Financial Research*, 11 (2003).
[435] Li, Y., "How to Promote the Diversification of the International Monetary System," *Financial Times*, December 29, 2008.
[436] Li, Y., "Reform of the International Monetary System and China's Opportunities," *China Finance* 13 (2008).
[437] Li, Y., "Calm Thinking on Promoting the Diversification of the International Monetary System," *Shanghai Finance* 4 (2009).
[438] Li, Y., "Examining Global Economic Imbalances," *Finance and Economics* 8 (2009).
[439] Yang, L., "Global Financial System Reform and Choices in Asia: We Need Deeper Thinking," *International Financial Research* 10 (2010).
[440] Yang, L. and B. Hu, *Global Financial Supervision Reform in the Context of the Financial Crisis*. Beijing: Social Science Literature Press, 2010.
[441] Li, Y. and W. Yu, "Global Economic Imbalances and Challenges Facing China," *International Finance Research* 2 (2006).
[442] Li, Y., "Non-international Currency, Currency Internationalization and Capital Account Convertibility," *Financial Research* 8 (2003).
[443] Li, Y., Runxiang Zheng and Minghao Huang, "Supersovereign Currency, Multicurrency System, RMB Internationalization and China's Core Interests," *International Finance Research* 7 (2010).
[444] Liang, Y. and L. Li, "Comment on the 'New Decision' of the International Monetary Fund's Exchange Rate Supervision," *International Trade* 7 (2008).
[445] Liao, F., "New Development of International Financial Supervision: From the Perspective of G20 and FSB," *Review of International Law of Wuhan University* 1 (2012).
[446] Li, D. and Y. Zhao, "Asymmetry and Symmetry in Sino-US Economic Interdependence," *International Economic Review* 2 (2008).
[447] Lin, J., *International Cooperation Mechanism for Financial Supervision*. Beijing: Social Science Literature Press, 2007.
[448] Lin, Y., *The Search for Prosperity: How the Developing Economy Rise*. Beijing: Peking University Press, 2012.
[449] Liu, W., "Adjustment of Global Economic Imbalance and China's Participation Strategy," *Journal of Wuhan University-Philosophy and Social Sciences* 4 (2008).
[450] Liu, J. and Z. Liu, "Dynamic Patterns and Causes of Real Output Volatility in China's Business Cycle Fluctuations," *Economic Research* 3 (2005).

[451] Liu, L. and B. Jiao, "Regional Monetary Cooperation in East Asia and China's Participation Countermeasures," *Northeast Asia Forum* 2 (2003).

[452] Liu, L. and S. Li, "On the Establishment of the East Asian Monetary Fund," *Northeast Asia Forum* 3 (2004).

[453] Liu, L. and C. Xie, "East Asian Currency Cooperation and the Choice of RMB Exchange Rate System," *Management World* 3 (2003).

[454] Liu, Q., "Regional Currency and World Currency: Judgment and Choice Analysis of RMB Prospects," *Academic Journal* 9 (2006).

[455] Liu, Z., *Research on East Asian Currency Cooperation and the Choice of RMB Exchange Rate System.* Beijing: China Economic Publishing House, 2006.

[456] Lu, J. and Y. Shu, "Long-term Currency Neutrality: Theory and Its Empirical Evidence in China," *Financial Research* 6 (2002).

[457] Lu, J. and Y. Shu, "Empirical Research on the Invalidity of Monetary Policy in China," *Economic Research* 3 (2002).

[458] Lu, Q., "On the Reform of the International Financial System and the Strategy of RMB Internationalization," *Social Sciences* 4 (2009).

[459] Lu, Q., "Dollar Hegemony and Reform of International Monetary System-Concurrently Discussing RMB Internationalization," *Journal of Shanghai University of Finance and Economics* 1 (2010).

[460] Luo, J. and S. Zhou, "Games and Competition between China and Japan in the Field of East Asian Currency," *Modern Japanese Economy* 1 (2008).

[461] Ma, R. and Y. Zhou, "Currency Swap: An Effective Tool for Participating in International Financial Rescue and Promoting the Internationalization of RMB," *China Finance* 4 (2009).

[462] Ma, X., "China's Current Industrial Structure Adjustment Difficulties and Optimized Development Roads," *China Development Watch* 6 (2010).

[463] Ou, M. and K. Zhang, "Research on the Double-layer Currency Basket Structure in East Asia," *International Finance Research* 6 (2010).

[464] Pan, L., "Reform of International Monetary System and RMB Internationalization," *East China Economic Management* 4 (2000).

[465] Qi, J., "Global Financial Crisis and Asia: Impact, Relevance and Challenges," In *Cooperation between Renminbi, Japanese Yen and Asian Currency: Dialogue between Chinese and Japanese Scholars,* edited by Xiao Li and Takao Kamikawa. Tsinghua: Tsinghua University Press, 2010.

[466] Qu, F., "Reform of the International Monetary System under the Financial Crisis," *Macroeconomic Management* 10 (2009).
[467] Ran, S., *Current International Monetary System and Reform of RMB Exchange Rate System*. Beijing: China Finance and Economic Publishing House, 2007.
[468] Ren, D., "Hegemonic Stability Theory in International Political Economy," *Strategy and Management* 6 (1995).
[469] Shao, Y., "The RMB Road (1949–2009): The Internal Logic of the Evolution of China's Exchange Rates," *Southwest Securities Special Report*, February 5, 2010.
[470] Shen, H. and L. Chen, "Research on East Asian Monetary and Financial Cooperation Mechanism and Its Characteristics," *Research on Nanyang Issues* 4 (2011).
[471] Shi, J., "East Asian Financial and Monetary Cooperation: Short, Medium and Long Term," *International Economic Review* 6 (2010).
[472] Shi, Z., Hongmei Huang and Chuang Deng, "Research on Impact of Trade on Sino-Japan-Korea Business Cycle Comovement," *Northeast Asia Forum* 4 (2009).
[473] Shi, J. and Y. Gao, "A Summary of the Research on Macroprudential Supervision Theory," *International Finance Research* 8 (2011).
[474] Song, H., "Explore the Experience of China's Opening to the Outside World and China's Economic Development," *International Trade* 5 (2012).
[475] Song, G., "China's Purchase of U.S. Treasury Bonds: Sources, Benefits and Impacts," *Fudan Journal* 3 (2008).
[476] Song, G., "Dollar Trap, Debt Weapon and Sino-US Financial Dilemma," *International Watch* 4 (2010).
[477] Song, X., "Multilateral Governance Mechanism of International Financial Supervision: A Multi-level Conceptual Framework," *Journal of Fujian Administration Institute* 3 (2009).
[478] Song, Y., "Research on the Influence of RMB Regionalization - An Analysis Based on Dynamic Distribution Lag Model," *International Trade Issues* 9 (2012).
[479] Sun, G. *et al.*, *Evolution and Development Trend of Contemporary International Financial System*. Beijing: Northwest University of Finance and Economics Press, 2004.
[480] Sun, L., "The Perplexity of Dual Identities: Trade 'Big Country' and Finance 'Small Country'," *World Economic Research* 1 (2007).
[481] Sun, L., "Financial Stability Board: True Stability? False Stability?" *International Financial News*, June 19, 2009.

[482] Sun, L., "Thoughts on Deepening East Asian Financial Cooperation in the Global Financial Crisis," *World Economic Research* 11 (2009).

[483] Sun, J., X. Wei and A. Tang, "Path Choice of RMB Internationalization Strategy from the Perspective of Three Major Currency Development Processes," *Asia Pacific Economics* 2 (2005).

[484] Sun, T., "Will the Asian Regional Foreign Exchange Reserves Be Established and Operate before the End of the Year?" *People's Daily*, May 4, 2009.

[485] Tan, Y., "Observation of US Dollar Efficiency and Strategy Refracted by American Financial Crisis," *Wuhan Finance* 8 (2009).

[486] Qin, Y., "Status Quo and Suggestions for the Development of RMB in ASEAN Regionalization," *Southern Finance* 9 (2004).

[487] Tan, R. and M. Li, "China and the United States' Responses to the Current Financial Crisis from the 'Great Depression'," *Journal of Shanghai University of Finance and Economics* 6 (2008).

[488] Tao, C., "Reform of the International Financial System and China's Role in the Subprime Crisis," *Economic Management and Research* 4 (2009).

[489] Tong, Y., "Research on Countermeasures to Improve the Independent Innovation Ability of Enterprises," *Economic and Social Perspective* 3 (2010).

[490] Wan, Z., "The Basis of Exchange Rate Cooperation in East Asia from the Perspective of Macroeconomic Symmetry," *Nankai Economic Research* 3 (2003).

[491] Wan, Z. and X. Chen, "Changes in Asian Regional Exchange Rates: A Test of the AMU Index of Asian Currency Units," *World Economy* 7 (2009).

[492] Wang, D., "The Current International Financial Regulatory Framework Led by the United States: Evolution, Defects and Reconstruction," *International Finance Research* 10, (2013).

[493] Wang, D. and D. Bai, "US Export Control Policy and Its Impact on US-China Trade," *Northeast Asia Forum* 5 (2012).

[494] Wang, D. and W. Xiang, "On the Latest Progress of International Financial Supervision Reform: Construction of the Global Financial Market LEI System," *World Economic Research* 1 (2013).

[495] Wang, D., W. Xiang and X. Liu, "On the Imbalance of Sino-US Economic Relations and Its Adjustment under the Global Financial Crisis," *Northeast Asia Forum* 1 (2011).

[496] Wang, J. and Y. Dong, "Evaluation and Analysis of IMF Loan Policy Disputes," *International Finance Research* 9 (2005).

[497] Wang, J., "The Prospect of the Subprime Debt Crisis and the International Monetary Capital Change Situation," *China Economic and Trade Herald* 10 (2008).

[498] Wang, L. and L. Liu, "China's Role in the Future Reform of the International Exchange Rate System," *Contemporary Economic Research* 12 (2012).

[499] Wang, L., J. Han and Y. Zhao, "Research on the Dynamic Correlation between Chinese and Foreign Business Cycles and the Forecast of China's Economic Growth," *Economic Developments* 9 (2009).

[500] Wang, S., "On the Reform of the International Monetary System," *The Banker* 4 (2009).

[501] Wang, Y., "Several Issues on Improving the Independent Innovation Ability of Enterprises," *China Soft Science* 7 (2005).

[502] Wang, Y., "Issues on the Effectiveness of International Mechanisms in East Asian Monetary Cooperation," *Northeast Asia Forum* 17, no. 4 (2008).

[503] Wang, Y., "The Imbalance of the World Economy is a Dynamic Equilibrium," *International Economic Review* 5–6 (2006).

[504] Wang, Y., "Strategy and Implementation of the Reform of the International Financial System," *Economic Theory and Economic Management* 9 (2009).

[505] Wu, J., "Touch the 'Fourth International Monetary System': RMB Becomes the International Currency Standard Currency after 8 Years," *Oriental Morning Post*, March 31, 2009.

[506] Wu, Z., "Unconventional Relationship between Money Supply and Prices: Theory and Empirical Analysis Based on China," *Management World* 12 (2002).

[507] Wu, G., "American Financial Crisis and International Monetary System," *Jiangxi Social Sciences* 5 (2009).

[508] Weng, D., "The Status Quo and Long-and Short-term Arrangements of Exchange Rate Cooperation in East Asia," *Asia Pacific Economics* 5 (2009).

[509] Xia, B., "Facing the Global Economic Imbalance," *Shanghai Economics* 6 (2008).

[510] Xia, B., "Macro-Prudential Supervision: The Framework and Its Improvement," *China Finance* 22 (2010).

[511] Xia, B., "2020: Main Thinking of China's Financial Strategy," *International Economic Review* 2 (2011).

[512] Xiang, S., "Reform of the International Monetary System: Thoughts and Strategies," *International Currency Review* 1 (2010).

[513] Xiang, W. and X. Liu, "The Issue of US Dollar Standard and Its Sustainability," *International Financial Research* 4 (2009).

[514] Xiang, W. and D. Wang, "On the Asymmetry in Sino-US Financial Interdependence," *World Economic Research* 7 (2011).

[515] Xiang, W. and D. Wang, *Research on the Corporate Governance Structure of State-owned Commercial Banks after Restructuring: How China Can Learn the Experiences and Lessons of Transition Countries in Central and Eastern Europe*. Beijing: Economic Science Press, 2012.

[516] Xie, L. and M. Huang, "Reflections on Asian Currency Units and Opportunities for China," *Jinan Finance* 3 (2006).

[517] Xiong, A., "Recent World Bank Reforms: Progress and Evaluation," *International Economic Cooperation* 1 (2010).

[518] Xiong, A. and J. Dai, "European Debt Crisis and Diversification of International Monetary System," *Social Sciences in Guangdong* 6 (2012).

[519] Xiong, A. and M. Huang, "An East-Asian Perspective on the Reform of the International Reserve Currency System," *Change Think Tank Global Macroeconomic Policy (GMEP) Series of Research Reports*, no. 2010-007.

[520] Xu, J. and Y. Yao, "New International Division of Labor, Development of Financial Markets and Global Imbalances," *World Economy* 3 (2010).

[521] Xu, M., "On the Reform of the International Financial System and the Reinvention of the Bretton Woods Institutions," *International Financial Research* 1 (2006).

[522] Xu, Q. and J. Li, "Currency Internationalization from the Perspective of International Division of Labor System: Typical Facts of the US Dollar and the Japanese Yen," *World Economy* 2 (2008).

[523] Xu, Q. and L. Liu, "Literature Review on China's Participation in International Regional Economic Integration," *Development Research* 1 (2006).

[524] Xu, Q. and L. Liu, "Estimation of Hong Kong's RMB Stock: An Investigation of M1 Caliber," *World Economy* 9 (2006).

[525] Xu, Q. and L. Liu, *Research on Exchange Rate Changes in the Process of RMB Internationalization*. Beijing: China Finance Press, 2009.

[526] Xu, Y., "East Asian Foreign Exchange Reserve will be Doubled when it is Gradually Decoupled IMF," *China Business News*, March 22, 2012.

[527] Xu, Z. and Q. Sun, "Financial Crisis, International Monetary System Reform and China's Choice," *World Economy* 4 (1999).

[528] Tong, L., *Research on RMB Internationalization*. Shanghai: East China Normal University, 2009.

[529] Yang, Q., "Development of Bilateral Currency Swap in East Asia under the Background of Global Financial Turmoil," *International Finance Research* 6 (2010).

[530] Yang, Q., "Member Benefits, Motivation and Supervision Mechanism of East Asia Reserve: Problems and Countermeasures," *Contemporary Asia-Pacific* 6 (2011).

[531] Yang, X., "Looking at the Future International Monetary System Reform from the Financial Crisis," *Contemporary Finance and Economics* 11 (2009).

[532] Yang, X., "The Realistic Choice of Exchange Rate Cooperation in East Asia — Based on the Study of Exchange Rate Dynamics," *World Economic Research* 7 (2009).

[533] Yao, Y., "World Significance of China's Roads," *International Economic Review* 1 (2010).

[534] Yao, Z., "Asymmetric Competition and the Asian Strategy of RMB," *World Economy and Politics* 7 (2004).

[535] Ye, H., "China Faces Different Periods of Strategic Opportunity," *International Economic Review* 5 (2012).

[536] Yi, G. and Z. Wang, "Monetary Policy and Financial Asset Prices," *Economic Research* 3 (2002).

[537] Yin, J., "Reform of the International Monetary System and China's Role Orientation," *Shanghai Finance* 10 (2009).

[538] Yu, Y., *Eliminating the Fear of RMB Appreciation and Suspense.* Beijing: China Youth Publishing House, 2004.

[539] Yu, Y., "Reform of the International Monetary System and Preservation of China's Foreign Exchange Reserve Assets," *International Economic Review* 5–6, (2009).

[540] Yu, Y., "Witness Imbalances-Double Surplus, RMB Exchange Rate and US Dollar Trap," *International Economic Review* 3 (2010).

[541] Yuan, Z. and Z. Cheng, "Chinese Banks: Dominoes Sold Off," *Economic Observer*, January 12, 2009.

[542] Yuan, Z., "International Monetary System in the Post-Crisis Era," *Wenhui Daily*, July 13, 2009.

[543] Zeng, Z., Z. Xie and W. Ding, "Analysis of Price Spillover Effects of US Financial Crisis on China's Trade," *International Finance Research* 2 (2012).

[544] Zhang, B., "East Asian Regional Exchange Rate Cooperation: A Chinese Perspective," *World Economy* 10 (2004).

[545] Zhang, B. and F. He, "Impact of Asian Currency Units on East Asian Currency Cooperation and RMB Exchange Rate Reform," *Management World* 4 (2006).

[546] Zhang, B. and F. He, "How to Adjust the RMB Exchange Rate Policy: Goals, Plans and Timing," *Doctor Coffee Website*, 2005. http://doctor-cafe.com/detail1.asp?id=3158.

[547] Zhang, C., "USD Standard, USD Circulation and USD Trap," *International Financial Research* 6, no. 4 (2008).

[548] Zhang, D., "Sino-Japan-Korea Relations and Feasibility of Establishing East Asia Free Trade Area," *Contemporary Asia-Pacific* 4 (2006).

[549] Zhang, H., "The Trend and Impact of the G20 Mechanism," *World Economic Research* 9 (2010).

[550] Zhang, H., L. Wang and Y. Xu, "Performance of Euro Zone's Unified Monetary Policy and Its Enlightenment to China," *Asia Pacific Economics* 2 (2008).

[551] Zhang, L., "The Attributes of the International Monetary System — A Study Based on the International Monetary Contract," *World Economic Research* 1 (2010).

[552] Zhang, M., "The Impact of the Subprime Crisis on the Current International Monetary System," *World Economy and Politics* 7 (2009).

[553] Zhang, M., "Reform of the International Monetary System under the Global Financial Crisis," *International Financial Research Center, Institute of World Economy and Politics, Chinese Academy of Social Sciences, Working Paper*, no. 0919 (2009).

[554] Zhang, M., "RMB Internationalization is Destined to Be a Long-term and Gradual Project," *International Financial Research Center, Institute of World Economics and Politics, Chinese Academy of Social Sciences, Policy Brief*, no. 09037 (May 25, 2009).

[555] Zhang, M., "Reform of the International Monetary System: Background, Reasons, Measures and China's Participation," *International Economic Review* 1 (2010).

[556] Zhang, M., "China is Still Long Away from Japan," *International Finance Research Center, Institute of World Economy and Politics, Chinese Academy of Social Sciences* Working Paper (2010).

[557] Zhang, M., "The Structural Transformation of Asian Countries is Easier Said than Done," *International Finance Research Center, Institute of World Economy and Politics, Chinese Academy of Social Sciences* Working Paper (2010).

[558] Zhang, M., "How Emerging Market Countries Cope with Capital Inflows: The Case of China," *International Economic Review* 2 (2011).

[559] Zhang, M., "Short-term International Capital Flows Facing China: Scale Measurement of Different Methods and Calibers," *World Economy* 2 (2011).

[560] Zhang, M., "Global Currency Swaps: Status Quo, Functions, and Potential Directions for the Reform of the International Monetary System," *International Economic Review* 6 (2012).

[561] Zhang, M., "RMB Internationalization: Policies, Progress, Problems and Prospects," *Financial Review* 5, no. 2 (2013).
[562] Zhang, M. and D. Qin, "Analysis on the Resource Flow of the Evolution of the International Monetary System," *World Economy and Politics* 12 (2005).
[563] Zhang, M. and L. Xiao, "Analysis of the Volatility of Emerging Market Economies Facing Short-term International Capital Flows," *Analysis and Forecast of the World Economic Situation in 2013*. Beijing: Social Science Literature Press, 2013.
[564] Zhang, M. and Y. Zheng, "Perspective on the New Wave of Capital Control: Causes, Tools and Implications for China," *International Finance Research Center, Institute of World Economy and Politics, Chinese Academy of Social Sciences, Working Paper* no. 2011.023 (2011).
[565] Zhang, Q., "Dollar Hegemony and RMB Internationalization," *Economic Survey* 2 (2008).
[566] Zhang, W. and Y. Wang, "The Classification, Country Distinction and Historical Evolution of the Exchange Rate System," *International Finance Research* 5 (2007).
[567] Zhang, Y. and L. Chen, "Analysis of the Endogenous Instability of the International Monetary System," *Modern International Relations* 12 (2003).
[568] Zhang, Y., "Internationalization of RMB Viewed from Internationalized Japanese Yen," *International Finance Guide* 4 (1994).
[569] Zhang, Y., "Research on Sino-ASEAN Free Trade Area and Regional Development of RMB," 8th ed., 2006.
[570] Zhang, Y., "Historical Impact of Factor Mobility and Global Economic Imbalances," *International Economic Review* 3/4 (2006).
[571] Zhang, Y., "RMB Internationalization: Agree or Oppose." *International Economic Review* 1 (2010).
[572] Zhang, Y. and T. Feng, "Definition of Emerging Economies and Their Position in the World Economic Structure," *International Economic Review* 10, no. 4 (2010).
[573] Zhang, Y. and Z. Li, *International Economics and Political Science*. Shanghai: Shanghai People's Publishing House, 2008.
[574] Zhang, Y. and J. Zhang, "The Nature of Currency and the Future Choice of RMB — Concurrently Discussing Asian Monetary Cooperation," *Contemporary Asia Pacific* 2 (2008).
[575] Zhang, Y., "China's Economic Integration and Cooperation with East Asia," *Contemporary Asia-Pacific* 1 (2006).

[576] Zhang, Z., "New Consensus of Exchange Rate Policy and 'The Disappearance Theory of Intermediate System'," *World Economy* 12 (2002).

[577] Zhao, G. and M. Huang, "An Overview of the Supervision Mechanism of the International Monetary Fund," *International Information* 9 (2005).

[578] Zhao, C. and X. Li, "Analysis of East-Asian Currency Cooperation and RMB Core Currency Status," *Contemporary Asia-Pacific* 2 (2007).

[579] Zhao, H., "On the RMB Which May Become one of the World Currencies," *Economic Research* 3 (2003).

[580] Zhao, J., "G20: New Mechanism, New Issues and China's Propositions and Actions," *International Economic Review* 5 (2010).

[581] Zhao, Z., "Investigation Report on the Circulation of RMB Cash in Sino-Mongolia Border Trade Ports," *North China Finance* 2 (2006).

[582] Zheng, H., "The Process of Asian Monetary Cooperation: A Chinese Perspective," *Asia Pacific Economics* 4 (2003).

[583] Zheng, H., *Research on the Design and Effect of East Asian Financial Cooperation System*. Shanghai: Fudan University, 2007.

[584] Zheng, H., "Regional Response to the Financial Crisis: East Asian Foreign Exchange Reserve Bank," *World Economic Research* 12 (2009).

[585] Zheng, L., "Progress, Prospects, and China's Policies of the Reserve Bank, Chiang Mai Initiative and East Asian Finance Cooperation," May 7 2009. Http://www.iwep.org.cn/info/content.asp?infoId=3908/.

[586] Zheng, L., "Shadow Banking System: Development, Connotation and Future," *Center for International Finance Research, Institute of World Economy and Politics, Chinese Academy of Social Sciences, Policy Brief*, no. 09035 (May 18 2009).

[587] Zheng, L., "Regionalization of RMB and Expansion of Local Currency Settlement Function of Border Trade," *International Trade* 7 (2006).

[588] Zheng, M., "On the Economic Effects of RMB Internationalization," *International Finance Research* 7 (1995).

[589] Joint research group of World Bank and Development Research Center of the State Council of China, *China in 2030: Building a Modern, Harmonious and Creative Society*. Beijing: China Finance and Economics Press, 2012.

[590] China 2020 Task Force, "2020: China's Position in the World," *International Economic Review* 3 (2013).

[591] People's Bank of China. "People's Bank of China Annual Report 2012," Http://www.pbc.gov.cn/image_public/UserFiles/chubanwu/upload/File/2012 People's Bank of China Annual Report.pdf.

[592] International Department of the People's Bank of China. "Brunei's Monetary System and Policy." 14 August 2009, 28 January 2013. http://www.pbc.gov.cn/publish/goujisi/3049/2010/20100324113408327311246/20100324113408327311246_html.

[593] Zhong, H., "Research on the Reform Direction of International Monetary System and China's Countermeasures," *International Finance Research* 10 (2006).

[594] Zhong, W., "On the Internationalization of RMB," *World Economy* 3 (2002).

[595] Zhong, W., "New Progress and Preliminary Impacts of Basel III," *Financial Reform*, edited by Pingping Xie *et al.* Beijing: China Economic Press, 2011.

[596] Zhou, L. and X. Wen, *Currency Internationalization.* Shanghai: Shanghai University of Finance and Economics Press, 2001.

[597] Zhou, X., "Thoughts on Reforming the International Monetary System," *Contemporary Economy* 4, no. 1 (2009).

[598] Zhou, Y., "On the Reform of the International Financial System," *World Economic Research* 5 (2009).

[599] Zhu, M., *International Coordination and Cooperation of Financial Supervision.* Beijing: China Finance Press, 2003.

[600] Zhu, M. and W. Chen, "Difficulties and Countermeasures of Exchange Rate System Selection in Developing Countries," *Asia Pacific Economy* 2 (2004).

[601] Zhu, F., "Analysis of the Conditions for Establishing Currency in East Asia Subregion," *Contemporary Asia-Pacific* 12 (2003).

[602] Zhu, X., "China's Strategic Research on Promoting East Asian Financial Cooperation," *World Economic Research* 4 (2007).

[603] Zong, L. and J. Li, "Historical Opportunities and Strategic Countermeasures of RMB Internationalization," *International Trade* 1 (2010).

[604] Zong, L. and J. Li, "Goals and Roadmap of RMB Internationalization," *China Finance* 13, (2012).

[605] Zong, L. and S. Liao, "Pattern of Capital Flow in Emerging Markets in Global Economic Rebalancing," *Banker* 6 (2010).

[606] [Japan] Murase, T., "East Asian Monetary and Financial Cooperation and the Role of China and Japan," In *East Asian Monetary and Financial Cooperation in the Post-Crisis Era*, edited by Li Xiao: Jilin: Jilin University Press, 2010.

[607] [Japan] Kawai, M., "International Monetary System and East Asian Monetary and Financial Cooperation," In *Post-crisis East Asian Monetary and Financial Cooperation*, edited by Li Xiao. Jilin: Jilin University Press, 2010.

[608] [Japan] Jinjing T., "Financial cooperation in East Asia: The Status Quo and Issues of the Chiang Mai Agreement," *Nanyang Data Translation Series* 2 (2011).

[609] [Japan] Kikuchi, Y., *International History of the Japanese Yen (Japanese Version)*. Xiulin: You Fei Pavilion, 2000.

[610] [Japan] Eiji, Y., "The Necessity of Establishing the Asian Edition of EMS and Joint Leadership Mechanism between Japan and China," *Post-Crisis East Asian Monetary and Financial Cooperation*, edited by Li Xiao. Jilin: Jilin University Press, 2010.

[611] [Japan] Ishida, K., "Stability, Internationalization of the RMB and the Future of the East Asian Monetary System," In *Post-Crisis East Asian Monetary and Financial Cooperation*, edited by Li Xiao. Jilin: Jilin University Press, 2010.

[612] [Japan] Shinohara, H., "Advances in East Asian Monetary Cooperation," *International Economic Review* 2 (2009).

[613] [Japan] Ogawa, E. and Z. Yao, "On the Exchange Rate System Pegged to a Basket of Currencies," *World Economy* 6 (2004).

[614] [France] Tirole, J., *Financial Crisis, Liquidity and International Monetary System*. Beijing: China Renmin University Press, 2003.

[615] [France] Condesou, M., "Towards a New International Financial Order," *China Finance* 2 (2010).

[616] [US] Brzezinski, *The Big Game: America's Primacy and Its Geopolitical Strategy*. Shanghai: Shanghai People's Publishing House, 2007.

[617] Daniel, J. B., *Americans: The Colonial Process*. Shanghai: Shanghai Translation Publishing House, 1997.

[618] Gavin, F., *Gold, the US Dollar and Power: The Politics of International Monetary Relations (1958 ~ 1971)*. Beijing: Social Science Literature Press, 2011.

[619] [US] Keohane, R. and J. Nai, *Power and Interdependence*. Beijing" Peking University Press, 2002.

[620] [US] Gilpin, R., *Challenges of Global Capitalism: The 21st Century World Economy*. Shanghai: Shanghai People's Publishing House, 2001.

[621] [US] Gilpin, R., *Transnational Corporations and American Hegemony*. Beijing: Oriental Press, 2011.

[622] [US] McKinnon, R., "Fall into the Trap of the International Dollar Standard," *New Finance* 7 (2005).

[623] [US] Schnabl, M., "Is China a Stabilizing Force or a Deflationary Pressure in East Asia," *Comparison* 7 (2003).

[624] [US] Mundell, *International Currency: Past, Present and Future, Mundell's Anthology of Economics*. Vol. 6. Beijing: China Finance Press, 2003.

[625] [US] Huntington, S. P., *The Third Wave: The Wave of Democratization in the Late 20th Century*. Renmin: China Renmin University of Press, 2013.

[626] [US] Roach, S., "The US Economy: Responding to a Different Recession," *New Finance* 3 (2008).

[627] [UK] Riverine, D. and C. Milner, *Frontier Issues in International Monetary Economics*. Beijing: China Tax Press, 2000.

[628] [UK] Gohn, P., *Global Gambling in Washington*. Jiangsu: Jiangsu People's Publishing House, 2003.

The Following References are in Japanese

[629] Takao, K. and X. Li ed., *World Financial Crisis: Dialogue between Japan and China: Yen, RMB, Asian Currency and Financial Cooperation*. [Japan] Spring Breeze Co., April 2010.

[630] Li, X. and H. Kenjiro, "Build the East Asian Currency System and Asianize the Yen," [*Japan*] *Review of the World Economics*, November/December 2001, January, April 2002.

[631] Li, X. and Y. Ding, "Build the East Asian Currency System," [*Japan*] *International Finance* 1 (2005).

[632] Li, X., "Yen Internationalization: from Failure to Strategic Adjustment," [*Japan*] *International Finance* 1 (2006).

[633] Li, X., "Japan-China Relations in the Economists Era," [*Japan*] *International Finance* 1 (2006).

[634] Li, X., "RMB Appreciation and Asian Strategy," [*Japan*] *International Finance* 1 (2007).

[635] Li, X. and Y. Ding, "East Asian Financial Cooperation under Global Financial Insecurity," [*Japan*] *International Finance* 1 (2008).

[636] Li, X., "Path choices of East Asian Monetary and Financial Cooperation under the Global Financial Crisis," [*Japan*] *International Finance* 1 October 2009.

Index

Lightning Source UK Ltd.
Milton Keynes UK
UKHW022230010721
386484UK00003B/144

9 789811 218866